AN ORKNEY ANTHOLOGY

★

*The Selected Works of
Ernest Walker Marwick*

Medieval burial service of a dignitary in the chancel of St Magnus Cathedral, 1885
Arthur Melville, RWS, RSW, RP, 1855-1904

AN ORKNEY ANTHOLOGY

*

*The Selected Works of
Ernest Walker Marwick*

★ ★ ★

Edited by
John D M Robertson

VOLUME
ONE

SCOTTISH ACADEMIC PRESS
Edinburgh
1991

Published by
Scottish Academic Press
56 Hanover Street
Edinburgh EH2 2DX

First published 1991
ISBN 0 7073 0574 8

© 1991 John D. M. Robertson

All rights reserved. No part of this
publication may be reproduced, stored in
a retrieval system, or transmitted in any
form or by any means, electronic, mechanical,
photocopying, recording or otherwise, without
the prior permission of Scottish Academic Press

Set in 'Monotype' Bembo by
Speedspools, Edinburgh
Printed in Great Britain by
Pillans & Wilson
Edinburgh and Glasgow
Bound by
Hunter & Foulis
Edinburgh

for my parents
JOHN AND RITA ROBERTSON

for my parents
JOHN AND RITA ROBERTSON

Contents

INTRODUCTION	xv
THE FAIR OF ST OLAF, KIRKWALL	xx
ACKNOWLEDGMENTS	xxiii

A WAY OF LIFE

THE DAY'S WORK—Farming	3
1 Farming in Orkney during the last two centuries	5
2 Farming freuteries	13
3 The horseman's word	16
4 The lore of harvest	19
5 The lore of plantikreus	26
THE DAY'S WORK—The Sea	29
1 Some sea superstitions	31
2 Tales of island smugglers	36
3 Our local pirate	42
4 Orkney's other pirate	44
5 The predicament of the grey seal	46
6 The first North Isles steamer	50
7 Orkney's back door	55
8 The story of the Stromness lifeboats 1867-1967	62
9 By bottle post	74
10 An odd fish	76
THE DAY'S WORK—Trades and Crafts	79
1 History from a day-book	81
2 The story of the Orkney chair	85
3 An Omond fiddle	88
DOMESTIC LIFE	93
1 The Orkney croft house	95
2 Domestic freuteries	98
3 Taking their medicine: some old-fashioned prescriptions	101
4 An ABC of Orkney food	103
5 Peat fire fancies	114
LIFE STAGES	117
1 Old ways at island weddings	119
2 Marriage and fertility freuteries	122
3 Funeral etiquette	124

CONTENTS

FESTIVALS	125
1 Yule in the north	127
2 New Year customs	129
3 Tailing day	133
4 Children's horse and plough festival in South Ronaldsay	134
5 Hallowe'en	137
6 Bonfire customs	139
PASTIMES	143
1 Games of a thousand years	145
2 The games we played	147
3 A cricket century	184
4 Entertaining galore	186
5 An Orkney concert in the 1920s	189
6 Orkney drinking	191
MEMORIES	201
1 The last Chief of Clan Macnab	203
2 Portrait of a vagabond	205
3 Peace's Orkney Almanac	207
4 Trials of a probationer	209
5 Electioneering	211
6 A Stromness childhood	214
7 When Stromness had a newspaper	216
8 Some annals of an Orkney parish	218
9 I remember rural poverty in Orkney	229
10 The water meedoo	231
11 Stone-breakers	235
12 Orkney 'feeders'	237
13 Motoring numbers preserve memories	239
14 The Kirkwall-Stromness bus	241
15 An islandman's war	242

LORE AND LEGEND

LEGENDARY CREATURES	255
1 Creatures of Orkney legend and their Norse ancestry	257
2 Tales of island fairies	279
3 Nessie's cousins	282
4 The man from nowhere	288
5 The peerie fool and the princess	290
ANIMAL STORIES	293
1 Seal stories	295
2 Days of the eagle	297

WELLS AND STONES — 299
1 Some ancient wells — 301
2 Strange stones — 307
3 The Stone of Odin — 309

TALL STORIES — 321
Tall Stories — 323

NORTHERN WITCHES
Northern Witches — 333

TALES FROM THE PAST
1 A memory of 1066 — 387
2 St Magnus — 389
3 The last sea-king — 392
4 When Orkney went to Bannockburn — 397
5 The belted knights of Stove — 399
6 Island of Dons and Angels — 401
7 The minister and the witch — 403
8 Orkney and 'the Englishes' — 406
9 Margaret Halcro of Evie—mother of a Scottish Church — 409
10 Kirkwall's flood — 411
11 Orkney memories of Nelson and Napoleon — 413
12 The day that Kitchener died — 419
13 The role of Scapa Flow — 424

ORKNEY MONUMENTS
1 Treasure troves — 443
2 The strongest hold in Britain — 446
3 Peterkirk—an island sanctuary — 448
4 Chiocchetti and the Italian Chapel — 453
5 Viking and saint — 457
6 The curious history of The Big Tree — 463

BIBLIOGRAPHY — 469

GLOSSARY — 471

INDEX — 483

Illustrations

COLOUR

1 Medieval burial service of a dignitary in the chancel of St Magnus Cathedral, 1885. Arthur Melville, RWS, RSW, RP, 1855-1904 *frontispiece*
2 Kirkwall Fair, 1874. Waller Hugh Paton, RSA, RSW, *facing page* xxii
3 Skippigeo, Birsay, c.1960. Stanley Cursiter, RSA, RSW, 1887-1976   64
4 Shore Street, Kirkwall, c.1955. Stanley Cursiter, RSA, RSW, 1887-1976   81
5 Selkies Hellier, The Home of the Seals, c.1955. Stanley Cursiter, RSA, RSW, 1887-1976   160
6 Finstown Old Church, 1949. Stanley Cursiter, RSA, RSW, 1887-1976   177
7 Cliffs at Yesnaby, 1950. Stanley Cursiter, RSA, RSW, 1887-1976   212
8 Kirkwall Harbour, 1872. Sam Bough, RSA, RSW, 1822-1878   221
9 Bisgeos, Westray, c.1929. Stanley Cursiter, RSA, RSW, 1887-1976   288
10 Scapa Flow in a Winter Gale, 1916. William Lionel Wyllie, RA, 1851-1931   305
11 Haymaking, Rackwick, Hoy, 1887. Robert Weir Allan, 1851-1942   340
12 Summer Storm, Yesnaby, c.1960. Stanley Cursiter, RSA, RSW, 1887-1976   349
13 Scapa Bay, 1869. Sam Bough, RSA, RSW, 1822-1878   372
14 The Big Tree, Albert Street, Kirkwall, 1888. Arthur Melville, RWS, RSW, RP, 1855-1904   381
15 Lobster Fishermen, Rousay, c.1950. Stanley Cursiter, RSA, RSW, 1887-1976   416
16 The Bridge of Brodgar, Stenness, 1875. Waller Hugh Paton, RSA, RSW, 1828-1895   433
17 Bowling in Tankerness House garden, 1885. Arthur Melville, RWS, RSW, RP, 1855-1904   452
18 North Aisle of St Magnus Cathedral, 1885. Arthur Melville, RWS, RSW, RP, 1855-1904   461

Plate 2 is reproduced with permission of Sheriff Alistair A. MacDonald. Plates 4 and 12 are reproduced with permission of Brigadier S. P. Robertson. Plates 14 and 17 are reproduced with permission of the late T. C. Wallace. The remaining colour illustrations are from the Robertson Family Collection.

Illustrations

BLACK AND WHITE

facing page

1	Scything and gathering the harvest, Deerness, c.1905	6
2	Cutting the harvest with a back delivery reaper, Orquil, St Ola, c.1900	6
3	Ox and cart Hoy, c.1880	7
4	A single-stilted plough used widely until the early nineteenth century. For several decades thereafter these implements were utilised in a limited way in some parishes	10
5	Singling turnips, Papdale, near Kirkwall, c.1900	11
6	Oxen yoked to an iron plough, c.1890	11
7	Feeding the hens, c.1900	16
8	Washing the horses' legs, Saverock, St Ola, c.1900	17
9	A plantikreu on the island of Swona, 1966	32
10	A plantikreu, Birsay 1987	32
11	This unusual summerhouse is located between St Catherine's Place and Bridge Street, Kirkwall	33
12	SS *Iona*, Dennison & Co, built in Shapinsay, 1893. Naval flotilla in background	36
13	SS *Iona* re-engined and refurbished in 1949. Wrecked in Elwick Bay, Shapinsay, 1964	36
14	SS *Orcadia*, 1868-1931, Orkney Steam Navigation Co Ltd, c.1900	37
15	SS *St Ola* I, 1892-1951, North of Scotland Orkney & Shetland Steam Navigation Co Ltd, c.1925	37
16	SS *Earl Thorfinn*, 1928-1962, Orkney Steam Navigation Co Ltd	44
17	SS *St Magnus* II, North of Scotland Orkney & Shetland Steam Navigation Co Ltd	44
18	Swona harbour, 1966	45
19	Stroma harbour, 1966	45
20	Stromness lifeboat *John A. Hay*, 1909-28	68
21	Stromness lifeboat *J.J.K.S.W.*, 1928-55	68
22	Kirkwall harbour, c.1890	69
23	Shaking nets, Stromness, c.1890	76
24	Herring fishing station, Burray, c.1900	76
25	Fish curing, Thomas Chalmer's fish store, Ayre Road, Kirkwall, c.1890	77
26	Gathering 'spoots' or razor fish, Scapa, c.1905	96
27	James Scarth Foubister, Newbanks, Deerness, baiting handlines, c.1900	97
28	A country blacksmith, c.1900	112
29	John Firth, cartwright, Finstown, c.1880	112
30	Making a straw caisie, c.1900	113

ILLUSTRATIONS

31	Spinning yarn for weaving, Westray, c.1900	132
32	Making a straw-backed Orkney chair, c.1920	132
33	An Orkney croft, Feolquoy, Stromness, c.1880	133
34	Interior of Craa'nest, Rackwick, Hoy, c.1880	133
35	Craa'nest, Rackwick, Hoy, c.1890	140
36	Travelling shop, c.1900	141
37	Tom Rendall, Longhouse, aak-swapping near Red Nev, Westray, c.1912	164
38	'Running the Lee', Copinsay, 1912	165
39	Islanders with swap-net, Westray c.1912	172
40	Aak (guillemot) eggs collected from 'The Lee', Copinsay, 1912	172
41	Balfour Hospital, Main Street, Kirkwall, c.1900	173
42	Balfour Hospital kitchen, c.1900	173
43	D. M. Wright, Chemist, Albert Street, Kirkwall, c.1920	192
44	Cutting peats, South Ronaldsay, c.1900	193
45	Transporting peats, Longhope, c.1900	193
46	Bringing home peats, Longhope, c.1890	208
47	Horse-drawn hearse, Sanday, used until the mid-1940s	208
48	The wedding of Mary Ann Smith Spence and William Mackie Taylor of Georth, Harray, at Makerhouse, Dounby, 24 May 1907	209
49	The throw-up, Christmas Day Ba', Kirkwall, 1988	224
50	The Ba' on Broad Street, Kirkwall, New Year's Day 1985	224
51	The Ba' at the Up-the-Gate goal, Kirkwall, New Year's Day 1913	225
52	The Ba' at the Down-the-Gate goal, Kirkwall, New Year's Day 1969	225
53	Trucking the Boys ba', Kirkwall harbour, New Year's Day 1906	240
54	A 'horse' parading in Cromarty Square, St Margaret's Hope, c.1980	241
55	Boys' Ploughing Match, South Ronaldsay, c.1980	241
56	Cattle Show, Dounby, 1912	260
57	Annual Show, Dounby, 1914	260
58	Putting on Junction Road, Kirkwall, c.1905	261
59	Hurdy-gurdy man with organ and monkey, Dundas Street, Stromness, c.1905	261
60	Children sailing boats in a rock pool, c.1905	268
61	Farm children at play, 1914	268
62	Concert programme, 1908	269
63	Band of Hope member's card, 1899	276
64	Advertisement for Old Orkney Whisky, distilled in Stromness, c.1900	276
65	Charter of the first Good Templar Lodge in Orkney—Star of Pomona, Stromness, 1872	277
66	Good Templar outing, Stromness, c.1905	284
67	Boys' Brigade and Independent Order of Good Templars, St Margaret's Hope, c.1910	284
68	Guides and Brownies, Tankerness House garden, June 1922	285

ILLUSTRATIONS

69	View of a small Druid Temple, 1760, by Richard Pococke	308
70	Circle of Loda in the Parish of Stenhouse in the Island of Pomona. Illustrated by Fred Herm Walden, 1772	309
71	A perspective view of the Standing Stones in the Parish of Stainhouse in Orkney, 1784, by Dr Robert Henry	316
72	Western Circle of the Stones of Stennis, 1805, by Elizabeth, Marchioness of Stafford	316
73	Stone of Power between the two Temples at Stenhouse, 1789, by John Thomas Stanley	316
74	View of a demisemicircle of Stones on the Banks of Stenhouse Lake in the Island of Pomona, 1772, by John Cleveley	317
75	Electioneering poster, 1880	352
76	*The Stromness News*, second issue, 7 March 1884	353
77	Tinker family near the old slaughterhouse, Cairston Road, Stromness, c.1900	368
78	Road workers breaking stones, c.1905	369
79	Steam-powered road roller, c.1905	369
80	The Evie coach setting out from John Street, Stromness, c.1900	388
81	The Orkney Motor Express leaving Harbour Street, Kirkwall for Stromness, c.1905	388
82	Orkney's first motor car in Harbour Street, Kirkwall, 1901	389
83	Early motor vehicles near the Kiln Corner, Kirkwall, c.1905	389
84	A Crossley tourer, BS 1 at Longhope, 1952. It had a canvas hood, and twin tyres on the rear	396
85	Carrying water from the pump in Broad Street, Kirkwall, c.1860	396
86	Pumping water from a country well, c.1900	397
87	The sacred well, Bigswell, Stenness, 1985	397
88	Demolition in Broad Street, Kirkwall, c.1884	420
89	The Earl of Mar and Kellie lays the foundation stone of Kirkwall Town Hall, 20 August 1884	420
90	The unveiling by Lord Horne of Kitchener's Memorial, 2 July 1926, Stirkoke, Caithness	421
91	Field Marshal Earl Kitchener	421
92	Kitchener Memorial, Marwick Head, Birsay	421
93	The battle cruiser *Hindenburg*, 1930	428
94	The battle cruiser *Seydlitz*, 1928	428
95	The *Royal Oak* sunk in Scapa Flow by German submarine U47 on 14 October 1939	429
96	Construction of No 1 Barrier looking from Lamb Holm towards St Mary's, 1943	429
97	St Peter's Church, South Ronaldsay, 1967	448
98	The Italian Chapel, Lamb Holm, Orkney, 1944	449

	ILLUSTRATIONS	
99	Italian prisoners-of-war at the inauguration of the statue of St George and the Dragon, 1943	449
100	The Tolbooth, Kirkwall, built 1740, and demolished 1890	464
101	St Magnus Cathedral, 1890	465

Plates 1, 2, 26, 27, 42, 58, 60, 61 and 86 come from the collection of the late David Horne and are reproduced by permission of Mrs Margaret Horne; plates 3, 6, 14, 22, 23, 25, 34, 35, 46, 100 and 101 are part of the George Washington Wilson Collection and appear by permission of Aberdeen University; plates 5, 7, 8, 30, 31, 32, 36, 41, 43, 44, 51, 53, 68, 78, 79, 81, 82, 83, 85 (copied), and 90 are from the Tom Kent Collection and are reproduced by permission of the Orkney Photographic Archive; plates 9, 18, 19, 92 and 97 are by Ernest Marwick; plates 10, 11 and 87 are by the photographer Charles Tait, and plates 50, 52, 54 and 55 are reproduced with his permission; plates 20 and 94 are by W. Hourston; plate 29 by W. Wood; plate 33 by J. Valentine; plates 37, 38, 39, 40, 59, 65, 66 and 77 by R. H. Robertson; plate 45 is part of the Ellison Collection, Stromness Museum; plate 47 is by Alastair Cormack; plate 48 by James Linklater; plate 49 by Donald Gillies; plates 56 and 57 by D. R. G. Ballantine; plate 69, 70 and 74 are reproduced by permission of the British Library, London; plate 71 is reproduced by permission of the Society of Antiquaries of Scotland; plate 72 is reproduced by permission of the Royal Commission on the Ancient and Historical Monuments of Scotland; plate 73 is reproduced by permission of the National Library of Iceland; plate 84 is by J. M. F. Groat; plate 95 is reproduced by permission of the Imperial War Museum.

Illustrations

LINE DRAWINGS

	page
Grinding grain with a quern, *c.*1900	2
Windmill, *c.*1900. These mills were used for threshing and grinding	15
Harvest knot	25
Iron pier, Kirkwall, *c.*1875	41
At the sillocks, Birsay, early twentieth century	43
James Leask, the Bellman, Stromness *c.*1905. He was known as 'Puffer'	73
Shore Street, Kirkwall, *c.*1880	84
South Ronaldshay Agricultural Society poster, 1845	136
Hallowe'en prank, Millhouse, Deerness, *c.*1900	138
Bowling at Dunnet's Hotel, Bridge Street, Kirkwall, *c.*1880	183
The Ba' at the harbour, Kirkwall, Christmas Day, 1978	188
William Laughton, an eccentric known locally at Skatehorn, *c.*1900	204
Tinker children, *c.*1900	234
Kirkwall Girl Guides Registration Form, 1919	252
Kirkwall Brownie Pack Registration Form, 1922	253
Troll wondering how old it is	254
Troll family pride	281
The princess and the troll	292
Kirkwall Company of the Orkney Volunteer Artillery, 1863	412
The Mercat Cross, Kirkwall, *c.*1900	440
The Watergate, Kirkwall, *c.*1870	445
The Big Tree, Albert Street, Kirkwall, *c.*1889	467

Introduction

ERNEST WALKER MARWICK was a distinguished Orcadian whose achievements touched and strengthened the life of his native culture at many points. His interests were wide and embraced Orcadian history, antiquities, dialect, literature, architecture, conservation and most of all, folklore. He was a writer of singular clarity, deftness and felicity, his work bearing the hallmark of scrupulous scholarship. Painstaking research into archival material was enlivened by the many contacts he made with fellow islanders, recording and documenting for posterity memories and stories often in a dialect in danger of being forgotten. Ernest Marwick's work is all the more notable for the way in which he conveys imagination and enthusiasm: the passing of the years did not dull his curiosity or affect his capacity to involve and delight the reader with all manner of subjects.

Brought up on the farm of Fursan, Evie where he was born in 1915, Ernest attended the parish school until the age of ten. Ill-health precluded further formal education and he was totally self-taught, apart from a short stay at Newbattle Abbey in 1953 and 1954, where he studied under the guidance of his friend Edwin Muir.

He began to write in his teens whilst working on the land. These early years farming the time-honoured way, and in the evenings listening to songs and stories, endowed Ernest with a profound knowledge of country things and stimulated a lifelong involvement in Orkney customs, traditions and history. In this period he absorbed in full measure the rich lore of his native parish. Little did the folk of Evie realise that this delicate youth possessed a burgeoning intellect which in the years ahead would earn international recognition.

Moving to Kirkwall in 1941 to work in a bookshop, he prepared articles on local history, folklore, literature and current affairs for both *The Orcadian* and *The Orkney Herald*. His appreciation of poetry prompted him to compile and edit *An Anthology of Orkney Verse* (1949), which includes some of the first material published by Robert Rendall and George Mackay Brown, and a selection of the oldest Orkney poems from the Norse era.

In the mid-1950s he joined the editorial staff of *The Orkney Herald*, writing many leaders, articles and reviews, as well as a weekly column, *Sooan Sids*,[1] which focused mainly on local folklife and culture. He marked

---

1. In his column Ernest Marwick made use of a variety of information which before publication might seem of little import to the casual observer. He transformed the material into delightful articles. Similarly sooans, a fine flour attached to the inner husk of sids (oats) and discarded by the uninformed, may be recovered and supped as a porridge or made into appetising sooan scones.

the centenary of *The Orcadian* in 1954 with a serial, *Journey from Serfdom—The Story of the Orkney People in the Nineteenth Century*. It is hoped that this magnificent work will be published in book form.

When he left *The Herald* in the early 1960s to work freelance, Ernest Marwick reached wider audiences through papers and magazines in Scotland, England, France, Germany, Scandinavia, the United States and the Commonwealth. He had a particular interest in Canada and in the Orcadians who worked and settled there, many of them connected with the Hudson's Bay Company. When Canada celebrated its Centenary of Confederation in 1967 he was chosen to broadcast Scotland's greetings to the Dominion. The even older links between Scandinavia and Orkney also fascinated him, and on visits to Norway he studied history and literature and recorded traditional music. In 1972 his folklore essay *Creatures of Orkney Legend and their Norse Ancestry* was published by *Norveg*, Oslo University's Journal of Folklife Research.

In this country, Ernest Marwick edited Walter Traill Dennison's *Orkney Folklore and Traditions* (1961) and contributed two chapters 'Age of Stagnation' and 'The Beginnings of Modern Orkney' to *The New Orkney Book* (1966), edited by Shearer, Groundwater and Mackay. He produced a section on Orkney, Shetland and Caithness for the Reader's Digest Association's *Folklore, Myths and Legends of Britain* (1973), published his own volume *The Folklore of Orkney and Shetland* (1975), and wrote a full and evocative introduction to a photographic essay by Chick Chalmers, *Life in the Orkney Islands* (1979). Shetland also meant a great deal to him and he knew the islands well. He provided a foreword for the anthology *New Shetlander Writing* (1973), compiled by John and Laurence Graham, and an introduction to the *Collected Poems* (1975) of his friend, the remarkably gifted Shetlander, T. A. Robertson—'Vagaland'. During this time he remained a luminary of the Orkney journalistic scene: his association with *The Orcadian* continued and for years his features and a weekly column, *Looking Around*, appeared in that newspaper.

Over a period of some thirty years he made more than eight hundred broadcasts, and in regular work with the BBC he covered topical matters in Orkney, Shetland and Caithness, as well as taking part in national and overseas programmes. In the 1960s a series of his features appeared in Scottish Television's *Talk of the Town*. Quick to appreciate the value of a local sound archive, his own collection of over two hundred tapes became the basis for the Orkney Sound Archive. He lectured for the Workers' Educational Association and for Aberdeen University Extra-Mural Department, and he was a popular guest speaker for numerous organisations throughout Orkney.

Ernest Marwick's love of his heritage led him to participate in many issues of public concern. He was the moving spirit in the formation of the Orkney Heritage Society, subsequently serving as its Chairman, and he campaigned vigorously on conservation issues, such as the preservation of

Papdale House, Kirkwall and against proposed uranium mining.

His work did not go unrewarded. People from all over the islands and farther away gathered in St Magnus Cathedral in 1975 when he was made an Honorary Freeman and Burgess of the City and Royal Burgh of Kirkwall 'in recognition of his distinguished contribution to and researches into the study of Orkney folklore, history and literature'. This was the accolade he treasured most, and Orcadians everywhere rejoiced—as they did again the following year when Edinburgh University made him an Honorary Master of Arts. In the last year of his life Ernest received a well-deserved Civil List pension. This recognition is given to distinguished people whose income has not matched their endeavour and ability.

He died in a road accident in July 1977 and his many friends in the islands and beyond were shocked and saddened by the tragedy. A feeling of loss pervaded the community.

> Genial in temper
> Quick in mind
> Ready in speech
> Generous in counsel
> To lovers of sound learning

Some years ago I read this epitaph on a tombstone in Winchester Cathedral and thought of my friend. At the time of his death he had taken a rightful place among the star cluster of Orcadians whose work has significantly benefited the culture of their native county. Ernest had a remarkable empathy with all things Orcadian and there were few aspects of island affairs past or present on which he could not talk and write with authority. He was certainly not sententious and although he told me that he could be pedantic I never found him so, his meticulous attention to detail seeming wholly admirable. Possessed of a calm diligence, he took great care in assembling his material and in presenting it without bias, illuminated only by clear judgement and compassionate vision. He had an extraordinary appetite for knowledge and a prodigious memory.

Throughout his life Ernest had a love of people, a contempt for hypocrisy and cant and remained entirely unpretentious. Living in quiet work, dedicated and thoughtful, he was an inspiration to his fellows, freely sharing the talents God had bestowed on him—indeed his generosity was legendary. His greatest joy was in qualities of mind and spirit and he totally discounted worldly success in the sure knowledge that there are powers in the universe more enduring than greed and materialism.

He treasured the old town of Kirkwall with its magnificent twelfth-century red sandstone cathedral, narrow flagstoned streets and grey architecture: every stone instinct with history. Stromness too he cherished and there spent happy holidays with Janette, a devoted and understanding wife through good times and bad.

Over the years many friends and visitors from various countries and walks of life came to his home, where all were welcomed with unfailing courtesy and charmed by his kindness and wisdom. Although essentially a quiet, gentle man, with a delightful sense of humour, he readily grasped the quiddity of any matter which might adversely affect Orkney and its environment, whereupon he became a fearless, indefatigable crusader.

Ernest pursued all things concerning his county that were lovely and of good report, and was foremost in guarding and revaluing our heritage. Indeed, the quickening awareness of the ethos of these islands can be ascribed to his unflagging efforts. Much of his writing is imbued with a perception and understanding of the past and of its relevance to the present and to the future.

Beset at times by adversity, Ernest's life and achievements demonstrate the dominance of character and ability over circumstance. He died at the height of his powers leaving an unquarried mine of information. Surprisingly he published little in book form during his lifetime, probably because he was too much of a perfectionist. A wide-ranging selection from a treasure trove of his hitherto unpublished papers has now been made available, together with material from broadcasts, lectures, newspapers and journals.

The first and largest section of this anthology, *A Way of Life*, contains material on the history of everyday life in Orkney (and to a lesser extent in Shetland), together with the traditions and superstitions entwined in the islands' culture. Much of the information is derived from interviews and correspondence with people throughout both island groups.

Belief in the supernatural led to many instances of Orkney witchcraft. The origins, practices and trials of witches form the subject of the following section *Northern Witches*—a fine example of Ernest's erudition and careful research. *Tales from the Past*, *Orkney Monuments*, *Explorers and Traders* and *Famous People with Orkney Links* (the latter two sections in Volume II) continue the entertaining and varied collage of Orkney history, extending to the many folk who ventured outside the islands. Careful historical assessments are included, together with old legends skilfully retold, sympathetic biographies and many fascinating scraps and curiosities.

Our island culture is closely associated with language and literature, and in Volume II, *Orkney Words and Expressions* includes a rich store of phraseology and sayings, names for birds and plants, and island and parish nicknames. Of particular note is Ernest's Orkney Word List which catalogues for posterity hundreds of old dialect words, none of which has appeared in works devoted to the Orkney language. Also in Volume II, *Orkney Writers and Orkney Literature* contains some of his best appraisals of early poems and of the lives and work of three important twentieth-century writers: Edwin Muir, Eric Linklater and George Mackay Brown. Examples of Ernest's own creative writing are to be found in the next section, *Short Stories and Poems*.

Any reader who has been captivated by Ernest Marwick's discoveries about his county and people will value the more personal views of the author in the final section in Volume II, *Essays and Comment*. There are articles, both light-hearted and serious, on aspects of life through the years, topical matters and the future of the islands.

Ernest told me in his modest way it was pleasant to reflect that when he departed this life he might perhaps leave some work of value and interest. His pamphlets, articles, recordings, broadcasts and books are evidence of an astonishing fecundity, and in them Ernest Walker Marwick has bequeathed to Orkney a legacy of inestimable value. This anthology contains examples of his many-faceted work and illustrates its range and depth. I hope that these two volumes will be read with enjoyment and enlightenment: they are a memorial for a remarkable man.

JOHN D. M. ROBERTSON
6 November 1990

Kirk and Fair
St Magnus 1873

In Volume III of *A Pen and Pencil Memoranda, 1874-1888* by Waller Hugh Paton, the artist describes the interesting events leading up to the painting of *The Fair of St Olaf, Extremes Meet*. This background information and the verse form the basis of the illustration. The following extracts from *The Memoranda* may be of interest:

By Dinah Mulock

    Candlelight, munelight & mirk
        Hurry & greed & prayer—
    Mony may gang to the Kirk
        Oure mony will gang to the Fair

★ ★ ★

By MP

    Saint Magnus was wont in days of old
    To gather his children within his fold;
    But now alas! his reign is o'er
    Orcadians flock to his shrine no more.
    And he looks from his dark & shadowy seat
    At the thoughtless crowds that play at his feet
    Nor heeding the time, nor heeding the place
    For 'Near to the Church is far from grace'!

★ ★ ★

By Hubert
29th Decr 1873

    High and black aloft it stands
    Foremost Church in the Orkney lands
    And below the people come
    to play upon the Kettle-drum
    They gamble, splutter, think it nice
    Take nothing but the Deil's advice

★ ★ ★

Kirk and Fair.
St. Magnus 1873

By Dinah Mulock

Candlelight, moonlight & mirk.
Hurry & greed & prayer —
Mony may gang to the Kirk
Sure mony will gang to the Fair.

By M. P.

Saint Magnus was wont in days of old
To gather his children within his fold;
But now alas! his reign is o'er
Orcadians flock to his shrine no more.
And he looks from his dark & shadowy seat
At the thoughtless crowds that play at his feet
Nor heeding the time, nor heeding the place.
For "near to the Church is far from grace."

By Hubert
29th Dec 1873

High and black aloft it stands
Foremost Church in the Orkney lands
And below the people come
To play upon the kettle-drum
They gamble, splutter, think it nice
Take nothing but the Devil's advice

The Fair of St Olaf, Kirkwall
'Extremes onect'

When on a visit to the Stills in Orkney in the autumn of 1873 I arrived one evening at Kirkwall, after a two days' journey with Mrs Still in a cart and saw the scene as I have tried to depict it. Though much impressed with the strange sight at the time I did not then think of painting it, so unfortunately made no studies. On coming home, however, the recollection grew upon me so much that I resolved to try it.

To enable me to do so I went to Kirkcaldy during the Fair time there and made a number of slight sketches of booths, etc. I also got some photographs of the Cathedral from Mr Davis, and with this very scant material I set to work and painted the picture during the winter in George Street Studios. I thought of many names and had many suggested to me until the one given was hit upon: amongst others were the three subjoined. It was exhibited in the RSA 1874, in the Smith Institute, Stirling 1874, in the Royal Manchester Institution 1875, in the Watt Institute, Greenock 1876 with the motto of

'Making good the saying odd
Near the Church and far from God'

in Glasgow 1873, in the Royal Albert Hall, South Kensington 1879.

It was purchased by Mrs Still, July 1883 for £200. Exhibited in the International Edin. 86 as her property.

Kirkwall Fair, 1874

Waller Hugh Paton, RSA, RSW, 1828-1895

Acknowledgments

I offer grateful thanks to the many people who helped in diverse ways during the editing of this book and in particular to:

Captain John Allan, Professor A. J. Aitken, Captain H. A. Banks, Miss Elaine R. Bullard, Alan Bullen, John L. Broom, George Bruce, Rev. H. W. M. Cant, Dr James I. Cromarty, Russell Croy, Professor Gordon Donaldson, Miss I. J. Eunson, Mr and Mrs Howie Firth, John Firth, Mr and Mrs Arthur W. Flett, Mrs Sibella Fraser, R. Garden & Co, John J. Graham, Mrs Enid Grant, J. M. F. Groat, Major Nigel Hadden-Paton, W. S. Hewison, Mrs W. G. Kent, Dr Raymond Lamb, Mrs J. J. Leith, Peter K. I. Leith, Mrs Ruby Leslie, the late James MacDonald, Mr and Mrs A. B. Marwick, Eric R. Meek, the late Miss Embla Mooney, David Murison, the late John G. Nicolson, Orkney Natural History Society, Lindsay Phillips, Dr J. N. Graham Ritchie, A. S. Robertson, John Scott, John G. Scott, the family of the late John Sinclair, Cecil Steer, Mrs Jenny Tait, Mrs W. I. Tait, *The Orcadian*, Albert J. Thomson, the late R. T. Tulloch, Eric Turner, the late T. C. Wallace, Marcus W. T. Wood, Captain Magnus Work.

David M. N. Tinch, the County Librarian, provided staunch support, and over the years I benefited greatly from the whole-hearted help of both Robert K. Leslie, the Depute Librarian, and Alison J. M. Fisher, the County Archivist. Bryce S. Wilson, the Orkney Museums Officer, gave aid on a variety of matters, not least in connection with old photographs, and the late Rev. Harald L. Mooney was generous with his time and erudition in clarifying words and passages in the old Scottish language and Orcadian dialect.

I should like to offer my gratitude to Colin Will for the perceptive care which had produced the Index. Also, I am greatly indebted to Mrs Marie E. Sutherland for research, typing the manuscript and checking proofs, and to Miss Connie V. Reid who kindly made herself available for typing and associated work.

The editorial advice which I have received from Dr Alison Parkes has been of an unusually high order. My sincere thanks to her for the consistent and imaginative assistance which she has so readily given.

The Coat-of-Arms of Orkney Islands Council is reproduced with the consent of the Council. The drawing is from *Scottish Civic Heraldry*, by R. M. Urquhart, published (1979) by Heraldry Today, Ramsbury, Wiltshire.

In correspondence and during my numerous visits to Edinburgh, The Scottish Academic Press in the person of Dr Douglas Grant was indefatigable in providing comment and constructive guidance, while the selection of the illustrations reflects the artistic perception of John McWilliam who also prepared the dust-jacket and the prospectus.

A WAY OF LIFE

THE DAY'S WORK—*Farming*

1 Farming in Orkney during the last two centuries   5
2 Farming freuteries   13
3 The horseman's word   16
4 The lore of harvest   19
5 The lore of plantikreus   26

I

Farming in Orkney during the last two centuries[1]

AGE OF STAGNATION

When we try to see what Orkney looked like for most of the two hundred years before our own twentieth century we almost feel as if we are looking through the wrong end of a telescope, for everything is a little smaller. Kirkwall is just a long straggling street and Stromness a village. Finstown and Dounby do not exist. In the country there are hardly any houses with a second storey. The fields are so small that they are little more than cultivated patches. Even the animals—horses, cows, pigs, and sheep—are a good deal smaller than those on our farms today. But there are a surprising number of those old-fashioned animals, and they seem to swarm over the hillsides, hungrily eating the rough herbage.

We are used to looking out over great stretches of cultivated land, especially in places like the West Mainland, so that we hardly know where farms begin and end, or where parishes meet. Our great-great-grandfathers saw a very different Orkney, farmed haphazardly and containing far greater areas of natural pasture and moorland.

The parishes all existed as they do now, and as they have done for a very long time. There was a parish minister. There should have been a parish school, although more often there was not. There was a laird, who owned a lot of the land; or even several lairds. But few of them lived for long periods in their native parishes. Life was more interesting for them somewhere else. The ordinary people for the most part spent their whole life in the parish, and were proud to be known as a Deerness man or an Orphir man, or whatever the parish was. But they took many of their surnames from districts that were once far more important than parishes. These districts were called *toonships*.

---

[1]. This article is an abridgement of two chapters 'Age of Stagnation' and 'The Beginnings of Modern Orkney' contributed by Ernest Marwick to *The New Orkney Book*, 1966.

THE DAY'S WORK—FARMING

Toonships

Surnames like Isbister, Hourston, Groundwater, Marwick, Corrigall, and a lot of others are toonship names. Toonships were areas of good, easily farmed land, which had been in use for centuries, perhaps even before the Norsemen came to Orkney. They varied in size according to the amount of useful land, and were situated wherever the good land had been found: along the shore or the loch, in a fertile valley drained by a burn, or perhaps on a hillside facing the sun. One thing they had in common—a boundary wall of turf and stones which separated them from the waste land outside. There would be quite a number of toonships in a parish, some adjacent, others with a good distance between them.

In some of the toonships, especially in Harray, the old Norse families had been so strong and firmly rooted in their land that the Scottish tyrants[1] could not displace them. These lived in what were practically family toonships. At the beginning of the eighteenth century some of them were still speaking the old Norn[2] language; and, as their land was divided equally among their children according to the udal law[3] of Norway which Orkney had inherited, without any need of papers to give them possession or to prove this and that, they were called *udallers*.

In the greater part of Orkney, however, udallers had almost ceased to exist. Other people had managed to get large portions of the toonships; sometimes because they were powerful, and related to the important Scottish families who now ruled the islands, or because they had money enough to buy the land from impoverished udallers. There were places, especially in the good, easily cultivated North Isles like Stronsay and Sanday, where the toonships were already broken up and large farms were making their appearance.

With it all, however, the way of life in the toonships was characteristic of Orkney right into the nineteenth century. Within the toonship was the very best land called the *toomal*, the not-so-good land, and some pasture land. Everyone owned a part of the toomal in one piece, but their land in other parts of the toonship was divided into little fields, scattered all over the place. This was so that their owners had equal shares of good land and poor land; but from the farming point of view it was a great nuisance. The narrow fields were drained by the earth being heaped up in ridges or *rigs*, and the method of farming was called *runrig*.

---

1. The Stewart Earls, 1564-1615.
2. The Norse dialect formerly spoken in Orkney.
3. Udal, or odal, land was held in freehold tenure and by uninterrupted succession. No original charter was required to substantiate possession, and the proprietor recognised no superior in the feudal sense.

1. Scything and gathering the harvest, Deerness, c.1905

2. Cutting the harvest with a back delivery reaper, Orquil, St Ola, c.1900

The farm

As there were no fences, cultivation could not be attempted in spring until the hordes of animals which had spent the winter roaming over the toonship, and making a hideous mess of the fields, had been sent outside to spend the summer on the moors and hills. Before this took place the dyke around the toonship was heightened and strengthened; but, even so, animals were always finding their way back and being chased out again by rough, yelping dogs. There were gates in the dyke so that travellers could pass through, and these had to be carefully closed. The gates were called *slaps* or *grinds*. The latter word lives here and there in Orkney farm names.

The Orkney farmer in the eighteenth century had a hard time, and he was an obstinate person. Because his way of farming was a poor one the land did not grow a great deal, but he firmly believed that it would be fatal to alter his methods. He grew oats and bere[1] year about, had never seen turnips, and would only manure his land with seaweed. The plough he used was much the same as people had in Old Testament days. He threshed his crop with a staff, hinged by leather to a handle, which was called a *flail*; and he ground his corn between round quern stones, such as are sometimes seen today ornamenting gardens.

Because the land was so poorly worked few people depended on it entirely for a living, or if they did they were often in sore straits. Some of the better-off lairds had ships with which they carried cargoes to and from Norway or the Baltic ports. They might take away meal, fish, rabbit skins, feathers, and tallow; and they might bring back sugar, tea, spices, calico, brandy, and gunpowder. The lairds also introduced *kelp-burning* to Orkney. All the spring, on suitable shores, people would carry up seaweed to be dried and burned. The residue that was left when the seaweed was burned produced iodine and other chemicals, as well as soda which was used for making glass, and the profit from kelp-burning was considerable. It was in the eighteenth century, too, that cod and herring fishing first became important to Orkney. These employments helped to keep people alive, but they prevented them from making full use of the land, which we now know is so rich and valuable.

In the kitchen the women worked at spinning and knitting, and, at a slightly later date, helped with the making of linen, for most of the clothes that people wore were made in their own homes or toonships. Men's jerseys and women's petticoats, for instance, were knitted at home; but the cloth for making into jackets, skirts, and trousers was manufactured by weavers, of which each parish had at least one, and sometimes two or three. The weavers occasionally built their own looms, and they worked very hard, but neither

---

1. Barley, specifically four- or six-row, hardier and coarser than ordinary two-row barley.

they nor the tailors were much thought of by the women of the parish, possibly because their crafts were considered to be too 'womanish' for a proper man.

THE BEGINNINGS OF MODERN ORKNEY

Although many interesting things happened to Orkney in the nineteenth century, the most important of them all was the change which took place in farming. Because the farmers were persuaded at last to try new methods, Orkney slowly became a county of green and fruitful fields. We owe so much to this revolution on the farms, to which is due the easier and pleasanter life we live today, that we ought to know how it took place. But before we read about the making of the new farms, we must look at what was happening at the beginning of the nineteenth century.

The wars with France

Agriculture was then poorly understood in Orkney. We have seen how badly the land was cultivated, and how people neglected their farms for kelp-burning and fishing. But it was not always of their own choice that men left the land for other jobs. Because Britain was at war with France men were required for the navy. Hundreds of Orkneymen served in Nelson's ships, some of them playing their part in great sea battles like Trafalgar. A proportion of these men may have volunteered to serve, but others had been caught and forced to enlist by the press gang.

It was the press gang's task to capture men for the fleet. Because it was difficult to persuade men to accept the sometimes brutal conditions at sea they had to be taken by force. Whenever constables were active in the districts pressing men to meet a quota imposed on the county, or a recruiting party was active, nearly every able-bodied man in Orkney found himself a hiding-place, perhaps in a cave, or in a hole below the floor, or in a hollowed-out peat stack. There were many exciting chases, and some clever escapes, but a lot of men were captured.

Each spring as many as fifty whaling ships came to Stromness, where they engaged hundreds of Orkneymen to go north to Greenland and Davis Strait as seamen and harpooners. Other men went to Canada with the Hudson's Bay Company to become labourers and fishermen and traders. These men were called *nor-wasters*, and although many of them came home after five or ten years a considerable number settled down in Canada. They sent orders to Stromness for much of the clothing, tools, and other articles they needed; and that town, which had by now grown a good deal bigger, was getting prosperous through trading and provisioning ships.

The need for improvement

With two thousand men, or perhaps even more, working or serving outside Orkney when they ought to have been at home cultivating their farms, things were in a sorry state. Many a little farm had no man on it to do the work, so women did ploughing, harrowing, and sowing as best they could. Where there were big properties the landlords tried to keep the men at home; but the cultivation of areas composed of very small properties for a time grew even worse than before. Folk often had to live on the money that their sons and daughters could manage to send them.

The only people who could help Orkney were the owners of large estates, of whom there were not a great number, for nearly three-quarters of Orkney was swallowed up in a dozen or so big estates. The most important of these properties was that which had once been the earldom estate, but which now belonged to Lord Dundas. Most of the tenants to whom the farms on the larger estates were let were content to carry on in the old-fashioned way, for they had neither the capital to bring about reforms nor leases of long enough duration to ensure that they would benefit from their labours. As for the landlords, they had other interests; and while trading, fishing, and kelp-burning helped to keep up their revenues it was hardly to be expected that they would tackle the very difficult task of turning the Orkney lands, divided into thousands of tiny patches by the old system, into modern farms. The people of Orkney were against this. Landlords who tried to reform their estates were sadly disliked.

The first steps

Nevertheless, even before the nineteenth century, small experiments in modern farming had been tried. Around 1760 one or two Kirkwall merchants became the owners of lands in Stronsay, which they tried to improve with a good measure of success. Before the end of the eighteenth century Stronsay had an agricultural society, the first in Orkney. In other islands—particularly in Burray, at the Bu—improved methods were being introduced. It was in the 1760s also that an attempt was made to destroy the runrig system, and to divide the land into fields; but the fields were so tiny, and still so intermingled, that little good came of it.

It may be that the wars in which Britain was engaged during the latter part of the eighteenth century, and the first decade or two of the nineteenth, impeded farming; for they made fishing in safe Orkney waters important, and increased the value of kelp, which rose from 45s a ton to £20 a ton. When peace came after Waterloo things began to change. In less than fifteen years kelp became almost unsaleable. Orkney's linen and straw-plait industries were in decline. Men came back from the navy looking for work. There was nothing left but the land.

New methods and ideas

Things were not easy for the landlords, many of whom had been brought to the brink of ruin by the depression in trade which followed the war, and by the failure of the kelp industry. But their only option was to improve their estates or give them up. Almost to a man they set to work, with new ideas from further south to guide them. A lead came from the owner of the earldom estate, who began to grant leases, and made his tenants follow a series of *Regulations*, which included a proper rotation of crops. Some proprietors had anticipated in a small way this example, others now began to follow it. They were helped by a series of *plankings*[1] (dividing the land into fields) which began in the 1830s, and which continued for the next thirty years. The fields were now of reasonable size, out of which real farms could be made.

To bring the new farms into being many things had to be done. The proprietors had to divide the land into holdings of various sizes, with new buildings and enclosures. They had to remove people from impossibly small crofts in the way of the improvements and find them somewhere else to live. They had to choose tenants who were willing to farm in the modern way. They had to bring in new and better breeds of cattle, horses, and sheep. They had to replace old implements like hooks and flails with reaping machines and threshing mills, or at least persuade their tenants to do so. And, most unpopular of all, they had to get permission to divide up the common land, which everyone had used for their geese and sheep for generation after generation.

Not all the improvements could be made without hardship. Some landlords were kind, and went to much trouble to see that people were not left homeless and helpless. Others carried through their reforms with less humanity, leaving a reputation for severity which is still remembered in the Orkney parishes. On the whole they relied on example. They engaged experienced farmers from the south to be the managers of their home farms, and brought others to Orkney as tenants. Although this policy was resented, its wisdom gradually became clear. It is obvious now that the rents were too high; and people living in poverty were angered when they saw fine new mansions going up on the big estates. Although landlords had to pay heavy duties, the worst of which was known as *superior duty*,[2] they doubtless passed on a proportion of the burden to their tenants.

1. See also 'The lore of harvest', p.21.
2. Feu-duty. The annual payment made to a superior. In Orkney it was another name for skatt.

5 Singling turnips, Papdale, near Kirkwall, *c*.1900

6 Oxen yoked to an iron plough, *c*.1890

When the new farms were made a lot of people were elbowed out. It was customary for these to be given twenty or thirty acres of waste land, which they cultivated with great toil, working early and late to reclaim their land. They made drains and built houses, creating from almost nothing the fertile little crofts which sprang up around the older farms.

It is astonishing how quickly agriculture began to flourish once the improvements were well under way. Owing to conflicting estimates we are unable to say quite how much arable land there was in Orkney when the improvements began, but there was at least two and a half times as much by the end of the century. The new breeds of cattle were far more valuable. By 1866 they sold for twice as much as they had in 1850, and four times as many were exported. The rise in the export of sheep was greater still. But the hen outstripped all competitors: from a hundred thousand dozen eggs sent out of Orkney in 1833 the figure mounted to one and a half million dozen by 1895. With the prosperity of the land increasing so quickly more people stayed at home; and this, with better conditions of health, brought the population of the islands to over 32,000 in 1861.[1]

The crofters' charter

Well before the end of the nineteenth century, Orcadians, apart from unfortunate people here and there, may be said to have achieved freedom from want. But there were other freedoms which, like people elsewhere in Britain, they were denied. We have noted that the land itself belonged largely to big proprietors. For the privilege of living on that land the ordinary small farmer or crofter had to pay dearly. He had to pay a rent, not necessarily in money but in grain, malt, butter, and so on; he often had to meet ancient taxes over and above his rent; and, in addition, he had to work at the busy periods of sowing, haymaking, and harvest on the landlord's own farms. Until 1889, when county councils came into being, the ordinary Orkneyman had little say in the running of the islands. The county's business was carried on by a body of people called Commissioners of Supply.[2] You could not be a Commissioner unless the yearly rental of the land you owned was over £100 Scots.[3] In practice these local rulers were the big landlords and their friends. We do not find that in the main they were tyrants, but we can understand what it felt like to be a crofter whose voice did not count for anything in Orkney affairs.

By far the greatest grievances of the crofters were the size of their rents

1. At the start of agricultural improvements in the 1760s the population of Orkney was approximately 23,500.
2. They were non-elected.
3. Scots currency was abolished by the Act of Union in 1707. It had lessened in value in the sixteenth and seventeenth centuries, and by 1700 the Scots pound was worth 1/12th of its English counterpart.

and the fact that they could be turned out of their homes when the landlord wished. They could never feel secure. There were many hundreds of such people in Orkney. On some estates they were treated honourably, but on a few the threat of eviction was always hanging over their heads. This applied to crofters in other parts of Scotland as well. It had been felt for a long time that the whole system was unfair and that the crofters should be protected by law. Many years passed before Parliament was willing to take action, but at last it came, with the Crofters Holdings (Scotland) Act of 1886. This for the rank and file of the Orkney people was probably the greatest event of the century: the Act has been called 'The Crofters' Magna Carta'.

From now on—those who framed the Act were saying—crofters must have fair rents and conditions, and they must be secure from eviction. In 1888 the persons appointed as the Crofters Commission came to Orkney to see that the changes which were necessary were carried out. Their coming had been eagerly awaited. They sat for the first time in Stromness Town Hall on the 14th of August. The hall was full, and the windows had to be opened so that people outside could hear. An Orkney lawyer, Mr Thomson, made a fine and moving speech on the crofters' behalf, then the business began. From the Mainland the Commission went to the islands. Day by day crofters were interviewed and their grievances heard. Most landlords acted with fairness and dignity when they were questioned. But the plight of the crofters had not been exaggerated; rents were greatly reduced, and much of the arrears of rent due to the landlords was cancelled altogether.

The time had come when the crofters of Orkney could regard their little holdings as homes in which they could live securely, and which their children could inherit. This meant, however, that the landlords were sometimes badly affected, especially if their incomes came mainly from their estates. These two factors, the increased security of the crofters and the growing insecurity of the landlords, between them set the stage for many of the great changes of the twentieth century.

2

Farming freuteries[1]

Never begin any task on a Friday. Never go to a new house on a Saturday— 'A Setterday flitting is a short sitting'.

Kirning

Before attempting to churn the milk, the guidwife would often place a cabbage leaf and a sixpence under the kirn. This was to prevent the hill-trows[2] from 'taking the profit'.[3] It was also important that an *erison*[4] should be said when churning, and a hand waved over the kirn to collect the butter. If butter refused to appear, it was considered necessary to drop a silver coin into the kirn.

Cow calving

Within living memory[5] a fire was lighted in a byre in the Velzian district of Sandwick when a cow was calving. This was to keep the 'peerie folk' away.[6] In Eday, when a cow dropped calf, the guidwife would pluck a live firebrand from the hearth, bring it quickly into the byre, and throw it several times to and fro over the cow's back, saying each time she did so 'Guid[7] be aboot thee'. The reason given was that the procedure 'scared the de'il', and prevented him from doing harm to cow or calf.

1. Also frooterys—superstitious beliefs, notions or customs.
2. For more information on trows, see 'Creatures of Orkney legend and their Norse ancestry', p.257.
3. Concerning 'taking the profit' by witches, see 'Northern Witches', pp.353-355 and Marwick's *The Folklore of Orkney and Shetland*, 1975, pp.51-52. Information on 'taking the profit of cattle' can be found in *The Old Lore Miscellany of Orkney, Shetland, Caithness and Sutherland*, 1909, Volume II, pp.133-134.
4. A short prayer for help.
5. This article was written c.1960.
6. For other methods of protecting cattle, see 'Creatures of Orkney legend and their Norse ancestry', p.257 and 'Bonfire customs', p.139.
7. God.

THE DAY'S WORK—FARMING

Hatching-time

Certain people were regarded as lucky in the matter of setting a hen on eggs. Not so long ago, a Longhope woman was in great request by her neighbours at hatching time, when she went from croft to croft performing the rite of arranging the eggs and placing the broody hen on them. The following incantation was sometimes said:

> I set me hen on fifteen eggs;
> Grace and luck atween her legs

For some reason, quite apart from the fact that it was rather late in the year, it was considered unlucky to set a hen at Beltane (the first day of May O.S.).[1] People said that if a hen was set 'between the Beltanes'[2] the chickens would be 'noathin' bit a lok o' June yappicks'.[3]

Before ploughing

Before the old-fashioned single-stilted plough[4] was put into the ground in spring, it was smeared with urine, as was also the plough harness. This was known as *straikan graith*,[5] and the practice was considered to be essential so that the field to be ploughed might be fruitful. To the plough was attached, by a horse-hair cord, a thin round disc of stone with a hole near one edge.

1. The Julian calendar, known as Old Style, treated all the centennial years as Leap Years. Towards the close of the sixteenth century there was a difference of ten days between the tropical and calendar years. In 1582 Pope Gregory adjusted the calendar by eliminating these ten days and ordained that henceforward every fourth year should be a Leap Year. The Gregorian calendar, called New Style, was adopted by Great Britain in 1752 when the difference between the Old and the New Style calendar was 11 days. This became 12 days after 1800 and has been 13 days since 1900.
    In many parts of Orkney until the First World War and even later the Julian calendar was observed, particularly in North Ronaldsay where it lingered on until the 1930s. It still survives in Foula, Shetland.
2. Perhaps this meant the days between Beltane O.S. and N.S.
3. Yappie—the sea term in fishermen's language for a hen. Jappie—to pipe, to cheep. Literally and in a derogative sense, 'nothing but a lot of June cheepers', i.e. hatching too late in the year to be productive. In certain districts they were referred to as June yalpies or naevelies. It is possible that the word comes from Yap—hungry.
4. It was little more than an ox or horse drawn digging stick controlled by a single handle, described thus by Shirreff in *General View of the Agriculture of the Orkney Islands*, 1814, p.51: 'The old Orkney plough, still too much used, has only one stilt . . . and the ploughman, when at work, leans his weight against one side of the plough.' p.60: '. . . an imperfect implement . . . without a mould board, by which the ground is rather pushed aside than turned over.' Later models had iron tipped shares, but broken parts of stone shares from older times may still occasionally be found in the land. Some of these old Orkney wooden ploughs were said to be in use in Rackwick, Hoy, in the 1880s—Tudor, *The Orkneys and Shetland*, 1883, p.95. See also a discussion paper *The Old Roman Plough* by George Marwick, read at Dounby on 8 October 1903.
5. Stale urine.

This stone, known as the *dian-stane*,[1] was obviously a sun symbol. It was hung from the plough-beam, and when the plough was turned at the end of a field it was moved across the beam to the sunny side. When not in use on the plough the *dian-stane* was hung from a nail projecting from the cottage wall, in full sunlight. The crofter, when going to sea, would hang it round his neck, in the hope of getting a good catch of fish.

A lucky scythe

If you fixed the grass-hook of your scythe to the handle with a horse-shoe nail, the scythe would be a lucky one.

Importance of numbers

A farmer liked to have the stock in his byre add up to an even number. It was not considered fortunate to have an odd number of animals, and the number 13 must be avoided at all costs, even if this meant buying or selling an animal.

On the other hand, horsemen invariably used odd numbers in their operations. For instance, when the plough rein was done up the procedure was 'seven hanks, then three wips, wi' a loop'.

1. Further information on the dian-stane can be found in Marwick's *The Folklore of Orkney and Shetland*, 1975, p.65.

3

The horseman's word

One of the best-kept secrets in rural Scotland was the 'horseman's word'. If you knew it you could do anything you liked with horses. Just whisper it in an awkward animal's ear—or so people said—and it became as docile as a kitten.

The mystery which surrounded this word (supposed to be a very shocking one) made the youthful farm servant avid for initiation. He would part with a considerable portion of his half-year's fee to learn it.[1] For a while he might be tantalized by hints and whispers, but sooner or later he would be offered, under a desperate oath of secrecy, the chance to become a member of the brotherhood.

For there was undoubtedly an actual secret society bearing the name of the Horseman's Word, just as there was another known as the Miller's Word. Such societies can sometimes be traced back to beliefs and observances that pre-date Christianity. But whatever its origin, the Horseman's Word once had the understandable function of passing on to the proper persons the distilled wisdom of generations of horsemen.

Like all the crafts, horsemanship had its jealously guarded secrets, not to be transferred to writing. If anyone divulged the slightest hint of them he was subjected to summary discipline. The discipline may have extended even further, for I have heard tales of farm lads being beaten up, although not members, just for casting ridicule on the society.

One should not, perhaps, speak of the society in the past tense, for there is some evidence that it still exists,[2] though not now as an organisation with any practical function. Be that as it may, there are still in many districts old men who are pointed out as initiates of the robust fraternity that the Horseman's Word is presumed to have been in its heyday.

I have spoken to several of them. Some will let fall scraps of information, but most feign ignorance or offer the name of a more knowledgeable

---

1. One version of the word was 'Both in one'.
2. An initiation took place in the parish of Sandwick, Orkney in 1989.

7 Feeding the hens, c.1900

8 Washing the horses' legs, Saverock, St Ola, c.1900

informant. It appears, however, that the 'word' itself is not really shocking, indeed not uncommon.

'It's in any good English dictionary,' one man told me, and went on, 'The important thing to learn was not the word but the psychology of its application.' Most definitely, I thought, the society moves with the times: that sounded to me a very modern phrase for a purveyor of magic!

'What about initiation?' was a question I persisted in asking. In a fit of confidence a friend said to me, his face lighting up with pleasurable reminiscence, 'I'll never forget the night when we initiated So-and-so and So-and-so.' He mentioned the names of two men whom I knew, and a place only a stone's throw from where I used to live. At the period of which he spoke I had never heard of the society, yet initiations were going on right under my nose. Usually the place chosen was as remote as possible from human dwellings. An old barn on a farm called Instabilie, near Scapa Flow, Orkney, was much used last century for initiations.

It is agreed that what happened was this—when the 'horsemen' consented to receive a new member, he was brought to them by one of their number prepared to act as his sponsor. Others made the necessary arrangements at the barn, which included sealing windows and every aperture about the building with divots and old sacks.

The initiation ceremony invariably took place in winter, and generally at midnight. At that hour, the whole brotherhood being assembled, the candidate arrived with his friend. They were met by 'guards', armed with flail handles, who demanded the necessary password. The candidate had to bring with him a loaf of bread and a bottle of whisky. This contribution was in addition to his initiation fee, which might be anything from five to 20 shillings.

The ceremony began with what was perhaps an unconscious travesty of older rites. The candidate was blindfolded. In an atmosphere as eerie as the 'horsemen' could contrive, sulphur was burned and plough chains clanked. Then the candidate was invited to shake hands with the Devil. As he extended his hand he grasped the cloven foot of an ox.[1] It was only when his nerve had been tested by such antics that he was instructed into the secrets of horsemanship. After the candidate had taken a solemn oath to bind him to secrecy, the whisky and bread were partaken. Whether they once had a ritual significance no one can say, but their presence was considered to be essential.

The actual value of the 'word' itself is difficult to determine, but recently I met a man who had seen it in action. His father had known it, but had always insisted that it was a secret. My informant went on to say, 'My father never actually forbade me to join the society, but I could see that he would be happier

---

1. The Devil's 'hand' could be a stick covered with a hairy skin, a rabbit's paw or a sheep's foot.

if I didn't. I remember that we once had a mare of uncertain temper, who used to fly at strangers if they crossed the field where she happened to be. One Sunday as we came home from church my father said, "We'll take the horses to the stable with us." He opened the gate, but the mare didn't know him in his Sunday clothes, and she came running at him fiercely. We never knew what he said, but in a moment the mare was rolling happily on her back on the grass. She got up and followed the other horses like a lamb. My father bluntly refused to tell us what had happened.'

* * *

Editor's Note

Members of the Horseman's Society have a distinctive handshake. The Society exists throughout Scotland and the form of oath is the same everywhere, with minor local variations. The oath used in Orkney is:

> I do now and ever swear before the Almighty God and all these witnesses that I shall always heal, conceal, and never reveal any part of the secret of horsemanship which is about to be revealed to me this night.
>
> Furthermore, I solemnly vow and swear that I will neither write it nor indite it, cut it nor carve it, nor engrave it on wood, sand, or snow, parchment, stone, brick, tile, clay, or anything movable under the whole canopy of Heaven, nor yet so much as wave one single letter with a finger in the air from which anything may become known therefrom.
>
> Furthermore, I vow and swear that I will never give it nor see it given to a tradesman of any kind except to a blacksmith or a veterinary surgeon or a horsesoldier. Likewise I shall never give it, nor see it given to a farmer or farmer's son, unless he be working his own or his father's horses.
>
> Furthermore, I will never give it or see it given to a fool or a madman, nor to a drunkard; nor to any man that would abuse his own or his master's horse with it; nor to anyone below the age of eighteen or above the age of forty-five; nor to my father, mother, sister or brother, wife nor witch; nor to any womankind.
>
> Furthermore, I will never give it or see it given to anyone after sunset on Saturday night nor before sunrise on Monday morning.
>
> Furthermore, I will neither abuse nor bad use any man's horses with it and if I see a brother do so I will tell him of his fault. Furthermore, I will never advise anyone to get it nor disadvise anyone from getting it but leave everyone to his own free will and accord.
>
> Furthermore, I will never see it given nor give it for less than £1 sterling, a loaf and a bottle of whisky and I will never see it given nor will give it unless there be three or more lawful sworn brethren present after finding them to be so by trying and examining them.
>
> Furthermore, I will never refuse to attend a meeting if warned within three days except in exceptional cases such as a house on fire, riding for a doctor, or a woman in travail.
>
> If I fail to keep these promises may my flesh be torn to pieces with a wild horse and my heart cut through with a horseman's knife and my bones buried on the sands of the seashore where the tide ebbs and flows every twenty-four hours so that there may be no remembrance of me amongst lawful brethren. So help me God to keep these promises.
>
> AMEN

4

The lore of harvest

It seems worth while, before our cereal harvest is merely a memory, to place on record some of its lore. In the old agriculture of Orkney, oats and bere followed each other in regular unbroken succession. The yield of grain so far north was never heavy, but the islands became famous for their bright acres of corn. The word corn, however, was applied specifically to bere—or bygg, as it was known earlier. Bygg is still the name given to barley in Norway, and I am told that, in some districts at least, it is referred to as *korn* in the same way as in Orkney.

The ale of James III's wedding feast was made with corn from the islands he had acquired with his bride. A sender of secret intelligence from Orkney in the mid-sixteenth century described the islands as 'the chief Nourishers and storers of the southland with Corne, victell and oil.' Grain went to Norway and the Baltic as well as to Scotland. Between April and July 1743, 2,414 quarters of bere were exported to Norway. In 1799, a record year, 8,835 bolls of bere were exported through Kirkwall to various destinations. Oats were exported mainly in the form of oatmeal: in the twenty years between 1780 and 1800 only four bolls of oats were exported as whole grain. Bere has been the staff of life in Orkney—in the form of bere bannocks and ale—from time immemorial. On pottery found in Unstan Cairn, perhaps 4,000 years old, Dr Hans Helbaek found impressions of ears of bere. It is not that oats were despised, or that they did not also have a long ancestry. As a Shetland poem by T. A. Robertson has it:

> A'm da aets, an I hae peerie bells:
> Mair as twinty ower da rip hings doon.
> Da crofter pat me ida grund fir maet—
> Göd bliss him, honest man, an sae his toon.[1]

---

1. I am the oats, and I have little bells:
   More than twenty over the oat head hangs down.
   The crofter put me into the ground for food—
   God bless him, honest man, and also his township.

In a legendary way Orkney farmers remembered that the Picts had most probably tilled their land long before the Norsemen came: they called a certain kind of wild oats 'Pickie aets'. Oatmeal was known in the sixteenth century as 'twice shelled meal'. It sold at £6 Scots[1] for a last, which was roughly 28½ hundredweights. Thomas Jamieson carried to Norway from Orkney in 1727 'one hundred and sixtie baggs or pocks of oatmeall each containing one hundred and eight pound Amsterdam weight.'

Basically, the technique in the harvest field remained much the same through the centuries, until the arrival of the mechanical reaper. The sickle (with the plough, one of the oldest farming tools) was known in Orkney as the 'heuk'. When cutting the crop with this, the shearer grasped a handful below the ears, severed it near the ground with a short sweep of the heuk, and laid it, handful by handful, on a band that a partner in the rig, often a child, had provided. Another method of cutting, described by James Omond,[2] was to swing the hook backward and slash forwards, as if one were using a scythe, 'the cut oats being gathered up on the arm, and when as much as could be conveniently lifted was cut, it was, with the help of the hook encircling it, lifted and turned over the arm on to the band.' This was called back-hand cutting. Sheaves were fairly thick and rather short, for the crop on the frequently impoverished rigs[3] did not grow tall, as in our day. It was the custom to spread out the end of the sheaf so that it could stand up by itself. Thus fields looked a little different, containing rows of single sheaves rather than stooks.

While the run-rig[4] system remained, the tiny strips of land in a toonship were so intermingled that it would have been easy for a dishonest farmer to place someone else's sheaves among his own. Even a high wind at the end of the cutting could have mixed them. To distinguish each farmer's crop, the bands of the sheaves were made, or tied, in a number of different ways.[5] By this means theft could be traced. Alister Watsone, of Grimness, South Ronaldsay, was convicted in October 1615 of 'the thifteous steilling of xviii sheaves of corne of uther menis bind pertening to his nychtbouris, quhilk wes fund in his skrow.'

1. Ten shillings sterling. Scots currency was abolished by the Act of Union in 1707. It had lessened in value in the sixteenth and seventeenth centuries, and by 1700 the Scots pound was worth 1/12th of its English counterpart.
2. *Orkney 80 Years Ago*, published in *The Orcadian* 8 April and 19 May 1911, recorded many facets of Orkney life in the 1830s. It was also published in booklet form.
3. For information on rigs, see 'Farming in Orkney during the last two centuries', p.6.
4. This was a communal system of land organisation with scattered, narrow strips of cultivated land shared among tenants, each getting a share of the good and the poor land. Run-rig holdings often became small, numerous and confused.
5. In 1988 differing bands were still being used in North Ronaldsay.

Apparently further precautions were considered necessary in some places, where old women or fatherless boys were detailed to watch that a farmer neither took bands out of his neighbour's crop nor encroached too far on the 'fur corn' that lay between their rigs. These watchers were called 'mullyos'. As a reward they were allowed to take the gleanings, also known as mullyos.

An old custom, common in the northern counties and probably in other parts of Scotland, was to 'cast the heuks' after the last rig was cut. One of the harvesters took hold of the heuks by their points and cast them one by one backwards over his shoulder. The direction in which a heuk pointed was thought to indicate in which direction its owner, often a servant, would next take up his abode. If a hook stuck with its point in the ground, the person to whom it belonged was certain to die, it was thought, before the next harvest.

Scythes began to replace heuks in Orkney in the early decades of the nineteenth century. We have a more definite date for the parish of Evie, where scythes were introduced in the late 1840s and had almost entirely superseded the heuk by 1856. The old-fashioned Orkney scythe was called a 'beyou'. It had a short broad blade, which, according to John Spence of Evrabist, was made at home by Orcadian smiths and tempered in a peat fire. Its main use was for cutting meadow hay. In most places it was really the modern scythe that followed the heuk.

On the bigger fields which followed the 'plankings'[1] of the 1830s and thereafter, the scythe could be used to good effect. Three, or even four scythes, might be engaged on a big field. Each man would have a woman partner to gather the cut corn and lay it on a band. Behind her might come someone to bind the sheaves and stook them. But a few women were so strong and agile that they would carry out the whole operation of gathering, binding and stooking themselves. When there were a number of couples at work on a field, 'kemping'—in other words, a struggle to see which couple could do the greatest amount of work—added to the fun, and was no doubt encouraged by the guidman of the farm.

Kemping between farms was also common in the days of heuk cutting. It got so intense at times that when a Sunday came in the middle of a period of clear moonlight people would secretly sharpen their heuks during the forbidden hours of the Sabbath, then, as soon as the clock struck midnight, hurry to the rig to continue cutting.

The daily wages for harvest hands at the end of the eighteenth century were, for women, 'sixpence a day besides three diets and plenty of drink.' A man might get rather more. One worker at Skaill (Sandwick) demanded to

---

1. A method of reallocating and dividing land into compact plots which swept away the old run-rig system. The usual Orkney plank was forty fathoms square: 6,400 square yards. From Old French *planche*, a measurement of land. See also 'Farming in Orkney during the last two centuries', p.10.

be 'well maintained in harvest, when cut off (finished reaping) a Shiling.' In the 1850s a man got £1 for a whole harvest.

A few of the words used in harvest came directly from the old Norwegian farmers. 'Bedded', to describe a lodged crop, was probably derived from Old Norse *bada*, which means to crush down. An 'oon' (from Nor. *ône*) could mean a scythe-cut's breadth (swathe), or the company of three who took a rig before them when shearing with hooks. 'Skare', applied even today to a swathe mown with a scythe, is the Old Norse *skári*. The word 'aff-shaering', the cutting-off, is practically the same as the modern Norwegian *avskjaering*. 'Rip', meaning a single straw complete with the head of grain, is related to *ripe*, a cluster of seed. The word 'diss', applied to a small stack of sheaves, could well come from *des*, used in Iceland in old times for a stack. 'Skroo', a corn-rick, is derived from the Old Norse *skrúfr*.

Reaping machines came to Orkney comparatively early. There were such machines at Huip and Holland, Stronsay, at Greentoft, Eday, and at (probably) Balfour Mains, Shapinsay, in 1861. In a three- or four-year period around 1872 something like 300 reapers were brought into the county. 'Wood's Mowing and Reaping Machine' was by far the most popular. The self-binder was introduced around 1890.

Customs of many kinds became linked with the period of harvest. In Sandwick, in the late 1850s, 'sheaf-getting' was still fairly common. When a man was about to begin farming on his own account, he visited his neighbours at harvest-time and received from each a gift of sheaves, which he could thresh, and so get seed for his first crop. Such a man was known as a 'sheaf-getter'.

More tenacious than any other tradition was that of the 'last sheaf' and 'last load'. The old veneration of the last sheaf, in which the spirit of the corn was thought to reside, or which embodied that spirit, was replaced by customs which only reflected it vaguely or which degenerated into horse-play sanctioned by tradition. Corn dollies were not known in Orkney, but a straw dog called a 'bikko'[1] was made from the last of the straw to be cut, and this would be hoisted in a prominent position in the stackyard or on one of the farm buildings.

Norwegian customs which may possibly have some relationship to this one are that of setting up a corn sheaf on the roof at Yule, to preserve the farm from the trolls (corn being regarded as holy), and that of making, during the cutting of the crop, goats out of the corn ears, which were hung up in the loft until Yule and then given to the goat kids. The latter custom was recorded in Saetesdal. In some parts of Scotland, although not in Orkney as far as can be ascertained, the last sheaf was kept until Christmas and then divided among the cattle so that they would 'thrive all the year round.'

1. Old Norse—*bikkja*, a bitch.

In Orkney the significance of the straw dog was gradually forgotten, until it became merely a means of annoying the man who was the last in the parish to finish his harvesting. I saw one once, around forty years ago, set up on the chimney of a farm which still had crop in the field when everyone else had it snugly built in the stackyard. This was a considerable insult, which was greatly resented. It has been stated that the 'strae bikko' was often tied on behind the cart of the man who brought in the last load of sheaves, and this may well be true. In Sanday this man, known as 'Drilty in the yard slap' (the man who came dragging along to the stackyard gate), was presented with the 'dog'. It happened in Rousay that a straw man, stuffed into old clothes like a scarecrow, was sometimes left at the home of the last person to 'cut off'. On one occasion last century the guidman o' Langskaill, who had a small piece of crop to cut when the others had finished (although he was usually one of the foremost farmers in the island), found such a straw man sitting on the seat of his reaping machine.

Traditions were sometimes run together in confusing ways. Another harvest custom was to bake and eat a bannock made from meal from the last sheaf. The original idea must have been that one was thus eating the 'corn spirit', and gaining in vigour and fruitfulness from doing so. In Gairsay until well into the second decade of the present century the traditions of the harvest bannock and the man with the last load were still remembered but had merged in an odd way. What happened was this: the man who brought the final load from field to stackyard was seized by his fellow workers, his bottom was bared, and then scrubbed vigorously with the rough butt end of a sheaf. Meanwhile, the master of the house went to the kitchen for a bannock which the women had baked from flour, melted butter and fruit. He brought this to the stackyard, and, taking aside the victim of the just-mentioned indignity, walked with him twenty to twenty-five paces from the other workers, then handed him the bannock and ordered him to run. Everyone set out in pursuit. If the man with the bannock outdistanced his pursuers, he was able to sit down and eat it in peace, but if they caught up with him they seized the bannock and devoured it among them, allowing the victim none of it.

An interesting variation of this odd procedure was carried out in Westray. There, when the last load of sheaves went through the stackyard gate, a sheaf was pulled out and laid in the gateway. This sheaf was known as 'Shytie in the gate.' The man who had brought in the final load immediately ran to the highest stack in the yard and tried to climb to the top. If he was caught by the other men before he reached it they pulled down his trousers and smeared his bottom with treacle. If, however, he got to the top in safety he was presented by his master with a harvest bannock (made from oatmeal) and a bottle of ale.

There is a significant passage in Omond: 'It is said that such was the poverty in some parts of Orkney that in harvest the breakfast was taken off the harvest field in the morning. Some sheaves of bere were taken into the barn, threshed with the flails, hammelled, and the corn dried in a big iron three-taed pot hung over the kitchen fire. It was then ground on the quern, sifted, and the meal made into porridge for breakfast.'[1]

No doubt poverty made such things necessary, but there may also have been a memory of the meal bannock made from the last of the grain to be cut. In Westray it was actually the first sheaf of the harvest which provided the grain for what in ancient times must have been a ritual meal. The grain from this sheaf was pounded in the knocking stone, and probably made into brose.

Sister Margaret Manson Graham[2] of Calabar, who belonged to Orphir, was once asked, as she sat quietly on the balcony of the governor's house after having acted as hostess at an important official dinner, what she was thinking about. She said: 'I was remembering coming home with the other children from school, and my mother saying, "Bairns, I have a treat for you." It was the first oatmeal of the season, and we ate it raw, and thought how good it was.'

In Rousay it is remembered that, until the early part of this century, a little triangular corner of the last field to be cut was left for 'the birds of the air.' I have placed the phrase in quotes, for it was one that people liked to use in this context. Sometimes a larger corner of a poor field with thin short oats would be left.

The last of the corn to be cut was used also in ways other than those described. A girl might take a handful of it to put under her pillow, in the belief that she would dream about her husband to be. Possibly also, harvest knots originated in straw taken from the last sheaf which was made into some kind of emblem representing the spirit of the corn. It is true that our traditional memory of their significance does not go so far back as this, and that in more modern times they were exchanged in much the same way as true lovers' knots. The only unusual custom attached to them in Orkney was this: if one of these 'hairst[3] roses', as they were called, was placed by one of the workers on the toe of the master's boot, the master was bound to provide the harvesters with a bottle of whisky. There are indications that the harvest knot was regarded in some places as a fertility symbol, but it is very difficult to discover its significance, for the few local people who know consider that it had a lewd connotation and are unwilling to divulge it.

1. *Orkney 80 Years Ago*, pp.21-22.
2. Born in Orphir in 1860 she devoted her life to nursing and missionary work in Nigeria, where she died in 1933.
3. Harvest.

At the end of harvest came the harvest feast. The name 'muckle supper' was given to it in Orkney, but apparently not in Scotland generally. 'Muckle' is taken to mean big, generous, plenteous, as applied to such an occasion, but it occurs to me that just possibly it was at one time the feast of Michael (Nor. *Mikkel*), which was celebrated on 29 September (or 12 October Old Style). In Sondmor, Norway, it was recorded in the eighteenth century that up to fifty years previously the head of a household would kill a sheep at Michaelmas (Old Style)[1] and share it very secretly with his workers without letting them make any reference to it. In Norway generally, Michaelmas Day was usually celebrated with a great feast for the servants. In Orkney, in olden times, a sheep was often killed for the muckle supper, and this was the feast to which all the workers were invited and the one at which they felt most at home. The correspondences I have noted may be illusory, but they seem worth placing on record in case some researcher with more knowledge should care to comment on them.

The muckle supper was a kind of family feast for workers, friends and neighbours in a sense in which the harvest home which succeeded it is not. A county harvest home was a far greater innovation than it seems to us today. The late Mr J. G. S. Flett once told me about a Birsay farmer of seventy or so who was so intrigued by descriptions of the Harvest Home at Kirkwall that he walked all the way from Birsay to see it, and, after it was over, walked home again.

1. Old Style—the Julian calendar. This was thirteen days later than the New Style (N.S.) Gregorian calendar. See also footnote 1, p.14.

5

The lore of plantikreus

There were once in every parish in Orkney, numbers of tiny walled enclosures known as *plantikreus*. Now, with only individual exceptions in islands like North Ronaldsay, they have disappeared. True, the name is still applied to small walled gardens situated some way from farm-house or farm-steading, by the sea or on the side of a hill: but these modern enclosures are usually larger than the old-fashioned plantikreu and have various functions, whereas the plantikreu proper only had one.

A plantikreu was used solely in the older Orkney economy for the raising of cabbage plants, which were transplanted in the spring to the more open kailyards or cabbage gardens. A traditional plantikreu was usually built in the form of a circle or round-cornered square, its walls—constructed of boulders from the beach or turf from the moor—being continuous with no break in them for a gate. The means of access to the interior were projecting stones, forming a rough stile. It might appear that anything so simple as an enclosure for growing cabbage plants could be accepted without comment; and so it has been, for there is no literature so far as I am aware on plantikreus, and scarcely a mention of them in the scores of Orkney books which have been published in the past two centuries. Yet, as I found recently when I began to ask questions about them, plantikreus have a curious lore of their own which is not without interest.

Their very name is tantalising. The old language of Orkney was a Norse dialect. *Plante* in Norwegian signifies a plant or herb, and *kreu* could mean either a pen or small enclosure. There is no evidence to suggest that plantikreus as such go back to the Norse period in the islands, although similar, but larger, enclosures were no doubt used for sheep from very early times. It is possible that when cabbage first came to Orkney it was raised in these sheep kreus.

When cabbage was actually introduced to the islands is a matter of conjecture. Earl Robert Stewart's late sixteenth-century palace at Birsay had a kailyard, as an old drawing testifies. James Wallace in his *A Description of the Isles of Orkney*, 1693 included cabbage among the vegetables which 'grow to a greater bigness here then [sic] I have seen them else where'.[1] In both Orkney and Shetland there exists the belief that Cromwell's soldiers[2] taught the people how to cultivate cabbage; the Shetlanders say specifically that the Englishmen initiated the sowing of the seed in plantikreus. It is difficult to decide how much credence, if any, can be given to this tradition.

Undoubtedly the Scots brought with them their 'kail', but there is a strong local tradition that the typical Orkney cabbage was first grown from seed obtained from Dutch fishing vessels. Some colour is given to the legend by the fact that the Orkney cabbage, which still persists in one or two districts where the seed has been preserved year after year for domestic use, is very like a Dutch winter cabbage: it is flat-polled, and the outer leaves are a harsh bluish-green, with pronounced veining; there is usually a touch of purple on the back of the leaf. So general was the dark-coloured cabbage that the appearance of a white or light-coloured cabbage stock among the others was regarded as a sign of certain death for someone in the household.

Orkney cabbages (always known locally as *kail*, as in Scotland generally) were credited with being very bitter, although the type of soil and the manure applied might account for this. Rabbits seemed to dislike them and seldom touched them. They were never considered to be fit to eat until they had been 'frosted'. In some places the Orkney variety was superseded first by 'Irish' cabbage and later by Drumheads. After the introduction of more palatable sorts, the original Orkney cabbage was occasionally referred to as *kye-kail*.[3]

Cabbage may indeed have been Orkney's original vegetable. The word *plant*, as understood in the countryside, was used specifically of cabbage, which is practically the only vegetable to be mentioned in traditional sayings and proverbs. Meat was formerly so scarce in the islands that the ordinary crofter was almost of necessity a vegetarian.[4] Thus cabbage was not so much a supplement to a meat dish as an article of diet on its own. It was frequently boiled in the same pot as potatoes, the two being eaten together. Occasionally boiled cabbage, with the water squeezed out of it, was supped with milk. It was usual to *brudge*, or shred, the cabbage before boiling.

The preparation of the soil inside the plantikreu varied from district to district, although it was quite common to begin by carting soil to the chosen site and making this up to a height of 18 inches. Enclosures near a beach were manured with seaweed. Dung, either cow or poultry, was frequently used; but a method of sterilising the soil and enriching it at the same time is remembered in several parishes. A couple of cart-loads of rough fibrous peats, known

1. *A Description of the Isles of Orkney*, 1693, p.12.
2. Mid-seventeenth century.
3. Cabbage suitable for cattle.
4. For an indication of the extent to which Orcadians relied on vegetarian dishes, see 'An ABC of Orkney food', pp.103-113.

locally as *yarpha-peats*, were placed on the surface of the soil and set on fire. The heat and flames killed weeds and injurious grubs, while the ash served as a fertiliser. This procedure, I am assured, served excellently, for an excess of manure made the plants too big and flabby to stand the winter.

The cabbage seed was dried in little brown paper parcels which were hung from the kitchen rafters, and this home-grown seed was sown in the plantikreu during August. The seed was sown for the most part in the normal way, but some veteran gardeners had their own methods. An old gentleman in the island of Rousay says that the custom there was to put some seed in the mouth and then take a sip of *kirn-milk*.[1] Seed and milk was spluttered out together on the ground. The seed-bed was always trodden down firmly after sowing. When the first frost was feared straw was scattered over the plants to keep them safe until spring.

There were several reasons why these little cabbage gardens were in outlying places. They might be built on a spot where the earth was deep and rich, or where the frost did not lie too badly. They were also remote from turnip fields so that the one or two plants which were left in them to seed should not be subject to cross-pollination. The absence of a gate, and the circular or oval shape of the plantikreus, helped to defeat the winter gales, sometimes strong enough to loosen the plants seriously in an ordinary garden.

The kailyard proper was usually in front or immediately behind the dwelling-house. To this the young plants were transferred at some appropriate period in spring. The necessity of a separate enclosure for raising the plants will be appreciated when it is realised that, at the time of sowing seed in August, the kailyard itself was full of cabbage 'hearts'.

During the present century plantikreus fell into disuse. In most places people began to buy their young cabbage plants from farmers or gardeners. Where the enclosures survived they were often given over to rhubarb or, if they were fairly large, to potatoes and root vegetables. They were provided with gates and became simply walled gardens. With the increased cultivation of the moors, dozens of the outlying ones fell before the plough. The very few genuine plantikreus which survive are merely decaying symbols of a simple domestic economy long since superseded.

---

1. Butter-milk.

THE DAY'S WORK—*The Sea*

1	Some sea superstitions	31
2	Tales of island smugglers	36
3	Our local pirate	42
4	Orkney's other pirate	44
5	The predicament of the grey seal	46
6	The first North Isles steamer	50
7	Orkney's back door	55
8	The story of the Stromness life-boats 1867-1967	62
9	By Bottle Post	74
10	An odd fish	76

I

Some sea superstitions

The *Flying Dutchman*, the phantom ship whose appearance is usually followed by tragedy, is one of the most tenacious of maritime myths. She is usually seen in the southern hemisphere, but in 1911 the whaler *Orkney Belle*, which was then near Iceland, had to reduce speed to avoid a collision with a sailing vessel that seemed to have neither captain nor crew. It was no modern ship, this spectre, but an ancient vessel with a high poop and carved stern.

In 1881 the late King George V, then a midshipman on H.M.S. *Bacchante*, recorded a sighting of the *Flying Dutchman* near the Cape of Good Hope. He wrote in his diary: 'At 4 a.m. the *Flying Dutchman* crossed our bows. The look-out man in the forecastle reported her as close to the port bow, where also officer of the watch clearly saw her ... A strange red light, as of a phantom ship all aglow, in the midst of which light the masts, spars and sails of a brig 200 yards distant stood out in strong relief as she came up.' That morning at 10.45 the seaman who had first called attention to the ghost-ship fell to his death from *Bacchante*'s cross-trees.

Some such ship was seen by several people in Deerness in the 1880s. It was, wrote Edwin Muir in his autobiography, a great three-masted vessel which made straight for the shore on a clear moonlight night and then, before it struck the cliffs, as it seemed bound to do, 'melted into a black mist on the water.'

If a vessel like this was observed to sail over dry land, either in a day-time vision or in a night-time dream, some imminent disaster was expected.

One afternoon in the latter part of the nineteenth century a close relative called in great distress on James Spence of Eastbank, to say that her husband had gone out with dog and gun to shoot over Wideford Hill. After he left, while she was resting in her chair, and sitting in a semi-conscious state, she saw quite clearly a splendid ship, painted black and with dark sails, travelling over dry land. She became aware, to her horror, that among a knot of persons standing on the quarter-deck was her own husband, looking strange and shadowy. When she came to herself she was so frightened that she ran, trembling, with her story to Eastbank. In an attempt to reassure her a search-party was sent out, equipped with lanterns, for it was dark. Kirkwall people remembered for a long time the host of lights glimmering and swinging that gloomy night on the hillside. After about an hour the missing man was found. He was dead, and his dog, which had not left him, lay whimpering at his side.

A somewhat different premonition of tragedy accompanied the loss in 1852 of an old sailing boat known as *The Luggage Boat*, or more frequently as *The Coffin*. This boat, manned by two local men, 'the twa Tammies', for both were named Thomas, was a somewhat crazy vessel which carried goods between Kirkwall and the North Isles. One Monday morning *The Coffin* left Kirkwall in good weather on her usual run. The wife of one of the men, with two of her daughters and a couple of neighbours, was sitting in a room in Erskine Square (overlooking the grottie-hoose[1]) around mid-day, when a weird sound, like the flapping of the wings of a gigantic bird, was heard at the very door. The door was opened but nothing could be seen. Once again the sound was heard, but fainter than before.

Late in the afternoon the minister and an elder came to say that *The Coffin* had overturned in a sudden squall, and that both men had been drowned. The tragedy had been seen from the shore. It had occurred at precisely the time that the strange sounds had been heard in Erskine Square.

At least one phantom ship has been seen in Scapa Flow within living memory. An Orkneyman, who himself told me the story, was talking at Scapa Pier to the mate of the *St Angus*, a small ship used by the Admiralty contractors Balfour and Beatty. Both men were looking out over the water. From where they stood they could see the whole expanse of Scapa Flow. Quite suddenly my friend saw a white ship of large size. 'She just seemed to glide along as if she was skimming on the top of the water.' He withdrew his eyes for a second or two. When he looked again the ship had completely disappeared. He turned to the mate and remarked, 'I was watching a big white ship out there just a moment ago.' 'So was I, but she's no there noo.' The ship did not reappear. There was no island behind which she could have sailed and nothing to explain her disappearance.

It was at Scapa Flow in the First World War that the well-known writer, Sir Stephen King-Hall, had a very striking experience of precognition. One afternoon in 1916 he was officer of the watch in the *Southampton*, which was nearing Scapa Flow. A small island lay a mile or so ahead. The sea was perfectly smooth, but he suddenly knew with a strange certainty that as the *Southampton* and her following ships passed the island a man would fall overboard.

The nearer they came to the island the stronger grew this feeling. He felt that he must act on it, and gave a number of orders—to put the lifebelts out

---

1. A small summerhouse built c.1730 with undressed stone from the ballast of Gow's ship *Revenge*. It is located on the west side of St Catherine's Place.

9   A plantikreu on the island of Swona, 1966

10   A plantikreu, Birsay, 1987

11 This unusual summerhouse constructed from the ballast of Gow's ship *The Revenge* is located between St Catherine's Place and Bridge Street, Kirkwall. Erected *c.*1730 by Provost James Traill of Woodwick. Photograph, 1990.

and muster the sea-boat crew, and so on. These orders were immediately challenged by the Commodore.

King-Hall, who sent the story to J. B. Priestley for his book *Man and Time* (Aldus Books, 1964), thus continued his account: 'We were abreast of the island. I had no answer. We were steaming at 20 knots and we passed the little island in a few seconds. Nothing happened! As I was struggling to say something, the cry went up, "Man overboard" from the *Nottingham* (the next ship in the line, 100 yards behind us), then level with the island. 30 seconds later "Man overboard" from the *Birmingham* (the 3rd ship in the line, and then abreast the island). We went full speed astern; our sea-boat was in the water almost at once and we picked up both men. I was then able to explain to a startled bridge why I had behaved as I had done....'

★ ★ ★

Sea superstitions were once almost unbelievably various. It is a pity that so few are recorded. The sea is such an uncertain element, and in the days of sailing ships men were so much at its mercy, that harbingers of good fortune and portents of ill luck were much heeded.

Boats were never counted before they put to sea: if this was done one would not return. The old whaling skippers were most unwilling to leave port just after a bird had flown between the masts.

If a ship was experiencing ill-fortune, and it was discovered that some Jonah on board was the cause, the only way to change the luck was to draw a picture of him and burn it. Sometimes, if the luck was extremely bad, two or three pictures had to be burned.

No skipper liked to put to sea with clean-faced sailors: beardless men were sure to be chicken-hearted.

Besides buying winds from persuasive old women, sailors would attempt to get a breeze from the right direction by whistling for it or by sticking a jack-knife into the mast. If a wind was heard whistling by itself in the lee-rail, when everything else was calm, a real snorter would follow.

Fishermen had even more superstitions than blue-water sailors. No man wanted to put to sea if a rat, an orange-coloured cat, or a pig crossed his path. An occasional woman also had the power to bring ill, not necessarily through malice but through some unfortunate quality she possessed, and to see her when on the way to the shore was disastrous.[1]

---

1. There was a widely held belief that it was unlucky to have a minister aboard a boat, and on the way to the fishing ministers were avoided. They brought bad luck. In some ports it was undesirable for a minister to come between a fisherman and the sea. Even in recent times, on his daily walk in Stromness an old salt resolutely favoured the seaward side of the main street. He was never seen to walk on the north of the road, thus ensuring there was no gap into which a divine might stray.
  The aversion to ministers may have arisen from the fish teind or tithe payable to the Church. This was a tenth part of the catch.

The boat must always be launched sunwise.[1] If, when it was launched it was discovered that some necessary article—such as an oar or the pail of bait—had been left on shore and had to be retrieved, exceptionally poor fishing could be expected. Limpets for bait were knocked off the rocks with any thin piece of stone that fitted nicely into the hand. When the bait was gathered, the stone was flung violently against the rocks. If it broke into a large number of fragments the fishing would be good; if it remained intact, 'You need never wet a line.'

Cuithes (coal-fish) had to have 'three drinks o' the Mey fleud'[2] before the fishers went after them. When fish were slow to take, things would improve if the fisherman succeeded in hooking three fish. By doing so he managed to 'free the aald wife'. The most acceptable explanation of this superstition is that, having hooked three fish (representing the number and power of the Trinity) the fisher was freed *from* the influence of 'the aald wife', meaning the particular witch whose sorcery was spoiling the fishing.

If fish bones were burned, those who burned them would be unsuccessful at fishing. Two cautionary jingles were quoted:

> Röst me an' boil me, bit dinno burn me beens,
> An' I'll come an' lie at thee hert-steens.

> Bait me an' haal me an' cairry me heem,
> Boil me an' röst me, bit dinno burn me been.

Taboo words were used at sea for familiar objects. It was unlucky to use the everyday name. When Robert Rendall went to sea as a boy with some Birsay fishermen he chanced to remark, 'It'll be fine if we catch a halibut.' Old Tom, in charge of the boat, was indignant. 'I shall never forget the slow hard look he gave me: "Boy, ye'll no see one the day noo."'

A knife was called a 'ragger' at sea; a clergyman (an old Stromness man told me) was spoken of as 'the bonnyman'; he could also be called 'the upstanda'. The kirk was 'the bonnyhoose'. A rat was 'the cold-iron child'. In Orkney, all but half-a-dozen of the old taboo words are forgotten. To give a better idea of their number and variety a little-known Shetland list, compiled last century by Arthur Laurenson, may be substituted. I have arranged it in tabular form.

Death on a fishing boat also brought bad luck. In the late 1920s the doctor accompanying a gravely ill man from Hoy to Stromness was questioned closely before departure by the two fishermen manning the yawl. They were fearful of the patient dying during passage and anxious that he should not expire on their boat. If this seemed likely they would not countenance the use of their craft.

1. With the sun; in the direction of the daily movement of the sun; in the Northern Hemisphere this is from left to right.
2. Three of May's flood tides should have occurred; these high tides normally come early in the month.

Everyday Word	Fisherman's Substitute
dog	bænie, bænibider
cat	kirser, venga, foodin, voaler, fitting
swine	mudveeties
hen	yunsie
dog-fish	heckla
turbot	baldung
minister	upstanda, hoydeen, prestingolva
minister's house	matratla-stilhod
church	büanhoos, banehoos
buried dead in the churchyard	kirksucken
young man	ungadrengur
girl	pirraina
wife	hemma, kunie
old woman	runk
lover	yink
witch	trulla-scud
to bewitch	vamm
sun	soolen, faigr
fire	birtick, finnie, funa
chimney crook	fisting
fire brand	taand
the tongs	clivan
kettle	ringrody or ringlody
bed	koy
a boat	farr
mast	steng
oars	rems, remmacks
a rope's end	damp
knife	skunie
mittens	hanlicks
dawn	riv
thunder	tevrdin
eye	soyndick
eyes	glouricks, suntags
cheek	keedin
ear	yera

My main purpose in printing these stories, superstitions and list of sea-words is to show readers the kind of thing which may still be collected in our islands.

2

Tales of island smugglers

Adam Smith called smuggling 'a crime which nature never meant to be so.' These were strange words for the son of the comptroller of the customs at Kirkcaldy, but Smith's eighteenth-century contemporaries probably found them lukewarm, for in Scotland the smuggler was a hero to whom all felt obliged to give succour and assistance. To inform on a smuggler was popularly regarded as a contemptible action, besides being a dangerous one.

It was after the Treaty of Union[1] with England that smuggling became almost a way of life in Scotland. None of the laws passed by the United Parliament was more deeply resented than that which forbade tea, brandy or wine to be imported without payment of a government duty. The new revenue system was all the more disliked because it originated in England, and because the new commissioners of excise and customs were to a large extent Englishmen, as were many of their subordinate officers. It became almost a patriotic duty to outwit them; a duty recognised not only by the common people, farmers and lairds (who considered they were fighting an unjust law which put a premium on the small luxuries that brightened their bleak lives) but very frequently too by county magnates, justices and ministers. Sympathy with smugglers often resulted in fierce clashes with the authorities, and indeed provoked one of the most famous and violent incidents in Scottish history, involving the so-called Porteous Mob.[2]

Economic conditions in Scotland probably made smuggling seem more lucrative and worthwhile than it did in England. The solidarity of the people also made it infinitely safer. Practically every house would offer sanctuary to the hard-pressed 'free-trader'. Even the geography of the country made it comparatively easy to find places where cargoes could be landed without being observed.

In all Scotland there were few places more perfectly fashioned by nature for a smugglers' paradise than Orkney and Shetland. To our islands with their

1. 1707.
2. In 1736 John Porteous, Captain of the City Guard in Edinburgh, ordered his men to fire on a noisy crowd demonstrating at the execution of a smuggler Andrew Wilson. Some thirty people were killed or wounded. Porteous was tried and sentenced to death but subsequently reprieved. A mob then broke into the tolbooth and hanged him.

12 SS *Iona*, Dennison & Co, built in Shapinsay, 1893. Naval flotilla in background, *c*.1910

13 SS *Iona* re-engined and refurbished in 1949. Wrecked in Elwick Bay, Shapinsay, 1964

14 SS *Orcadia*, 1868-1931, Orkney Steam Navigation Co Ltd, *c.*1900

15 SS *St Ola* I, 1892-1951, North of Scotland Orkney & Shetland Steam Navigation Co Ltd, *c.*1925

sheltered bays, and cliffs bountifully supplied with caves, cargoes of illicit goods could be taken with impunity. Local lairds and merchants (these were often the same people) sent their own ships to Hamburg and Holland, and they did not scruple to conceal barrels of rum and brandy among the sugar, salt, tar, gunpowder, glassware and muslins with which the holds were to all appearances filled. French and Dutch luggers, which came north in great numbers to fish, usually carried a keg or two of spirits to sell in the islands.

It is not surprising, then, that many tales of the smugglers and their adventures are remembered, or that more or less open smuggling persisted round our shores for a very long time. It is generally admitted that a limited amount of smuggling was still carried on in Orkney at the beginning of this century. Much later than that, however, there were rumours of free-trading, the authenticity of which it is difficult to determine.

Some of the earliest ventures were on a considerable scale. In 1723 a group of Orkney merchants brought a cargo from St Martins in France which included 35 hogsheads of claret, 4 hogsheads of white wine, 48 quarter casks and 20 smaller casks of brandy. The net profit on the whole cargo was around £1,414 Scots.[1] The immunity of the merchants from seizure and arrest was not so much the result of good fortune as of good public relations. They were prudent enough to allow '32 pints ... gratis' to the landlord who supplied landing facilities, and to make a generous allowance 'for wine to treat the Customs officers.'

The island lairds in their grey weather-scarred mansions fortified themselves with Hollands[2] which had escaped duty. They were secure in the knowledge that the justices around them and the magistrates in Kirkwall were also deeply implicated. Even the ministers were complaisant. A traveller wrote, 'It is a shame that the clergy in the Shetland and Orkney Isles should so often wink at their churches being made depositories of smuggled goods, chiefly foreign spirits.' One Seceder minister felt called upon to denounce the trade. His church officer remarked afterwards, 'I think oor minister is no' very consistent, for at the very time he was preaching, he had six kegs o' as guid brandy under his pulpit as was ever smuggled.'

The situation was often Gilbertian. A respectable merchant, George Eunson,[3] known by his friends to be a veritable prince of smugglers, cashed

1. The value of £1 Scots was 1/12th of its English counterpart.
2. A grain spirit manufactured in Holland.
3. Ernest Marwick has been a little kind to George Eunson who was not a particularly respectable merchant. Indeed at one stage in his career he was described as 'going about the country without employment and like a vagabond ... of such a turbulent disposition that he would be ready to enter into anything that was mischievous to his Neighbour'. The article does not make entirely clear that Eunson was the 'notorious smuggler' who was found a place as Extraordinary Officer of Customs. See B. H. Hossack, *Kirkwall in the Orkneys*, 1900, pp.128, 242 and 387-390. Also R. P. Fereday, *The Orkney Balfours, 1749-99*, 1990, pp.102-104, 107-108.

bills for the Collector of Customs at Kirkwall, and he used this much-needed medium of exchange to pay his own agent for supplies of gin and rum. A notorious smuggler, he was found a place as 'Extraordinary Officer of Customs', with instructions to harry his patron's political enemies and to protect his friends. Only when this zealous turncoat decided to indict most of the magistrates and councillors did he run into such grave trouble that he found it more prudent to return to smuggling. He occupied some of his leisure in writing a book on Orkney which is now a collector's rarity, and in compiling a chart which was adopted by the Admiralty. His book contained harsh criticisms of the magistrates, who:

> With loads of grain send out their sloops to roam,
> And bring the curst pernicious *liquors* home;
> Defraud the revenue, nor care a pin,
> Whoever lose, so they themselves but win;
> Over all, their pride or avarice controuls,
> They poison bodies, as they poison souls.[1]

The magistrates were in an excellent position to smuggle safely, for the Town Council of Kirkwall made a habit of offering generous entertainment to customs officials who arrived in the town. In this way they were able to listen blandly to the confidences of many an officer who, in an excess of conviviality, confided his plans to the interested councillors.

The Collector of the Stamp Duties at Kirkwall in the late seventeenth century was an amiable local gentleman, who granted licences to sell liquor to those who applied, but who considered it no part of his duty to inconvenience those who did not. A new clerk, bristling with importance and ambition, who had access to the collector's correspondence, wrote to the authorities in Edinburgh, 'I am not ashamed to be the Informer agst. *Hundreds* in the County of Orkney who are most Notorious Smugglers and Retailers of all kinds of Foreign Spirits, and what is more extraordinary, not one of them has a licence.' This was not strictly accurate, *one* of them did have a licence; those who did not, numbered, as was later ascertained, one hundred and two. Although the clerk got a dusty answer from his superiors, the collector was quietly and politely replaced.

With so many kinds and classes of people engaged in smuggling, the sale of spirits was not confined to hotels and dram shops. As late as the 1860s, the customers of a certain Kirkwall bank could buy smuggled gin quite publicly over the counter.

Where it was at all possible, the authorities liked to arrange things so as not to arouse popular emotion. In the Napoleonic War, H.M.S. *Norfolk*,

---

1. G. Eunson, *The Ancient and Present State of Orkney*, 1788, p.127.

commanded by an Orcadian,[1] ran many a contraband cask. Eventually, when she was lying at Kirkwall, a Collector of Excise[2] found a pretext for searching her. He discovered that even her guns were loaded with tea and tobacco. The ship was condemned and became the property of the Excise, but her captain was allowed to retire gracefully.

Courtesy as shown on the higher levels, or should one say 'diplomacy', did not operate on the lower levels, where hard-boiled and determined men would take any risk to prevent capture and seizure of goods. The tale is still told of a crew who, after a rendezvous with a French lugger well north of Orkney, were laboriously rowing their boat in the direction of an often-used cave when they spotted the coastguard cutter near by. The unlucky proximity of the preventive vessel made a long and tiring detour necessary, and the men only arrived at another possible hide-out many miles away long after darkness had fallen. They sent one of their number to alert a sympathiser in the neighbourhood, and nodded over their oars as they awaited his return. Soon someone stepped into the boat. Without looking up, the crew waited for their friend's instructions. Then it dawned on them that their visitor was a customs man. Their reaction was frighteningly primitive; they were tired, frustrated, apprehensive; so, in the words of a descendant of one of them, 'They just shoved him ower the side and droondid him.'

Right up to the end of last century several Orkney merchants owned their own schooners, manned by local crews. These could very conveniently carry moderate amounts of contraband goods with their legitimate cargoes, and could be so adapted that the hiding places of tobacco and gin could not easily be discovered. The most famous island smuggler of modern times was not an Orkneyman, however, but a Yorkshire man—Captain Askham of the *Julia*. One of his methods of procedure was to take cargoes of spirits, quite legally, from Grimsby to North Faroe, where they were publicly landed. He then took on board a consignment of fish, oil, and ponies, and quietly re-shipped the spirits. On his way back to Kirkwall he landed the casks at some outlying island, such as Westray, and proceeded with the rest of his cargo to the home port. The spirits were brought in later by a small boat hired for the purpose. Once, in 1876, the receivers of such a cargo were caught and prosecuted, and Captain Askham, safely and good-humouredly turned Queen's evidence, described his part in the venture with the utmost frankness and relish.

Four years later a cargo which he handled was landed at Walls. The Customs officers were informed of the episode by a disgruntled member of the crew, but they were too late. They ransacked houses, pulled down peat-

1. Captain William Richan.
2. Robert Pringle.

stacks, and probed middens without finding anything. So safe did the receivers feel that a joiner whose workshop had been painstakingly explored offered the discomfited searchers a glass of the spirits whose hiding-place they had so signally failed to discover.

While the merchants might rely on their own ships, and people like Captain Askham, for supplies, the ordinary islander more frequently had recourse to the foreign fishing vessels which offered their wares throughout the North Isles. A local gentleman, still very much alive, remembers well when 'Frenchmen' and 'Dutchmen' anchored in the bay near his home. He was a child then, and was sent early to bed while his father and mother made their way to the shore with loads of eggs, butter and cheese, which they bartered for rum and 'black gin', the latter a liquor never now seen, whose nature it would be interesting to discover. He was aware that in the late evening hurried digging took place in the cabbage garden. When he asked his mother what she had been doing, she replied that she had been getting flowers from the beach, which would only grow if planted after dark.

The Frenchmen, in particular, took great risks, and their effrontery was the subject of many a tale. During a period of very foggy weather a French lugger anchored in a bay near Kirkwall. At a large farm close to the shore the dairymaids were surprised that the cattle seemed suddenly to give very little milk. It was only afterwards that they realised what had happened. Under cover of the fog, the Frenchmen had been landing to milk the cows and convey the milk back to the ship.

The Dutchmen almost always accepted capture philosophically, but the more volatile Frenchmen became very angry when a Customs officer discovered contraband goods in their vessels. In June 1900 five fishermen from a Gravelines lugger were sentenced at Kirkwall for striking a Customs man with lethal weapons and endeavouring to throw him into the sea. Less than a month later, another French lugger, *Le Dieu Jesus*, set out for the open sea with the Principal Customs Officer at Thurso, who had discovered tobacco and spirits on board. She was captured by a volunteer crew, who chased her in a steamer which was lying at Scrabster, and the Frenchmen were brought back for trial.

Islanders who did business with the Frenchmen soon discovered that they had to be most circumspect in their dealings. Some of them got a bad fright in the summer of 1877. One Sunday evening a lugger anchored off one of our islands. Among those who went on board was a teetotaller, who refused to drink a friendly glass with the Frenchmen. The latter were so incensed that the unfortunate water drinker was assaulted and almost choked. He considered himself lucky to escape with unbroken bones.

Worse was to come. On the following evening the same ship visited another island. A party of men on the island, who were helping a tradesman to manoeuvre a log over a sawpit, noticed that a boat-load of Frenchmen were coming to land. They seemed to be greatly excited: one of them carried a large knife, which he brandished furiously, while another had armed himself with an ancient-looking blunderbuss. They bore down on the sawpit, and the islanders could only conjecture that they had mistaken the swinging log for a piece of ordnance directed towards their ship. The man with the knife seized one of the islanders and declared that he would drive his weapon through his heart. The wielder of the blunderbuss declared in broken, but effective, English that he would 'shoot them dead'. Panic seized the group and a general flight ensued, each doing his best to get out of range. Some escaped by the links, astonishing even the rabbits with their speed, but others were more unfortunate. One scared individual plunged into an old sack lustily shouting 'Murder!'

It turned out that the cause of the Frenchmen's displeasure was that a keg of spirits had been stolen from the deck of the lugger; the raid was made for the purpose of regaining this property. Search was made in several houses, but the missing spirits could not be discovered. After hair-raising threats, and shouts of 'vagabond'—a word common to both languages—the Frenchmen's passions cooled somewhat and overtures of peace were made and accepted.

3

Our local pirate

My father once acquired a pirate's telescope when the contents of an old island mansion were put on sale. It cost him sixpence.

The telescope was nearly two feet long—almost twice that when fully extended. It was green with verdigris, and the lenses were covered with dust. But my father refurbished it, and it served us for some twenty years. The last time I used it was to watch a German bomber spiralling earthwards in smoke. That was on Christmas Day 1940. Afterwards, the object glass unaccountably got broken. I was away from home for many years; and when I looked again for the pirate's telescope it had disappeared.

We were assured of the telescope's identity by the parish antiquarian, a thin, olive-skinned person of considerable eccentricity who brought out tags of Latin whenever he could. The pirate was a local man, John Gow. Born in Wick, Caithness, he had been brought up in the seaport of Stromness, which lies to the south-west of the Orkney Mainland. One fine day he sailed away, and came back years later as a full-blown pirate. He even had the effrontery to re-christen his ship with the famous name of *The Revenge*.

For a time he acted the part of the honest, prosperous trader returning to his native town, but it seems that his crew did not quite live up to this innocent role. After they had abducted three girls and plundered a large country house, their real character was evident.

These doings were in sad contrast to the gallantry of John Gow. He had been making himself agreeable to the best families, and he had engaged the affections of a romantic girl, Miss Gordon. One day the two of them rode over the moors on Shetland ponies and plighted their troth at the Stone of Odin,[1] a prehistoric monolith with a hole through it. Any promise made with hands clasped through this hole was binding.

But it was by now too dangerous for the self-declared pirates to remain in port, so John Gow put to sea on the pretext of paying a visit to an old school-fellow on Eday, one of the outer isles of Orkney. This man, James Fea, had already suggested that Gow should be apprehended, so it may be

1. See also article 'Strange stones', p.307.

that *The Revenge* was sailing on a punitive, rather than a friendly, mission. However that may be, the ship ran ashore on the Calf Holm, a little island near his acquaintance's residence, and in the ensuing battle of wits it was James Fea who won. He managed to capture all the pirates.

They were sent to London for trial, and John Gow and nine of his crew were executed.

It was a somewhat ordinary, sordid story, and John Gow might well have remained unknown, like many another pirate. But it happened that the journalist who wrote up the trial, and made a book about it, was Daniel Defoe, author of *Robinson Crusoe*. By another strange coincidence, Sir Walter Scott heard the story when in Orkney in August 1814 and Gow was quickly transfigured by Scott's imagination into the charming Captain Cleveland, hero of his novel *The Pirate*.

What became of poor Miss Gordon, saddled with the vow of Odin? The tradition is that she travelled to London and after the trial and execution of the pirates she obtained permission to see the body of Gow. Holding his dead hand in hers she redeemed the pledge given so gladly one winter day on an Orkney moor.

4

Orkney's other pirate

On one occasion I was rash enough to speak of John Gow as 'Orkney's solitary pirate'. As a newspaper man, I should have learned that when you describe anything as the only one of its kind, instances of other things of the same kind are immediately pointed out by aggrieved readers. I thought I was safe with the Pirate Gow—his reputation has always seemed unique in Orkney—but not a bit of it! We actually produced another pirate so bloodthirsty that Gow's villainies look like the delinquencies of a teddy-boy when compared with the atrocities this man committed.

His name, it seems, was John Fullarton. What part of Orkney he hailed from is uncertain: some say Stromness, but I will not insist, for it seems a bit unfair to saddle Stromness with two such rogues as Gow and Fullarton. The name Fullarton was also found in Orphir around this date, but again I should not like to draw conclusions.

What does seem certain is that John Fullarton, an Orkney master mariner, had a run of bad luck around the middle of the eighteenth century. To retrieve his fortunes, he did some smuggling, choosing as the most suitable place the Channel Islands, then the centre of a great smuggling organisation. He must have done well (or badly, depending how you look at it) for he soon had enough money to equip a privateer.

Privateering has had a bad press, but it was a respectable occupation in its day. There was a government licence, which allowed privateers in time of war to harry and rob enemy vessels at sea. There was the great danger, of course, that if enemy ships were too infrequent, or if the war stopped, the privateer might be tempted to attack peaceful merchant shipping.

Fullarton made a deal of money as a privateer, but he was overcome with greed; and, casting in his lot with a Royal Navy captain named Keppel, he fitted out a pirate ship. This partnership was infamous. Keppel and Fullarton raided a whole series of peaceful traders, often beating or killing their crews. Keppel was soon out of the business, for he fell in love with the wife of a Frenchman. The husband resented this so strongly that he ran his sword through Keppel; and Fullarton was left to carry on alone as a professional pirate.

He was unbelievably successful, but his cruelty increased with the scope

16 SS *Earl Thorfinn*, 1928-1962, Orkney Steam Navigation Co Ltd

17 SS *St Magnus* II, North of Scotland Orkney & Shetland Steam Navigation Co Ltd. Built 1912, sunk by enemy action off Peterhead, 12 February 1918.

18 Swona harbour, 1966

19 Stroma harbour, 1966

of his operations. The 'Orkney Pirate' was a name which made men shudder anywhere in the North Sea. With several vessels under his command, he was a scourge to lawful traders. Money came to him quickly, and accumulated to his account in Leith. With some part of it he bought an estate in Orkney, where he sent some of his local relatives—entirely respectable people—to live and await his homecoming. He actually visited this place, and stayed for a time with his mother, without being apprehended.

He could not bring himself to settle however; but he confined his piracies to waters nearer home, particularly the Firth of Forth. It was at this stage of his career that his downfall came. He ordered a Scottish packet, the *Isabella*, heavily laden with cargo, to lay to, but the captain, a gallant man, refused. A running fight followed—Captain Jones of the *Isabella* returning Fullarton's broadside. The packet put up strong opposition to Fullarton for about two hours, then her mast was shot away and she was boarded. Fullarton, livid with anger at the man who had opposed him, shot Captain Jones, then turned to haul down the *Isabella*'s colours. He had not reckoned with the captain's wife; and crazed with grief she seized a pistol, pushed it against Fullarton's temple, and fired. With the 'Orkney Pirate' dead, the crew of the *Isabella* took courage, turned on their attackers, and captured both pirates and pirate ship.

'Mary Jones, the Pirate Slayer', as the chap-books[1] called her, was awarded a pension from the Edinburgh Guild of Merchants, and lived to be an old woman.

There, then, is the story of Orkney's second pirate. I hope for the sake of our reputation that no-one knows of any others.

---

1. Small pamphlets of popular tales, ballads, tracts, etc.

5

The predicament of the grey seal

In Scotland generally, but particularly in Orkney, the war goes on between determined protectors of the grey seal and a hydra-headed enemy, identified more or less with the Nature Conservancy Council, the Scottish Salmon Net Fishing Association, the Ministry of Agriculture and Fisheries, and local holders of permits to kill seals (nearly a score of them in Orkney).[1]

Readers of local newspapers are familiar with arguments from both sides, or more accurately all sides; for there are marked deviations of opinion.

At one extreme are people who would not have a single seal destroyed; at the other are hunters keen to cash in on the scheme for controlled killing. These latter are known, through a recent admission by the Secretary of State for Scotland, to have exceeded their quota by at least a quarter.

Unwillingly caught up between the contestants, scolded by the protectors and lobbied by the salmon fishers, are scientists whose job it is to ascertain the facts about those large colonies of grey seals now known, somewhat to the surprise of the average Orcadian, to have their breeding grounds in Orkney.

There is a certain dualism in the islander's thinking about, or it might be more appropriate to say his feeling for, the seal. With his innocent round eyes, unbounded curiosity, love of play, and sheer grace of movement when in the water, he easily captivates the watcher.

The killing of seals has always seemed somewhat repulsive, as it is a difficult, even a skilled, operation, and inexpert attempts may be attended by suffering not easy to condone. This aspect has been particularly stressed recently with regard to killings in the Farne Islands and Orkney.

A keen sportsman once confessed that he had come back more than once from a seal-hunt without firing a shot, 'the ways of the selkie having made everybody altogether forget to begin to think of killing him.' Yet Samuel Hibbert, writing of Shetland in 1822, told of a boat's crew who 'lamented'

---

1. This article appeared in *The Glasgow Herald*, 22 February 1964.

that they could not shoot a grey seal, who was watching them curiously, because it was Sunday; and another Shetlander, Edmondston, wrote, 'Seal-hunting is splendid sport—superior, I affirm, to every other species of sport in this country, not excepting deer-stalking and fox-hunting.'

Because of his taste for human society, his almost 'human' expression, and his ability to live either in the sea or out of it, the seal, as such, has gathered around himself a greater mass of legend than any other sea creature. Indeed, most of the legends are so familiar that they do not need to be retold.

The mysterious being who is 'a man apo' de land . . . a selkie i'de sea,' and who had a tragic *affaire* with the wife left behind by a Crusader, found his way into Orkney's finest traditional ballad.[1] It was more common, however, for roles to be reversed, and for earth-bound males to marry seal-women. This is the form of the legend found most often in the Western and Northern Isles.

Since such relationships could occur it was obvious that a kinship existed between seals and men which should be recognised. A snatch of Orkney verse declares:

> The selkies are Orkney folks' cousins—
> So the selkies are sib[2] too tae me.

The rational explanation seemed to be that the seal was a human being under a magic spell. This accounted for his reputed wisdom, for his love of music (a characteristic frequently noted), and for his habit of frequenting, in the case of the common seal, places very accessible to man.

Obviously it was desirable to act with propriety towards the seals and there have always been islanders who could not bring themselves to kill one. Yet, more especially at earlier times, harsh necessity intervened, overcoming sentiment and prejudice, for the seal was a valuable source of oil and its skin had many uses.

At the complex site of Jarlshof, in Shetland, bones of the grey seal have been found at both Bronze and Iron Age levels, as well as in ninth- and tenth-century Viking dwellings.

The Orkney earls used to go to Suleskerry to hunt the seal. Even the monks of Iona, who had to grapple with grim realities like other men, had their seal preserve, as a story in Adamnan's Life of St Columba makes clear.

In the eighteenth century the commercial interest in seals was accentuated. Hitherto the seal-hunter had killed seals mainly for his own use, even if the skins were exportable. But now the demand was at its height. The naturalist

---

1. The Play o' de Lathie Odivere.
2. Related by blood or descent.

Pennant explained why in his *Arctic Zoology*, published in 1784:

> Seals are now become a great article of commerce. The oil from the vast Whales is no longer equal to the demand for supplying the magnificent profusion of lamps in and round our capital. The chase of these animals is redoubled for that purpose; and the skins, properly tanned, are in considerable use in the manufactory of boots and shoes.

With new methods of lighting, and the discovery of sources of mineral oil, seal oil was little prized; and in addition the demand from fashion houses for skins was irregular.

Indeed, the trade in skins either declined rapidly or Orkney seamen were too busy fighting Napoleon to bother about seals, for the annual export of seal skins from Orkney in the early years of the nineteenth century only once exceeded four dozen. Nowadays the market is brisk again, and local papers carry advertisements offering 'Highest Prices for Seal Skins'.

In Orkney and Shetland seal flesh was scarcely regarded as edible; but in the Western Isles it was eaten, as Martin[1] tells us:

> The Natives Salt the Seals with the ashes of burnt Sea-ware, and say they are good Food, the vulgar eat them commonly in the Spring time with a long pointed Stick instead of a Fork, to prevent the strong smell which their hands would otherwise have for several Hours after.

It was used by the people in the springtime, and eaten with a pointed stick instead of a fork, because of the strong smell that would have remained on the hands.

The allusion to springtime may mean that seal meat was eaten only during Lent, as happened in Roman Catholic districts, where it was argued, says our author, that seals were fish and not flesh.

The mystery and legend which surrounded the seal gave rise to the belief that seal oil was a valuable specific. It was taken until recent times in the Highlands for chest diseases, and rubbed into the joints to relieve rheumatic pains. Broth made from the flesh of young seals was also considered to have medicinal value.

For diarrhoeal disorders a medicine was compounded from seal liver and whisky; although it must have harried the emotions of the islander to see the 'craitur' so destroyed. The skin also had some curative virtues: girdles of seal skin were sometimes worn by persons who suffered from sciatica.

There were many other purposes for which the skin could be used.

---

1. *A Description of the Western Islands of Scotland*, 1703, M. Martin, p.64.

The phrase 'seal-skin trousers' really refers to the seal-man legend; but skin waistcoats were common, and most men had a *spleuchan*, or tobacco pouch, made from the same material. Skin cut into thongs was used to harness the horses to the primitive side-ploughs. In Shetland skin shoes, or *rivlins*, were sometimes made from seal skin.

The grey seal (*Halichoerus grypus*) whose welfare is causing so much genuine concern, even among those who adopt (in the view of those who advocate total protection during the breeding season) a 'midway attitude', was not until recent times regarded as plentiful in the Northern Isles, where nowadays such a sizable part of the world grey seal population is located.

Perhaps the best summary of moderate opinion in the islands was made recently by *The Orcadian*'s nature correspondent:

> If the grey seal must be controlled by culling, Orcadians should demand a rigid system of control, a rigid system of inspection, a minimum number of known permit-holders, specific times of supervised killings, and rigid checking of skin exports.[1]

---

1. 9 January 1964. The last seal cull took place in 1984-85. From then until 1988 common seals were afforded protection during the period 1 June to 31 August, when shooting could take place only on licence. Due to the seal virus, in 1988 the protection for common seals was extended throughout the year. No licences have been issued since that date. Grey seals are protected during the period 1 September to 31 December, when a licence is required to shoot them. Since 1970 a defensive power has been available to fish farmers. This allows them, without seeking a licence, to shoot seals which endanger their stocks.

6

The first North Isles steamer

On 3 April 1965 there is a centenary which the North Isles of Orkney have particular reason to remember, for on that date in 1865 regular steam communication between them and Kirkwall began. It may be gratifying to the self-esteem of the various islands to mention that the service was inaugurated *from* them, and not *to* them; for the pioneer of steam transport, Captain George Robertson, was brought up in Stronsay, and the first official trip of his privately purchased steamer the *Orcadia* was made from Sanday, Stronsay and Eday to Kirkwall.

The importance of this event can best be realised if we try to see what communications were like before Captain Robertson started his steamer service.

The islands were visited by all kinds of sailing ships: smacks of every description, sloops, cutters and occasional schooners. The smaller ships were usually owned by their masters, or by some local laird. They carried whatever cargo they could pick up, bringing wood, coal, guano and like things to the islands and taking away fish, grain or potatoes. Such passengers as could fit in with their uncertain departures might sail with them. Most people depended, however, on the packet boats, small vessels which carried passengers and light cargo. A number of these seem to have belonged to their particular islands, for we read of the 'North Ronaldsay packet', the 'Sanday packet' and others.

They were supposed to run more or less regularly between Kirkwall and the islands, but they seldom managed to adhere to a strict timetable, partly because of the weather and partly because they did not scruple to interrupt the service when they were asked to flit[1] a farmer from one island to another or to do any other remunerative job. There were constant complaints about them. A newspaper of the period said that there were many boats coming into Kirkwall 'which ought to be prevented from going to sea and not allowed to become man-traps.' This was a warning in no way extravagant, for in the two years 1862 and 1863, three North Isles packets and a luggage boat were wrecked. The arrivals of mail could be erratic. Thomas Davidson, the

1. Move.

famous 'Scottish Probationer',[1] wrote from Westray in January 1866, 'for the first time since my arrival, the post-boat has ventured into Kirkwall,' which meant that the mails were at least eight days overdue.

Undecked cattle boats, heavy-timbered, but slow, comfortless and ungainly, were often to be seen, carrying along with the cattle one or two hardy passengers. Travel, as can easily be imagined, was not the simple, straightforward thing it is now. Anyone journeying to the North Isles, unless he hired a boat for himself, might spend quite a while at Kirkwall looking for a passage on whatever ship might be calling at a particular island.

These remarks apply to conditions prevailing before the mid-nineteenth century, but things had changed very little when, in the early months of 1865, the local newspapers announced that at long last a steamer was going to sail regularly to the North Isles.

The *Orcadia*, first of the name, arrived at Kirkwall around the beginning of March, after a stormy passage from the south. Formerly the *Quarry Maid*, she was a small wooden screw steamer. Her size has been variously stated in local publications, but from a fleet list printed in *Marine News* of February 1961, and compiled from official sources, the following figures are taken. She was eighty-three feet in length, with twenty feet of beam. Her tonnage was sixty-two net register (one hundred and one tons gross).

The speed of the *Orcadia* was estimated at eight knots. There was accommodation for an unspecified number of passengers—she frequently carried a hundred or more—and, quite as important, she had room for sixty cattle.

To those who were inured to conditions on the packets, the new ship was the last word in luxury. She had a comfortable cabin where thirty people could sit; she was provided with a lifeboat, lifebuoys and rocket apparatus. The packets had never had a single lifebuoy between them and their bulwarks were so low as to be extremely dangerous.

Some time was spent after the *Orcadia*'s arrival in making plans for the service and in securing storage accommodation in the isles. On 3 April the steamer made her first historic run. At six o'clock in the morning she left Sanday, steamed somewhat heavily through white-capped waves in Sanday Sound, but reached Stronsay on time, to find the luggage boat and passenger boat waiting for her. From Stronsay the *Orcadia* steamed to Millbounds in Eday where more passengers and cargo were taken aboard. Despite the fact that wind and tide were right ahead, the ship responded well to the promptings of her engine, showed a sceptical disregard for the fact that there were three ministers in the cabin (which had not gone unnoticed among the superstitious), picked up more passengers from two open boats, and set course for Kirkwall. 'The best packet,' wrote a reporter, 'would have had to wait the turn of the

1. See also 'Trials of a probationer', p.209.

tide,' but the *Orcadia* just 'glided along'. The quay heads at Kirkwall were crowded with people, whose enthusiasm was so aroused by the brave sight of the incoming steamer that they let loose a salvo of cheers.

Captain Robertson intended to devote four days a week to regular island traffic, leaving two days on hand for special runs and excursions. The early schedules were not so very different from those with which we are familiar today; and the *Orcadia* maintained a very consistent service, helped out for a time by a little paddle steamer named the *Rover*.

It is difficult for modern Orcadians to realise that the coming of the steamer added a new dimension to island life. Before that time, people travelled little from island to island, and seldom visited Kirkwall except at Lammas.[1] Only a small minority of people on the Mainland had ever set foot on any of the North Isles. Plenty of people in the isles themselves, especially the women, had never set eyes on Kirkwall, and had the quaintest ideas about the town.

Now, things were different. It became the fashion, especially among the gentlemen and ladies of the capital, to travel for 'pleasure'—the word had never been mentioned in connection with the sailing ships—and men in travellers' caps and thick great-coats, accompanied by women much petticoated and beshawled made excursions to places like Westray, to gaze on the ruins of Noltland Castle and picnic at Pierowall. Conversely, parties from one or other of the islands came to spend a day in Kirkwall. Mr Horne, factor for the laird of Eday, set the fashion by announcing that he intended to give the farm servants and people in his employment a holiday trip to the city.

Even at a time when money was worth much more than now, the fares were astonishingly moderate. A cabin passage to Sanday or Westray cost 2/6d or 1/3d steerage. The fares to Eday and Stronsay were 2/- cabin and 1/- steerage. In the 1870s the cost was little more—3/- cabin, 1/6d on deck.

That same summer of 1865 an excursion to Fair Isle was advertised. The *Orcadia* set off from Kirkwall at 4 o'clock on the morning of 23 June. Her passengers were almost all men. It was a cold morning with leaden skies and mist-covered hills, but the spirits of the pleasure-seekers were kept up by the Volunteer Brass Band, who drowned the protestations of the engine with lively airs. Two and a half hours later, twenty self-conscious travellers came aboard at Stronsay. But the weather was getting worse, and the *Orcadia* wallowed in the swell before reaching the rendezvous off Sanday where she was to collect the passengers from that island, along with those who had come from Westray and Eday on the *Rover*.

---

1. The Lammas Market held in August was a great annual event when folk from all over Orkney came to Kirkwall.

In the unpleasant conditions it was decided that the steamers should change their rôles, so it was actually the *Rover*, whose churning paddles made her somewhat more stable than the *Orcadia*, that steamed northwards, with both captains on her bridge. The excursionists held out until they were opposite Start Point, then those who were still able to make decisions sent a deputation to Captain Robertson, begging him to turn back. A compromise was reached: the *Rover* returned to Kettletoft, then made her way through more sheltered waters to Westray, where her reanimated passengers spent the day. Even Westray at that date was unfamiliar territory to the majority.

It does not appear that this *Orcadia* ever got to Fair Isle, but it was one of the first places outside Orkney to be visited by the second *Orcadia*, and, oddly enough, also by the third *Orcadia*, the present beautifully appointed ship which bears the distinguished name.

As notable as the first *Orcadia*'s contribution to the social life of the isles was the fillip she gave to agriculture and trade. She brought livestock quickly to the market in Kirkwall. Sometimes she made direct runs to Fraserburgh with cattle or sheep. Wholesale houses in Kirkwall found that they could now have a regular and much increased trade with the North Isles. Indeed, it has been said that in the first two years the volume of cargo increased fourfold.

When all is said that can be said to celebrate Captain Robertson's achievement, it must be admitted that the ship had her faults, the chief of them too little power, a defect not greatly rectified by additions to her boilers. She also rolled in bad weather more than was pleasant. But these defects were regarded as trifling in comparison to the benefits she conferred.

Two years went past, during which time it became evident that the financial demands of the service and the task of administration were more than a private individual should be expected to carry. Near the end of 1867, with Captain Robertson's concurrence, the Orkney Steam Navigation Company Ltd was formed, the deed of co-partnery being signed at a meeting in Kirkwall on 26 November. Two local lairds—David Balfour of Balfour and Trenaby and Thomas Traill of Holland—were present, along with several merchants, farmers and shipowners. 1,760 shares of £5 were taken up (rather less than had been hoped), and about half of these were subscribed for by Mr Balfour, the Earl of Zetland, Mr Traill of Rattar and other landowners. The directors chose Mr Balfour as their convener, and Captain Robertson became the company's manager.

The first necessity was felt to be a new ship, a need which must surely have been anticipated before the company's formation, for the second *Orcadia*, specially built at Shields, arrived at Kirkwall late on Thursday evening, 21 May 1868. She was 120 feet long, and her engines were rated at sixty horsepower. There were two holds, the forehold being constructed to carry about ninety tons and the afterhold thirty-five tons. The saloon offered a degree of comfort never seen before in the inter-island vessels. Reporters were quick to notice that it even contained an umbrella stand.

The ship, familiar to hosts of people still living in the Mainland and North Isles, remained in the company's service for over sixty years. Although a smart new steamer, the *Earl Thorfinn*, was placed on the route on 3 May 1928, the *Orcadia* (second) was kept in operation until the arrival of the *Earl Sigurd*, early in 1931.

Captain George Robertson, who inaugurated the service, was a man of wide knowledge, massive determination and rugged personality. He was born in South Ronaldsay in 1832, reared in Stronsay, to which his family moved shortly after his birth, and ran away to sea at the age of sixteen. He sailed on various ships, obtaining his master's certificate in 1854, when he was still under twenty-two.

Besides transporting cargo, Captain Robertson did a great deal of salvage work. Presumably it was from the profits made on salvage that he financed the Orkney service. As manager of 'Orkney Steam' he was efficient, enterprising and, if need be, ruthless. His energy was so great that he was able to devote time to private adventures. In 1868 he was successful in obtaining the Post Office contract to convey the mails between Scrabster and Stromness, placing on the route a new steamer, the *Express*, the following April. He held the contract continuously for nine years. Salvage work still interested him, and besides operating nearer home, he employed a salvage tug, of which he was owner, in Mediterranean waters.

The Orkney Steam Navigation Company was in sight of its first half-century, and Captain Robertson was a veteran of eighty-one when he, so to speak, let go of the tiller. He died in Kirkwall two years later, on 16 June 1916.

7

Orkney's back door

My friend Alec is a farmer by vocation, but an adventurer by instinct. He is one of the dwindling band of farmers in Orkney who are as much at home on the sea as on the land. When he is tired of ploughing and attending cattle sales he finds an excuse to launch his motor boat; and several times a year he crosses the Pentland Firth to Caithness, ostensibly to collect agricultural supplies, but actually, I am sure, for the sheer love of the voyage and its possible hazards. Before setting off on one of those trips, he was good enough to suggest that I should join the party, knowing full well that it was just the sort of adventure to appeal to me.

The Pentland Firth has always been regarded as one of the most treacherous pieces of water in the world. Its recorded wrecks run, I suppose, into many hundreds. Even passengers on the large mail steamer *St Ola*, which runs daily between Scrabster in Caithness and Stromness in Orkney (that is, weather permitting) are sometimes heartily relieved when the vessel ties up at their port.

But there is a back door to Orkney, which was used extensively before the days of steam. From some of the little harbours that lie along the Caithness coast between the Ness of Duncansby and St John's Point it is only from seven to nine miles to the most southerly point in South Ronaldsay in Orkney. It is amazing how frequently it is possible for men who know the geography of the Pentland Firth, and all about its tides and the complexity of its currents, to make the passage in quite small boats.

There is a tradition that one of the earliest pilots of the Pentland was John de Groot[1] who settled down on the Caithness coast in the late fifteenth

---

1. John de Groot and his two brothers were Dutchmen who settled in Caithness during the reign of James IV of Scotland and duly took up employment as ferrymen plying between Caithness and Orkney. Certainly a charter was granted in 1496 to 'John Grot (sic) son to Hugh Grot', by the Earl of Caithness. A picturesque tale recounts that at a later date when eight members of the family met to celebrate the anniversary of their arrival in Caithness there was considerable disagreement regarding seniority. To restore harmony John built a house in octagonal form, with eight doors and eight windows, and he also provided an oak table of the same shape. This contrived to resolve any dispute about rank. John o' Groat's House later became an inn and although the building no longer exists, the octagonal tower of the present hotel perpetuates the story. There seems to be no substance in the tradition that the surname derives from a Pentland Firth ferryman whose fare was a *groat* (roughly fourpence) for each passenger transported.

century with two brothers, Malcolm and Gavin, to run the Orkney ferry. At a later date the Caithness end of the ferry was at Huna, from whose comfortable inn the traveller departed for the South. From 1747 onwards, for well over a century, the mail route to Orkney was from Huna to Burwick in South Ronaldsay. The service was maintained with four-oared or six-oared boats. Only once was there an accident, around 1815, when the post boat was run down by a ship.

For a considerable period after steam communication across the Pentland Firth was established in 1856, the ferry service was kept in operation, since, as a traveller to Orkney wrote in 1860, 'when the weather prevents the steamer running, a ferry-boat carries the mails between South Ronaldsha and Scotland.' Could there have been a better tribute to the courage and skill of the Pentland Firth boatmen?

A few farmers and lobster fishermen in the South Isles of Orkney still have the reputation of knowing the Firth as intimately as if it were their own backyard—which in a sense it is—so I had no hesitation when Alec telephoned to say that the *Cecilia* would be leaving Herston in South Ronaldsay in the early afternoon for John o' Groats.

In the days of the post-runners of last century I should have had to cross two separate ferries between leaving my home in Kirkwall and joining Alec and his crew. The Churchill Barriers have altered that, adding for all practical purposes eleven miles to the length of the Orkney mainland by joining up to it, through a series of causeways over the eastern entrances to Scapa Flow, four of the South Isles. On my little motorcycle I covered the twenty miles to Herston in about three-quarters of an hour. It is exhilarating to ride over the narrow ribbons of road which form the top of the causeways, with the great inland harbour of Scapa Flow, surrounded by blue hills, on the one side, and the open North Sea on the other.

Alec had said that I would recognise his boat-slip by the wreck of the Canadian drifter *Monarch*, which has been beached at Herston for many years. The *Monarch* was built by the women of Chicago during the latter years of the First World War, under the supervision of shipbuilders from Buckie. Lying there beside that lovely bay of Widewall, below the eighteenth-century houses with their old-fashioned flower gardens, the wreck was as conspicuous as the tall mansion-house of Roeberry on the opposite skyline, or the Howe of Hoxa, reputed grave of that terrible viking Thorfinn Skull-splitter, further east.

The *Cecilia* was pulled up well above the tide-mark a little to the lee of the wreck. She was quite small as motor-boats go, and undecked, but how the five of us who had assembled were going to get her into the water over fifteen yards of stony beach I could not see. Alec went on talking—for he had begun a monologue on the nature and history of the Firth, based on the most exact knowledge, which went on all the way to John o' Groats. But during the recitation he was directing the placing of over a dozen wooden rollers at four-foot intervals from the boat to the sea. One of the young lads took a bucket and splashed each roller with water. All we had to do was to steady the boat as she glided over the wet rollers. Never was there a faster launch; within minutes we were afloat.

We slipped out of the bay past Hoxa Head, which is surmounted by the empty concrete gun-emplacements that once guarded the southern entrance to Scapa Flow, and which will perhaps be there in all their ugliness a century from now. At the other side of the sound was Stanger Head, similarly disfigured. We have our vandals in Orkney, but none on the scale of the War Department. Happily, from sea-level these blemishes on the landscape did not bother us much.

I sat in the stern, beside Alec at the helm, as we ran down the long grey coast of South Ronaldsay; he pointing out landmarks—the positions of wrecks with name and year, and giving me so much information about tides that my non-nautical mind became fuddled, lost in admiration of expertise from which it was too ignorant to benefit.

I gathered that we were going down to Scotland (we preserve the distinction between Orkney and Scotland) on the flood, and so would steer well to the west to make allowance for the force of the tide. We left with blue skies and sunshine, but soon the sky over Caithness and Sutherland was filled with gunmetal-grey clouds which gradually drifted over the Firth. What I feared at first as marring the beauty, added to its loveliness; the muted greys of land, sea, and sky were incredibly subtle. When a steamer passed us, as nine did, its black sides seemed to break into the slow movement with cacophonous stridency. Ahead of us lay Swona like a couchant animal, with a long, curved back. I had never visited it, but Alec assured me that we had all the time in the world. We could go ashore and perhaps collect his brother-in-law James;[1] perhaps even borrow his boat for the rest of the journey. He was sure I would like to see the Wells of Swona. We were on the edge of them almost before I knew, and I was having a ringside view of the dark whirlpools which look as if they could suck anything that got into them to the bottom of the sea. We had an engine to keep us clear, but in a really rough sea a row-boat would have been whirled round interminably until it got swamped.

The little natural harbour on the east of the island was hidden in the wall of rocks. One could have passed it several times without noticing. And just to make access seem more difficult, there were reefs around the entrance. Alec laughed when I commented on the delicacy of steering which was required. 'Some people make a hard job of it,' he said, 'but the boat can find the way herself.' He let go of the helm and proved his point.

1. James Rosie.

We pulled into the rocks on the left-hand side and scrambled ashore. One of the lads set off across the island to the only inhabited house to look for James. Swona is a singularly attractive island, one-and-a-quarter miles long, but narrow. It had on that summer afternoon the sweet smell and quiet atmosphere—a kind of honeyed drowsing—which is always associated with thick natural pasture. Close to the harbour were the uninhabited houses, some settling quietly into decay, but one, a decent two-storey house, looking as if a family could move in tomorrow. When we went inside we saw that a considerable part of it was warmly lined with wood. There is one family of three persons on Swona now,[1] but James has a picture, taken in his boyhood, of busy people at a sheep-dipping, when the inhabitants numbered twenty and more.

The harbour is on an isthmus. At the other side seals were lying on the flat rocks. I was almost near enough to photograph them when they tumbled clumsily into the sea; but they kept close in, their heads turned resolutely towards me. The same thing happened with the fulmars, which were sitting on the tumble-down chimneys of an old croft house. I was just abreast of them on the roof when they glided away.

I had often heard of James. It was a privilege to meet him, and we shook hands with mutual regard. He decided that we should transfer our gear to his boat, the *Hood*, which was larger and more powerful, although like the *Cecilia*, without a cabin.

We kept close to the east coast of Swona, with Alec, now freed from the burden of navigation, pointing out the caves and the Gloup,[2] through the top of which the light was streaming. At one point we ran into an excited mass of gulls fishing busily. They opened for the boat and closed again behind us. Near the south of the island the boat rocked for five minutes with the swift current. The coast looked ugly, with long ridges of 'rocks like bayonets', as Maurice Lindsay has described them; the same rocks on which the *Johanna Thorden* was wrecked on 9 January 1937, with a loss of thirty-six men, women and children. That night a woman in South Ronaldsay dreamed that she saw a fair-haired lady with gold earrings lying on the rocks. Next day news came of the disaster, and of the finding of just such a victim.

James and Alec, with the most unselfish concern for my entertainment, decided that we should put in to Stroma harbour. Once again we veered well to the west, right out in the open Firth now, in the path of the big ships. The first to pass our bows was the *Pass of Kildrummy*, on her way to the Western Isles. I asked one of our crew, a young man who farms on the very edge of the Pentland Firth, how many vessels go through it in a day. He said that an

1. The article was written in 1966. James Rosie, the last permanent resident on Swona, left the island on 26 March 1974.
2. A cave which has collapsed at the inner end making the sea visible from above.

average of thirty in summer would be a reasonable guess. It is different in winter, when they often delay in the Atlantic until conditions improve in the Firth, and then come through more or less together.[1]

The Firth was deceptively smooth this summer day, but I had seen it during many a storm, in particular on that famous occasion when the crew of the *Dovrefjell*, wrecked on the Pentland Skerries, were taken to safety from her deck by helicopters. As we approached Stroma, the Skerries (there is a nasty ring of them like an open-mouthed trap into which you can run) were directly to the east, low and unremarkable except for their lighthouse.

There are parts of Stroma rising to perhaps 170 feet, but in the great storm of 1862 a remarkable tide climbed the cliffs and swept over the island, washing cabbages out of the soil and compelling some people to leave their homes. In Orkney a hundred small boats were knocked to pieces. Away to the west in Lewis forty-two fishermen were drowned.

Conditions were quiet enough as we ran down the east side of the island, and then turned south to the harbour. Facing us from the ridge of the hill were a succession of two-roomed and three-roomed houses. It was like many a small island in Orkney and Shetland, apart from the fact that not a soul moved around these houses, which seem in years following the evacuation to have deteriorated little outwardly. I was amazed at the excellence of Stroma harbour; almost totally enclosed, with its entrance protected by a breakwater. It cost thousands of pounds, and in the end was ready only for the evacuation of the island.

James summed up the situation in one quiet comment, 'It came sixty years too late.' That is the simple truth. The Stroma men, led by the redoubtable William Bremner, fought for generations to get the pier which would have saved the island. But by the time it came some had died, a number had to leave for health and other reasons, and there were not enough men left to work the land and bring in stores. It is an injustice to the Stroma folk to suggest that they left the island carelessly or light-heartedly; the community perished because the life-belt was thrown to it too late.

The younger men of our crew decided to look for the rare plant *Primula scotica*,[1] of which there is a patch or two. James, Alec and I walked across the fields, raising a rabbit now and then out of the thick pasture dotted sparsely with sheep. We looked through the broken windows of what I presume was the Baptist Church, to find the interior a wreck, with pews and woodwork

---

1. In 1989 the number of vessels passing daily through the Pentland Firth remains approximately thirty, and the difference between summer and winter ship movements is negligible.
2. Scottish primrose. A very small, rare purple flowering plant with a rich yellow eye. Found on grassy sea-cliff tops, the plant is peculiar to Orkney, Caithness and north Sutherland, and thrives only in its natural surroundings. Colonies flower in May and again from July onwards.

torn out. Below us on the sea edge was the kirkyard, with the square tower of the Kennedys' Tomb. This dates from the latter part of the seventeenth century, and once, to judge from old photographs I have seen, had a roof with crow-step gables. The lower part is a vault, around eighteen feet by ten. The upper part was a dove-cot with a great number—some say 366—square pigeon boxes made of flagstone.

Stroma has a curious but long-established reputation for mummies. In 1792 Bishop Forbes wrote:

> This island is famous for having dead Bodies of Men, Women, and Children above Ground, entire, and to be seen for 70 or 80 years, free of all corruption, without embalming or any art qtsoever, but owing, it is thought, to the plenty of Nitre that is there. The Bodies become very brownish through length of Time; but so as that the Visage is discernable by any Friend or acquaintance that ever had seen the person alive.[1]

As we looked around the kirkyard we saw, close to the landward wall, a new grave. Another of the older folk, who had been so reluctant to leave Stroma, had come home.

We were only a hundred yards from the harbour when someone said, 'Look behind you.' Right on my heels was a huge, well-horned goat. We both stopped, but the look in his eye was agreeably mild. He seemed for all the world like the companionable goat in one of the colour plates of my boyhood edition of *Robinson Crusoe*, and he was very lonely, grateful for overtures of friendship. He was at my heels all the way to the boat. He stood there as we set out on the last two-mile stretch of our trip to Caithness, huge and heraldic against the sombre sky.

There are two places to avoid within four miles of each other in this area of the Pentland Firth. One is the whirlpool called the Swelkie, off the northwest corner of Stroma, where, according to Norse legend, the magical quern Grotti is forever grinding. The waters fall through the eye of the quern, which grinds the white salt that gives the sea its saltness. The other place is the Boars of Duncansby, whose breakers are created by the sunken reefs off Duncansby Head.

It was raining slightly when we drew in to the harbour at John o' Groats, whose dead-white hotel with its octagonal tower is one of the landmarks of this coast. A few yards from the hotel is a mound with a flagstaff. This is reputed to be the position of the home of the original John o' Groat.

While Alec borrowed a van from a friendly Caithness man to collect some cans of weed-killer for his farm, the rest of us arranged for tea. Obviously,

---

1. *A History of the Episcopal Church in the Diocese of Caithness*, Rev. J. B. Craven, DD, 1908, p.265.

to the visitors whose cars stood outside the tea-room, and to the Caithness girls who served us, our Orkney accents sounded strange. One of the crew told me that on a previous occasion an American handed him half-a-crown and implored him to go on talking.

At the pier a dozen Caithnessians watched as we prepared to depart, making jocular remarks about Orcadian seamanship and asking after old friends in the islands. It was eight o'clock before we got away, for the younger men had made a rendezvous with one or two of the local girls. James and Alec waited tolerantly until the high-spirited dialogue ended.

We were going home on the ebb, which meant we had to veer well to the east, out past Duncansby Head. The cliffs loomed above us, surmounted by a lighthouse which looks more like an exclusive hotel. Close by, a box floated on the water. One of the lads pulled it on board with a boat-hook. In the water trapped inside was a perfect little herring, only an inch and a quarter long.

The ships were still coming through. Two large ones, almost exactly alike, passed within a mile of each other. Alec thought they might be ore-carriers, or perhaps grain ships taking part of the big purchase of American grain to Russia.

We made a quick run to Orkney through the gathering dusk—an hour and three-quarters from John o' Groats to Herston. Soon the islands were all around us, and I was saying good-bye to the friends who had given me such an enjoyable day, and setting out on my motorcycle to run through the fine rain over the Churchill Barriers to Kirkwall.

8

The story of the Stromness lifeboats 1867-1967

The celebration of the centenary of Stromness Lifeboat Station in October 1967 helped vividly to recall the bravery and self-sacrifice our island seamen have so frequently exhibited. This commemoration of a hundred years of achievement by Stromness lifeboats and lifeboatmen—at which the Royal National Lifeboat Institution was represented by the Duke of Atholl—touched a responsive chord in the hearts of Orcadians, for life-saving at sea is among our few experiences of the heroic in an age that has become safe and complacent.

Lifeboats came into being largely as the result of a great shock to the public conscience when the *Adventure* of Newcastle, stranded only 300 yards from the shore in a raging sea, could not be reached by ordinary craft, and thousands of spectators saw her crew perish. That was in 1789. Although numbers of lifeboats were built and donated by private philanthropists in the next three decades, it was not until the founding, in 1824, of the Royal National Institution for the Preservation of Life from Shipwreck (later the Royal National Lifeboat Institution) that the saving of life at sea became a matter of wide public interest and concern. Within a year the Institution had built twelve boats and had placed them at strategic stations around the coast. The RNLI began as an independent organisation, and so it has continued: it has always been one of the most efficient, and in conception one of the grandest, of our benevolent Institutions.

The manner in which the national imagination was stirred in 1789 had a parallel in Orkney in 1866, when, on New Year's Day, the emigrant ship *Albion* became a total wreck on the Point of Oxan, Graemsay. Although boats, hurriedly launched from Graemsay, saved most of the 100 passengers and crew, one boat-load of eleven were drowned.[1]

It was suddenly realised that a lifeboat was a necessity on such a perilous coast, and a petition asking for a boat was sent to the RNLI. From the Institution came a quick and sympathetic response. The formation of a broadly-

---

1. A Graemsay man and ten people from the *Albion* were drowned when a local yole was holed by the paddle of the *Royal Mail* which was assisting in the rescue.

based lifeboat committee at Stromness was, however, essential. This had its first meeting on 30 July 1866. Included in its ranks were ministers and professional men, merchants and practical seamen.

Some provision had to be made for the working expenses of the promised lifeboat, so it was decided that contributions should be solicited throughout the county. The committee's first responsibility was to build a boat-house. They deliberated for some time on where it could best be placed. Three sites were available: at Breckness, at the beach of Ness, and within the harbour at the Town House. The position on the beach of Ness was finally chosen, on the advice of Captain Robertson of the RNLI, as the best the coast had to offer. The site was leased from Mr Stanger for a small annual payment, and the boat-house (which still stands) was erected, together with a slipway, for £200.

Its situation soon proved to be completely unsuitable, but one can understand why it was chosen. With only a sailing-and-pulling life-boat available, the aim was to have the station as near the open sea as practicable, to save time when a call came. For twenty years the Ness station was a worry to the committee. Even the 'roadway from boat-house to low-water mark', completed in 1870, and the 'extension of Boat Slipway', added in 1874, did not help matters much; launching at certain states of the tide remained a difficult operation.

The position of the boat-house was responsible for the only blot on the escutcheon of the Stromness station, the tale of which may be frankly related before the heroic saga of the five lifeboats is begun. Some time during the early morning of 13 October 1881, the barque *Arcturus* struck on Braga, then on Pulseskerry, before stranding on the Outer Kirk Rocks, where she became a total wreck. The alarm was given, but the lifeboat was not launched. The coxswain, 2nd coxswain, and eight of the crew turned up but with low water at the time they were helpless. They calculated that it would have taken thirty men to get the boat afloat within an hour. They declared, too, that when the flood had made in the Sound the boat could not have reached the wreck without the aid of steam.

The crew of the *Arcturus* were rescued by the men of the rocket brigade,[1] who showed splendid courage and resource; but a week later a meeting was held in the Masonic Hall, Stromness, to enquire into the causes of the lifeboat's inaction. The inadequacy of Ness beach as a launching place was fully realised, but the members of the lifeboat's crew who had not turned up were censured. The meeting recorded this uncompromising verdict: 'We consider that the boat ought to have been afloat and an attempt made to get to the

---

1. The section of men in HM Coastguards whose duty it was to assist ships in distress by firing a rocket carrying a light rope to which was attached a heavier rope and a breeches buoy. The Stromness Brigade in 1881 was manned by volunteers.

westward.' Probably the worst punishment the defaulters received was a scathing article in *The Orcadian*, which, with the over-righteousness of the arm-chair critic, denounced them as 'cowards' and 'skulks'.

It was no doubt this event that brought home to the lifeboatmen what the public demanded of them. They were, in all fairness, simply hard-pressed fishermen who had consented without much consideration to become members of the lifeboat crew. They had not imagined that they might be asked to put their lives at risk in an open boat in impossible conditions. They exercised individual judgement about what could be done and what could not be done. Now they learned that the service demanded utter dedication. No matter how poor the chances of rescue, or how dangerous the attempt, every call must be answered. Stromness rose to the challenge. On no future occasion was there any question of the readiness of the lifeboat or the devotion of her crew.

Even so, the difficulty of launching the boat remained a problem and for some time the committee toyed with the idea of a 'land-carriage'. Finally, they made the decision to dispose with the boat-house. In 1890 the lifeboat was anchored at the north-end of the harbour and remained there until the construction of a new lifeboat house and slipway in 1901.

The first boat

The first Stromness lifeboat arrived during October 1867. She was paid for out of a legacy from Sir Titus Salt, of Methley Hall, Leeds, and named the *Saltaire*. Her period of service lasted from 1867 to 1891. She was a self-righting boat, thirty-five feet long.

Such a boat had a limited range, she could not beat to windward, and in a gale the men at the oars on the lee side had their legs soaked by the water which she took aboard. The crew often suffered greatly from exposure. On one occasion they searched the whole of the coast to Birsay for a fishing boat lost in a gale. It was a terrible night, and their misery was increased by a snowstorm. They managed at last to reach Skippigeo in Birsay, where they rested until the SS *St Olaf* which had been sent to search for them, discovered their whereabouts and took them home.

Exposure was no less of a problem in the *Saltaire*'s successor. In 1902 a sum of £15 was voted for the relief of the widow of George Campbell who had died as a result of exposure while out on service on 19 December 1898. This is an occasion not noted on the service board at the station.

A year after she arrived in Stromness the *Saltaire* rescued five men from the schooner *Victor* of Grimsby. She also helped to save the vessel. Never again in her twenty-four years' service was this vessel credited with saving life, although she endured some heavy seas.

Skippigeo, Birsay, c.1960 Stanley Cursiter, RSA, RSW, 1887-1976

'The Good Shepherd'

The next lifeboat, *The Good Shepherd*, counted only a total of eighteen lives saved, one for each year of her service. As has been said, these boats had a very restricted range, unlike the powerful motor lifeboats of today, but they gave opportunities for feats of endurance and heroism that have not been surpassed. It must be remembered, too, that ships in those days were different, and that navigation was perhaps more expertly studied by the masters of fishing craft than it has been since. By far the most regular clients of the Stromness station have been steam trawlers, to at least thirty of which assistance has been given. Next to trawlers have come Scandinavian vessels, ten of which have required help.

Like her predecessor, *The Good Shepherd* was a sailing and rowing boat, but she was appreciably larger than the *Saltaire*, measuring forty-two feet by eleven feet. She was the gift of the Loyal Order of Ancient Shepherds, hence her name. Her cost, which seems ludicrous today, was £519. She arrived at Stromness on 15 June 1891.

In 1892 the RNLI inspector asked the local committee to enrol a double crew so that there would always be sufficient men when needed, but the lifeboat coxswain reported that he could only muster twenty good men. This was well short of the number desired as *The Good Shepherd* needed a crew of fifteen. When she put to sea she had ten rowers—five on either side—pulling the great sixteen-feet oars, which were ballasted with lead in the shafts to make them easier to handle. She was an open boat, affording no shelter for the crew or for those whom they rescued.

Around the end of the nineteenth century and the beginning of the twentieth she gave assistance to several fishing boats and drifters; then, on the morning of 11 December 1907, her hour of glory arrived.

Early on that dark winter morning the fishermen were gathered around the harbour and in the street trying to decide whether to go to sea. They were still deliberating when the order came to launch *The Good Shepherd*, securely housed in the building which had once been the Salvation Army barracks. The farmer at Breckness, David Clouston, had galloped over the hill on horseback to say that a trawler was wrecked on the Point of Spoil, and in extreme danger.

The launching of the lifeboat went without a hitch, the swiftest that Stromness had ever seen. Soon the rowers had taken her past Ness and Warebeth and had come within sight of the trawler, which proved to be the *Shakespeare* of Hull. The trawler was in a desperate situation. Her hull, which lay about fifty yards from the shore, was entirely submerged, with head to the sea and an outward list. The sea was breaking over the vessel constantly, and she was surrounded by broken water. Only her masts and part of the funnel were in sight. To the foremast two men were clinging; another hung on to the funnel. On the mizzen mast were three more men. Four men had already been drowned: two had been washed away and two had fallen exhausted from the mizzen mast, one of them when the lifeboat was within sight.

It was obvious that the work of rescue would be exceedingly difficult and dangerous, but there was little time left for calculation. Coxswain Robert Greig made up his mind quickly. He was described later as the most capable man who ever held a tiller. Everything depended on his superb seamanship. He anchored some way ahead of the *Shakespeare*, then, sure of the co-operation of his crew, manoeuvred into the lee of the wreck, until he was only twelve yards away. From there, with the lifeboat often standing on end in the boiling surf, and with the black rocks of the shore a constant menace, the grapnel was thrown to the trawler, taking hold on the fore-rigging, and a lifebuoy was passed to the men clinging to the mast. Once they were safely on board, a line was thrown to the man on the funnel, who was saved with difficulty, as the line jammed and he was very exhausted. The three men on the mizzen mast were taken ashore by the rocket brigade, which had arrived about the same time as the lifeboat.

For his conduct in the *Shakespeare* rescue Coxswain Robert Greig was awarded the Silver Medal of the Institution, a decoration reserved for supreme gallantry. It had come once before to Stromness, having been voted to Robert Leask, who put off in squally November weather in 1872 and saved two out of three people whose craft had capsized.

'The John A. Hay'

For five years, beginning in 1904, the RNLI deliberated on a new lifeboat for the Stromness station. By this time the crew had grown so fond of their old boat, which had proved her seaworthiness on several notable occasions, that they were loth to part with her. When pressed, they asked for a boat of the same size and type with two feet more rake on the stern post.

But motor lifeboats were very obviously the craft of the future and the Institution decided to build one for Stromness. This boat, the *John A. Hay*, named after the man whose legacy covered the building cost of £2,895, was actually the first lifeboat to be built as a motor lifeboat; previous ones had been converted from sailing craft. She arrived at her station on 30 April 1909, under the command of Commander H. J. Rowley, RN.

The *John A. Hay* was the same length as *The Good Shepherd* (forty-two feet) but she had more beam (twelve-and-a-half feet). Her crew quickly came to appreciate the advantages of a boat with a powerful engine. The new lifeboat greatly extended their radius of action. She had an active life of nineteen years, only being replaced in 1928. During that time, which included several wartime years of enforced inaction, 102 lives were saved. The boat more than once went to the extreme limits of the North Isles.

In 1916 the lifeboat, although kept ready for immediate service, was prevented from performing what might have been her greatest task. On the evening of 5 June, shortly after eight o'clock, the *Hampshire*, on her way to Russia with Lord Kitchener, sank off Marwick Head.[1] Several rafts loaded with men were seen to leave the ship before she disappeared.

By some means news of the disaster came shortly afterwards to the lifeboatmen of Stromness. The honorary secretary of the Stromness branch of the RNLI, G. L. Thomson, telephoned to Stromness Naval HQ to offer the services of the lifeboat. He received a cold reply, to the effect that warship movements could not be discussed and that nothing was known about a cruiser in distress. Nevertheless, he alerted the lifeboat crew and had the boat prepared for sea. He himself went to see Commander Walker, Commander Western Patrol, who absolutely refused to have the lifeboat launched, and who treated him with such extreme discourtesy that the matter rankled in his mind until the day of his death.

Mr Thomson well knew that the Stromness lifeboat, manned by seamen who knew every mile of the coast, was the only craft likely to get to the scene of the disaster in time, and the only one which could take the risk of exploring the waters close to the shore. In the event, only twelve members of the *Hampshire*'s crew survived. The thought of the two hundred men on the rafts who perished because they could not get help in time greatly troubled the lifeboatmen, who were convinced that they could have given effective service even in the heavy seas then running.

The RNLI have placed it on record that they notified the Admiralty that no information was given to the Lifeboat authorities with regard to the loss of HMS *Hampshire* and they add: 'It is the belief of the people of Stromness that if their lifeboat had been called out large numbers of the crew of the *Hampshire* would have been saved.'

The late Major John Mackay, Orkney RGA (T), who himself did his best to provide help on that dreadful night, wrote afterwards: 'The Stromness motor lifeboat, a fine vessel of its class, could easily have weathered the breeze. . . . The falling darkness could scarcely have hindered the lifeboat's work as practically all the Naval rafts were fitted with lights which ignited on touching the water. Personally, I saw many lights on the sea that night. I could not understand their meaning at first—but there they were, the guiding signals from the rafts to the rescuers, had they been permitted to proceed on their errand of mercy.'

The lifeboat had to wait nearly four years before she was called out on

1. See also 'The day that Kitchener died', p.419.

service again. On 27-28 June 1920, she landed ten men from the SS *Ulster* of Aberdeen, and helped to save the vessel. Between then and 1928 she had rescued seventy-one men in the course of six launches.

Her coxswain, William Johnston, was voted the Bronze Medal for the rescue of two men clinging to a raft in Eynhallow Sound. Their vessel, the steam trawler *Freesia* of Grimsby, was wrecked on Costa Head on New Year's Day. The lifeboat was operating twenty-five miles from her station in particularly severe weather conditions. Nine members of the trawler's crew perished.

A new type of boat, the 'JJKSW'

The Stromness committee were notified in 1921 that a more powerful motor lifeboat would be supplied, possibly one similar to a sixty-feet boat which was being built for New Brighton. The New Brighton boat actually visited Stromness in 1923 and was tested by members of the committee and crew in a whole gale. A little later the honorary secretary, coxswain and 2nd coxswain visited Tenby to see a smaller, very modern, lifeboat stationed there. Something in between the forty-five feet Tenby boat and the large New Brighton boat seemed to be most suitable for Stromness.

Mr G. L. Thomson went to London with a handful of suggestions. Stromness felt that its boat should be capable of being housed; that she should be around fifty feet long, with twin engines and a speed of not less than nine knots; that she should have increased sheer, a higher bow and more flare; that protection of the crew should be provided in a forward cock-pit; that she should have sail power; and, finally, that she should be fitted with a low foot rail below the railings on deck. All these things were discussed by Mr Thomson and the naval architect, and the suggestions were incorporated into the ultimate design.

The result was the *Barnett* (Stromness) type motor lifeboat, named after the designer J. R. Barnett. This became a standard design, supplied to stations in many parts of Great Britain. Some years later, at a meeting of the Council in 1933, the secretary of the RNLI reported: 'The most interesting recent developments have been in filling all the gaps on the Lifeboat map. This has been mainly due to the work done by two officials who are sitting together here today: Mr J. R. Barnett and Mr Thomson of Stromness, who have invented the 51-feet twin-screw *Barnett* (Stromness) type. Mr Barnett will admit how much help he got from Mr Thomson and the fine crew at Stromness in bringing the boat to its present perfection.'

It was not until 1928 that the Stromness boat was ready. Meanwhile, accommodation for her had to be provided, so, on 3 October 1925, the contract for a new house and slipway was given to Melville, Dundas and Whitsun of Glasgow.

20 Stromness lifeboat *John A. Hay*, 1909-28

21 Stromness lifeboat *J.J.K.S.W.*, 1928-55

22 Kirkwall harbour, c.1890

Over the years the cost of producing a modern lifeboat had increased greatly. The new boat, named the *JJKSW*, cost nearly five times as much as her predecessor, the final figure being £13,642. She was provided by the combined legacies of Miss J. Moody, Mr J. P. Traill, Mr W. M. Aitken, Mr E. J. Hanson and Mr W. W. Notting. The initials *JJKSW* represented an extraordinarily long name for her full title was, *The John and Ann Moody, J. P. Traill, Kate MacFarlane Aitken, Sam Wood and William Notting*. The The builders were Saunders & Co., of Cowes, Isle of Wight. She made the thousand-mile journey to Orkney at the end of February and the beginning of March 1928, arriving at Stromness on 3 March. A week later the veteran *John A. Hay* left for Belfast.

The first test came in a little over a fortnight when the *JJKSW* was called to the assistance of the steam trawler *Lord Devonport* of Hull, wrecked at Hoy Head. Before the lifeboat got to the vessel several members of her crew had been drowned, but she was in time to respond to a piece of cool and daring seamanship, during which six men were rescued. Her excellent behaviour in dangerous conditions greatly impressed the lifeboatmen, who did not hesitate to take her to Shetland some two years later when a trawler was reported to be in extreme peril on the Vee Skerries. Unfortunately, she was called too late, but this long journey in foul weather was a memorable feat which put to the test the splendid qualities of both the boat and her crew.

It had been decided that the *JJKSW* should have the honour of a royal christening. This took place on 6 June 1928, when HRH Prince George came to Stromness for the naming ceremony, which he performed with a fine dignity and simplicity.

Less than a year later Prince George sent a telegram (still to be seen in the lifeboat house) congratulating the Stromness lifeboat crew on their gallantry. The occasion was the rescue, on 14 February 1929, of the entire crew of the steam trawler *Carmania II* of Grimsby, stranded on the Kirk Rocks. The trawler was returning home from Iceland with a large catch of fish. As she was passing through Hoy Sound about 3.30 in the morning her steering gear jammed. A stream tide was running and snow was falling thickly when a heavy sea struck the unmanageable vessel and drove her on the rocks. Signals from her siren roused people in the neighbourhood, and the lifeboat was launched.

The situation was so dangerous that nothing could be done until daylight. The first light came at last, and about the same time came the turn of the tide, which swung the trawler completely around. The lifeboat, which had been standing by, put out a kedge anchor and dropped down through the surf. At times she seemed to watchers on shore to be completely enveloped by the sea. But action was now essential, for the trawler was being swept by waves from stem to stern, and the men clung desperately to the wheel-house as she rolled and shuddered on the rocks.

Coxswain Johnston showed consummate judgement. He brought the lifeboat so near to the wreck that a line could be thrown over her. Whenever the sea allowed, a man was pulled aboard, until five soaking trawlermen had been rescued. Then came seeming disaster.

So great was the strain that the wire hawser to the kedge snapped and the lifeboat was no longer able to maintain her position. The situation of the men remaining on the wreck was very grave. There was one hope left. During the storm the trawler's small boat had been swept off her deck and was floating alongside, attached to the trawler by her painter. The seven men on the heaving ship managed to pull the small boat alongside and fall into it without capsizing. This was the lifeboat crew's opportunity. They manoeuvred their boat until they came up to the trawler's boat, from which five men scrambled into safety.

Again the sea took command. The painter of the trawler's boat snapped, and she was adrift and helpless in the boiling surf. One of the two men still on board managed to keep her head to the sea. The lifeboat took a last calculated risk. She ran between the trawler and the beach, reached the boat, and pulled its occupants aboard.

The helpless spectators on the open beach at the cemetery vowed that they had never seen such superb seamanship. The comment made to reporters by the coxswain remains in the memory: 'We have a grand boat, and we are afraid of nothing above water if we have plenty o' water below us. I like no' when we see the redware[1] churning up alongside of us.'

William Johnston did not like publicity; but that episode entailed a trip across the Firth to Scrabster, where he received from the Duchess of Portland the Bronze Second Service Clasp of the RNLI.

The *JJKSW* had many another exciting trip, for she was launched, according to the Institution's records, ninety-two times, and saved in all 139 lives. Famous among her exploits was the rescue of three men from the ill-fated *Leicester City* on 22 March 1953. Her crew had received, among other commendations, a letter of appreciation from the Danish Government in 1939, in respect of a launch to the aid of the schooner *Nordstennan* of Marstal. In 1928 her usefulness was increased by the installation of a wireless receiving set. This was replaced by a transmitting and receiving set in 1937.

From the end of the First World War until the time when wireless was installed, the late Mr G. L. Thomson, Mr John Rae and Mr J. G. Sinclair always endeavoured to keep in touch with the lifeboat when she was operating off the coast of the Mainland by means of Morse signals or, in event of recall, by Very pistol, and later on by small rocket. The two survivors of this trio can remember wild nights spent on the cliff tops when the boat was at sea.

---

1. A broad-leafed seaweed which grows under water.

It was during the period of service of this lifeboat that the honorary secretary, G. L. Thomson, a man of splendid character and devotion, received national recognition. In June 1941 he was awarded the MBE. The RNLI had recognised his unique qualities many years before—in 1924—when it appointed him a life governor. He died in May 1944. In a tribute to Mr Thomson, C. R. Satterthwaite, Secretary of the RNLI, wrote: 'I can safely say that there is not a lifeboat station in the British Isles which has been more efficiently organised than the Stromness station under Mr Thomson's care.'

The last services given to Orkney by the *JJKSW* before she was superseded were unusual and important ones. In January 1955 all transport in Orkney was brought to a standstill by heavy falls of snow. On one route twenty to thirty stranded vehicles were snowed up to the roof. Roads were only cleared to fill up again. Aircraft dropped food and animal fodder to some isolated farms. The lifeboat played her part in the emergency. On 14 January she took a Graemsay lightkeeper's wife to hospital in Kirkwall, landing her at Scapa. Her record for three days ran: 18 January—Took provisions to Quoyloo; 19 January—Took hospital case to Scapa; 20 January—Took medical party to Hoy.

The present lifeboat

A new lifeboat (the present one),[1] again of the *Barnett* (Stromness) type, had been on order for the station for a considerable time. Like her predecessor, she was built in the Isle of Wight. By May 1955 she was ready. On the 21st of the month she was met in Scapa Flow by the *JJKSW* and escorted into Stromness Harbour. A 52-feet twin-screw motor lifeboat, with two 60 h.p. diesels, she is still in excellent condition. If need be she can carry over a hundred passengers, and is capable of travelling well over two hundred miles at nine knots without refuelling. Her engines are water-tight and could continue running even if the engine-room were flooded.

This boat was the gift of Miss Margaret M. Paterson, of St Petersburg, Florida, who presented the money to the RNLI in memory of her brothers, uncle and grandfather. The boat is named the *Archibald and Alexander M. Paterson*. She cost £36,000.

The actual naming ceremony did not take place until 25 August. It was performed by Miss Chris McKinnon, a cousin of the American donor.

In the decade that she has been in service the present lifeboat has been called out at least thirty times and has saved many lives. She has had the usual tally of trawlers, but has also had to give help several times to smaller fishing boats.

1. It was replaced in October 1984 by *The Joseph Rothwell Sykes and Hilda M*, an Arun class lifeboat.

For a long time now the efficiency of the crew[1] has been proverbial. As Admiral Sir Angus Cunninghame Grahame said in 1955, 'The Stromness Lifeboat has a tradition to be proud of.' There is no possible doubt that it will be maintained.

An integral part of the Stromness tradition has been length of service. There have been only nine coxswains in the past hundred years, and individual lifeboatmen have had wonderful records. Perhaps one should not name particular men where so many have given decades of unstinting devotion, but surely the late John W. Folster's period of service, which covered fifty-one years, has seldom been equalled anywhere.

Always solidly behind the crew has been a faithful and efficient local committee.[2] Here, too, length of service has been conspicuous. From thirty to forty years has been such a usual period as to pass almost unnoticed. Mr G. L. Thomson was honorary secretary and treasurer for over forty years, and had been a member of the committee before that. The present chairman of the Stromness branch of the RNLI, Mr John Rae, has been a member of committee for thirty-nine years and chairman for twenty-three years.[3] He was presented with the Silver Badge of the RNLI ten years ago.

For the record a list is given of coxswains and honorary secretaries:

COXSWAINS		HONORARY SECRETARIES	
William Flett	1867-1878	James R. Garrioch	to 1879
James Shearer	1878-1898	Captain George Bilton	1879-1888
Robert Greig	1898-1915	Captain George Bailie	1888-1903
William Johnston	1915-1930	George L. Thomson	1903-1944
William Linklater	1930-1938	John G. Sinclair	1944-1945
Robert Greig	1938-1940	Thomas S. Harvey	1945-1962
William Sinclair	1940-1953	Captain John Allan[5]	1962-
James Adam	1953-1963		
Alfred Sinclair[4]	1963-		

1. Alfred Sinclair, coxswain; Jack Leslie, 2nd coxswain; Robert Scott, bowman; Edward Wilson, motor mechanic; William Sinclair, assistant motor mechanic; Ivor Donaldson, George Skinner, Leslie Halcrow, James Mowat, deck hands.
2. John Rae, chairman; Captain John Allan, honorary secretary; William Halcrow, honorary treasurer; Dr James Cromarty, honorary medical officer; Thomas S. Craigie, Capt. John Hourie, George Ireland, William E. Knight, John E. P. Robertson, Capt. John Stevenson, James Wishart.
3. John Rae remained chairman until 1983.
4. He retired in 1983 and was succeeded by William Sinclair.
5. He retired in 1985. William Craigie then became honorary secretary.

A lifeboat station was opened at Longhope in 1874 and one at Stronsay in 1909.[1] Although the above is solely the story of the Stromness lifeboats, written for the centenary year, the other stations have histories that are no less worthy of being related, and in the celebrations which marked the hundred years of the lifeboat service in Orkney they were not forgotten. Between them the lifeboats belonging to the three stations have saved a total of 934 lives.

1. It operated until 1915. The station reopened in October 1952 and finally closed on 30 May 1972.

9

By bottle post

Among the commonest finds on Orkney shores are bottles with messages. Just recently, as listeners heard at the time on the news, a bottle message brought a Westrayman a free holiday in Norway. But for a century or more, bottles of all shapes and sizes, carrying serious messages and fantastic messages, have been brought in by the sea.

One of the fastest travelling bottles of all time was picked up by two Birsay men, William Moar and Peter Slater, just north of Skaill on Friday, 9 February 1877. It was attached to a lifebuoy, which perhaps accounts for its speed. Anyway, when the message inside the bottle was read, it was found to be a letter written in St Kilda on 22 January. In something like seventeen days, perhaps less, the bottle had travelled 185 nautical miles—which is roughly 212 miles as we calculate them on land.

But the message the bottle contained was no casual one. It was a call for help. The writer was John Sands of Ormiston who was on one of his visits to the island. Six months earlier he had brought the islanders the gift of a large open boat. For the whole of the autumn and into winter he was storm-stayed on St Kilda. But the situation really got complicated when, on 17 January, an Austrian barque, the *Peti Dubrovacki*, was wrecked near St Kilda, and the captain with eight of his crew became the guests of the islanders. They were welcome enough, but they were hungry; and provisions got shorter and shorter. To summon help Mr Sands wrote his letter, put it in a bottle, and consigned it to the sea.

He could hardly have anticipated that just over a fortnight later a telegram would be speeding from Orkney to the Austrian consul in Glasgow. The consul sent the news to the Admiralty and on 22 February the gunboat HMS *Jackal* was on her way to St Kilda. She made the island, most fortunately, during a break in the storms. No sooner had she taken Mr Sands and the Austrians on board than the island was swept by one of the severest gales of the winter.

But the seventy-one St Kildans in their black houses were happy. They had cheerfully shared their dried fish, fulmars and eggs with their guests. Now the gunboat had brought them in exchange some meal, hard tack in the form of ship's biscuits, and, to wash it all down, a barrel of rum.[1] And Mr Sands was happy. He was already planning his book about St Kilda, which had a good sale. He called it *Out of the World or Life in St Kilda*. So, you see, a good many people owed a lot to a record-breaking bottle.

---

1. It is said that despite these gifts the islanders temporarily had to do without porridge and bread. In May 1877 grain, sugar, tea, salt and other foodstuffs arrived by the naval vessel HMS *Flirt*. These items were purchased with a donation of £100 given by the Austrian government to the St Kildans in recognition of their kindness to the shipwrecked Austrians.

10

An odd fish

From January to April, at new moon or full moon, an amiable madness seizes many Orcadians. They muffle themselves up in their oldest clothes, with caps over their ears and jerseys up to their chins. Stuck away in poacher's pockets or the legs of rubber boots, they carry long, ugly knives. If you see a bunch of these people together, they look like revolutionaries in a vintage film.

Yet they are the most harmless people on earth. You might call them fishers, but books on the gentle art of angling have no place for them, even in appendices. Nor will the long knives ever be fleshed in shark or whale. Their quarry is in the sand—a shell-fish that looks for all the world like the handle of an old-fashioned razor, and which prefers to live at the extreme seaward margin of a sandy beach. In text-books these odd molluscs are called *razor-fish*, but everyone in Orkney knows them as *spoots*.

For most of the year the spoots are safe, buried away in chilly comradeship below the tide-line. But with the spring tides (hence the tie-up with the moon) the sea goes out so far that for an hour or two the stretches of sand inhabited by the spoots are uncovered. Then you have, unless an awkward wind interferes, a *spoot ebb*.

Every enthusiast who can get away takes advantage of such an ebb, for conditions of weather and tide seldom make the sport possible for more than twenty or thirty hours in a whole year.

At places like the Sands of Ness in St Andrews and the Echna Loch in Burray, cars arrive with loads of bemuffled fishers, some of them townsfolk from Kirkwall and Stromness. On one beach recently, a prominent Kirkwall businessman and the captain of Orkney's best-known steamer could be recognised.

They wait patiently for the sea to ebb, fortifying themselves from the cold with spirits or hot tea, pulling on rubber boots, looking out knife and bucket.

When conditions are right, each fisher finds what he considers the best place, then moves slowly backwards, knife clutched firmly in his hand, eyes

23 Shaking nets, Stromness, *c*.1890

24 Herring fishing station, Burray, *c*.1900

25 Fish curing, Thomas Chalmers' fish store, Ayre Road, Kirkwall, c.1890

glued to the sand. As the spoot feels him coming it burrows furiously downwards, leaving a characteristic hole, or hollow, in the surface. That is what the man with the knife is waiting for. He plunges his weapon quickly into the sand with a sideways sweep, so that he makes contact with the shell and prevents the spoot from escaping. Then with his free hand he scoops away the surface sand, digging down until he can seize the shell and draw it triumphantly forth.

He may with luck take home several dozen spoots in his bucket. To the true Orkney epicure those yellowish-brown shells contain manna from heaven, but some people regard the spoot with distaste, and liken the fish to a pale piece of guttapercha. I am told by a Kirkwall expert that it should not be like that at all—what makes the delectable mollusc tough and indigestible is over-cooking. Instead of boiling and then frying the spoots, as the uninitiated do, one should steam them in a pan with either no water or a mere tablespoonful. Then the fish should be taken out of the opened shells and dropped into hot melted butter.

There is no export trade in spoots, but local shops occasionally sell them when a good ebb has brought a surplus. In fact, just recently, a Kirkwall chip shop tried them out as an experiment on its patrons, who included youngsters and some non-Orcadians who had never seen them before, with the result that so many asked for more that the spoots were sold out half way through the evening.

THE DAY'S WORK—
Trades and Crafts[1]

1 History from a day-book	81
2 The story of the Orkney chair	85
3 An Omond fiddle	88
4 The story of the provost's chain	90

1. This section highlights a few Orkney trades and crafts. Others are described in *Some Annals of an Orkney Parish* and *Stone Breakers*—both articles are to be found in the section 'Memories'.

Shore Street, Kirkwall, c.1925

Stanley Cursiter, RSA, RSW, 1887-1976

I

History from a day-book

Once upon a time we thought that history was all about kings and queens and battles. Indeed, until fairly recently there was a tendency in Orkney to consider that our own history began and ended with the *Orkneyinga Saga*. We have now learned to appreciate that the way ordinary people lived and laboured is also history.

Where do we find the sources of this? Well, to take an obvious one, Mr Evan MacGillivray[1] has in the County Library something like 200,000 documents: estate papers, reports, letters, memoranda; all the kinds of things that accumulate over the years in busy households. Some day local historians will analyse and study these, and fascinating facts will emerge.

Mr John D. M. Robertson has given us another excellent example[2] of how a game can be made to throw a revealing light on the life of town and country.

But have you ever thought that in your own offices and places of business you may have the raw material of history? Indeed you may; and that is why I am calling this short piece *History from a day-book*. From the fading pages of day-book, letter book or ledger a social historian may be able to resurrect the past and make it live. So first of all, may I make a plea for the preservation of your records, no matter how unimportant they may seem to you at the moment.

A Stromness merchant's day-book is at present being studied. It gives a picture of the last years of the trade between Stromness and Hudson Bay. For the men of the Nor'-Wast dealt directly with merchants in Stromness until 1913. From the day-book we can discover who these men were, at what forts and trading-posts they were stationed, what kinds of articles they needed in their new homes in Canada, and much else.

But a day-book from a small rural community can be just as interesting. I was given on loan recently a day-book covering the period from May 1884 to November 1906, kept by John Spence, Beaquoy, Birsay. I can remember

---

1. A distinguished Orcadian, he retired to Sweden where he continued to write scholarly articles on Orkney. He died in 1987.
2. *Uppies & Doonies*, The Story of the Kirkwall Ba' Game, 1967.

John Spence as he appeared to me as a boy: a kindly man with a big beard, continually peering into watches with a glass screwed to his eye. In his latter days he seemed to be mainly a watchmaker. In 1923 he built himself a wonderful regulator clock, which still keeps splendid time.

In the time covered by the day-book, however, when John Spence was a younger, more active man, the trades of which he was master were many. He was a joiner, wheelwright, millwright, cabinet-maker, decorator, commission agent, cycle-mender, a watchmaker even then, and an undertaker.

In communities like the area of Birsay in which he lived, the clever neat-handed tradesman had to tackle every kind of craft. People were often too poor to buy readymade articles from the shops, and the local man made them for next to nothing. For most of this period John Spence's charge for his work was 2/- a day, and that was for a full day, from eight in the morning to seven, or even eight, at night. Into a tradesman's hands came a little money, and he was often petitioned for loans by people in extremity. There are a number of references to this in the day-book—loans varying from a shilling to a pound. Fancy a loan of a shilling making a difference to a poor family. The loans were almost always repaid, with not a penny of interest charged.

You may be interested to hear what some articles cost eighty years ago and how much people paid for specific jobs. One man built a new house, and John Spence did all the woodwork, including roof, windows, doors and beds. The wood, which was his customer's, probably drifted in from the sea or was salved from a wreck, but John Spence sawed it, dressed it, and fitted it—all by hand—and his total bill was £5, 12s. To take two items only: To making twenty couples 5/-; to laying parlour beams and floor 1/10d.

He made a new cream churn for a woman and charged her 2/6d. She disputed the cost, and they compromised for 2/-. But she bought three clothes poles, for which she paid 2/9d.

I mentioned that he was asked to do all kinds of jobs. There is a note: 'To framing a Gospel compass' (whatever that may be) 3/0¼d. Someone from Abune-the-hill, perhaps a sailor, wanted a parrot cage. John got tinned wire and zinc and produced one, for 7/6d. The schoolmaster at Costa needed a pitch-pine bookcase—a large one. It cost him £2, 9s. 9d. Another man required a windmill. John Spence made that too, cutting the big sails from canvas.

America was regarded as the most progressive of all places at that time in Orkney. American clocks were very popular. Red cheese was American cheese; oil-cloth was American cloth; a textile with a fake leather surface was American leather. So we find John Spence making a Californian pump and an American pattern mill.

Speaking about mills, it was just at this period, the 'eighties and 'nineties, that people were putting in horse-gear to drive their mills. There is evidence of this in the day-book. Between 1885 and 1895 John Spence fitted up seventeen horse-mills. The gears and machinery for a horse-mill cost £5, 2s, with 6/- extra for the wooden lever. On more than one occasion he made a complete water-mill, including wheel and trough, and the cost was from £10 to £12.

Just a glance at what tools and material cost him. A chisel was 4d, nails were 3d a pound, paint 6d a pound, a wooden batten 6 inches by 4 inches was 1½d a foot.

I said that John Spence was an undertaker. He made on an average seven coffins in a year—156 coffins in the period covered by the day-book. What was called a 'full mounted coffin', with handles, name-plate, cords and tassels; covered with black crêpe outside and unbleached cotton inside, and with lace round the edge, cost 25/-. Most of the cost was material; John Spence charged for his work from 4/3d to 5/-. When a pauper died, the parochial board ordered an economy type coffin for which they paid 20/-.

Refreshments were a necessity at funerals then. Sometimes John obtained these for his clients, supplying port wine at 1/6d a half bottle and rum at 1/4d.

As a commission agent, he obtained sewing machines for the local dress-makers, for all the women's outfits were made in the parish. When it was a White's machine the cost was £4, but a Wheeler and Wilson cost £4, 13s. He supplied tobacco at 3d an ounce. A clock for the Hope of the West Good Templar Lodge (8-day, walnut case) was 15/-. Don't be surprised when I tell you that one of the requests made to him was for a microscope. The student was William Linklater of Halbreck. He bought the microscope in 1893 for £3, 10s—a big sum in those days. It was no passing fancy; five years later he was still ordering books on microscopy. The Birsay folk were an astonishing race, especially the Spences. Nicol Spence around this time was provost of Kirkwall; John Spence of Evrabist was collecting his folklore and compiling his flora of Birsay; Peter Spence of Eastabist was settling down once again to read through Gibbon's *Decline and Fall of the Roman Empire* (he read it eight times in all). Our John Spence was studying astronomy.

A lot of the man gets into his day-book. His honesty, for instance. He writes, 'This charge is too much' then makes a reduction. His willingness to make interest-free loans to his neighbours. His philosophy—between bills for mending watches he wrote, 'Not every great work is a good work, but every good work is a great work.' He pasted in his book a prayer. 'Strengthen our hands to ready deeds of kindness,' it ran.

We see in the bills the men who were his clients, some well-off, paying a sizeable bill at once; others making payments on account for sums that seem to us very small, usually under a pound. There are house-names which have disappeared—Jerusalem and Reekie Brae, the latter becoming Canada.

John had his own ideas about medicine which I pass on to you. For drowsiness or dullness take one pennyworth of Bicarbonate of Potash in a black bottle of water. Cabbage contains dangerous oils, boil it in two waters. Brimstone kills every species of fungus in man, beast or plant in a few minutes. A sulphur gargle is a certain cure for diphtheria. For gout take a teaspoonful three times a day of a mixture of sweet nitre, sulphur and honey.

I don't suppose you enter such things in your own day-books, but even without them you can perhaps glimpse the picture that such a simple source of material can give of a man and his time.

2

The story of the Orkney chair[1]

This is the story of the Orkney chair—a very special type of chair, which, you could say, has made its way in the world.

For many generations the Orkney chair was a humble piece of furniture, only to be found at the side of the open hearth in island cottages, where its high, rounded back of closely-knit straw kept off the draughts and fitted comfortably the tired body of the goodman after a long day on land or sea. But the basic design of the chair was so good that nowadays examples made by a craftsman who specializes in its manufacture are to be found in many a stately home.

If you've never seen an Orkney chair, let me describe it for you. It has a square framework of wood, of fairly generous proportions, with short side-arms, and a back that rises to head level. This back is made of oat-straw, built up in beautifully regular courses of straw rather less than an inch thick. All the courses, about forty-five of them, are bound together with thin, straw-coloured cord made nowadays of raffia, but in the old days fashioned out of bent grass. The craftsman shapes the back as he builds it up. When finished it is very strong and a joy to the eye.

It is said that the original Orkney chair was made entirely of straw, its lower part being like an inverted tub of straw on which the back was super-imposed. Then, somewhere around two hundred years ago, a North Ronaldsay man made the first Orkney chair with a wooden frame. His chair was probably put together from driftwood, which at that date was strewn on shores every winter. His invention was soon adopted throughout Orkney, the straw back being sewn tightly to wooden uprights.

Two kinds of chair (in those days it was called a 'steul'—using the old Norwegian word) became common: the goodman's chair and the goodwife's. The difference was that the goodman's steul had a higher back and underneath its seat a shallow drawer was added in which the owner kept his tobacco, fish-hooks, Bible and boot-nails.

1. This was broadcast c.1966. Reynold Eunson, master craftsman, died in 1978 at the age of 47. Orkney chairs are still made locally by skilled craftsmen.

If you had told that old North Ronaldsay man of the 1760s that one day his chairs would be considered suitable gifts for two reigning monarchs, a Queen mother, and a princess, and that they would be coveted by people in a dozen different countries, he would have laughed derisively; but this is all part of the saga of the Orkney chair.

The chair of today has evolved to its present technical perfection through the genius of an island craftsman, David M. Kirkness, who went to Kirkwall as a young man to make his way as a carpenter. It occurred to him that the rough country steuls might be so improved in design that, without losing any essential feature, they might be welcome in the drawing-rooms of people who liked fine furniture. In 1876, or thereabout, Kirkness opened his workshop, and during the next half century—indeed right up to the end of his working life in the 1930s—he was continually adjusting his design, improving its balance, perfecting its finish. Orcadians all over the world became his customers, and he was supremely happy when his extraordinary skill was recognised by royalty. He treasured a coloured photograph—still displayed in the workshop—of Princess Mary in her golden-haired girlhood sitting in one of his chairs.

The Second World War came and went, and David Kirkness's templates lay unused in the workshop in Palace Road, in the shadow of St Magnus Cathedral. Then, in 1956, Orkney had the honour of a visit from the Queen Mother; and it was decided that, like royal visitors of the past, she should be given an Orkney chair. About this time, a young Kirkwall craftsman, named Reynold Eunson, bought the carpentry business, in which chair-making had once predominated. He was asked to construct the royal chair. He consented with considerable misgivings, but, in turning out a job which compared favourably with the best examples of the past, he discovered such a love of the craft, that he decided to orientate the business once again towards chair-making.

The rest of the story for the past decade—for he has just celebrated his tenth anniversary as a chair-maker—is Reynold Eunson's. Year by year his orders have increased, but he has never been tempted to skimp his workmanship. The oak is selected with the utmost care, coloured by fuming with ammonia, and finished with many coats of linseed oil, giving a surface of rare beauty. The chair backs are made at their cottage firesides by islanders of long experience, willing to work hour after hour so that the result is as perfect as they can make it.

Who purchases Orkney chairs today? When I asked Reynold Eunson this question he hardly knew where to begin. His straw-back chairs have gone over the oceans to Canada, Africa and Australia; they have found their way to France, Norway and Sweden; twenty-eight of them stand round the tables at the Scotch Club at Aachen in Germany; recently the German

Ambassador to Great Britain called at the Kirkwall workshop and ordered one for himself. Other individuals in many countries have had them made—for instance, a few months ago one of the chairs was jolted along a dirt road in an ancient truck to Amen Farm, Brooklin, Maine, the latest of a long series to go to the United States.

The world of fine furniture has caught up at last with Mr Eunson. He recently had an order for eighteen chairs from a famous English furniture firm. If you see a dignified straw-backed chair in a modern hotel, or in an old country mansion, look for Reynold Eunson's trademark: the initials R.E. on either side of a Scotch thistle.

3

An Omond fiddle

The furnishings of the old-fashioned Orkney home used to be spartan in the extreme—a table, some chairs, a meal-girnel[1]—but in hundreds of homes there was one luxury: a violin. In the evenings, bleak little cots, lit only by a reed lamp,[2] would resound with music. Many of the tunes must have come down through the centuries, but are forgotten.

Probably, with violins so much beyond the average man's means, a number of people would have liked to try their hand at violin-making, but lack of proper materials and tools frustrated them. Nevertheless, a few Orcadians became good violin-makers and one man became notable. His name was James Omond. While his work was nearly all done last century, every knowledgeable Orkney violinist knows what you mean when you speak of an 'Omond fiddle'.

James Omond was born in 1833. After many struggles he equipped himself for the profession of a schoolmaster. He became a country dominie, teaching at a small school in the parish of Stromness. But his enthusiasm was such that he overtaxed his physical powers, lost his voice for eight years, and had to spend the remainder of his life in bed. Life was hard for the family, and James Omond was not the man to escape from his obligations. He tried to be a watchmaker, but did not discover an aptitude for the craft, so determined to teach himself violin-making. With some inherited skill in the use of tools, he quickly found that he was able to produce good instruments.

He studied the work of the masters—Giovanni Paolo, Antonio Stradivari, Jacob Stainer—endeavouring to learn their secrets. He also corresponded with the authorities of his day, people like Horace Petheridge and George Hart.

Although he was so greatly hampered by his physical malady, he often managed to get lovely pieces of old sycamore and pine. In the best of his instruments the finish is very fine. Acoustically, their leading characteristic is *sweetness*. Indeed, the professional magazine *The Strad* said of him: 'For subtle insinuating intoxicating sweetness, no modern make beats Omond.' In the

1. A storage chest for meal.
2. Cruisie.

eighties and nineties of last century he won medals and diplomas in places as far apart as Glasgow and Melbourne. In all, he made well over two hundred instruments, selling them at prices as low as £3, and never over £10. It is amazing that not until he started to make violins had he ever played a note on one, but he became a good violin-player.

At one time there were twenty of his violins in Wales. In these islands many an Orcadian bought one; and even now there must be violins in various parts of the islands with his label gummed to the neck block inside.

4

The story of the provost's chain

The Kirkwall Provost's Badge and Chain of Office was recently returned from Edinburgh, where it was one of the most beautiful exhibits at Messrs Hamilton & Inches' Centenary Exhibition. It was given to the town as a memorial to a Kirkwall lady, Margaret Loutit,[1] and was made by the Edinburgh firm in 1956. This lovely chain of fine gold, which Orcadians see on such colourful occasions as the 'Kirking'[2] of Kirkwall Town Council, has an interesting story behind it, connecting it with an Orkney craftsman of perhaps eight or nine hundred years ago.

But before I tell that story, let me describe the chain. The badge has the arms of the City and Royal Burgh in gold and enamel, a galleon with furled sails, with red flags bearing the St Andrew's Cross on a field of blue and gold, and the motto 'Si Deus Nobiscum'. These arms, in an oval setting, are encircled with pearls. The enclosing frame carries viking figures, to show the town's Norse origin, and mermaids, dolphins and sea-birds as symbols of our dependence on the sea. The central link from which the badge hangs is made in the form of linked ovals, containing the figures of our three northern saints—St Olaf, St Magnus and St Rognvald.[3]

The link at the centre of the back carries a Norse galley with furled sail and a cross on the masthead: the arms of the County of Orkney. These pieces are beautifully designed, and are the main glories of the chain, but it is on the lovely, unusual intermediate links that our story depends.

The complete design was the work of the Kirkwall born artist, Dr Stanley Cursiter.[4] His fertile imagination soon found ways of incorporating the

---

1. By her daughter Mrs Helen Gordon Gibson.
2. Ceremonial attendance at church.
3. St Olaf, King of Norway, brought Christianity to the north, and to the islands, largely by offering an immediate choice of baptism or execution. For information on St Magnus and St Rognvald see the articles 'St Magnus', p.389 and 'Viking and saint', p.457.
4. Her Majesty's Painter and Limner in Scotland from 1948 until his death in 1976. He was a Freeman of the Burgh. Dr Cursiter designed St Rognvald Chapel in St Magnus Cathedral—see 'Viking and saint', p.457.

symbolical devices into the chain, but he cast around for a while for a satisfying and unhackneyed design for the links.

Then he remembered a little carved wooden box which used to stand on the drawing-room table of his uncle's house in Kirkwall. It was very old, and the carvings on it had always fascinated him. The pattern on one of its long sides supplied, so many years afterwards, the inspiration that the artist was seeking. You can still see the box in the National Museum of Antiquities in Edinburgh.

Anyone who knows Dr Cursiter's extremely sensitive mind is bound to think that the story of the box inspired him no less than the pattern. It was found one day in 1885 in the borderland between Evie and Birsay, in a peat-bog, by men cutting peats, and became one of the most prized possessions of Stanley Cursiter's uncle. In it were the handles of tools made of wood, bone and horn—their blades had rusted away—as well as a worn pumice stone, a pointed tine of deer horn, a bone pin, a piece of cut bone, and scraps of leather. It was thought that the box was lost by a wood carver hundreds of years ago as he crossed the sodden bog between Birsay and Evie, perhaps on a bleak windy day, when it fell into a brown peaty pool and disappeared.

An Orkney crafts-specialist living in Edinburgh examined the box. He was William Kirkness, whose father was the famous maker of Orkney chairs.[1] He knew woodworking tools when he saw them, and he was quite sure that the tool handles could not have belonged to a wood-carver; they were too short. They were those employed by a worker in leather.

The story became apparent. The route over the peat-bog was the way from the monastery on Eynhallow to the religious establishment on the Brough of Birsay. Out of the past came the picture of a monk, walking on a wild day, and carrying the box of tools that he used for binding the carefully written manuscripts from the scriptorium on Eynhallow, then, for some reason, losing the box for ever. . . . A humble artist who would never know that the box he decorated would inspire another Orkney artist, and that his design would be recorded in gold.

---

1. See 'The story of the Orkney chair', pp.85-87.

DOMESTIC LIFE

1 The Orkney croft house   95
2 Domestic freuteries   98
3 Taking their medicine some old-fashioned prescriptions   101
4 An ABC of Orkney food   103
5 Peat fire fancies   114

I

The Orkney croft house

The Orkney farmhouse of the older style[1] would seem to resemble in its basic plan the Norse longhouse of the ninth and tenth centuries, but its appointments, because of the widespread use of stone for furnishings, are reminiscent in an odd way of stone-age settlements like Skara Brae.

Often the dwelling-house was built in line with the byre, barn and stable, each opening into the other—an obvious convenience in the dark, windy winter, when the light to be carried was a *koly* (little iron open lamp, often known as a *kruisie*).

Few houses of this kind are now to be seen, and those that still stand with their recessed beds of stone (*neuk beds*) and their stone cupboards, or aumbries, are (except for a notable exception at Kirbister, Birsay) more or less ruinous.

The very oldest houses, unlike the small croft houses of the last century or two, were built irregularly, large stones and small ones being used in such a way (with characteristic 'pinning') that courses of masonry are hardly to be identified. They were also built 'with the rig' (i.e. end-on to the slope) to allow for easy drainage of byre and stable. Most of them consisted of two rooms, known at one time as *firehouse* and *sellar*, but later on as *but-hoose* and *ben-hoose*.

Somewhere near the middle of the beaten clay or flagged floor of the *fire-house* was built a low isolated wall called the *back*, against which the peat fire was built. This room had an outer door on the side wall near the gable, which the animals, in going into the adjoining byre, also used. All the space between this door and the fire was called *oot-by*. It was partly occupied by hens on their *hallan* or roosting bars below the roof, calves in tiny *beuls* or stalls, or by the brood sow. With the smoke hole, or *lum*, overhead, with the droppings of animals on the floor, and with the heap of ashes pushed through a hole in the fire wall, it was hardly salubrious. Any comfort the house had to offer was to be found *in-by*, between the fire and the inner wall. Here stood

[1]. This article was written as a guide to an exhibition in Stromness Museum in 1972. The Kirbister and Corrigall Farm Museum, Orkney's Museum of Farming and Rural Life, now exhibits most of the details described in the following article.

the straw-backed stools of the master and mistress, with perhaps low *creepies* for the children.

A smooth flagstone, resting on upright stones or a wooden frame, was known as the *bink* and served the purpose of a dresser. The water tub, or *sae*, was placed on a shelf of stone at the bottom of a rounded recess in the front wall. Food was stored in the *ammery*,[1] a cupboard with stone shelves, which was frequently lined neatly with flagstones. Near the floor might be goose nests, three or four square recesses. Over the fire was a beam called the *pauntree*, from which as occasion demanded the *three-taed* pot, or iron kettle, or *yetlin* (griddle) were suspended, often by a thick rope of straw. One or two *neuk beds* in a stone-built lean-to, partially screened by upright flagstones, were let into the back wall and shared the genial warmth of the fire, which in old times was never allowed to go out. A dead hearth meant bad luck.

In the adjoining room, or *sellar*, there was normally a stone shelf (*quern ledder*) for the *quern* (hand-mill) for grinding meal and malt. Also in this room were the *girnel* (meal-chest), the stores of potatoes and ale, and a box-bed for the guid-man and his wife. A *plout kirn*, for churning butter, and the *ale-kirn* were frequently stored in the *sellar*.

Much used in the house were baskets of straw of various sizes, called *cubbies*. These might include 'peat-cubbie', 'ass-cubbie' (for the ashes), 'hen-cubbies' (for the fowls to lay in), and the tiny 'speun-cubbie' for the family's horn spoons. An inner 'door' consisted sometimes of a straw mat, called a *flackie*.

From straw ropes stretched across the house might be suspended half-dried fish and pieces of pork and mutton. There was so much smoke among the beams *oot-by* that mutton or geese hung there could be *reestid*, or smoked.

Frequently, the only windows were skylights let into the roof. The roof itself was occasionally of thatch but often of large flagstones covered with turf. It was supported by the minimum of couples (rafters) owing to the scarcity and dearness of timber.

Sometimes a more modern house would replace the traditional dwelling, but it was quite customary to adapt the old house to later needs. Many of the interiors which found their way into photographs were of the adapted house, whose fairly commodious original rooms might be divided by intrusive gables (one of them containing fireplace and chimney to replace the old *back*) or by an arrangement of box-beds set back to back to partition off separate little chambers. Windows were inserted in the walls, and some wooden furniture introduced, such as a wooden table and a plate-rack or *range*. Such things as *sae-binks* and *ammeries* were considered to be obsolete and they were built up when the walls were plastered over. Many of the new cottages which

---

1. Also almery.

26 Gathering 'spoots', or razor fish, Scapa, c.1905

27 James Scarth Foubister, Newbanks, Deerness, baiting handlines, *c*.1900

were built last century had no interior walls of stones, but were divided into *but*, *ben* and *closet* by box-beds.

When the original house grew too small for a large family, extra sleeping accommodation in the form of a *chaumer* was built directly in front of the house. This, with an *orra-house*, or shed, gave some shelter in stormy weather. The passage between the houses was called a *kloss*.

2

Domestic freuteries[1]

Never let the *restid*[2] fire go out. If you go to a neighbour's house for kindling, you bring bad luck to that house.

If peats fall off a burning fire replace them quickly: they are visitors, bid them welcome.

When the cat washes her face or cleans her fur, visitors are coming. If she washes over her ear the minister will come.

If your right palm is hot you are going to shake hands with a stranger. If your left palm is hot you are going to get money.

If a kitten follows you home you will have the best of luck.

To see the new moon through glass signifies ill-fortune.

Never borrow salt.

It is unlucky to see your first *teeack*[3] in spring on the ground. It is lucky to see the bird in flight, and even luckier to see a flock on the wing.

The number of crows one happens to see at one time is also significant. The rhyme embodying the superstition runs:

> Wan for sorrow,
> Twa for mirth,
> Three a waddeen,[4]
> Four a birth,
> Five a christneen,
> Six a daith.
> Seven for heaven
>   and
> Eight for hell
>   and
> Nine the devil, his ain sel'.

1. Also frooterys—superstitious beliefs, notions or customs.
2. Banked.
3. Lapwing.
4. Wedding.

Health and disease[1]

Never lift anything off the road: the person you give it to will not live long.

Do not lift a tinker's clothes left at a crossroads. Tinkers leave their clothes there when they are ill, in the belief that the person who takes them will get the disease, and the tinker will get well.

If you find money, give it to the first person you meet.

If your ears burn, someone is speaking about you, probably an ill-wisher, so you should say:

> Me right lug[2] burns and me left lug scads,[3]
> Ill may he deu that me ill-wads,[4]
> If hid be me true love, burn lug, burn,
> Bit if hid be me enemy, upon him may he turn:
> Mad may he go, like a rae[5] apon a hill,
> Till he spaeks as much guid o' me as he's spoken ill.

If you have a blister on your tongue, it has probably been caused by someone telling lies about you. To remove the blister from your tongue to the tongue of the slanderer, repeat this formula three times:

> Blether aff o' me tong an' on tae the
> tong that's leean[6] on me.

After each repetition you must spit, as if you were spitting the blister off your tongue.

To cure *fissies*[7] apply a poultice of oatmeal and kirn-milk, and get the dog to lick it. You could escape having chilblains if, when your feet were cold and wet, you persuaded a dog to lick them.

A wart could be charmed away by pointing a straw at it and then at the moon, saying all the while the appropriate incantation. This incantation, like so many others, has been forgotten.

To prevent cramp, skins stripped from eels were worn around the ankles.

For the cure of toothache one had to possess a curious pamphlet, once common in Orkney, which was entitled, *A copy of a Letter containing the Commandments of our blessed Lord and Saviour Jesus Christ, Written by Himself. To which is added King Agbarus's Letter to our Blessed Saviour: Likewise our Saviour's Answer*. It cost one penny, and was 'printed for Isabel Johnston,

---

1. See also superstitions and curses in 'Northern witches', p.333.
2. Ear.
3. Hurts.
4. Ill-wills.
5. Roe-deer.
6. Lying.
7. Chilblains.

near the Old Palace, Kirkwall, Orkney, 1784.' The printing was done at Newcastle-upon-Tyne.

Long ago the pamphlet was used as a charm. A gentleman in Stromness remembered that a girl, who was tormented by toothache, received from an old woman a little paper parcel which, if worn round the neck, was guaranteed to effect a cure. On no account, however, must it be opened and examined. The girl obeyed the instructions and was immediately cured. Unfortunately, her curiosity proved too much for her, and she opened the packet. In it was the pamphlet, containing an account of a miracle, ascribed to Christ, but not to be found in the New Testament. No sooner had the girl looked at this than the toothache came back more fiercely than before. As a result of her broken promise, the charm had also lost its efficacy.

Jennie Fea was a herbalist who lived in the Palace Road Houses, Kirkwall, over seventy years ago. A Stromness woman (still alive, as this is written)[1] told me that when she was a girl she had some kind of skin infection. Her mother would not send for a doctor, but asked the driver of the Stromness coach to call on Jennie Fea and ask for a suitable *saa*.[2]

1. Mid-1960s.
2. Salve or ointment.

3

Taking their medicine: some old-fashioned prescriptions

It would be interesting to see how our great-great-grandfathers would have reacted to a typical modern doctor's prescription of a few tiny pills. Not well, I think; for they demanded prescriptions which were more spectacular, both in substance and quantity.

Only last century, a patient in South Ronaldsay who had jaundice was treated in a very interesting way by his doctor, a local person and presumably self-taught. This magic worker gave the patient a draught, the nature of which I had better not name, then placed a meal sieve on his head. In the sieve were a bunch of keys, a comb, a pair of shears and a basin of water. Lead[1] was melted and poured into the water three times. The third time the lead took the shape of a heart. The patient had to carry this heart in his pocket. He had, also, to eat bere meal cakes cooked between the flat points of the tongs, along with the egg of a black hen, each day until he was better.

This remedy was clearly pure magic and might almost have come from the fairies, who were thought to be excellent doctors. There was once, so tradition says, a fairy doctor in Shapinsay, who was frequently called by patients in the other islands. The only stipulation he made was that he must be paid in 'white money', in other words, silver.

But to come back to real doctors... I have lying in front of me a doctor's bill from the eighteenth century. There are pages of it, dating from 1781 to 1785; for these old doctors did not bother to send out their bills at fixed intervals, and the lady mentioned most must have been a proper hypochondriac. She had everything prescribed for her that you could imagine. Let us look at an item or two:

One drop saffron	6d
One ounce powder of Peruvian bark	1/6d
Nervous drops	1/-
4½ ounces Spirits of iron and champhor	1/4d
A phyal Carminative drops	9d

1. For more information about the use of lead as a healing agent, see article 'Northern witches', p.333.

And so on. The doctor was certainly a useful person, for he supplied in addition to medicine such things as 'Bitter materials for 8 pints Ale . . . 1s', and 'A Chopin bottle best Spirits of Turpentine by your orders for mixing with paint for the raills of your house . . . 3s'.

Country doctors until quite recently made up their own prescriptions, and I suppose some do so still. I remember an old Orkney doctor telling me that his patients insisted on medicine with a nasty taste. Within limits, the more obnoxious the mixture the greater the reputation of the doctor. Old ladies, he told me, used to come to him with large lemonade bottles, which he obligingly filled for them. When I asked him what he put in them, he just smiled and shook his head. 'That's my secret,' he said.

Another doctor, who is still remembered[1] in Orkney by people whose parents or grandparents he treated, had a tremendous reputation as a purveyor of potent and effective medicines. People said that the stuff was 'gey siccar'[2] to take, but that it worked wonders. When he died, he left behind him in his surgery a big barrel, still half-full of Epsom Salts.

---

1. This broadcast took place in the mid-1960s.
2. Very strong.

4

An A.B.C. of Orkney food

Maet an' drink—A Gloondie's[1] alphabet

AAKS (common guillemots), COOTER-NEBS (razorbills) and TAMMY-NORIES (puffins) were caught on the cliffs by means of *swap-nets* (nets with a triangular frame, mounted on the end of a long, thin bamboo pole, or *waand*). The birds were killed and eaten. The custom was to hang them for some time in a cool stone shed, by pushing their *nebs* (beaks) into interstices in the wall. There is a tradition (for which I cannot vouch) that they were considered ready for eating when they were so 'high' that the neck gave way and the body of the bird fell to the ground. They were skinned before being cooked.

ALE[2]. Genuine Orkney home-brewed ale was prepared as follows:

To make the maat (*malt*)

Take good Orkney bere, dress it well, and see that it is free from *stoor* (dust). Put it into sacks—a bushel or so in each two-bushel sack—and tie them near the top to give the bere room to swell. Place the sacks under water in a quarry-hole or loch for two days and nights, then take them out and let them *sype* (drain) for another two days or more.

When white rootlets begin to appear, spread the bere nine or ten inches deep on the floor of the barn loft. So that the growth stays fairly even, turn it twice a day—or more often if the roots grow too quickly. The bere will have to be spread out thinner as time goes on, especially if the weather is mild or *muggy* (close and foggy), and there is a tendency for the grain to heat. Winter is by far the best time to make *maat*.

After a week or a little longer on the floor, the young shoot inside the *mettins* (seeds of grain) should have grown about two-thirds the length of the *mettin*. You should break single *mettins* every now and then

---

1. Glutton.
2. See also article 'Orkney drinking', p.191.

to find out, cracking them with your thumb-nail. This is just about the right length for the shoot in making *maat* for ale, and by this time, too, withering of the roots should have begun. If you have turned the grain properly and the young shoot does not grow appreciably longer, the grain should be left on the floor for another day or two to let the withering of the roots continue.

The bere is then piled into a heap called the *sweet-haep* or *sweet-bed*, where it becomes warm, and reaches the right stage of sweetness, which can only be judged after much experience. The *sweep-haep* will need to be turned over now and then to prevent it from getting too hot and to promote evenness in the heating and mellowing of the grain. It may be necessary to start the process by sprinkling water over the *sweet-haep*.

When the bere leaves the *sweet-haep* it is shovelled into sacks and sent to the grinding mill to be dried. This is a critical process. Some millers used to put it on the warm kiln plates immediately after oats had been removed from them. The kiln was gradually allowed to grow warmer. When the bere was nearly dry it was given an extra burst of heat to finish it off. It must be winnowed[1] after it comes from the kiln to remove the withered roots.

The process of making *maat*, which will have taken about three weeks, is now completed, but it needs to be crushed or very lightly bruised before it is used. In old times it was crushed in a hand quern, set so as merely to 'nick the corn'. Ale makers used to crush just enough *maat* for the amount they intended to brew, the rest being kept in a dry place, often in sacks suspended from beams in the kitchen.

To brew the ale

First of all put a stone (the old miller's stone of $17\frac{1}{2}$ lbs) or more of the *maat* into the brewing kirn. Over this pour five or six gallons of very hot water.[2] This is to mask, or infuse, the brew. The resulting liquor, or *wort*, should be left for two hours before being strained and drawn off into pails. In most of the old ale kirns the tap was merely a wooden plug, and the liquor was strained through straw placed on the bottom of the kirn with a flat stone on top of it.

To the strained *wort* is added a quantity of hops[3]—four ounces

1. Separated from chaff or other refuse material by wind.
2. Water actually boiling may swell the *maat* into a glutinous mass.
3. Before the introduction of hops to Orkney, and for quite a while afterwards if there was difficulty in obtaining them, the leaves of bogbean, *Menyanthes trifoliata*, known as 'craw-shoe' to Orcadians, were used to add the necessary bitterness to the *wort*. In some places they were also put into the ale after it had been brewed, to flavour it. Orkney's average annual import of hops in the early years of the nineteenth century was a little under four tons. (E.W.M.)

perhaps—in a muslin bag. The amount is determined by the flavour desired: the more hops, the more bitter will be the brew. The *wort* is then boiled for an hour and a half to two hours, strained once again and cooled to blood heat. A bucketful, or rather less, is returned to the kirn. At this stage a small quantity of *barm*, or yeast, is introduced. When the *wort* in the kirn has begun to *work*, or ferment, properly, a little more of the *wort* is added, and so on until all the liquor is in the kirn. You must now wait until the *barm* has sunk to the bottom of the kirn and the ale is clear, which will take a couple of days. When bottling, use for preference 5-gill bottles with an ordinary cork; rubber or composition corks are unsatisfactory.[1]

To strengthen the brew

To make the ale dangerously 'heady' was the aim of some brewers. This was accomplished in earlier days by adding *saave* (the tops or blooms of heather or common ling) to the *maat*, usually under a stone at the bottom of the kirn, where it also acted as a strainer. Another way of strengthening the liquor was by allowing an oat-sheaf, with the ears of grain set downwards in the kirn, to *mask* with the *maat*. In more modern times oatmeal was sometimes added to the *maat*, or double-brewing was resorted to. This meant that another lot of *maat* was *masked* in the *wort*, making the resulting liquor very strong indeed.

In most modern recipes, sugar is added to the boiling liquor, but brewers of the traditional Orkney Ale would never have added sugar—indeed they were most scornful of such an innovation. Sweetness was controlled first of all in the *sweet-bed*, when the *maat* was being made, and later on when the ale was brewed by the amount of hops introduced into it.

Ale warmed by having a red-hot poker thrust into it was called *nugged ale*, or mulled ale.

A brewing of ale was known as a *broust*.

Porridge was supped with ale when milk was in short supply.

New Year's Day and the peat-cutting were the occasions for which ale was brewed in large quantities. There were also, in some places, brewings for haytime and harvest, but these brewings were more casual, and the ale was considered to be of inferior quality.

ALE-Y SCONES. See under *whey scones*.

BACK-FEAST: an entertainment given at one time by the 'best man' in return for the wedding feast provided by the parents and friends of the bride.

1. The ale should be bottled and left for at least a fortnight. It begins to deteriorate after approximately six months.

BEESMILK: the first milk given by a cow after she calved. This could be made into cheese by putting it into a bowl and steaming it. A little salt was added. The cheese was much improved by mixing some skimmed milk with the *beesmilk*. A 'crowdie' cheese could be made by heating *beesmilk* in an oven; this became a *beesmilk pudding* if sultanas and cinnamon were added.

BERE BANNOCKS: thick, round scones made from Orkney barley, which was known as bere or *bygg* (the name still used in Norway).

The bannock is made by mixing (for a family baking; half quantities for a small household) two pounds of beremeal with half a pound of flour and a teaspoonful of salt. When the dry mixture is ready, a pint and a half of buttermilk is put into a jug and stirred up quickly with a good tablespoonful of baking soda. While it is still effervescing, the buttermilk is poured into the dry mixture. With as little working as possible a soft dough is prepared, which is rolled out lightly on a floured board until it is roughly half an inch in thickness. This is cut into large rounds, and baked at a moderate pace on a hot girdle, being turned when sufficiently browned on the first side.

An account of the way to make Bere Bannocks
by Mrs Johina Leith, Stenness. October 1975

Take two parts of beremeal and one of flour. Mix together with baking soda, and add butter-milk.

Mix in the baking bowl quickly, then place the mixture on the baking board and give it a good kneading. Bere bannocks are the better of a good kneading (while floury bannocks are not).

Take enough of the dough to make a bannock, roll it into a ball, and flatten it on the baking board with the *liv* (palm) of the hand. Rolling it out is optional. Mrs Leith was always able to flatten the bannock sufficiently with her hand. During the operation of rolling into a ball, kneading etc., you have to keep the bannock floured. Before putting the bannock on to the girdle, hold it lightly between the palms of the hands and knock off excess flour. Firing, which should be moderate, is a matter of experiment, as is the correct quantity of baking soda.

BLAAN FISH: fish partly dried by exposure to wind and sun. Putrefaction was only partially arrested, and the sour taste of the fish was enjoyed by those who were used to it.

BLAND: a drink made from buttermilk and boiling water.

BLATHIC or BLATHEW: new buttermilk, but sometimes applied to thin watery buttermilk.

BLIDEMAET: food and drink offered to visitors after the birth of a child.

BLOWN MILK.[1] I have found memories in Rousay of a dish which was made as follows: warm milk from the cow was put into a bowl, with just a little rennet to curdle it. This was 'switched' with a home-made instrument, consisting of a rounded stick, about a foot long, with a kind of wheel at the end with a series of spokes. To the ends of the spokes was fixed a thick rim of cow-hair, which was carefully washed before being used. The 'wheel' was suspended in the bowl, and the stick was rotated quickly between the palms of the hands until the milk was sufficiently 'blown', i.e. aerated. It was maintained that only cow's hair was suitable for the operation, which could not be performed without it.

BRAM: a dish of oatmeal and milk (or buttermilk) eaten uncooked. Oatmeal mixed with hot buttermilk was sometimes called *Leepid gibbo*.[2]

BRAND-IRON: gridiron.

BREEKS: roe of cod; this was boiled in a piece of muslin, then cut into slices and eaten with potatoes.

BRIDESCAKE.[3] At one time the bridescake used in Orkney was made of oatmeal, butter, sugar and caraway seeds. It always contained a ring and a button. Originally, the cake was marked on one side with a cross enclosed in a circle. Sometimes the cake was thrown over the bride's head as she returned from the wedding walk; at other times it was actually broken over her head. The guests scrambled eagerly for pieces. To get the piece with the ring in it was very fortunate: to find the button presaged bachelordom or spinsterhood. In later times, the cake was a large thick round of shortbread, containing a ring and a thimble.

BRIDESCOG[4]: drinking vessel, used at weddings, shaped like a small tub and usually made of alternate staves of light and dark wood, secured with *girds* (hoops) of wood or metal. The cog may have either two or three handles (called *horns*), which are prolonged staves. At an earlier period, the bride was always the first person to drink from the cog, which was then passed round the wedding company. Nowadays, it is quite as common for the person who proposes the bride's health to take the first drink, after which the cog passes from hand to hand round the bride's table, moving *sungates*, i.e. in a clockwise direction. If there are several tables, a number of cogs may be in use. Even after the tables are cleared,

---

1. In the Highlands of Scotland a somewhat similar dish was called frothed milk. 'The stick used in preparing frothed milk was called a *Loineid* (in Badenoch a *frohstick*) ...', Dr Isabel F. Grant, *Highland Folk Ways*, 1961, p.298. Mrs Wylie of Blossom, Rousay (interviewed in 1966, when she was 83) told me that she was familiar with blown milk when she was a girl. (E.W.M.)
2. Scalded cat.
3. See also 'bridescake' in 'Old ways at island weddings', p.119.
4. See also 'bridescog' in 'Old ways at island weddings', p.119.

the cog may circulate for hours among the thirsty dancers, being constantly replenished. Traditionally, the cog contains a mixture of hot ale, spirits (whisky, gin, rum, or all three) and eggs, but amounts, and actual ingredients, may be varied by the expert who prepares the cog. Often pieces of pancake were dropped into the cog, and fished out with a long-handled spoon.

BROCHAN: thin oatmeal gruel.

BROSE 'fae the lee side o' the broth pot'. This was the term used for a dish made with oatmeal and salt and a spoonful or two of the fat that boiled to one side of the pot when soup was being made.

BURSTIN: bere dried in a pot until brown, then ground in a quern. It was mixed with buttermilk and supped with a spoon. As will be noted, it was meal made from scorched grain. The art of drying consisted in scorching the outside husk without burning the grain, so that when ground the husk went to powder among the meal, giving it a dark colour and a pleasantly burnt flavour.

CARVEY BISCUIT: a hard ship's biscuit with *carvey* (caraway) seeds baked into it, and containing salt but not sugar. Still a favourite in Orkney, and obtainable from bakers.

CHIZZEN-MAET: It was once customary, on the day after a birth, for the women who had been present at the delivery to bring the mother a present of food, which generally consisted of *eggalourie* (q.v.) and bannocks. This *chizzen-maet* had to be brought into the house secretly.

CLAPSHOT: to make this dish, turnips and potatoes were peeled and boiled together in a pot. They were then mashed together, with the addition of salt and pepper, and—if it was available—a little butter.

CUTTY: a very thick oatmeal bannock, frequently baked on hot embers.

DAGON: a large piece of anything edible, especially a large piece of cheese.

DAICH: oatmeal and water mixed to form a stiff dough, also *sooans*, (q.v.), mixed with oatmeal to form a dough dry enough to be carried in the pocket. It was eaten as required. Sometimes this was called *rolly-o-daich*, referring to the fact that it was rolled into a ball. Fishermen occasionally mixed the oatmeal with whisky instead of water.

DARROW: a large slice or lump.

DOG-FISH. These were eaten in some parishes and islands, but in other places were regarded as unfit for human consumption. One way of using them was to dry them in the sun on the side-wall of a house until the oil was oozing out of them. They were cut into strips, and these strips were made edible, when required, by roasting them '*owre the kols*', i.e. over glowing peats in an open fire.

I have the following instructions for curing and cooking the dog-fish from Birsay.

First catch your dog. Use fresh bait, which may be cuithes,[1] but preferably a piece of dog-fish. Having caught the fish, remove his 'horns' immediately. When you get to shore remove the head and belly fins. Split open down the back from head to tail, keeping the bone to the right-hand side of the knife. When you get to about four inches off the tail, turn the knife and cut along the other side of the bone, after which you will be able to pull the bone out. Remove the guts and internal organs at the same time. Wash well in salt water.

Next morning hang the fish against a wall in the wind and sun, but take care that no rain or dew falls on them. When you take them in at night, stack them on top of each other, placing a heavy weight on the pile. Each morning, before you hang the fish up to resume curing, wash them in fresh water to remove any fly eggs that may have been laid on them. In good conditions the drying will take a week or a little more. The fish are cooked by being boiled, but be sure to boil in well-salted water. When you can, eat them with new potatoes.

At one time pieces of dog-fish skin were kept handy for scouring knitting needles.

DROONDIN' THE MILLER: putting too much liquid into the mixture when baking. The reverse, putting in too little, was termed *hangin' the baker*.

DULSE: an edible seaweed, *Rhodymenia palmata*. It was often collected in Orkney and eaten raw. Another seaweed which was used to a limited extent was that known as *carageen*, a purplish-red alga which was used for making a kind of jelly or custard. It was valued as an aid to 'setting' long before the use of seaweed derivatives in so-called 'instant' jellies was thought of. I have heard of carageen being collected from rocks at Melsetter and dried on a window-sill.

EBB MAET: shell fish such as whelks and limpets gathered from the rocks at low tide. In times of dearth, *ebb maet* was often the only food available.

EGGALOURIE: eggs and milk boiled together.

FAA: the heart, lungs and other internal organs of a slaughtered animal. From these a host of tasty dishes were made, and a *guid faa* was much prized.

FITLESS COCK: the remains of stuffing, made into a dumpling and boiled in a pot of soup, but often specially made to take the place of meat.

FOAL: The term was used in more than one way. A small bannock, made from the last of the mixture at the end of baking, was called a foal. The name was given to a dough of oatmeal and water, salted and peppered, which was rolled to the shape of a thick little bannock and attached firmly to the inside of a pot in which cabbage was boiling. The 'foal' was cooked with the cabbage and eaten with it.

---

1. Saithe or coal-fish.

Garry-Skons: a kind of pancake, or crumpet, sticky to the touch, the recipe for which seems to be forgotten.

Glaary Kleppo: a sticky, ill-cooked bere bannock.

Glunt: to swallow food ravenously, and without chewing it.

Hamefare: a feast held to celebrate a move into a new house.

Hansel: a refreshment of bread and cheese offered to the guests at a wedding as they returned from the wedding walk, and before they entered the wedding house. The *hansel* was handed out by the hansel-wife, some elderly woman renowned for generosity. In later times, *hansel* sometimes referred to a paper packet containing a little bit of each of the cakes at the wedding, together with cheese, which was handed to each guest to be taken home.

Kail Breu: the water in which cabbage is boiled, left to cool and drunk as a thirst quencher.

Kilts: cod roe; see under *breeks*.

Kirn milk: buttermilk.

Klagum or Clagum: toffee.[1]

Klineoo: a buttered bannock given as a perquisite to the herd when a cow was served by the bull. The word *kline* is still used in the sense 'to cover thickly', as with butter. In Rousay *klined* meant pregnant. It is difficult to decide from which meaning of the word the *kline* in *klineoo* is derived.[2]

Klounk: the noise made by swallowing a liquid hurriedly and in quantity.

Knockit Corn: bere pounded in a hollow in a large stone (the *knocking stone*) with a rounded stone held in the hand. The *knockit corn* was used in soup, taking the place of pot barley.

Krackans. The dish is made in this way: when melting suet, take what remains after the tallow is extracted; put it into a pot with oatmeal, stir together, and cook until the oatmeal is brown.

Krang: the flesh of a whale.

Krappin Banno: cod livers kneaded into bere meal and boiled in a pot along with fish.

Liveren: flour or meal put into soup to thicken it.

Liver Heids: cod heads and livers, boiled together with potatoes. After boiling, the big bones were removed from the cod heads, and the whole mixture was mashed with a 'tattie chapper'.[3]

Liversoakie: a gutted sillock (young coal-fish), filled with livers and roasted.

1. Sometimes pulled into strips or sticks, it was made from syrup or treacle, and brown sugar. Also known as *Gundy*.
2. In some districts of Norway a flat bannock (*lefse*) spread with butter was called *kling* or *klining*.
3. Potato masher.

LOWTS: sour (ripened) cream, ready for churning, collected in the *lowty-jar* or *lowty-cag*.

MELDER SILLOCKS: sillocks dried in the kiln on the top of straw.

MERT: an animal killed in the fall of the year and salted down for household use over the winter.

MOUGELDEN or MUDYELIN: a small sillock rolled in meal and roasted, without being gutted.

NAPP: oatmeal and milk mixed together until the mixture was of the consistency of dough.

NIP-A-DOONS: bere bread broken into a bowl of sweet milk, and eaten like sops. This frequently formed a supper dish.

NOGAL: a large piece, a chunk. Also *whuggal*.

OVEN POT: a shallow pot, either flat-bottomed or having three toes. In cooking, *gleeds* (live coals) were laid on the metal lid. Also called *camp-oven*.

PARTAN: an edible crab.

PEUCHIS: tripe.

PURDO IN A KLOOT: boiled pudding.

PURR or SALT PURR: boiled salt herrings.

RAME: cream.

RANZE: the roe of a fish; *ran* was specifically herring roe.

REESTID: smoked—of pork or geese hung from the roof and partly cured by the smoke of the fire.

ROST PEEDIE: roasted sucking pig.

RUMBLY THUMP: potatoes and kail boiled together in one pot.

SARGAS: an unpalatable mass of food, e.g. cold porridge.

SHORN: curdled. Cream in the gathering jar had to be *shorn* before it was churned.

SKIRLIES: fried onions or shallots, with oatmeal sprinkled over them. Dinner often consisted of *skirlies* eaten with potatoes, or even more frequently *clapshot* (q.v.).

SKRAE: two-year-old coal-fish split and dried.

SNODDY: a very thick oatcake, not baked too hard, and much smaller in diameter than the ordinary oatcake.

SOOANS: the fine flour that clings to the inner husks of oats (sids) which have been separated from the meal in the process of milling. To remove the *sooans* from the husks or *suids* it is necessary to steep them in water for at least a week, during which time fermentation will take place. The vessel containing the *suids* should be placed near a fire, or in some place where the air is warm.

It was customary to steep the *suids* in a tub or barrel, and to *sye*, or strain, the *sooans* when ready through a skin sieve full of fine holes into a large earthenware jar, but any large *syer* will do. The *suids* must be squeezed well by hand, and finally washed in water and returned to the *syer* to remove all the *sooans*. It will take a day or two before the *sooans* will sink to the bottom of the jar, leaving the liquor, or *swats*, on top. If the *sooans* are to be preserved over a prolonged period, the *swats* must be poured off and clean cold water added.

Sooans may be supped raw with sugar, or may be made into a porridge by putting them in a pan with some water and a little salt, and boiling for a quarter of an hour, stirring constantly until the porridge thickens.

SOOAN SCONES: these may be made in the following way: Take a pound of flour, a teaspoonful of sugar, and a teaspoonful of baking soda, and mix together. Add a small amount of *sooans*, and mix the whole together with some *sooan* liquor (*swats*) into a thin batter. Drop in spoonfuls on to a hot girdle which has just been well greased with suet, and manipulate the girdle until an extremely thin pancake or crumpet results. As soon as the underside is ready, turn quickly with a knife and allow the other side to brown *Sooan scones* are usually spread with butter or jam, while hot, in a narrow band down the middle, and are then rolled into a cylinder.

SOOR-DOOK: buttermilk, or sometimes sour milk.

SOOROS: green leaves of sorrel, eaten raw.

SPLOOTER PIECE or SPLOOTERO. When knives were scarce, bread was sometimes buttered by putting a lump of butter into the mouth, and, as it melted, *splootering* it on to the bread. I suppose every parish in Orkney has a story about an innocent (sometimes said to be a minister new to the place, at other times a herd lad) who, on being asked by an old woman whether he would 'like his piece *thoombed* or *splootered*', looked at her dirt-grimed hands and decided unwisely that the unknown option must be the less unpleasant.

SPOOTS[1]: razor-fish.

SWEETIE-FOLLS: a sweet biscuit containing ginger and treacle, and decorated on the top only with sugared caraway seeds in assorted colours. This biscuit was baked traditionally as a Lammas 'fairing',[2] and some are still baked commercially at market-time (early August).

TATTIES AND POINT: potatoes, especially new potatoes, dipped in butter, this forming the entire meal.

The local explanation of the term is this: at a time when people in Orkney were very poor indeed, and potatoes occasionally the main meal, they would be eaten without any accompanying relish. If a guest were

---

1. A description of how to catch and cook spoots is to be found in 'An odd fish', p.76.
2. Present.

28 A country blacksmith, *c.*1900

29 John Firth, cartwright, Finstown, *c.*1880

30 Making a straw caisie, c.1900

present, a dish with butter, or fat, would be placed in the centre of the table, into which he would be invited to dip his potatoes. The members of the household would make a semblance of joining him, but would merely point their potatoes at the dish of butter. In later times, potatoes were dipped in butter placed on the side of the plate (by then people had individual plates) and this kind of meal continued to be called *tatties and point*.

An old man of fifty years ago used to say, when reminiscing about his boyhood,[1] that his family were often so poor that dinner would consist of 'three times roond the table and a spit at the *reuf* (roof)', a comical exaggeration. It was not unusual, where people were nearly destitute, to take a sheaf for the evening meal. The grain would probably be roughly cleaned, toasted, crushed, and eaten with milk.

TYNO SILLOCKS: sillocks dried by being hung on a *tyno* (skewer or thin wire) until they were very dry and hard.

One could also speak of *tyno herring*, which were usually salt herrings tethered under the running water of a burn to remove a good deal of the salt. They were then put on a *tyno* to drip until dry, after which they were fried.

TOOM or THOOMB PIECE: a piece of bread, usually bannock or oatcake, spread with butter, the thumb being used as spreader. Such a 'piece' was often given to a child or a hungry 'herdie boy'.[2]

WENTID MILK: sour milk.

WHEY SCONES: large pancakes—like crumpets—baked of oatmeal soaked in cheese whey until soft. Sometimes *carvey* (caraway seeds) was added to the mixture. If no cheese whey was available, the oatmeal was soaked in water. The oatmeal could be soaked in ale, to make *ale-y scones*.

YETLIN: an iron girdle.

YIRNING(S): part of the stomach (fourth stomach) of a calf, salted and dried, and afterwards soaked in water. The liquid was used to curdle milk or make cheese.

---

1. This would have been in the mid-nineteenth century.
2. A lad employed in summer time to control stock and in particular to keep animals on grazing and off unfenced, cultivated land and crops. Girls were similarly employed.

5

Peat fire fancies

The very nicest thing I can think of on cold winter nights is to sit before a peat fire listening to a good Orkney yarn. The imagination seems to burgeon in peat reek: it is as if history and legend flow out of the ancient burning hearts of the peats themselves. As indeed they do; for peats have been burned in Orkney for over a thousand years.

It is said that the first peats used in the islands were an export from Scotland. Torf-Einar[1] is alleged to have discovered on some unidentified Turfness, perhaps in Caithness or Sutherland, that peat could be burned. He didn't know then that there were many rich mosses in Orkney; so he ferried his peats across the Pentland Firth. The story is probably untrue but it makes a peaceful picture: the tall, very ugly, one-eyed earl coming slowly up Scapa Flow with a longship full of peats.

As years went on, peat became one of the most important commodities in the isles. There were laws about peat-cutting in the old Orkney law book, which was irretrievably lost. One of these laws, however, remained in men's minds: 'The poor may take as many peats from the nearest moss as will keep them warm, but not to sell.'

When peats at last became merchandise, they were sold very cheaply. In the sixteenth century, a fathom of peats, which would be at least 500 cubic feet, was worth six shillings Scots—sixpence of our money. Before coal became cheap and plentiful, Edinburgh was a valuable market for Orkney peats. In the summer, ship-loads were sent to the Forth. People set aside the best peats for export, and burned on their own hearths the rough sods which they called *yarpha* peats or *flaymeurs*.

But within living memory peats went further afield than Edinburgh. Quite by chance the other day, when I was looking for something totally different in the 1893 file of *The Orkney Herald*, I came across this news item:

---

1. 'Torf'—O.N. peat. *The Orkneyinga Saga* alleges that this Norse Earl was the first man to cut peat for fuel, firewood being very scarce in the Islands. The Saga records that he took the peat from Tarbat Ness, Scotland. There must be uncertainty as to just how he acquired the name.

> Ten tons of peats were shipped by the *Fawn* at Rousay on Monday by General Burroughs, and transhipped at Kirkwall yesterday for Australia.

Do as I would, I could not find a hint of what the peats were to be used for—ten tons of them! Were they being sent for some great gathering? Or for distribution to island exiles? Or to flavour whisky? It just doesn't make sense.

Peats are little valued now. Could the great peat mosses of Caithness, Sutherland and Orkney ever be a source of wealth?

'Of course they could,' said a German economist to me last summer. 'Sell them to the Americans. Cut squares of peat, and pack them in polythene bags with a lovely tartan design. Advertise them as 'Peat from the Scottish Moors for your Yule Fire', and price them at two-and-six each. The Americans, with their great big romantic hearts, would fill their suitcases with them.'

It seemed a sound scheme. At least, I thought so for nearly a whole day. Until I remembered—centrally-heated Americans have no open hearths where peat from the Scottish moors could blaze and sputter.

LIFE STAGES

1 Old ways at island weddings 119
2 Marriage and fertility freuteries 122
3 Funeral etiquette 124

I

Old ways at island weddings

Even today at weddings all over the country amusing little superstitions of the 'something old, something new' variety are common. But you will agree that they are the merest remnants of old beliefs when I tell you about the wedding customs that existed in my great-great-grandmother's day in the Northern Isles.

Weddings were not private family functions then: they involved the whole community; and an elaborate ritual of preparation before the ceremony, and conduct after the ceremony, was insisted on.

The evening on which the bridegroom and his friends visited the minister to arrange for the proclamation of banns was also 'foot-washing night'. While the men were away, a number of the local girls prepared a tub of water in which to wash the bride's feet. The bride had to sit on a stool beside this tub, with her right side next to it. Her father removed her shoes, then her mother took off her stockings, and pulled her feet over the water in a sunwise direction (which was very important). The mother patted each foot, pronounced a blessing on her daughter, then plunged her feet beneath the water. This was the sign for all the girls to surround the tub and help to scrub the bride's feet. As they did so, they searched for a ring which the mother had dropped into the water. The one who found it was inevitably the first who would marry. In the scramble everyone got wet, but it was splendid fun.

In some districts, at an earlier period, the bridegroom also took part in this ceremony, the roots of which originate many centuries ago. Sun worship and water worship entered into it. The empty tub had to stand in the sunlight for twelve hours, and no dog must look into it; so all the dogs in the neighbourhood were shut up for a day. Then into the tub went a pailful of fresh water from a well and a pailful of water from the sea. The man and woman sat on opposite sides of the tub with their feet in the water, but so placed that the growing moon could shine between them.

Sometimes the water was kept until the night before the wedding, to allow the couple to wash their hair. Thereafter the liquid could not be thrown away in the ordinary way, but was poured into a round hole dug in the earth. The oldest woman in the house said a certain form of words over it, the hole was filled and covered with turf.

After all this was over, the young couple had to eat the 'kissing meat', which traditionally consisted of limpets boiled in milk and water before sunset. The couple had to kiss before and after eating.

The wedding day ceremonies usually began in the forenoon, with the guests arriving at the bride's house. The marriage might take place there, but more often there was a wedding walk, with the party forming into couples and marching to the church, preceded by a piper or fiddler. On the way to the church, or manse, the bridegroom led the best-maid, and the bride walked with the best-man. Returning home, the groom had the bride on his arm, and the best-man escorted the best-maid. A wedding walk had to cross running water twice and during the walk guns were fired to scare away the 'peerie folk'.

Waiting to meet the party was one of the oldest and most respected women in the neighbourhood, who acted as the 'hansel-wife', and who offered bread and cheese with a generous hand. In the midst of this another woman would slip out of the house with the bridescake[1]—made from oatmeal, butter and caraway seed—and fling it over the bride's head. Everyone present scrambled for a bit, and it was very lucky to secure the largest piece.

Sometimes, in the more distant past, the 'hansel-wife' had with her a 'hansel-bairn', who was always the youngest child in the district. She placed this child in the bride's arms, while everyone watched anxiously to see which foot it would raise first; if the left, boys would predominate among the bride's children, if the right, then girls would be more numerous.

Among the earliest customs of which there is any record was the watching of the wedding house, usually by two stalwart young men. They were on guard outside to see that no ill-disposed person, carrying dried fish, walked round it in an anti-clockwise direction, that is 'against the sun'. If this happened, great harm or sorrow might come to the bride; for instance she might be barren or have no milk for her child. The bride was regarded as being very vulnerable from the time of her marriage to the first sunrise. In those days it was not uncommon for a bridegroom to keep his left arm around his bride with his left hand over her heart, until the danger from supernatural beings who might spirit her away had passed. One man's bride was replaced, according to an Orkney story, by a sea-woman; but he made the best of a bad job, and had a large family, the descendants of whom are reputed to be with us still.

The bride's home was always emptied of furniture so that long tables could be set up for the wedding guests. The feast consisted, in earlier days,

1. See also 'bridescake' in 'An ABC of Orkney food', p.103.

of boiled geese and barley-meal bannocks, washed down with home-brewed ale. The ale was always drunk from an ale-cog. This vessel, known as the bridescog,[1] has handles rising from the rim. The drink it contains is potent, made up from hot ale, gin, brandy or whisky, the whole well-peppered. The bride is the first to drink, and the cog is then handed round the gathering.

Apart from some traditional dances, the passing round of the bridescog is the only one of the old ceremonies that survives, but the festivities frequently go on until near sunrise. In more leisurely and less colourful times, people were loth to give up their feasting and dancing too soon, and an Orkney wedding could last three or four days: until all the food was eaten and all the ale drunk. This was not such an imposition on the bride's parents as might be supposed, for the guests brought a considerable amount of the food and drink with them.

It is said that it was the privilege of some of the bride's most intimate women friends to undress her on her wedding night; and very secretly some of the older women of the party performed a ceremony known as 'the burning of the snood'. The snood was a narrow ribbon used for tying up hair—the badge of virginity. The bride's mother removed it when she dressed the girl for the wedding. When all the household was silent, the mother and her close friends took a hot stone from the fire and placed on it the bride's snood. From the shape it took when burning, these wise women thought they could gain some knowledge of the bride's future, especially in relation to fecundity and material prosperity.

These are only a few of the customs associated once upon a time with island weddings, but you will see that the marriage period must have been a nerve-racking time for our great-great-grandmothers. That is, if they really believed in all the signs and portents that their own grandmothers watched for so avidly.

---

[1]. See also 'bridescog' in 'An ABC of Orkney food', p.103.

2

Marriage and fertility freuteries[1]

It is dangerous to let water boil alone in a pot. If it does, the girls in that house will lose their sweethearts. A Rendall woman was visiting 'a neebor hoose'. While she was there a pot of water began to boil. The woman of the house called out excitedly to her daughter, 'For mercy's sake pit a clod in the pot or else thoo'll lose thee lad.' The girl obeyed at once.

As a girl and her young man sat by the open fire in winter, they, or their friends, would place two short straws—which had been given the names of the lad and the lass—on a glowing peat. On one straw was a knot. Soon the heat caused this straw to jump slightly. If it jumped towards the other straw the named pair would wed, but it might jump away . . .

Weddings were commonly held in winter and Thursday was the lucky day on which to marry, with Tuesday and Sunday the best alternatives. It was important to marry with the moon waxing, that is between a new moon and a full moon, and with the tide flowing. It was regarded as extremely unlucky to marry when the moon was waning.

Young brides frequently went to drink the water of the Muckle Spring (about twelve feet from the right-hand side of the old road to Rackwick, Hoy, just where it entered that valley) to ensure fertility in childbearing.

It was firmly believed in some parts of Orkney, notably in Evie, that a married woman who assisted at a birth would herself conceive almost immediately.

Pregnant women were kept out of the byre when a cow was calving, because it was thought that if they were present when this occurred they risked a miscarriage.[2]

Preparations for the coming baby must be made in secret, and no indication of its presence must be hinted at in conversation, otherwise the

---

1. Also frooterys—superstitious beliefs, notions or customs.
2. Still births or miscarriages in humans can result from contact with an infection which causes enzootic abortion in sheep. At present, vaccination of the animals does not prevent spread of the disease. Pregnant women should have no contact with sheep during the lambing season.

trows[1] and other supernatural beings might get to know and cause trouble.

When the hill-trows went to a house to steal a mother after birth (to suckle some puling[2] infant of their own) they sang this song:

> Spinnan yet, spinnan yet?
> Go tae bed, go tae bed!
> Cutty speun an' tree laidle,
> Gaad[3] horse an' riven saiddle,
> Strae-i an' strae-boggan:
> > Tae hi dal doodle, an'
> > tae hi del doo-dee.[4]

---

1. For more information on trows, see 'Creatures of Orkney legend and their Norse ancestry', p.257 *et seq.*
2. Sickly.
3. *Gaad* comes from 'gaw' a defect, or 'gall' a sore, such as a saddle sore. The meaning of the final line is obscure. *In the strae* means 'in childbed', and *boggan* may well mean 'bochan', to vomit.
4.
> Spinning yet, spinning yet?
> Go to bed, go to bed!
> Short spoon and wooden ladle,
> Unsound horse and torn saddle,
> In childbed and unwell:
> > To hi dal doodle, and
> > to hi del doo-dee.

3

Funeral etiquette

A. Harryman recalled to our notice the other day the sharp division there is in the Orkney parishes concerning funeral etiquette. In his own parish it is considered right and proper that women should attend funerals, just as the men do, and there is seldom a funeral without some female mourners. Yet in many other parishes no woman would dream of attending a funeral, and her presence at the graveside would be considered strange, and almost a breach of etiquette. Why should this be so? he asked, and we can only repeat the question. No answer we can think of seems wholly satisfactory, although the most probable may be that certain parishes in previous centuries were almost wholly denuded of their able-bodied male population for large parts of the year, when the whaling and other seasonal occupations called them away, and women had to deputise at funerals.

Prior to the First World War a young Kirkwall man, John Flett, worked for a time as a joiner in Hoy. While there he attended a funeral. He told me that the coffin had to be carried a long way and at the outset each bearer was supplied with a clay pipe and some tobacco.

FESTIVALS

1 Yule in the north   127
2 New Year customs   129
3 Tailing day   133
4 Children's horse and plough festival in South Ronaldsay   134
5 Hallowe'en   137
6 Bonfire customs   139

I

Yule in the north

All over Orkney and Shetland and in Caithness we used to speak of Yule, never Christmas. In the long history of the winter festival in the north, the holy message of Christmas was, until recently, overshadowed by memories of Yule.

Yule was not just one festival. It was perhaps, at its very earliest, a feast of the dead. It was, too, the festival of the winter solstice, when people celebrated the returning sun, and tried to see what the New Year would bring them. It was this aspect of the celebration—that of homage to the sun— which the Church with great wisdom began to celebrate as the birthday of Christ, the Son (sun) of Righteousness.

The ancient festival of Yule was the one which our Norwegian fore-fathers took with them to the north of Scotland; and there are amazing correspondences between the customs of medieval Norway and those which are still dimly remembered in the islands, particularly in Shetland.

For instance, Yule was not just a single day, but a festival lasting some three weeks, during which ordinary work was not undertaken. Woe to any-one who broke the Yule peace. It began at Thomas-mass (21 December)—a day which was also regarded as particularly holy in Shetland—and ended on 13 January. The festival was sometimes called 'the Yules', in the plural.

It was thought in Norway that as Yule approached, the spirits from the grave-mounds came into the houses to share the Yule fare. In Shetland and Orkney it was the trows who came in, and people had to be careful to sain[1] themselves when these dangerous beings were around.

During Yule one was not permitted to bake or brew. A Norwegian stanza beginning 'Ikke brygga, ikke baka'[2] is almost completely echoed by the old Shetland verse:

> Nedder bake nor brew,
> Shape nor shew,[3]
> Upon gude Yule...

1. To make the sign of the cross.
2. Neither brew nor bake.
3. Cut nor sew.

All the brewing was done beforehand, for in Norway, as indeed in the isles, Yule was the greatest ale-feast of the year. Ale was regarded as holy. In the old Gulathing law, which the Norwegians brought to us, a man who refused to have an ale-drinking on Holy Night[1] for three years running forfeited his goods to the last penny.

In Norway the Yule-candle was left burning all night before Yule Day. It was taken into the byre on Yule morning, and, to help them to thrive, all the cattle were singed with it. In old Shetland a light was also left burning all night. The guidman took the candle into the byre on Yule morning when he fed the animals.

There had to be plenty of food at Yule. In Orkney and Shetland people carefully saved 'flesh meat'[2] for the festival.

One custom which the Greeks knew—that of chasing out the hunger spirit—was observed by the Norwegians. On the second day of Yule, in Norway, everyone, big and small, armed themselves with sticks and poles, and struck with them under the beds and chairs, chasing out unseen beings. Almost exactly the same custom was followed in Shetland, but there it was on 'Twenty-fourth night'. The idea was to chase out the spirits of danger and misfortune and to usher in the good and fruitful spirits.

To keep the house and its occupants safe at Yule, people in Shetland made crosses of straw, and carried blazing brands through barn and outhouses. In Norway they burned torches of birch twigs, set a cross over the food and ale casks, and placed a sheaf of corn on the roof, for corn, like ale, was holy.

There were various sun symbols used at Yule in Norway. In Shetland, a round bannock was baked, and its edges were pinched to represent the rays of the sun. Football was the great sport on Yule Day in Norway, Orkney and Shetland. Some people think that the ball represented the sun, and the opposing sides the powers of light and darkness.

Two things about Yule in Orkney were, I think, very pleasant. Extra rations were given to the animals and a place was laid at the table for a stranger. These things surely presaged the holy festival of Christmas as we know it today.

---

1. Christmas Eve.
2. Animal meat, as opposed to fish or 'ebb meat' (shellfish).

2

New Year customs

If you ask ninety-nine per cent of Orcadians whether Orkney still has any traditional New Year customs, they will mention the Kirkwall Ba',[1] but will assure you that all the others are long forgotten.

This is a mistake that arises because of our lamentable lack of knowledge of the Orkney which exists outside our own parish or island. For instance, a year or two ago a Norwegian visitor called on various people who had lived all their lives in a certain Mainland parish and asked them to name the farms that were lying in clear view on an island just a mile or two across the sound. Not one of them could. People on the Mainland are particularly ignorant of the South Isles, which are undoubtedly one of the most fascinating parts of our far-flung county. They are rich in tradition, and in the character of their folk.

It is in Burray, not surprisingly, that one of our oldest New Year customs survives—the singing of the New Year Song. There was a time when nearly every parish and island had groups of young men who went from house to house on New Year's Eve, singing the ancient ballad, and receiving gifts of seasonable fare and draughts of ale. The North Ronaldsay version of the New Year Song was fifty stanzas long, and contained part of an ancient poem relating the fortunes of King Henry II and his mistress Rosamond. There were slightly different versions of the Song and its tune, but, in nearly all of them the second line of each verse ran, 'We're a' St Mary's men,' and the last line of the verse was, 'Before our Lady'.

The Song was still sung in a number of places earlier in the century, but the custom gradually died out, and it is only in Burray, of all our islands, that a version of it is remembered. There, at the village, a few children still go round on Hogmanay to the neighbouring houses, singing the song and receiving gifts of cakes and money. Alas, there are few children now in Burray—it is all the more to their credit that a little group of them never fail to carry on the tradition. Long may they be able to do so.[2]

1. Information on the Ba' can be found in 'The games we played', p.147.
2. The custom is still observed in Burray.

The Burray Song, as I heard it sung in 1969, went like this:

> This is the last night of our old year,
> Peace and joy may a' hae here—
>   And that's before oor Lady.
>
> A three-legged cog was standing by,
> Full of cake and apple pie—
>   And that's before oor Lady.
>
> May a' your mares be weel tae foal,
> An' every een a big fat foal—
>   And that's before oor Lady.
>
> May a' your coos be weel tae calf,
> An' every een a big fat calf—
>   And that's before oor Lady.
>
> May a' your sheep be weel tae lamb,
> An' every een a big fat lamb—
>   And that's before oor Lady.
>
> May a' your hens be weel tae lay,
> An' every een a dizen a day—
>   And that's before oor Lady.
>
> Get up, aald wife, an' shak' your feathers,
> Ye needna think that we are beggars;
> We're only boys and girls come round
> To sing our Hogmanay.
>
> CAKES, CAKES!
> SCONES, SCONES!
> MONEY! MONEY! MONEY!

The interesting thing about this song is that the first six verses seem to stem from the old New Year Song, as it was remembered in Orkney, but the last part closely resembles a song that was sung by children at the New Year in Findochty, Banffshire, and probably in other places along the East Coast. The first four lines of the Findochty version ran:

> Rise up gweedwife an' shak' your feathers,
> Dinna think that we are beggars,
> We're only children come to play,
> Rise up and gae's oor Hogmanay.

There was a time, in the days when the fishing industry was at its height, that a number of people from the East Coast found their way to Burray, where some of them settled. Is it possible that the two songs were 'married' when some of the newcomers added their verses to the traditional Orkney song?

I knew that the Findochty song had been sung until the 1950s, perhaps a little later, so I telephoned the Findochty postmistress about it. She told me that she remembered the song well, but that for a while past it had not been heard. Instead, Findochty children sing carols on Hogmanay. They go around the houses 'all dressed up', and singing lustily, regardless of the fact that they are a little behind the rest of the world in their celebration of Christmas. It looks as if strong-minded people who did not like the traditional song have triumphed.

It was interesting to hear that the children are 'all dressed up', for in various places the singers of the New Year Song wore guizing costumes, sometimes made of straw, but often of oddments of brightly coloured clothing ornamented with ribbons.

★ ★ ★

Editor's note

T. A. Robertson, the Shetland poet 'Vagaland', sent to Ernest Marwick his memories of the song in Shetland:

> The New Year Song was known in several places on the West Side of Shetland. I have heard of it in Skeld and Foula, as well as in Waas.
>
> In the parish of Waas, where I lived when I was a boy, we used to go round the houses on the 12th of January (New Year's Eve by the old style calendar) and in each house that we visited we sang the New Year Song, which we called 'Da Huggeranonie Sang'. (The word 'Huggeranonie' may be connected with Hogmanay, but I have never heard the word Hogmanay used in Shetland. People always spoke about Newr Even.)
>
> The song would, I suppose, have been in English originally, but it had become a mixture of English and dialect. The verses which I can recall were as follows:

Dis is god Newr Even's Nicht,
  Sant Mary's men are we;
An we're come here ta crave wir richt
  Before Our Ladye!
	This is good New Year's Eve Night,
	  Saint Mary's men are we;
	And we've come here to crave our right
	  Before Our Lady!

God wife, geng ta your butter-kit An gi'es a spon or twa o hit.	Good wife go to your butter tub And give us a spoon or two of it.
God man geng i your beef barrel An gi'es da bit lies neist da sparrel.	Good man go to your beef barrel And give us the bit which lies next the small intestine.

Geng apo your mutton-reest	Go to your smoked dried mutton
An gi'es da bit at's neist da breest.	And give us the bit that's nearest the breast.
Cut wide, an cut roond,	Cut thick, and cut round,
An be sure your dunna cut your toom.	And be sure you don't cut your thumb.
Here we hae a kyerrin-horse,	Here we have a carrying horse,
Da deil sits atil his corse.	The devil sits within his corpse.

We were dressed in guizing-suits and wore masks. The guizing-suits were fancy dresses, made up of anything we could get or borrow for the occasion. We tried to get things that were brightly coloured. The masks, or 'faase-faces', were usually made out of bits of cotton with eye pieces cut in them.

The Kyerrin Horse was supposed to carry the gifts we got, and in the old days would have carried a kishie[1] to put things in, but we did not get beef or mutton. Instead we got pieces of cake, or apples, which we ate, and pennies, which the Kyerrin Horse collected and shared out afterwards.

In the old days I expect the Guizers would have worn the traditional guizing-dress—a hat made of straw, decorated with coloured ribbons, and a kind of cape and kilt also made of straw.

The New Year Song seems to be very old and may be connected with a Christianised version of some pre-Christian celebration.

Professor Holbourn, in his book *The Isle of Foula*, gives an interesting account of the New Year Song, as remembered in Foula, and gives his opinion that it is the surviving part of what was originally a Medieval Mummers' Play. He says that the Guizers used to end their performance by dancing round the fire, which in the old houses was in the middle of the floor.

In *The Folklore of Orkney and Shetland*, p.102, Ernest Marwick comments that at the outset the singers invoked blessings on the house itself:

> Guid be tae this buirdly biggin ...
> Fae the steid-stane tae the riggin[2] ...

---

1. Straw basket.
2. May good befall this sturdy building ...
   From the foundation-stone to the ridge of the roof ...

31 Spinning yarn for weaving, Westray, c.1900

32 Making a straw-backed Orkney chair, c.1920

33 An Orkney croft, Feolquoy, Stromness, c.1880

34 Interior of Craa'nest, Rackwick, Hoy, c.1880

3

Tailing day

Young folk in Orkney, as in other places, love the First of April, 'goaking day'. Here it is not a time for freshly invented humour, but a day on which the hoary traditional jokes are once more trotted out. In Kirkwall, as I suppose in other places, apprentices are still sent shopping for 'tins of elbow grease' and 'striped paint', or even to the Bank to request 'a long stand for coppers'. They get it too, poor boys.

In Orkney, however, we used to do things not in single days but in threes. There were three days of feasting during the three weeks of Yule, and any respectable wedding lasted three days. So it was with April fooling, and so it has continued. We have, first, 'goaking day', then 'tailing day', and finally 'borrowing day'. The last of the three, 'borrowing day', when anything anyone was foolish enough to lend could be regarded as a gift, has almost disappeared. It doesn't fit into the modern Orkney idea of economics. By far the most highly regarded of these days is 'tailing day'.

On that day, 2 April, it is legitimate to pin a tail on any passer-by. Children haunt the streets of Kirkwall, barely concealing handfuls of paper tails, each with a pin at the end twisted into a hook. Some over-enthusiastic kids bring tails by the basketful, but are rightly dealt with by the more discriminating, as so much enthusiasm is apt to put people, who once indulged in the practice themselves, on the alert.

Officially, adults deplore tailing day. So do I, until I see the local teacher or minister unsuspectingly walking down the street with a long tail hanging conspicuously from the seat of his black coat. And I am afraid I cannot resist the look of inquiry on the face of a stranger as he walks through Kirkwall and becomes aware that the whole population is laughing at him. What can be amiss?

The biggest game I ever saw stalked and tailed was a very, very important official from the Ministry of Agriculture. Some farmers watched his progress with open appreciation. It made their day. In fact, it added something to their lives.

4

Children's horse and plough festival in South Ronaldsay

For most children the Easter holiday is a period of indeterminate leisure, with only the brief excitement of Easter eggs to enliven it. But in South Ronaldsay, Orkney, there is a traditional event which makes the spring holiday the most colourful period of the year.

This is the Boys' Ploughing Match; but its name gives no indication of the delightful richness of the spectacle, which brings enthusiastic amateur photographers from every corner of the islands. The festival normally takes place on the first Wednesday in April,[1] tide permitting—surely the strangest of all requirements for a ploughing match.

Boys of school age are the ploughmen and they use perfectly proportioned model ploughs on fields of sand at a convenient beach. The ploughmen with their clean, scrubbed faces and knees, grey shorts or blue denims, look workman-like but undistinguished. It is their 'horses' that give the event something of the splendour of a Mediterranean carnival.

The 'horses' are mainly little girls, although small boys are admissible.[2] The costumes are their glory—rich outfits handed down from child to child, which become richer with each year. It is difficult to describe the effect of fifteen to twenty children so gorgeously dressed.

Think of outfits that begin with the appearance of the more showy Norwegian national costumes (although there is no connection); bespangle them with medals, coins, beads, sequins, brooches, anything brightly coloured and glittering; then remember that the children represent horses, and add to the outfits silver-painted hooves and hairy fetlocks, neat blinkers, and tall collars and hames covered with bells which tinkle as the children move. The result may be more like a Cockney pearly king than a horse, but it is at least

---

1. The event is now held on a Saturday in mid-August. It is a popular tourist attraction, enjoying an additional title *The Festival of the Horse*.
2. Before 1939 only boys took part, smaller lads being the horses. After the war girls became involved.

as magnificent. Nothing comes amiss, so dads with war medals and mums with sequinned dresses had better keep them under lock and key.

On the afternoon of the match the children gather at the Cromarty Hall in St Margaret's Hope.[1] The village is a place of grey walls and muted colours; against this background the splendour of the 'horses' has a fairy tale unreality. The ploughmen, each grasping his miniature plough, assemble on the stage inside the hall.[2] The 'horses', standing shyly in a circle, take the floor. Mothers, fathers, the folk of the village, sightseers from the Mainland of Orkney and visitors crowd the seats.

They are all there for the first part of the show, which is the judging of costumes and model ploughs. The judges are not imported pop stars or anything like that; they are two or three of the most respected men in the community. Nothing could exceed the solemnity and deliberation of their appraisal. For ten or twenty minutes their sober, low-voiced comments are exchanged. Then with grave finality, lightened by a quick joke here and there, the secretary of The Management Committee reads the placings.

There is a rush out into the open. The children are photographed again and again. And only then can the ploughing match proper begin.

Cars and buses in a long procession set out for the chosen beach,[3] where the sea has retreated, leaving a long stretch of damp firm sand. Here the 'field' is marked in 'flats',[4] and the boys, pushing their ploughs with all the skill they can command, try to fill their squares of sand with smooth, even furrows.

The 'horses' have disappeared; they were decorative only, and have no part in this stage of the contest. The arena is surrounded by spectators, three deep, pulling up coat collars against the chill wind from the sea.

Ploughing is judged with the same deliberation as costumes. In the evening in the Cromarty Hall, when the children have fed hugely and cheered their hosts, the prizes are presented.

No one has any idea when the Boys' Ploughing Match began. It was once a simpler event, with the boys trying their skill in the soft earth of a potato field. Ploughs could be crude in the old days, sometimes only the hoof of a cow on a length of stick. Costumes too were much less elaborate: braid,

1. Before the Second World War ploughing matches were also held by pupils of Grimness and Widewall schools. At Widewall, ploughing continued into the mid-1960s when the school was closed. The catchment area was Widewall, Herston and Eastside and the proceedings were concluded with a party at Widewall farm.
2. Now the judging takes place outside the Cromarty Hall. Only if the weather is inclement is the event held inside. Before the war the East End Hall, now a house, was used.
3. For many years the location was the Sand of Wright, Hoxa and this is still the preferred beach. Ploughing sometimes takes place at Kirkhouse of Widewall or at Sandwick, depending on the condition and availability of sand.
4. This is undertaken by the Field Committee, and the boys draw lots for rigs—plots of land, each four feet square.

ribbons and badges were sewn or pinned on to Sunday suits in the morning and hastily removed in time for the evening party.

But the tradition was so strong that the match grew bigger and bigger, limited only by the number of South Ronaldsay boys and girls. Many of the ploughs, like the costumes, are works of art.

THE SOUTH RONALDSHAY AGRICULTURAL SOCIETY'S
HORSE & CATTLE SHEW.

The following *Premiums* will be awarded for Stock at a Horse and Cattle Shew to be held at St. Margaret's Hope, on the 12th *November* 1845. viz.—

	£ s d
For the best STALLION, not exceeding 5 years old	0 10 0
For the best MARE	0 10 0
For the best BULL, not exceeding 4 years old	0 10 0
For the second best Ditto. ditto	0 5 0
For the best COW	0 10 0
For the second best Ditto	0 5 0
For the best STOT, not exceeding 4 years old	0 8 0
For the second best Ditto ditto	0 4 0
For the best QUEY, not exceeding 3 years old	0 8 0
For the second best Ditto- ditto	0 5 0
For the best Crossed CALF	0 6 0
For the best CALF not crossed	0 4 0
For the best BOAR	0 7 0
For the best SOW	0 6 0
For the best TUP	0 7 8
For the best EWE	0 6 0

At the same time will be awarded, other PREMIUMS as follows:—

	£ s d
For the best TURNIPS	0 8 0
For the second best Ditto	0 6 0
For the best SOWN GRASS	0 8 0
For the second best Ditto	0 5 0
For the greatest extent of Thorough DRAINING	0 8 0
For the second greatest Ditto	0 4 0

N.B. Those Persons who intend Stock for the Competition, must have them on the Ground before 12 o'Clock noon, on the day of the Shew.

South Ronaldshay, 18th October, 1845.

KIRKWALL PRESS

5

Hallowe'en

... Turnip lanterns again.... Well, it's a long time since I made one, but the youngsters are as keen as ever. They were at my door weeks ahead of Hallowe'en, and not all the witches and warlocks who are supposed to be abroad will keep them in on Hallowe'en itself. We shall hear that request—A PENNY FOR THE LANTERN, PLEASE—several times before tonight and tomorrow are over.

It's entirely the children's festival now, but in the old days in Orkney it was the night above all others charged with significance for the young women: for it was the one night in the year when by courage and craft a girl might catch a glimpse of her future husband, or at least get a glimmer of a clue to his identity.

There were of course all over Scotland well-known ways of thus peeping into the future. Burns tells of several in his poem *Hallowe'en*, but some of the Orkney methods were perhaps unique to the islands.

Not long ago I came across one new to me. The girl simply ate a salt herring before retiring to rest, in the assurance that her future husband, or his apparition, would appear sometime that night with a draught of water.

In Orphir, in the old days, the girls had recourse to another method of foretelling the future. A live coal was taken from the fire, put into water, and when extinguished placed under a piece of turf. In the morning the turf was broken in two. If a hair was found, it would undoubtedly be the same colour as that of the husband-to-be.

These were comparatively easy and safe methods. But some took courage. How would you like to sit in a dark barn, with both the doors open, when all the bogles were around, winnowing with an empty sieve on which you placed a knife, and knowing that an apparition having the appearance of your future partner would pass the door? Or how would you like to go out into the eerie stackyard, and fathom one of the screws: that is, span the corn-rick all round with your extended arms, knowing that at the full circle you would embrace the apparition of an unknown man, even if you had a good idea who it ought to be. Then there was a spell that had to be completed in the kailyard.

There were other beliefs associated with Hallowe'en. As late as 1930 in the island of Burray it was whispered that if you went into a dim room holding a fork with an apple impaled on the end and looked into a mirror you would see the devil rising through the floor.

. . . WHAT DID I TELL YOU. . . . There's the kids again!

6

Bonfire customs

For the past month every shopkeeper in Kirkwall has been asked time and time again, 'Ha'e you any bruck[1] for the bonfire?'. Everything that would wheel was brought into use, from bicycles to lumbering hand-barrows. Children staggered to every corner of the town with loads of paper. There was hardly a garage or shed that was not filled to the roof with inflammable materials. And the culmination on Saturday night was superb. The sky was a vivid crimson in every airt.[2] Great bonfires flamed, and the bairns were delirious with delight. Even sober folk like myself were thrilled.

Nowadays, no one quite knows why the bonfires are lit. The English tradition has superseded the older Orkney ceremonies, Guy Fawkes' Day has been chosen as an appropriate date, although the children gathering 'bruck' and pennies mix Hallowe'en and Guy Fawkes in their minds in a glorious jumble. But there is something in the Orcadian blood which responds to the appeal of the bonfire in a way that the alien adventures of poor Mr Fawkes cannot account for. The ritual bonfire goes back to the very beginnings of our history, and even before.

The old bonfires were lit on four occasions in the year, the festivals at Yule, Beltane,[3] Midsummer and Hallowmas,[4] but gradually three of the festivals ceased to be commemorated in this particular way, and bonfires were lit only at Midsummer, or Johnsmas.[5] Every parish, or it may be truer to say every township, had its bonfire. Vast heaps of heather, peats, straw, and any wood that was expendable, were piled up. It was an unwritten rule that the lads who collected the combustibles might carry away from any peatstack as many peats as could be built on a barrow. The site chosen had generally been used from time immemorial.

1. Rubbish.
2. Direction.
3. The first day of May.
4. The first day of November.
5. It was declared by some that the purpose of the Johnsmas bonfires, held then on 24 June, and continued until the second half of the nineteenth century, was to prevent witches from cutting the corn.

When the fire was lit in the evening the fun began. People thrust great bunches of heather into the flames, and ran around with the blazing torches. Young men vied with each other in leaping through the bonfire. In some places a bone was either built into the pile, or thrown into the flames when the fire was at its height. The significance of this is now forgotten, but some of the other rites are remembered. In his splendid book, *Reminiscences of an Orkney Parish,* John Firth wrote:

> The farmers who wished a bountiful crop the ensuing harvest, had large heathery torches made, lit them at the John's Mass fire, and never allowed them to get extinguished till the whole circumference of the fields had been traversed. This ceremony was gone through with the utmost gravity, after a solemn procession had circled round the blazing pile for some time.[1]

In some places people carried the blazing torches into the byres among the cattle, encircling them where possible so that they would thrive.

Young people in the parishes of Stromness and Sandwick used to climb to the top of Kringlafiold for three mornings at midsummer to herald the rising sun with uplifted hands. They would dance in the summer dawn, then eat the food they had brought with them.

No doubt it all went back to the days of sun-worship, but the whole subject is so involved, and has been so bedevilled by unfounded theories and rash speculations, that an amateur like me is wiser to keep his opinions to himself.

In Kirkwall, the midsummer bonfire had its date changed at an early period to commemorate the Royal birthday, probably, according to Hossack,[2] in the reign of George I. The bonfire on the Kirk Green was once provided by the town, but later it was put there by the townsfolk themselves. A mast, or pole, was built into the middle of the bonfire, and the Up-the-Gates and Down-the-Gates[3] were there to see in what direction it would fall. It was a good omen for that part of the town towards which the burning pole inclined when the fire fell away. As in the Ba', however, the factions left nothing to chance, and the object of the opposing parties was to snatch the burning pole and bear it to their own end of the town. It was forced either to Burgar's Bay or into the harbour. Finally, the embers of the fire were kicked all over the Kirk Green and into the street by the more foolhardy of the spectators, who did not seem to mind singeing their clothes or burning their legs.

Eventually the bonfire on the Kirk Green became too big and too hot for

---

1. p.125.
2. *Kirkwall In The Orkneys,* 1900, p.465.
3. For further information on Up-the-Gates, Down-the-Gates and the Ba' see 'The games we played', pp.180-182.

35 Craa'nest, Rackwick, Hoy, c.1890

36. Travelling shop, c.1900

the safety of the town. After a particularly fierce blaze scorched the paint on the doors and windows of the houses in Broad Street, the Authorities decreed that future bonfires must be held at Gallowha.[1] Alas, this was too far out of the town to attract the citizens and Kirkwall lost its traditional blaze. But, as I said, bonfires are in the very blood of Orcadians—witness the big heather fires each year which legislation seems powerless to stop—and the custom has risen like the phoenix to renewed youth, by virtue of the interest that the children have created by their increasingly massive fires.

In my own life-time, I think the finest bonfires I have seen were those that blazed from Orkney hilltops on the silver jubilee of King George V. I had something to do with preparing one of them, and I can remember the little hillock of rubbish that was assembled. In the centre was a tar barrel and masses of old rubber tyres. The central core was surrounded by several cartloads of peats and straw, and masses of wood. The whole was saturated with gallons of paraffin. It made a glorious blaze. After all these years I can still find the spot where it stood, for it burned so deeply into the ground. It was thrilling to stand on the hilltop and watch the fires on every eminence within sight.

I have doubtless given myself away as a frustrated incendiary; but I have managed at last to sublimate my instincts—simply by striking innumerable matches to light a pipe that is continually going out.

---

1. Warrenfield.

PASTIMES

1 Games of a thousand years — 145
2 The games we played — 147
3 A cricket century — 184
4 Entertainment galore — 186
5 An Orkney concert in the 1920s — 189
6 Orkney drinking — 191

I

Games of a thousand years

Now that the dark evenings are here, quite a lot of Orkney people (in spite of TV and other distractions) will be doing something which their ancestors have done for a thousand years: they will be taking their draughts boards from their place on the top of the kitchen cupboard, and settling down to a long evening of intense companionable silence. How I used to enjoy those nights forty years[1] ago—the interminable waiting, when the game got tense, for one's opponent to make a move; the prompting of him with the remark, 'It's your shift'; and the satisfaction with which each *crooner*—not a pop singer, but a king in our language—was finally created. It was something of a ritual. I think I felt this even as a boy, although I did not know then that the great sagas, like *Grettir the Strong*, have many references to draughts, and that our own Earl Rognvald played the game so well that he boasted, 'I'm a master of draughts.'

While I was thinking of the honourable history of the game in Orkney, I began to wonder if the Vikings and their contemporaries, who seem so barbarous in our history books, had left us any other evidence of their more human activities. Of course I remembered at once the exciting discovery of my friend Robert Rendall that children's games with shells, which were still remembered when he and I were young, were a direct inheritance from Norse children playing on our Orkney sea shore. I can recall his enthusiasm when he first told me that popular shell names like *smurslin*,[2] *coo-shell*,[3] *kraeno*,[4] *soo-shell*[5] and *sholtie*[6] went back to the days when the children who lived on our coastal farms (which still keep their Norse names) used shells to represent animals when they built their pebble-stone enclosures on the beaches and played at

---

1. The late 1920s.
2. *Mya truncata*, the truncated gaper-shell.
3. *Dosinia exoleta*, the rayed artemis, and *Phacoides borealis*, the larger white bi-valve shell.
4. *Mytilus edulis*, the common mussel.
5. Probably *Mya truncata*, the truncated gaper-shell.
6. *Calliostoma zizyphinum*, the common top-shell.

farms. A finely ribbed cockle suggested a sheep's fleece, a gaper shell a pig's snout, and so on.[1]

It is possible that these Norse children started a form of noughts and crosses[2] on the flat white sand of beaches in islands like Stronsay and Sanday, using sticks or pointed stones to form their diagrams. We even have the name of the game—*Trip-trap-truisky*, which is near enough to the present day Norwegian *Tripp-trap-tresko*. In Orkney the name also became the winner's shout of triumph.

In Sanday, probably one of the earliest islands to be settled by the Norsemen, Dr Hugh Marwick found a game which, although I have no Norse parallel, seems so like the kind of thing which would have delighted Viking boys that I am inclined to accept it as a survival. Each player removed the turf from a small area of ground leaving within the area a narrow strip of grass untouched. Then each, with a skilful twist of his hand, threw up his knife so that it fell point downwards into the earth. The distance which the point penetrated the earth was measured, and that distance cut away from the player's strip of grass. The first player to have his strip completely cut away was the winner. Sanday boys played this game with their pocket knives, but it is easy to imagine bright-bladed viking knives turning somersaults in the Orkney air.

Other missiles also hurtled through the air in a 'faely[3] fight', a popular game when I first went to school in one of our Mainland parishes. We pelted each other with pieces of wet turf dug from the ground on the toes of our boots, and I often arrived home with thick muddy marks on the back of my jacket. But the game was exciting, and my father had played it too. So, I find, had his fathers before him. For the Norsemen included it in their list of popular games and called it *Torfleikr*, which means 'turf-play'.

Of all these games, however, the only one which survives is draughts, a game which the Norsemen shared with the whole of Europe. We still play earnestly in the islands, and win national correspondence competitions. But I sometimes wonder if I am destined to see disappear this last happy memory of Norse life in Orkney.[4]

---

1. For further information see 'Orkney Shell Names and Shell Games' by Robert Rendall, *Orkney Miscellany*, Vol.II, 1954.
2. See also 'The games we played', p.147.
3. Fael—sod or turf.
4. Draughts is still a popular game throughout Orkney.

2

The games we played

Only a handful of indigenous Orkney games have been recognised. It is not intended to repeat these here, but rather to record some games of wider provenance which were popular with the children of yesterday. A few of these were remembered up to the beginning of the Second World War, but others have been out of favour for half a century and more.[1]

The great majority of our games were imported from much further south. They frequently found their way to Kirkwall from the streets of London, especially the singing games. These were bought from Jewish book vendors at the Lammas Market, and were eagerly hunted for among piles of penny broadsheets containing the songs and diversions of the age. No sooner had Orkney children learned them than they began to adapt them to their own tastes. Although it is easy, even now, to recognise some games, others have been altered out of recognition.

★ ★ ★

SINGING GAMES

These had simple tunes which were sometimes transferred to new games, with the words roughly tailored to fit them.

SEE THE ROBBERS PASSING BY

> See the robbers passing by, passing by, passing by:
> See the robbers passing by, my fair lady.
>
> What's the robbers done to you, done to you, done to you?
> What's the robbers done to you, my fair lady?
>
> Broke my locks and stole my gold, stole my gold, stole my gold:
> Broke my locks and stole my gold, my fair lady.
>
> We shall go and capture them, capture them, capture them:
> We shall go and capture them, my fair lady.

1. The article was written c.1955.

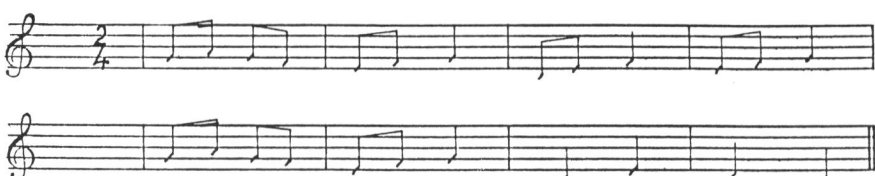

This was a tug-o'-war played by girls, but the greater part of the game and the best of the fun consisted in selecting the teams. To head the teams the two tallest girls among the players were chosen. These two decided in secret conclave which of them should lead the apple team and which the orange team, the other players being kept in ignorance. They then stood facing each other, just far enough apart for the other players to pass between them. They raised their arms and clasped their hands to form a double arch, through which the rest of the children passed in Indian file, each holding the belt or dress of the girl in front. As they passed through they all sang the above song, wheeling round one of the leaders in a circle to catch up with the back of the queue, from which, however, the foremost girl kept separate by not holding on as the others did. As she passed through the second time the foremost girl wheeled the queue round the second leader, and this figure-of-eight progress round the leaders was continued until the last word of the last verse was sung, at which point the leaders forming the gateway lowered their arms and caught between them the girl who was passing underneath at that moment.

They rushed the captive to one side, asking in a whisper whether she would like an orange or an apple. If she chose an apple she had to stand, when the game was continued, behind the girl who had decided to lead the apple team. If she chose an orange she stood behind the other leader. The same procedure was followed until all the players had been caught, questioned, and placed in the respective teams, when an arms-round-waist-in-front tug-o'-war ended the game.

HAVE YOU ANY BREAD AND WINE?
(The tune is the same as that for 'See the robbers passing by')

>   Have you any bread and wine, bread and wine, bread and wine?
>   Have you any bread and wine, my fair lady?
>   Yes, we have some bread and wine . . .
>   We shall have a loaf of bread . . .
>   A loaf of bread you shall not have . . .
>   And we shall have a bottle of wine . . .
>   A bottle of wine you shall not have . . .
>   What kind o' men are ye ava'? . . .
>   We are all King George's men . . .
>   An' we are all King James's men . . .
>   Then you'll have to fight for it . . .

The players formed two equal lines which faced each other some distance apart. The first line then advanced towards the second, singing the first verse of the song. Their progress forward was made while singing the first line and their retreat backward while singing the second. The opposing players then took up the challenge, advancing and retreating while singing the second verse. This was done alternately until the end of the final verse, when both lines advanced on each other hopping on one foot. As they met, the players tried to bump their opposite numbers off balance so that they had to put both feet on the ground. Both sides continued to hop and bump each other until all had been forced to put their feet down.

JOHN, JOHN, THE GUNDYMAN

> John, John, the gundyman[1]
> Washed his face in the frying-pan,
> Combed his hair wi' the leg o' the chair:
> John, John, the gundyman.

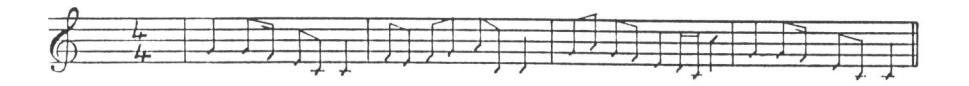

The child was held on the knee, and the actions of washing and combing were simulated while the appropriate words were being sung.

TILLIE WUPLAN, HIGHLAND JOHN

> Tillie Wuplan, Highland John,
> Went to bed wi' his trousers on,
> Wan buit[2] aff an' the ither wan on:
> Tillie, Willie Wuplan, Highland John.

The Orkney version of a rhyme known all over the country. Kirkwall children sang it in all good faith, believing that it referred to a well-known and somewhat eccentric local gentlemen.

1. Toffee seller.
2. Boot.

They're all so black and browsy

> They're all so black an' so browsy,[1]
> They sit on the hills o' Rousay,
> Wi' five gold chains aboot their necks—
> An' they're all so black an' so browsy.

Another example of the adaptation of a far-travelled original.

My name is Queen Mary

Part one

> My name is Queen Mary, my age is sixteen,
> My father's a farmer on yonder green;
> With plenty of money to dress me sae braw,[2]
> Yet no bonnie laddie will tak' me awa'.

> One morning I rose an' I looked in the glass,
> Says I to myself, 'What a handsome young lass!'
> My hands by my sides as I gave a 'Ha, ha',
> Yet no bonnie laddie will tak' me awa'.

Part two

> Clean the brazen candlesticks, clean the fireside,
> Draw back the curtains an' let us see your bride:
> For a' the men in Orkney live a happy life,
> Except (Andrew Brodie) for he wants[3] a wife.

1. Plump, well fed.
2. Fine.
3. Lacks.

> A wife shall he have an' a widower shall he be,
> For look at (Mary Halcro) sittan on his knee.
> He paints her cheek an' he curls her hair,
> An' he kisses her twice at the feet o' the stair.

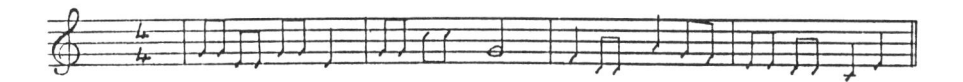

As the children sing the first part of the song, they dance in a ring around the girl chosen as Queen Mary. As the second verse ends she chooses a partner, and in the pause between the two parts of the game the one chosen goes inside the ring with her. The tune changes, and the children dance around singing the second set of verses, while the two in the centre skip or dance as they will. They must kiss each other as the game ends; when the one chosen remains in the centre and the other joins the ring. The game is repeated for as long as interest and energy last.

This is a very curious game, made up from at least two games once played in London and elsewhere. The original of the first part (I quote from 'London Street Games' by Norman Douglas) went like this:

> My name is sweet (Jennie), my age is sixteen,
> My father's a (farmer) and I am a Queen.
> Got plenty of money to dress me in silk,
> But nobody loves me but (Gladys) dear.

The second part echoes a game which runs:

> All the boys in our town, eating apple-pie,
> Excepting (Georgie Groves), he wants a wife—
> A wife he shall have, according he shall go
> Along with (Rosie Taylor), because he loves her so.
> He kisses her and cuddles her, and sits her on his knee,
> And says, my dear, do you love me?
> I love you, and you love me.
> Next Sunday morning, the wedding will be,
> Up goes the doctor, up goes the cat,
> Up goes a little boy in a white straw hat.

In one version of the Orkney game, the children who were in the centre of the ring during the singing of the second part joined hands, put their toes together, and whirled round like a teetotum.

Round apples

(The tune is the same as that for 'My name is Queen Mary')

> Round apples, round apples by night and by day:
> There stands a poor (Mollie) by yonder the way.
> Her cheeks were like roses, but now they're like snow:
> Oh (*choose partner*) (Nellie), Oh, Nellie, you're dying I know.
>
> I'll wash you in milk and I'll dry you in silk,
> And I'll write down your name with a gold pen and ink.

The first player (Mollie) who is in the centre of the ring at the beginning, having chosen her partner, rejoins the ring during the singing of the last line, and the second girl (Nellie) remains in the centre to choose the next partner. And that is all there is to it. The game was popular because it was fast moving, giving most of the children a chance to get into the centre.

The words of the Orkney version are again very different at the outset from the London one (once more I quote from Norman Douglas):

> Green gravel, green gravel,
> Your grass is so green (or: Your voice is not heard)
> I'll send you a letter
> To call (Florrie) in.
>
> I'll wash you in milk, and dress you in silk,
> And write down your name with a gold pen and ink.

Comarinkle tinkle

> As I was walking down the street an Irish lady I did meet,
> With patent slippers on her feet and a gold ring on her finger.
> Comarinkle tinkle, fah lah lah, fah lah lah, fah lah lah.
> Comarinkle tinkle, fah lah lah, on board a man-o'-war ship.
>
> I can wash a sailor's shirt, I can wash it clean,
> I can wash a sailor's shirt and bleach it on the green.
> Comarinkle tinkle, fah lah lah, etc.
>
> I can chew tobacco, I can smoke a pipe,
> I can kiss a bonnie lass at ten o'clock at night.
> Comarinkle tinkle, fah lah lah, etc.

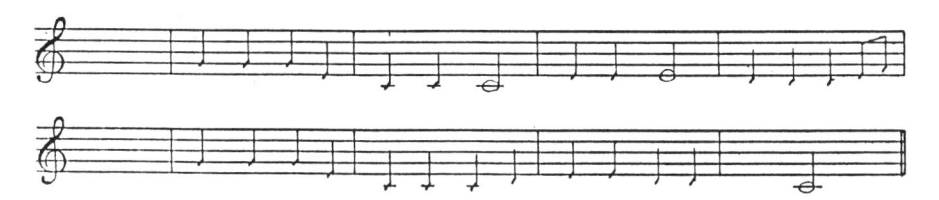

Another simple ring game. The child in the centre makes her choice of partner at the end of the first verse. All the children dance around until the last verse is sung, after which the game is repeated.

HERE'S A POOR WIDOW

> Here's a poor widow, she's left alone,
> She has no one to marry upon:
> Come choose to the east, and choose to the west,
> And choose to the one that you love best.
>
> Now she's got married, I hope she'll enjoy
> Every year a girl and a boy,
> Loving each other like sister and brother:
> I pray you come, come kiss together.
>
> Tea and sugar for aald wives,
> Corn and hay for horses,
> Cheese and bread for gentlemen,
> And bonnie lads for lasses.

This was played in the same way as the former game; but the couple were expected to kiss at the end of the second verse. It was usual, I think, for the child who did the choosing to rejoin the ring at this point, and to dance around with the others during the singing of the last verse, which is almost certainly an addition to the original game.

In some parts of Orkney the first verse began:

> There was a poor widow of Sandilands,
> Who had no daughter to marry her son . . .

and there were other differences. There are many variants of the game, and those who are interested may refer to pages 80 and 82 of *Children's Games*

Throughout The Year by Leslie Daiken, who also has versions of 'Have you any Bread and Wine?' (with English and Roman soldiers)—page 19; 'Round Apples'—page 64; and 'Green Gravel'—page 81 (there is inextricable confusion between these two in Orkney); 'Queen Mary'—page 88 (printed as 'A Scottish Courtship Poem' with almost the same words as the Orkney version); and 'In and Out the Windows'—page 153. For the last word on children's language, lore and recreations, turn to the works of Iona and Peter Opie, whose examples are usually too complete and voluminous to quote.

DAVIE DASKAL

    Davie, Davie Daskal,
    A'm on yer Castal.[1]

This was a hopping game. The children hopped on and off the pavement singing the words over and over. The child who was Davie Daskal pretended that he was not interested until a player was so near that he could attempt to knock him off balance. A player was 'caught' by Davie when he had to put both feet on the ground. He then became Davie Daskal.

In other parts of the country this is a 'King of the Castle' game, with the words:

    Willie, Willie Wastell
    I am on your Castle,
    A' the dogs in the toon
    Winna pu' Willie doon.

RING-A-RING, A-ROSEY

    Ring-a-ring, a-rosey,
    Sat upon a posey.
    Station, station, all fall down!

The players dance around in a ring. At the command, they all fall (or sit) down. The last one to get up again goes into the centre. The game is repeated until all are in the centre.

 1. Castle.

ROUND AND ROUND THE VILLAGE

Go round and round the village,
Go round and round the village,
Go round and round the village,
As you have done before.

Go in and out the windows, etc.

Stand up and face your lover, etc.

Come follow me to London (or Dublin), etc.

The children stand in a circle with a space between each. The player who begins the game walks around outside the circle during the singing of the first verse. He varies this during the second verse by making his way through the spaces between the players, passing in front of the first, behind the next, and so on. Throughout the third verse he stands in front of the player he chooses. He leads her around the circle while the last verse is sung, after which he joins the players in the circle, and the game begins all over again.

I have the words of two interesting singing games, but not, alas, the tunes. They are 'The gallant, gallant ship' and 'A soldier lay dead'.

THE GALLANT, GALLANT, SHIP

Three times around went the gallant, gallant ship,
And three times around went she;
And three times around went the gallant, gallant ship,
Till she sank to the bottom of the sea,
The sea, the sea,
Till she sank to the bottom of the sea.

Pull her up, pull her up, cried the poor sailor boy,
Pull her up, pull her up, cried he;
Pull her up, pull her up, cried the poor sailor boy,
Pull her up from the bottom of the sea,
The sea, the sea,
Pull her up from the bottom of the sea.

The players formed a ring, linking hands. As they sang the first two lines of the first verse they danced around in a clockwise direction, reversing this to anti-clockwise at the beginning of the third line. At the end of the verse all sank down, and the second verse was sung sitting. The child in the centre of the ring went to one of the sitting players and pulled him up. This player then helped to pull up others, and so it continued until all were pulled up. The first player to be pulled up went inside the ring when the game was started again.

A SOLDIER LAY DEAD

> There was a soldier lay dead in his grave,
> Dead in his grave, dead in his grave;
> Heigh-ho, dead in his grave.

The 'soldier' lies 'dead'. The children sing around him.

> They planted an apple tree over his head, etc.

The planting of the apple tree was suggested in Orkney by the children holding one closed fist in front of them and hitting it with the other.

> The apples grew ripe and they all fell off, etc.

With a sweeping movement of the hands, the children fell to the ground, taking up positions as ridiculous as they could think of.

> There was a poor woman came picking them up, etc.

The girls lifted up their pinafores by the hems, and pretended to fill them with apples.

> The soldier got up and gave her a kick, etc.

At this the 'dead soldier' got up and chased the girls, who ran away screaming. The first to be caught and firmly held then became the 'soldier'.

Other familiar games like 'Oranges and lemons', 'Nuts in May', 'The farmer's in his den' also had their local versions, but those printed above are perhaps representative of the singing games.

★ ★ ★

THE GAMES WE PLAYED

FAVOURITE SONGS

Three songs loved by generations of children, dancing with delight on the knees of the singers, were 'Cock-a-Bendy', 'Kyetty Beardo' and 'Jenny Nettle'. Here are the local versions:

COCK-A-BENDY

> Cock-a-Bendy's lyan seek[1]
> Guess ye what'll mend him—
> Twenty kisses in a cloot,[2]
> That's what we'll send him.
> A penny's worth o' green peas,
> A hapney's[3] worth o' pepper,
> An' a drink o' buttermilk,
> An' that'll mak' him better.

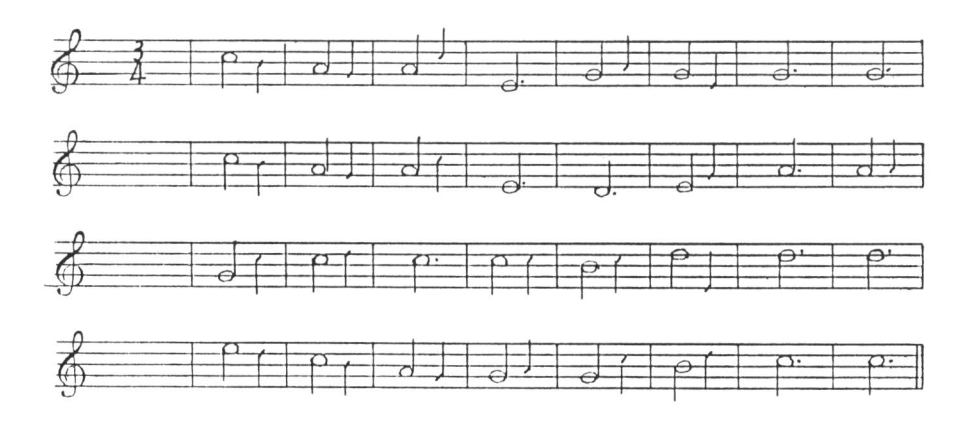

KYETTY BEARDO

> Kyetty Beardo hed a hen,
> Shae could toddle but an' ben,[4]
> Wisna that a denty[5] hen?
>   Dance Kyetty Beardo.
> Kyetty Beardo hed a duck,
> Shae could grub amang the muck,
> Wisna that a denty duck?
>   Dance Kyetty Beardo.

1. Sick.
2. Cloth.
3. Halfpenny's.
4. But—kitchen, Ben—parlour, i.e. through the house.
5. Remarkable.

Kyetty Beardo hed a coo,
Spotted white aboot the moo,[1]
Wisna that a denty coo?
   Dance Kyetty Beardo.
Kyetty Beardo hed a rabbit,
A' the heid o' hid wis scabbit,[2]
Wisna that a denty rabbit?
   Dance Kyetty Beardo.

Kyetty Beardo hed a cat,
Hid could fight a muckle[3] rat,
Wisna that a denty cat?
   Dance Kyetty Beardo.
Kyetty Beardo hed a dog,
Hid could guide her through the fog,
Wisna that a denty dog?
   Dance Kyetty Beardo.

Kyetty Beardo hed a fan,
A' shae hedna' wis a man,[4]
Wisna that a denty fan?
   Dance Kyetty Beardo.
Kyetty Beardo hed a plan
For tae get hersel' a man,
Wisna that a denty plan?
   Dance Kyetty Beardo.

1. Mouth.
2. Scabbed.
3. Large.
4. All she had not was a man.

JENNY NETTLE
(A nursing song)

>Jenny Nettle, Jenny Nettle,
>Coman' fae the market;
>A poke[1] o' mael apin her back,
>A bairn in a blanket;
>A pint o' eel[2] in every hand,
>An' shae sat doon an' drank it. } Repeat

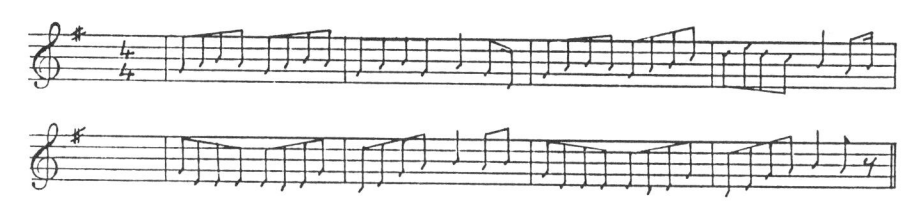

Another version is:

>Saa thoo no'[3] me Jenny Nettle,
> Jenny Nettle, Jenny Nettle,
>Saa thoo no' me Jenny Nettle
> Coman' fae the market,
>Bearan a peerie bairn,
>Bearan a peerie bairn,
>Bearan a peerie bairn
> Rowed[4] in a blanket?

* * *

RHYME AND ACTION GAMES

TWO LITTLE BLACKBIRDS

>Two little blackbirds sat on a hill:
>One was named Jack, the other was named Jill.
>Fly away Jack! Fly away Jill!
>Come back Jack! Come back Jill!

Small pieces of paper (sometimes with faces, or blackbirds, drawn on them) are stuck on the nails of both forefingers. Then, with the forefingers extended and the rest of the hand closed, the paper 'blackbirds' are moved rhythmically up and down while the first part of the verse is repeated. At the words 'Fly

1. Bag.
2. Ale.
3. Did you not see me.
4. Wrapped.

away Jack', the right forefinger is lifted quickly up to the head. While this is being done, the middle finger is deftly substituted and the forefinger tucked into the hand, so that when the finger comes down for the child to see, 'Jack' has disappeared. This same thing happens with 'Jill'. At the words, 'Come back', the fingers are changed again (the raising and lowering movement continuing all the while) and first 'Jack' and then 'Jill' reappear. A young child finds the disappearance of the 'blackbirds' very puzzling.

With the Bairn on your Knee

GETTING A RIDE

    This is the way the old man rides—
      Trot ... Trot ... Trot ... Trot ...
              (slowly and heavily)
    This is the way the lady rides—
      Trip-trot ... Trip-trot ... Trip-trot.
              (gently)
    This is the way the gentleman rides—
      Gallop, Gallop, Gallop, Gallop.
              (quickly)
    But this is the way the donkey rides—
      Hobbledehoy, Hobbledehoy, Hobbledehoy.
              (heaving from side to side,
              and lifting the child off
              your knee on to the floor)

MILL DOGS

    Twa peerie penny-dogs aff tae the mill,
    Ae feet afore the tither—hill, trill, trill.
    Lickan oot o' every man's pockie[1] o' meal,
    Home again, home again—hill, trill, trill.
    Twa peerie penny-dogs aff tae the fair,
    Home again, home again—nobody there.

---

1. A small sack.

Selkies Hellier, The Home of the Seals, c.1955

Stanley Cursiter, RSA, RSW, 1887-1976

The Dogs o' Holm

>This is the wey the dogs o' Holm,
>The dogs o' Holm, the dogs o' Holm,
>This is the wey the dogs o' Holm
>Go runnin' tae the mill—
>>Ae feet afore the ither,
>>Ae feet afore the ither,
>>Ae feet afore the ither,
>Hobble ... Hobble ... Hobble.

You grasped the child's ankles, and moved its feet in time to the tune, to imitate a dog running. The teu-name[1] of the people of Holm was *Hobblers*.

Leuk up ... Leuk doon

>Leuk up there an' thoo'll see Jock Manson;
>Leuk doon there an' thoo'll see the dog dancin'.

Said to a fretful child to take its attention from its woes.

Fun with the Face

>Chin, chin, cherry,
>Mou', mou' merry,
>Eye, eye winkie,
>Broo, broo brinkie,[2]
>An' ower the hill tae get a drinkie.

Me broo brinkie,	(touch forehead)
Me eye o' life,	(touch eye)
Me bubbly ocean,	(touch nose)
Me pen knife,	(touch mouth)
Me chin cherry,	(touch chin)
Me trapple kirry, kirry, kirry.	(tickle throat)
Chap on the door,	(tap on forehead)
Peep in,	(lift an eyelid)
Lift the sneck,[3]	(twig the nose)
Walk in.	(put a finger in the mouth)[4]

1. Nickname.
2. The edge or brink of the brow.
3. Latch.
4. An extension is:
Sit doon on the chair	(touch the chest)
Brak the buddom oot o' the chair	(tickle the tummy)

As the following rhymes were said, playful or teasing passes were made at the child: who was the cat, the calf, the victim of the crow, or whatever the rhyme suggested.

> A B Buff,
> Gi'e the cat a cuff:
> Gi'e her een,
> Gi'e her twa,
> Knock her heid tae the wa'.[1]

> A'll tell thee a story
> Aboot the reid calf's lug[2]—
> Thoo'll bore the hole
> An' A'll pit in the plug.

> Pit thee fingar in the craw's nest—
> The craw's no' home.

A Paddy Dreel—this is the humorous term given to the act of taking a person by the ear (such as a child from his seat to the front of the schoolroom) and marching him along against his inclination.

Five Fingers

A SANDAY HAND

> Thumb--Toomikin.
> Index finger—Loomikin.
> Middle finger—Langman.
> Third finger—Lickpot.
> Little finger—Peedieman.

A NORTH RONALDSAY FIVE

> Little finger—Peedie Peedie.
> Third finger—Paddy Luddy.
> Middle finger—Lady Whisle.
> Index finger—Lodey Whusle.
> Thumb—Great Odomondod.

---

1. Knock her head to the wall.
2. About the red calf's ear.

This is the Man

> That's the ane 'at breuk the barn,
> That's the ane 'at staeled the corn,
> That's the ane 'at beur hid awa',
> That's the ane 'at telled on them a',
> An peerie, weery Winkie, fell i' the gutter an' paid for 'em a'.

A Kittly Hand

> Lady, Lady o' the land,
> Can thoo bear a kittly hand?[1]
> If thoo laughs, or if thoo smiles,
> Thoo'll never be a lady o' the land.

The little game consisted of tickling the liv, or palm, of the child's left hand, while the child did its best not to laugh.

Haet a Wummle

> Haet[2] a wummle,
> Bore a hole,
> Whar peece[3] whar peece?
> Cheust dere,[4] dere, dere!

The forefinger of the reciter, which was the wummle, or auger, described circles nearer and nearer the victim, until the final prod into some tickly part of the child's anatomy produced squeals of laughter.

Breaking the Fiddle

> Me faither hed a fiddle,
> He breuk hid here, he breuk hid there,
> He breuk hid right i' the middle.

The action of breaking the fiddle was demonstrated on the child's arm, which was struck with the side of the hand first on the forearm, then on the upper arm, and finally in the middle, causing the arm to double up at the elbow.

★ ★ ★

---

1. Can you bear a tickly hand.
2. Heat.
3. What place.
4. Just there.

BAIRNS' RHYMES, SAETROS AND RIDDLES

Bairns' Rhymes

STROMNESS PORRIDGE

> The man o' Myre
> Pat on the fire,
> The man o' Clook
> Made hid smook,[1]
> The man o' Pow
> Made hid lowe,[2]
> The man o' Creuk
> Pat on the heuk,[3]
> The man o' Cott
> Pat on the pot,
> The man o' Ratter
> Pat in the watter,
> Tammy Watt
> Pat in the saat,[4]
> The man o' Dale
> Steered in the mael,[5]
> An' Jessie Omond
> Supped uncommon.

The houses named in this rhyme were actual houses in Innertown, Stromness.

DAVIE DUNDERLEGS

> Davie, Davie Dunderlegs,
> Boil him in a pot,
> Salt him an' pepper him
> An' aet him while he's hot.

DANCE, DUSTY FEET

> Dance, dance, dusty feet,
> Sing Andrew Young;
> The dog's heid's i' the pot,
> An' thoo'll get the tongue.

1. Smoke.
2. Burn.
3. Hook.
4. Salt.
5. Stirred in the meal.

37 Tom Rendall, Longhouse, aak-swapping near Red Nev, Westray, c.1912

38 'Running the Lee', Copinsay, 1912

Jamie Seatter, dirty craeter

Jamie Seatter, dirty craeter,[1]
Killed a coo an' couldno' aet her;
Laid her in a tub tae steep,[2]
Hang her in the barn tae dreep;[3]
An' eftir a' he couldno' aet her:
Jamie Seatter ... puir craeter!

A sillock for tea

Robbie Tullock
Caught a sillock[4]
In the Peerie Sea;
He teuk hid home
An' fried hid
An' hed hid for his tea.

Catching a scorrie

Tammie Norrie
Catched a scorrie[5]
On the Peerie Sea;
Hid gaed him a nip
On the hip,
An' then he let hid be.

Clumsy Geordie[6]

Geordie Loggie, puir body,
Caa'd his tae in a curl-doddy;[7]
Ap he got, doon he fell,
Caa'd his tae in a cockle shell;
Ap he raise, then he ran,
An' caa'd his tae in a frying pan.

---

1. Creature.
2. Soak.
3. Drip.
4. Young coal-fish.
5. Young gull.
6. Another version is:
    Henry Noddie puir auld body
    Knocked his heid on a curly-doddy,
    Up he got, doon he fell,
    Knocked his heid on a tattie-bell*
    (* the flower seed formed on potatoes)
7. Caught his toe in a clover head.

The Wey the Tirlie Runs[1]

>Peter o' Winds
>Cocks his tail an' then he rins
>Up by Mooterhoose an' doon by Winds—
>That's the wey the tirlie rins.

Mooterhoose and Winds were two houses in Stronsay, and Old Peter was kiln-man at the Stronsay mill for many a long day.

Ride Awa' tae Rousam

>Ride awa' tae Rousam[2]
>An' flay the aald mare,
>Jock'll get the fetleens[3]
>An' Jean the meil o' bere.[4]

Cripple Dick

>Cripple Dick apin a stick,
>Sandy on a soo,[5]
>Ride awa' tae Gallowha'
>For a pund o' 'oo'.[6]

This rhyme may go back to the time when executions for sheep stealing were common.

Tell-pie

>Tell-pie, Picky Tord,
>Sat apin the byre board[7]
>Dellan[8] doon hen-dirt for bawbees.[9]

---

1. Something whirled around, usually by wind.
2. The local pronounciation for the district of Rothiesholm, Stronsay.
3. Possibly fetlocks.
4. The measure of bere—old Orkney barley.
5. Sow.
6. Wool.
7. A wooden shelf in the byre on which the hens sat.
8. Shovelling.
9. Another version of the last line is:
    Pickan ap hen-dirt, an wadna be forbidden.

Poor Paddy

Poor Paddy lay so domiless,[1]
The snow moored ower his tomiless,[2]
An' then he got rheumatees
Intae his tammileerie.[3]

Poor tailors

The rumples o' a soor skate,[4]
The haggis[5] o' a hen,
Are good enough for tailors,
For they're no men.

Skillo folk

Ceutikin[6] hose an' grey leather sheun,[7]
The Skillo folk mix their cheese wi' a speun.

Skillo is a local pronounciation of Skelwick, Westray.

A lazy man

The Rousay man said tae his mare,
'I wis' I wur i' thee for faer o' the ware:[8]
If I wur i' thee wi'oot a doot
Hid wid be Mertinmas or I wid come oot.'

This should probably be Lammas. A man who sought to avoid the kelp-burning would want to hide until Lammas, after which no kelp was burned.

Davie Dip

Davie Dip, Davie Dip,
Fell i' the fire an brunt[9] his hip:
He's no' very weel, but he's brawly[10] yet.

1. Listless.
2. The snow drifted over his body.
3. Possibly private parts.
4. The backbone of a sour skate.
5. Stomach.
6. Stockings without feet.
7. Shoes.
8. I wish I was in you for fear of the seaweed.
9. Burnt.
10. Well enough.

The Keeng o' the Jews

> Jeemie Bews, the Keeng o' the Jews,
> Selt his wife for a pair o' shoes;
> Whin the shoes began tae wear,
> Jeemie Bews began tae swear.

Two peats and a clod

> Two peats and a clod
> Spell Nebuchadnod,
> Two rings and a razor
> Spell Nebuchadnezzar,
> Two pairs of boots
> And two pairs of shoes
> Spell Nebuchadnezzar
> The king of the Jews.

This rhyme is probably known outside Orkney. The fact that Nebuchadnezzar was really King of Babylon need not worry us.

Hupple-dupple

> Hupple-dupple-deezo,
> Me bonnie Leezo;
> Hupple-dupple-dilso,
> Me peedie trilso.[1]

The wan that tells on me

> Tell-pie Picky Terno
> Sat apo' a tree;
> Knock doon aipples,
> Wan, two, three:
> Wan for baby,
> An' wan for the lady,
> Bit none for the wan that tells on me.

---

1. Obscure—probably toddler.

A PIECE O' BRUCK[1]

> I sat in me cheerum-charum
> An' luiked oot trou me leerum-larum,
> An' I saw a ree-raa
> Kairryan me ranty-pipes awa',
> Said I tae me breety-brattikin
> If I hed bit me wheety-whattikin
> I wad mak the ree-raa
> Let me ranty-pipes fa'.[2]

WHY DID YOU?

> For fun an' for folly,
> As the coo kissed Molly.
> *or*
> For fun an' for fancy,
> As the coo kissed Mansie.

Answers to persistent questioning.

WHICH HAND?

> Neek-a-tee Nack,
> Whit hand will thoo tak'?
> The right or the left—
> I'll beguile thee if I can.

---

1. Nonsense.
2.   I sat in my chair
    And looked out through my window,
    And I saw a crow
    Carrying away my ducklings,
    Said I to my servant
    If I had but my gun
    I would make that crow
    Let my ducklings fall.
For a slightly different version see Marwick's *The Orkney Norn*, 1929, p.139.

Saetros

It is not pretended that any of these counting-out rhymes are genuinely Orcadian, but as variations, and in some instances possibly the only survivals of rhymes once familiar to children everywhere, they seem worth preserving. The origin of the word *saetro*, which appears to have been the local name, is obscure. It is possible that this was the name once given to a formula for counting animals, and was borrowed by the children.

> Eesisey, Orsisey, Sukersey Ann,
> Pots o' vinegar as I began;
> Halaby, crackaby, tenaby, leefen,
> Peen pan, musket man,
> Teet tat, moose fat,
> Cara riddle, bom fiddle,
> Stink hole, fizz OOT.

★

> Eentie, feentie, fickity, fegg,
> Elf, delf, doman egg,
> Oriam, borkam, storam rock,
> An, tan, toosh, ock.

★

> Eetam, peetam, penny pie,
> Popa larum, chinkim, chie,
> White puddin', black troot,[1]
> I choice (choose) thee first OOT.

★

> Eetum, peetum, penny pie,
> Popum, lorum, chinkum chie,
> Eese ose, small rolls
> In a dish-cloot;[2]
> Two times two is a tuppenny loaf,
> An' two times two you're OOT.

★

---

1. Trout.
2. Dish cloth.

Eetem, peetem, penny pie,
Popin, larim, chinkim chie,
Ees, ass, ees, sink,
Peas pottage, small drink,
Count one, two, three,
And OUT goes she.

★

Eesy, oosy, eggers an,
Popsy, vinegar, abegan,
Teet tat, moose fat,
Cat a riddle, bump, fiddle,
I choice thee first OOT.

★

Eenity, twaity, tuckety, teven,
Malaba, creukaba, ten upa leven,
Ping pang, muskietang,
Eetle um, ottle um, twenty-wan.

★

Wanery, twoery, dickery seven,
Ella MacCrackery, nine, ten, eleven,
Peeng pang, muskey dang,
Tweedledum, twiddledum, twenty-wan.

★

Eetle ottle, black bottle,
Eetle ottle, out;
Tea and sugar is my delight,
Tea and sugar you're OUT.

★

Eetle ottle, black bottle,
Eetle ottle, out;
If you want a piece
Of bread and jam,
Please walk OUT.

When children could not agree on some point in their games, such as who should be the leader, they would insist that 'We'll say a saetro'. A saetro was sometimes prefaced by an old local rhyme:

> Cripple Dick on a stick,
> Sandy on a soo,[1]
> Ride awa' tae Gallowha'
> Tae buy a pund o' 'oo'.[2]
>
> Wi' a One an' a Two
> The 'oo' wis ower coorse,[3]
> Wi' a Three an' a Four
> The 'oo' wis ower thick,
> Wi' a Five an' a Six
> The 'oo' wis ower thin,
> Wi' a Seven an' a Eight
> The 'oo' hid widna spin,
> Wi' a Nine an' a Ten
> The 'oo' widna mak' a skin
> Wi' a 'Leven an' a Twelve
> Tae a humpie-backid loose,[4]
> But the sheep were safe in their den, o.

When an eel was caught in a burn, it was held to see whether it would tie itself into a knot, and apostrophised with what seems a variation of a well-known counting-out rhyme:

> Eeny, meeny, minny, mo,
> Cast a knot apin yer tail
> An' then we'll let you go.[5]

---

1. Sow.
2. Wool.
3. Over coarse.
4. A hump-backed louse.
5. A variation was:
    > Eelie, eelie, o,
    > Tie/Cast a knot apin yer tail
    > An' then I'll let you go.

    There was an old belief that horse hair dropped in water would turn into eels. In Orkney a young eel was known as a 'hair eel'.

39 Islanders with swap-net, Westray c.1912

40 Aak (guillemot) eggs collected from 'The Lee', Copinsay, 1912.
Standing back: James Groat, David Foubister, Robert Skea, James Hourie, Robert Foubister, Thomas Foubister, James Skea, Thomas Spence.
Seated front: William Tait, James Craigie.

41 Balfour Hospital, Main Street, Kirkwall, *c.*1900.

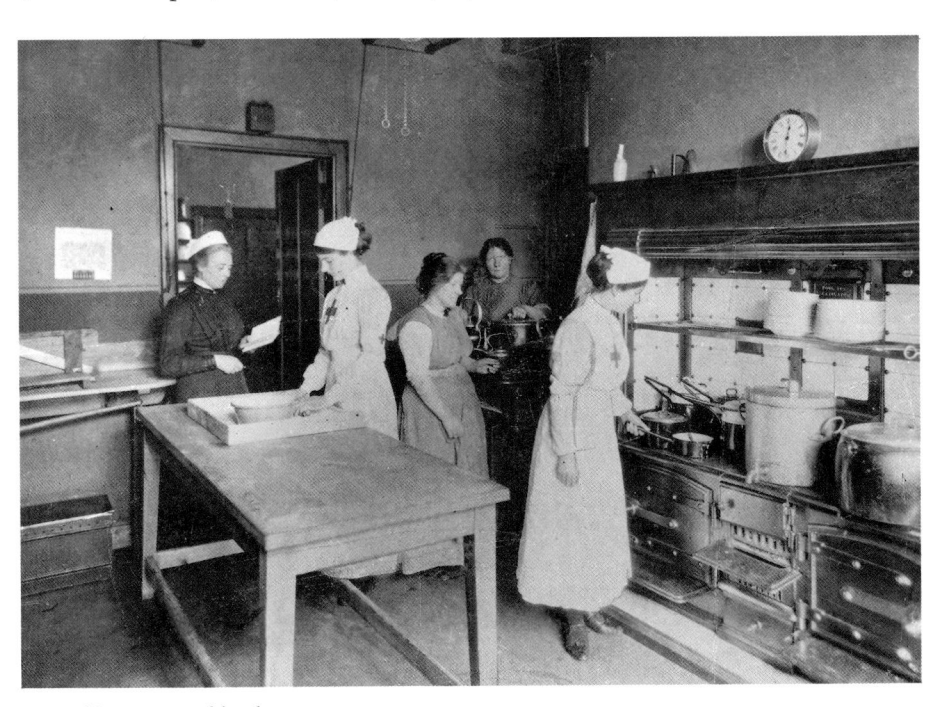

42 Balfour Hospital kitchen, *c.*1900

Riddles

HOITY-TOITY

    Hitty-titty within the dyke,
    Hitty-titty withoot the dyke—
    If ye touch Hitty-titty,
    Hitty-titty'll bite you . . .   . . . A THISTLE

FOWER AND TWENTY WHITE BOYS

    Fower and twenty white boys
    Playan wi' a ba',
    By cam' a red wife
    An' tuik the ba' awa' . . .   . . . A BITE OF BREAD

'White boys' are the teeth, and 'red wife' the tongue.

BODIED LIKE A BOGIE

    Heided like a mill pick,[1]
    Buited[2] like a sheul,[3]
    Bodied like a bogie,[4]
    An' yet hid's no feul[5] . . .   . . . A GOOSE

TEENK TANK

    Teenk, tank, under a bank,
    Ten apae fower[6] . . .   . . . MILKING A COW

AS WHITE AS MILK

    As white as milk,
    As fine as silk,
    Wi' feet as black
    As a coal peat stack . . .   . . . A SWAN

---

1. A tool used for dressing mill stones.
2. Booted.
3. Shovel.
4. Ghost.
5. Fool.
6. Ten (fingers) over four (teats).

HE'LL DEE O' CAULD WATTER

  Muckle Willie, peerie[1] Willie
   sittan in a staa,[2]
  Gi'e him little, gi'e him muckle,
   he'll tak' hid a',
  Bit gi'e him a drink o' cauld watter
   an' he'll dee awa' ...   ... A FIRE

GREY GRUNKIES

  Twa grey grunkies[3]
  Lyan in a sty,
  The more they get
  The more they cry ...   ... QUERN STONES

LANG LEGS

  Lang legs, creuked thighs,
  Peedie[4] heid an' no eyes.
  or
  Lang legs, wi'oot knees,
  Roond feet like bawbees ...   ... A PAIR OF TONGS

'THAT' IN ORKNEY WORDS

  Babbie o' Bomisty
  Bore a bairn tae the back o' the Bu;
  The boys o' the Bu made a baste[5] o' the bairn—
  Noo, hoo many B's are in THAT?[6]

    ★   ★   ★

---

1. Small.
2. Stall.
3. Grunters, i.e. pigs.
4. Small.
5. Beast or animal.
6. John Firth, author of *Reminiscences of an Orkney Parish*, published in 1920, records additional tongue-twisters in his lecture pamphlet:

  The swan swam ower the loch—   The rattan louped ower the rape,*
  Weel swam swan;   Loup, rattan, loup.
  The swan swam back again—   The rattan louped back again,
  Better swam swan.   A weel louped rattan.
                 (*The rat leaped over the rope)
    The red cock sat on the red kail stock;
    While the red cock cocked, the red stock rocked.

THE GAMES WE PLAYED

Editor's note

John Firth, 1838-1922, the remarkable Finstown ethnologist who was a repository of much lore of nineteenth-century rural Orkney, gave a Lecture on 25 December 1918 to Firth United Free Church Guild, entitled *Old Orkney Words, Riddles and Proverbs*. The following additional riddles are contained in the Lecture pamphlet:

    Woo' withoot, an' woo' within,
    Not a single bit o' skin;
    Lift thee leg an' shove it in ...   ... A STOCKING

    Hid rins on the land,
    Hid swims on the sea,
    Fire wonna burn it,
    What can it be? ...   ... MIST

Heuketie, crueketie, whar rins thoo? ...   ... THE BURN

Clipped tail every year, whit wants thoo? ...   ... THE MEADOW

    A mooth like a mill-door,
    An' lugs[1] like a cat;
    Guess thoo a' the day,
    Thoo'll no guess that ...   ... A LUGGED SHEU[2]

    As I cam' ower the hill o' heather,
    There I met a man o' leather;
    Throwe a rock, throwe a reel,
    Throwe an auld spinning-wheel,
    Throwe a sheep's shank-bone,
    Sic a man was never known ...   ... A WOOD-WORM

Whit is it that rins best when its leg is broken? ...
     ... A HEATHER COWE[3]

The head o' the living in the mooth o' the dead,
If thoo guesses this, thoo'll get butter wi' thee bread ...
     ... A MAN WITH HIS HEAD IN A POT

What are they that tear the faces o' ane anither a' day,
an' lie in bosoms a' night? ...   ... A PAIR OF WOOL CARDS

1. Ears.
2. A shoe with raised or extended sides.
3. A stalk of heather.

> There is a thing was one month old
> When Adam was no more;
> And still this thing was one month old
> When Adam was four score... ...THE MOON

* * *

OUTDOOR GAMES

THE COBBLER'S DANCE

The 'cobbler' sits on his haunches, keeping as low as possible, and crossing his arms. He then attempts to walk quickly, without rising, shooting out his legs smartly in front of him. There is an even more difficult variation in which the legs are directed outwards at an angle from the body. The fun consists in keeping one's balance while carrying on a steady forward 'walk'.

FITTY-GO-MASH

An exercise used to gain warmth in cold weather. A couple stand up facing each other. With a little hop they bring their right feet together. They continue with their left feet, matching each other's movements, and hopping from one foot to the other.

SEESAWING

The Orkney name for a seesaw, or more precisely the sport of seesawing, was *Happy Killy Donkey*.

PICKO

Picko[1] was the Orkney name for *Tig*. This was often played on a cold day as the children came home from school. The child who 'had it on' had to catch one of the other players by touching him and getting clear without being touched in return. Then the next child (the one who was touched) 'had it on', and had to catch someone else to 'get it off'.

LEE-LO-LAY

Lee-lo-Lay[2] was played by a mixed band of boys and girls. Equal numbers stood at either side of the street. The child who 'had it on' stood between them in the middle of the street. When he called 'Lee-lo-Lay' the players rushed across to exchange sides. As they did so, the child in the middle tried to 'catch' as many as possible by touching them before they reached the safety of the

---

1. Known in North Ronaldsay as 'Fidro'.
2. Known in Rousay as 'Come-a-lee-a-Laulie', and in Birsay as 'King-come-a-lee-lo-lee'.

Finstown Old Church, 1949

Stanley Cursiter, RSA, RSW, 1887–1976

opposite kerb. All those touched became catchers. It usually happened that when the catchers became numerous and the runners few, the latter were unwilling to run immediately they heard the call. When this occurred, the catchers could call 'Lee-lo-Lay, Bound' a summons the runners had to obey even if their chances of escaping the catchers were almost non-existent.

GAMES WITH MARBLES

Knock-Out Marbles (I think this game was also called *Roopie*). The players each laid down one marble to form a group. With a larger marble each tried to knock out of the group as many marbles as possible. The winner kept the marbles he knocked out, while the owners of these laid down another marble to keep the game going.

Bowley. Three holes were made in the ground, and from a determined distance the players tried to roll a marble into each successive hole without a miss. The victor was sometimes known as 'Keelie'.

Check Stones. The player had four 'checks', usually silver buckies[1] or, if these could not be had, four suitable small stones. Squatting on the pavement, he held the four buckies in one hand and threw up a marble. This was allowed to 'stot', or bounce, once only on the ground before being caught. On the first throw, the buckies had to be scattered in the interval before the marble was caught. During the next four throws of the marble one buckie was caught up each time. When all had been retrieved they were scattered again, and were now lifted two at a time in the interval during which the marble fell, bounced, and was caught. After the second scattering, they were retrieved in two throws—three during the first and one during the second. After the final scattering, all four buckies had to be caught up during a single throw of the marble.

Sometimes the game was varied and made more difficult by spreading out the fingers of the left hand and resting their tips on the pavement. When the buckies were being retrieved, they were placed successively into the spaces between the fingers. This was called 'putting the horses into their stables'.

Compare with this last game the Shell Games described in Robert Rendall's *Orkney Shore*, pp. 17-20.

BALL ON THE SHED

The ball was thrown on to the sloping roof of a low house or shed. During the time that it took to return, the hands were clapped together once; after which the ball was batted back by the hand. Before it returned next time, two claps (one in front and one behind the back) had to be made. Each time an extra clap had to be got in before batting back the ball. When the first player

---

1. Whelks.

failed to get in the full number of claps before it was necessary to bat back the ball, the next child took over. Often several players used the same roof, keeping an adequate distance between them.

Skipping

Girls could vary the recreation of skipping more resourcefully than is sometimes realised. There was regular slow skipping, with the skipper sometimes counting as many as 200 skips over the rope before she became too tired to continue. Then there was the fast variety, called a 'Nicky-Tober'. In this the girl waved the rope as fast as she possibly could, trying breathlessly to see how many skips she could do before she tripped herself up.

Another variation was to run a race while skipping, measuring the distance run before fouling the rope. With a long rope, two children could act as 'wavers', while the rest ran in and began to jump in time to the rope. If one got caught by the rope she changed places with a 'waver'.

A progressive skipping game for several children was played in this way. Each girl in turn ran into the circle of waving rope, skipped over it once and ran out. The second time each did two skips, the third time three skips, and so on, gradually increasing the number of skips until all the players had been caught by the rope.

Kites

Kite-flying used to be popular in Orkney, particularly in Kirkwall. I found a reference to kite-flying at Easthill in October 1897. There were fifty children with kites, and a serious committee of grown-ups to judge their performances and award prizes. The most popular kite was the diamond-shaped variety, because it was the easiest to make. Two pieces of wood, in the shape of a cross, had a piece of stout string stretched around their ends to form a 'diamond'. To the string was glued the paper which covered the kite. A 'tail' of string had twists of folded paper knotted into it every foot or so. 'Guides' or 'steadiers' of paper were tied to the ends of the cross-piece.

A 'message' was sometimes sent up to a high-flying kite. It consisted of a circle of thin card with a penny-sized hole cut in the centre. When this was threaded on to the string, and thrown vigorously, it whirled up quickly towards the kite.

Sooker

A sooker consisted of a small circle of soft, well-soaked leather, to the centre of which a length of string was attached. The sooker was trodden down hard on a flat, wet stone. If the stone was not too large, the suction was sufficient to allow it to be lifted, otherwise the sooker would leave it with a 'pop' when pulled. A good sooker was much envied.

WOGGIE CATTIE MATTIE

This was a local name for the game of 'noughts and crosses'[1] which was sometimes played on the beach. Other Orkney names for the same game were *Trip-trap-truisky* and *Trip-trap-trullyo*. The person who began the game cried out:

>Trip-trap-truisky, here we go,
>Tae get three crosses in a row.

The winner's cry of triumph was:
>Trip-trap-truisky, the coo's creuked horn,
>A'm won the day, see thoo wins the morn.

Favourite games, universally familiar, were Blindy-Bockey (Blind-man's Buff), Diggie-Doo (Hide-and-Seek played around the stacks in the cornyard), Peevers (Hop-Scotch), Hares and Hounds,[2] Bat-and-Ba' (a variety of Rounders) and, of course, football....

FOOTBALL CUSTOMS

A crude form of football was celebrated by the men of every parish, from the youngest to the oldest, who spent most of New Year's Day on the Ba' Green. The men and women started the day by getting weighed. Then the men went on with their rough and tumble football, refreshing themselves now and then with ale and sooan scones brought to the field by girls.

Football could get mixed up with weddings. John Miller of Monthooly in Evie testified in 1852: 'There was a custom when an Evie man was married to a Birsay woman that the Bridegroom paid for or gave a foot Ball to the School of Birsay and when my father who was an Evie man was married in the Church of Birsay the foot Ball was played for from the Church to the House of the wedding in Birsay'. William Halcro of Gairngreena remembered that 'if the foot Ball was not given or paid for the people of the Bride's parish took off the Bride's shoe.' But the custom was older and more deeply-rooted than even these references would suggest, for the Cathedral Session resolved on 7 December 1684 'that ther is non in toun and paroch that marries but shall pay a foot ball to the scholers of the grammour school.'

Yet Kirkwall Town Council issued an edict against football playing through the streets and liberties in the winter of 1825, and it was Kirkwall that was always having misgivings about the propriety of the New Year's Day Ba'....

1. See also 'Games of a thousand years, p.145.
2. The hare sets out and after a suitable interval is pursued by the hounds. In some parts of the country the hare sometimes laid a trail of paper to indicate the direction of his run and then the sport was known as 'The Paper Chase'.

The Ba'

Kirkwall has had many Ba' games; but the Boys' Ba's, and the Christmas Day Ba' are really excrescences which have deprived the New Year's Day Ba' of some of its unique interest. The ball itself, specially made for the occasion, is stuffed very tightly with the fragmented cork used for packing grapes. It has narrow panels of dark brown and light brown leather. The word 'Ba'' applies both to the ball and to the game in general. It is convenient to use a capital letter only when referring to the game.

A prominent Kirkwallian is chosen to throw the ba' into the assembled crowd from the steps of the Mercat Cross at one o'clock on New Year's Day. In the crowd are two or three score of determined men, representing the two sides: the Up-the-Gates who are all those born to the south of the Cross or who first entered Kirkwall from that side, and the Down-the-Gates, who represent in the same way that part of the town which lies to the north, the dividing line being the lane which runs from the front of the Cathedral to Junction Road.[1] It is the aim of each side to take the ba' to the extreme limit of its own territory. For the 'Uppies' this limit or goal is the corner where Main Street meets Junction Road; for the 'Doonies' it is the harbour, where there is the additional hazard of retrieving the ba' from the waters of the Basin.

Nowadays the game is played like this: someone among the players grabs the ba' and hugs it in his arms. The others huddle around him, sorting themselves out so that they are pushing in the direction in which they wish the ba' to go. Each side is concerned with pushing the opposing players, and with them the ba', backwards; or, at the least, in halting the progress of the game until it has regained its energies. To halt the game's progress requires that the whole huddle of players jams itself tightly against a wall. For most of the three or four hours which the game may last (although it has sometimes ended in ten or fifteen minutes when a fleet-footed person made a break-away with the ba') the players seem to be glued to this wall or that. The drama consists in the sudden spurts forward, which may take the players five yards on or fifty, or which may in the end become a triumphant progress.

A halt may easily take place before a door or a shop window, so it is essential that these should be heavily barricaded. Kirkwall on New Year's Day looks like a beleaguered city. To complete the picture, the contestants soon begin to wear the marks of battle, in the form of bruises, scratches and torn clothes. There are no rules; but the tradition that pushing is the only offensive action allowable is strictly maintained. Serious accidents are few,

---

1. With all births now taking place in the Balfour Hospital situated in Up-the-Gate territory, the expected custom is for players to follow the persuasion of their family and in particular the allegiance of their father.

but people are said to have died[1] in the scrum and broken limbs are not unknown. At the end, the ba' is awarded to a player by popular acclaim. He is usually someone who has played in the Ba' for several years, and who has shown outstanding prowess. The winner is seldom agreed on without a preliminary, and sometimes lengthy and acrimonious, argument.

Some local historians speculate that the Ba' had its origin in the rivalry between the Bishop's men from The Laverock, or upper part of the town, and the Earl's men from The Burgh, or lower part. Others suggest that wandering vikings may have observed rites in the Mediterranean which involved a struggle for a human head, and that they brought back to Kirkwall their reminiscences of that agreeable diversion. The truth is that there is a lack of documentary or traditional evidence, which frustrates serious inquiry. I am not aware that there is any written mention of the game until well through the nineteenth century.[2]

Sometime in the early eighteen-forties,[3] the resident sheriff issued an edict abolishing the Ba'. The ba' was then, according to the local historian Benjamin Hossack, 'kicked or dribbled, but never held'.[4] If this is true, as it almost certainly is, it raises the question of whether the Ba' is much more than an adaptation of the old-fashioned street football, without antecedent mystery. But to get back to the sheriff—even in his time this New Year's Day game seems to have been a venerable institution, for his edict was flouted by the whole townspeople, including the Earldom Chamberlain and the Town Clerk.

In 1863, *The Orkney Herald*, the voice of 'respectable' Kirkwall, decided that the Ba' was an irrational amusement; the following year the game was described as 'unsightly'; in subsequent years it was designated 'barbarous', and finally—strongest adjective of all—'out-of-date'. Local notabilities, moved by journalistic condemnation of 'The Foot Ball Fight', dangled attractive carrots before the noses of the 'Uppies' and 'Doonies'. Mr Traill

1. There is no record of anyone dying in the scrum but Captain William Cooper of the smack 'Caleb', who had been playing for the Down-the-Gates on New Year's Day 1903 and was having a rest outside the scrum, collapsed and died. The game was allowed to continue.
2. The first written account of the Ba' in roughly its present form is contained in a letter by Thomas Campbell, Kirkwall, to David Scott, a Sanday man, then living at Mungoswells near Haddington, and is dated February 1845. On New Year's Day 1845 the Down-the-Gates had an unexpected win, prior to which they had suffered a long run of disappointment: 'I am hapy to inform you that the bal went down the Street on new years day She was not on the broad Street above ten minuts when She was played up the Straind and went in to the Street at Mr Robertsons and went then down to the harbour and was put up to the top of the Brendo and you may consider the Steat of the up Streets as theay thought She would never go down again bu the down Street players Stood very trusty and determined'.
3. 1845.
4. *Kirkwall in the Orkneys*, 1900, p.465.

offered the combatants the use of a field, and unlimited refreshments, if they would get off the streets. The magistrates tried to seduce them with elaborate Christmas games, complete with 'elegant pavilion and grandstand'. It was pointed out that the highly civilised people of Shapinsay now substituted 'Tossing the Caber, Throwing the Hammer, and Leaping and Running', for the New Year's Day football, and that Stromness engaged in target shooting. Kirkwall was obdurate: the game went on—as it has done to this day, apart from war-time interruptions.

The Ba' has a book to itself: *Uppies and Doonies* by John D. M. Robertson. This book tells in the most fascinating way, and with a wealth of patiently accumulated detail, all that is known of the game.

GENTLEMANLY SPORTS

If football was the sport of the common people, what about their betters?

The lairds' sons and professional gentlemen did prefer more sophisticated amusements. In intervals of drinking ale and smuggled brandy in the winter they put on plays; once a crowd of them performed Addison's *Cato* in the ruinous Noltland Castle in Westray. In the seventeenth century they played golf at Kirkwall. They celebrated St Magnus Day—16 April—by taking a vacation to the island of Sanday and playing golf on the plain of Fidge. Each year the whole crowd was billeted in one of the four mansion houses on the island. Horse-racing was sometimes engaged in around Kirkwall, usually on the side of Wideford hill, but seldom with much zest, or for very long periods. Cock-fighting was not frowned on: in 1787 Orkney game cocks were said to be 'not inferior to those of England in point of spirit and courage'. 'Our bull-dogs,' the writer boasted, 'are equally fierce.'[1]

Then there was archery—we have place-names like Buttquoy to prove it—and bowling, fishing and fowling. The winters must have been much colder, for curling was frequent. One of our bishops got into some trouble because he 'was a great curler upon the Lord's Day.' Even at the end of the nineteenth century there was skating in winter.

Three cricket[2] clubs were founded in Kirkwall in 1864 and the game was played also in Stromness and South Ronaldsay. It continued intermittently in Orkney until the Second World War.

Before being ousted by soccer, rugby had a short life during the latter part of the nineteenth century, games being played at Wick (1876), in Kirkwall against Thurso (1878) and Lerwick (1879). On Christmas Day 1875, as an alternative to the Ba', a game of rugby was held in a field at Soulisquoy.

---

1. *Considerations of the Fisheries in the Scotch Islands*, James Fea, 1787, pp.20, 21.
2. See article 'A cricket century', p.184.

This the Doonies won by a goal to their opponents' try. It is good to witness the revival of rugby in recent winters, for soccer in Orkney is a summer game.

WALKING

Walking was one of the chief amusements of young men, in days before cars were common. It was the boast of the very fit and energetic that they had walked round the Orkney Mainland. I knew one old man who had walked fifty miles each weekend, in going to see his sweetheart and in returning home. Dr John Rae, a splendidly developed Orcadian, when in North West Canada once covered on snowshoes one hundred miles in twenty-four hours.

Kirkwall boys used to walk on summer afternoons to the top of Keelilang Hill in Orphir—five miles each way as the crow flies, but more difficult going than would at first appear. There was a rhyme which cautioned them:

    Whin thoo gangs tae Keelilang,
    Tak' a binnack[1] in thee han';
    Thoo may tak' ane, thoo may tak' twa,
    Keelilang'll tak' them a'.

1. Bannock.

3

A cricket century

It is a hundred years this week since Orkney first heard the sound of leather striking wood, to an accompaniment of 'Well played, Sir', for our earliest cricket club, the St Magnus, which had just been formed, played its opening game at Grainbank, near Kirkwall, during the first week of May 1864.

St Magnus Cricket Club started life with thirty-seven members, and a complete set of balls, bats and wickets— the gift of the Member of Parliament, Frederick Dundas. It was more or less a gentleman's club. Before the end of the summer two other clubs, a little more representative perhaps of the young men of Kirkwall, had been formed. This meant that in a mere two months a hundred men were learning to play cricket.

Perhaps to assert its seniority, St Magnus Cricket Club issued a challenge and arranged an away match only four months after its inception. This was unwise; and it was more unwise still to take on Thurso's John o' Groat Cricket Club, which had several years' experience.

The two teams met on 10 August in a park beyond the Thurso River. One team was to be distinguished by light blue caps, the other by dark blue. A big crowd gathered; the scorers sat down at a table on the edge of the field; and the Thurso men, who had won the toss, went into bat. Before they were dismissed they had scored 95. Then St Magnus took over the batting. The Orcadians were bowled out with indecent speed, and with a total score of 12.

The return match took place near Kirkwall in July 1865. St Magnus had improved a little by then, but not enough. When the match ended, Kirkwall had scored 42 runs and Thurso 85.

It was left to the most juvenile of the Orkney clubs, the St Ola Cricket Club, to retrieve the good name of Orkney two years later, when it met Thurso St Peter's Cricket Club, and defeated the Caithnessians by a single run.

That was the beginning of Orkney cricket's very chequered story. Although there was much enthusiasm, which became evident again and again, the weather was continually dampening it down. Clubs came and went. The St Magnus was the most tenacious: in May 1886 it divided itself into Up-the-Gates and Down-the-Gates.[1] After putting together 80 runs, the Uppies bowled out their opponents for 47. The club survived its early rivals, and also Kirkwall Trades Cricket Club and the Norseman Cricket Club, but I cannot find any mention of it after the turn of the century.

Twentieth-century cricket was mainly in the hands of a new club—Kirkwall Cricket and Athletic Club—which with some degree of success played Naval teams during the First World War, and then quietly expired. It was brought back to life in June 1926. That was Orkney cricket's Indian summer, with five teams (St Magnus, St Olaf, St Clair, St Rognvald and St Ninian) in the field. That month there was another game between Up-the-Gates and Down-the-Gates, which this time the Doonies won by 32 runs.

From then until 1939 the club remained in being, playing when it could in the Bignold Park, but struggling unequally against the attractions of golf and football, which were somewhat less vulnerable to the Orkney weather. Orkney cricket, alas, did not survive the Second World War.[2]

---

1. See 'The games we played', pp.180-182.
2. Inter-County cricket, Orkney v Shetland, commenced in Kirkwall on Saturday, 1 June 1985.

4

Entertainment galore

With the nights getting dark and long, numbers of the people I know are looking about for means of entertainment, and I have actually heard some of them say, 'Goodness only knows what people did before these days to amuse themselves. It must have been pathetic.'

Well, actually, it was not pathetic in the least. It seems to me that there is less purely communal entertainment today than there has been for generations. To prove my point, let me take you back to the Kirkwall of nearly a century and a half ago to see what was happening in the entertainment world. The year I have in mind is 1829-30.

The season started in September. Right through the winter there were assemblies in the great hall of the Tolbooth.[1] These assemblies consisted of dances for the young people and card playing for the old. The girls who attended the dances, although they may have been fond of their escorts, sons of merchants and professional men, were always waiting for a greater thrill, for sometimes the sons of those landlords who had town houses—dashing young men in scarlet vests and top boots—would look in condescendingly for half an hour and whirl the girls around, intoxicating them with their fine manners and grand talk.

For the music lovers there were song recitals; some of them in the Grammar School where the resident men, Mr Moir and Mr Hunter, were accompanied by the famous Mr Boyle of London, 'Professor of the Science of Singing and the Theory of Music'. They would sing up to twenty songs, some of them forgotten, but a number well known even today. No recital seems to have been possible without, 'Draw the Sword, Scotland' and 'The Death of Nelson'.

On a very slightly lower social level were the Vocal Concerts of Miss

---

1. It stood on the edge of the Kirk Green, fronting Broad Street and Palace Road. New municipal buildings including a spacious Sheriff Court were erected in 1877 at The Watergate. For some years the Tolbooth, which had stood for over one hundred and fifty years, continued to be used for Burgh Courts and Town Council meetings. It was demolished in 1890.

Gunn (billed as a professional pupil of the celebrated Mr Boyle) which took place in the Assembly Room. Miss Gunn's clear contralto voice alternated with Mr Moir's assured and pleasant tenor and her mother's shattering soprano. Miss Gunn was a singing teacher, by no means the only one in Kirkwall, and her terms were most modest—10/6d a month, with a lesson a day. That, if my arithmetic is right, is 4d a lesson. On the other hand, admission to the recitals was fairly high at 2/6d per person.

A Mr McDonald, who was in Kirkwall at the time, gave far better value. Lectures were the rage, and for a shilling you could hear him speak on ... and I'm afraid I must give you the title in full: 'AN ATTEMPT TO RECONCILE THE MOSAIC ACCOUNT OF THE CREATION, AS STATED IN THE FIRST CHAPTER OF GENESIS, WITH THE PRESENT IMPROVED STATE OF PHILOSOPHY: AND A CURSORY AND COMPREHENSIVE VIEW OF THE ORIGIN AND DISTRIBUTION OF THE NERVOUS SYSTEM, FROM THE LOWEST ANIMALS IN THE SCALE OF CREATION TO MAN.' Phew! ... and all for a shilling. Mr McDonald wisely avoided too great a rush of enthusiasts: 'To prevent the room from being inconveniently crowded, a certain number of tickets only will be issued.' He was versatile. If you wished he would give PRIVATE DEMONSTRATION IN CHEMISTRY, with the pupils undertaking the experiments. In case the elements and gases were naughty, he very properly segregated the sexes. 'LADIES,' he advertised, 'may have an hour appropriated to themselves.'

But this is only building up to the big event of the spring of 1830: the visit of Mr Mullender[1] and his Theatrical Company. A whole month of them, change of play twice a week, PIT 2/-, GALLERY 1/-. And what plays! WALLACE, REGENT OF SCOTLAND; MACBETH, KING OF SCOTLAND; PATRICK, EARL OF ORKNEY (written specially for the local audience); HEART OF MIDLOTHIAN; GIRNIGOE CASTLE ('performed for the first time at Wick to a fashionable and overflowing audience'); ROMEO AND JULIET. And because these plays were not long enough they were followed by farces, ballets, operas, recitals, and so on. What spectacles they must have been, with broadsword combats, the burning of a Highland clan, who may be seen 'enveloped in flames of REAL FIRE'. As for glamour, think of Miss E. Mullender as Lord Ramsay and Miss M. Mullender as Lord de Clifford, coyly attired in gentlemen's clothing.... What did people do before these days to amuse themselves? What didn't they do?

Entertainers of all kinds found their way to Orkney, and not always at the time of the Lammas Market, when they were most in evidence. Boxers and German acrobats were common. Richard Reidman, a quack doctor, who visited Kirkwall in January 1887, attracted patients by putting up a stage near the cathedral on which two negroes performed their tribal dances. Reidman also erected a tight-rope high over the end of Broad Street, where for a couple

---

1. Possibly Mulliner.

of months one of the negroes would walk every now and then 'seven stories high, with his pumps on'. Reidman advertised: 'The Nobility and Gentry shall be kindly entertained with a variety of divertissements, and those that are really poor shall be entertained for God's sake.'

5

An Orkney concert in the 1920s

Just recently, Andrew Johnston (formerly of Vetquoy), whom I have known for as long as I can remember, fished out of his wallet a single pink sheet of paper fifty-one years old. This turned out to be the programme of a 'Grand Concert' held in the Drill Hall, Evie on 31 March 1922. A simple thing, you might say, but it brought back a vanished world.

First of all, it was a salutary reminder that the Orkney of half-a-century ago was not unaware of what was happening in other parts of the globe. Evie had produced its 'Grand Concert', for which it had practised a good part of that winter, in aid of the Russian Famine Relief Fund. It would be fine if present-day Russians could know of the simple goodwill behind that gesture, and behind a host of similar efforts all over Britain.

It is easy to reconstruct that evening of half-a-century ago. The externals remain unchanged in the mind's eye: the stage hastily improvised, with curtains that stuck at least twice at awkward moments; the gleaming brass oil lamps, with the one nearest to the door blackening its glass chimney as it flickered with the draught; the seats with backs to them occupying the front part of the hall and holding a dozen comfortable and consequential families; the rows of planks supported on egg-boxes providing seating for the generality, including plenty of boisterous but good-natured young men.

Outside the hall there would be a couple of gigs, and a line of bicycles leaning against the side of the ditch, while beyond them would stand a gaunt-looking motor-cycle with a gear-lever fastened to its long angular tank.

Musical instruments were few, merely a piano and two fiddles. Most of the programme was supplied by unsophisticated human voices, but people were still happy to listen to songs and recitations. The first solo came from the minister, whose pleasant, flexible voice must have been heard at its best in 'Lament for Maclean of Ardgour'.

If you imagined that the Evie people in 1922 merely came to listen to romantic and comic songs, how wrong you would be. That audience enjoyed Shakespeare's 'I know a bank whereon the wild thyme blows' just as much as 'Blue Bird' or 'Finnegan's Ball'. But how many of the songs are known today?

Let me list a few: 'The Romany Lass', 'Mrs Jean Macfarlane', 'Locket and the hair', 'She's the lass for me', 'Dream Boat'.

We were extremely correct, I seem to remember, when it came to formal occasions. We might sit with perfect contentment on our rough planks; throughout the week we might call each other Jessie and Maggie or Peter, Andrew and Bob; but we expected the printed programme to designate us correctly as Mr, Miss or Master. Yet how gloriously relaxed everyone was. When it came to 'Mr Stevenson's' song or recitation, everyone cheered and shouted, 'Come on, Bob!'; and Bob, rising from a seat near the back of the building, would make his way, cap in hand, to the platform, which he mounted from the front with a comedian's agility.

The audience, buoyed up on a great wave of liking and laughter, would hardly let him leave the stage—encore followed encore. We had heard his repertoire unnumbered times . . . 'The Mountains of Mourne', 'The Old Rustic Bridge', 'The Terrible, Terrible Cake', 'The Lady Sold by Auction', 'Poor Old Joe' . . . but Bob's individual gifts as a performer made each piece seem new and delightful. His range included everything from romantic pathos to boisterous fun. In comic songs his voice made the hall resound, while the audience laughed themselves to tears over his antics. Only Andrew himself had the same power over the audience, but as a younger man he was tactful enough not to steal the thunder from Bob.

We were formal again when it came to dress. It was nice to see the Misses B—— and Miss L—— in evening gowns and Mr M—— with a black bow tie.

At that period, what we called a 'sketch' (in essence a little play or conversation piece) was extremely popular. The two sketches in the 'Grand Concert' were 'Lodgings for Single Ladies' and 'Minding the Babies'. If their titles were suggestive, their dialogue was innocuous; if they implied that single ladies might possibly be flirtatious or that babies occasionally needed a change of diapers, that, no doubt, was the extreme limit of their daring. Would anyone laugh at them today?

There were twenty-four items in the 'Grand Concert', which was divided into two parts. I suppose it was still in progress around eleven-thirty. Probably the minister and Master G—— Y—— left during the interval; the former, an ascetic man, to collect some material for the sermon which would have to be written the following day; the latter to be tucked into bed at a time suitable for a ten-year-old who had just recited with marked success 'He's no' born yet!'

6

Orkney drinking

I notice that a local organisation has sponsored a lecture on home-brewing. This appears to have become the hobby of a great number of thirsty Orcadians. Many of the shops I patronise stock packs of ingredients for brewing; and in certain homes I stumble over buckets of pale, uninspiring liquid that pretends, somewhat unsuccessfully, to be Orkney ale.

With a packet of do-it-yourself materials, some extract of malt, and a little sugar, you can hardly expect to produce the full-bodied liquor that used to be the result of weeks of work (from the beginning of the malt-making to the bottling of the ale);[1] but if people would stick to their weak brews, instead of consuming excessive amounts of spirits, Orkney would be a happier and more salutary place than it threatens to become.

It seems to me that when people had to decide how much of their hard-won crop of bere they could spare for brewing; when they only had ale at peat-cutting time and harvest, or for weddings and such festivals as Yule; and when time and skill were spent on preparing an acceptable brew, Orkney ale was part of the pattern of local life in a way that it most decidedly is not today. Easy money makes for easy drinking, and easy drinking becomes a pernicious fashion that only those with more important things to devote their lives to can resist.

A controversial writer, now dead, declared that the further north you travelled in Scotland the greater was the amount of liquor that you saw consumed, and the less the joy the consumer seemed to get from it. It is difficult for an Orcadian to accept such a criticism; and he is amazed when told that centuries ago we were regarded as being among the hardest drinkers to be found anywhere.

In Hollinshead's *Chronicles*, which were printed in London in 1570 (and of which Shakespeare made such notable use), the section devoted to Orkney asserts:

> There is great abundance of barley whereof they make the strongest ale that is to be found in Albion, and thereto knowne, that they

---

1. See also description of Ale in 'An ABC of Orkney food', p.103.

are the greatest drinkers of anie men in the world; yet was there never drunken or man disguised with drinke seene there, neither anie foole, or person otherwise bereft of his wits through frensie or madnes.

Richard James, Master of Arts at Oxford,[1] observed in 1616 of the gentlemen of Orkney: 'All in generally given excessively to drinke in which they quarrell and cut and stab with their durkes and swoardes and pots.'[2]

The nature of the climate requires strong liquor—pleaded the minister of St Magnus Cathedral, the Rev. James Wallace, in 1693.[3] This seemed to remain so at the beginning of the nineteenth century, when in one year (1803) there were legal imports of 1,584 gallons rum, 127 gallons brandy, 1,108 gallons gin, and 3,533 gallons British Spirit (presumably whisky). The amounts of smuggled spirits would probably have exceeded these figures.

In an old book entitled *The Ancient and Present State of Orkney*, published in 1788, the writer, George Eunson, declared:

> ... several of the inhabitants of Orkney, having contracted a pernicious taste for drinking, consume a vast quantity of spirits; and there are, so many *public-houses*, where such liquor is to be had, that it is as free to them as the water; the price being no more than three halfpence each *gill*. Some of the most indolent people, and those that are particularly subject to excessive drinking, spend what they gain one day, in hopes that the other will provide for itself; and being thereby put in the situation of fools or madmen; and their bodies become either burnt up, or emaciated, according to the constitution of the persons so addicted.

Later in the nineteenth century, a strong temperance movement took root in Orkney. Eday, whose proprietor had made that island officially 'dry', the fact with a song (of which, I imagine, there can hardly be a celebrated parallel):

> Ye sons of Eday, stout and strong,
> Come join with me the joyful song,
> And swell the chorus loud and long—
> We have no public houses.
>
> No dram-shop stands upon our shore,
> The drunkard's voice is heard no more,
> Where all was grief and woe before—
> We have no public houses.

---

1. Bodleian Library, MS James 43**.
2. Steel helmets.
3. *A Description of the Isles of Orkney*, pp.83, 84.

43 D. M. Wright, Chemist, Albert Street, Kirkwall, c.1920

44 Cutting peats, South Ronaldsay, c.1900

45 Transporting peats, Longhope, c.1900

In 1872 the Good Templars came north—the first lodge being the Star of Pomona (Stromness).[1] The lodges had plenty of positive things to do, besides opposing the drink trade. The Kirkwall lodges formed a Choral Union during their early days. In 1876 the Excelsior Lodge recorded a notable declaration of principle:

> That the lodge believing in the universal brotherhood of man and deploring the differences that have so long existed between the negro and the white man hails with satisfaction every step taken in the direction of elevating this down-trodden race.

But I am far away from home-brewed ale, with which I began and whose origin is legendary. The Picts were supposed to be experts and to have the recipe of a marvellous beverage called heather ale. The story is that the Norsemen were desperately anxious to obtain the recipe, but were never able to wrest it from the conquered race. At last only two Picts who knew it, a man and his son, were left. They were to be tortured to make them reveal the ingredients. The old man said that he would never bring himself to give the secret away and bear the scorn of his son, but that if the boy was killed he would make it known. Without pity, the younger man was murdered, whereupon the father said proudly that at last the secret was safe. His son might have parted with the information under torture, but he himself would never do so.

Perhaps the secret of Pictish heather ale was lost, but heather was used until comparatively recently in certain Orkney recipes. The late Henrietta Groundwater told me that when she was a girl, she was sometimes sent out at four o'clock on a summer morning to gather the young green heads of heather for a brew.

There is another tale of Pictish ale, or rather of ale made from the wild oats once common in Orkney, and called 'Pight aits'. This was said to make a good brew by itself; but if mixed in the bere which was normally used, it had the amazing quality of preventing the drinker from ever getting drunk. If we could grow it today, would we use it?

---

1. Star of Pomona Lodge No.789 met weekly in the Town Hall, 52 Albert Street until 1904 when the Temperance Hall was built in Hellihole Road. It is difficult to imagine how powerful Good Templarism was at one time in the islands. Perhaps a list of some of the adult lodges at work around 1900 will give a rough idea: Hope of the West, No.1044, Birsay; St Lawrence, No.338, Burray; Star of the East, No.826, Deerness; Victoria, No.910, Finstown; Rose of St Mary's, No.87, Holm; Emblem of Love, No.89, Holm; St Magnus, No.787, Kirkwall; Excelsior, No.817, Kirkwall; Norseman's Home, No.964, Kirkwall; Ward Hill, No.1064, Orphir; Flower of St Andrew's, No.861; John Paul, No.862, Sanday; Maeshowe, No.1050, Stenness; Star of Stromness, No.883; Philanthropic, No.385, Westray; Noltland, No.594, Westray.

* * *

Editor's Note

The following two sets of verses, written by a carpenter named Bews, were found in a notebook kept by a William Leslie in 1893. They are held within the Stromness Museum. Bews, who worked at Stanger's boatyard, Ness, Stromness, was a Good Templar and a native of Kirkwall.

The lines are important as evidence of the emotional power which the Good Templars, working within the Temperance Movement, were able to generate. Along with Holm, Stromness voted to go 'dry' in November 1920 and despite polls in 1923 and 1926 licensed premises there were closed until November 1947. (JDMR)

1. Ye Stromness Templars stand
    And work together with your might
    To save your native land
    From Alcohol the nations curse
    For ever, set it free
    No more let Stromness Street resound
    With drunken revelry

2. Unfurl your banner to the breeze
    And march throughout the town
    The first you've got to do is put
    McPherson Brothers down
    Twill be a feather in your cap
    A thing of lasting joy
    When you have slain in fair good fight
    The whisky 'Man O' Hoy'

3. Close to the whisky 'Man O' Hoy'
    There is a drinking shop
    But put a noble effort forth
    Its whisky trade to stop
    All Christian people in the town
    Approvingly will hear
    The name of Clouston's will no more
    On Licensed lists appear

4. That's held by Sandy Flett
    We hope to see the premises
    For better purpose let
    And in a noble business way
    A better trade begin
    No more let any market green
    Behold his tent of sin

5. The gentry of the White Horse Inn
    Have held sway long enough
    And many a reeking hogshead sold
    Of the accursed stuff
    And in their house full many a seed
    Of evil has been sown
    We trust that Marwick's licensed house
    Will soon become unknown

6. Commercial and the Mason's Arms
    Of whisky sweep them clear
    That from their bars, may jolly tars
    Have nothing more to fear
    Instead of sickening whisky fumes
    And song and ribald jest
    May in those stately buildings reign
    Peace, Quietness, and Rest

7. Another drinkshop by the way
    You must entirely snub
    And that is Ernest Robertson
    The licensed grocer's pub
    For ever in the way of right
    Good Templars onward press
    Till not a public house remains
    Twixt Hamjavoe [sic] and Ness

Song of the Kirkwall Viking Templars

KIRKWALL PUBS

1. Kirkwall Templars sons of Vikings
   Some hard work before you lies
   To push the Temperance movement on
   Rise, every Templar, rise
   Go burnish well your armour
   As your fathers did of yore
   Work for the right with all your might
   To close the drinkshop doors

2. Mobilize the Temprance army
   Fully man the Temprance bark
   And with united forces go
   And shut the Highland Park
   Then sweeping on past Crantit
   Use your arms with tact and skill
   And do not rest, till you have stopped
   The Scapa Whisky Still

3. Our sailors long have felt the scourge
   Oft have their heads been sore
   But we shall help them all we can
   To close up Dunnet's door
   No more our worthy fishermen
   Will roll in dirt and smut
   And Harbour Street will happy be
   When Geddes' door is shut

4. Our foes are numerous and strong
   But gird ye for the fight
   No more let William Stratham's wine
   Make anybody 'tight'
   No more let the wives of Albert Street
   Their drunken sots deplore
   For we shall have the victory
   And close up Mitchell's door

5. More foes have we to conquer
   As we march up the street
   We hear the women wailing
   And we hear the bairnies greet
   We'll take the fallen by the hand
   As we have done before
   And make a bold determined stand
   And close John Tinch's door

6. Although the fighting has been hard
   We shall not give it o'er
   We'll put our forces in array
   And march unto the shore
   And with another victory
   Our song of triumph swell
   We'll for our friends and brethren's sake
   Shut Hewison's Hotel

7. The enemy still hold redoubts
   But they shall all go down
   And victory's triumphant shout
   Shall ring throughout the town
   Such glorious times in Kirkwall
   Were never seen before
   When might and right unite to close
   The Licensed Grocers door

LOCAL VETO POLL, 1947

TO THE ELECTORS OF THE BURGH OF STROMNESS

Ladies and Gentlemen,
As you are aware, a Poll, under the " Temperance (Scotland) Act, 1913," will be held in the Burgh of Stromness on **Tuesday, 25th November 1947.**

IMPORTANT CONSIDERATIONS

As the future prosperity of our town will, to a large extent, depend upon the way you exercise your Vote, we respectfully invite your careful consideration of the following questions :—

1. Apart from the artificial prosperity of the War Years, can it be **truthfully** said that Stromness has been a thriving town since it became " Dry " in 1921 ?

IS STROMNESS AS IMPORTANT A BUSINESS AND SHOPPING CENTRE AS IT WAS PRIOR TO MAY, 1921 ?

(a) We submit that it is not ! **The Farming Community** on whose patronage the Stromness shopkeepers so largely depended now do most of their shopping and other business elsewhere.

(b) **Shipping,** excluding regular call steamers, does not now use the Port for the replenishing of stores, etc., to anything like the extent it used to before 1921.

Before Stromness went " Dry," about **FIVE** trawlers came in for repairs each week ; now we have only about **TEN IN A YEAR,** and even when running for shelter they now avoid our harbour and make for the other Pentland Ports. When they frequented this Port, their stay often lasted several days, much to the advantage of all classes of shopkeepers.

NOT LEAST IMPORTANT, in this connection, **IS THE FACT THAT THE HARBOUR REVENUE HAS BEEN SERIOUSLY AFFECTED.**

(c) Owing to its beautiful situation and its nearness to most of the Mainland places of Archæological and other interest, Stromness was, prior to 1921, the centre of Orkney's Tourist Industry ; much to the benefit of the whole community.

2. In 1920, the No-Licence Party promoted Polls in 584 Burgh and Parish areas. Of these **508 Voted NO-CHANGE,** 35 Voted **LIMITATION,** and **411 Voted NO-LICENCE.** Of the Limitation and No-Licence areas **33 HAVE REALISED THE MISTAKE OF 1920 AND HAVE REPEALED THEIR FORMER RESOLUTION.** Notable among the 33 are your nearer Burghs—**KIRKWALL, WICK,** and **LERWICK** ; the last two, together with **ST MONANCE, FIFE,** voted **REPEAL** last December by large majorities.

THE ELECTORS OF STROMNESS SHOULD FOLLOW THE EXAMPLE OF THESE THIRTY-THREE BURGHS AND PARISHES AND

VOTE REPEAL

3. The alleged object of the 1913 Act is to "promote Temperance." Can any unbiased Elector believe that by driving people out of town in order to obtain their requirements, the cause of "Temperance" is promoted ? No ! **The reverse is the case ! Such restrictions are a fruitful cause of INTEMPERANCE !** True Temperance cannot be imposed from without ; it can, and will, be promoted by individual self-control and self-respect !

PROMISES AND PERFORMANCES

4. During the 1920 No-Licence Campaign throughout Scotland, the No-Licence Party were profuse with their promises to provide social and recreational centres in such Towns and Parishes as would become "Dry." **WHAT HAVE THEY DONE IN STROMNESS ON THESE LINES ? NOTHING ! ! !**

They predicted happiness and prosperity for all if the Town went "Dry." Apart from the War Years, **has Stromness been prosperous since 1921 ?** Is happiness being promoted by driving people, by the bus load, to Kirkwall and Isew here, if they desire to meet their friends ?

FELLOW ELECTORS — WE ASK YOU TO END THE FARCE CREATED BY THE PRESENT SITUATION by VOTING REPEAL on the 25th November, AND THUS RESTORE THE FAIR FAME OF STROMNESS !

IMPROVED AMENITIES

5. If a **REPEAL RESOLUTION** is carried in Stromness, the inhabitants and visitors can rest assure that such premises as will be licensed <u>shall be planned on modern lines and provided with comfortable sitting accommodation.</u> The Hotel and Public-house Bars of former generations are of the past !

CONCLUSION

6. Finally, if you are a Teetotaler, or one able to have a stock of <u>excisable liquors at home</u>, we would ask you, on the 25th November, to remember that, <u>if you vote CONTINUANCE you will imply that the men and women who stood between you and death during the years of 1939-1945 could be entrusted with the defence of your life and liberty, but are not to be trusted to make reasonable use of licensed premises.</u>

THE MAN OR WOMAN WHO WOULD, BY THEIR VOTE, SUGGEST THIS, IS NOT WORTHY OF THE SACRIFICES MADE BY THOSE WHO, UNDER PROVIDENCE, MADE IT POSSIBLE FOR US TO ACT AS FREE MEN AND WOMEN.

We appeal to the Electors of Stromness to ponder the foregoing facts and **RESTORE THE LIBERTIES OF THE INDIVIDUAL IN OUR TOWN.**

Yours faithfully,

STROMNESS REPEAL COMMITTEE.

73 Victoria Street,
   Stromness, Orkney.

YOUR POLLING PLACE IS AT THE TOWN HALL.

POLLING HOURS—Eight a.m. to Eight p.m.

HOW TO VOTE

PLACE YOUR X IN THE SPACE ON THE BALLOT PAPER OPPOSITE THE WORDS

"REPEAL RESOLUTION"

1	**Continuance Resolution** (Means that the position remains the same as if this poll had not taken place, i.e., the No-licence resolution continues in force)	
2	**Repeal Resolution** (Means that the licensing courts shall have the same powers and discretions as before the coming into force of the No-licence resolution now in force)	X

Put No Other Mark.

Indicate your Vote by making a X in the right-hand space opposite the Resolution for which you vote. You have one vote, and may vote for one Resolution only.

Write nothing on the Ballot Paper except your X.

VOTE
REPEAL

Published by the Anti-Prohibition Campaign Council, 46 Melville Street, Edinburgh.

Hugh Paton & Sons Ltd., Printers, 5 St James Square, Edinburgh.

MEMORIES

1 The last Chief of Clan Macnab   203
2 Portrait of a vagabond   205
3 Peace's Orkney Almanac   207
4 Trials of a probationer   209
5 Electioneering   211
6 A Stromness childhood   214
7 When Stromness had a newspaper   216
8 Some annals of an Orkney parish   218
9 I remember rural poverty in Orkney   228
10 The water meedoo   231
11 Stone-breakers   235
12 Orkney 'feeders'   237
13 Motoring numbers preserve memories   239
14 The Kirkwall-Stromness bus   241
15 An islandman's war   242

I

The last Chief of Clan Macnab

Orkney, with its Norse inheritance, has never had much to do with the Highlands, and though redoubtable clansmen have occasionally found their way to the islands even the kilt has been little in evidence: the Orkney gales may account for that. To my mind the most picturesque Highlander who ever found his way to Orkney was Archibald the last acknowledged Chieftain of Clan Macnab, who lived for several years in the White House of Breck in the parish of Rendall.

I found his picture the other day in a massive History of the Highlands; and a mighty figure he seems, tall and dignified in his highland dress. He brought all his dignity and authority of manner to Orkney, despite the fact that his great days as a despot were over.

Archibald Macnab, nephew of the Twelfth (or some say Sixteenth) Laird, succeeded to a scattered inheritance. He had to sell his property to satisfy his creditors, keeping only the old graveyard of the Macnabs on the islet of Innis Buie. There seemed no future in Scotland for the Macnabs. Over three hundred of them emigrated to Canada in 1817, and in 1821 the Chief himself with more of the clan sailed to that country. He was in Canada for thirty-two years. During that time he sought to rule his transplanted clan like a feudal lord, but democracy triumphed, and his claims were at last spurned by the scattered clansmen.

In his middle seventies, discredited and poor, he was glad to accept help from his wife whom he had left over thirty years earlier. What she offered was a small income and a lodging in the White House of Breck. And so it was that Archibald Macnab's connection with Orkney began.

At Breck he lived in gloomy state, discouraged by his failure to lord it over the people of Rendall, who cared little for his still dictatorial pretensions. His only intimate was a piper Angus MacInnes, who was almost as eccentric as his master.

Both these men existed in semi-poverty, despite their ability to come by whisky in large quantities. Each evening the piper, Angus, paraded round the dining-room playing highland airs, while The Macnab took his frugal meal.

So it went on for some years until The Macnab once more fell in love at the age of seventy-nine. The object of his fancy, a middle-aged Yorkshire woman, Elizabeth Marshall, also moved into the White House, and she bore him a daughter when he was in his eightieth year.

Although Rendall could stand the bagpipes and was tolerant of whisky, it frowned darkly on irregular love affairs. Its hostility was made so plain that The MacNab, his mistress and his piper felt it expedient to leave the parish. They went first to Paris and then to Lannion in Brittany, where the fiery chieftain died at the age of eighty-three.

Although a hundred years have passed there are still vague traditions in Rendall about the Last Chief of the Macnabs. Beaten by the world, and living in enforced seclusion in Orkney, he still had the dignity of the abbot who was the supposed founder of the Clan, and the fierceness of his forebears who fought against Robert the Bruce and who loved above all else 'a bonny fight'.

2

Portrait of a vagabond

Until the day before yesterday homeless vagrants were a part of the Orkney scene. But they were not the drab anonymous tramps, forever moving on, who flitted across the larger landscapes of the South. Our vagabonds had distinctive personalities. They were accepted as legitimate citizens, treated with the respect which should be shown to fellow human beings, and addressed by their Christian names. Not that they did not have popular nicknames, or eeknames,[1] as well!

Of them all, the best known—a man whose name is still completely familiar in the Orkney parishes after half a century—was William Laughton, otherwise known as Skatehorn. Thus it is possible for me to draw a portrait of a man whom I never saw, except in picture postcards (sold by the hundred earlier this century) in which he was photographed holding the handlebars of a penny-farthing, something I am sure he was never rich enough to own.

Skatehorn was born around 1840. His father and mother were pedlars, who had their home in Burgar's Bay, High Street, Kirkwall. How the boy got his nickname no one seems to know; but it implied a certain irresponsibility, a more or less amiable lunacy. Not that Skatehorn lacked ability. He served for some years in the Naval Coast Volunteers (a body long extinct); but the accomplishments he acquired were characteristic of him: they were boxing, fencing, dancing, and swimming. As a youngish man, he taught a number of Kirkwall boys to swim. An old lady in Harray, now dead, told me that it was a sheer joy to see Skatehorn dancing.

Quite early in life, he seems to have decided that work was obnoxious, and that a life of jobless wandering was the one which suited him best. He preferred to sleep outside in summer, but he took care to do it comfortably. Having selected a sheltering stone dyke, he made a bed of grass or heather, then spent a long time filling the chinks in the dyke with grass and moss to keep out the draughts. In winter, he slept in barns. There was not a parish where he did not get a welcome and a bed of straw.

---

1. Teu-name was the Orkney word for nickname, but in Stronsay it was eekname.

The kindly country folk went even further. Often, in the morning, the woman of the house would go to the barn with a bowl of porridge and milk, rousing him with a cheery shout, 'Rising time, Willie.' Skatehorn would take the bowl with solemn deference—but almost as a right.

The children loved him; his mischievous conspiratorial grin was irresistible. As he sat in a farm kitchen with a cup of tea[1] and a half of a buttered bere bannock in his hands, he would put on that comical grin and say, 'You know, bairns, this is very good for a disease I have.'

Skatehorn's dress consisted of cast-offs he had been given. When a hole appeared in his clothing, he filled it with a wisp of grass. He liked to wear a hat—one of the hard, round, black hats that people in those days wore of a Sunday. But he did not leave it untouched. Once, when he was given a hat in good condition, he was profuse in his thanks, but he said, 'Before that hat is suitable for a person in my condition it must be renovated.' Next time he appeared it was—by the addition of a hole in the crown and the characteristic wisp of straw.

The left shoulder and back of Skatehorn's jacket were always white with the dust of the meal from his meal poke. This poke, or sack, he left in some conspicuous position when he visited a house, studiously avoiding it with his eye, but very conscious, nevertheless, that the housewife was slipping a cheese, or a few bannocks, into it. One day when a dog ran off with his meal poke, his air of indifference disappeared and his anger was terrible.

I can not pretend that Skatehorn's character was wholly admirable. Once, a sharp-tongued woman, who told him that he was a filthy vagabond and counselled him to wash, afterwards found him doing so—in the farm well. Another woman, who was gravely concerned with Skatehorn's spiritual well-being, gave him a handful of tracts. When she asked him later if he had read them, he said, with an air of bland innocence, 'As a matter of fact, I distributed them.' Which he had—with the aid of the wind.

During Skatehorn's last years he spent the winters in Orkney County Home, but went wandering in summer. A man who met him, after having lost sight of him for months, said, 'Willie, I heard you were dead.' 'I heard that myself,' said Skatehorn, 'but I didn't believe it.' When he did die,[2] there were many who didn't believe it. He had become more than just a person; he was an Orkney institution.

---

1. He referred to it as *tea water*.
2. He died, unmarried, in the County Home, Old Scapa Road, Kirkwall on 2 August 1913, aged 72.

3

Peace's Orkney Almanac

Many people wonder why Orkney's once popular publication, *Peace's Orkney Almanac*, does not appear nowadays. The answer is that it was a casualty of the last war, and that the manpower shortage and other factors since then have made the compiling and printing of a comprehensive local almanac well-nigh impossible. No one regrets its disappearance more than its publishers.

We were talking about this matter one day, when a friend offered to provide us with a copy of the first almanac ever issued by *The Orkney Herald*, and a day or two after he very kindly made good his promise. It was a very slim pamphlet, dated 1861, and had the title *Peace's Household Almanac*. It cost one penny.

The calendar with its little snippets of historical and other information was a feature even of that first almanac. This was expanded and localised later. It was based on the Christian Year, and this continued right down to the last issue.

The local lists were rather scanty, including only Kirkwall and Stromness, but in their second issue the publishers included all the parishes and islands. Apart from these lists, the almanac gave the principal markets in Orkney, which in addition to the town markets were at Hosen, Stenness, Sanday, Shapinsay, South Ronaldsay, Toab and Wasdale.

In Kirkwall there were five schools: Grammar School, Subscription School, Infant School, Society School and a Charity School. There was an Orkney Library linked with the Literary and Scientific Association, and each church had a library of its own. Dr Paterson was at the height of his ministry at the United Presbyterian Church; there were two ministers at the Cathedral; one at the Free Church, but the Independent Chapel at Mill Street, the Temperance Hall[1] of today, was vacant.

Advertisers were prominent. The Kirkwall Co-operative Society, started by the 'Working Men of Kirkwall', was still doing business hopefully. It offered three qualities of flour, bere meal and brose meal, tusk,[2] ling, cod,

1. Now Kirkwall Arts Theatre.
2. A ling-like fish of the cod family.

saithe and red-herrings, for ready money only. Six months before it had started with a capital of £65. J. and J. Smith were in business, advertising trousering, vestings, mantles, merinos, plaids, falls, muslins and stays[1]; and Thomas Warren at the foot of Broad Street could execute the orders, 'so largely bestowed on him' because he had purchased an 'excellent PATENT SEWING-MACHINE'.

The main material of the almanac consisted of articles either practical or moral. There was a page on 'How to Get on in the World' (the answer was Thrift); another on how to 'Overcome the Difficulties of life' (the answer this time was Courage); still another on 'The Uses of adversity' (the writer was a little hazy, but the answer seemed to be Character). There were a few words on servants—very apposite to the time, when servants had mostly a raw deal—'God gives us servants. Did you ever look on them in that light? As gifts, and very precious ones—more valuable than you can fully appreciate, unless you meet a reverse which will compel you to be your own servant—then you will understand how much you owed them. . . .'

A medical page had 'receipts' for some ghastly potions made from rhubarb and ipecacuanha; senna and ginger; Epsom salts, sulphuric acid, quassia chips—the latter described as a 'tonic aperient'.

There are some very smug 'Hints for Home Happiness'. A good wife 'never tells other people that he (her husband) does not bring home money enough to keep the house in food, clothe her and the children, pay the rent and appear respectable.' She never questions the ability of her husband to earn sufficient money in his trade or in his business. She must not 'interfere with her husband's arrangement of any articles of use, or alter the disposition of his books, papers, &c.' She was advised 'never to create a commotion in the household while your husband is at home; but defer all domestic operations, such as washing, dusting furniture etc., until he goes out, and bring your labours to a conclusion before he returns.' Nostalgic reminders of the authority the male exercised in the Victorian home.

In strong contrast to the moralistic left-hand pages of the almanac are the factual and 'newsy' right-hand pages. These relate blythely details of executions, frauds, intrigues, poisonings, battles, forgeries, tortures, burnings alive, whippings, love elixirs, and so on. The duality of the Victorian mind is strongly apparent.

All in all, our great-grandfathers got a good penny-worth.

---

1. Trousering and vestings—serge cloth for trousers and waistcoats; mantles—ladies coats; merinos—fine quality knitted wool underwear; plaids—men's coats of a type similar to a cloak; falls—collars, at that time usually with more than one layer; muslins—open lace material; stays—corsets.

46 Bringing home peats, Longhope, c.1890

47 Horse-drawn hearse, Sanday, used until the mid-1940s for funerals from the North End to Lady Parish cemetery.

48 The wedding of Mary Ann Smith Spence and William Mackie Taylor of Georth, Harray, at Makerhouse, Dounby, 24 May 1907. In the centre front of the lower illustration is the hansel-wife, traditionally an elderly woman in the parish renowned for her generosity. She offered a refreshment of bread and cheese to the guests on their return from the wedding walk and before they entered the wedding house.

4

Trials of a probationer

I have on my shelves an almost forgotten book. It has what may seem an unpromising title—*The Life of a Scottish Probationer*[1]—but it is full of humour, courage and fine old-fashioned virtue. Its hero is Thomas Davidson, a young man from the Scottish Borders who died at the age of thirty-two.

Davidson studied divinity and became a probationer of the United Presbyterian Church. At that time (the 1860s) probationers were sent on an almost mechanical rota to preach in vacant churches in all parts of the country. They gathered experience prior to ordination; but for a year or two they had an arduous life. A hundred years ago, Davidson's journeyings took him to Orkney, which he saw through amused and perceptive eyes. He arrived here late in November 1865 by the Holm Ferry route. His first impressions, recollected as he sat in Mrs Stewart's smoky parlour in Holm, were that he could 'see no reason for Orkney holding the evil reputation among us that it does hold.'

He was even prepared to see the bright side when he had to walk the sixteen miles from Kirkwall to Sandwick on 'a cruel bad road' sometimes 'half-a-foot deep of mud and water'. The darkness fell before he completed that journey. He ended his march to the Sandwick manse by crossing a moor full of holes and ditches and stumbling across ploughed fields. He did not become reconciled to Sandwick. The people were kind, but he speculated as to what he 'should do in the scarcely conceivable event of being settled in this waste place. I would, first of all, grow idle . . . then moody, then mad, and perhaps wind up with murdering my wife.' When he looked at the bleak kirkyard he thought of Keats 'feeling the daisies growing over him'. There were compensations: he had time to read Wordsworth; and one day he walked to Birsay where 'a very intelligent Mr Leask' showed him a Pictish tower and 'the old palace of Robert Stuart who was executed for bad Latin'.

In late December and early January Davidson was in Shapinsay, sitting in the manse with his greatcoat on to make life tolerable. The weather was so wild that he did not venture out for three days on end. His companion was a

[1]. James Brown, DD, Glasgow, 1889.

housekeeper named Eliza, of whom he paints a most diverting picture. Eliza's tales went on and on. In them were mixed up a disreputable old grey cat, a pet ewe who furnished material for five pairs of blankets, the pet ewe's 'brither' who fetched two pounds five shillings, and a minister who inadvisedly made friends with the pet ewe and who talked to it in such a way that the local Morrisonians (a rival sect) cast doubts on the man's mental capacity. Into these tales came a church elder, a very tall man, who married the smallest woman in the island. On the day the elder was *kirket*[1] he marched to church with the little wife on one arm and her little sister on the other. The islanders remarked gleefully that 'he looked like a man wi' twa pails of water'. Orkney humour has not changed.

At Pierowall, Westray, on 12 January, Davidson was given treacle scones and ale, for the people were observing New Year's Eve—Old Style.[2] Next day was their New Year's Day, and all the young fellows were out playing football, in indescribable slush. Indoors, wrote the probationer, 'the day has been celebrated chiefly by eating; cakes and scones, and buns and shortbread forming the staple food.'

He found that on Sundays the Westray people were most attentive listeners. The weather was still very mixed, so Davidson read Wordsworth, The Golden Treasury, and Sir Robert Peel. On Thursday evenings 'the arrival of the *Orkney Herald*'—a newspaper then only five years old—'let in a gleam of light from the outside world'.

The probationer enjoyed his stay on Westray. He left there at eight o'clock on Monday morning, 22 January, in company with three ministers and a magician, and after 'a pretty fair passage' arrived in Kirkwall at seven o'clock that evening. Such was a fair passage a hundred years ago.

---

1. To attend church on the first Sunday after marriage.
2. The Julian Calendar. This was thirteen days later than the New Style Gregorian Calendar. See also footnote 1, p.14.

5

Electioneering

I accumulate paper very happily, and sometimes excitedly. Among the miscellaneous bundles and folders are special treasures, including a collection of local parliamentary election posters from last century. I am writing this column on the day that the 1974 election has been declared, and by the oddest coincidence the postman brought me this morning a grand election poster which I did not previously have. It is a gift from my good friend John Graham, co-editor of *The New Shetlander*.

The poster, addressed TO THE ELECTORS OF ORKNEY, is undated, but it is clear at a glance that it was part of the fun and games at the election of 1880. It consists of a long letter, signed in the boldest of type by JINGO ROWDY BADENOUGH, LLD (Lying Liberal Detractor). It did not take the voters of the day a second to realise that this signature parodied the name of the Conservative candidate, J. R. Badenoch, who had the temerity to fight the mighty and magistral Samuel Laing the Younger on his home ground. Poor Mr Badenoch was made to say, in defence of his party:

> I consider that the prudent and far-seeing policy of Her Majesty's Government in Foreign Affairs has restored our Country, as a Christian Kingdom, to its rightful condition among the nations of the earth. This has been accomplished by picking a quarrel with and slaughtering 10,000 Zulus (who have no souls)—by breaking the faith of our Treaty with the Dutch Boers in the Transvaal—by requisitioning the Indian Famine Fund, and compelling India to pay for a war thrust upon her against her will—by destroying a neighbour with whom we were at peace, and turning Afghanistan into a determined enemy. All these acts, in my opinion, prove that our Christianity is unimpeachable.

All fair enough; but Mr Badenoch was also required in this skit to say of himself, 'My own Party were bound to gratefully accept whatever was sent to them, whether man or monkey.' Standards of mutual courtesy between the parties were not very high. The poster was printed in aid of the Liberal cause at *The Orkney Herald*.

In the 1873 by-election, when the *Herald* supported the radical Sir Peter Tait against Samuel Laing, then a Liberal Conservative, that newspaper was even more fiercely lampooned in a wonderfully printed poster headed (it was only by consummate art that the printer got the heading in), 'THE PRINCE OF THE ISLES and the VISION OF THE BEAST with the GREAT CABBAGE STOCK CLOTHED IN SHODDY.' The text beneath was written in the form and manner of the Book of Revelation. The Prince of the Isles was, needless to say, Samuel Laing; the rest of the heading was, I should imagine, an unkind reference to Sir Peter Tait's coat of arms and the fact that he had made his money from the manufacture of clothing.

> And, lo! as I looked toward the Little City, a Contagious
> Diseased *Herald*, lately doctored up, lean and ill-favoured, with
> legs like a grasshopper, came towards the beast, with his eye
> fixed on the great bag.

That was, no doubt, *The Orcadian* having its own back on *The Herald* for many former insults. The bag was Sir Peter's money bag. Great play was made of Sir Peter's riches in election skits.

> He came on the *Queen* with a wonderful freight,
> With a couple of cabs for driving in state . . .

In another poster, probably of a previous election, Samuel Laing was the target. He (that is, Samuel the Younger) was Chairman of the London, Brighton and South Coast Railway. The Railway had run excursion trains from London to Brighton on the Sabbath Day! This had made 'DOUBLE WORK FOR RAILWAY SERVANTS ON SABBATH ONLY.' On the strength of it, Samuel was shown driving a railway engine with a dragon's head over the bodies of working men, in a large line drawing. Underneath was the caption, 'PORTRAIT, AS TAKEN IN BRIGHTON IN 1868, OF MR SAMUEL LAING, THE OPPRESSOR OF WORKING MEN, AND THE BETRAYER OF THE LIBERAL CAUSE!'

The 1873 election, however, was exceedingly productive of posters. I have another which says in the blackest of black type:

> ELECTORS OF ORKNEY! EXERCISE YOUR INTELLIGENCE! You have
> two Candidates craving your Suffrages, the one a fellow-
> countryman of the highest intelligence and mental training,
> having in his University career at Cambridge carried off the
> highest honours, who is acknowledged by men of all shades of
> opinion to be an able statesman and a great financier, who has
> filled offices of the highest trust and responsibility with honour
> to himself and benefit to his country: *the other* an individual who
> by accident got a handle to his name (a knighthood and not a
> baronetcy, as stated in *The Orkney Herald*) while serving as a
> Magistrate in the most Roman Catholic town of all Roman

Cliffs at Yesnaby, 1950

Stanley Cursiter, RSA, RSW, 1887–1976

Catholic Ireland, and whose effigy was burned by the Protestants as a mark of disapproval.

People say this will be one of the dirtiest elections ever fought. Nonsense! As compared with, for instance, the election of 1833, it will be kid-glove stuff, full of postures but essentially bloodless. When Kirkwall heard in 1833 that Shetlanders, exercising the franchise for the first time, had defeated Samuel Laing (the Elder) of Papdale, there was a free fight as the sheriff tried to announce the result and proclaim the winner from the hustings on Broad Street. The story was well told in *Orkney Miscellany*, *I*, by the late P. N. Sutherland Graeme:

> Captain Baikie turned out to help his party; but in coming down his steps, he was met in the face by the fist of Skipper John Dearness. Mr Traill Urquhart was doubled up by a blow under the ribs and died soon afterwards as a result of it. . . . The sad fate of Captain Balfour during the fracas is recounted. He fell into an open drain and was only just saved from being trampled to death; but he lost the tails of his coat!

A howling mob brandished sticks and threw peats at the sheriff and his escort. After he had pantingly declared the election result, the sheriff did not leave his home for a fortnight, but prudently held his court in his dining-room.

In Orkney, surely, the Age of Violence was long before the Age of Affluence. It was all very regrettable, no doubt; but are our present flabbiness and apathy to be admired?

6

A Stromness childhood

One of the joys of being a correspondent of *Town and Country*[1] is the opportunity it gives you of making new friends and of entering interesting and delightful homes. I want to tell you about a visit I paid the other day to two ladies in Stromness, one of whom has recently celebrated her ninetieth birthday—a fact difficult to believe when you look at her alert figure and listen to her crisp conversation, flavoured with an endearing combination of pungent directness and sweet old-world civility.

My new friends were sitting in front of a wide window, which gave a view of a great area of Stromness harbour. Eight generations of the family had lived in the house, and had looked out on the shipping and the birds. They had seen the whalers come and go, and the Hudson's Bay ships, and the trading smacks—many of them built in a yard at the other end of the town, and owned by far-sighted Stromness merchants.

As a child in the 1880s, the older lady had paddled on hot summer days in the clear water on the slipway. Later she learned to row a boat, as did every Stromness child. On a calm day the harbour was full of children in boats and canoes; the only parental prohibition being that they must not tie a sail. It was an uninhibited childhood, spent partly on the water and partly on the streets, still safe for old-fashioned games like 'picky' and 'diggy-doo'.[2] Eventually a young lady had to go to Miss Newsome's school to learn French and deportment, and to become acquainted with a rigid code of good manners, but all her childhood days were free and exciting.

The little girl's friends were the shopkeepers and the boatmen, the tailor sitting cross-legged sewing trousers, which he flung down in unbearable excitement when he heard the Salvation Army band, and the red-faced fisherman bringing his newly-caught haddocks and cod to the door, where he sold for ninepence a dinner for the whole large family. Food was different in those days, but how good it tasted! In a cupboard were stored tongues which

---

1. BBC radio programme.
2. 'Picky' was tig and 'diggy-doo' was hide and seek. For further examples of old-fashioned games, see 'The games we played', p.147.

had been pickled, and then dried until they were as hard as flint. It took days of soaking to soften them, but when cooked they were delicious. Every year a sack of new oatmeal was brought in, to be stored in a large barrel. It was trodden down, until packed tightly enough for preservation, by one of the boys who had to put on white socks for the purpose. Hanging from the rafters upstairs were cured cod brought in for sale by men from Hoy.

Every article in that spacious room in Stromness had some story attached. The family, like so many in that seafaring town, had travelled to all parts of the earth. In a cupboard was some exquisite Limoges china, which had been brought back from France. A portrait in the hall was painted by an Orkney-man who had studied under Sir Joshua Reynolds, and had then become painter to the Great Mogul in India.[1] Two fabulous Chinese vases were given to one of the family—a sea-captain—by a mandarin whose daughter he saved from death. I studied the degree certificates of two Orkney women who were among the earliest women to enter a Scottish university.

Through the eyes of my friends I saw the picture of a family fulfilling itself generation after generation ... children growing up in the gracious old house, doing their lessons before a great fire in the parlour, sitting very upright at their reading, with their books on the table—no sloppy curling up in chairs. And it was good reading too, food for the mind and the imagination.

How perfectly appropriate, how delightfully in character, was the verse the older lady quoted to me, remembered over half a century:

> A sweet disorder in the dress
> Kindles in clothes a wantonness;
> A winning wave, deserving note,
> In the tempestuous petticoat;
> A careless shoe-string, in whose tie
> I see a wild civility.

That verse made me see a happy little girl playing by a Stromness slipway in those halcyon days before our tumultuous, war-ridden, twentieth century.

---

1. Charles Smith, born at Tormiston, Stenness c.1749, worked in the West Indies before travelling to India c.1783 where for a short time he enjoyed the patronage of the Great Mogul, Shah Allum.

7

When Stromness had a newspaper

We shall be hearing a good deal about Stromness this year,[1] for the town will be celebrating in June the 150th anniversary of its elevation into a Burgh of Barony.[2] There has already been much probing into the town's history. Among the interesting things I have seen, through the kindness of a friend who delights in such things, is a file of a Stromness newspaper; an ambitious weekly journal which, sad to say, ran for less than six months.

The Stromness News put out its first issue on Leap Year Day, February 1884. For one penny it offered its readers eight large pages of closely packed matter. It proclaimed that it would be independent of Church and State, but in the same breath it tactfully promised to 'advocate the interests of the Presbyterian Church'. It saw as one of its duties the task of defending the town from 'hostile and unfriendly attacks'—from whom, I wonder, if not perfidious Kirkwall! It called itself a 'strictly local paper', but this must be understood in terms of its day and age, even perhaps in a Pickwickian sense, for there were times when local material did not fill out two of its columns.

That, it seems to me, was the tragedy of *The Stromness News*: it was only local in the most limited way. Although one can see from looking over the file that it saw its sphere of influence extending over half the Orkney Mainland and the islands of Hoy and Flotta, it never made a serious attempt to gather local news and views. It filled its columns with reports on Parliament, London Society, a serial story, Ladies' columns, City topics, a famous divorce case, and, most dreadful to modern eyes, lashings of what it called 'Wit and Humour' or 'Facetiae'. When it folded up, on 1 August 1884, it complained bitterly of meagre support.

The modern reader naturally confines himself to the paragraphs which tell about Stromness during that short period of publication eighty-three years ago. The tone of the paper may be gathered best from the obituaries. That of Willie Nowlan, King of the Orkney Tinkers, declares loftily, he was

---

1. 1967.
2. A corporation analogous to a Royal Burgh. From its elevation to this status various advantages accrued to the town such as the raising of taxes, the holding of a regular market, an annual fair, etc.

'famed more for his hardiness of nature and longevity, than for his acts of philanthropy, scholarship or daring.' Poor old Willie, that was surely somewhat gratuitous! Another subject was 'Whisky Jock', departing this life when at least thirty years old. Day by day, he had passed 'along our streets, dragging his "spiritual" burden, with patient mien and unshod feet.' In other words— the distillery horse. But it was difficult to renounce the grand style once you started.

Stromness was genuinely worried in those days about its young people; far more so than it needs to be now. Young boys all over the place were smoking 'dirty cutty pipes',[1] and thus 'ruining themselves both morally and physically.' Three boys, under the age of ten, had been seen in an 'advanced state of intoxication'.

The most notable events chronicled in the paper's short life were the arrival of the Hudson's Bay Company's ships in June—taking fifteen local men away to the Norwast[2]—and the visit of the 'royal conjurer and humorist', Dr Ormond, who with 'his wonderful family', gave an entertainment of an 'enjoyable and refined character'.

Refinement was the key-note of *The Stromness News*; it was choked by refinement. Stromness at that date was robust, exciting, full of life. A born journalist could have found fascinating material in the town and its hinterland. Instead, the honest Stromnessians were fobbed off with horrible little essays, like one on the Charms of Change, which had this passage: 'day with its sunshine and night with its stars, present marvellous contrasts in aspect, just as summer and winter do, and man cannot, therefore have the presumption to lay the blame upon his Creator if he finds monotony in human life.'

Stromness quickly said to the unfortunate publisher, as it had once said to the tax-gatherers of Kirkwall, 'This will not do,' then found itself without the gallant journal, which, strangely enough, had never had to repel any 'hostile and unfriendly attacks' on its native town.

1. Short, stumpy clay pipes.
2. North-West Canada.

8

Some annals of an Orkney parish

The parish, as I first remember it, was three hours' journey from Kirkwall. You reached it by climbing into an oblong box on wheels, dignified by the name of a coach. This vehicle was drawn by two sturdy little horses who knew every foot of the road. In the early winter darkness they picked their way unerringly, neither helped nor impeded by the beam from the flickering coach lamps. In those days driving at times was made difficult on parts of the road by reason of great blocks of wood disposed at intervals over its surface. The position of these blocks was changed daily, with the object of making wheel traffic use a new track, thus preventing the formation of ruts on the rough and thinly surfaced highways.

As the coach topped the last rise you could see our valley spread out. There is fertile land in the valley and the big farms with their good houses and well-appointed steadings are there. Clustered around the smaller hill is a pretty little township, and higher up, across the broad marsh which lies at the base of the main range of hills, are the crofts, laboriously wrested from the heather and boulder clay of the upper slopes. Just outside the valley to the north, are the church and the school; at its southern end are the smithy and the carpenter's shop.

Nowadays the houses stand out gauntly from the landscape with their white-harled walls. Even the crofts have been rebuilt, thanks to a housing grant. It is altogether a much more comfortable and hygenic countryside than the one you viewed from the top of the horse-coach. It is also more integrated, but alas much more materialistic than it was then.

The 'big hoose' which occupies the lower part of the valley, into whose policies the hill burn babbles pleasantly, has not changed much, except that it is now a country hotel, whereas, in the days of which I speak, it was the home of the family who owned the district. It dominated the valley then; up its drive the young ladies' horses would canter; and from its gates in August would issue a party of determined gentlemen with dogs and guns. Now the family is scattered, and their home has seen many vicissitudes in these later years. It has been let to rich tradespeople who landed their own aeroplane on the home farm. It has also sheltered within its walls parties of Americans, and, not so long ago, men whose minds and bodies were broken by the ardours of seafaring in wartime.

As far as I can remember, no lime-washed walls spoiled the colour harmonies of the landscape when I viewed it from the coach. The larger houses had heavy roofs of Orkney slate, mellowed by time, and the crofts were all covered with green sods, or thatched with heather. In those days each house had a garden filled with old-fashioned flowers—honesty, mignonette, red poppies, lupins and white roses. I notice that in other places gardens bloom as never before, but in this valley the delight in gardens has disappeared. Most of the gardens I knew as a boy are derelict. There are still wild flowers in abundance—more perhaps than there used to be. In summer the marsh is covered with meadow sweet and bogcotton, and the ditches are full of primroses and marsh-marigolds. A few small trout still dart to and fro in the dark brown water of the burn.

With it all, I must admit that the changes in the landscape are relatively unimportant. It is in the way of life, and in the spiritual climate of the countryside that a revolution has taken place. For one thing, the district is now so democratic that you cannot tell the man who comes from the croft high up the hill from the man who has the big farm in the valley. This was certainly not the case as I recollect it. There were then two nations, as it were, existing side by side. The hill folk viewed the valley folk with suspicion, sometimes soured by active dislike. They were very poor, and the valley folk were affluent by comparison. The hill folk were the people of the land—generation by generation they had lived on their few barren acres—whereas the big farmers shifted from farm to farm and from parish to parish, never taking root for more than a decade or two. The old lore of the district was preserved among the hill-folk; they knew all the legends of their race, the efficacy of charms and the baleful meaning of omens and portents. They felt that the dwellers in the valley, who were obviously unconscious of the need to propitiate vengeful spirits or to act upon a favourable omen, secretly ridiculed this faith in the supernatural, as many of them doubtless did, and they resented this attitude of unbelief as deeply as any puritan reacted to the light scepticism of the cavaliers.

Such animosity as existed was all on the side of the hill-folk. It was a veiled animosity, however. Only a person who had been brought up in the district could have been aware of it. Why these feelings were kept hidden is partly explained by the fact that the crofters were economically dependent on the farmers. They eked out their existence by working at seasonal jobs on the bigger farms. They also got frequent gifts of meal, and the loan of farm implements and horses when these were needed. But I remember vividly the awe with which I listened to old crofters criticising the way things were done by some go-ahead farmer. He had probably ridden rough-shod over some of their cherished superstitions. 'Does he no' ken,' they would say, shaking their heads ominously, 'that there kin only be wan end tae hid?' What that end might be, I could not tell, but that it was a terrible one I had no doubt whatever.

It was a way of life that was doubtless good for the soul, but sometimes hard enough on the body. It was a way of life too in which culture had no place. There were one or two 'mute inglorious Miltons' (I shall write of them presently), but their talent for literature, music or whatever it might be, was stunted from the beginning. They had no access to books; they had never heard great pieces of music well performed (how the wireless has revolutionised that); they had never seen an original picture. I know that opinions differ widely about the values of the fine arts; I will content myself with saying that people with an itch to create found very little scope. There was a time when every parish had its celebrated liar. I am rather uncertain whether this is still the case, but these unblushing spinners of yarns supplied a real cultural need—they were novelists who had been nipped in the bud; and were in the true tradition of our imaginative ancestors, who invented such personalities as the Walliwa and the Mester Muckle Stour-worm. The same, I am sure, applies to those diverting mimics, usually women, who added to the social gaiety of the countryside: they were natural actors, whose gift for characterisation had not found a legitimate outlet.

I am in no doubt concerning the hardness of the economic life of the average farmer prior to the recent war, but I feel sure also that the social life of the parishes compensated greatly for the lack of creature comforts. In the cities we pay our duty calls, we are polite and even suave to one another, we go to the pictures and are either tolerably amused or frankly bored, but there is no 'abandon' in our enjoyment of social occasions or public entertainments. In my childhood in the country it was very different. We enjoyed people, we felt a sense of impending pleasure in the realisation that 'Jock' was going to drop in tonight, or that we had been invited out to 'Beunaquoy', and that Peggy and her sister the teacher were also going to be there. There would be no special entertainment provided; we would discuss the affairs of the farm, rag the girls unmercifully, especially when we found that Peggy's sister's extended education had not spoiled her sense of fun, then the cards, a much-fingered pack, would be produced, and game after game of 'batchie'[1] would ensue, each game more fun than the last.

---

1. A card game, the object of which is to avoid being left with any cards. A few cards (usually five) are distributed to each player and the remainder face down are drawn as required to enable participants to follow suit at each hand. When the pack is exhausted play continues with the cards held. Those who manage to discard all their cards drop out, and the last person with cards becomes *batchie* and is sent out of the room or 'behind the door'. The four King (or Queen) cards are shuffled, laid face down and named. Batchie is summoned, selects one and the card determines his (or

Kirkwall Harbour, 1872　　　　　　　　Sam Bough, RSA, RSW, 1822–1878

Our crying need today is gusto. In the country they used to have it in plenty: at the weddings, at the muckle suppers,[1] at Hogmanay. But sophistication kills gusto, and even the rural areas are becoming sophisticated now.

If a country district is to achieve any sort of integration, all its affairs must become common property, even affairs that individuals in larger communities would regard as strictly personal. I am all against spiteful gossip, but I believe that the minute investigation of other people's doings which went on in the country was astonishingly detached and free from rancour. A country man cannot camouflage his character as a townsman can. All the district knows whether he is a good neighbour or the reverse, whether he is tight-fisted or generous, whether he is moral, immoral or amoral, whether he is rich or poor, and whether or not he gets on with his wife. To become 'au fait' with the affairs of the community, people had to get together, and in many districts, ours included, the local shop became a kind of social club. In the evenings people gathered there ostensibly for business, but also for the agreeable purpose of discussing local events. Saturday night was the favourite night. There were, of course, provisions to get for Sunday.

New bread had come out of the town; several boxes, for we had pronounced tastes; some liked Garden's bread for it was baked right through; some liked Arthur's because the children did not object to its less vigorously fired crusts; others would only eat Finstown bread for undefined reasons of their own. We all bought 'heaters',[2] a sugary ring of them, although butter scones were occasionally substituted. The shopping done, we withdrew from the counter, set down our baskets, found a seat on a box if we could, and waited for an opportunity to join in the conversation. The shop-man would have been in town all day. Often he had interesting news to tell about doings in Kirkwall. We did not approve of a great many of the follies of that ancient city. We thought that the townsfolk were a bit light and that they did not take life as seriously as seemed desirable. We also thought that a lot of them were making too much money at our expense, but I think we rather admired them for that. Our interest in their concerns soon waned, however, and we got back to the much more interesting task of discussing our own.

We did not wear our working clothes on Saturday night. We put on our second-best suits, although a collar could be dispensed with. The

---

her) marital prospects. The choice was often attended by much hilarity. In earlier times the more credulous believed that the suit of the card chosen gave an indication of the person's future. Clubs signified hard work, diamonds were a sign of good luck and money, hearts were associated with love, and spades brought ill luck. The game was also known as *Batchie behind the door*.

1. A harvest home celebration.
2. Wedge-shaped buns usually baked in rings of eight. Sugared and glazed on top, these sections resembled the cast iron inserts, or *heaters*, used in laundering irons and by tailors.

grown-ups had shaved; with luck the shave would last over Sunday, unless one happened to be a kirk elder, when the painful process would need to be renewed the following morning.

We all met again at the kirk on Sunday; but under much more formal circumstances. We were all more uncomfortably dressed, and a bit conscious of the elegance of our 'Sunday best'. Frivolous conversation was felt to be out of place. We stood at the corner of the church in little groups discussing the weather, the crops, and any parochial affairs that were of a sufficiently serious nature. We watched the gigs bowling up, saw the horses being unharnessed and tethered out on a piece of common land outside the churchyard dyke. There was Erchie Halcro's well-varnished governess car, the high-gig from Millquoy with the clumsy grey pony, the rather muddy dog-cart from Netherabist, which had come seven miles. Carlyle writes somewhere about 'gigs and gig-mania'. 'Gig-mania' was common in our parish, until the onset of 'motorists'. To be able to offer a lift on your gig to some humble pedestrian plodding along to church was one of the most snobbish of delights, especially if the pedestrian had the good sense to extol his good fortune and the comfort of the gig, when he might be asked to join the party again on the homeward journey. When a person of particularly generous proportions was accommodated, everyone had to get up while drastic adjustments were made to the seat, but all with great decorum. It was correct on the return journey to discuss the sermon. Not the ethical implications of it, of course, but its general effect as an essay in sermon-making. We would agree that the minister had 'a fine wey of pittin' things', or that 'hid wis an awful bonny bit at the end', or that we had never 'heard hid worked oot that wey afore,' but we allowed no intrusions on our spiritual reticence. The lack of such reticence in the few extreme evangelicals in our parish offended our sense of decency.

On the way home we met the congregation from the opposition church (there was no church union in those days to destroy the element of competition). We nodded to them in a superior kind of way, and a little frostily to their minister, who walked along with his wife a hundred yards or so behind his flock, grasping tightly a small brown attaché case, said by his congregation to contain his hymn book and sermon notes, but known by us (without evidence) to conceal a little bottle of the best, which we knew had not a little to do with his fiery eloquence in the pulpit. Our own minister was strict T.T., and rather uninspired as a public speaker.

During the afternoon we took advantage of our respectable turnout to pay a visit to relatives in another parish, or to call on a neighbour. Such calls had no hint of the secular, we never forgot that it was Sunday, but we often managed to observe the proprieties, while watching Sandy's new mare going through her paces, or while paying a call on the fat cattle which were almost ready for marketing.

During week-nights the younger men of the parish met each other at some convenient place, usually the bothy belonging to some popular farm-hand. Ten or a dozen could always be found there, indulging in conversation or argument, or playing a rough and ready game of whist. There are few subjects which have not been touched on in bothy arguments, I should imagine. I have heard unending discussions of theology, some of them much more subtle than an outsider would suppose. In fact the conversation might be about anything from the price of potatoes to the exploration of the supernatural. It would stop as suddenly and inconclusively as it began, and the animal spirits of the youngsters would find expression in a bout of fisticuffs or in some daft ploy. These country 'ploys' were notorious. Very stupid tricks were played on unoffending people. Acts of vandalism were considered funny. But the reason for some of these poor jokes was the lack of creative interests for the adolescents. The youth clubs should do much to correct such tendencies today.

What I miss most in the county today are those virile personalities I used to know as a boy. Our valley had then a wealth of rugged characters who were so intensely individual that they made an indelible impression on my mind. Men and women today are far too obviously out of a common mould. They lack the supremely personal attitude to life which characterised their grandfathers.

The first of such individuals to leap to my mind is the local comedian, James. He was a little man, but burly, with a large head which had gone prematurely bald. His face was creased with humorous lines and his eyes were very blue. I have never heard a man laugh as he used to laugh, tears falling from his eyes, his whole body contorted. Like many other humorists, he was deeply serious at times, inclined to despise his own mirth, and in his last years very doubtful of his reception at the end of the road. Dear old James. I have no doubt that St Peter met him quite a way from the gate, and that the two of them went in laughing happily over some new joke. In all the years I knew him, I never heard him speak ill of a living soul, and I never saw him raise his hand or use a harsh word to a child or an animal.

In his hey-day no merrymaking in the parish was complete without James. He sang, he recited, or told stories, and everyone enjoyed his efforts, not least because he enjoyed them so obviously himself. His songs were gathered from sources I have never been able to discover. Most of them I have never heard anyone else sing. They were good, rollicking songs. As for the recitations, they were often inoffensively Rabelaisian, full of incident and colour. He was a master of effective gesture, but his gestures had little bearing on the sense of the recitation, they were comic in the best sense.

At public concerts he would sit among the audience, he would refuse to have his name placed officially on the bills, he would regret his inability to do anything worthwhile to assist. The producers took all that for granted; they put his name in the chairman's programme nevertheless, and waited on events. When his name was read out, James would sink a little deeper into the shadows, but by this time the whole audience were shouting 'James' at the pitch of their voices. A few burly young fellows would help him to his feet, give him a push, and all was well. He would not mount the platform in the orthodox way, but took a flying leap on to the boards, cap in hand, his bald head glistening. He would stop a minute, as if in doubt, then he would sing. At times his voice was a subdued murmur, at others nervous old ladies looked apprehensively at the roof and held tightly to their seats. He would go on and on, for encore followed encore. He would fill the audience with intolerable mirth, or, quite suddenly, bring tears to their eyes that were not caused by laughter. At last, when one felt that this ought to go on for ever, he would stop very decisively, clutch his cap more firmly, and descend from the platform in the same way as he had approached it.

I have heard many comedians since, but never one like James.

Another lovable personality was David, the poet. I find it difficult to describe him. He never seemed to belong securely to this world. He was a rather wraith-like individual, tall and extremely thin with a wiry moustache and over-hanging eyebrows. He seldom spoke, and preferred to work by himself in the fields. Although extremely gentle, he could never be swayed by anyone else's opinion. He was a regular churchgoer, and his Bible was much thumbed. Some people thought him dreadfully unorthodox, for he found the limitations of Presbyterian thought unsupportable. He could seldom be induced to argue, but when he did his eyes would gleam and he would talk disconcertingly of a religion wide enough to include 'the folk on the Pleiades and the Bear.' Everyone liked him, but such talk confirmed the impression that he was very, very strange mentally.

David's poems were mostly composed while lying on his back among the straw in the barn. He never wrote down any of them, but he never forgot a line he had composed. In the right kind of company he could often be induced to repeat some of his verses. People with retentive memories (people's memories were much more effective then) would write them down, and so they gained circulation. They were always much admired. As for their quality, what can I say? They were very bad poems, but, nevertheless, they were inspired poems. This seems a contradiction in terms, but I would hold to this definition. The badness of their form and substance was due to the crippling burden that an almost complete lack of education had placed on the poet. All the same, they were composed at white heat, and under the genuine creative impulse. The badness of David's verses was no index of the enthusiasm which inspired him.

An ubiquitous character, who always appealed to my sense of humour

49 The throw-up, Christmas Day Ba', Kirkwall, 1988

50 The Ba' on Broad Street, Kirkwall, New Year's Day 1985

51 The Ba' at the Up-the-Gate goal, Kirkwall, New Year's Day 1913

52 The Ba' at the Down-the-Gate goal, Kirkwall, New Year's Day 1969

was the savant. He was getting rather old when I knew him, but he had not submitted to the cramping limitations of work for a decade or so. How he lived was a mystery, but he existed somehow. His self-imposed task was to spread enlightenment in our parish. He sought to do this with a missionary fervour, but he was not unmindful of his own reputation as an intellectual, and he never lost an opportunity of adding something to the legend. He was keenly interested in science, but his science stopped short where the radio and motor-car began.

More because of the fine opportunities he gained for arguments than from any spiritual compulsion, he affected a peculiar comprehension of the mysteries of theology. A new minister was a godsend to him, for sooner or later he would find an opportunity of involving the unwary cleric in a discussion on some deep ethical problem. The wise minister would have sized up his man, and led him back to more practical issues, but few of the savant's victims were wise. He invariably became the devil's advocate in such discussions. The old specious arguments for free-thinking were at his finger-tips. Some of his antagonists became angry at being confronted with such feeble rationalistic sophistry; others sought earnestly to correct his errors, and it was they who afforded him his chiefest joy.

Only once was the savant entirely disconcerted. This is how it happened. He managed to get into conversation one day with a visiting clergyman, and after a few preliminary remarks, began to make a concentrated attack on what he imagined was the stranger's position, only to find that the clergyman was also an agnostic, and glad of a chance to air his own scepticism. It was no agreement that our savant was seeking, however, and he immediately turned right about, contriving to put up such a telling defence of the faith that both his opponent and himself were shaken by it. This incident had its repercussions, for the clergyman told several people about his experience, and the parish, which had long doubted the quality of the savant's rationalism, never took him quite seriously again.

If space allowed, I could tell of many more such characters; of the antiquarian, who unwittingly added a beautiful fake to the collection of the Society of Antiquaries in Edinburgh, where it is still exhibited; of the old pedlar with the long beard and the box of oddments on his back, who shared our dinner every fortnight or so, and repaid us with shrewd comment and witty observation; and of the twisted old gangrel with the crutches who used to boil his tea-can on our stove—we shall never see the like of that man again; very fierce and dirty he looked, and he carried all his earthly possessions in the pockets of his manifold clothes, his most fascinating possession being a great gleaming gully with a greasy handle, with which he attacked his food. It was that gully which gained him access to our stove, for my mother had long made up her mind that it was safer in the hand of a friend than of an enemy.

The 'characters' have mostly gone their way, and another fraternity seems likely to follow them. I shall call them the 'local specialists'. I can remember a time when every second man had something he could do superbly well. If you were at a loss during sheep-shearing, you sent to Hammersquoy for Sandy, if it was peat-cutting, then your man was Tammy o' Windyhill. Perhaps you had a difficult colt to break; if so Big Jamie would see you through. If you had an exasperating form to fill in, you took it one evening to Erchie o' Midbanks. So it went on. For every job there was the man. How these people loved their self-acquired skill. The knowledge of their expertise gave them self-respect and real mental satisfaction.

In my time local boys loved more than anything else to watch the official craftsmen of the parish—the blacksmith and the joiner. I maintain that to see the making of a wheel was one of the finest cultural experiences that any boy could have. Our joiner was a pleasant man, direct in speech, but too kindly to give offence. The odd things I remember about his appearance are insufficient, I'm afraid, to give much of a picture of him. One can still see the smudges of paint on his clothes, the way the pockets of his jacket hung down from carrying heavy tools, his corduroy trousers, much-bagged at the knees, his hands, very strong and flexible, but smothered beneath a coat of grime grown very shiny through contact with putty. One can remember the condition of his tools—surely no one but he could put such an edge on a piece of good steel. And one will always remember with affection the way he would stop an important job to look out odd pieces of wood for some aspiring young craftsman, and when the price was asked, reply gruffly, 'Tak' hid awa' oot o' me road,' and get back to his work.

In these days of shoddy materials, it is good to think of the care he exercised when selecting wood for one of his famous cart-wheels—the tough, long-seasoned block of elm for the heart, the straight-grained oak for the spokes. How beautifully biased, to take the strain, was the finished wheel, and how gay in its conventional red paint, for nothing stands the weather like red lead.

The blacksmith, also, loved to put a good job out of his smithy. Farmers in a hurry would sometimes complain of the care he exercised, but if any suggested that a rougher job would do, he would draw a sinewy arm across his brow, straighten his back, and say exactly what he thought of them. He did not mince his words, either.

So far I have written mainly about the grown-ups and their doings. Where did the child come into the picture? It is true that the country child identifies himself from a very early age with the life of his elders. Most people have noticed little boys coming into town, who are in their own minds already grown-up. They are most serious individuals, their talk is already of crops and animals, and they are most knowledgeable about the finer points of stock-rearing. They have, even at nine and ten, a deep scorn of toys. Offer them a bat and a ball or a train set, and they will blush furiously. They will say coldly, 'Hid's no yeuse tae me.' Games, except football, are also beneath their dignity.

The country child is not to be put off with imitations of the real thing such as delight a town child. No toy horse for Geordie; he can get astride 'Prince' any day and take him home from the plough. No furry lamb either for his little sister, Mary Ellen; she has a special sheep among the flock, which will have two real lambs in March. No toy gun either for Robbie, the older boy; he has an old twelve bore, which he got from his uncle. The gun is pretty rusty by now, but it has never had a licence in its history, and it never will.

Perhaps the country child comes into contact with the realities of life too soon, perhaps his imaginative life never gets a chance to develop, perhaps he is denied many of the more subtle pleasures of life. You may put all these things on the debit side, but there is quite as much or more to outweigh them on the credit side.

It is one of the tragedies of urban life that so many people who do brain-work are almost 'physically illiterate', as Rex Knight, the psychologist, has described this condition. They can enter figures correctly in their ledgers, but when they come to grips with a loose slate, or a broken gate, they are helpless. Here the countryman scores, for he has a genius for improvisation. Certainly the ability to use one's hands is one of the major pleasures of life. A man who can use his head only is not a completely educated man. My advice to the educationalists would be: Teach the country to use its head and the town to use its hands!

9

I remember rural poverty in Orkney

Nicknames, a Norse legacy, used to be common in Orkney. One man was called 'Puir Times', after his recurring theme. This was in the late nineteen-twenties, when conditions were undoubtedly bad. How bad I have often attempted to work out in my mind, but it is difficult to put boyhood memories into perspective. The best I can do—as I mean to do now—is to set down some of the things I remember and see how they add up.

I was brought up on a 40-acre hill croft. Some of the ground was poor. To save fodder we kept only one horse. A relative with a croft of similar size kept another, and we used the two horses as a team on both crofts. We had three milk cows on our own croft. If we were lucky there would be three calves. If not, we might have to buy one. Thus we hoped to sell each year three two-year-olds. There were also a few sheep and 100 hens.

Roughly, the amount of money we could expect to bring in each year might be calculated as follows:

Three cattle at £18	£54
Six lambs at £2	12
600 dozen eggs at 1/-	30
Milk, oats and potatoes might bring	10
Total	£106

To that amount was to be added £14, which my father got for spare-time jobs—in all £120.

Out of this gross income of £120, feeding-stuffs, manures and seeds had to be bought. If these, and other expenses like horse-shoeing, took £50, there was £70 left for food, clothing, and all other necessities for a family of four. We grew a large part of our food, spending perhaps £45 a year on the rest. That left £25. This was enough for working clothes and all the sundry expenses; and it brought each of us on an average a new Sunday outfit every three years.

This was not poverty. If there were no disastrous losses we could live healthily and happily on our income—but with no luxuries. We did not have a wireless until 1935, when an outside source made its purchase possible. The constant fear was the death of a cow, or of one of the young beasts. A loss of £20 on that narrow budget did not mean complete ruin, but it made life grim and naked of comfort. We experienced such losses twice in 15 years, and each time it took three years to recoup them. Savings were non-existent, and such things as life or accident insurance were unknown among the crofting population.

The bigger farmers, with 80 to 150 acres of land, lived more easily and put some money into the bank. A few had begun to use cheque books, but the majority distrusted them. A good number of the crofters would not accept cheques, so cattle dealers had to carry large sums in notes.

One could call our situation, as I have described it, a midway one. When I think of poverty, I do not think of my own experiences, but of the life led by people with crofts of eight to twelve acres—places too small to keep a horse. There were around ten of these which I knew personally.

The houses were mostly roofed with flagstones covered with sods, although about a third of them had tarred roofs. (I am referring to the poorest croft houses.) Their windows and doors deteriorated for lack of paint. The small amount of furniture grew yearly shabbier.

Wallpaper (at 3d a roll) was too dear for some folk. Ochred interior walls were common, a harsh blue being popular in our neighbourhood. One house, which I liked to visit because of the welcome I got, had its walls papered with pages of old magazines, the pictures being pasted over the mantelpiece and the text pages around the rest of the room.

The local merchants kept the poorest of the crofters going. They accepted eggs and butter as payment for groceries. I have seen an old man gathering together a few duck eggs so that he could purchase four ounces of tea. Merchants frequently forgave debts of a pound or two, and farmers supplied meal and potatoes against a few days' work in the harvest field.

Even from such poor homes, people turned out to church on Sunday in decent clothes. There was a prodigious amount of wear in one of the blue serge suits made by the parish tailor. Some of these suits obviously dated from the early manhood of the wearers, when they had made a bit of money as unmarried farm servants. The natural desire to marry and have a croft of their own set the seal on their future condition. Henceforth, too many children and too little money kept them in lifelong servitude.

Clothing for the children had to be made out of unorthodox materials. A month or two ago a woman (not much over 50) told me that as a child she constantly wore vests and knickers made out of bleached flour sacks.

Parents were grateful for old clothes and hand-me-downs from any source. It was not considered a disgrace if the discarded suits of minister or doctor could be distinguished in their transmogrifications. To the delight of the neighbourhood, one woman wore under her petticoats, rather than waste them, plus-four trousers sent home by a brother in the city.

An old man, whom I knew personally, cut himself trousers out of the heavier type of hessian bag and dyed them a purple colour with a decoction he made from heather. This same man often said that if he could only make £100—his idea of wealth—he would never do another stroke of work. He was thin and under-nourished, and had never in his life, I am sure, possessed a £5 note.

As poor as the poorest crofters, but more miserable because less settled, were the married farm servants, or 'bow-men'. A few of them never stayed more than a term, or at most two, at any farm—partly because they incurred debts they could not meet, and partly because, Micawber-like, they hoped the next situation would be better. Carts carrying wives, children, and some rickety furniture were to be seen every term, taking the wanderers to a new farm or to a new parish.

Poverty was, of course, commonplace in the nineteenth century, but there is reason to believe that the sufferings of the rural poor in the 1920s and early 1930s were hardly less acute than those of their great-grandfathers sixty to eighty years earlier. There was a good period from perhaps 1890 until the First World War. More than one old man assures me that this was the best period he lived through, not excluding the past fifteen years.

'Wages were small, but everything was so cheap that you really didn't need money,' one man told me. He was a crofter and spare-time postman. His postman's pay was 7/6d a week. He spent 2/6d of this on tobacco, repairs to his bicycle, and new tyres when needed. The remaining 5/- he paid into savings.

10

The water meedoo

The whole floor of our valley was filled with a marsh which we called 'the meedoo'. If a fairly wide burn at the extreme edge of the marsh had not carried a deal of water away to sea, our meedoo would have been a shallow loch. Even so, apart from a short period in summer, it was not wise to cross the bog, the depth of which had never been plumbed. In it had been deposited during the centuries soil, peat and vegetation, washed down from the hills. Those who tried to dig deep draining ditches found the earth thick and sticky and black, sometimes resting on a blue clay, sometimes coloured to a dark brown with iron. On the top of this soggy soil, grass was so thickly matted that a lightfooted person could often pass over without sinking, but cattle and horses would have mired at once. Hence, although the sweet marsh grasses grew profusely all summer, the meedoo could not be used for grazing.

The only way to utilise the grass was to cut it for hay. To make this possible very deep drains were dug, with an outlet to the burn. Sufficient water ran out of the spongy marsh in summer to make certain parts stable enough for haymaking. The hay was cut with a scythe, which had to be very sharp, as the soft grasses did not stand up strongly against the blade—like oats or rye. In summer the meedoo seemed to draw the heat, and mowing could be very warm work; after every few swings of the scythe the mower paused to draw a shirt-sleeve across his forehead.

The hay was called 'bog-hay' to distinguish the crop from hay reaped from the fields. It was very soft and had a sweet, heavy scent. The airing process was similar to that used for ordinary hay—tossed several times, then built into tiny coles.[1] It had often to be carried long distances to the stackyard, because no vehicle could cross the bog. Most people seemed to use big four-pronged forks, like byre-forks; but I am told that in earlier days people often carried great quantities in a double loop of rope slung from their shoulders. Cattle were very partial to bog-hay, but I have heard that although valuable as part of a mixed diet, it was not good if used exclusively.

1. Haycocks.

Fodder at one time was so scarce in winter that, even in my time,[1] the meedoo was held in common. Each croft for some distance around had a share. Although there were no distinguishing marks or boundary lines visible to my eye, the older people seemed to know perfectly which part was 'Erwick's Meedoo', 'Bisgar's Meedoo', or 'Creya's Meedoo'. The parts available to each croft were comparatively small. Perhaps six people were still cutting bog-hay when I was a boy. Maddo Person came down from the hill farm, from whose little fields she seemed to be gathering stones all day long. Clad in her heavy brown shawl and sack apron, she swung her scythe with the skill and strength of a man. Robert, at the far side of the valley, cut neat, narrow swathes which dried quickly. Young Duncan from Burgar seemed determined to cut all his hay in one long afternoon and evening.

Plenty of straw and turnips, the fruit of better farming, soon meant that only those on the very fringe of the meedoo continued to cut bog-hay. These were freely encouraged by the defaulters to use their lots as well, so that I doubt if anyone could now define the boundaries. One of the last people to harvest his whole crop of bog-hay was my uncle Peter. As a younger man he had dug a ditch all round his portion of the meedoo—a really colossal undertaking, for the ditch was two feet wide and six feet deep. He was a short man, and to heave out the heavy, wet earth must have been peculiarly exhausting. When he had finished he planted raspberries along a length of the ditch. These grew well and were a perennial attraction to small boys, who rarely, if ever, tasted fresh fruit.

To a child the meedoo was rather awesome. The prohibition against attempting to cross was sufficient to invest the area with mystery; particularly the insistence that it contained quagmires so deep that anyone who set foot in them would be sucked down into the bowels of the earth. Then the thick mat of grass on the meedoo, so unlike the sparse ankle-deep grass on the fields, might contain all kinds of unusual things. On the edge I once captured a coot, whose bald crown seemed very odd. Water hens darted quickly, almost before you had a chance to see them, from the sides of the ditches. In one corner I came across a toad, and was repelled; although tadpoles collected in a jam-jar from a slimy ditch were fascinating, children took them to school, and the teacher tolerantly displayed up to half-a-dozen jam-jars along the window ledge. There were voles in a slightly drier part of the meedoo. It was full too of snipe, whose drumming in the twilight is to me the loveliest natural sound in the world.

Few farmers bothered to grow any but the most common garden flowers, so the meedoo was our garden. Pink lady's smock grew profusely all over its

---

1. Ernest Marwick was born in 1915.

surface. The ditches were full of marsh marigolds, so intensely bright to a child's eye that they looked like a golden mirror. Here and there were very large water forget-me-nots of such a soft, pure blue that they made the other flowers seem flamboyant. In a part of the bog, almost encircled by the burn, there was a great quantity of yellow irises, valued in my younger days more for leaf than flower, for the leaves made excellent boats, known as 'seggie-boats'. Blood-drops, or musk, grew freely; but of a quite fantastic beauty in certain lights were the pale expanses of bog-cotton.

There is more to say about the most characteristic of all the marsh-flowers, meedoo-sweet. This plant was not so very noticeable when I first remember the meedoo, for the annual mowing of the hay kept it down. But when patches of bog were left unmown meedoo-sweet gradually took over, until it completely covered them. At times the scent became intense, and I had the impression of being drugged—a sensation so pleasant that I must try to describe it.

I well remember returning to the meedoo after many years and wandering over the ground. It was a day of sun and wind, both subdued and intermingled until they seemed like a single element. And over the wind came powerfully the scent of meedoo-sweet, a heavy perfume that would have lain along the ground, if the wind had not shaken it free to fill the whole valley. I experienced such remarkable sensations as I stood in the meedoo breathing that heady scent that I can hardly believe they were not in some degree due to it.

The most noticeable was a sense of complete timelessness. The soft wind blowing with the sun in it had, I felt, blown from the beginning and would blow on for ever, carrying utter relaxation and complete peace of mind. Something, I am not sure what, had happened also to space. Nothing existed outside the tiny valley, where everything was rounded and complete. The only phrase I have ever come across that can in any way describe my sensations is Edwin Muir's 'deep in the diamond of the day'; but that gives a hard feeling of too intense light and clarity, whereas I was conscious of a calm fluidity in which all elements became one. It seemed as if one's spirit—which is always struggling in alien territory, where it is bruised and battered—was suddenly returned to its proper element. Here, like a seal returned to the water, it could plunge and glide with no sense of effort, and hardly distinguish between itself and the element in which it swam. I was in no way unconscious of the scene around me—the white road, the low hills, the fields, the little farms, the flat, brown marsh—but they all became dear to me in a way that had never happened before. I do not think that visually they appeared any different; but I seemed suddenly to be aware of their nature—the very essence of its quotation of stone and grass and water—and absorb these into my own nature while I was being absorbed into theirs.

All this is inadequate; but the sensation was of such blissful awareness, that it seemed to offer some clue to the mystery of being.

A companion guided me home, telling me that I seemed in a 'dwaam'—in other words, a light-headed dream. I felt drugged all that day.

II

Stone-breakers

The other day I passed on the road a diesel road roller and a stone-crusher. I know that we have to thank these powerful machines for the present fine condition of our Orkney roads; yet I thought a little sadly of the stone-breakers who were the friends of my boyhood.

I lived only a hundred yards from a stone-quarry—an awesome cavern, with grass growing green on its upper ledges and yellow vetches straggling over its rim. It was out-of-bounds until I was six years old; and I had, until then, to imagine what kind of life went on in its depths, from which day-long came the steady 'chap-chap' of hammers.

It was never actually with my parents' permission that I haunted the quarry, but as soon as I found that I could do so without getting into trouble, I spent nearly all my spare time there. At first I merely lay among the vetches, hearing the little insects chirring in the hot sun, and watching the men quarrying and breaking the stones. Some of the holes where they raised the blue whin were very deep, and as the great slabs were lifted by the crowbars, I had a little spasm of fear in case the quarrymen would go right through the world's shell. I was hazy about what would happen: if the world was hollow they would fall in, down and down; but it might be that it was not hollow, and that great flames would pour out.

That period passed. I got to know the men who worked in the quarry, their faces almost hidden by dusty caps and black goggles. When sufficient stone was quarried the breaking began. Each man chose a fairly level place on the floor of the quarry, barrowed a pile of stones to the vicinity, then sat down on an old sack filled with straw and started to break. It was a difficult thing to swing the long-handled hammer with the maximum effect. Occasionally a man would let me try, and I would pound at a stone with no result whatever. The others would stop work and grin as they watched me. One intelligent man tried to interest me in stones that had a pattern of black specks and scales. He told me that these were from a fish that had lived millions of years ago; but my leg had been pulled so often that I looked wise and turned away.

There was a certain size to which the stones had to be broken; probably they had not to exceed two or two and a half inches. My friends the stone-breakers built the broken stone—road metal it was called—into lovely oblong heaps. Every now and then an inspector from Kirkwall came to measure the heaps, so that the men could be paid; for they were on piece-work and the stone was purchased by the cubic yard. The inspector was a frequent subject of conversation. He was hated on principle. Not only did he measure the road metal, but also made certain that it had been broken small enough. Even I had to admit that the men sometimes surfaced their heaps with stone broken specially small, while larger carelessly broken stones lurked underneath. The inspector had an instinct for this: sometimes he would pull down a heap and, with scathing words, say what he thought of the work.

When he had gone, the 'chap-chap' of the hammers stopped, and the air was full of other sounds. I heard curious words. When I tried these out at the tea-table that night there was a shocked silence, then I was hurried off to what I still consider unmerited retribution. With my heart pounding, I had heard the quarrymen discuss what they were going to do to the inspector next time he came; and the prospect was so exciting that I made a point of being on the spot. But my fears, or was it my hopes, came to nothing. My outraged stone-breakers merely said 'Yes' and 'No' and 'Weel, weel, sir'. They had wives and big families to keep, did Willie and James and Davat.

All of them are gone now, but somewhere under the surface of every Orkney road are the stones that they and their mates broke so patiently and painfully.

12

Orkney 'feeders'

It is a feature of life in Orkney and Shetland today that all kinds of interesting men and women, tired of their way of life in the busy south, are coming to live in the islands. A few of these people seem a bit exotic to sober-minded country folk. There was a time, however, when eccentrics of all kinds found a haven here, and were accepted. In my own boyhood these eccentrics, or 'feeders' as they were usually known, were not uncommon. But I had better explain.

Until well into the twentieth century, distinguished, or at least well-off families, who had anyone—son, uncle, nephew—who was an embarrassment, sent him to a quiet farm in Orkney. He would get board and clothing, small luxuries like tobacco, but no money. As he grew plump on Orkney eggs and butter, he was called, like the shining animals which were putting on weight in the farm byre, 'a feeder'. The term was not meant to be cruel, but it was wickedly apt.

Not far from my childhood home three 'feeders' lived—humorous, likeable young men, well known to my father. The reason for their banishment to Orkney was an addiction to the bottle, coupled with a distaste for such mundane things as university examinations, or what their parents called 'honourable careers'. In a country parish they lived a life so unremarkably virtuous as to be almost frightening: tramping the hills, fishing for trout, and singing romantic ballads in farm kitchens.

Only once did they make a bid for freedom. By various means, such as writing letters for those unhandy with a pen and giving some mild help to neighbours in harvest, they had acquired a few shillings. They borrowed a gig and a good-natured farm horse and trotted briskly along the rough waterbound road to Kirkwall, fifteen miles away. The farmer who was their host and keeper discovered their absence with comical dismay. He thought they had gone forever. But they returned, along with the gig, in the dark of the evening, to meet their distressed host, who had walked several miles with a byre lantern. They hoisted him into the vehicle, exaggerating with many a wanton song their inebriety; and they spent the rest of the winter singing a ballad they called 'The Drunken Feeders' in the less straightlaced homes of the parish.

In one of our towns local 'feeders' had an understanding with the merchants. When a 'feeder' came into a shop, ostensibly to make a purchase, it was instantly recognised that his real need was ready cash for refreshments. He was given the money, and his family in the south were debited with 'a dozen paper collars', 'a pair of socks', or anything similar that would not occasion remark. An elderly 'feeder' in a certain island was a courtly man dressed always in a brown Inverness cape. He had been a designer of table linen before taking to opium. Among his few possessions was a paint box, and he had a passion for painting flies on doors, windows, and crockery. With the most inoffensive but nevertheless loudly expressed appreciation, he would watch the housewife swatting them unavailingly. Orcadians were poor at that time, and this urbane, perfectly mannered gentleman had the task of collecting limpets to be boiled as food for ducks. Of just such another 'feeder'—beloved in a landlord ridden district—the postman said when he heard of his death, 'The Almighty made a terrible error o' judgment whin he took Robertson an' left the Laird.'

13

Motoring numbers preserve memories

Not long ago, a Caithness correspondent had something to say about old motor cars and registration numbers. His talk created so much interest here that I was encouraged to find out whether Orkney has a record of its first motor vehicles.

Some odd things turned up.

The Orkney registration letters are B.S. We have had them for sixty years, but at the end of 1964 another letter will be added.

The first car to run in Orkney belonged to tourists who stayed in Kirkwall for a week in the latter part of 1903. It was a Daimler-Benz.

The first Orkney registered car was not, as one might think, BS1, but BS7. In those days one could, more or less, choose one's number; and Mr W. R. Tullock of Kirkwall, having a liking for seven, selected it for his $3\frac{1}{2}$ hp Daimler-Benz four-seater. It was a rear-engined car which was started by hand, pulling the fly-wheel. It took the road on 3 March 1904.

BS1, however, was close behind—an 8 hp Peugeot, belonging to Mr William MacLennan, factor of the earldom estate, which was registered only twelve days afterwards. The number BS1 was transferred to several cars, and its last Orkney owner was Mr J. M. F. Groat of Longhope. It then belonged to a canvas-topped 1916 Crossley Tourer. Mr Groat had the number until three or four years ago.[1] It is now held somewhere in the south. The number of the first car, BS7, can still be seen in Bristol.

BS2 and BS3, like many other Orkney registered cars of the period, belonged at the outset to people in the south of England; for you were allowed then to register in any part of the country. The first holder of BS2, a Werner motor-cycle, was Michael O'Ryan of Sussex, and of BS3, a Rudge motor-cycle, Noel Byron of Kent. Both numbers later came back to Orkney.

It has become a fashion to have registration letters to match your initials. For instance, Billy Smart, the circus proprietor, has, or had recently, four

---

1. c.1958.

BS numbers—56, 57, 58 and 59. As in so many other things, however, he was anticipated by Bernard Shaw,[1] who obtained in November 1908 the number BS73. Shaw was then living at Adelphi Terrace, off The Strand. He had a wonderful car: a side entrance phaeton, with the back part detachable, which could be converted into a two-seater. The contraption was decorated with stripes of light green and dark green paint. It weighed twenty-nine hundredweights.

Another unusual vehicle was the motor bus put on the road by Robert Nicolson of Kirkwall in 1920. It was a horse-coach mounted on a Ford Model T truck chassis—it accommodated eleven passengers and its number was BS88. His son John G. Nicolson, who remembers the bus with sentimental affection, still holds the number on his latest car.[2]

Other early numbers to be seen in Orkney are BS5, BS6, BS21, BS25, BS32, BS43, BS84 and BS113, all of which were registered prior to 1912.

---

1. George Bernard Shaw, Irish dramatist and critic, 1856-1950.
2. The number was sold outwith Orkney in 1984.

53 Trucking the Boys ba', Kirkwall harbour, New Year's Day 1906.
   The game started at 8.30 am, the photograph was taken at 9 am and, the game over, the ba' has been hoisted to the top of the taller mast, that of the smack *Thomas Henry*.

55 Boys' Ploughing Match, South Ronaldsay, c.1980

54 A 'horse' parading in Cromarty Square, St Margaret's Hope, c.1980

14

The Kirkwall-Stromness bus

Someone reminded me the other day that it is now over fifty years[1] since motor buses appeared on the Orkney roads.

The first bus service between Kirkwall and Stromness started in July 1905 and was called *The Orkney Motor Express*. The conveyances, two Stirling single-deck buses, each capable of carrying sixteen passengers were owned by William Grant, proprietor of the Castle Hotel, Kirkwall, and operated by Mr W. R. Tullock. There was a time, earlier than that, when it looked as if a railway line would encircle the Mainland, but despite a lot of local interest, the proposal came to nothing.[2]

A double-deck bus came into service on 14 August 1906. It was an open top Leyland which seated forty-three passengers. On its first visit to Stromness it knocked down a gas lamp at the narrow entry to the town whereupon Stromness Town Council sued *The Orkney Motor Express* for the cost of a replacement.

It was ahead of its time, for farmers, among others, disliked the bus too much to make use of it. Running at a top speed of twelve to fourteen miles an hour, it filled horses and their drivers with dread. There is a story, for the truth of which I cannot vouch, that one frightened farmer, seeing its unimaginably fast and inexorable advance, tied his horse to a telegraph pole and jumped over a dyke to safety. This ultra-modern vehicle had solid tyres. On a hot day these were inclined to expand, so that the driver might suddenly see one of his tyres careering down the road in front of him. Considering the condition of roads, and the terrible solidness of these tyres, a ride on the topdeck must have been something of an adventure. Kirkwall used to brag that it had a motor bus before Edinburgh, but refrained from pointing out that its patronage of this vehicle was insufficient to keep it long on the road.

---

1. The article was written in 1958.
2. This was in 1873.

15

An islandman's war[1]

There are strategic areas in Northern Britain which, in time of peace, are allowed to forget their potentialities. Their great land-locked anchorages lie nakedly beneath the uninquisitive sky. On shore an unemphatic but prosperous rural community gravely pursues its concerns.

How well we know in the islands what happens when the country finally presents an ultimatum on behalf of the fifth or sixth little state whose integrity we have guaranteed. Even before Big Ben has boomed out the dead-line, and a tired Prime Minister has said something which he hopes will sound well in history books, the trek northwards has begun.

First of all, a dozen or two unlovely grey ships slink quietly into the shelter of our bays,[2] then our town, which is the capital of the area, grows bright with recently acquired gold braid. Pompous authorities commandeer our hotels and public buildings. Awkward lads in ill-fitting khaki greatcoats stand guard over our pier. Flirtatious Wrens, as cocky and inconsequent as their cheery namesake, make life bearable for their country's defenders. All over the place nissen huts are being built; camps, batteries and army laundries constructed. And everywhere troops with broad north-country accents are making contact with the farm folk, and endeavouring to dispossess them of their eggs and butter.

In the shop, where in peace-time we sell newspapers and cigarettes, books and stationery, toys and games, wallpaper and kitchen kettles, we make frantic efforts to grapple with war-time requirements. The order for Sunday 'pipers',[3] essential to home-based troops, must be increased by roughly five hundred per cent.

We discover that, in spite of educational statistics, men read comic papers up to the age of twenty-five or so. Suddenly a dozen different tobaccos,

> 1. This article was based on Ernest Marwick's own experiences working in Stevenson's Bookshop at the junction of Bridge Street and Albert Street. He uses pen names throughout, but the last character mentioned, Benetto, clearly is his friend Chiocchetti.
> 2. See 'The rôle of Scapa Flow', p.424.
> 3. Papers.

which our normal clientele would not touch with a barge pole, are in constant demand. It becomes clear that young ladies in service uniform have developed tastes in stationery that we are unable to satisfy, so delicate pinks and greens and mauves find a place among our azure woves and superfines. There is a shortage of cosmetics, so we gatecrash on this complicated line, and become familiar with pancake make-up, cream rouge, setting lotions and what not.

Fragile war-time friendships between the sexes demand suitable expression. Thus a good deal of service pay finds its way into our fancy goods section. All day our counters are besieged by strangers who outnumber the residents by two to one.

During most of the week our book counter is the Cinderella of the shop. While the stationery department is dispensing much beribboned birthday cards by the dozen, and the cosmetic corner is rationing unsuccessfully the latest consignment of cheap lipstick, the book counter, looking like a pathetic step-child of the newspaper department, sells only an odd copy of *No Mean City*, *Miss Blandish*,[1] or their equivalents. True, the illusion of normality returns when a country clergyman comes to spend a pound or two on prizes for his Sunday School, or when the local spinster of uncertain age asks sweetly for the latest 'romance stories', but the illusion is quickly dispelled by the alien Cockney voice at one's ear, demanding 'Somethink by Joan Butler, chum.'[2]

There is one day, however, when the book counter comes into its own. On Saturday, for some reason best known to itself, the army is conspicuous by its absence from our streets. Its place is taken by the Senior Service. From ships at the base, from Fleet Air Arm messes, from hush-hush establishments, from wreneries, from commandeered hotels, gallant and self-conscious lieutenants, captains and other officers of both sexes pour into the town. The shop becomes filled with pleasant people, talking what our assistants call high English, and acting in a slightly unnatural way in their highly unnatural circumstances. These aristocrats of the base have from the first been conscious of their status as intellectuals. They are flying the flag of culture in an outpost of the Empire. So they are reading extensively, and very seriously and critically, all the things which the highbrow war-time reviews sententiously discuss. Poetry, as always in war-time, is read widely, and new fashions in esoteric religion are frequent. Knapsack anthologies come out by the dozen: *The Spirit of Man*[3] is reprinted and finds its way on to our shelves.

★ ★ ★

1. *No Mean City* was written by Alexander McArthur and H. Kingsley Long; *No Orchids for Miss Blandish* was the work of James Hadley Chase.
2. A writer of humorous fiction.
3. By F. J. Allsopp.

All Saturday, with other duties delegated or postponed, I stand at the book counter and traffic with these earnest young people, who have so lately aspired to the glory of uniform. Wren officers, with presents for masculine opposite numbers in mind, try to cajole from me books which are in short supply. Brilliant displays of dentures hail the production of some elusive *Oxford Book* or *The Snow Goose*, or Peter Scott's handsome, if rather thin, *Wild Chorus* and *Morning Flight*. Freshly-fledged intellectuals repair their lack of T. S. Eliot and Edith Sitwell. Students of another type ask innocently for *Ulysses* or *The Well of Loneliness*. Then there is a percentage of aggressive low-brows who slap down their eight and sixpence for Peter Cheyney and Gerald Kersh.[1] These, exploiting a mental as well as a physical masculinity, are not without their feminine counterpart.

As Saturday succeeds Saturday, certain faces become familiar. The freckled Wren with the Irish accent, from the Fleet Mail Office, is always adding fresh volumes to her set of Kipling. Lieut. T—— of the FAA asks regularly for his Left Book Club choice two weeks before it is due. The rather austere young lady, who was the peace-time secretary of a famous poet, becomes more friendly, and shares an enthusiasm for Donne, eagerly and ingenuously. The old Commander, who merely wants 'a rattling good yarn' and hates to choose it for himself, becomes a crony and a confederate. He loves to relate the humours of the base, without giving a fig for the Official Secrets Act. All these people and a hundred more impress their features on one's mind and often revisit the memory. But there are others, richly individual, of whom one thinks deliberately and gratefully.

★ ★ ★

Such a one, chosen from several worthy runners-up, was Lieutenant Brown. This unlikely representative of the Silent Service was just over the minimum height, his features were non-patrician, unfairly so, and his hair, a reddish-brown, escaped untidily from his naval cap. An air of tired cynicism affected his features when he remembered to assume it. His greatcoat was a couple of inches too long, but this was apparently ignored by the educational unit into which a cherished university degree had carried him. Lieutenant Brown's appearance was soon familiar to me. Every Saturday he turned up about mid-afternoon, and spent half an hour or so browsing among the books. His literary wants were apparently few, for we never did any business together, and he consistently ignored my presence. Once I saw him looking enviously at a new volume of verse by a snob poet much in vogue. I was feeling very good-natured that day, also a little sorry for Brown, who was obviously an odd stick. I went up to him and suggested—a thing which I

---

1. Peter Cheyney wrote crime stories, and Gerald Kersh produced thrillers.

could seldom risk doing—that he might care to take a loan of my own copy and return it to me the following Saturday. He looked me up and down with ineffable contempt, replied 'Not really, thank you,' and walked away.

He did not return again for three weeks. Had I offended him? I had not. For when he appeared again he had acquired a Mrs Brown. How he managed to find anyone so like himself in features was a miracle. I soon found out, however, that Mrs Brown was very different in temperament; she was docile to a fault. It also began to appear that Mrs B's poetical education had been neglected. For, every Saturday, Lieutenant Brown brought her to the shop, and, esconcing himself with her in a not too public corner of the book department, read to her from one of the immortals. He would seat himself comfortably on the edge of a table. With Mrs Brown standing before him, he read and commented. His wife's look of total non-comprehension was bewildering, but the Lieutenant did not seem to notice. She must have been a very pleasant pupil after the rough bunch of practical jokers he tried vainly to educate at the base.

As I passed I would hear him say: ' "Life like a dome of many coloured glass stains the white radiance of eternity"—you see, darling, the poet is making an allusion to the spectroscope.' And Mrs Brown would reply obediently, 'Yes, dear.' This went on for about three months. Never during this time did the Lieutenant make a purchase; never did he condescend to notice my presence. But I had my reward at last.

On the occasion of his last visit—he had been posted—I heard him say, 'Darling, I adore this shop. It's so frankly commercial!'

* * *

As the war went on, other voices, a trifle uncertain at first, began to be heard through the tumult of British and neo-British accents. To begin with, these were the voices of allies; then, in the later stages, the voices of erstwhile enemies, captured, bewildered, and harmless. All this ill-assorted fraternity, at one time or another, found their way into the bookshop, some of them many times. A few became friends, in that queer inexplicable war-time way.

There was Paddy, whose grey face betokened the first morning I saw him, although I only knew this months later, that he had just brought in his little ship from a brush with the enemy, with her captain lying dead beside him in the wheel-house.

The tall, olive-skinned, saturnine figure who accompanied Paddy on his visits to the book-shop had become well-known to me, but I had never had a single glimpse of his personality. He talked in monosyllables. He was very aloof to everyone, but Paddy seemed to understand him perfectly. It was for Paddy's sake we agreed when our disreputable friend asked if he might take a Norwegian, Bertel, to the house one day. On his first visit

Bertel was a little stiff and awkward, his English showed up badly: two years without the amenities of home life had made him shy of teacups and small talk. But it was clear to us at once that his natural environment was the home and family. We liked him enough to ask him back, and were pleased and a little surprised when we found that he reciprocated the feeling sufficiently to take us very much at our word. Soon Bertel was a frequent visitor. Presently he adopted us. On his regular monthly week-ends ashore he made his home with us. He had his own particular chair and his own particular place in the family. He would come and go quite happily without the necessity of entertainment. Probably our friendship was possible because we could appreciate the honesty of some of his devastatingly direct statements and laugh often at their incongruity. In such laughter he would sometimes join us, although never very sure of its import.

As time went on, he would tell us a little about the grim life which he lived on the clumsy vessel he commanded. But, like most of his comrades of the North Patrol, his respect for the tradition of silence was strong. The reason for a week-end of taciturnity might not become apparent until months later, when the need for secrecy had gone. He would talk freely about his crew, most of whom we knew. The majority of the men were simply 'All right', and no amount of scrapes on shore could affect this judgment: in fact he relished very much as a man some of the naughty escapades he had to punish as an officer. But woe betide the man of whom he said simply, 'He ees no goot.' Nothing atoned in his eyes for the lack of seamanship and courage. His dislike of the Germans was particularly strong at this date, incidents which he was prohibited from relating had filled him with a chilling disgust. He professed to approve strongly of the action of a Polish ship with which he had made contact on his latest patrol. The crew of this vessel had picked up a boat filled with shipwrecked Germans. These had been 'rescued', tried by a grim and unlawfully constituted court on shipboard, and hanged individually from the ship's bowsprit. 'Dey deed quite right,' said Bertel. ' I would haf done de same.' We would shake our heads unbelievingly. 'No, perhaps not,' he would agree, 'but dey deserve eet all de same.' Then a sick dislike of the whole sad business would cloud his eyes. He would rise hastily and go in search of Mhari, whose schoolgirl enthusiasms he was able to share and sometimes surpass.

Mhari and he were comrades from the first. He easily detected a likeness in temperament if not in features to little Anna, just a hundred miles away in Evjafiord. Mhari loved to see Anna's photograph and to hear stories of her. Then she would ask for more tales, and Bertel would rack his brains for exciting incidents from the sagas, with which he had grown very familiar, reading them on his long spells at sea. We were not sorry that Mhari should become as familiar with Gretir and Bui and Rognvald, or with the mythical

Baldur, as most little girls are with Snow White or Rumpelstiltskin. Often she would sit silently on his knee, while he sang verses of the Norwegian National Hymn. This song has the undoubted merit of recalling the country's heroes and its reasons for pride. I gave Bertel a copy of William Ellery Leonard's translation, which he liked. He would repeat its opening lines approvingly:

> Yes, we love this land together,
> Where the wild sea foams,
> Furrowed, beat by wind and weather,
> With the thousand homes.
> Yes, we love her; with her blending
> Father, mother, birth,
> And that saga-twilight sending
> Dreams upon our earth.

He also approved the lines, 'Women too stood up that day, Smote as they were men,' but over those immediately following he would shake his head irritably—'Others could but weep and pray, Nor was that in vain.' 'Dat is not right, dat is not vat ve say,' he repeated, 'Dese crying women vere no use.' Bertel's idea of heroism, like that of many of his countrymen, was derived from the nation's war-like past. The sweet and gentle ladies of English romance annoyed him. Mhari, whose temperament was at the moment belligerent, and whose favourite heroine was St Joan, agreed with him heartily. During the discussion, Bertel inadvertently let slip that he sometimes found it necessary to spank his wife Sölven. Later, he plainly regretted that admission, but his tremendous regard for truth would not allow him to repudiate it.

How greatly Bertel's toughness was undermined by sentiment, and by very strong emotion, we already knew. With some future project in mind, he had taken to learning German. He appropriated the gramophone, which mostly stood silent during those busy, anxious days. With his portfolio of Linguaphone records open beside him, he would stand for hours over the whirling turntable, repeating after the mechanical instructor: 'Vater . . . mutter . . . grossevater . . . grossemutter. . . .' But he always ended by playing a record he had somehow acquired, one of John MacCormack singing, 'I'll Walk Beside You.' How often that record was played I cannot pretend to guess. It must have been many times, for my clearest recollection of Bertel is of him standing silently while it played, his face sad, his eyes entirely expressionless. The song has become imperishably associated for us with thoughts of Sölven and little Anna. It was the complete contradiction to Bertel's pretended cynicism. One day he burst in like a happy boy, his whole leathery face shining like a soft, well-polished old boot, and his eyes dancing. A letter had reached him from Evjafiord, through the activities of the Red

Cross. It contained a recent snap of his wife and daughter. Sölven looked grave but was boldly trying to smile. Little Anna, with four years on her head, was no longer little Anna. She was a self-conscious young lady of fourteen, very correct, very prim, but very lovable. Bertel had two enlarged copies of this snap made for him: one he tacked up above his bunk in the *Nordala*, the other he gave to Mhari.

How much a part of the family Bertel had become, we did not realise until he had left us. He had become familiar with the dates of birthdays, and with the inwardness of many little family anniversaries. He was accepted by gruff, playful old Jock, who loved to take a mouthful of his trouser leg and to persuade him to take a walk on the moors in the dry windy days of March, or to swim with him in summer. Bertel and Jock put the devil into each other. Away out on the moors they would wrestle together, with entire abandon on the part of Bertel and growling delight on the part of Jock. I shall never forget the look of blank astonishment on the faces of two sober young sailors when they came suddenly on their taciturn captain and old Jock in the middle of one of their high-spirited frolics. They saluted and went on hastily. 'I make dem scrub out my cabin with cold water,' said Bertel afterwards, 'to show dem dat my head is all right.'

It looked as if our friendship might be permanent, although we ought to have known better. But the war ended at last. In quick succession came the victories in Italy, D-Day, and the sordid end of the mad chancellor in a cellar in Berlin. Once more the *Nordala* went on patrol. Then she was ordered to Chatham. One letter came from England, to be followed by one from Norway. Bertel's Linguaphone conversations had become useful: he was given a task in making his country's navy Norwegian again, and in speeding the parting Germans. There was a snapshot in his letter, taken on the harbour-front at Oslo. Standing proudly against a background of masts and funnels were Sölven and Anna.

★ ★ ★

Of a very different type was Monsieur X. We called him that, for his real name we never knew. A quiet-voiced French naval officer, cultured and gracious, he first made our acquaintance when he was looking, in his fastidious way, for *un livre de cadeau*. The book was for his daughter, a charming young damsel (he had her picture) of just *dix-sept*—'seventeen, you say. She know your Scott and Deekens. O yes, we read them mooch. *Jane Eyre* and your *Pride and Préjudice* we do not know. Are they to be read by *jeune filles*? Do they have anything that *ma fillette* should not know till she marry?' Our belief in the precocity of French *demoiselles* was shattered by this quiet gentleman. He decided at last that Poppée should have a copy of *Alice*.

On subsequent visits he confided to me that his wife was a well-known writer, but not a *femme savante*, 'blue-stocking, I think. O no!' Which modern French writers did we sell most easily? Francois Mauriac and André Maurois. 'O, but Maurois he is, what you say, friend of my heart, *ami de coeur*. But he is not French, he is English we tell heem. I shall see heem soon. Shall I give heem your salutations?' How ready he was to forget the war, and all its implications; charming, anonymous Monsieur X.

There was an interlude of Russians; for the long submarine-infested route to Murmansk was being kept open, although at great cost. Tall, heavily-fleshed and friendly, with grave, stoical faces, these sailors from the north were innocent of a single word of English. They developed a sign-language which they repeated, or varied when necessary, with infinite patience, until they were understood. This primitive form of communication was adequate only at first for denoting the simpler commodities, but its range and intelligibility increased until it could refer to such complex things as typewriter ribbons or treasury tags. These likeable and unsophisticated allies had heard many tales of the poverty of the British proletariat. With embarrassing generosity they would slip a rouble into the hand of anyone who did them a trifling service, and wave off refusals and explanations with beneficent non-comprehension.

★ ★ ★

At last the Allied armies began to creep slowly up the coast of Italy. There were several mass surrenders, for the Latins had by this time only one definite war aim—an entirely pacific one. The necessary camps for the detention of those prisoners were difficult to find, so it occurred to the authorities that one group could be usefully accommodated on a remote Scottish island, where constructional work of high importance was being carried on.

This island's supreme distinction was its total lack of amenities. It was as bare as a billiard table, uncultivated and uninhabited. In ugly huts in this wilderness several hundred men, fresh from the warmth and colour of the Mediterranean, were billeted. At first the contrast numbed them. 'Eet ees so cold,' sighed Guilio. Life was not worth a *bajocco*.

But the slow spring gave place to summer. With the sun, gaiety and light-heartedness returned. Angelo, on his frequent visits to our town, fell in love with the pretty wife of a naval officer, who presided over our Stationery Department. It fell to me to explain to him the hopelessness of his passion. Angelo was apologetic and miserable, but he felt that his advances had met with some response. However, women were like that—*cosi fan tutte* —and Angelo soon found new worlds to conquer. The prophecy in his dictionary-compiled letter: 'If you love me not, I die immediately soon,' did not come to pass.

Months passed before I became acquainted with Benetto. He was unlike the others, very tall and brown-haired, very quiet and shy—very un-Italian, one would have said. But Benetto was Italian all right, of that type, rare enough perhaps, who have made their country the aesthetic home of civilised men. He used to purchase with his meagre earnings—made from the sale of little pictures on wood—paints and brushes and paper.

He had little English, but on the interchange of simple ideas in this primitive currency a friendship grew, until we discovered by accident, in Latin, an easy gateway into each other's minds. The barriers had fallen. One day Benetto confided to me his great project. He meant to build a church. I gasped. We were standing together in the Cathedral, examining a flake or two of fresco which still remain. Benetto quoted proudly but with a little embarrassment, Corregio's famous '*anch' io son pittore*'. Then his idea was let loose on a torrent of words.

I thought at first that he was building cloud-castles around what might happen when the war was over, and he had returned to the architect's office in Naples. But not a bit of it. His church was to be built on the lonely holm where he and his compatriots were confined.

'There is nothing there, my good Edmund, to praise God. The concrete and the bulldozers do not praise Him. The bare rocks do not know him.'

'The seas praise Him, Benetto, and the larks know Him.'

'True, my friend, but man was created to praise Him, his hands were made to glorify Him. It is there I shall build my church.'

'But the materials, Benetto? The hewn stones, the coloured glass, the carved oak?'

'They are not of this age,' he said sadly. 'Of this age are cement and corrugated iron.'

As he went away, I watched him with strange emotions, the slim figure in the green battle-dress with the brown diamond on its back, who had been possessed by an overmastering idea.

How that idea was realised I still find it difficult to understand. But realised it was. That barren island, which has not heard the argot of the Mediterranean for over six years, has a church in which no one worships, but which still stands to the glory of God.

The wind and rain beat on it harshly, but, although vulnerable to the elements, it is still beautiful; an object lesson in what the human spirit can do with concrete and corrugated iron. For its skeleton is a nissen hut, clothed with cement. Its interior is rich with the skilful painting which imitates carved reliefs and primitive frescoes. The plain glass of its windows has been transformed with brightly-hued saints. Rusty iron from the sea-bed was forged and beaten until a chaste screen of metalwork emerged.

Over the altar is Benetto's masterpiece, the Madonna, on which he lavished so much care and skill. The sweet features may be those of Gabrielle in Florence or of Beatrice in Turin, but the spirit in the picture is that of simple adoration. One feels grateful to the generous young officer in charge of the camp who permitted the constant inroads on his cement and the persistent demands on the paint-shop. And one is sad and angry that there are people who can visit the place and chalk up crude anti-Roman slogans on its walls.

But the predominant feeling is one of pride, that men reduced to poverty and imprisonment can create from ugly materials a shrine for the spirit of eternal beauty.[1]

---

1. See also 'The Italian Chapel', p.453.

THIS FORM IS FOR THE SOLE USE OF THE HEADQUARTERS.

FORM "A."

THE GIRL GUIDES ORGANISATION.

County _Orkney_

Commissioner _None_

Local Committee _Kirkwall, consisting of 15 names of representative ladies in Kirkwall_

REGISTRATION FORM.

Name of Company _1st Kirkw~~ar~~ 1st Kirkwall Company._

Address of Company Headquarters _None - At present the Guides meet once a week in the Burgh School, Kirkwall, which the funds pay for, but all communications are sent to me as Sec.y_

Name of Captain _Miss Rose Alice Leith_

Address _Rognvalsey, Dundas Crescent, Kirkwall_

1. Name of Lieutenants _Miss Meta Sinclair, 14 Queen Street, Kirkwall;_

Address _↑ Miss Lila Garrioch, Bridge St, Kirkwall_

Date of formation of Company or Patrol _September, 1916_

Date of registration _17th June, 1919_

Total strength of Guides _60 (8 Patrols)_

(1.) Is the Company an independent one raised by an individual Captain, or is it under the control of some Church, School, or other body specified in Girl Guide Regulations? ... _Independent, raised principally by Captain_

(2.) If the latter, who is responsible for the management of the Company and the appointment of the Captain? ... _The Local Committee_

Signed _Rose A. Leith_ Captain.

Date _16th June, 1919_

(Mrs) _Katherine W. Heddle_ County Secretary.

Approved _by Local Committee_ ~~Commissioner~~

Kirkwall District.

* In cases where there is not a Local Committee this form must be accompanied by letters of personal recommendation from three well-known Ladies of Local Standing and returned to Headquarters, 76, Victoria Street, London, S.W.

Date of Final Approval _17th June, 1919_ _Margaret Trotter_

The Girl Guides
(INCORPORATED).

REGISTRATION FORM.
FOR ~~GUIDE OR RANGER COMPANIES OR~~ BROWNIE PACKS.

Fee 1/-

(*In order to ensure accuracy, please write in BLOCK LETTERS.*)

County _Orkney_
Division
District _Kirkwall_
Name of Company or Pack _1st Kirkwall Company's Brownie Pack_

Name of ~~Captain or~~ Brown Owl _Miss Rita Wright_
Address _Hopemount Kirkwall_
Name of ~~Lieutenant or~~ Tawny Owl _Miss Ruby Johnston_
Address _Marston Kirkwall_
Total strength of ~~Guides~~ _Brownies_ _36_
Date of formation of (Company, Patrol or) Pack _6th May 1922_

*Date of Registration (*To be filled in by Headquarters only*)

(1.) Is the Company raised by the Local Association or a Guider in conjunction with them? ... _by a Guider trained by Capt. 1st K'wa Coy & approved by Local Assoc._

(2.) Is the Company attached specially to any Church, Chapel, School, Factory, Kindred Society or other body? ... _no_

(Please state particulars fully) ...

(3.) If the Company is an attached one, will the representative of the body sign this form, recommending the appointment of the Guider, and agreeing to work in conjunction with the Local G.G. Association, according to the Rules of the Girl Guides ...

(Signed) _Rose A. Leith_
Representing _1st Kirkwall G.G._
Approved _Norah Martin Laing_
~~District~~ County Commissioner.
Katherine W. Heddle
County Secretary.

*Where there is not a Local Committee this form must be accompanied by letters of personal recommendation from three well-known Ladies of Local Standing and returned to Headquarters, 25, Buckingham Palace Road, S.W. 1.

Harrison & Sons, Ltd.

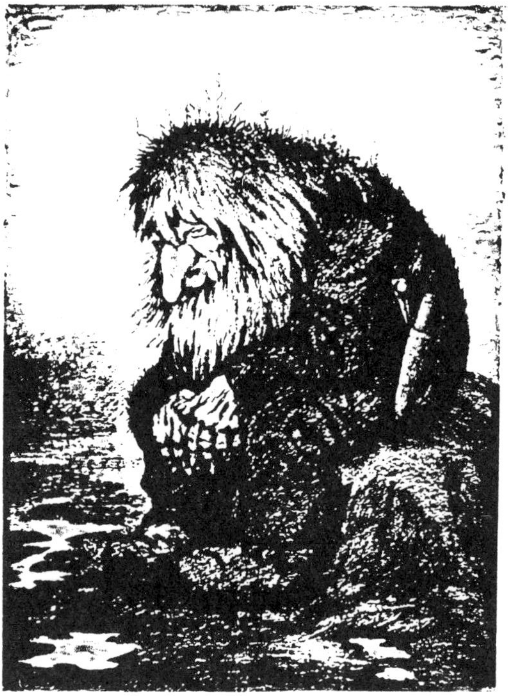

LORE AND LEGEND

LEGENDARY CREATURES

1 Creatures of Orkney legend and their Norse ancestry	257
2 Tales of island fairies	279
3 Nessie's cousins	282
4 The man from nowhere	288
5 The peerie fool and the princess	290

I

Creatures of Orkney Legend and their Norse ancestry

Numbers indicate sources appearing at end of article, on p.278.
Letters indicate explanatory footnotes on relative pages: *Editor*.

Up to now no attempt has been made in Orkney to compare the legendary creatures which come into our folk tales with Norwegian originals. I make such an attempt in this essay. Even if it is not successful it may have the merit of preserving some unfamiliar lore. It cannot be pretended that there is a great deal of Orcadian traditional material which has not been recorded in one form or another, but for such a survey as this it is necessary to use both the well known and the little known. In using this material with care and gratitude one may, I think, show one's faith in the work of former Orkney folklorists, and thus pay them the best compliment one can offer.

The most primitive, most elemental beings in Norwegian folklore were the *jotner*, or giants. These lived in the mountains and partook of their nature. They were of immense bulk and grotesque shape. Just as a mountain may have several peaks, giants could have several heads. Three, six or nine were common, and one fantastic *jotun* mentioned in the *Edda* was endowed with 900 heads. Their huge eyes were blank and deep, like mountain tarns.

It seems that these giants had their own peculiar territories. When they quarrelled they threw things at each other: the Rendal *jotun*, for example, flung his great stone axe over the valley at the Glaamdal *jotun* who fell dead. They were creatures of the night. An Eddic poem tells of a giantess named Rimgjerd who was turned into a stone when struck by the rays of the rising sun. The *jotner* built bridges, *jotulbroer*. Sometimes these took the form of a long shoal across a bay or inlet, or a ridge of beach cutting off a lagoon, called an 'ayre' in Orkney.

Despite the fact that the lack of mountains in Orkney would have made it difficult to give the giant legends the credibility that they had at home in Norway, there are traces of them in Orkney folklore. The word *jotun* appears, if infrequently, in place-names. A pool enclosed by rocks on the coast of Papa

Westray is called Ettan's Pow. There is a standing stone known as the Yetna-steen in Rousay, and in Burray there is the Echna Loch. The late Dr Hugh Marwick derived Trussins Geo in Papa Westray from Old Norse *þursinn*, 'the giant'.

One can easily discover the legend of the giant turned into stone in the Yetna-steen, which goes down immediately after midnight on New Year morning to the Loch of Scockness for a drink. In the parish of Birsay there is a similar legend about the Stone of Quoyboon, which finds its way each New Year morning to the Loch of Boardhouse, but is always back in its place *before dawn*. The *jotun* bridge is conspicuous at the Echna Loch, where a perfect 'bridge' of shingle and sand has been piled up by the sea. Stone-flinging, a propensity of the *jotner*, comes into various Orkney legends. There is a large boulder in Copinsay known as the Giant Stone. The legend is that a giant flung it from Stembister in Toab, St Andrews. It is interesting to know that the name of this farm comes from Old Norse *stein-bólstaðr*, 'stone-farm'.

Standing-stone legends more explicit than the Orkney ones were remembered in Shetland. In a footnote to his account of the parishes of Sandsting and Aithsting in the *New Statistical Account* of 1841, the Rev. John Bryden wrote:

> I may mention the tradition respecting two standing stones in the neighbourhood of West Skeld [now Wester Skeld]. . . . These two stones are said to be the metamorphosis of two wizards or giants, who were on their way to plunder and murder the inhabitants of West Skeld; but not having calculated their time with sufficient accuracy, before they could accomplish their purpose, or retrace their steps to their dark abodes, the first rays of the morning sun appeared, and they were immediately transformed, and remain to the present time in the shape of two tall moss-grown stones of ten feet in height.

In a way which has many parallels in folklore a mass of *jotun* legends were transferred in Orkney to an actual person, the Norse chieftain Kolbein Hruga, who had his home in Wyre and who is referred to in the most specific way in the Orkneyinga Saga. In local tradition he became Cubbie Roo, a giant so big that he used the islands as stepping stones. He was, when angry, an accomplished stone thrower; a boulder which he threw from Fitty Hill in Westray at a giant on Kierfea Hill in Rousay fell short and lies beside the Wasbister shore. It is known as the Finger-steen,[A] for Cubbie Roo's finger marks are supposed to be visible in it. They are visible too in the Cubbie Roo Stone lying in the Evie Hills north of the Dale of Woodwick. There is

---

[A]. Situated in the Lower Leean, which runs up to the Wasbister-Sourin boundary. There are other such stones, with the reputed finger-marks of Cubbie Roo, at Marlaryar in the Rousay hills and in the hill near Onziebust. (EWM)

another boulder bearing his name in Stronsay, said to have been thrown to waken a brother giant who was slow to get up in the morning.

Several bridge-building exploits, none of them successful, are attributed to Cubbie Roo. He began to build a bridge from Rousay to Wyre, and carried some of the stones in a kaesy, or heather basket, on his back, but the band of the basket broke and the stones were deposited in a mound still known as Cubbie Roo's Burden. Other story-tellers identified the contents of the gigantic kaesy with the Skerry o' the Soond in Eynhallow Sound. In Sanday it was related that the bridge was intended to join the Red Head of Eday with Weatherness in Westray, and the tumbling stones formed the Red Holm. The Danes Pier in Stronsay was also identified with the discarded 'burden'. Here the bridge was to extend from Stronsay to Auskerry.

In the West Mainland of Orkney the tale of the giant losing his load was conceived on a much grander scale than in the North Isles. This giant was a Scottish one, who waded across the Pentland Firth to collect a kaesy-full of earth from Orkney. The depressions from which he scooped up the soil and rock became the Stenness and Harray Lochs. As the giant left the Orkney shore to go home a sod fell off his heaped kaesy, which still remains as the island of Graemsay. He had gone only a little further when the fettle (carrying rope) of the kaesy broke, and the whole vast load tumbled into the sea, to become the Hills of Hoy.

Possibly we can see in these local tales a dim memory of the giant Ymir, out of whose body, according to the Scandinavian myth, Odin and his brothers built the world, making the seas and lakes of his blood, earth of his flesh, and the sky of his skull.[1]

In the older Norwegian legends the *jotner* and the huge mountain trolls are hardly distinguishable. The latter liked to spirit away beautiful girls, princesses in particular, whom they forced to spin all day and to scratch the troll's head all night. The Rousay story of Peerie Fool[2] contains some of these elements. A giant seizes in turn three princesses, and each girl has to 'take wool and wash and tease it, and comb and card and spin, and make claith.'[A] The low intelligence of the giant, or troll, insisted on in some Norwegian tales, is also evident: he is outwitted by the third princess and meets his death when a boiler of scalding water is emptied over him.

Hoy, with its high hills and deep valleys was, like Rousay, an obvious place for the *jotner* to inhabit. Two huge rocks on the slopes of the Ward Hill above the Nowt Bield were said to be the home of a giant who attacked anyone who ventured on to the hill after dark.

Giantesses also come into the picture. Two of these were bond-maids to a Danish king called Frodi. Their names were Fenia and Menia, and Frodi kept them at work turning a magic quern of massive size, called Grotti, which

A. Cloth.

would grind out whatever it was asked to grind. The giantesses were held so mercilessly to their task of grinding out gold for Frodi that they rebelled, and ground out an army to free them from this rigorous servitude. The result was that a sea-rover named Mysing overthrew and killed Frodi, helped himself to his gold and possessions, and sailed away with Fenia, Menia and the magic quern. The song which these giant-maidens sang as they ground out the army will be found in my *Anthology of Orkney Verse*,[3] together with a fuller account of the legend. The reason why it is mentioned here is that Mysing was supposed, according to some of the old story-tellers, to have sailed through the Pentland Firth. At sea he commanded the giantesses to grind salt and the ship became so heavy with it that it sank near Stroma, creating the whirlpool known as the Swelchie, at the bottom of which is the quern Grotti, turning endlessly and making the sea salt.

When Dr Jakob Jakobsen, the Faroese philologist was in Orkney in the autumn of 1909, he met a woman who said that she had heard in South Ronaldsay the story of the salt-grinding quern in the Pentland Firth. A tale he had heard a decade or so before, taken apparently from Orkney to Fair Isle, concerned two witches known as Grotti Finnie and Grotti Minnie.[4] John Spence of Evrabist put on record in 1911 a Birsay saying: 'As lang as Lucky Minnie sat i' Fusbar, an' hid was seevan year o' Yule daes!'[A, 5]

In Orkney the Norwegian trolls became diminished in size owing to the greatly reduced scale of the landscape. The word troll was also changed to trow, possibly at a time well after the first Norse settlement of the islands, for in Shetland many of the associated names begin with troll (Trolladale, Trolla skerries, Trolligart, Trollhoulland, and so on) and in Orkney we have Trollawatten (loch of the trolls) in North Ronaldsay, and fishing rocks in Birsay known as the Ooter and Inner Troola. There are, however, a number of trow names as well, the best known being the Trowie Glen in Hoy. Most of the others are known only locally, such as Trowswal, near Westerhouse in Birsay, and the Trow's Chest, Trow's Kettle and Trow's Chair on the coast of Deerness.[6] What I suggest about the comparative age of these names seems to be borne out by the fact that the 'troll' names are compounded with Norse words, while the 'trow' names are used in conjunction with Scots (or English) words.

But even more remarkable, there are several Stronsay people living today who can tell you still the names of several of the island trows. Here is the list I have collected: Eelick (or Alick), Bollick (or Dollick), Gimp, Kork, Tring, Keelbrue, Bellia, Horny and Barnifeet or Bannafeet. Kork and Tring were said to have been Eday trows who had changed their abode.[7]

From trow we have the word 'trowy', meaning sickly when it applies to a person, or of poor quality when it refers to an object. The classic story

A. As long as Lucky Minnie sat in Fusbar, and it was seven years of Yule days!

56 Cattle Show, Dounby, 1912

57 Annual Show, Dounby, 1914

58 Putting on Junction Road, Kirkwall, c.1905

59 Hurdy-gurdy man with organ and monkey, Dundas Street, Stromness, c.1905

relating to this use of the word has been retold more than once, but here is how John Spence of Evrabist told it originally to Provost Nicol Spence of Kirkwall in a letter dated 22 November 1897:

> John Spence of Millbrig [flourished c.1800] sat down one summer evening on the green earth dyke at the Owlidens not far from his house to herd cattle. Another old man came along and sat beside him and they began to talk. The stranger pulled out his snuff-box and offered old John Spence a snuff. John took the snuff-box, but found it to be a sorry specimen, all 'chawed' and frayed at the end. 'Ah man,' he said, 'ye hae a vera trowy snuff-box.' No sooner had he uttered the word 'trow' than off the old man vanished in glowing spunks of fire away out into the Moss of Teamora.

Here the trow looked like any old man, and latter-day Norwegian trolls could also take on the appearance of human beings. In Norway, as in Orkney, the distinctions between the different kinds of legendary creatures grew somewhat blurred, but not nearly so blurred as in these islands, where people now know of only two kinds, trows and fairies, and use the terms indiscriminately. If at this late date we are to make any distinction at all between the vague beings who appear in our traditional tales we must become familiar with their originals in Norwegian folklore, which generations of folklorists have more or less sorted out. There can be no hard and fast distinctions, however, for the mountain trolls and the various types of underworld people, the *underjordiske*, had various things in common, in particular a propensity for courting personable young women.

It is not my intention here to trespass on, far less attempt to retell, the sea myths collected by Walter Traill Dennison, and printed in *Orkney Folklore and Traditions*,[8] and I shall only advert to them where they overlap with my present material or where I can add a few facts from other sources. Creatures which are fully described in the book mentioned, such as the Stoor Worm, Nuckelavee, the Mither o' the Sea, Terran, and in large measure the Selkie Folk, have therefore no place in this collection. The Fin Folk I shall have a special reason for discussing.

My plan is to take a group of mythical creatures from Norse legend, pick out their most characteristic features, and then try to discover any parallels that Orkney folklore may offer. The beings I have in mind are trolls, *dverger* (dwarfs), *huldrefolk*, the *nisse*, *alver* and *tusser* (elves, fairies), and the *nøkk*. The few things one can suggest about the Orkney *jotner* have already been said.

To return, then, to the trolls. They were monstrously ugly, covered with hair, and had very long noses. They were nocturnal creatures to whom sunlight was fatal. They lived inside mountains, where they frequently had hoards of treasure. All high mountains had a special troll. They often had a foul smell, but in their turn disliked intensely the smell of Christians. For the most part they were peaceable, stupid and slow to act, but were savage when teased. The only weapon man had against them when they were roused to fury was his superior intelligence. There is a decided likeness between these creatures and bears, and one is not surprised to learn that they kept bears as pets. Among refinements allowed them in later legends were an ability to travel rapidly through the air and to transform themselves into what looked like human beings. In the older mythology thunder was the scourge of the trolls. It was believed that they were struck down during a thunder storm by 'thunder-stones'—round smooth stones of rock crystal or common quartz. The thunder-god (Thor) was thus acting for the good of human beings and it was said that without thunder, the whole world would be poisoned by the trolls.

In Orkney thunder was known until recent times as 'Geud's weather' (God's, i.e. Thor's weather). In Hedemark, in Norway, it was said that, 'if thunder strikes down in the open furrow during the spring work it will be a good year for the farm.' Similarly in Orkney there was a proverb: 'February thunder is a world's wonder.' Thunder-stone was not a term used in Orkney, but quartz pebbles were called 'haley-stones' (holy stones). I can remember gathering these as a boy on a piece of rough hillside which had just been ploughed. Numbers of them can be found in the walls of most old houses, for it was considered that they kept the occupants safe from danger and warded off the lightning.

Trolls in Orkney were said to be of two kinds, hill-trows and sea-trows. The sea-trow is remembered vaguely and does not quite seem to correspond with anything in Norwegian folklore. Like the Nordland merman, its head was covered with seaweed, so that the sea-trow was sometimes known as Tangy; but this creature was monstrous whereas the merman was supposed to be either extremely little or at least not bigger than a human being. In fact the Orkney sea-trow was more like a mountain trow which had suffered a sea-change: he was most ungainly, with a pointed head, miserably clumsy arms and legs, a lean, wizened body, and round, shuffling feet. It may be symptomatic of a change in the tradition, necessitated by the Orkney landscape, that—as Dennison emphasises[9]—he was banished to the sea by the land trows, but this is not a theory I would care to carry further on such slight evidence.

Nowadays it is extremely difficult to distinguish the land trow, or hill-trow, from various other creatures, often called generically 'hill-folk' or 'hillyans' (Papa Westray). A very broad generalisation might be made on the analogy of a saying once common among amateur bird-watchers: 'If you see a lot of crows together they're rooks; if you see a single rook it's a crow.'

Modify that to: 'If you find a tale with a whole crowd of mythical creatures in it, they are not trows; if you discover a story with a single one, or only a few, you are more likely to have a genuine trow story.' Even then, you must not forget that the Devil himself was frequently called 'The Trow'.

A story in which the trow of the classic tradition may be seen was related by William Smith, of Newark in Sandwick.[10] It concerned a bridegroom who was taken by trows from the farmhouse of Sowie, in Sandwick, and conveyed to Suleskerry. After what seemed to him only a few hours' absence he was returned to the farmhouse, only to find that he had been away seven years and that his bride was married to another man. His body was covered all over with hair, so that his friends could hardly recognise him. Here we have a faint memory of the hairy nature of the trolls, and probably of their ability to fly through the air. The latter aspect comes through much more clearly in a Shetland story, in which some trows, who had plotted to steal the bride from a wedding-house in Norway, cut themselves bulrushes at Cunningsburgh, each of which became a horse and conveyed its rider to Norway in a moment of time.

Duncan J. Robertson, who added so much to Orkney lore, heard in Rousay a tale which immediately strikes one as authentic:[11]

> In a twa-built hoose[A] in Rousay there was once a peerie boy that had to go from the wan hoose to the ither every night. One night he did not come in. He was sent for, but could not be found; he had left his daily dwelling as usual. They went and began to cry for him 'Johnny, boy, what's come o' thee?' After a while he cried out that he was on the back 'o' the trow'. Then the 'ould trow woman' dropped him and gave him a clour[B] on the head that took the hair off him, and he was bald for the rest of his life. I got this story from people who remembered the man.

A man of over eighty told me that he remembered when he was a boy at Huip the folks there used to go out in the evening with old pails and other implements, and make a great din in order to 'buil'[C] the trows who were supposed to do a great deal of mischief about the house. Their 'buil' was a green mound west of the house. And that must have taken place no longer ago than 1850![12]

There was, in addition to the hill- and sea-trows, a kind of mill-stream troll, equivalent to the Norwegian *kvernknurr*. In Norway he was regarded as a pleasant creature on the whole, who supplied the means of good and generous measurement. At Yule he was given a buttered bannock and ale (dropped through the eye of the millstone) so that he would increase the meal.

A. A long building consisting of two farm houses with their stables etc. built end-to-end.
B. A blow.
C. To gather together and enclose for the night; also an enclosure.

But he could be mischievous, and would sometimes seize and stop the mill-wheel. A story, widespread in Norway, tells how a *kvernknurr* kept on stopping the water-wheel of a certain mill until the miller became exasperated. He heated pitch and tar in a pot, then opened a door looking on to the mill-wheel, to find the *kvernknurr* standing in the middle of it yawning. 'And his mouth was so big that his nether jaw was on the threshold and his upper jaw at the door lintel.' The miller reached for the boiling pot and thrust it into his tormentor's mouth. The *kvernknurr* raised a terrible bellow and was never seen again.

A somewhat similar story comes from Birsay. A mill called the Mill of Skelday—wrote John Spence of Evrabist—stood at one time below the present Klik Mill in the Hillside. 'There was once a miller of this mill called Johnnie Sinclair, a *gavellous*[A] body, who sometimes when the *tirl*[B] refused to go, would take a *teeng o' brands*[C] and run out to throw it underneath in the water, where it came boiling out from the *tirl*, in the dark evening, to make "knappy"—a trow or water spirit—let go his hold of the wheel.'[13]

Tales of mischievous and provoking water trows are told in nearly every parish in Orkney. In the toonship of Kirkness, in Sandwick, they made a habit of putting out the kiln fire in the local mill.[D] The incensed miller hid himself under some straw. Two trows came in and sat beside the fire. One noticed a movement in the straw, and said '*Strae's gae'n*'[E] but his fellow trow replied, 'Sit still and warm thee wame.[F] Weel kens thoo strae canna gang.' The miller sprang from his hiding place and belaboured both with a flail.[14]

In Westray, the tale goes, a thief was in a barn at Tuquoy stealing corn. He was near the kiln door, and there he saw a fairy lying under a lot o' gloy.[G] 'Oh,' he said, 'gloy ga'an.' 'Haud ee still,' said the wife, 'gloy canna' gang.'[15]

The Papa Westray version relates to the farm of Shorehouse, where two Peights (Picts), a man and a woman, came in to warm themselves at the kiln fire. The farmer, overcome by fear, crept into a heap of straw. When it rustled the female Peight got up in alarm, but the male Peight reassured her by saying:

> Sit thee still, Skeenglo,
> And warm thee weel thee wame;
> For weel kens Skeengles
> That gloy canna gang.[16]

A. Awkward, and drawling in speech.
B. The wheel; the act of rotating, turning, twirling.
C. Burning peat held in the tongs.
D. These were water trows from a neighbouring loch. The story should really apply to a barn with a kiln for drying corn, rather than to a mill. (EWM)
E. Straw's moving.
F. Belly.
G. Straw.

Another, but more doubtful, kind of troll was recognised in Orkney and Shetland by Dr Jakobsen. This was a *keddhontla*, which word he defined in his famous dictionary of the Shetland Norn as 'the name of a kind of ogress, probably belonging to a certain class of troll.' He had found that in the island of Yell a distinction was made in former days between three kinds of trolls—*Gruelis*, *Skeltas* and *Ketthuntlas*. He guessed from the form of the word that the creature was half she-cat and half bitch. With these Shetland examples in mind, he had no hesitation in explaining the name Kithuntlins—a place high up in the Birsay-Harray hills—as 'the Troll-hill'. It had occurred to people even before Dr Jakobsen's time that the story of Kate Huntly, who brewed heather ale in that remote spot, had merely been invented to account for the unusual place-name, but there is no story I know of which brings in that strange cat-and-dog apparition the *Keddhontla*. The Quholmsley dog, which scared some people almost out of their wits, and which has been seen within recent memory, is probably a much later phenomenon.

There is no well-defined tradition of Orkney trows being the guardians of treasure, but in Shetland people who had communed with the trows were allowed to enter the howe[A] at Trolhoulland, and were, Hibbert says, 'dazzled by the splendour exhibited within the recesses through which they have passed . . . all the interior walls are adorned with gold and silver. . . .'[17]

As old as the trows in folk tradition, but very different in size, were the *dverger*, or dwarfs. In the Eddic poems and some of the sagas they were said to 'brew the mead of poetry'. They were splendid smiths. Had they not forged Thor's hammer Mjöllnir, Odin's spear, and the great sword Dáinsleif? In later tradition they became somewhat more ordinary, but they retained their skill as smiths. They lived in stones or in cliffs on the sides of mountains. They talked a lot, and the echo from the mountainside was called 'dwarf talk'.

The dwarfs are remembered in Orkney in place-names only. Most interestingly, perhaps, in the name of a little hill in Woodwick, Evie, which is called Dwarmo. I remember how puzzled the late Dr Hugh Marwick was by the name, until he made the brilliant assumption (which I as a former dweller in the neighbourhood could confirm) that the hill must have a notable echo. This echo comes from the hammars, or cliffs, on the side which faces the island of Rousay. On the strength of this information Dr Marwick decided that Dwarmo is a corruption of the Old Norse *dverg-mál*, which literally means 'dwarf talk'.

In Hoy the cliffs on the hillside south of the Dwarfie Stane are known as the Dwarfie Hammars. They would have been one of the most obvious places

A. A hillock or mound.

anywhere in the islands for dwarfs to live in, and when the Norsemen found just below them a great stone hollowed out as if into a tiny house for dwarfs, the legends they brought with them from Norway about dwarfs living in stones must have been spectacularly confirmed. It became at once the *Dvergasteinn*. The name is not unique, for the place-name Dvergasteinn (Dwarfstone) is recorded both in Norway and in Iceland.[18]

A creature I want to mention in some detail is the *nisse*, because he may possibly appear in stories told me by my friend Walter Meil, of Work, near Kirkwall. *Nisser* are seen nowadays, much sentimentalised, on Norwegian Christmas Cards, but the *nisse* as he was described in the remote valleys of Norway was small and hairy, with pointed ears, and no thumbs. He wore a beard. His eyes were yellow and slanting, and shone in the dark. He hissed when he spoke. His dress included knee breeches, buckled shoes and a red cap. The *nisse* had an odd temperament. On the one hand he was cross-grained and peevish, mischievous and full of tricks, while, on the other, he could become very attached to the people he stayed with (he usually lived in the barn) and nearly always went with them to any new farm they might choose to inhabit. He took great care of the farm animals, particularly the horses, and had no hesitation stealing fodder from a neighbouring farm if it was in short supply on his own. The girls were completely safe with him for he was a hermit and recluse. If a troll came to do mischief he would attack him most manfully.

In Norway the *nisse* went under various names—*vett, gardvor, godbonden, tuftekall* . . . perhaps some of the names are older than others. But it is pretty clear that, whatever his name, his descent can be traced from the *haug-bui* or *haugbonde*, the dweller in the mound. In pagan times each farmer was buried on his own farm. If he was a wealthy, powerful man a large mound would be raised over his grave. Sometimes people coming to a farm would find a prehistoric barrow or natural mound on the place, and would give it the same veneration as if it were the grave of the original owner. There was a certain importance attached to this (beyond the impelling force of superstition) for under udal law landowners needed no written title, but simply the fact of continuous possession, vouched for when necessary by honest men in the neighbourhood. One could point, however, to the mound in which the remote ancestor who had cleared the land still lived as evidence of the family's ancient possession. In the oldest times the *haugbonde* was a very real person, maintaining a lively interest in the farm, and looking for generous entertainment, either in the mound or when he came out of it, particularly at Christmas. At some stage in Norwegian folklore, and in a diversity of places, he left the mound altogether, moved into the farm buildings, and became the *nisse*.

We have traces in Orkney of the *haug-bui* in both guises. In Skelwick,

Westray, milk and meal were poured[A] through a hole in the top of a large hillock when the cows calved, and there is a record of milk being poured down a hole in a mound at Pierowall.[19] It is probable that these offerings were still being made at the end of the eighteenth century or even into the nineteenth century. They were by then supposed to be for the fairies, but the parallel between them and the offerings made in Norway to the *vett*, or guardian spirit of the farm, is evident. There is even better evidence that a belief in the *haug-bui* was taken to Orkney by the Norwegian settlers, for it was common until very recent times to associate a being known as 'the hogboy' with any large mound.[B] The excavator of Maeshowe, James Farrer, wrote in his privately printed *Maes-Howe* in 1862, 'The country people state that the building was formerly inhabited by a person named Hogboy, possessing great strength.' And in an account of Stenness J. T. Smith Leask wrote (1931), 'Seventy years ago there were many stories in the district regarding the "Hug Boy", but they are now forgotten.'[20] In Hoy, too, the tradition lingered on. But it was in Sanday, where this creature was called the 'hogboon', that a few resemblances to the Norwegian *nisse* remained.

Mr Meil (whom I mentioned earlier) could not quite make up his mind, the legend having grown somewhat vague, whether his Sanday stories applied to the 'hogboon' or to hill-trows, but I think it very obvious that it is the former being who can be dimly discerned in them. The first story concerns a farmer who was awakened at three o'clock in the morning by a little fellow who stood in front of the box bed and asked for the loan of a 'piftan piv'. The farmer grunted that he had no intention of getting up at that time of the morning, and told his visitor to look around for it himself. This the little fellow did. When he found it he disappeared with it, 'in a blue lowe',[C] through the smoke-hole in the roof. The odd thing about the story is that the nocturnal visitor's speech (although remembered as somewhat unusual) has a defect precisely opposite to that usually attributed to him: the hissing sounds of 'siftan sieve' have been replaced by 'piftan piv', as if the 'hogboon' (or *nisse*) lisped rather than hissed.

The sieve in that tale would have been of sheepskin, stretched on a frame, and covered with fine holes made with a red-hot wire. The forgotten *nisse*

A. A character in Walter Traill Dennison's *Orkney Weddings and Wedding Customs*, 1905, p.41, is made to say: 'I meant to pour the wine on the house-know [a hillock or mound associated with a particular house], whar the Hogboon bides, for good luck to the wedding.' (EWM)

B. At a house in Rousay, when a spinning-wheel refused to work because its driving band had become dry and loose, the woman who owned it would place it at night on a nearby mound, in the certainty that it would be all right in the morning. No doubt the night-dew shrank the band, but just as obviously the woman was performing an age-old custom which began when the guardian spirit of the farm was expected to give practical help if asked to do so. (EWM)

C. Glow.

was even more apparent when I asked Mr Meil what these creatures looked like, and he replied that they were small, with long ears 'standing near the tops of their heads'. The second story has already been made familiar by Dr Marwick (who also had it from Walter Meil), but I shall give Mr Meil's version as I recorded it recently:

> There was a house, and it was a bit outlandish. They called it Hellihowe. It was away on a point, and there were a lot of hill-trows [sic] who inhabited the country round about, where there were knowes and braes. They came to be very troublesome, so bad that the man and wife and family decided they would have to flit,[A] and leave them: they weren't too honest, and they were always borrowing stuff. One fine day the family got under way with the flitting. They had some ponies, and they got cubbies[B] on their backs, and gathered together the furniture and whatever they had, and started out early in the morning. It was a lovely day, and when the family were a long way from their old house they felt they were safe now anyway. But just then one of the hill-trows set his head up out of a kirn and said, 'We're gettan a fine day tae flit on, guidman.'[C]

Here again the *nisse* is evident: in his size (he could get inside a kirn), in his mischievous disposition which had exasperated his human neighbours, but most particularly in his attachment to the family, so that he had no hesitation in moving house with them. The fact that these beings lived in 'knowes and braes' is also revealing.

While our minds are occupied with mounds it may be placed on record, although it has no strict relevance in the present context, that there were in Orkney small mounds called 'assie-knowes', which when opened contained nothing but ashes. The only thing I know which can throw any light on the matter is a tradition that at one time every young girl within a mile of Maeshowe had to take a kaesy of ashes to the top of the mound each full moon, empty it there and urinate on the ashes. As far as I am aware none of the excavators of Maeshowe has called attention to an admixture of ashes with the earth on the top of the mound, and I set down the local story with extreme reserve.

A very different being from the *nisse*, but easy to confuse with him, is the elf. Norwegian *alver* are sometimes portrayed in folklore as small naked boys

---

A. Move.
B. Straw baskets.
C. In another version of the story of the Hellihowe hogboon, it is told that he became exasperated with the family when a young woman, who came to the house as its new mistress, neglected to carry on the family tradition of 'feeding the trows'. She did not leave meal for them, and she scraped the cooking pots clean instead of leaving them overnight with plenty of food adhering and available. (EWM)

60 Children sailing boats in a rock pool, *c.*1905

61 Farm children at play, 1914

KIRKWALL ❊ BOWLING ❊ CLUB.

Concert.

**TEMPERANCE HALL,
= = = KIRKWALL, = = =
Friday, Feb. 7, 1908.**

Chairman—Colonel PEACE.
Conductor—Mr G. D. BAIN.
Accomp.—Miss DAVIDSON.

Remainder of Gallery. WM. PEACE & SON, PRINTERS, KIRKWALL.

62 Concert programme, 1908

with a big hat. They lived under the earth, could inflict injury on men and animals, and were responsible for many kinds of disease. If they breathed on a person his body became covered with blisters. Their women frequently had great difficulty in labour and required a mortal woman for a midwife. Sometimes at night they would be seen dancing round a fire. In the morning a dark ring which had been formed by the dancing could be seen. It is difficult even in Norway to make fixed distinctions between elves and *tusser* (a kind of fairy), for both were malicious, and could steal food or kidnap children. The *tusser* were all dressed in blue. One can just glimpse them in local legend, for on two occasions I have found blue-clad fairies in Orkney stories. The best we can do, however, in respect of most of our old tales is to think of Norwegian fairies as having the attributes described above, and to try to survey the field of Orkney fairy lore with these in mind. This has been made a somewhat arbitrary exercise by the fact that all kinds of fairy stories have come to us from Scotland and England and have been incorporated into our folklore. The one sure 'note' in the older stories is the dangerous nature of the northern elves and fairies.

Tales of changelings are so familiar in all fairy folklore, and have a depressing sameness. A woman in childbed was in great danger, and every effort was made to protect her and her child. A knife and a bible were placed in the bed, she was 'sained' (signed with the cross), and a constant watch was kept over her by the family. I have heard of a woman being circled three times with a piece of burning rag. It was important to show no preparations for the coming baby, for 'the peerie folk might ken'. Even when the midwife slept with the expectant mother—as happened in Orphir—the child, born during the night, had disappeared before morning. Midwives were themselves convinced that they were in danger: a Costa woman who was called to help a woman at childbirth carried in her hands a pair of tongs with a glowing peat held firmly in them to scare away the fairies. Children were told when they went anywhere after dark to hold the left thumb in the palm of the hand with the fingers folded firmly over it; if they did this the fairies, although they might annoy them, could not do them any harm. Some people wore for their protection 'elfbelts' made of silver. On 3 April 1644, the North Isles Presbytery ordained 'that *Elfbelt* be destroyed, in respect it had been a monument of superstition, as was declared by Mr George Graham and Mr James Aitkin, and the silver of it being melted, payment to be given out of the box to the owner of the same.'

The belief that fairies could 'shoot' cattle with what were known as elf-arrows was widespread. 'Fairy-shot' was apparently a condition in which the animal's skin, especially around the chest, seemed to be full of small hard lumps. (This reminds one of the power of elves to raise blisters.) There were old women in every parish who professed to be able to diagnose the condition and sometimes cure it. They would examine the cow carefully, then excitedly point to a place devoid of hair as the spot where the arrow had struck.

A newly calved cow was a favourite victim of the fairies. To protect her, a cat was set on her neck and drawn by the tail towards her hindquarters. This done, the cat was set on the middle of the cow's back and pulled—again by the tail—down one side, under the belly, and up the other side. When this was done the cow was safely 'enclosed'.

One method of curing an elf-shot cow, told me by a woman in Rendall, was to recite a charm over the animal (she could not remember what it was), then to secure in the hair on its hide a needle folded into the leaf of a psalm-book. Another remedy was to give the cow a drink, after having placed a silver coin in the water.

Rather than repeat traditions sufficiently known already, I shall tell two stories which were told to me by dependable old men in different parts of Orkney. The first relates to Rousay. My informant there said that when his uncle was a boy a farmer in the neighbourhood decided to take a cow which had been elf-shot to a house on the hill where an old woman who was supposed to be skilful in such matters had her home. The cow was taken into the byre, and the woman went in also. The boy, who had accompanied the farmer, was left outside, but he put his eye to a chink in the door to see what the old woman did. She rubbed the cow with some kind of stone (the boy was not sure if she was rubbing, or making the mark of the cross) muttering an incantation as she did so. She would murmur every now and then, as if with regard to the cow's condition, 'Just riddled like a sieve.'

A woman in Hoy had a cow which became very ill, so sent her son to a benevolent old woman in the neighbourhood who came at once. This person put her hand two or three times over the cow's back, then told the owner not to be afraid if she took the disease upon herself for a few minutes. Before the boy and his mother could say anything, she was rolling in the muck behind the cow and sweating profusely. In a short time she came out of her fit or trance, and the cow too was well.

If one found an elf-arrow (which was often a prehistoric flint arrow-head, but sometimes just a sharp splinter of wood) it was considered to be a fortunate occurrence. The arrow was treasured by the finder both as a luck bringer and amulet. A farmer in Tankerness, who was still remembered at the beginning of the century, kept a wooden elf-arrow among his most precious possessions in an old chest, where it was found after his death. He would never allow anyone to look at or handle it.

Numberless stories have been told of people who went dancing with the fairies, or who entered a fairy mound, lured by beautiful music. The main features of such stories are always the same: the dancer comes back to his human friends, thinking he has only been away for a few minutes; or he has not been enthralled by the fairies, either because he carried steel, usually a knife, or took care not to eat the fairies' food.

The most amusing and unusual fairy story I have heard was told by the late John Bremner of Hoy. I shall summarise it, but shall preserve essential details. It concerns a Rackwick man named Magnus Ritch, who found himself drawn inexorably one night to the Trowie Glen. He suddenly realised that he was not alone, but had an escort of little people, the tallest not more than a foot high. The procession stopped at a cave half-way down the glen, while the leader went in to report to a personage known as 'Himsel'. After some minutes Magnus was told to enter. He found himself in a richly appointed and elaborately furnished hall, where a dance was in progress. Magnus was ushered into an anteroom, where 'Himsel' came to greet him. This personage was rather taller than the others; he was dressed in pale blue and had a white beard. On his head was a blue turban. He seated himself on a throne which two of his people had carried into the room. Addressing Magnus in the Orcadian dialect he said, 'Boy, dis thoo ken wha I am?'

Magnus said courageously that he did not, but added, 'I'm no faerd for thee a' the sam'.'

'Weel, thoo're a brave man,' said his host, 'I'm the head chield[A] here in the Trowie Glen.' He went on to say that Magnus should have had a passport before entering the king's palace, but that he would give him one; then he invited him to have a drink of ale, saying, 'Thoo niver tasted ale like hid.' It was heather ale, wonderful stuff that made Magnus feel light on his feet. He began to prance gaily among the dancers, of whom there were some thirty couples on the floor. The little ladies, dressed in white, were very beautiful, and everyone applauded while Magnus danced, although the dances were unfamiliar to him. He felt so much at home that he asked the king's permission to light his pipe. Everyone gathered round in great curiosity to see this strange ritual. Magnus filled his clay pipe with the tabacco known as Bogie Roll, and blew out happily its pungent fumes. Then a dreadful thing happened. All the little people turned a ghastly white, and one after the other fell to the floor, the king being the last to succumb. As the little man in blue toppled over, Magnus found himself at the entrance of a rabbit burrow with not a fairy in sight.

Although the story has picked up in the course of telling an amusing modern twist and some of the furniture of the story-book narrative, it is interesting to find the king of the fairies dressed in blue, the traditional colour of the *tusse*.

Rather story-bookish too, and not so far as I know in the Norwegian tradition, are the accounts of how the fairies died out in Orkney. One tale is that they decided to move from the Mainland, which had grown too dangerous to hold them, to live among the hills of Hoy. Their flitting was to

A. Child.

take place at midnight, when there was a full moon. They gathered at the Black Craig near Stromness, with an immensely long 'simmany rape' (rope of straw) which they had plaited. One end of this was fixed to the top of the craig. An extremely agile fairy took the other end and jumped with it across the sound to Hoy. He landed safely and secured the rope, over which the fairies scrambled. When they were half-way over it broke and they were all drowned in the stormy waters. The solitary fairy on the opposite shore, observing what had happened, threw himself into the sea and was also carried away. In other legends the fairies were drowned when travelling from one island to another in boats made of eggshells.

Anything unusual which was found near their reputed haunts was thought to belong to the fairies. Robert Stevenson, the famous lighthouse engineer, lost a hundred-foot box-measuring-line when he visited the Standing Stones with Sir Walter Scott in 1814. Some years afterwards one of his assistants noticed the tape in a cottage window. The woman to whom he applied for it said, 'O sir, ane o' the bairns fun it lang syne at the Stanes, and when we pulled it oot we took fright, thinking it had belonged to the fairies, and we threw it into the bottom of the window, and it's been there ever since.'

As for fairy rings, I had them pointed out to me more than once as a child. One, an almost perfect circle of short grass forming a path less than a foot wide and perhaps twenty feet in circumference, could be seen in the rough moorland pasture not far from the ancient kirk of Norrisdale high up the Woodwick Burn.

It is worth pointing out perhaps, in relation to the martial qualities said to belong to the *huldrefolk*, that Orkney 'fairies' are occasionally seen in warlike panoply. The Rev. John Brand, who published a description of Orkney in 1701, wrote, 'Evil Spirits also called Fairies are frequently seen in several of the Isles dancing and making merry, and sometimes seen in Armour.'[21]

A writer in the *Old-Lore Miscellany* in October 1910, who signed himself D.S., told with the utmost seriousness a story of what he had seen in Greenie, in Birsay. One morning he heard the tramp of marching feet, and all at once saw a troop of men 'six deep, and about seventy yards in length marching past with guns on their shoulders, and officers with drawn swords. They all passed about 60 yards from where the writer was standing, and marched to a dyke at the public road, and as each rank came to the dyke it disappeared.' Around this time 'whether it was the same day, or some time afterwards or before, a farmer standing on the rising ground above the knowes of Furse-a-Kelda, saw a body of men coming out of a small knoll on the farm of Norton, marching direct for the knowes of Furse-a-Kelda. When about half the distance was covered, a number of men came out of the knowes of Furse-a-Kelda and met the other company. He described it as an awful fight—lots of men were killed on both sides and wounded. Both armies drew off and marched back to their respective knolls, while a number were engaged in carrying the dead off the field of battle.'

Two glimpses now of 'fairies' and their livestock. A boy, riding home on horseback behind an old man in Sandwick, saw the valley near Housegarth full of fairy riders driving a cow before them. Next day a cow was found dead in a Sandwick byre. A letter in *The Orcadian* of 27 March 1924, by an anonymous writer, told a story from much the same district. It had happened over a hundred years before:

> One night (he wrote) when my grandfather, then a lad in his teens, and his brother had retired to rest in the 'but'[A] bed, they were awakened by a tremendous knocking at the outer door and a voice crying 'For God's sake, boys, let me in!' He sprang out of bed and opened the door and a man rushed in with white face and shaking limbs. After he had recovered a little he told them that he had been visiting some friends in Birsay and had stayed late, forgetful of the lonely hill-road he had to traverse in order to reach his home in Sandwick. However, all went well until he reached the top of the Sandwick Hill, when he discovered to his horror that the fairies were out on their midnight ride. Right across his path they came, riding furiously on white horses with their faces to the tails. He stood trembling and waiting for a break in the line, but on and on they came in endless procession. Suddenly he remembered that cold steel and holy name were said to be a sure safeguard from fairies. So, taking his pocket knife and opening it he shouted as loud as his shaking voice would let him, 'In the name of the Lord let me through.' The next moment he stood on the top of the hill alone, and he added: 'Oh, boys, I tell you I ran is I niver ran i' me life afore, an' I were aye coonted brave and swack.'[B] The two lads had to accompany him to his home, half a mile distant, and saw him inside the door before he would let them go, while all the time he vowed that never, never would he cross Sandwick Hill at midnight again.

A rather vicious creature which appears in Norwegian folklore, and which can be discovered in one or two places in Orkney, is the *nøkk*. The *nøkk* could assume many forms, but was commonly regarded as the water-horse; indeed in Iceland this was his name—*vatnhestr*. His chief aim in life was to lure people into the water so that they would drown. In one Norwegian tale he assumed the form of a raft of logs. If one were to choose a classic instance, however, from Norwegian folklore, it could be the story of

---

A. The bed in the kitchen or living-room.
B. Oh, boys, I tell you I ran as I never ran in my life before, and I was always thought brave and active.

the three small boys who were playing beside a stream. Out of the water came a grey horse, who laid himself on his back between them. The eldest two crept up on to the horse; the third child came and said, 'I should have got up there also.' But the horse rose with the two upon his back and plunged into the river with them.

The *nøkk* was well known in Shetland, where he became the *njuggle*. Scalloway's reservoir is Njuggle's Water. There is a Njildigrind beside Snarravoe loch, and quite a number of small lochans have his name in some form. He could appear beside mill-dams and burns ('Du'll kyin[A] the Njugl by da burn'—T. A. Robertson), usually taking the form of an ordinary Shetland pony. But if he was mounted he would plunge in the twinkling of an eye into the nearest burn.

At one time it was thought that (apart from Nuckelavee, who lived in the sea and became a creature of terrifying ugliness and monstrous malignity) Orkney had no *nøkk* tradition. It was when studying a place-name, the Loch of Knitchen in Rousay, that Dr Marwick suggested it might represent the Old Norse *nykartjorn*. He wrote in his *Rousay Place-Names*, 'Nykar was a fabulous monster supposed to emerge from lakes etc. in the form of a horse . . . but I must admit I am aware of no such legend in connection with the Loch of Knitchen.' Since Dr Marwick wrote the above, Kathleen Harcus, of Rousay, has done some excellent research on my behalf, and has found two versions of a *nøkk* (or *nykar*) tradition attached to the Loch of Knitchen. The first version tells that a wonderful black water-horse came out of the loch when all the farmers around had their animals on the hill nearby. This horse joined the flock, but never allowed himself to be caught. In the second version of the tale the horse did allow himself to be caught, but anyone who got on his back was taken into the loch and drowned.

Several haunts of the water-horse have been named in Hoy, mainly around the Water of Hoy, the Pegal Burn and the Little Loch, but I have found no extant place-name which points to the *nøkk*.

I have purposely left until the last, to be arrived at by a process of elimination, the *huldu-folk* (Old Norse) or *huldrefolk* (Norwegian). These are the beings who appear, I think, most interestingly in Orkney tradition, but so allusively and tantalisingly that anything I write must be taken as completely tentative and exploratory. In order that little scraps of local tradition may be recognised for what they are, it is necessary to give a fairly full account of the *huldrefolk* as it can be pieced together from Norwegian folklore.[22]

The male *hulder* was rather ugly, with a long nose, but the women when young were beautiful and ingratiating, with good singing voices. They were strong enough to bend a horseshoe with their bare hands. The cross the female *hulder* had to bear was a long tail like a cow's, which she did her best

---

A. You'll know.

to conceal under her skirt. It was no wonder that with this blemish on her charms she was moody and dangerous. The greatest desire of the *huldrefolk* was to achieve equality with human beings, and the *huldre* girls tried desperately to marry ordinary men, often flinging themselves at them in the most immodest way. If a man was unwise enough to jilt a *hulder* she was ruthless in pursuing and punishing him. She tried if possible to get married in church, for if she could do so her tail fell off and she became like an ordinary woman. The *hulder* quickly became wizened and ugly, but her temper improved greatly as she grew older.

Huldrefolk are thought of as farmers, and very good ones, having bigger and better livestock than other people. *Huldre* girls were excellent at milking cows and keeping house. People took care not to trespass on farms belonging to the *huldrefolk* or to build their houses on the place where they were believed to live. A man whose animals were dying one after another found that he had built his byre right over the cradle of a *huldre* child, where the filth from the byre fell on it. He quickly moved his byre, and was left in peace. On many farms a stall was left empty in the byre so that a *hulder* could have a place for his cattle there.

Though the *huldrefolk* lived mainly on farms and in the forests, there were *huldre* islands which in the ordinary way were invisible, but which sometimes rose from the sea. Tales were told of splendid farms on *huldre* islands. If anyone could cast steel over them they became the finder's property, and were therefore called *findegaarder*.[23]

Although most usually the *huldrefolk* lived in harmony with the human farmers, having their farms on the rough pastures, they occasionally spirited people away. These were then said to be *berglat* (i.e. spirited off into the hill). People to whom this had happened, and who were afterwards sick in mind, were called *huldre-elsk*.

Sometimes, it was said, the *huldrefolk* would appear in the guise of soldiers, and would fight for their human friends in the forefront of the battle.

It is possible that the word *hulder* is known in Orkney in the form of 'hilderbogie' (recorded in Firth), and in the place-name Hildival, in Westray (O.N. *huldu-fjall*).

The strongest link we have with the *huldre* legend is the belief, once general in Orkney, that people suffering from some kind of mental illness which made them sickly and lethargic were 'in the hill'. In other words, their souls had been taken away by the hillfolk and only their bodies were left behind. The phrase, if not the belief, was quite common when I was a boy. I remember being told by the late Auda Macrae, of Grindelay, Orphir, that in his younger days her brother made a trip in a sailing boat with two companions around the North Isles of Orkney.[A] They anchored at Rousay and

---

A. A cruise made by John Macrae c.1910.

called at a house for provisions. There they found a young girl, pale and entirely listless, lying in a box-bed in the kitchen. She seemed entirely apathetic and only semi-conscious. Her family were convinced that she was 'in the hill'. Mr Macrae made enquiries later on. He was told that after many weeks the girl gradually came to herself and got well again. There is a story of an old man, also in Rousay, who was extremely peeved and frustrated because his friends would not take him 'oot o' the hill', even when he had told them the exact place where he could be found.

We have no exact equivalents of the tales of people losing cattle or other livestock because they had built their houses over a *huldre* homestead but we most certainly know something about the *huldre* islands. It is a subject that bristles with difficulties.

I shall have to repeat very briefly stories that are well known in Orkney. The first relates to Eynhallow, which was once a vanishing island, but which was won from the waters when someone managed to land on it with steel in his hand, having never taken his eyes off the island since he had first observed it. Walter Traill Dennison tells a much more picturesque and detailed story,[24] which is confirmed as a genuine myth by tales once current in Evie. I shall only select the points which are pertinent to this enquiry. These are: Eynhallow was once called Hildaland; the wife of the man who finally freed Eynhallow had been spirited away; among the creatures which tried to divert the man from his purpose were two beautiful sirens (Dennison calls them mermaids), who stood on the shore singing most melodiously; the cattle belonging to the former owners of the island ran helter-skelter into the sea.

Dennison says that the owners of Eynhallow were Fin Folk. It seems to me that the Fin Folk and the *huldrefolk* have become quite mixed up in Orkney. The mermaids singing on the island remind one irresistibly of *huldre* maidens, and there seems to be even a stronger connection when we learn that if a man fell in love with a mermaid she had the power of laying aside her tail. What was more, like the *hulder* she became wrinkled, wizened, and repulsive in form very quickly. It has sometimes occurred to me, but I am not a good enough philologist to say whether this is possible, that the term *findegaarder* applied to the *huldrefolk's* island farms could have led to the idea that the islands belonged to the Fin Folk. But we must not get involved in barren speculation, for our Orkney folklore, as we have it, is a rich and rare development. A search for Norse originals, such as the present, should be kept within bounds, and should not delude us into thinking that the Orkney legends have no right to exist on their own, but should conform to some hypothetical original pattern.

With that caution very much in mind, we can turn to the name itself—Hildaland. This has been identified with the *hilder*, the place on the horizon where sky and sea seem to meet, and where a *hildring*, or mirage, can sometimes be seen. The idea would apply perfectly to the mythical island of Hether

63 Band of Hope member's card, 1899. Formally founded in England in 1847, the first Bands of Hope appeared in Scotland in the 1850s. They were established within existing Sunday schools and membership was open to all children under sixteen.

64 Advertisement for Old Orkney Whisky, distilled in Stromness, c.1900

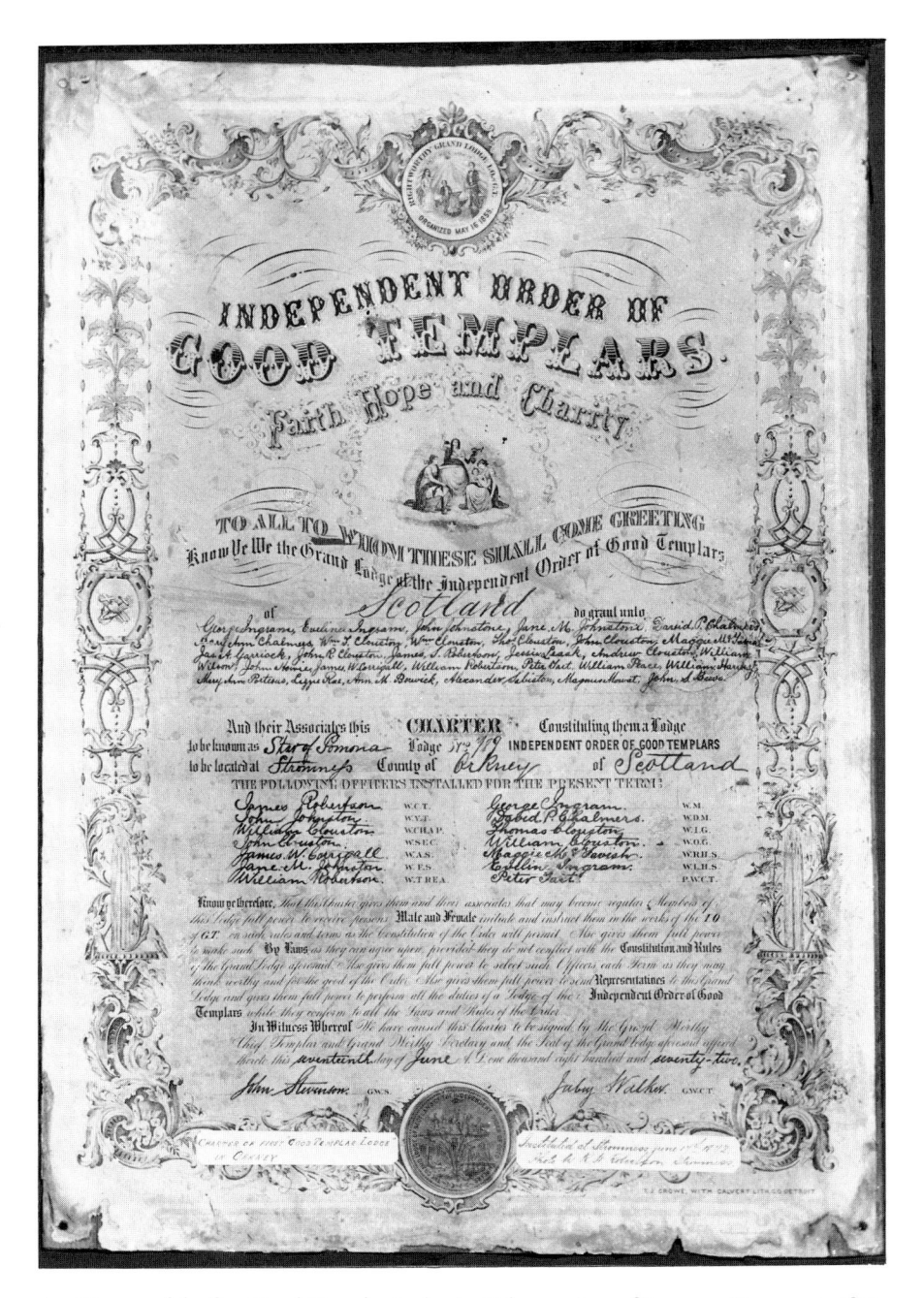

65 Charter of the first Good Templar Lodge in Orkney—Star of Pomona, Stromness, 1872

Blether, of which I shall write presently, but it would not apply to Eynhallow, only a mile from the Evie and Rousay shores, which is named specifically Hilda-land. Everything would seem to point to a legendary *Huldreland*, inhabited by the *huldrefolk*, with *huldre* maidens and *huldre* cattle, over which some mythical Orcadian cast steel. How and when the legend became elaborated we cannot even guess. There are numerous isolated legends of sea cows coming to live on shore, having several calves, and at last taking them back into the sea.

The idea of the *huldre* island can be seen most clearly in the stories of Hether Blether, which is supposed to rise from the sea in the Atlantic beyond Eynhallow, right on the horizon's rim. The legend runs thus. . . . A Rousay girl disappeared, and was looked for all over the island without success. Many years later the girl's father and three brothers were at sea when they became enveloped in fog. They sailed on in what they hoped was the direction of Rousay, when their boat grounded on a strange island. I shall give the rest of the story as it was told to me by a Rousay woman a year or two ago:

> There was a white beach and white houses on the island. They pulled to the shore, and there the missing girl came to meet them with three bairns. She had been married to a man on Hether Blether all this time and she was delighted to see them. They wanted her to go back with them, but she wouldn't leave her husband. But she gave them an iron stake and told them that if they kept it safely they could always come back and see her. After food and rest they set sail again for Rousay, but in the excitement of bidding goodbye they dropped the stake overboard and Hether Blether sank below the sea. It has been seen a few times since then, but no-one has ever reached it.

There are more elaborate versions, but that is the essential story. Dennison describes such an enchanted island. 'Many a burn ran rollicking down the hillsides, and sparkling in the sunshine on the green valleys below. Each bonnie burn sang its own little song as it wimpled to the sea, and Our Lady's hens (skylarks) sang so that ye would have thought the sunny lift (sky) was showering music down. To the weary and tempest-tossed mariner this calm bay with its fair surroundings seemed a haven of bliss.'[25]

Compare what has been written with what the great Norwegian folklorist P. Chr. Asbjornsen had to tell:[26]

> It happened not seldom to the Nordland fishermen when they were coming home that they found corn straw fastened to the helm, or barley corn in the fishes' stomachs. Then it was said that they had sailed over Utrøst, or one of the *huldre* lands about which there are legends in the Northlands. These islands show themselves only to pious and foresighted people who are in mortal danger at sea, and rise up where otherwise no land is

found. The underworld folk who live there have agriculture and cattle-breeding, fishing and hunting, like other folk. But here the sun shines over greener grass and richer fields than in any other place in the Northlands; and happy is he who comes to, or can see, one of these sunlit islands . . .

The Utrøst referred to is supposed to lie outside Røst on the southern spit of Lofoten. I have been very impressed by the similarity between some of the Orkney legends and those of the Lofoten Islands.

★ ★ ★

I must emphasise in concluding this essay that it is a pioneer attempt to systematise some of our Orkney folklore, and I have taken the risk every local folklorist must take, namely, of being proved wrong in certain of my conclusions.

1. See E. O. G. Turville-Petre, *Myth and Religion of the North* London, 1964, pp.275-276.
2. Told by an old Rousay woman to Duncan J. Robertson, and communicated by him in *Longmans Magazine* in 1889 and the *Proceedings of The Orkney Antiquarian Society*, Vol. II, 1923-1924, p.42.
3. Kirkwall 1949.
4. *Old-Lore Miscellany of Orkney, Shetland, Caithness and Sutherland*, Vol. III, 1910, pp.8-9.
5. Ibid., Vol. IV, 1911, p.187.
6. The trow place-names of Deerness were taken from *Round the Shores of Deerness*, an article by Mrs R. Eunson, printed in *The Orcadian* on various dates during September 1936.
7. *Proceedings of The Orkney Antiquarian Society*, Dr Hugh Marwick, Vol. V, 1926-1927, p.71.
8. Kirkwall 1961.
9. *Orkney Folklore and Traditions*, Walter Traill Dennison, 1961, p.15.
10. *Old-Lore Miscellany*, op. cit., Vol. VII, 1914, pp.98-99.
11. Ibid., Vol. II, 1909, pp.108-109.
12. *Proceedings of The Orkney Antiquarian Society*, Dr Hugh Marwick, Vol. V, 1926-1927, p.71.
13. *Old-Lore Miscellany*, op. cit., Vol. II, p.131.
14. *Old-Lore Miscellany*, William Smith, Vol. IV, p.3.
15. *Proceedings of The Orkney Antiquarian Society*, op. cit., Duncan J. Robertson, Vol. II, 1923-1924, p.39.
16. John D. Mackay: unpublished paper on 'Social and Economic Conditions in Papa Westray during the nineteenth century'.
17. *A Description of the Shetland Islands*, 1822, p.191.
18. *Myth and Religion of the North*, op. cit., p.234.
19. *Old-Lore Miscellany*, op. cit., Vol. II, pp.22-23.
20. *A Peculiar People and Other Orkney Tales*, Kirkwall 1931, p.59.
21. *A Brief Description of Orkney, Zetland, Pightland-Firth and Caithness*, 1701, p.63.
22. There is an excellent account of *huldrefolk* in *Draugen Skreik* by Dagmar Blix, Norsk Folkeminnelags Skrifter 93 Universitetsforlaget, Oslo, 1965.
23. Kristofer Visted, *Vor gamle bondekultur*, Kristiania, 1923, p.122.
24. *Orkney Folklore*, op. cit., pp.55-61.
25. Ibid., p.49.
26. *Norsk Huldre-Eventyr og Folkesagn*.

2

Tales of island fairies

An old woman told me when I was a child: 'The fairies only left Orkney when folk stopped seekin' them.' And she shook her head wisely for some seconds.

I thought then she was merely suggesting that the fairies had grown lonely through neglect, or even resentful, and had gone where they could find a better welcome. But, as I realise now, she really meant that the fairies depended for their very existence on being believed in—the suspension of belief meant extinction. And I am sure she had never heard of Peter Pan or Tinker Bell.

The countryfolk of Orkney took pains to propitiate the fairies. They called them 'wir good neebors', for fairies had an uncanny way of discovering what people said about them. They also made them gifts. At Skelwick in Westray it was the custom to pour milk from a newly calved cow through a hole in a nearby hillock.[1] Fairies were fond of milk. When it was not given freely, they helped themselves. Occasionally a fairy lived in close contact with a household, establishing a friendly relationship with its people: here we can just recognise the fundamentally peaceable *nisse*.

Despite a family's most anxious vigilance, the fairies managed every now and then to steal a child and leave a changeling. In the West Mainland many years ago lived a woman who was a very tiny individual, not much more than three feet high, and most people were sure she was a fairy child. The father had heard the fairies conversing outside the house as the mother was being delivered. He had said immediately, 'Guid save the mither,' but had neglected to include the child. So the fairies had been able to effect the exchange. People were careful not to get on bad terms with the 'fairy'. A man who was frequently intoxicated, and who at such times teased other children unmercifully, always showed her the most careful respect, being convinced that she had occult powers.

Human children who had been abducted were sometimes allowed to live and grow up among the fairy folk. A man who joined in a fairy dance was

1. See also 'Creatures of Orkney legend and their Norse ancestry', p.267.

warned by one of the fairies not to accept any food or drink if he wanted to see his home again. He knew he had been cautioned by a human changeling who had been stolen many years before from a house at the other side of the loch.[1]

People working by themselves in lonely places, in the peat mosses in particular, sometimes found themselves surrounded by fairies. An Orphir man named Tammy Hay, scared out of his wits by such an appearance, plunged his knife into a fairy and took to his heels. He got home safely; and next day a neighbour found Tammy's knife embedded in a small heap of peats where he had been working.

I remember an amusing story told me by a Stenness man. It concerned a woman who was busily raising peats, when she discovered that she was encircled by fairies. She was very frightened, but she knew what should be done in such a predicament—she crossed herself and murmured a prayer. To her surprise and concern this had no effect: the fairies came still closer. The woman, who was a forceful individual, suddenly acted in character. She swore roundly at the fairies. Almost before her mouth was shut they had disappeared. I am afraid this is a profoundly immoral tale, but I still chuckle when I think of it.

It was not unnatural that in an island county like Orkney the power of the fairies should have extended to the sea as well as the land. They were accomplished wreckers. If human beings were not extremely careful they might unwittingly assist them. For instance, an egg-shell was never put into the fire without being broken into little bits. If a whole egg-shell was thrown on the fire, the fairies would use it as a boat[2] and sail out to sea to wreck the first ship they met.

It is pleasanter to record the more amusing pranks of the 'peerie folk'—how they kept on tripping up Billy Spence as he passed the Dell of Keldereddie, and then almost split their sides laughing at him.

It is pleasant, too, to remember their love of music. Many an Orcadian in the old days declared that he had never heard finer music in his life than that which came out of the knowes in the dim of a summer twilight. It was almost invariably pipe music. Not that the fairies did not appreciate 'human' music: for example, there was a Harray man, known as Davie o' Teeveth, who played for them.

A man who frequently danced with the fairies was the Shapinsay 'fairy doctor'. He had uncanny skill, and could always cure his patients, provided that they paid him in advance with 'white money'.[3]

While there are many tales about mounds, there is no description in the

1. See also 'Creatures of Orkney legend and their Norse ancestry', pp.270-271.
2. Ibid., p.272.
3. Silver.

legends with which I am personally familiar of fairyland as such—that is, as a place corresponding to the pre-Christian abode of the dead. But there is a hint of it in the writings of an itinerant priest, known as Jo Ben (1529). Referring to the island of Stronsay, he says: 'Some here worship God purely, others not. Many believe in the fairies (the ferries), and relate that men dying suddenly afterwards live with them, which I do not believe.'

As time has gone on the Scottish (or English) fairy has appealed more to the Orkney imagination than the Teutonic one. Two Orkney ministers wrote charming laments for the fairies. In his 'The Death of the Fairy Queen', John Sparke saw her:

> In robes of green
> With royal mein

—the accepted fairy colour at last. And David Yair, departing slightly from the romantic tradition, described her as:

> ... wrapt in golden sheen
> Of her own loved flowers the plunder.

I did not realise how strongly this more pleasing concept had taken root in Orkney until I lifted my telephone to confirm with a well-known local writer a point mentioned earlier. We were about to say goodnight, when my friend suddenly remarked, 'You know I once saw a fairy as a child of three,' and went on: 'I had been visiting my granny, who lived at one end of our house, and was coming back through a passage, when I saw a little man in green with a peaked cap emerge from a deep wall-cupboard. He was about eighteen inches high and carried a cane. He came up to me and poked me playfully in the stomach with his cane. I screamed and he disappeared. He is as vivid in my memory today as he was then.'

3

Nessie's cousins

If Nessie, celebrating her one hundredth, two hundredth or even three hundredth birthday, seven hundred feet below the surface of Loch Ness, has come to regard herself as unique, you could hardly blame her. She used to be all quiet and friendly, coming to the surface for an occasional chat with a passing monk or shepherd. But soon she won't be able to take a breath of fresh air without television cameras staring down her throat and batteries of computers starting to analyse her. It's enough to make anyone think that they are somewhat singular, especially one cut off for so long from the outside world as Nessie.

Even if it shatters this illusion, it might be good for her to know that away up north in the islands—where we have no Celtic twilight, and where the light is strong and clear—we would not dream of entering the foolish debate about whether Nessie is fabulous or not. We have been acquainted with her cousins for the past thousand years, and we can see in her the family likeness.

Of course the likeness is a bit distorted in the earliest pictures. Such ancestors as the Stoor Worm, the Kraken and the Fin King were so overdrawn that their presence seemed to fill the mysterious canvas of sea and sky. The world was such a magical place to our ancestors anyway, that, if you wanted them to visualize a monster, your description had to be of a kind that strikes modern readers as eccentric.

The Stoor Worm, or great sea serpent, was the most terrible being of all. He was thousands of miles long, and his forked tongue could sweep a village into the sea. Ships ran into his ever-open mouth and disappeared. He was, however, a dainty feeder, and always had seven maidens for breakfast on Saturday morning.

Now the David and Goliath story is older than history; and the northern world was freed from the Stoor Worm by a little man called Assipattle, who entered the monster's mouth with his boat, rowed down his gullet, and set fire to his liver. In his dying agony Stoor Worm shed his teeth, which became the islands of Orkney and Shetland.

I live in a comfortable position on one of these teeth, which are certainly black enough and venomous looking at the edge; so you can understand my interest in monsters.

The Kraken was very different from the Stoor Worm; not sinuous and swift and unpredictable, but round and flat and uninteresting, like a featureless island or a gigantic cuttlefish. The good Norwegian bishop Pontoppidan said that he was about a mile and a half in circumference, and had arms long enough to enclose the largest ship. For good measure he surrounded himself with an inky black excrement. Obviously a very remote ancestor of Nessie's and an unlikeable one.

Far more in the family tradition was the Fin King, who like the Stoor Worm had a taste for personable girls, but for reasons of companionship rather than diet. Girls were relatively plentiful, and it was only when the Fin King, who was the virtual ruler of the sea, prohibited the Orcadians from catching any fish that they became seriously annoyed. They consulted a witch, who sent out a picked crew with the instructions necessary to lure the monster shorewards and then destroy him. Any old man would have told you that there was nothing mythical about this. The pile of stones on the shore at Sandwick where the carcase of the Fin King was burned could be pointed out; and it was remembered that the man who owned the boat which lured him ashore was named Thomas Marwick.

While all this is real enough to me, I am well aware that there are people who will not believe in anything unless they measure it with a foot rule, cut it into pieces, and look at little slivers of it through a microscope. They go securely through life on the assumption that no one has ever met a monster and measured him.

Well, they are wrong. A number of completely truthful and intelligent people did just this on the island of Stronsay, Orkney in the year 1808. The monster was exactly fifty-five feet long from the junction of head and neck to the tail; its neck, carefully measured by a Kirkwall carpenter, was ten feet three inches long. It resembled a giant eel, thickening at the middle to a circumference of perhaps ten feet, and tapering greatly towards head and tail. Its head was not unlike that of a sheep, with eyes bigger than a seal's; and it had six limbs (arms, legs or fins—people called them various names): three on either side, jointed to the body near the ridge of the back, the foremost limbs being four-and-a-half feet long.

There was a mane, with bristles about fourteen inches long, extending from the shoulders to the tail. These bristles were silvery in colour, and particularly luminous in the dark. On either side of the neck were blow holes. The skin was grey, and felt rough to the touch when the hand was drawn over it towards the head, but smooth as velvet when stroked in the opposite direction.

The monster was first seen by John Peace, tenant in Dounatoun, Rothiesholm, lying on some sunken rocks, on 26 September 1808 when he went fishing off Rothiesholm Head. Ten days later a south-east gale drove it ashore, and he was able to see the carcase at close range, and almost undamaged. Thomas Fotheringhame, a house-carpenter from Kirkwall who was in Stronsay at the time heard of it, and did great work with his foot rule. George Sherar, tacksman[1] of Rothiesholm, measured it as well, and examined it until every detail had fixed itself in his mind. William Folsetter, tacksman of Whitehall, came to see the monster on 28 October but by then corruption and sea birds had done their work and it was a grisly mess.

All four men were brought to Kirkwall, where on 10 November 1808, before Malcolm Laing, MP, the Scottish historian, and Robert Groat, physician in Kirkwall, two of His Majesty's Justices of the Peace for the County of Orkney, they swore to the above facts ... so help them God.

The matter was reported to the Wernerian Natural History Society of Edinburgh who got an expert to examine parts of the animal. You can read an exact technical description by beginning at page 418 of the first volume of the Society's *Transactions*; but it may be beyond you, as it was beyond me.

It may have been a brother of the Stronsay monster that Alec Groundwater saw one summer day in the 1830s, rising out of Scapa Flow. I'll tell you the story exactly as Alec's daughter told it to me. He was a boy at the time, she said, and was sitting on one of the high banks at the 'Binks o' Birnorvie' in Orphir. It was an afternoon of calm sunshine; the water below him was lippering gently on the rocks; when suddenly it seemed to come to a boil a stone's throw from where he was sitting, and the strangest sea creature he had ever seen raised its head out of the sea and glared at him. After regarding him thus for a few seconds, it reared itself up and tried to catch hold of his bare dangling feet. It was fortunate for Alec that he was out of reach, for he was rooted to the spot by fear and surprise.

The creature had a broad head, and a wide mouth with large teeth or tusks, and cold baleful eyes. There was a long mane down the back of its neck that reminded Alec of a horse's mane. It made several attempts to reach him, bouncing up from the water. When at last it gave up, it plunged beneath the sea, rose once more to shake its head and mane till the water cascaded from it on all sides, then dived and disappeared. Alec went back many times, hoping and fearing, but he never saw the creature or its like again.

For a dead-pan factual account of a meeting with a sea-serpent, nothing can surpass that written by Captain William Taylor of South Ronaldsay in the log of the ship *British Banner*, sailing off Australia on 25 April 1859:

> I saw an enormous serpent shaking the bowsprit with his mouth. There was about 30 feet of the serpent out of the water, and I could

---

1. A leaseholder or tenant.

66 Good Templar outing, Stromness, c.1905

67 Boys' Brigade and Independent Order of Good Templars, St Margaret's Hope, c.1910

68 Guides and Brownies, Tankerness House garden, June 1922. Founded nationally in 1910, the Kirkwall Guides were established in 1916. The Brownies, initially known as the Rosebuds, were formed in 1914, and the first Kirkwall Brownie pack met in May 1922.

see his tail in the water abaft of our stern. It must have been about 300 feet long; was about the circumference of a very wide crinoline petticoat, with black back, shaggy mane, horn on forehead, and large glaring eye placed rather near the nose, and jaws about eight feet long.... The serpent was powerful enough, although the ship was carrying all sail, and going about ten knots at the time he attacked us, to stop her way completely. When the bowsprit, with the jib-boom, sails and rigging went by the board, the monster swallowed the foretopmast-staysail, jib and flying-jib with the greatest apparent ease. He also snapped the thickest of the rigging asunder like a thread. He shoved off a little while after this, and returned, apparently to scratch himself against the side of the ship, making an extraordinary noise, resembling that on board a steamer when the boilers are blown off. A whale broached within a mile of the ship at this time, and the serpent darted off after it like a flash of lightning, striking the vessel with its tail, and staving in all the starboard quarter gallery.

That monster was obviously a playful fellow; but our local newspaper was not being playful when it described Captain Taylor as 'a gentleman of unimpeachable veracity and great intelligence'.

Would you class a mermaid among monsters? Surely not. Yet I cannot help saying that among Nessie's cousins are more attractive creatures than those I have mentioned. Such a one was the Deerness Mermaid, which for several summers around 1890 appeared in Newark Bay. People came by gig and cycle from all parts of the Mainland to see her. The best description I can find of her is in—rather unromantically—*The Fish Trades Gazette*. The writer says:

It is about six to seven feet in length, has a little black head, white neck, a snow-white body and two arms, and in swimming it just appears like a human being. At times it will appear to be sitting on a sunken rock, and will wave and work its hands.

She achieved much local fame. A pantomime was written, called *The Deerness Mermaid*, and it played to enthusiastic audiences. The reactions of those who watched the mermaid from the shore were as mixed as those of the observers of Nessie. Some sportsmen wanted to shoot her, and had to be forcibly prevented by local farmers. One eccentric local poet swore that if she was captured he would marry her. The Mermaid, thank goodness, was never captured. She disappeared after a season or two, to remain with us forever as a legend.

Monsters, you see, don't just belong to the legendary past. In fact, a little way up the hill from me lives my neighbour Bill Hutchison, who has had the experience of seeing two monsters—one alive in the sea; one washed ashore dead after war-time depth-charging in Scapa Flow. I asked Bill first of all to tell me about the strange creature he saw in the sea off Orkney:

In August 1910 a cousin of mine, my father and I, took the boat to go to the Skerries of Work to shoot duck and plover. It was a beautiful day, the sun shining and the sea sparkling—it was just a perfect Orkney summer day. We got the sails on the boat, went out past the Head of Holland on a fine sailing breeze, enjoying the weather, sunshine and all.

We got round the Head of Holland and were about half-way between the Skerries of Work where we were going to shoot and the north point of the Head of Holland when we spotted a school of whales—I reckon maybe twenty to thirty—the biggest would have been about 60 feet, jumping clean out of the water. They were making in the direction of Auskerry, and they were jumping out of the sea so high that we could see Shapinsay below them. And when they came down on the water it made the spray stand up. It was a most extraordinary sight—I've never seen the like before or since. We watched these whales until they got out past Rerwick, and then my father who was steering looked ahead and I heard him say 'My God boys, what's that?' So I looked and there was something, a creature standing out of the sea. We reckoned it would be, when we came to consider it, about 18 feet straight up, with a head like a horse, a slender neck and it gradually tapered down to the sea surface. There was no body to be seen, no humps at all, but just this giraffe-like neck and head. It was a dark brown colour and appeared to have stripes running down its neck. It was looking at the whales when we first spotted it. My father took the boat off to port to get as quick as we could into shallow water where we thought the thing, by the size of it, wouldn't follow us, and I jumped for a Martini-Henry rifle. My cousin grabbed a 12-bore shotgun and we were ready if it did attack. We saw it for about five minutes and it was looking at us now, and as we headed in for the land it gradually sank down and the water closed over its head without a single ripple. We kept expecting it to attack us but never saw it again. We got close inshore in shallow water watching out for this monster all the time. We didn't see it. We went to the Skerries of Work but got no duck and no plover. My father was sort of nervous about this thing, so we stayed in along the land in at the Bay of Meal, out round the Head of Holland and close inshore until we got back to the mooring. That was the last we saw of it, and I've never seen anything on the sea like it in all my life experience either at home or abroad.

Nothing more was seen of that odd creature; but three decades later, in 1942, another monster was washed up below the farm of Deepdale on the east side of Scapa Flow. Bill Hutchison was one of the first people to see it:

> I think it was 1942 at Deepdale. A friend, Mr Spence, came here one afternoon and he told me that there was a strange sea monster washed ashore below the farm of Deepdale in Holm. A party of us, my wife included, got in the car and went out to Deepdale. We got down to the beach and I looked at this creature and the first thing I said to my friend was: 'This looks to me like the young of the creature we saw in the Bay of Meal.' It had a body shaped something like a seal, a long neck which was about five feet long from the shoulder to the head, and it would have been about twenty feet I reckon overall. The head of it was like a Shetland pony without ears, the birds had picked the eyes out of it. Even at that time it was quite fresh except for the smell of its guts. It was battleship grey in colour, and had a streamlined body like a seal. There were no flippers that I could see or can remember seeing, except two enormous big flippers on the tail end. They were shaped very much like frogmens' flippers, only far wider and broader. I wanted to get a piece of this monster as it was a curiosity to me and was not a basking shark. My friend had a sheath knife. I got the knife, we both lifted the tail flipper and I cut a chunk off it, meaning to dry it and have it as a curiosity. I took it home and after a week or so the whole thing seemed to go away to a jelly. I put no salt on it or anything else, just thought it would dry, but it became a sort of jelly substance.
>
> I think that if Nessie ever comes ashore or is ever seen dead, or can be photographed the body will be absolutely like what I would say the Deepdale monster's outline would have been.
>
> Now there is the surgeon's photograph[1] taken of the Loch Ness monster and if we had had a camera aboard in the Bay of Meal that day we saw that giraffe-like creature, with a neck like a giraffe, our camera would have shown a photograph very similar to the photograph of Nessie.

EWM: At this point I think we should make it quite clear that long before there was a furore about Nessie you had made a report of this monster you had seen. I mean, we make it quite clear you are not being wise after the event, that this story had been told to many people by your father and you from 1910 onwards.

Bill Hutchison: That's absolutely correct.

1. In April 1934 Robert Kenneth Wilson, a London surgeon, is said to have photographed the monster from 150 yards.

4

The man from nowhere

One of the most mysterious figures in folklore is the person with more than human powers who comes, as it were, from nowhere and lives for a short time with ordinary men.

The tale of such an uncanny person was once told in the island of Stronsay. A farmer there was having a terrible series of misfortunes, with people falling sick in the house and animals dying in the stable and the byre, when a young man came to the place seeking work. The farmer asked him who he was and whence he came, but his answers were so vague that they did not commend themselves to the prospective employer. The guidwife,[1] however, had taken to the lad, and with true Stronsay generosity she said, 'What does it matter where he comes from; let him alone and be good to him.'

Her husband took the advice and set him to work. Soon the whole situation began to improve. Cattle ceased to die, crops were abundant, and a feeling of well-being once more pervaded the farm.

All the work-people, except one, were tolerant of the stranger, who was easy to get on with, but insisted on one unusual privilege. He asked to be allowed to eat his meals in private, and he desired what appeared to be a more than adequate amount of food. The farm folk might be sympathetic, but they were inquisitive as well. They began to keep a watch on him and what they saw amazed them. In the midst of his eating, the young man would constantly hand some food over his shoulder, from where it seemed to be immediately snatched away by some invisible being who shared the meal. No-one dared to mention what they had seen to the stranger, for his personality completely overawed them.

One day, when the fishing season was over, a crowd of neighbours gathered on the beach near the farm to help the farmer to haul up his herring boat. It was a heavy boat, and they tugged and strained without getting it very far. Even the usual generous dram made no difference, so it was decided to send someone to get additional assistance. It was here that the stranger suddenly intervened. He asked that everyone should immediately go away

1. Mistress.

Bisgeos, Westray, c.1929

Stanley Cursiter, RSA, RSW, 1887-1976

and leave him with the boat. The neighbours laughed and grumbled, but the farmer, who knew his man, persuaded them to leave the beach. They had hardly got beyond the banks at the shore when they discovered that the lad was close on their heels. 'Go down and shore up your boat, boys' he advised them, and they returned to find the herring-boat snug in its noust.[1]

As I said, nearly everyone treated the mysterious stranger kindly. The exception was one morose, spiteful ploughman who resented the attention that was given to the newcomer, and who did all in his power to make his stay at the farm disagreeable. This lout was jealous too of the languishing glances the servant lasses directed, quite unavailingly, at the well-favoured lad.

The ploughman often set off on amatory adventures to other farms where there were girls. One beautiful morning, just before sunrise, he was returning from one of his expeditions, when he got a clout on the ear which tumbled him into the ditch. He got up in a foul rage to look for his assailant, only to get a heavier clout on the other ear. No attacker could be seen, but out of the empty air came a fusillade of blows and kicks. The ploughman could not escape. If he retreated he was whacked; if he ran forward he met a barrage of unseen fists. Shouting for help, tumbling, being kicked on to his feet again, he reached the farm at last and staggered into the kitchen, where his lamentations roused the family and his fellow servants. There were many interjections of amazement and sympathy as he blubbered out his tale. Only the stranger listened silently, a contemptuous, knowing smile on his face.

Probably he was settling accounts, for a morning or two later he was nowhere to be found, and no-one on the island had seen him. He had come without warning, and disappeared without trace. What happened afterwards to the ploughman has never been told, but the farm continued to prosper, as it does, I have heard, to this very day.

---

1. A hollow or recess at the edge of a beach into which a boat is drawn up and secured.

5

The peerie fool and the princess

A long time ago a Queen lived on Rousay wi' her three dowters. The King had died, so they had tae bide in a peerie[1] hoose, wi' little that wis their ain bit a coo an' a kail-yard.[2]

What made things worse, someone began tae tak' their kail in the night. The owldest Princess, a bonnie, brave lass, said that she wad pit a blanket aroond her an' watch fur the thief. She hadno' watched long in the dark night afore a muckle giant cam' intae the kail-yard an' began tae fill a muckle big basket, that wis caa'd a caisie, wi' the kail.

The Princess said tae him what right had he tae tak' her mither's kail, bit he said that if she wisno' quiet he wad tak' her too. Weel, what woman could ever be quiet? So he slung her on the top o' the kail in his caisie an' took her tae his ain hoose.

He said she must do all the wark: milk the coo an' send her tae the hill; an' she must taize,[3] comb, caird an' spin the wool, an' waive hid intae claith.

As soon as the giant gaed awa' she milked the coo an' sent her tae the hill. Then she made some porridge. While she wis sittan suppin' the porridge, she saw all aroond her a host o' peerie yellow-headed folk, tizing[4] her tae gae them some porridge. Bit she said tae them:

> Hid's little fur ane an' less fur twa,
> An' niver a grain I'll gae awa'.

Then a funny thing happened, fur she fan that she could do nothing wi' the wool at all. The giant wis so mad whin he cam' hame that he started at her head, an' fleeped[5] aff all her skin right doon tae her feet, an' flung her ower a couple-back[6] beside the hens.

1. Small.
2. Cabbage yard.
3. Tease.
4. Coaxing.
5. Peeled.
6. Cross-beam.

Noo, exactly the same thing happened tae the second Princess, who wis watchan the kail-yard the next night. The giant fleeped aff her skin too an' flung her ower the couple-back beside her sister.

An' the third night the last Princess, a bonny peerie ting, wis carried aff by the giant. Bit there wis this difference: whin the peerie folk cam' an' asked her fur porridge, she said tae come wi' something tae sup hid wi', an' they all cam' wi' bits o' heather-cows[1] an' broken leam[2] an' supped as hard as they could.

Whin the porridge wis deun the peerie folk disappeared, except fur wan sma' yellow-headed boy who asked if he could help wi' the wool. She said she had nothing tae pay him wi'; bit he said that all he wanted wis fur her tae guess his name. She thowt that wis aisy enough, so she gaed him the wool an' he took hid awa'.

The day wore on, an' in the grimmelins[3] an owld wife cam' an' asked fur a place tae sleep. The Princess said she had no place fur her, bit she asked the owld wife fur the news o' the isle. The owld wife could think o' no news ava,[4] so she gaed tae sleep under a big mound that they caa'd a knowe, near the hoose.

Hid wis warm there, an' deu as she wad, the owld wife fan hersel' climan tae the top. Whin she got there she heard some-ane cryan:

> Taize, taizers, taize;
> Caird, cairders, caird;
> Spin, spinners, spin;
> Fur Peerie Fool, Peerie Fool is me name.

There wis a crack in the knowe, an' the owld wife saa a whole host o' peerie folk workan inside, an' a sma' yellow-headed boy urgan them on.

The owld wife thowt that this news wis surely worth a bed fur the night, so she gaed back wi' hid tae the Princess. The Princess repeated hid ower an' ower again, till the peerie yellow-headed boy cam' back wi' the claith. Whin he asked her what his name wis, she gave a haep o' wrong answers, bit at last she said, 'Peerie Fool'. The boy wis so mad that he could hardly speak, bit he threw the wabs o' claith[5] at her an' ran awa'.

As the giant cam' hame, he met a lok o' peerie folk. They were that tired some had their eyes hingin' doon their cheeks an' some had their tongues hingin' doon their breists. They said they had been workan hard makin' fine wool intae claith. This scared the giant, an' he said that if his gude wife wis all right he wad never ask her tae work at the wool again. He wis

1. A twig or tufted stem of heather.
2. Earthenware.
3. Twilight.
4. At all.
5. Webs of homespun cloth.

geyly[1] plaised whin he fan the Princess wis just fine, an' all the wabs o' claith ready, an' he wis very good tae her.

The Princess wis reddan[2] up the hoose next day whin she cam' across her sisters an' took them doon fae the roof. She pulled their skins on again, an' told the owldest sister tae step intae the giant's big caisie. Then she pit lots o' fine things fae the giant's hoose on top o' her, an' covered everything wi' grass.

Whin the giant got hame she asked him tae tak' the load o' grass tae her mither the Queen tae feed her coo. The giant wis so muckle in love wi' the Princess that he did hid at once.

Next day, she pit her second sister in the caisie, an' covered her up in the same way, an' the giant cairried her hame. At last the Princess said that she wis goan oot fur a peeric while, bit she wad ha'e the last o' the grass fur her mither's coo ready that night, an' wad he tak' hid tae the Queen?

Whin the giant's back wis turned, the Princess got intae the caisie, an' covered hersel' wi' a lok o' fine things fae the giant's hoose, an' pit grass on the top o' hid all. The giant lifted the caisie an' took hid once again tae the Queen's hoose.

Bit the Queen an' her dowters had a great pot filled wi' boilan water. As the giant cam' under the window, they couped the boilan water on top o' him, an' that wis the end o' the giant.

Wi' all the fine things they had got fae the giant's hoose, the Queen an' the three Princesses were as happy as could be.

1. Well.
2. Cleaning.

ANIMAL STORIES

1 Seal stories 295
2 Days of the eagle 297

I

Seal stories

The sight of a curious seal apparently following my movements a little way from the shore brought to my mind the very close links between human beings and seals that are taken for granted in Orkney folklore. These have been frequently discussed elsewhere, but it occurred to me that I might place on record seal stories told to me which have not found their way into print.

It was from Sanday that we got the classic story *The Selkie that deud no' Forget*, about a seal that saved the life of a fisherman who many years before had resisted the temptation to kill her pups. A story from the same island about a seal with a long memory was related to me by a much respected friend. This man assured me that an uncle of his was going along the beach one dark winter morning around seven o'clock, when he came across a seal pup and killed it. He threw the pup into a field of turnips, intending to collect it on the way home and skin it. As he returned, the mother seal set up her head a little distance from the shore and followed him round the beach to his home. It seemed that the seal never left the place where her pup was killed, for every time that the man made his way round the shore, the sad presence in the water followed him all the way to his house, which was right on the edge of the coast. This preyed considerably on his nerves. 'Although there were,' my friend said, 'plenty of "seal burds"' (as pups were known locally) 'to be found on the beach he never killed one again.'

One often hears of dogs and cats which return to their former homes after being taken a long distance away. From South Ronaldsay I once heard such a story, but it concerned a homing seal. Before young William Sutherland of Knockhall went to sea—around the eighteen-fifties—he had a tame seal. When he was about to leave home, his mother said, 'You'll have to get rid of that seal. I almost fell over it last night, and it may learn to bite people.' William was most unwilling to part with the creature, but his mother insisted. The skipper of a local ship took it on board and put it in the sea to the west of Hoy. Almost next day the seal was back at Knockhall.

William declared that the seal had shown such an affection for its home that it ought to be allowed to stay, but he was overruled. There was a ship at South Ronaldsay that carried salt from Runcorn to the fishing station at Cara. Her captain was asked to take the seal and dump it overboard at the furthest point from Orkney that he reached. He did this. In two months the seal was back again at Knockhall, but in poor condition, with––my informant said—'the skin just hanging on it.' There is no memory of what happened to it after that.

The mystery inherent in a true folk tale permeates a story about the Holms of Ire, north-west of Sanday. The holms are little tidal islands, and the crofters in the neighbourhood had grazing rights on the outer holm, which is the bigger one. In summer, when all the ewes had lambed, they put sheep there. One man, the story goes, put seven ewes and their followers there one year. On his way over with this little flock, he killed a seal burd. That night all his sheep disappeared without trace. All the rest of the sheep on the holm were completely safe. This occurred in good summer weather, when there was no question of the sheep being swept away. Moreover, the ewes were well-used to being on the holm in summer. Local opinion attributed the disappearance of the sheep to the vengeance of the seal-folk.

2

Days of the eagle

It is a long time since a nesting eagle hovered over our hills; but there was a time when the sea eagle at least was not uncommon, and when Orkney had a store of legends concerning these birds.

I must tell you at the outset that, although I am fascinated by the lore of the eagle, I have no exact knowledge. My bird-watching friends are for the most part sceptical about some of our most often repeated traditions, especially the one without which for more than a hundred years no description of Orkney was complete: the tale of how an infant in the parish of Orphir was lifted by an eagle and carried over the sea to its eyrie on the island of Hoy. The child was retrieved safe and sound by people who had immediately set out to look for it.

One must agree with the bird-men that this is a tall story, but it was told by sober clergymen, by at least one eminent local naturalist, and by Sir Walter Scott. Indeed, Scott capped it by relating that the individual who had been picked up by the eagle while in his swaddling clothes was living in Orkney not long before his 1814 visit to the islands.

Scott also told a story he had heard from a parish minister, of how a piglet squealing with terror was carried away in the talons of a large eagle. As late as October 1861, there is an eye witness account in *The Orkney Herald* of a duck being lifted from a mill-dam in Rendall, and being devoured at a safe distance in full view of its owners.

An inveterate egg collector named Bullock said in 1812 that, 'In the isle of Hoy we discovered all the species of British eagle except the osprey.[1]

---

1. Only two species of eagle have ever bred in Britain, the golden eagle and the white-tailed (sea) eagle.

    In Orkney, golden eagles probably only nested on Hoy and never more than one pair at any time. They disappeared in the nineteenth century, possibly as early as 1844. A pair was again found there in 1966 and it seems likely that the same birds continued to breed until 1982. Since then occurrences have been rare and restricted to single birds.

    White-tailed eagles were more common with sites on Hoy, at Costa Head and Mull Head on the Mainland, in South Ronaldsay, Eday and Switha. Occupation of

They are extremely numerous, and one of the greatest pests to the poor inhabitants, frequently carrying off their lambs, pigs and poultry. Near the nest we found the remains of several lambs; and the legs of 48 fowls were found near another.' These observations are, I know, contrary to the beliefs held today by some of the best authorities on the eagle—but there it is.

In Orkney all species of eagle were given the old name of Erne. As early as 1625 an Act of Bailiary was passed for the County of Orkney, under which it was provided that any person slaying an 'earn' or eagle was to get 8d from 'every reik[1] within the parochine, except from cottars that have no sheep.' Another law allowed the killer of an eagle a hen from every house in the parish. Around the middle of last century collectors for museums were offering a guinea for an eagle.

Despite these tempting rewards, it was never found easy to kill an eagle. It was left to the egg collectors to destroy the nesting population, which they did with great thoroughness. In 1839 there were four eagles' nests on Hoy, two of the golden and two of the white-tailed eagle, and all were robbed, cragsmen taking considerable risks to obtain the eggs. The eggs of the two species being very similar in appearance, it is said that Hoy men sold what came their way as golden eagle eggs to obtain a higher price.

Probably the golden eagle was never very common in Orkney. It is very curious therefore that, in his book *Nature and a Camera*—published around 1897—such an authority as Richard Kearton should write:

> Twice—and both times, as it curiously happened, on a Christmas Day—we have seen a golden eagle perched upon the spire of
> St Magnus Cathedral, Kirkwall.

What actually happened? Was the light at the dark of the year deceiving? Was the ale which Orkney brewed for Yule and offered to its guests too potent? Or was truth stranger than fiction, and Kearton right?

It is a nice thought, anyhow, that the king of birds came to watch our Christmas Day Ba'[2] game on two separate occasions.

---

      all these locations had ceased by 1873 and only in recent years has the species been seen again as birds from the re-introduction scheme on Rhum have found their way north.

      Having mentioned the osprey in his 'eagles' context, Bullock presumably grouped other large birds of prey in this category. Thus he may have included both the buzzard and the hen harrier. The latter has a long tradition of nesting in some numbers in Orkney, and Low, writing in 1774 mentioned the hen harrier as being 'very frequent'. In contrast, past records suggest that the buzzard was rare and that it did not breed until the 1960s. There is no evidence that any other broad-winged raptors such as the red kite, marsh harrier or Montagu's harrier have been other than very rare vagrants to these islands.

1. Also reek: a dwellinghouse.
2. For more information on the Ba', see 'The games we played', pp.180-182.

WELLS AND STONES

1 Some ancient wells 301
2 Strange stones 307
3 The Stone of Odin 309

I

Some ancient wells

There was a time when water was regarded as a very precious thing. People did not have any scientific means of locating springs or the tools to dig deeply until water was found. Hence, any spring trickling out of the rocks or welling up from the ground, particularly in a district remote from lochs and streams, was a treasure. People who know their Bible well will remember how often water is mentioned. In that great poem which we call 'The Revelation of St John the Divine' the writer imagines 'a pure river of water of life, clear as crystal' flowing from the throne of God.

Even in pagan times certain wells were regarded as sacred, just as others, which may at one time have been contaminated, were thought of as evil and feared intensely. It is possible that some of the 'holy wells', of which there are examples all over Britain and Europe, are ancient wells once regarded with terror, which the Church blessed to remove the attitude of fear and loathing they inspired in people who lived near them. Other wells became sacred through transferred virtue: they might, for example, have been used by a much venerated local saint or by a brotherhood of monks; or, again, they might have been used for cleansing sacred vessels. There is at least one St Magnus Well in Orkney, Manswal in Birsay (not far from Boardhouse, beside the road at Mill Cottage), which was regarded as medicinal because the relics of the saint were supposed to have rested there. A tradition once current in the parish, but advanced somewhat tentatively by a few of the older people, was that Magnus' bones were washed in the well before their enshrinement. Manswal once supplied water to many farms in the Barony, and the reason for the tall iron pump on its stone base, which surmounted it, was to allow water-barrels or water-carts to be filled easily. This well was mentioned, with a forgotten St Ninian's Well (which was apparently in Sandwick), in a List of the Holy Wells of Scotland published by the Catholic Truth Society.

In a few places the original Norse word *kelda* (meaning spring or fountain, in Orkney spring-well) remained—as in Rousay, where Keldro is a well at the hammars[1] behind Tratland, and in Holm, where the place name Kelday

---

1. A mass of stone, or a crag, jutting out of the face of a hill or slope.

must have had its origin in an important well. It is likely that from this place name our Orkney families of Keldays and Keldies derived their surnames. Farm names were not infrequently taken from an old well on the property. Examples from Holm are Hestikelday, 'the horse well', and Backakelday, 'the well on the slope'. Vinikelday, in St Andrews, means 'the well on the pasture land'.[1]

One or two powerful Orkney springs have a name whose origin must remain a mystery. They are known as *teeve wells*. There is a Teevick Well at Horries, in Deerness; and the Teeve Well in Holm—beside the road which runs from Greenwall to the Kink at the shore—was such an important feature that the road became the Teeve Road; *Tee* or *teev* occurs as a place-name element in various wet or marshy parts of the Orkney Mainland.

A mineral well could very easily become a holy well. A case in point is the place once known as the Wells of Kildinguie, where three adjacent springs were to be found among the rocks at the edge of the Links of Hunton in Stronsay. Owing to a certain amount of quarrying in this area in recent times the water is now reduced to a trickle, but can still be identified. It was a weak chalybeate,[2] but its properties were so exaggerated that there was a traditional saying: 'The well o' Kildinguie, and the dulse o' Geo Odin, can cure all maladies but the Black Death.' That such claims can still influence modern men was demonstrated a few years ago when an elderly German gentleman, suffering from Parkinson's disease, found his way, with extreme physical difficulty, to Stronsay, and collected bottles of water.

He was the last of the pilgrims, born out of his time as it were, for in the Norse period sufferers came to Kildinguie from as far away as Norway and Denmark. They doubtless prayed first of all in the little chapel on the bank above the well, then made their way to the place where a priest sat on his stony seat, dipping a stoup into the water and blessing it as he handed it to the drinker. To whom the chapel was dedicated is not now known. Keldraseed in Sandwick had a more localised reputation as a holy well. People in the neighbourhood insisted that water from it must be used when a child was christened.

Another mineral well of ancient repute is situated beside the road near

1. Other *kelda* well names still remembered include Keldraseed, in Voystoon, near the north-west corner of the Loch of Stenness; Crossikeld in Yesnaby; the Well o' Keldereddie, near the south-east end of the Loch of Hundland, Birsay, and Mussakelda, on the land of the Glebe in the same parish; Sinniekelda, near Backatoon, in the district of Redland, Firth; Keldamurra and Kairi Kelda on Eynhallow; Backakeldie, in North Ronaldsay, near the north-west corner of the Loch Park of Holland; Cutkelday, in Rothiesholm, Stronsay; Greenakilda, west of the entrance to the Oyce of Huip, Stronsay; Hammerykeldo on the farm of Testaquoy, Wyre; Randiekeldie, below Ervadale, Rousay; and Tookeldy, near Edge-a-riggs, Papa Westray. The last named island had a Kelday-gates, or 'well road'. (EWM)

2. A spring impregnated or flavoured with iron.

Brownstown, Stromness. It had, apparently, two periods of fame: the one when, as the 'Haley Hole', it was visited by pilgrims from all over Orkney, who regarded it as a miracle well; and the other when, around the middle of last century, it was advertised as 'The Mineral Well' and had a well-house built over it to protect the water from birds and animals.[1] In its first phase it was famed as a specific for scurvy and similar disorders, which it may have alleviated. Later, it was valued as a more general tonic which visitors and townsfolk frequently drank. An analysis of water collected on Christmas Day 1862 showed a high percentage of sulphate of lime, chloride of magnesium and sulphate of iron, and a moderate percentage of chloride of sodium. The analyst was Dr Murray Thomson, who wrote a book on the mineral wells of Scotland.

For a long time the well-house has been without door or window, and the well has been unprotected from surface water. But even in the days of my own youth it was thought to have health-giving properties. Once, when my father had a protracted illness, friends in Stromness sent him weekly an earthenware jar full of the water.

A chalybeate, once celebrated and known as Blakeley's Well, was situated on the Glenorkney property in St Ola. Another, below Grainbank, was recommended to his patients by Dr Duguid, a noted Kirkwall physician of last century. The mineral well was, in fact, one of the popular fads of the time. At a somewhat earlier period the 'Water of Scoridale', in Orphir, was much in vogue, as was Winster's (or Wunster's) Well, near the shore at Villigar on the northern arm of Flotta.[2] Water from the last-named well had to be collected by a person able to remain silent; if he spoke to anyone when carrying the vessel which contained the water all its virtue was lost.

Crossikeld in Yesnaby had the reputation of having been blessed by the Church. An alternative tradition—an odd one—was that survivors from the Spanish Armada dipped a silver cross for a certain time each day into the well, thus making its water an elixir for all diseases. Like so many traditional stories, this was merely a way of providing an explanation of a name whose meaning had been forgotten. Up to perhaps a hundred years ago old people still came to Crossikeld for water when there was an illness in the family.

The well on the Brough of Deerness, close to the chapel, was used in the performance of an odd ritual. When pilgrims climbed to the summit of the Brough they circled the chapel three times, every now and then throwing stones and water behind their backs. This practice does not seem to have been

---

1. '... local magnates of half a century ago erected a stone structure with a wooden door. A ladle was attached so that all and sundry might drink their fill....'—*The Orcadian*, 19 May 1927.
2. There is a field named Hellywell near The Witter, Flotta. This is the highest land on the island.

unique; in Caithness around the middle of the seventeenth century several people were reproved by the Kirk Session of Canisbay for having crept on their bare knees round the ruined chapel of St Moddan, after which they had gone to a nearby stream and thrown two handfuls of water over their heads.

Wells named after the Virgin Mary were common. Boats used to pull in to the shore at Brough on the west side of Rousay to collect water from the Well of St Mary, near the old Mary Kirk. North Ronaldsay has a Well o' Lady, about two hundred yards from an old chapel site at the north end of the island. At the other end of Orkney, at Kirbuster, in South Walls, there is a Lady Well, situated less than a quarter of a mile from Myres Bay and a short way to the east of the Myres Burn. Water pouring out of a square opening in the sea-wall between the Weyland Bay houses and Craigiefield, in St Ola, comes, it is said, from a spring formerly known as The Lady's Well.

The people of Orkney were not always content with their own miracle-working wells. Sometimes invalids from the islands went to Loch Manaar, in Strathnaver, Sutherland. There were definite times when the waters of this loch were efficacious: the first Monday in February, May, August and November (Old Style).[1] Obviously because of the weather, the most popular times were May and August. The cure was something of an ordeal. The patient was bound and given little to eat for about twenty-four hours. Immediately after sunset on the appropriate day he was taken to the middle of the loch and immersed in the water. After this, his wet clothes were exchanged for dry ones and he was allowed to his home.[2]

The ritual described was very similar to that once followed at Bigswell in Stenness. The well there does not have a name, for the second element of Bigswell is actually a corruption of the Old Norse *vollr*, a field, while the whole name means either 'the barley field' or 'the field of a man named Bygg'. There are two wells in the Bigswell area with a claim to be regarded as the old sacred well: one in the marsh below Mid Bigswell, and the other (still used as the farm well) about fifty yards from the farmhouse on the slope above the road. Earlier antiquaries preferred the well in the marsh because of certain supposed alignments with the standing stones. Their argument is not very impressive; indeed from every point of view the well beside the old road which led through the valley from Orphir past the battlefield of Summerdale is the more likely. To the Norse mind, wells springing out of a hillside had a heightened power and were regarded with special reverence. The name given in Norway to a well with a reputation for curing disease was *sundhetskilde*, literally 'health well'. We may even regard Rendall's Sinniekelda as an example (only slightly corrupted) of this term.

1. Old Style—the Julian calendar. This was thirteen days later than the New Style (N.S.) Gregorian calendar. See also footnote 1, p.14.
2. MacKinlay, *Folklore of Scottish Lochs and Springs*, 1893, pp.249-250.

Scapa Flow in a Winter Gale, 1916

William Lionel Wyllie, RA, 1851-1931

Patients visited the well at Bigswell at Beltane (Old May Day) and Midsummer. They circled it sunwise before drinking the water. Children were bathed in it and then carried for further ceremonies to the Stone of Odin.[1] Lovers knelt to taste the water before going to the same stone to take their vows. Men and women subject to epilepsy, or of unsound mind, were plunged into the well and then tied all night to a post erected beside it. If they appeared to be cured, their ordeal was over; if not, the ritual was repeated on the next occasion when the well was considered to be effective.

A number of wells, such as Keldraseed, although their waters were valued, do not seem to have any special legends attached to them. But it is impressive to consider that such a well, which overflows into a pool, and which is enclosed by a wall of horseshoe shape, may have provided drink for man and beast for the best part of a thousand years. Keldereddie in Hundland was a haunt of fairies, but this may have been incidental, for Birsay was noted for its fairy legends. Fairies also appeared in legions at Fursakelda, below the farm of Nether Bigging.

Of the wells on Eynhallow, Keldamurra may mean 'the well in the marsh'. Kairi Kelda is more difficult. Can it possibly mean 'the beloved well', affectionately named by the monks? I first heard the later, and sadder, tradition about this well from an old man in Evie. Eynhallow was ravaged by a fever, probably typhoid, in 1851. Several people died and the remainder left the island. My informant said that the source of the infection was this well of Kairi Kelda, which he spoke of gloomily as 'the well o' daith'. Inquiries in Rousay have shown that contamination of the well was also regarded there as the cause of the fatal epidemic.

A well which had an unusual connection with death was situated at the Back Burn, near the pier of the now deserted island of South Fara in Scapa Flow. It was generally believed in the island that if a very sick person suddenly desired a drink from this well it was a sure sign that he would not recover. Even so, the request was always gratified and the water brought to the sufferer. It was a fine pure well full of clear, ice-cold water.[2]

It used to be a fairly common practice in Orkney to put a trout in the farm well. The reason always given was that the trout kept the well clean by consuming flies and insects. Children—myself included—were cautioned that never must we harm the trout. When he was inadvertently lifted out in a bucket he was returned to the water immediately. Sometimes in winter a small handful of crumbs was scattered over the surface of the well after the necessary amount of water had been drawn from it. It is not without interest

---

1. For more information on the Stone of Odin, see 'Strange stones', p.307.
2. Miss Annie Brown who was a somewhat eccentric schoolmistress on South Fara from 1909 to 1932 believed that the water was wholesome and had beneficial properties. She and her pupils used it freely.

that people used to say, when hinting that a woman was pregnant—'There's a troot in the well.'

There may have been nothing more in this custom of keeping fish in wells than appears on the surface, but one cannot help remembering that consecrated fish were once preserved in pools and streams. In Scotland there were several springs which contained consecrated fish. M. Martin in *A Description of the Western Islands of Scotland* wrote, 'I saw a little Well in Kilbride in the South of Sky, with one Trout only in it, the Natives are very tender (to) it, and tho' they often chance to catch it in their wooden Pales, they are very careful to preserve it from being destroy'd, it has been seen there for many Years.'[1] The people of Kilmore, in Lorne, in the seventeenth century, called two fishes, which were preserved in a well near the church, *Easg Seant*, or 'holy fishes'.[2] Quite late in the nineteenth century there was a trout in a well at Glenquithel, in the parish of Aberdour, which was treated with great respect. McPherson in *Primitive Beliefs in the North-East of Scotland* declared 'To destroy it would have been sacrilege.'[3]

The fish could be an eel. An old Westray lady wrote to me: 'Our well, beautifully clear water from a spring in the rocks, was cleaned out twice yearly. In it lived a huge fat eel, and while cleaning was taking place he (or she) was placed in a tub of water, and then put back in the well again.'

Although it is not strictly a well, it seems worth while to place on record the Devil's Well at the Hammars o' Syraday,[4] in Firth. This is a small bowl-shaped depression in one of the flat ledges of rock where the burn tumbles steeply down the hillside, doubtless created over a long period of time by a drip from the ledge above. Local people believed that this 'well' could cure toothache. The sufferer came to Syraday with a pin inserted between the aching tooth and its neighbour. On reaching the well he dropped the pin (and, if he was fortunate, the ache!) into the water.

1. P.141.
2. MacKinlay, *op. cit.*, pp.249-250.
3. P.58.
4. Syradale on the O.S. and other maps. This is one of many place names that ignorant cartographers have distorted. The second element is not the Old Norse *dalr*, a valley, but *dý*, a bog. Informed residents of the district, like the remarkable John Firth, author of *Reminiscences of an Orkney Parish*, took care to write Syraday. (EWM)

2

Strange stones

If you look over a northern landscape, probably the only thing you will see to remind you of the past is a grey standing stone. It is amazing the feeling of awe that such a stone can still excite, and it was the aura of mystery that preserved them from vandals in times past. In Orkney, apart from the great ring of Brodgar and the semi-circle of Stenness, there are forty-one individual standing stones—twenty-three of them on the Mainland and eighteen in the isles.

The most interesting of them, to my mind, is the North Ronaldsay one.[1] Less than two centuries ago crowds of islanders used to dance round it in the moonlight, singing lustily, on the first day of the year. I have sometimes wondered if this custom has anything in common with the Shetland one of 'Rinnan aroon da Winter Stane'. When a Shetland girl in the old days saw the first new moon of the winter, she would go to an 'earth-fast stane' and run around it three times sunwise and three times 'against the sun'. As she circled the stone she sang:

> New meun, new meun, tell me true
> Whether my love be fause or true;
> If he be true, the first time I him see,
> His face to me and his back to the sea;
> If he be fause, the first time I him see,
> His back to me and his face to the sea.

There are three erect stones on the island of Eday in Orkney. One of them, which stands at the upper end of the Mill Loch, and which is called Sator's Stone,[2] is connected with a very curious, relatively modern story. When the clergyman, George Low, was making his eighteenth-century tour of Orkney, he came on this stone and found that it had a Latin inscription: *Andreas Matheson hucusque fugit a Veneficiis Ducis Weller 1755* (Andrew Matheson fled here from the sorcerer Captain Weller in 1755). It seems that

1. Sited near Holland House, it has a hole.
2. Stone of Setter.

Matheson, who was a ship's surgeon, imagined that his captain was a powerful wizard, whose spells were affecting him badly. He fled in terror to Eday but even there he sometimes felt that the sorcerer's spells were reaching him. It could well be that Andrew Matheson put his trust in the power of the ancient stone to avert evil. The stone must have been transported some two miles before being erected, and the story is that it was set up by a local laird. He dug a deep hole, heaping the earth into a steep slope at the edge. The stone was laid on its side on this slope and gradually see-sawed by those handling it so that it would eventually slide end-on into the hole. To help to over-balance the stone, the laird made his wife sit on the bottom end. During the final heave she fell off, tumbling to the bottom of the hole with the huge stone on top of her. The laird had disliked her intensely, and no attempt was made to get her out. The monolith was gradually brought to the vertical and made firm with rocks and earth. It is useless to speculate whether or not this quaint and ridiculous tale carries in it a memory of human sacrifice connected with the planting of such stones.

Many writers have mentioned the Stone of Odin and its powers. It is clear that the stone held a position of importance in the life of the islands. Indeed of all the perforated monoliths, the Stone of Odin was the most venerated. A full description of its history may be found in the next article, *The Stone of Odin*.

69   *View of a small Druid Temple* by Richard Pococke.
    British Library, London. Add MS 14257, f79v (245 mm by 205 mm).
This pen and ink wash provides an unusual view of the Stenness promontory from the north side of the causeway between the lochs; it shows the four stones of the circle, the Watch Stone, the Stone of Odin and an irregular, but apparently holed, boulder closer to the shore of the Loch of Harray. The drawing formed the basis for the less successful lithograph, which is published in Kemp's edition of Pococke's *Tours* (Pococke 1887, xxix, 143). Drawn in 1760, it is the earliest known illustration of the site.

70   *A Plan of the Circle of Loda in the Parish of Stenhouse in the Island of Pomona with the country adjacent taken from an actual Survey by Fred. Herm. Walden.*
     British Library, London. Add MS 15511, f3 670 mm by 470 mm.
The map and watercolour were done by members of Sir Joseph Banks's party during his visit to Orkney in 1772 (Lysaght 1974, pls 8 and 6). The map seems to be the clearest indication of the position of the Stone of Odin (Stone of Sacrifice), and of its relationship to the Stones of Stenness (Crescent) and to the Watch Stone. The decorated title to the map has a picture of a stone that can only be interpreted as the Stone of Odin—the perforation is to one side and there is a worn area between it and the edge of the stone. The highest point on the stone is on the edge with the perforation.

3

The Stone of Odin[1]

Introduction

The Stone of Odin, though broken into pieces in December 1814, had such a hold on local imagination that an outline of its story is still familiar to Orcadians. The stone was pierced by a hole and this was associated with two distinct traditions—one curative and the other contractual. Through the hole, it is recorded, were passed the bodies of infants, to prevent them from taking specific diseases, and the palsied limbs and pain-racked heads of older men and women seeking a cure. It was also used by all kinds of people in making vows, particularly by lovers, who stood on either side, clasped hands inside the hole and swore an oath known as the Oath of Odin. Several visitors to Orkney in the eighteenth and early nineteenth centuries described and illustrated the stone and these accounts provide an impression of it and of its situation. The circumstances surrounding its felling in 1814 are those already discussed[2] for the desecration of the Stones of Stenness, but the stone was not completely destroyed and it may here be put on record for the first time that a part of the Stone of Odin survived till 1940. Finally some of the traditions associated with the Stone may be presented in order to complete the story from prehistoric to modern times.

Description

The earliest mention of the stone—briefly and without being specifically named—was by the Rev. James Wallace in *A Description of the Isles of Orkney* in 1693 (Wallace 1883, 26). Rev. John Brand, 'one of a Commission appointed by the General Assembly of his Church to inquire into the state of religion and morals in these parts' visited Stenness in 1700, perhaps because of the

---

1. Because of Ernest Marwick's illness, this paper was prepared for publication by Dr J. N. Graham Ritchie as an appendix to his report on *The Stones of Stenness, Orkney*, and was published in the *Proceedings of The Society of Antiquaries of Scotland*, Vol. 107, 1975-1976, pp.28-34. The paper includes a Catalogue of early illustrations.
2. Ibid., p.5.

traditions associated with the Stone of Odin, and his account is given in the first person (Brand 1883, 66). Bishop Pococke visited Orkney in 1760 and described the situation of the stone (1887, 144, *facing* p.308)[1]. Sir Joseph Banks visited Orkney in 1772 and the view of the Stones of Stenness completed by his draughtsman (*facing* p.317) is shown; it gives a good impression of the openness of the promontories and shows the stone approximately to the north of the circle, standing on a slight rise, and with the perforation clearly marked about one-third of the way up the stone on the west side. The survey of the area done by another of Banks's draughtsmen, F. H. Walden, a naval architect and surveyor, is perhaps even more important in pinpointing its position about 92 metres north of the circle and 76 metres south-east of the Watch Stone; it also contains an illustration of the stone to one side of the ornamental title (*facing* p.309).

Five other ministers of religion make mention of the stone: G. Low (1879, xxii); A. Gordon (1792, 263); R. Henry, minister of Greyfriars Church, Edinburgh, who presented a drawing of the Stones of Stenness to the Society of Antiquaries of Scotland in 1784 (Low 1879, xxiii-xxvi); J. Malcolm, minister of Firth and Stenness between 1785 and 1807, who wrote the parish entry for the Statistical Account (*Stat. Acct.*, 14 (1795), 125-138); finally G. Barry, minister of Kirkwall between 1782 and 1793, who makes a brief allusion to the Stone of Odin (1805, 209). But perhaps more useful are those accounts by visitors to Orkney who were taken to Stenness as part of the northern tour and who recorded what they saw in their day-books or journals. The immediacy of Ker's Naval Log of 1780 makes it an important source about the contractual associations of the Stone of Odin (National Library of Scotland, MS 1083). Ker visited the stones with a shooting party in the company of a Kirkwall doctor, Dr Groat; he describes the outlying stones to the north of the Stones of Stenness:

> near this are two large Stones standing singly, the shortest perforated with a hole near the Edge large enough to admit a Man's Head, thought to have been used to bind the Victims to and called therefore the Stone of Sacrifice, the other which has nothing remarkable about it is named the Stone of Power.
> Dr Groat says that about 20 years ago he remembers it customary with Lovers, when Circumstances did not admitt of their marrying immediately in a publick manner: to put their Hands thro' on opposite Sides and joining them Swear Fidelity to each other, likewise that whenever Circumstances would admitt their marriage should be publicky solemnised. He adds, that after this they proceeded to Consummation without further Ceremony & that no Instance was ever known of their refusing to keep their

1. See footnote 1, p.309 and illustration *facing* p.308.

agreement afterwards. The Situation of these Remains of Antiquity would be highly picturesque had it the addition of Trees but alas not so much as a Shrub is to be seen!

Other distinguished visitors to the area before the fateful day in December in 1814 when the stone was broken to pieces were Thomas Stanley in 1789, Dr Patrick Neill the eminent botanist (1806, 18), and Sir Walter Scott, as recorded in his *Memoirs* for 16 August 1814. Some of the more traditional names (the 'Temples of the Sun and Moon'), first recorded by Martin Martin (1716, 365), were apparently still current when the area was visited by Edward Fitzgerald in 1841 (Ross 1933).

What can be learned of the likely position, size and appearance of the stone as presented to us from the pre-1814 evidence? Wallace in comparing it with the Stones of Stenness describes the stone as of the 'same largeness with the rest' (1883, 26); Brand also considered it to be of a 'like bigness' (1883, 66), but he appears in this matter to echo Wallace, and what he says need not be accepted as confirmatory evidence. Neill speaks of 'a solitary stone of great size' (1806, 18). Unfortunately, not all the observers are in agreement: Low refers to it in 1774 as 'pretty broad stone, probably broke from its original height' (1879, xxii), and both Gordon (1792, 263) and Stanley estimated its height at 8 feet, an estimate accepted by Thomas, whose informant was a local man named Leisk. Peterkin, with the adjacent circle in mind, calls it 'a similar detached pillar' (1822, 20-21).

A number of illustrations of the stone are known, but those of Pococke and Aberdeen cannot help us to visualise the Stone of Odin. The drawing by Cleveley (*facing* p.317) seems to give a good impression of the general appearance of the stone and of the position of the perforation, and that by Stanley (*facing* p.316) in 1789 also seems to give a reliable and deliberate representation of the stone. The notes to the drawing confirm parts of Low's observations, Gordon's measurements and Thomas's informant; it is 8 feet in height, 3 feet 6 inches in breadth and the perforation is 3 feet from the ground. One of Stanley's companions, James Wright, records that the perforated stone 'would admit a hand'. Malcolm, who as the local incumbent should be a reliable source, says that the oval hole was large enough to admit a man's head, and that the part between the hole and the edge of the stone had the appearance of being worn (*Stat. Acct.*, 14 (1795), 134-135); a worn area between the hole and the edge is clearly indicated by the picture of what must be the Stone of Odin in the ornamental title to Banks's map (*facing* p.309).

The exact position of the stone would be uncertain if we had to rely on the contradictory and confusing evidence of most of the observers, but Banks's map, a plan in Register House, Edinburgh (RHP 4002), and the information collected by Thomas (1852, 101), whose local informant 'had looked through it in his youth', seem to confirm the approximate site indicated above (p.310). The Register House plan is of the common land in the parish of Stenness as it was divided proportionately between the heritors in 1812 and was surveyed by James Chapman and Alexander Gibbs of Inverness. The four stones of the circle and the Stone of Odin are indicated rather schematically but the measurements and compass bearing of this map tend to confirm the position suggested by Banks's map. This is practically the same situation as that shown on a sketch map of Orkney in 1774 by George Low, a skilled and painstaking observer.[1]

Destruction

On Christmas Day 1814, the historian Malcolm Laing was entertaining friends to dinner in Papdale House, near Kirkwall, when he was informed that Captain MacKay, the tenant of lands in Stenness, had begun to demolish some of the Stones of Stenness. Laing was much perturbed and entreated a guest, Alexander Peterkin, who had been appointed Sheriff Substitute of Orkney a couple of months before, to intervene. On Peterkin's advice Provost Riddoch of Kirkwall and Laing, as Justices of the Peace, made application to the Procurator Fiscal, who executed a Sist and Suspension against MacKay in order that the matter be discussed by the Sheriff and the Trustees of the Estate. The felling of the stones, however, was, as Hossack clearly relates, just one strand of a series of disagreements between Rae, the factor to the estates on which Stenness lay, and the Town of Kirkwall and its chief citizens (1900, 396-400). Archaeologically the damage was quickly wrought—the Stone of Odin was felled and broken to pieces; of the stones of the circle, no. 5 was toppled and no. 6 completely destroyed. As has been related earlier, no further stones were felled, but local feeling against MacKay was greatly increased by the destruction of the stones and for other reasons too, as Peterkin commented a few years later that the offending farmer 'has indeed suffered a mean persecution ever since. The peasantry who were removed by his landlord when he entered to this farm, availing themselves of the prejudice which had risen against him, partly at least as a *Ferry Louper* (the name by which all persons not natives of Orkney are designated by the vulgar), were loud in their complaints against him. Various conspiracies were basely formed to injure him, and two different attempts were made to set fire to his dwellings and his property, happily with little effect' (1822, 21).

> 1. In May 1988 Mr Colin Richards and his team, who were engaged in a rescue excavation of a neolithic settlement at the margin of the Loch of Harray in the field adjacent to the Stones of Stenness, located by resistivity and subsequently excavated a deep socket-hole, at a point about 100 metres NNW of the Stones of Stenness and 65 metres SSE of the modern bungalow named 'Odin' (NGR 30631261). The size, shape, orientation and location are consistent with what is recorded about the Stone of Odin.

Later history

The explanation made on MacKay's behalf was that his pasture was being spoiled by people who walked over it to the stones; this is hardly credible for most of this area was still undivided into fields in 1849 (Thomas 1852), and could only have been rough pasture in 1814. Another explanation of MacKay's action is that he wanted stones for building byres or a pigsty, and it has been assumed that large pieces of the broken-up stones were incorporated in the farm buildings in Barnhouse. The writer has explored the walls of that steading without finding any large stones of this type. Contrary to the accepted account, the fragments of the Stone of Odin were not used for building purposes; it appears that the Stone of Odin was completely broken up in 1814, but that a piece roughly five feet long, which contained the actual hole, remained in the neighbourhood of Barnhouse for a considerable time.

Later in the century—the exact date is uncertain—a horse-mill was installed at the farm, and the very heavy piece of stone with the hole in it was sunk into the ground to anchor the outside gear wheels. The end of the 'crown-wheel' shaft seems to have rotated in a bush fixed into the hole by running molten lead into the space between the outside of the bush and the interior edge of the hole. This short vertical shaft was a substantial one, for the mill had four wooden levers to which horses were harnessed. The horse-mill at Barnhouse was replaced a number of years later by a water-mill. This mill, on the testimony of a Stenness man who once lived at Barnhouse, was certainly in operation by 1895, and perhaps a good deal earlier. The redundant horse-mill was bought by a neighbour and taken to the farm of Overbigging. With the mill went the piece of stone, which continued to be used for the purpose to which it had been adapted. The whole of the gear, including the stone, was moved once again when the farmer of Overbigging bought a nearby farm and settled there.

At this farm the ancient horse-mill was in use until the early 1940s, when it was replaced by a threshing mill powered by an oil engine. The gear was pulled up from the 'mill-course'. Together with the massive stone it lay around the farmyard. One day when the owner of the farm was away from home, his son decided to tidy away the scrapped machinery. He found the stone impossible to move. Knowing nothing of its history, he took a large hammer and broke the stone into tiny pieces. Only when his father returned and exclaimed angrily, 'You had no damned business to break that stone: that was the Stone of Odin that came from Barnhouse', did he realise what the discarded stone had actually been.

This farmer, who is still alive, has given the writer the most complete co-operation in his efforts to gain a clear impression of the appearance of the stone. It is due to his excellent memory and powers of observation that it has been possible to form an idea of what the main part of the stone looked like. He is sad that an accident deprived us of the remaining part of what was, without much doubt, the Stone of Odin, when it had existed for a century and a quarter unknown to the general public and the antiquaries alike. The farmer, who was the last person to look upon what we may regard as the main portion of the stone, said that the hole was a fairly large one, but he could not remember if it was near to one side. The block of stone which he broke up was roughly 5 feet long and tapered in width from at least 2 feet 6 inches to something over 2 feet. The thickness at one end could have been 'a good bit more than a foot' but the stone got thinner towards the hole, which was considerably bevelled around the edge, but whether this resulted from its original 'work' condition, as described by several authors, or was the result of later trimming it is impossible to say. I handed the farmer a copy of Lady Stafford's drawing (*facing* p.316) and he thought that the stone he had seen could well have been part of the monolith she illustrated. It was, he said, a hard blue rock very different from that quarried in the neighbourhood. Mr G. H. Collins of the Geological Survey has kindly commented on the blue colour of the flagstone; the 'blue' nature of the flagstone indicates that it is rich in calcite and Mr Collins considers that it would be possible to derive slabs which were grey with a bluish tinge from beds of the Stromness Flags.

Folklore and tradition

The Stone of Odin is connected in the earlier accounts with ceremonies carried out at the group of standing stones nearby. The following is Henry's account as given in Anderson's introduction to Low's Tour (Low 1879, xxvi) and accompanied the illustration (*facing* p.316).

> There was a custom among the lower class of people in this country which has entirely subsided within these 20 or 30 years. Upon the first day of every new year the common people, from all parts of the country, met at the Kirk of Stainhouse, each person having provision for four or five days; they continued there for that time dancing and feasting in the kirk. This meeting gave the young people an opportunity of seeing each other, which seldom failed in making four or five marriages every year; and to secure each other's love, till an opportunity of celebrating their nuptials, they had recourse to the following solemn engagements—The parties agreed stole from the rest of their companions, and went to the Temple of the Moon, where the woman, in presence of the man, fell down on her knees and

prayed the god Wodden (for such was the name of the god they addressed upon this occasion) that he would enable her to perform all the promises and obligations she had and was to make to the young man present, after which they both went to the Temple of the Sun, where the man prayed in like manner before the woman, then they repaired from this to the stone marked D [the stone of Odin], and the man being on the one side and the woman on the other, they took hold of each other's right hand through the hole (mentioned above), and there swore to be constant and faithful to each other. This ceremony was held so very sacred in those times that the person who dared to break the engagements made here was counted infamous, and excluded all society.

It was likewise usual, when husband and wife could not agree, that they both came to the Kirk of Stainhouse, and after entering into the kirk the one went out at the south and the other at the north door, by which they were holden legally divorced, and free to make another choice.

Thomas believed that this account was extremely exaggerated, but gave no good grounds for thinking so. Gordon (1792, 263) was the first to put the term 'Promise of Odin' on record. He asserted that the original design of the hole was unknown (he must have meant to people who were not native Orcadians) 'till about twenty years ago, it was discovered by the following circumstance: A young man had seduced a girl under promise of marriage, and she proving with child, was deserted by him. The young man was called before the session; the elders were particularly severe. Being asked by the minister the cause of so much rigour, they answered, "You do not know what a bad man this is, he has broke the promise of Odin." Being further asked what they meant by the promise of Odin, they put him in mind of the Stone at Stenhouse with a round hole in it, and added that it was customary when promises were made for the contracting parties to join hands through the hole, and the promises so made were called the promises of Odin'. Baine wrote in his diary during the Stanley expedition of 1789: 'We were told that the young Country Lovers meet here and join hands thro this hole, and having agreed to go together, for Life they consider the ceremony equally binding as that by the Priest himself, no instances being found of infidelity on either side after this' (West 1965).

Neill (1806, 18-19) made only two comments worth noting in this context: the first was that the hole 'it has been supposed, was intended for tying the sacrifices offered at this rude, but magnificent temple . . .', and the second was that 'The more superstitious of the natives also are of opinion, that if, when they are young, they pass their head through this hole, they will never shake with palsy in their old age.' 'Up to the time of its destruction,'

A Perspective View of the Standing Stones in the Parish of Stenhouse in Orkney.

This drawing, now lost, was presented to the Society of Antiquaries of Scotland in 1784 by Dr Robert Henry, minister of Greyfriars Church, Edinburgh; it is published in Anderson's edition of Low's *Tour*, along with Henry's notes which accompanied the presentation (Low 1879, xxiii-xxvi). The whole archaeological vista between Stenness Kirk and Maes Howe across to the Ring of Brodgar is illustrated in foreshortened perspective. The drawing is peopled and may be the earliest illustration of the Oath of Odin, but is not very helpful archaeologically. The accompanying notes for C (the Stones of Stenness) and D (the Stone of Odin) read (Low 1879, xxv):

> C.—Standing Stones, called by the inhabitants of Orkney the Temple of the Moon; they are formed into a semicircle, the curve whereof is to the south; they are from 12 to 14 feet high, $3\frac{1}{2}$ feet broad, and 18 inches thick.
>
> D.—A stone which is supposed to have been used for tying the sacrifice to, it is distant north-east from the Temple of the Moon about 100 yards, and has a round hole cut artificially through it, six inches in diameter 3 feet from the ground.

A rather different copy of the drawing presented by Henry is published by Hibbert in his paper on the 'Tings of Orkney and Shetland' (1831, 122); only the central part of the view appears on the wood-cut. See also Thomas 1852.

Western Circle of the Stones of Stennis.

Elizabeth, Marchioness of Stafford (Duchess—Countess of Sutherland).

An etching executed in 1805, and published privately in 1807 (218 mm by 107 mm and 216 mm by 110 mm) as *Views in Orkney and on the North-Eastern Coast of Scotland*. The first illustrates the Stones of Stenness, and the second the Watch Stone and the Stone of Odin with the Ring of Brodgar in the distance. Four stones of the Stenness circle (and the stump of no. 8) are shown, with the hills of Hoy forming an impressive background. The second is important as a close-up view of the Stone of Odin, with a clear view of the perforation and the vein or line of weakness (shown also on Stanley's sketch), which may have made it easier for MacKay's men to break the stone to pieces.

Stone of Power between the two Temples at Stenhouse signed JTS. 1789.

National Library of Iceland, Reykjavik. Lbs. 3886, 4to—307 and 299.

This view was drawn during Stanley's visit to Stenness in 1789; the former is a unique panoramic view from the west with the Ring of Brodgar as the focus, rather hillfort-like, the stones to the south-east are less successfully shown. This illustration of the stone of Odin is particularly interesting, giving the dimensions: height 8 feet, breadth 3 feet 6 inches, the hole 3 feet from the ground. The proportions of the stone are very close to those shown in Lady Stafford's etching, but Stanley's more slab-like stone gives perhaps a better impresssion of Orkney geology.

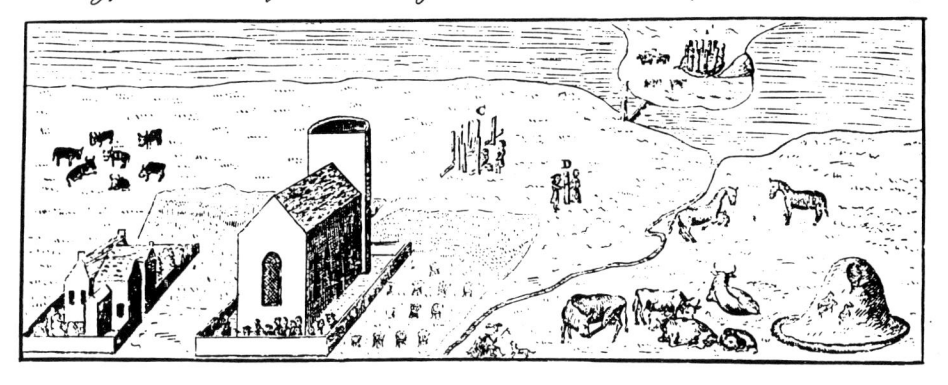

71 A perspective view of the Standing Stones in the Parish of Stainhouse in Orkney, 1784, by Dr Robert Henry.

72 Western Circle of the Stones of Stennis, 1805, by Elizabeth, Marchioness of Stafford

73 Stone of Power between the two Temples at Stenhouse, 1789, by John Thomas Stanley

74 View of a semicircle of Stones on the Banks of Stenhouse Lake in the Island of Pomona, 1772, by John Cleveley

wrote Thomas, 'it was customary to leave some offering on visiting the stone, such as a piece of bread, or cheese, or a rag, or even a stone' (1852, 101). Magnus Spence found, as late as the 1880s, traditions connecting the stone with the well at Bigswell, about two miles to the SE (1974).

Tudor gives an instance of how binding the Oath of Odin was considered to be. In telling some of the adventures of the pirate John Gow, he writes, 'Whilst lying off Stromness he fell in love with a Miss Gordon, who, according to tradition, pledged her troth to him at the Stone of Odin.... So binding did she consider this engagement, that, in order to be released from it, she considered it necessary to journey all the way to London to shake his hand after his execution in 1729' (1883, 295).

We have seen that the Stone of Odin had two distinct traditional aspects —one curative and the other contractual. It shared a curative function with a number of similar stones which have been discussed by Grinsell (1976, 15-16, 89, 91-92, 142-143), one of the best-known examples being Men-an-tol in Cornwall (Burl 1976, 332). The contractual function of the holed stone has also been recorded (Grinsell 1976, 15), but no other instance of a stone in which both curative and contractual functions were combined has been traced. A tradition of handfasting through a perforated stone, in this case of runaway couples, was recorded by Cuthbert Bede at the church of Kilchousland in Kintyre (1861, 206-207), but White, while recounting the tradition, also suggests that the stone was no more than 'a common grinding stone' (1873, 112-113). Grant seems to imply, however, that 'handfasting' at a perforated stone was not altogether a rare occurrence (1975, 362; *see also* Vernon 1911). The close association of such stones with betrothals, and the binding character of the promise, has made one wonder if consummation of the token marriage took place immediately after the ritual at the Stone of Odin; and in Ker's Naval Log one finds the assertion that 'after this they proceeded to Consummation without further Ceremony.'

There is a tendency to suppose that the name Odin Stone and the term Oath of Odin may not be of ancient provenance, but fairly modern, and perhaps fanciful inventions. Important among the considerations that have given rise to this assumption is the fact that the Odin attributions appear at a very late stage in written or printed records. There is also a belief that there is little sign of an awareness of the god Odin in Orkney history or folklore, far less any suggestion of an Odinic cult. To those who have confined their investigation of Orkney folk-belief to the *Orkneyinga Saga* it has seemed significant that there is only one reference to Odin in that work (Taylor 1938, 142). While there is obviously no way of proving that Odin's Stone was the name given to the stone by the first Norse settlers, the argument against this being so because of the late appearance of the name has no validity whatsoever. Written accounts of Orkney in the seventeenth, eighteenth and even nineteenth centuries were produced almost entirely by strangers, who had little idea of what Orcadians believed and talked about among themselves. The other assumption—that Odin hardly appears in local folklore—is based on lack of knowledge, due to the strange reluctance of historians to collect and evaluate their own island traditions.

Odin in a place name would hardly excite comment (even though there are no more than twelve with this name element in the whole of Norway; Turville Petre 1964, 66, 295), and there are certain place names in Orkney's North Isles which may well be compounded with the name of the god: Odinsgarth and Odinswick (the old name of Otterswick) in Sanday, Odin in Shapinsay, Odin's Ness and possibly Guuden in Stronsay, and a mound known as God-Odina—this is just below the house of Odness.

Memories of old myths relating to Odin were to be found last century in the two North Isles of Sanday and Stronsay and in the West Mainland of Orkney. There remains a remarkable tale, whose full significance has not been recognised. It was written down in the latter part of the nineteenth century by a Sandwick man named George Marwick, whose collected folklore, containing a wealth of local traditions, but requiring extensive and critical editing, the writer has been allowed to read. The story (related very diffusely and with extensive corruption of place and personal names) tells how Odin (Oddie), with a servant named Hermoð (Har Mowat), went to Hel (Huli) to look for Baldur (Ballie). They had a number of adventures, but brought Baldur back to life by means of the charm of the old Æsir, Mistletoe. From internal evidence, this would seem to be an authentic myth, remembered for centuries in Orkney, and owing nothing to literary sources.

Another Orkney folk-tale, related at some length by Walter Traill Dennison (1961, 55-61), tells how the man Thorodale, who freed the island of Eynhallow (Hilda-land) from the Fin Folk, acquired the power to see the still invisible island: 'For nine moons, at midnight, when the moon was full, he went nine times on his bare knees around the Odin Stone of Stainness. And for nine moons, at full moon, he looked through the hole in the Odin Stone, and wished he might get the power of seeing Hilda-land.'

This tale, which must be very old, and which was remembered in large part by an old man, born in Evie, who had not seen Dennison's printed version, has one of the unmistakable marks of Odin: the association with the number nine. Odin hung on the tree for nine nights. As the Shetland folk-rhyme has it:

> Nine lang nichts i' da nippin rime,
> Hange he dare wi' naked limb.[1]

1. Nine long nights in the biting hoar frost,
   Hung he there with naked limb.

He learned nine mighty songs from the son of the giant Bolthor; he could perform eighteen spells (twice nine); when sacrifice was made to him the number nine was important. 'According to Adam of Bremen, the notorious festival at Uppsala was held every nine years, and continued for nine days. Nine head of every living thing was sacrificed; and the bodies were hung on trees surrounding the temple. . . . We could believe that the hanged victims were dedicated to Odinn . . .' (Turville Petre 1964, 49-50). What was extremely important was that Odin was the master of magic; and very strong magic was needed by the man who had sworn to free Eynhallow. When he finally set foot on the island, he cut nine crosses in its turf, and caused it to be encircled with nine rings of salt. As for the Oath of Odin, it comes quite clearly into a curious Orkney ballad, 'The Play o' de Lathie Odivere', reconstructed from fragments in oral tradition by Dennison (1894, 53-58; but see also Bruford 1974, 71-72). A man named Odivere courted a Norwegian lady, 'An swore bae him dat hang on tree' to marry her. When he was successful, 'he bragged near and far He wan his wife bae Odin's Aith.' The story ends in misfortune and Odivere 'rues de day/He ever tuk de Odin Aith'. In discussing the ballad, Dennison describes as its 'moral' the belief that to swear the Oath of Odin was sure to bring success to the swearer in the first place, but was most certain to bring him bitter disappointment in the end.

★   ★   ★

REFERENCES

Barry, G. 1805. *The History of the Orkney Islands*. Edinburgh.
Bede, C. 1861. *Glencreggan: or a Highland Home in Cantire*. London.
Brand, J. 1883. *A Brief Description of Orkney, Zetland, Pightland-Firth and Caithness*. Edinburgh (reprint of 1701 edition).
Bruford, A. 1974. 'The Grey Selkie', *Scottish Studies*, 18 (1974), 63-81.
Burl, A. 1976. *The Stone Circles of the British Isles*. New Haven and London.
Dennison, W. T. 1894. 'Orkney Folklore: Sea Myths', *Scot. Antiquary*, 8 (1894), 53-58.
— 1961. *Orkney Folklore and Traditions*. Kirkwall. (Reprint of articles in *Scottish Antiquary* between 1891 and 1894.)
Gordon, A. 1792. 'Remarks made in a Journey to the Orkney Islands', *Archaeol. Scotica*, 1 (1792), 256-268.
Grant, I. F. 1975. *Highland Folk Ways*. London.
Grinsell, L. V. 1976. *Folklore of Prehistoric Sites in Britain*. Newton Abbot and London.
Hibbert, S. 1831. 'Memoir on the Tings of Orkney and Shetland', *Archaeol. Scotica*, 3 (1831), 103-210.
Hossack, B. H. 1900. *Kirkwall in the Orkneys*. Kirkwall.
Low, G. 1879. *A Tour through the Islands of Orkney and Schetland in 1774*, Anderson, J. (ed.). Kirkwall.
Lysaght, A. 1974. 'Joseph Banks at Skara Brae and Stennis, Orkney, 1772', *Notes Records Roy. Soc. London*, 28 (1974), 221-234.
Martin, M. 1716. *A Description of the Western Islands of Scotland*. London. (Second edition, reprinted in 1970, Edinburgh.)
Neill, P. 1806. *A Tour through some of the Islands of Orkney and Shetland*. Edinburgh.
Peterkin, A. 1822. *Notes on Orkney and Zetland*. Edinburgh.

Pocock, R. 1887. *Tours in Scotland, 1747, 1750, 1760*, Kemp, D. W. (ed.), Scottish History Society, Edinburgh.
Ross, C. 1933. 'Edward Fitzgerald in Shetland and Orkney', *Scot. Notes Queries*, 11 (1933), 161-162.
Spence, M. 1974. *Standing Stones and Maeshowe of Stenness*. Reprint by the Research into Lost Knowledge Organisation.
Taylor, A. B. 1938. *The Orkneyinga Saga*. Edinburgh.
Thomas, F. W. L. 1852. 'An Account of some of the Celtic Antiquities of Orkney, including the Stones of Stenness . . .', *Archaeologia*, 34 (1852), 88-136.
Tudor, J. R. 1883. *The Orkneys and Shetland: their Past and Present State*. London.
Turville-Petre, E. O. G. 1964. *Myth and Religion of the North*. London.
Vernon, J. J. 1911. 'Betrothal and Other Perforated Stones', *Trans. Hawick Archaeol. Soc.*, 1911, 57-59.
Wallace, J. 1883. *A Description of the Isle of Orkney*. Reprinted 1883. Edinburgh.
West, J. F. 1965. 'A Student Expedition visits Orkney in 1789' and 'The Pleasures of Orkney in 1789', *The Orcadian*, 10 and 17 June 1965.
White, T. P. 1873. *Archaeological Sketches in Scotland: District of Kintyre*. Edinburgh and London.

TALL STORIES

Tall stories

A friend with whom I was chatting the other day made what will seem an astonishing assertion, in tones of the deepest regret. 'Orkney,' he said, 'does not have one really good liar left.'

Despite the obliquity and brevity of the observation, I knew what he meant. He was referring to those magnificent 'liars'—far better call them fabulists or romancers—who, in an older Orkney, were masters of the tall tale. All such, my friend asserted, have been routed by the square-eyed monster, the greatest deceiver of all.

Story-telling is indeed the oldest of the arts; and it is sad that such an ar tform as the tall tale should have degenerated to the point where it is only represented by the shabby little stories people tell to illustrate their own importance.

Our Norse ancestors boasted of battles with giants and trolls, or exaggerated splendidly the feats of their heroes. But they also told tall tales by the winter fire, for the sheer fun of it, vieing with each other to invent additions to a tale that were consonant with its spirit and character.

Possibly the oldest of the tall tales that have come down to us is that of the Mester Ship, whose size had to be postulated before any new fictions concerning her were told. A hundred years ago (in Walter Traill Dennison's day), she was so big that her stern would be 'lying off Stronsay taking in peats from Rothiesholm, while she was taking in wood on midships at the same time off Norway.' But she grew even bigger before she sailed forever out of our ken. According to Willie Newlands, who was possibly the last man to speak of her with an imagination so vivid that she seemed actually to exist, 'her bows were stuck in the redware on the Banks of Newfoundland while her rudder was fouling the tang at the Rock of Gibraltar.'

To illustrate further her vast dimensions, this grand old storyteller would say: 'The skipper's family sailed with him, you see. One day one of his boys was working some devilment, and he ran up the rigging with the old man after him. The old man didna go very high, but the young lad went right up to the top of the mast; and when he looked doon and saw his father wasno there he started to come doon again. ... And afore he got doon, so help me, he had a beard that he could tuck into the band o' his troosers.'

Once the moon took the wind out of the Mester Ship's topsails. She had been heeling under a smart gale, and she righted herself so suddenly that the foretop-gallant mast struck the bottom of the moon. Then, as she sped on, the maintop-gallant mast struck the side of the moon. Part of it was left on the moon, along with two men who were sitting on the cross-trees mending their rivlins.[1]

The ship's bible was as big as a barn, and it took four men with hand-spikes to turn over a leaf. The Mester Ship was remembered in Shetland as well as in Orkney; and to my friend Mr Tom Henderson I am indebted for some additional details: 'When they wanted to put her about a man galloped fore and aft on a race-horse shouting "Ready about, Tiesday comes eicht days!"[2] And when she eventually came around her rudder would be stirring up the waar cowes[3] on the Banks of Newfoundland while her jib-boom knocked sheep off the Hills of Hoy. A minor detail: she had a bonnie green park on her foretop with 40 owsen[4] grazing.'

Wind and sea came into many a tall tale. An ancient mariner of South Ronaldsay came through a storm so terrifying that when his ship was on the crest of a wave he was looking down on the Kame of Hoy, while between seas the smack was lying on the sea bottom. Bad as the storm was, he did not lose such a precious opportunity: during the periods when they were on the bottom he sent men overboard with buckets to gather the cockles and mussels off the seabed.

Of earlier vintage was a tale of the great three-day storm in 1742, which destroyed nearly every growing crop in Orkney. The wind was so strong that a very fine bell which belonged to the Sandwick Kirk was carried up into the air and suspended there for two days, ringing for all it was worth. When the storm subsided, the bell fell on the Kirk Brae at Breckness, just missing a woman who was milking a cow. It made a deep hole in the ground, which was pointed out for many a long day.

That story reminded a good Orkney story-teller of a chimney in a West Mainland parish which had a vicious draw on it in windy weather. One evening when the wind rose, the people seated by the fire saw the ashes being whirled up the lum. The gale increased, and soon peerie clods, and then muckle clods, were swept up from the hearth. The watchers thought they heard a scratching noise, and, when they looked, they saw a cat being drawn stern-first by the suction from under the box bed. It held on desperately with

1. Shoes made of untanned hide.
2. This is a nonsense saying.
3. Lengths of large broad-leaved seaweed.
4. Oxen.

its claws—hence the scratching—but it was unsuccessful, and went flying up the lum and out into the night.

Many an Orkneyman spent his youth in the United States. One of them used to tell a story of two men who were employed in a city by a boot and shoe company. They had their living quarters on the seventh floor of the warehouse. Unhappily, the building went on fire. The stair was a mass of flames before the men cou d descend. Their situation seemed desperate, but one of them had an idea. There was a room close to them full of rubber boots. They broke into this room and began to pull on rubber boots, first of normal size, and then bigger and bigger, until each was wearing seven pairs. With these to cushion his fall, the first of the two jumped, followed in a minute by the other. But they had not reckoned with the spring that was in the boots. As the first man bounced high into the air, he passed the other man coming down; and as he came down again he passed the other man coming up. They bounced like this interminably so that 'They had tae shoot them doon, for they wad hae died for want o' maet.'

The interesting thing about this last tale is that it has been found in at least seven different versions between the Mid West and the Far West. For instance, 'The super-cowboy Pecos Bill had to shoot his first wife Slue-Foot Sue when her horse threw her and she bounced for ten days on her steel bustle.' The tale is even recorded from Somerset, where the victim is a little fat fellow who is blown by the wind over a cliff. ''E bounced up a 'undred feet, 'e come down and 'e bounced up fifty feet. And what's more the poor little fellow, 'e went on a-bouncing and a-bouncing for a week, and they 'ad to shoot 'un.'

★ ★ ★

There are tales that, in their imaginative quality, seem to echo the old northern myths. . . . Like the one about the Orkney seaman who bragged that he had been all over the world and to the end of it. 'What did you see there?' he was asked. 'O, there wis a great muckle dyke,' he answered, 'and whin I luiked ower, they were braakan up owld meuns and stars.'

Most stories, however, are more mundane; and it seems that at some period even the shaggy dog type of story reached Orkney. Here is an example. There is an East Mainland man who is noted for two things: his love of the game of checkers and his ability to train dogs. One night a neighbour rattled on the sneck[1] and stepped in, to find a game in progress. Seated on the top of the kitchen table, with a paw on the edge of the checker board which lay there, was the man's favourite dog, Glen. It was obviously a tense moment in the game, and the man motioned to his visiting neighbour to sit down and be silent. The dog had only three men left on the board; so had the man. The

1. Latch.

man made a move, and the dog quickly snapped up the piece, without realising that he had fallen into a trap. With a great look of satisfaction, the man 'jumped' over the dog's remaining men and swept them from the board. Able at last to speak, the neighbour said, 'My, that's an aafil clever dog thoo has, Androo.' 'Him! Whit's clever aboot him?' said the man in a weary, contemptuous tone. 'He's lost the last four games, wan efter the ither.'

The farm provides the greatest number of stories. There are several versions of the tale relating to the Harra-man and the horse. This, I think, is the best. The Harra-man had a gift of brewing ale of incredible potency. Once he hid a kirn of it in an empty 'sta' in the stable, covering it with the wooden lid and a quantity of straw. One night the man was away, and his horse, which had been tethered out on the grass, was taken in by the wife. She knew nothing about the barrel of ale, and tied the horse in the stall where the liquor was hidden. When the man went to give the horse his feed next morning, he found the animal lying stiff on the floor and showing no sign of life. The man was much vexed, but he decided to salvage as much from the tragedy as he could, and the horse was pulled out of the stable and skinned. The operation had just been completed, when the horse, which had merely been dead drunk from the amount of ale it had consumed, stood up and began to nip at the grass on the edge of the green. But the poor animal was shivering with the cold. Seeing this, the man ran into a shed for a number of sheep-skins from sheep that had recently been killed and covered his horse with them. By a miracle of nature, the skins stuck to the horse and grew on it as if they had been the animal's own skin. And each year, for a long number of years, the man got such an amazing clip of wool from the horse that he had bags more of it than any neighbour.

A Stronsay farmer lost one of his sheep. There was no trace of it throughout a winter noted for its heavy falls of snow. Only with the thaw in spring did it come to light. One day the farmer was carting turnips when he came across the ewe—now with three lambs—inside a hollow turnip which it had used throughout the winter as both food and shelter. The sagacity of the ewe was as great as that of a certain West Mainland dog, which, when sent out to caa in the ducks in the evening, only took in those ducks that were going to lay that night.

Before the reaping machines and self-binders (far less the combines) came to make harvesting easier, men could boast of great feats with the scythe. One scythe-man reckoned that he could 'tak a scare fifteen feet across.' Another notable scythe-man was very poor at sharpening his blade, but he was such a powerful man that it made little difference, for he just forced the implement through the crop. After a long day he would set his scythe against the field dyke and go home. On a particular evening, a servant-man, walking past the field, noticed the scythe. This servant-man took a pride in his ability to sharpen a scythe, and he put an edge on it like a razor. When the owner started work in the morning, he gave as usual one of his muscular swings, 'but the scythe was so sharp that he turned twice aroond afore he got stoppid.'

This scythe-man would have found his equal in a South Ronaldsay man who boasted of his strength. But this man fell ill and was laid-up for a time. When he got back on his feet, someone asked him how he was feeling. 'O, I'm waek, waek,' he answered. 'I'm as strong as an ordinary man yet though. But, O my, I'm waek, waek.'

It is interesting that the farm stories, which must be relatively late, are set mostly in the dominions. For example, many young Orcadians emigrated to Canada and came home with accounts of the wide prairies. A good story-teller who sited his farm in the vastness of Manitoba, as it might be, could achieve a temporary suspension of doubt in his audience; which would not have accepted that such an extensive farm might be discovered in Evie or Egilsay.

At the outset a general idea of the farm's size had to be given. 'The barn had twenty couples, every ane a mile fae the next een.' 'The haystack wis that big that id teuk a greyhound three weeks tae run roond id.' 'The peeriest field wis the size o' Sandwick; they cheust used id tae tether twa sheep on. Wan day we sterted intae ane o' the fields of wheat wae a binder, an' whin we stopped that night we still hadno' turned a corner.' When the story-teller had given a sufficient picture of the extensiveness of the place, he could bring in the human element: 'The foreman wis a faerful size o' a faloo. Wan day he wis pittan on his buits, whin he felt something in the tae. He tuik the buit, an' gaed id a shak', an' the herdie-boy fell oot o'd.' Needless to say, the very rodents were fiercer than in Orkney. A man jumped on to a stack on a Canadian farm to fork sheaves, and immediately fell into a great hole the rats had made in the centre. He was conscious that down below him the rats were at their work . . . 'An' fork as hard as he could, whin he wis feenished there wis nothing left o' his buits but the iron heels an' tae-pieces.'

In Stenness, some people remember a man who lived for several years in New Zealand, and who, when he returned to his native parish, could always cap any local tale with a recital of his 'experiences' in the dominion. One who knew him writes, 'He said the grass was often very bare. He once saw a lone cow in a twenty-acre field take off at speed for the other end as she had spied a daisy.'

Someone said to him, 'There would not be very strong winds in New Zealand.' 'Boy,' he answered, 'It could blow there. On the farm where I worked there was a huge barn; it was full of sheaves—the mill was enormous and driven by wind. The boss ordered all hands to start threshing. As the wind rose the mill went faster. "Thresh all the stacks in the yard," he shouted. Still the wind increased. "Fork in the midden," he yelled. As the last forkful went in, such was the velocity of the wind that the drum flew out and circled the square for a fortnight.'

Still speaking of the wind, the same man would tell that one season it was so strong that the boss ordered the kye to be tethered, and they were all like kites in the air at the end of their tethers.

I have heard the same story told, with relation to the Orkney hurricane of 15 January 1952, but with the picturesque addition that, 'The kye didno' hiv muckle tae aet, but *my*, they hed a bonnie view.' It was just such a storm that blew off the horns of cattle tethered in Rackwick; they were standing head-on to the gale and became the first polled cattle in Orkney.

One Orkneyman stood at the end of his house to watch what was happening during the hurricane. He saw about half of a corn stack going past, with a man on the side of it, hanging on grimly to the stack-net. Much later in the day, when the wind had gone down, a man came walking by with a stack-net under his arm. He paused for a moment to ask if he was far from Watten in Caithness.

One of the difficulties about the hurricane as a theme is that such fantastic things happened that it is difficult to distinguish the actual event from the imaginative fiction. In one of the best accounts of the hurricane (compiled for the April 1952 issue of *Weather* by R. G. Ross) there is this delightful tale: A farmer tells how the roof of his dwelling house, a wooden erection, was carried away. It was replaced, however, in a few moments by another roof. The farmer telling the tale says it showed how the Lord was kind. Later in the morning he and his family did their best to fasten it down, although it was not too good a fit. A day or two later, while talking to a neighbour who lived over the hill to the southward, he learned that his neighbour had completely lost a pig house, and it had a good roof on it too!

★ ★ ★

Presence of mind was the quality illustrated in a tale of personal adventure told by a West Mainland man. He was walking along the great cliffs on our Atlantic seaboard when he slipped and fell over the edge. He was greatly worried when he discovered that he was falling feet first; 'But I cheust steadied mesel, an' turned ower, an' made a clean dive intae the sea.'

A Deerness man used to tell that he once lit his pipe with a piece of ice. It happened during a particularly fierce winter early in the century. He was badly needing a smoke and had no matches. So he took a lump of ice, trimmed it into a lens, gave it a polish, and used it as a burning glass. The same man had a great misfortune during a snow-storm so deep that it buried all the houses in the parish. He was trudging over the white waste with a horse when he saw a post sticking out of the snow. He tied the horse to the post and went on. But there came a prodigiously quick thaw, and when he went back he found his poor horse hanging from the chimney of one of the highest houses in the neighbourhood.

Once a man who lived in the Scapa district shot two hares, standing in line, with a ball of roset[1] that he pushed into the gun for want of a shot; but his sporting activities could not compare with those of a Birsay man called Mansie who owned an old muzzle-loader. One day this elderly sportsman was out with his gun but found that it refused to fire. Each time it clicked, and didn't go off, he shoved in some more powder and shot. 'I hed deun that a lokk o' times,' he said, 'whin I raised a whole dizzen o' meur-hens. This time the owld musket gaed aff with a terrible roar, an' there wis so much shot in her that I waved her roond an' roond an' I got every wan o' them. But what wae deuan this, an' the recoil sheu gaed, hid caa'd me ower, an' as I fell I clubbed a hare that wis runnan cheust ahint me wae the stock. For some raison I haed left the ramrod in the gun, an' hid gaed sailan intae the Loch o' Hundland an' speared as fine a fry o' troot as I ever taisted.'

In another exploit, Mansie saw two 'doos' in the stackyard. The end of one of the houses, he considered, was within shooting distance of his prey. But he knew that if he appeared round the end of the house the 'doos' would see him and fly away. He hit upon a plan: using his knee as a fulcrum, and pushing with a hand one either side, he succeeded in bending the barrel of the gun. The rest was easy. Mansie was in hiding behind the house, so all he had to do was to poke the muzzle round the corner and shoot. Mansie got both birds.

Mansie straightened his gun. The bending did not impair its accuracy in any way. Not long afterwards he saw a flock of starlings packed tightly along the ridge of a house. He aimed at one end of the row, and as he fired he swept the gun along in an arc and shot the whole flock.

That brings me to the tale of a Westrayman who claimed to have killed 999 sparrows with one shot. When asked why he didn't make it a nice round thousand, he replied, 'Wha wad be a leear fur wan spurro?'

A Mainland farmer on the way to the hill for a load of peats was sitting on the fore-breest of the cart when two moorhens flew low over him. He had a whip in his hand and he made a cut with it. The whip encircled their necks, and he was able to pull both birds, already dead, down into his cart. Sometimes people who heard the farmer telling the story would take the liberty of doubting its truth. On such occasions the old man would retort vehemently, 'It's true enough!' and expectorate so voluminously that the spittle landed (says my informant) 'with a clep on the floor and spread out like a cow-pat on the grass.'

Sometimes a serviceman brought home a good story. An Orkneyman who was in Archangel at some period of the last war described the tremendous

1. Resin.

snow-storms he had to endure. On one occasion the snow was so thick in the sky that bombs released from a German Heinkel bomber, high above the storm, only came down when the snow ceased.

A tale of the Second World War that one islandman loved to tell was this. Some time during the war he left St John's, Newfoundland, on a ship loaded with wheat and potatoes for Britain. In mid-Atlantic the ship was torpedoed, but the story-teller was picked up by one of the United States destroyers which were with the convoy. The shock and immersion did his health no good, and he had to stay a month or two in hospital in the States before he was fit to go home. He had been torpedoed in the spring. It was summer when he sailed home in another ship. This time it was a peaceful voyage; but when, said the story-teller, they reached the part of the Atlantic where his ship had been torpedoed, they started to run into 'breer'[1] and 'sailed for two whole days through nothing but growan wheat breer.' After that, for another two days, they made little headway in a sea covered with 'tattie-shaws'.[2]

Here is a final tale, about the beverage out of whose foaming strength (some people suggest) many a fantastical narrative sprang. A West Mainland man found a neighbour somewhat downhearted because 'the barm[3] wadno go on the ale.' The visitor knew where there was some 'good-gaun barm', so he set off and got some for his friend. Next day the visitor went back to investigate. In telling of it afterwards, he said, 'Cheust whit I expected wis happenan: he hid the ale-kirn tied tae the chair tae keep her fae jumpan aff.'

And with that, my collection of tall tales has run out. There will be no more instalments of them unless a few expert 'liars' come to my aid!

---

1. The first shoots (of a crop).
2. The stalks and leaves of potato plants.
3. Yeast.

NORTHERN
WITCHES

Northern Witches
*with some account of
the Orkney Witchcraft Trials*

Numbers indicate sources appearing at end of article on pp.381-383.
Letters indicate explanatory footnotes on relative pages: *Editor*

The Norwegian background

Witchcraft has a long history in Orkney. How long we cannot even guess, for we know nothing of the beliefs of the ancient races. Nevertheless, it is certain that the Norsemen, who began to settle in the islands in the eighth century or even earlier, believed firmly in what may conveniently be termed witchcraft, if we use the term in a fairly broad sense.

If we look into Northern literature we shall find that magic, or sorcery, is a skill belonging to certain of the gods and goddesses: to Odin unquestionably, who was called the father of magic, having learned, some said, his secret wisdom from the dead, whom he called from their graves, while others declared that he was instructed by the goddess Freyja, once his mistress. Odin had many of the powers traditionally ascribed to witches: he could see into the future, bring on sickness and cause death, raise and calm tempests, and make men powerless or insane.

To think of witchcraft in the Norwegian context is to remember that there was a mythical background of intercourse between gods and men, and that in their immense mountain solitudes people felt they were surrounded by a host of supernatural beings. These beings had more than human powers. One might learn from certain of them and become wise. This idea was present in a crude form in old Norse stories. When Sigurd Favnesbane killed the dragon he roasted its heart, and when he tasted it he understood the language of birds. There was a mystical serpent called the White Worm; if one could get a piece of it to eat, and drink some of the water in which it was cooked, one was sure to acquire great wisdom and understanding. It was better still to drink some of the water which boiled over during cooking, for then one was able to see what went on all over the world.[1]

Many an ancient fiddler claimed to have learned his best tunes from the trolls, or even insisted that his fiddle was a gift from the *fossegrim*, the waterfall troll. Sometimes a girl would boast in all seriousness that her bridal crown was stolen from the trolls.

According to Zinken Hopp, the distinguished Bergen folklorist, there were at least three kinds of Norwegian witches, and the troll-woman was one of them. Another was the long-nosed witch of the fairy tales, neither good nor evil, who dabbled in magic and would do favours when asked. The third type was the witch of the theological treatises and witch-purges, to all appearance an ordinary human being, but actually in thrall to the Devil.

It was, of course, only rarely that someone acquired magical powers or became a witch. Most people were sure that the creatures of the mountains and the seas—trolls, *nisser*, *nokker*, *tusser*, *huldrefolk*, *dverger* (to name only a few)—were hostile to them. So they were always looking for ways to propitiate them, or seeking for charms or spells that would render them harmless.

A sickly condition of mind was thought to be the work of the *huldrefolk*, and rickets, called 'the English sickness', was also supposed to come from the underworld people (*de underjordiske*). One had to have recourse to a wise person to learn how to deal with such things.

The Finns—a race of witches

Now, the Norwegians never considered themselves to be good at witchcraft, but there lived in their country a race of aborigines endowed, they believed, with magical powers. These were known as Finns (though only distantly related to the present-day inhabitants of Finland) and they were so named by the Norwegians, who still use the word as the equivalent of Lapp. Shakespeare, who seems to have known most things, wrote:

> Sure these are but imaginary wiles,
> And Lapland sorcerors inhabit here.[2]

The Finns were not then confined to the far north—known as Finmark. There is little doubt that they were to be found in most parts of Norway, particularly in the mountains and islands, until historical times. A 'Finnaland', which may be located in South Norway, is mentioned in the old English poem *Beowulf*. Moreover, as Dame Bertha Phillpotts pointed out, the ancient laws of this region forbade the practice of visiting the 'Finns' to obtain knowledge of the future.[3] Some evidence was collected by Dr Nansen,[A]

[A]. Fridtjof Nansen, 1861-1930. An explorer, oceanographer, statesman and humanitarian, who made several expeditions to the Arctic.

showing that a population of Finns, noted as fortune-tellers, may have occupied certain districts of South Norway as late as the twelfth century.

Snorri Sturluson tells in *Heimskringla* how Eyvind Kellda—whose grandfather Rognvald Rettilbein was a wizard and the son of a Lapland witch—came to Kormt island with a well-manned longship, 'of which the whole crew consisted of sorcerors and other dealers with evil spirits'. In *Heimskringla* too we have the notorious Queen Gunnhild, who was found in a Finnmark cot studying wizardry. Snorri describes her as wise and cunning in witchcraft.

It is most probable that many of the Finns became thralls of the Norwegians (that is, of the Teutonic population which we know by that name).[A] Early Norse settlers in Orkney and Shetland, we may reasonably imagine, brought with them their Finnish thralls.[B] There are no place names in Orkney which can confidently be said to contain the word 'Finn', but in Shetland, as Dr Jakob Jakobsen noted,[4] there are traces of a prehistoric wall across the island of Fetlar from north to south which was known as the Finnigord, the Finn wall. The story is that the farmer of Kolbinstoft, who wished to build an enclosure round his property, promised to sacrifice his best cow if the wall was built in the course of the night. The following morning the wall had been built and the cow had disappeared. Here the attribution to the Finns of magical powers is clearly evident.

Another Shetland place name is Finnister Hadds. It is tempting to suppose that this may have meant 'the hiding-place of the Finns'. 'Hadd' was used until recently in Orkney with the meaning of shelter: an old man of my acquaintance would always say, 'Tak' hadd fur the shoo'er'.[C]

A story remembered in Fetlar by William Laurenson tells how a 'Norway Finn', rescued by an Aith man when his little boat was caught in a storm, rewarded the local people by showing them an excellent fishing ground known later as Aith's Bank. The Finn remained in Fetlar and was buried at last in the township of Aith. 'Many a stone was added to his cairn by the grateful inhabitants'.

A. A well-known Norwegian scholar told me that his grandmother was very superstitious and believed strongly in the wisdom of the Finns. When a daughter of this woman (my informant's aunt) was a little girl she upset a kettle of boiling water over her face and neck. Her mother called a Finn woman, who produced some kind of medicine compounded of herbs. This was applied to the face, but not to the neck. The face healed with practically no trace, but the neck was badly marked. The little girl, now an elderly woman, was alive when I heard the story in 1968. (EWM)

B. Earl Einar, 'Turf-Einar', of Orkney was half Norse and half thrall, tall, ugly and one-eyed.

C. Shower.

Jessie M. E. Saxby wrote in *Shetland Traditional Lore*[5]:

> I remember seeing a woman who went by the name of 'Finnie'. She was very short, less than five feet in height, and very broad in the body. She had black hair and black eyes, and it was said that she 'could do things we canna name', but her doings were always of a kindly nature, 'just the way o' a' the Finns'.

At one time it was not uncommon for members of certain Shetland families to claim descent from the Finns.

In Orkney there lived in Sanday at the beginning of the present century an old woman, reputed to have strange powers, who was known locally as Baabie Finn, and her neighbours asserted that her ancestors were Finns. There was also a considerable folklore concerning a sea-abiding community known as the Finn Folk whose home, Finfolkaheem, was situated at the bottom of the ocean. As a whole section of Walter Traill Dennison's *Orkney Folklore and Traditions*[6] is devoted to them, it is only necessary to stress here the correspondences that may be noted between this mythical community and the Finns of Norwegian history. The Finn Man was a lithe active man with a dark gloomy expression. He was the very embodiment of sorcery and magic. As a boatman he was superb, being able to pass from Orkney to Norway with seven strokes of an oar. He dearly loved 'white' (silver) money and would do all kinds of services to human beings to obtain it. The Finn Wife 'when she became old and ugly, was often sent on shore to collect white money by the practice of witchcraft among men'.[7] She could cure diseases in man and cattle. Her familiar was a black cat which, changing into a fish, carried messages to her kinsfolk in Finfolkaheem.

It is odd that in Orkney the cat should have been black. In Norway it was light grey. Troll-cats came into being in this way: the witch took cream and cow-dung and mixed them with blood from her little finger into a dough. This she rolled into an oblong and flung to the floor, exclaiming: 'I have given you flesh and blood, now may the Devil give you life and breath!' Immediately the troll-cat sprang up and went about the witch's business. The white spit on grasses in summer was called in Norway 'troll-cap spit'.

A very human touch in the Orkney stories is the observation that, if the Finn Wife did not send home enough white money to satisfy her husband, he turned up and gave her a hearty thrashing. Can we see in this a habit of later vagabonds whose wives pretended to a knowledge of witchcraft and who were identified by the country people as Finns?

There was a strong tradition in Orkney that parts of the islands were once the property of the Finn Folk. The last place to hold out against the human invaders was Eynhallow. The man who finally won it from the Finn

Folk used very potent magic. For nine moons, at midnight, when the moon was full, he went nine times around the Odin Stane[A] in Stenness on his bare knees, and looked through the hole into the stone, wishing all the time that he might get the power to see Hildaland—for such was the old name of the realm to which the then invisible island belonged. When, after many adventures, the human conqueror landed on Eynhallow he cut nine crosses on the turf of the island and sent his three sons three times round the island sowing salt. Thus there were nine rings of salt, except that the salt gave out and the ninth ring was not completed. That is why cats, rats and mice cannot live on Eynhallow.[8] Under some of the older houses in Kirkwall is earth taken from Eynhallow for the express purpose of keeping out rodents.

The continued existence of the Finns in Orkney tradition may have been substantiated by the occasional appearance, far off course, of an Eskimo or Lapp in a kayak. The Rev. James Wallace, Minister of Kirkwall, wrote in his *Description of the Isles of Orkney*:

> Sometimes about this Country, are seen these men they call *Finn-men*. In the year 1682, one was seen in his little Boat, at the South end of the Isle of *Eda*, most of the people of the Isle flock'd to see him, and when they adventur'd to put out a Boat with Men to see if they could apprehend him, he presently fled away most swiftly. And in the year 1684 another was seen from *Westra*; I must acknowledge it seems a little unaccountable, how these Finn-men should come on this coast, but they must probably be driven by Storms from home, and cannot tell when they are any way at Sea, how to make their way home again . . .[9]

One of their kayaks, according to Wallace, which was 'catched in *Orkney*,' was sent from thence to *Edinburgh*, and is to be seen in the Physicians Hall, with the Oar and Dart he makes use of for killing Fish. There is another of their Boats in the Church of *Burra* in *Orkney*'.[10] An English clergyman named Gastrel saw in Kings College, Old Aberdeen, on 12 October 1760, 'a canoe about seven yards long by two feet wide, which, about thirty-two years since, he was driven into the Don with a man in it who was all over hairy and spoke a language which no person there could interpret. He lived but three days though all possible care was taken to recover him'.[11]

There is a passage in *Heimskringla*, in the section relating to the Sons of Harald, where boats made by Laplanders 'with deer sinews, without nails, and with withes of willow instead of knees' are described:

A. See also *Strange stones*, p.307.

These boats were so light that no ship could overtake them in the water, according to what was sung at the time [1139]:

> Our skin-sewed Fin-boats lightly swim,
> Over the sea like wind they skim.
> Our ships are built without a nail;
> Few ships like ours can row or sail.[12]

The powers of Norwegian witches

An interesting story which illustrates the nature of early Norwegian witchcraft is to be found in the *Orkneyinga Saga*.[13] Somewhere around the 1090s, Hakon, Earl Paul's son, made such a nuisance of himself in Orkney that he was sent off to pay a round of visits to his relatives in Norway and Sweden. He stayed in Sweden for a while, where King Ingi was good to him. The sagaman goes on to say, 'Christianity was then young in Sweden. There were still many men who dabbled in the black art and believed they got by that means certain foreknowledge of many future events'. Hakon was attracted by this, and when he heard that there was a wizard in a little forest township who could foretell the future, he went to him and asked what his prospects were. The wizard fell into a sort of trance; he breathed heavily, stroked his brow, and said it was a painful thing to attain to this knowledge of the future. Among other things, he told Hakon that one day he would be sole ruler of Orkney, although he might grow tired of waiting for this to happen. It is possible that the inevitability of the wizard's prophecy coming true was in Hakon's mind when he confronted his cousin Magnus on Egilsay nearly a quarter of a century later, and assented to his death.

Another Norseman mentioned in the Saga,[14] Sweyn Breastrope, was 'deeply versed in the black art and had often engaged in out-sittings', The purpose of these out-sittings, that is sitting out all night in the open, was to enter into communication with the trolls. When Bishop William heard after Mass one Christmas Eve that Sweyn Breastrope had been slain, he remarked to the slayer with understandable, if not very Christian, enthusiasm that it was a good riddance. Out-sitting (*uti setid*) was, by the old Gulathing law, a crime which could be punished by outlawry. It strikes one as ironical that the slayer, Sweyn Asleifsson, is declared to have had 'the second sight in many things'.[15]

The official attitude to sorcery and witchcraft was repressive in Norway, as elsewhere, and the Gulathing Law decreed that a man convicted of having practised soothsaying or of having told fortunes 'shall be an outlaw and shorn of all personal rights; and all his chattels to the last penny shall go one half to the king and one half to the bishop'. He could, however, refute the charge by taking the sixfold oath.[A] In the Court Book of Shetland for 1602-1604 we find the sixfold oath still being imposed in serious cases of witchcraft, at least in the first instance. The Orkney rentals for roughly the same period show several portions of land 'escheat'[B] for witchcraft.

Despite the law's prohibitions, written into it by the Church (sorcery is dealt with in the Church law section of the Gulathing Law), one feels tolerably certain that the average person did not regard witchcraft as intrinsically evil. Even in later times, when supposed witches were savagely sought out, tortured and condemned to death in many parts of Western Europe, Norway was reluctant to proceed against those who were accused of the crime unless the most complete and damning evidence was produced. Witch trials in that country were amazingly few, numbering, it is thought, less than two dozen.

This was not through any lack of practitioners, or through dubiety about the sources of their power. The central idea, that one learned the secrets of sorcery from supernatural beings (more especially the trolls, or from human exponents of the arts who had themselves been in communication with such beings), was undoubtedly widespread. But it seems as if witchcraft was regarded as a legitimate and necessary accomplishment for which certain people, and even certain races, had a peculiar aptitude. Thus, all Finns were considered to be gifted sorcerers. The ordinary man and woman had need of their help to avert or neutralise the evil by which they were constantly threatened.

Evil, in the form of disease, disaster or death was the work of malevolent beings of immense variety, who exercised their magic on human beings either specifically, when someone angered them, or in a broad, general, often blundering way. Some of these beings were most dangerous to mortals at certain periods of life, and young brides or women in childbed had to be watched over solicitously. The only way to counter magic was with more powerful magic, so one function of witches was to provide protection against the peculiar hazards that beset mankind. That was why the witch's treatment in cases of sickness was not primarily a draught or potion, but a magic formula, or ritual, in which actions and words played correlative parts.

Although as has been suggested, the witch's powers were not thought of as inherently evil, they were, nevertheless, dangerous if possessed by the

A. Compurgation or oath-helping was in general use in Shetland until 1611. This was a system by which an accused person produced three, six or twelve witnesses to swear to his innocence. The *larycht aith*, the *saxter aith* and the *twalter aith* can be equated with the Norwegian *trimannseid*, *settareid* and *tylvtareid*. However, in Norwegian usage the different oaths depended on the gravity of the offence or the severity of the punishment, and discounted the significance of first offence or repeated offence, which seems to have been a development in Shetland.
B. Forfeited.

wrong kind of person. A troll-woman was a witch per se; the common Norwegian word for witch is to this day *trollkjerring*. On the whole, unless adroitly handled, the *trollkjerring* was malicious; but she was also stupid and clumsy and less of a risk perhaps than some more intelligent human witches.

If I am right in my reading of the sagas and Norse folklore, the dangerous woman was not the person with a natural gift for witchcraft, but the woman who studied sorcery for evil ends, such as Queen Gunnhild, briefly mentioned earlier, who was the reputed poisoner of King Halfdan the Black. She spent her life in plotting and mischief. She was twice in Orkney, the first time during the reign of Thorfinn Skullsplitter. On that occasion Gunnhild's daughter Ragnhild became the wife of Thorfinn's son Arnfinn. The daughter was worse than the mother. She arranged the murder of her husband Arnfinn, married his brother Harvard, and then connived at his death at the hands of his nephew Einar, whom she had promised to wed. She went on to break her promise to Einar, and had him put out of the way by one of his cousins, leaving her free to marry the third brother Ljot, who in turn killed the avenging cousin.

There were plenty of male sorcerers; like Svan of Svanhill in *Njal's Saga*, who was 'a very unpleasant person to have any dealings with', and Sorcerer-Hedin of Kerlingardale, who caused a great chasm to open under the evangelist Thangbrand.[16]

Wise-women (the term is almost a technical one) who appear in the *Orkneyinga Saga* include Eithne, mother of Sigurd the Stout, who made her son the famous magic banner which he was bearing when he fell at Clontarf, and Ragna of North Ronaldsay, a very gifted person who seems to have stayed at what is now Kirbist, in the toonship of Busta. It was Ragna who persuaded Earl Rognvald to allow the Icelandic poet Hall Thorarinson to join his court. The two poets collaborated in writing the *Hattalykill*. No stigma was attached to such people as Eithne and Ragna, who probably possessed what we call second-sight.

In the *Saga of Eirik the Red* there is a description of a wise-woman, who was more a priestess than a witch:

> She was dressed in a blue cloak, held together with straps and ornamented over its whole length with stones. Round her neck she wore glass beads, and on her head a covering of black lambskin, which had white cat's-fur inside. The stick she carried had a knob covered with brass and set with stones. Her girdle was made of amadou. A large purse was suspended from it, and this purse contained the charms she used in her sorcery. Her shoes were made of calfskin, with the hair left on it, and were tied

Haymaking, Rackwick, Hoy, 1887   Robert Weir Allan, 1851-1942

with thick laces ending in large tin knobs. Her gloves were of white catskin with the fur inside. Everyone greeted her with the greatest respect when she came into the room, and she acknowledged their greetings in accordance with the esteem she had for each individual.[A]

This type of woman, of whom there were representatives in Orkney until comparatively recent times, was believed, according to Traill Dennison[17] 'to possess all the supernatural wisdom, some of the supernatural power, without any of the malignant spirit of witches. The women of this class were mighty in counsel, in medicine and surgery, in dreams, in foresight and second sight, and in forestalling the evil influence of witchcraft. Such women were looked upon with a kind of holy respect'.

The gift of second-sight was of frequent occurrence. Its exercise was considered to be one of the essential functions of a wizard. Men who possessed it seem to have been consulted much as astrologers are consulted today.[B]

When one investigates the early days of Christianity in the North it is difficult at times to decide where paganism and magic end and Christian faith begins, as there is such an overlap. The charms drop the name of Odin and substitute that of Christ; the sign of the Cross becomes potent magic. Several notable churches in Norway were said to have been built by the trolls, among them the great stave church at Hiterdal in Telemark, Trondenaes Kirk, and even Trondheim Cathedral. The story of the erection of the Hiterdal stave church is typical.[18]

The farmers in the valley decided to build a church. To Raud Rygi, their leader, came a stranger who promised to erect it if Raud would do one of three things: get him the sun and moon from heaven, 'let his heart-blood run', or find out the stranger's name. Raud agreed, but the church began to rise so quickly that it was clear it would be completed on the third day. The farmer began to fear for his life. Then he heard someone sing inside the mountain:

> Hush, hush, little child,
> Tomorrow comes Finn with the moon
> Sun and a Christian heart; I will spare them
> For fun and playthings for the child.

It was clear that the master-builder's name was Finn. When he invited Raud to inspect the church on the third day, the farmer struck the main-post with his hand and remarked, 'This stands askew, Finn'. On hearing his name,

---

A. *Eirik the Red* and other Icelandic Sagas, Gwyn Jones, 1961, p.134.
B. In his translation of the *Orkneyinga Saga*, Dasent describes such a person as a *spaeman*, but Taylor prefers the word *soothsayer*. (EWM)

Finn replied, 'More askew will it be', and rushed out of the kirk into the mountain.

Once more the association of the name Finn with magic will be noted. But what is even more interesting is that the tale told about the church is far older than northern Christianity. A giant offered to build a wall around Asgard, the stronghold of the gods. As his reward for building it in the space of one winter, a thing the gods considered impossible, he asked for Freyja to be his wife. In addition he was promised the sun and moon. It looked as if he was going to finish his task in time. The gods were terrified that they would lose Freyja (a symbol of fertility as well as the goddess who had taught the Aesir[A] witchcraft) and be plunged into perpetual darkness. By the cunning of Loki the wall remained unfinished and Thor slew the giant with his hammer.[B] Another story of giant slaying by Thor which involves Freyja is told in the *The Thrymsquidha*, one of the poems of the Elder Edda. A translation was made by Henry Leask[C] of Boardhouse, Birsay, and published in Kirkwall in 1872.[19]

The purpose of this seeming digression has been to show that the concept of witchcraft and magic the Norsemen took with them to Orkney was one which arose out of centuries of folklore and tradition. There were no hard and fast definitions. A witch might be man, woman or troll, good or bad, possessed of tremendous powers or only limited ones. Among the many strange beings which inhabited land and sea the witch did not stand out starkly. It would be possible to tell endless stories to show how naturally the witch fitted into the legendary and psychological background, but that would be needlessly to expand this essay.

From the folklore that survives in Orkney it is clear that certain of the mythical beings, and a vast number of the beliefs which were common in Norway, found their way to our islands.

OTHER INFLUENCES ON ORKNEY WITCHCRAFT

The pure Norse traditions were constantly being modified and augmented by ideas coming in from Scotland. Among those who spread the knowledge of spells and witchcraft were the vagabonds called in Orkney, as elsewhere in Scotland, 'the Egyptians'. Whether these were genuine gypsies or not is never made clear.

- A. A race of Scandinavian gods. Odin was their chief, with Thor, Balder, Bragi, Heimdall, and Loki next in importance; the chief goddesses were Freyja, Frigga, and Idun.
- B. In other versions of the story it is Odin who destroys the giant by placing his shield Svalin in the eastern sky to hide the rising sun and then withdrawing it, so that the sun suddenly shines on the giant and turns him to stone. (EWM)
- C. It is possible that the translation was by Mr A. Laurenson.

Geillis Sclaitter was accused with her husband Magnus Linay in 1616 of having accompanied the Egyptians, and of having 'learned to take the profit from their neighbours corn and cattle by the said Egyptians, as the leader of them declared'.[20]

A few years earlier (1612) at a trial in Scalloway[A] the vocation of the Egyptians was asserted to be, after common theft, the 'geving of thame selffis furth for Sorcereris givearis of weirdis declareris of fortownis And that they can help or hinder in the proffeit of the milk of bestiall'.[B, 21]

A good example of diablerie which does not seem to fit completely into either the Norse or Scottish tradition is a formula for acquiring the infernal knowledge which was collected in Sanday last century by Walter Traill Dennison:[22]

> The person wishing to acquire the witch's knowledge must go down to the sea-shore at midnight, must as he goes turn three times against the course of the sun, must lie flat on his back with his head to the south, and on ground between the lines of high and low water. He must grasp a stone in each hand, have a stone at the side of each foot, a stone at his head, a flat stone on his chest, and another over his heart; and must lie with arms and legs stretched out. He will then shut his eyes, and slowly repeat the Incantation—
>
>> O, Mester King o' a' that's ill,
>> Come fill me wi' the warlock skill,
>> An' I sall serve wi' a' me will.
>>> Trow tak' me gin I sinno![C]
>>> Trow tak' me gin I winno![D]
>>> Trow tak' me whin I cinno![E]
>> Come tak' me noo, an' tak' me a',
>> Tak' lights an' liver, pluck an' ga',[F]
>> Tak' me, tak' me, noo, I say,
>> Fae de how o' de head tae de tip o' de tae;
>> Tak' a' dat's oot an' in o' me,

A. Of Faws, or Faas, a family well known on the Borders as the Royal Faas, who ruled in Northumberland, Berwickshire and Roxburghshire. They claimed Egyptian and Jewish blood and descent from Pharaoh's daughter. Many of their words seem to have been akin to Hindustani. (EWM)
B. 'giving of themselves forth for sorcerers, givers of weirds, declarers of fortunes, And that they can help or hinder in the profit of the milk of beasts'.
C. If I shall not.
D. If I will not.
E. When I can not.
F. The internal organs.

> Tak' hide an' hair an' a' tae thee:
> Tak' hert an' harns, flesh, bleud, an' banes,
> Tak' a' atween de seeven stanes,
> I' de name o' de muckle black Wallawa!

The person must lie quiet for a little time after repeating the Incantation. Then opening his eyes he should turn on his left side, arise, and fling the stones used in the operation into the sea. Each stone must be flung singly; and with the throwing of each a certain malediction was said.

What is one to make of this? Walter Traill Dennison was our most notable folklorist. Where his material can be checked it is impressively accurate. He was, I think, only tempted to 'improve' when he found verses that were clumsy and incomplete. His prose folklore (as distinct from his long, more literary, stories), although written in a somewhat stilted English (e.g., 'Begone!, or, by my father's head, I'll defile Hilda-land with your nasty blood!') is a good enough approximation of the tales he was told in the dialect. But one has sometimes to question the complete verbal authenticity of his spells and charms.

In the formula quoted above, the directions which insist on the person who wants to become a witch turning withershins three times, lying between the tidemarks, and placing stones at the extremities and over the heart, have the ring of truth. The Incantation, on the other hand, seems too long and too literary. It may well have been given to Dennison in its present form; but sentiments like

> O' Mester King o' a' that's ill,
> Come fill me wi' the warlock skill . . .

have a modern sound. To my ear, the kernel of the Incantation lies in these five lines:

> Tak' me noo, an' tak' me a',
> Tak' lights an' liver, pluck an' ga',
> Tak' a' dat's oot an' in o' me,
> Tak' hide an' hair an' a' tae thee,
> I'de name o' de muckle black Wallawa!

By such a reduction, certain inconsistencies seem to be eliminated. 'Mester King o' a' that's ill' is a sophisticated conception of the Devil which does not chime with the 'Trow' lines that follow. Then there is the question of what kind of being Wallawa is? Edmondston,[23] in his *Glossary*, says 'the devil', and Jamieson,[24] following Edmondston in the belief that 'Walawa' is an interjection of sorrow or disgust, suggests that the Devil is thus nominated 'the Sorrow'. Even if we accept the word as being an expression of noisy grief (as we must, for does not Lindsay[25] write of witches gathering 'with mony wofull Wallaway', and the English form 'wellaway' is familiar enough), there is still no certainty that the Wallawa of island legend is the same word, or even that it refers to the Devil. Could it not be a corruption of the Old Norse *volva*, which means prophetess or witch? Then the 'muckle black Wallawa' would become 'the great dark witch'. But anyhow, the mention of Wallawa, whatever may be the meaning and derivation, seems to relate the formula to an earlier period than the first lines of the Incantation would suggest.

Whatever the truth, we have in it a more familiar conception of witchcraft than we have discovered so far in our somewhat sketchy survey of Northern beliefs. It is true that Dr Margaret Murray[26] offers a wide definition of a witch as anyone who worships a non-Christian god and claims strange powers to heal or to cast magic spells for good or evil. But if we are to understand the nature of the Orkney witch trials as legalistic exercises which were conducted according to Scottish law (itself a reflection of the prevailing climate of opinion in the sixteenth century, when it was passed by the parliament in Edinburgh) we must think of a witch as a person who has dealings with the Devil or evil spirits, and who is able by their co-operation to perform supernatural acts. In popular phraseology, the witch sold her soul to the Devil. Dennison's formula shows us one way in which she tried to seal the bargain.

To a certain extent it would be true to say that a perverted theology, laws framed to fit it, and a murky residuum of folk belief, produced the witches. Any number of men and women were continually dabbling with recipes for curing diseases. It was a profitable activity at a time when mortality was high and legitimate medicine ineffectual. Hunger induced people to pretend to powers that they did not possess, in order that they might be paid to exercise them. Superstition was so rife that a word spoken in malice might be held responsible for any subsequent disaster. Farming was so poorly understood that crops failed frequently and cattle died regularly, without the real causes being apparent; and odd, half insane, or malevolent women got the blame. A wide-meshed net would have sufficed to catch these pathetic, ignorant creatures, but the trap devised by the lawyers, at the instigation of the clergy, had a strong spring and cruel teeth.

WITCHCRAFT AND THE LAW

The act against witchcraft was passed in 1563 by the ninth parliament of Queen Mary.

It is important to know how the Law of Scotland, which applied to Orkney after 1611, regarded witchcraft. To my mind, the best interpretation of it is contained in *The Laws and Customs of Scotland in Matters Criminal* by Sir George Mackenzie of Rose-haugh. My copy is dated 1678, and was given to me by an Orkney lawyer. Mackenzie was an expert on witchcraft. As a 'justice-depute' he was ordered by parliament in 1661 to repair, with his colleagues, 'once in the week at least, to Musselburgh and Dalkeith, and to try and judge such persons as are there or thereabouts delate[A] of witchcraft'. His book has twenty-nine pages on the subject of witches.

Although the tone of *Laws and Customs* is sober and judicial, and Mackenzie urges on kirk sessions and justices the utmost caution so that 'poor ignorant creatures' are not apprehended, himself giving instances of miscarriages of justice, he nevertheless believes sincerely in the existence of witchcraft. His prejudice is evident in his first sentence:

> That there are Witches, Divines[B] cannot doubt, since the Word of God hath ordain'd that no Witch shall live; nor Lawyers in *Scotland*, seing our Law ordains it to be punished with death.

This experienced lawyer, unable to break through the prejudices of his time, and capable as king's advocate of such harsh judgments that he has been named 'the bloody Mackenzie', nevertheless sees some aspects of the witch-hunt very clearly. The ignorance of the so-called witches he takes for granted: 'It is dangerous that these who are of all others the most simple, should be tryed for a Crime, which of all others is most mysterious. I condemn next to the Witches themselves, those cruel and too forward Judges, who burn persons by thousands as guilty of this Crime.' He is convinced that most of the 'poor creatures' are tortured by their jailers in order to extract confessions. He describes his personal examination of a woman who told him under secrecy 'that she had not confest because she was guilty, but being a poor creature, who wrought for her meat, and being defam'd for a Witch she knew she would starve, for no person thereafter would either give her meat or lodging, and that all men would beat her, and hound Dogs at her, and that therefore she desired to be out of the World.'

Mackenzie looked on what he regarded as genuine witchcraft as 'the greatest of Crimes, since it includes in it the grosses of Heresies, and Blasphemies, and Treasons against God, in preferring to the Almighty his rebel and enemy, and in thinking the Devil worthier of being served and reverenced...' Over half a century later, in 1733, (just three years before the

---

A. Accused.
B. Ministers.

old Scottish Act against witchcraft was abolished), William Forbes showed in his *Institutes of Scots Law* that proof by law was allowed that a woman was currently reputed to be a witch, that she could not shed tears, was capable of repeating the Lord's Prayer, and had the Devil's marks on her body.

In seventeenth-century Scotland the Privy Council exercised supreme authority in all questions relating to the public peace, and by the order of the Privy Council special courts, known as commissions, composed of eight local men of good standing and reputation, were often set up to inquire into charges of witchcraft. If a charge appeared to have sufficient foundation, the commissioners instructed the sheriff to summon an assize. Up to forty-five men got the summons, of whom fifteen were chosen as jurors. The commissioners presided over the subsequent trial. It was apparently permissible in Scotland for the accused person to be represented by a lawyer, but poverty, and the difficulty of finding anyone who would undertake the defence, made nonsense of this single concession to fair play.

Some historians have held that a commission, however good in theory, could hardly fail to be biased, in that all those serving on it (together with the jury) were local men, as deeply prejudiced perhaps as their more ignorant neighbours. But commissioners were very often dispensed with, and the alternative was no better, for such was the power and zeal of the Kirk,[A] on which was placed a special injunction to seek out witches, that minister and kirk session frequently acted as their own court of inquiry, interviewing witnesses, receiving confessions, and formulating the charges. In such cases there was little left for the civil court to do but pass sentence and see that it was carried out. Mackenzie was uneasy about the power of kirk sessions: '... since so much weight is laid upon the depositions there emitted, Kirk-sessions should be very cautious in their procedors (sic)'. I have not come across an instance of a Privy Council commission sitting in Orkney, but there are several records of examination by kirk session or presbytery. The fully reported trials I have examined, beginning in 1615, were all brought before the sheriff court at the instance of the procurator fiscal.

We have the most meagre records of what happened at Orkney trials before 1612, but it would seem from the slightly fuller evidence available from Shetland that the Norwegian laws in force until 1611 were not nearly so severe as Scots law, which in the matter of witchcraft was soon felt here in its fullest rigour, unlike other laws which were tempered somewhat to former usages.[B]

    A. The General Assembly passed Condemnatory Acts in 1640, 1643, 1644, 1645 and 1649, 'and with each successive act, cases and convictions increased'. Thomas Davidson, 'Rowan Tree and Red Thread' (Edinburgh, 1949), p.24. (EWM)
    B. See *The Minister and the witch* for the trial of Alysoun Balfour in 1594 which was, one feels, a complete perversion of the Norwegian code. (EWM)

If possible, under the Scots system, the accusers tried to bring evidence, no matter how fantastic, of the witch's association with the Devil, which was theologically and legally the very heart of the crime. Mysterious happenings were alleged, with the intention of showing that she was using powers not normally given to mankind. If she could be connected in any way with the illness or death of men or animals, this was done. Even the curing of disease was described as 'devilrie and witchcraft'.

The general indictment which followed the citation of evidence usually ran thus:

> And generallie, ye, the said ———, are indyted and accusit for contravening the tenour of the said act of parliament, and for airt and pairt of the using and practising of the Witchcraftis, Sorceries, and Superstitioun above specifiet, and geving your self to have sick craft and knowledge, expresslie against the tenour of the said act of parliament, thairby abusing the people; and that, by your cursingis and superstitiouns, ye wrang and hurt men and beastis; and quhilkis evillis is broght to pas be your divilrie, and working of the divill your master: And thairfoir, aught and sould underly the law, and be adjudgit to the death thairfor, in example to utheris to do the lyk.

Many, although not all, of the trials took place in St Magnus Cathedral. A ladder stored in that building, which has two sets of rungs, is supposed to be the Kirkwall hangman's ladder, but on what authority cannot now be determined. There is also in existence what seems to be the cross-beam of the town gallows, with shallow grooves which could have been made by a cord.

Accounts of the proceedings at a number of Orkney witch trials are available. Some have been copied from manuscript records of the Sheriff Court of Orkney preserved in Edinburgh. Others were transcribed last century in Kirkwall by George Petrie. Several are contained in a Maitland Club Miscellany published in 1840.[27] Very complete records of six trials and one kirk session examination are printed in the *Miscellany of the Abbotsford Club*.[28] The revised text of a 1615 trial appears in *The Court Books of Orkney and Shetland 1614-1615*, edited by Robert S. Barclay.[29] A large number of extracts from trials between 1616 and 1643 are contained in *The Darker Superstitions of Scotland* by G. Dalyell.[30] Accounts, long and short, have been reprinted in a number of general works on Orkney, and in *Social Life in Scotland from Early to Recent Times* by the Rev. Charles Rogers.[31]

Summer Storm, Yesnaby, c.1960   Stanley Cursiter, RSA, RSW, 1887-1976

Witches and the Devil

It was only by inference than the relationship between most Orkney witches and the Devil was decided, but a few were seen in his company, or confessed that they served him. (From now on there will be many references to supposed witches[A] and the trial date, if known, will follow the first reference to any individual witch).

Marion Richart (1633) was seen in the old house of Howing Greinay in Sanday, in company with the Devil 'in likeness of a black man.'[32] Jonet Reid (1643) dried corn for the Devil at Pow, in Sandwick.[33] He appeared to Janet Rendal (1629) 'clad in white clothes, with a white head and a grey beard'.[34] He taught Jonet Irving (1616) 'if she bore ill-will to anybody' to look on them 'with open eyes and pray evil for them in his name that she should get her heart's desire'.[35]

Very little is heard about covens of witches, so notorious in parts of Scotland, but Marable Couper (1624), of Birsay, confessed that 'when you lay in gissing[B] of your sone Robie, your companie came and tuk you away, and that they fetche you, and ye are with thame every moon since'.[36] Barbara Boundie was questioned by the Presbytery on 9 November 1943.[37] 'Being asked if she having been requested by Mr patrick weemse,[C] to tell if she was one of the fourscore and nynteen who danced on the links of Muness in Hoy? At first denied, but thereafter confessed that she said it, which being compared with her first words in saying that it was but six years, since the Devil deceived her, is found to vary in her speeches, for it is eleven years, or thereby, since the dancers in Muness were first spoken of'.

At a place less than a mile away from the links of Muness a coven was dispersed by John Pitcairne (Minister of Hoy 1714-1740). A crofter saw on the Green o' Gear one moonlight night a great concourse of women with a strangely clad individual in their midst. He realised that it was a coven of witches, complete with the Devil, and hurried with his news to the manse. His earnestness impressed the minister, who seized his bible and went back with him to the place. True enough, the whole brood was still there. Pitcairne advanced boldly into the centre of the ring, the open bible in his hand, and exclaimed loudly, 'Get thee behind me, Satan'. At once the Devil vanished in a sheet of flame, and the witches departed with supernatural haste.[38]

It is of interest that witches were said to convene at these places, just under the shadow of the Ward Hill, Orkney's highest mountain. One recalls

---

A. For ease of reading, in many cases I have modernised the old Scottish forms.
B. Childbed.
C. Patrick Wemis AM translated to Ladykirk, Sanday in 1647.

that the northern witches were always partial to mountains as meeting places.^A The Kirk of Hoy in the same vicinity had also some occult significance. John Sinclair (1633), under silence and cloud of night, took his ailing sister with him, and 'horsed her backwards from where she lay, to the Kirk of Hoy, where he met the kirk sevin fathoms;^B at that tyme a voice appeared saying, "sevin is ower many for one sin". Thaireftir, he tuik hir, and layed hir at the north side . . . by directioun of the devill: and in the morning, the first thing she saw, was a boat with fyve men, whereof four perished, and one was saved—by which devillry the woman became well'.[39]

Where the Devil had not made an appearance, the courts were quite willing to settle for fairies. Jonet Drever (1615) was declared to be 'convicted and guilty of the fostering of a child in the hill of Westray to the fairy folk called by her "our good neighbours" and in having carnal dealings with her and having conversation with the fairies 26 years before'.[40] Issobell Sinclair (1633) was accused that during seven years 'six times at the quarters of the year, she has been controlled by the fairies; and that by them, she has the second sight'.[41] A poor demented creature named Elspeth Reoch (1616) confessed to various meetings with the Devil in the shape of a fairy. On one occasion he had told her, as well he might, that Orkney was Priestgone,^C as there were too many ministers in it.[42]

The witch's cat

Apart from the tradition about the Finn Wife already mentioned, the idea of a witch having a familiar seldom comes into Orkney witchcraft. But the cat plays some part in the story. Thomas Logie, coming past the Cross Kirk, in Sanday, on 3 September 1616, late in the evening, 'and meeting a number of cats within the dyke of Colzigar, upon the brae, among the bere sheaves, which surrounded him', the said Thomas saw Anie Tailzeour's (1624) face on one of the cats. He challenged old Anie afterwards, and immediately contracted a sickness which lasted two years. When his wife confronted the witch, the sickness was placed on her, 'who yet continues sick and not likely to live'.[43]

There is a memory of an old woman, known as Recchel, who often appeared when fishermen were returning from sea in the form of a black cat

---

A. The German and Scandinavian witches congregated on mountains to conduct their wild orgies. In Germany such a mountain was Blocksberg, in Iceland Heckla, and in Norway one of the so-called seven mountains around Bergen, the Lyderhorn. (EWM)

B. He circled the kirk seven times fathoming it with his outstretched arms against the wall.

C. Priest ridden.

with a white spot on her face. She would mew piteously in the hope of being thrown a fish. Another person told me that her father's aunt was as a girl a fellow servant with Recchel at Elsness in Sanday. One evening both girls were sitting together by the fire in the kitchen, when Recchel said 'Would you like to see me change into a cat?' She disappeared immediately, and there was a black cat standing beside her chair. She turned back almost at once into a girl.

When two young men fell ill with a dangerous and infectious fever at a house near the Cross Kirk, no-one was brave enough to go and look after them. It was said that food was taken to them by Recchel in the form of a cat. At this very time a cat was caught in a trap on Backaskaill Links. Its leg was broken, or was broken by the trapper, but it was allowed to go away otherwise unharmed. Soon it became known that Recchel was confined to bed with a broken leg.

One day a fisherman kicked the cat in the face when she got in his way, and next day Recchel had a black eye and a bruised nose. The old woman was eventually found dead in her cottage by the mother of a good friend of mine.

The circumstances struck the discoverer as most peculiar. 'There', said my informant, 'was Recchel lying dead in bed. All around her were bunches of everlasting grass (in Orkney tradition this was associated with witchcraft); the fire was full of burnt copper—pennies and halfpennies—the clock had stopped; and Recchel's black cat lay dead on the top of the box bed.'

Householders in a certain part of Kirkwall were always having something or other stolen from their gardens during the night. Although they kept watch, they could never discover a likely thief. But they noticed frequently a big grey cat prowling in the vicinity. It was rumoured that an old woman changed herself into a cat so that she could see in the dark and roam around unsuspected. One night, after his own garden had been severely raided, a man armed himself with a stick and went out to look for this cat. He found it at last sitting on a garden wall, glaring balefully. Seemingly aware of the stick in his hand as a menace to itself, the cat sprang on the man and tried desperately to get at his throat, around which he had folded as a precaution a thick woollen cravat. At last, the man managed to grasp the cat by the nape of the neck and tear it off him. He flung it with all his strength to the ground, and so belaboured the cat with his stick that he imagined he had broken every bone in its body, then went home satisfied. The next day the old woman on whom suspicion had rested was reported to be very ill in bed, and a doctor was called in to set some broken bones. There was no more pilfering from gardens after that episode.

The cat was a potent factor in certain magical formulae. When a fisherman failed over a period to get any fish, the remedy was to wash the cat's head and feet in the water in which he kept his bait. This water was then poured over the fisherman, his bait cubbie,[A] and his sea kaizie.[B] Marion Richart was accused of carrying out this procedure twice in Sanday in the first part of the seventeenth century.[44]

Katherine Cragie of Rousay (1643) advised a bride who was going to set up house on the neigbouring island of Egilsay to take with her to her new home the wash cog[C] and the cat.[45] The reason for this is not made clear in Katherine's trial, but in J. M. McPherson's *Primitive Beliefs in the North-East of Scotland* he writes, 'An Orkney woman, on marriage, took the cat with her to her new home. If there was evil in the house, it fell upon the cat and it died, saving the lives of the family'.[46] The many superstitions about the cat, not directly connected with witchcraft, cannot be related here. Its taboo name[D] was 'the thing that goes about the fire'.

Witches' activities

There was little of enterprising and hair-raising devilry in the Orkney witches' activities. One of the few macabre incidents related was from Westray, where Katherene Bigland (1615) stood 'on the style of the kirk yard of the Cross Kirk of Westray with drawn knives in her hand while Marioun Tailyeour, her mother, and others who were in her company, came out of the said kirk, for most part of a night'.[47] This is an obscure statement. It may mean that Katherene stood on guard while a coven was in progress, but my interpretation is that Katherene was accused of raising a procession of the dead.

Unusual occurrences were at times attributed to witches. During the Lisbon earthquake of 1 November 1755, coasts all round the British Isles were swept by a tidal wave. The laird of Breckness, in Stromness parish, made a race for his life on horseback, accompanied by the ranzelman, or parish constable, on foot. The latter, as he struggled to safety, saw a local witch, Annie Caird, dancing around him. Blaming her for the terrifying occurrence, the ranzelman dealt her such a heavy blow that, as he afterwards declared, she flew away in a 'blue lowe'.[E,48]

A farmer in Tankerness had a small boat in which he frequently went fishing when his day's work was done. He was usually accompanied by some of his neighbours. One evening this farmer planned to go out to fish, but

A. A small basket made of straw or heather.
B. A larger carrying basket made of straw or heather.
C. A small wooden basin.
D. A substitute name used to avoid misfortune.
E. Blue flame.

TO THE
ELECTORS
OF
ORKNEY.

GENTLEMEN,—

No one invited me to come among you. My coming is the result of having all my expenses paid out of Mr Dalrymple's Election Fund, and more particularly of the supreme conviction I have always entertained as to my own capacity to fill any situation, from that of a mere Pamphleteer—as I have been hitherto—to that of an M.P., or even a Premier. I did not think it necessary to announce my coming, knowing that my own Party were bound to gratefully accept whatever was sent to them, whether man or monkey. Without wasting time in the mere courtesy of calling on Electors in Kirkwall, I therefore pushed on to Shetland in the first instance, trusting that the greater ignorance which I expected to find in these extreme northern regions would be most easily imposed upon—a hope which, I regret to say, has not been *quite* fulfilled.

"The present political condition of our Country is momentous. I consider that the prudent and far-seeing policy of Her Majesty's Government in Foreign Affairs has restored our Country, as a Christian Kingdom, to its rightful condition among the nations of the earth." This has been accomplished by picking a quarrel with and slaughtering 10,000 Zulus —(who have no souls)—by breaking the faith of our Treaty with the Dutch Boers in the Transvaal—by requisitioning the Indian Famine Fund, and compelling India to pay for a war thrust upon her against her will—by destroying a neighbour with whom we were at peace, and turning Afghanistan into a determined enemy. All these acts, in my opinion, prove that our Christianity is unimpeachable.

I am of opinion that dissenters from the State Church of England have no right to Christian interment, but should be "buried with the burial of an ass." I am likewise of opinion that the Scotch Church should continue to be Established and Endowed, that she may be used as a political engine by the Christian Conservative Party, through their mutual "Consolidation of Co-operation."

I believe that great advances towards the general enlightenment and progress of humanity were made by gagging the press of India, and refusing necessary information to Parliament, thereby "dishing the Liberals."

I consider that our national honour and morals are to be maintained in their purity, and I therefore have no scruple in slandering the Liberal Party, whenever possible, by stating that they have combined with the Home Rulers to subvert the Church and State. Although both parties join in declaring that this is not true, I still continue to reiterate it.

I believe that the most powerful political weapon is brag, and I will therefore support the present Christian Government whenever they go in search of "Peace with honour," whether in Cyprus, Asia Minor, or Berlin.

The highest Foreign Policy of this Empire is self-aggrandisement; and I therefore regard the surreptitious acquisition of the unhealthy and useless island of Cyprus as a great national triumph.

My opinions regarding Finance are a little hazy, but I feel certain that the proper direction of taxation is to burden the Tenants and relieve the Proprietors, as has just been done through the Inventory Duties and otherwise, by the Conservatives.

I greatly regret that the Ballot secures absolute secrecy, and thus prevents voters from being coerced, and I also regret that "Faggot Votes" cannot be more rapidly manufactured to meet cases of necessity such as at present existing in Mid-Lothian. If I am elected, I will be glad to assist in putting these matters on a very different footing.

Gentlemen, I am above giving pledges, but if you do me the honour to elect me as your Representative, you may rest assured that for any—*any*—Conservative requirement I will always be found,

Very truly, a

JINGO ROWDY BAD-ENOUGH, LL.D.

(Lying Liberal Detractor.)

75 Electioneering poster, 1880

The Stromness News, second issue, 7 March 1884

found that the arrangement did not suit one of his neighbours. The neighbour in question asked the others to put off the expedition until he could go with them. This the party were reluctant to do, and prepared to go to sea without him. The man who was going to be left behind had a queer reputation in the parish. He immediately declared that if the others were fishing by themselves they would catch nothing. One of the men replied laughingly, 'Jeust thoo go home an' sit on thee shells[A] an' deu a' thoo can, bit we're gaun tae hae a try onywey'. The man went off, muttering angrily to himself, while his neighbours went to the fishing ground. When they threw their lines on the water, however, they were dismayed to see their lead sinkers floating on the top. They had to go home empty-handed that night; but the next time that the man accompanied them the sinkers acted naturally and they had a good haul of fish.

A party of men in Rousay wanted to salve goods from a wreck before the proper officials arrived to take it over. These men had gathered a large pile together, but had to carry the articles some distance to the place where they had determined to hide them. The night was a lovely one with very bright moonlight. The men stood in a group in a dark spot, grumbling about the danger of being seen on such a clear night. One of their number stepped forward and berated them for doing nothing. He would guarantee, he said, that they would get all the stuff away without being seen. They set to work, each man taking as much as he could carry. As they started off from the shore a heavy mist enveloped the whole party, and travelled with them as they went back and forth with fresh loads from the wreck. As soon as they had everything safely stowed away the mist lifted and the moon shone as brightly as before. Enquiries made next day confirmed that no mist had been seen by anyone else on any part of the island that night.

Agents of death and disease

Causing death, and bringing on disease or curing it, were the most frequent allegations made against witches. In charges made during the first half of the seventeenth century against twenty local witches, whose cases I have studied, there were fourteen concerned with bringing death to human beings and thirteen with causing animals to die.

The causation of sickness in men and women was alleged ten times, and in animals four times. The same twenty witches were said to have cured twenty-four persons of various kinds of sickness, and seven cattle (or horses). They had been responsible for what was known technically as 'loss of profit' thirteen times.

[A]. The derisory suggestion was that the reluctant man went home and sat on his bait, which would have been limpets and whelks.

Often when a person died, a woman's vague threats or general animosity were remembered against her. But sometimes cause and effect were linked more closely. Katherine Cragie was reminded that she said, 'Henrie Zorstoun hes bein making reportis of me, but ere one year be at ane end he sall find it.'[A] Henrie died within the year, and Essen Corse, who was to have been examined on his knowledge of this incident by the kirk session, ere the session day came, was caught, when fishing from the rocks, 'with ane swelling sea, and drouned'.[49] When Jonet Rendall was refused lodging at Christmas, she said, 'it was guid to know if ever the guidman of the house should make another yule banquet'. Within fifteen days he was dead.[50]

If cattle died, it was sufficient if the reputed witch had walked over the fields or looked into the byre. Some women, however, made specific threats. Annie Tailzeour, mentioned above, seems to have been a sour, short-tempered person, many of whose threats were remembered at her trial: 'About mid somer, fyve zeiris syne, James Ego, smyth, his wyff haueing tane ane loik of zour beir, ze said scho sould repent it, and immediatlie ane meir deit to hir worth xx lib.: And becaus scho wald not geue zou ane soup milk of ane new callowit kow, ze said so sould scho find it; and presentlie the kow deit: And in winter last, ane foill of the said James, haueing eatten ane schave of zouris, ze prayed God nor the foill burst and beall; quhilk schortlie came to pas, and the foill deit be zour witchcraft and diuelrie.'[B,51] This kind of thing was so typical that no further instances need be cited.

A well vouched Sanday story is about a prominent farmer who kept a stallion which was made available to farmers in one part of the island. This farmer was incensed when he heard that a man in another district had just bought a stallion with which he intended to tour the whole island. Determined to prevent this intrusion into what he considered his territory, the farmer went to see a woman in one of his cottages who was reputed to have the witch's knowledge. He found this woman (who was named Anno Swanney) milking a cow, halted her in the task, and asked if she could do anything. She answered that she might well be able to help, but said that the farmer must first of all put some money into her milk-pail. He agreed, dropped several coins into the pail, and went away. In due course the newly bought stallion was put on the road by its owner, but as it passed the church which the farmer regarded as the boundary of his territory it became lame, and eventually had to be destroyed.

    A. He shall come to grief.
    B. About midsummer, five years ago, James Ego, smith, his wife having taken a lot of your bere, you said she should repent it, and immediately a mare died to her worth £20: And because she would not give you a sup of milk of a new calved cow, you said so should she find it; and presently the cow died: And in winter last, a foal of the said James, having eaten a sheaf of yours, you prayed God that the foal burst and fester; which shortly came to pass, and the foal died by your witchcraft and devilry.

On a croft in Orphir a certain cow was regarded as an exceptionally good milker, and at the same time an excellent cow for butter. A neighbour of the owner wanted to buy her, but the owner did not want to sell, even for a good price. The would-be purchaser seemed to accept his dismissal, but asked if he could have a pint of the cow's milk. This was willingly given. From that time onwards no one could get a drop of milk from the cow, although her swollen udder showed how badly she needed to be relieved of her milk. The owner told a friend of the strange circumstance and was advised to sell the cow at once. As soon as the buyer began to lead the cow away the milk began to flow from her and continued to do so all the way to her new home. There was no longer any difficulty in getting her to give her milk. By obtaining some of her milk, it was supposed, the purchaser had been able to put a spell on the cow, which lasted until he had concluded his purchase.

A cousin of mine, who died only recently, remembered seeing a hen's foot tied to the door of a small croft house in the Evie hills. He asked about its purpose from the old woman who lived there. She explained that a neighbour had bewitched her hens. To remove the spell it had been necessary to kill a hen and hang up one of its feet in the way he had noticed.

This same informant remembered hearing a woman tell the story of how all the 'profit' on her household's butter vanished. Try as she would, the milk did not yield the amount of butter it ought to. A little distance away, however, a crofter was selling an amount of butter much in excess of what the number of his cattle warranted. One dark night some members of the woman's family went to the house of this crofter. Stealing up to the window, they watched him churning. He was dressed only in his shirt, and worked in a wild frenzy. The watchers firmly believed that he was demon-possessed and knew a spell which brought him the 'profit' of other people's milk as well as his own.

After a late-nineteenth century division of common land in Evie, two women who lived in a small house called Linday saw the ground on which their geese had ranged freely become the property of a neighbouring farm. They declared in their anger that it would never be of any value to anyone. To ensure that it would be unproductive they took egg shells, in which were placed little pieces of butter, and set these at various places on the surface of the common, muttering some unrecorded malediction as they did so.

Curing disease with charms and spells

The means taken to cure people or animals of their distempers are far more interesting. A classic example of using stones as healing agents was alleged against Katherine Cragie. The indictment is wordy and involved, but, briefly, what Katherine did was this:

> She brought three stones, which she laid at three corners of the hearth for a whole day. At night she laid these stones behind the door, until early morning, when she put them individually into a vessel of water. They seemed to seethe in the water ('chirme and churle'). Katherine then used the water to wash her patient, Thomas Irving. She went through the whole process on three separate occasions, washing Thomas each morning. The evening immediately following the third washing, she commanded Thomas to rise from his bed 'under silence and cloud of night', and forbidding him to speak until he had returned home, caused him to follow her to the bridge at Saviskaill (Rousay) at the seashore, where she took three 'loofsfull'[A] of water and threw over his head. Together witch and patient returned silently to his home, where he daily recovered his health. Katherine had diagnosed that 'it was the sea trow or spirit that was lying upon him'.[52]

Katherine Caray (1616) also took three stones, one for the hill-spirit, one for the kirkyard-spirit, and one for the sea-spirit. From her divining she concluded that it was the spirit of the sea which troubled her patient.[53] Margaret Sandieson (1635) touched Margaret Mure's head three times with each of three small stones (i.e., nine times), which cured her speedily.[54] Jonet Reid, of Sandwick, used a variation of the formula, with 'nine blue stones'. She touched the joints of a woman who had 'boneshaw'[B] with each of the stones, then washed her with water from the vessel in which the stones had lain.[55]

A deep significance attaches itself to the number nine, because it multiplies thrice the power of three. A charm for toothache used in Orkney until last century ran:

> T'ree Finnmen cam' fae deir heem i'de sea
> Fae de weary worm[C] de folk for tae free,
> An' dey s'all be paid wi' de white monie[D]
>   Oot o' de flesh an' oot o' de bane;
>   Oot o' de sinew an' oot o' de skin;
>   Oot o' de skin an' in tae de stane;

A. Handfuls.
B. Sciatica.
C. Toothache was believed to be caused by a worm.
D. Silver money.

An' dere may du remain!
An' dere may du remain!
An' dere may du remain!

The charm is usually printed without spaces, but I have set it out thus to show its form. There are nine lines, forming three distinct groups of three lines. Each line in the first two groups has nine words, and each of these groups contains a total of twenty-seven words (a most powerful combination). In the last group the lines only contain five words each, but the total of fifteen words is again divisible by three. This may be pure coincidence, but I can hardly believe it.

Take, for instance, another charm used for curing sprains:

Oor Saviour rade,[A]
His foal slade;[B]
Oor Saviour lichtit doon.[C]
Sinew tae sinew,
Vein tae vein,
Joint tae joint,
Bane tae bane.
    Mend du i' Geud's neem!

Twenty-seven words—three nines. The accepted Shetland version is slightly different, but it has the same number of words.

This charm is the oldest and most widespread that I know. It was recited in more than one local witchcraft trial. It was used all over Scotland. Gaelic versions have been obtained in North Uist, Arasaig and Birneray, Lewis. It was employed in Devon in a somewhat corrupt form. In an eighth century German version the rider is Odin. The old Norwegian version is very like the Orkney one, except that it contains forty-five words; another number that one could play about with: e.g., it is made up of three fifteens, each divisible into five threes.

It is of course possible to read these combinations of numbers into charms where they only exist by pure chance, but countless instances of the numbers three and nine being used in witchcraft could be adduced. In charms nine is often insisted on:

Nine knots upo' di treed,[D]
Nine blissings on dee heid . . .

A. Rode.
B. Slid.
C. Alighted.
D. Thread.

As evidence of the importance placed on these numbers in ancient times, a charm mentioned by Pliny may be cited. As a cure for spleen ailments, take fresh sheep's milt[A] and apply to the patient's body. The person doing so must say twenty-seven (3 × 9) times, 'This I do for the cure of the spleen'. Then he must plaster the milt into the bedroom wall and seal it with a ring.[56]

Jonet Reid seems to have been accomplished in the old magic techniques. On another occasion she said that one of Alexander Linklater's children in Housgar had the 'hart cake',[B] 'and that if you pleased you would cast the hart cake, and see what would become of him'. She took a pot with water in it, and laid the fire-tongs across the mouth of the pot. Putting a pillow over the tongs, she placed the child on it, with the pot beneath him. Then she took a sieve and supported it on the child's head. A wooden cog, full of water, was placed inside the sieve, and on top of the cog a pair of shears. Jonet now took some lead,[C] melted it in an iron lamp, and poured it through the 'boul'[D] of the shears into the water three separate times. She pretended to divine from the lead whether the child would live or not, gave him a drink of water from the cog, and said all would be well.[57]

This technique of 'casting the heart'[E] was performed in South Ronaldsay in the nineteenth century, with the following variations: a bunch of keys, comb and knife were placed in the sieve beside the bowl of water. A lead 'heart' was found in the water after the third pouring. The patient had to carry this in his pocket until he lost it, when he would be cured.[F] Small cakes of bere meal and water were cooked between the heated flat points of the tongs. A dozen had to be eaten on the first day, and a decreasing number each succeeding day. Each morning until the patient was better the egg of a black hen had to be eaten.[58]

In Orkney salt water was considered an effective medicine. Katherine Cragie used it, as we have seen. Katherene Bigland took her master under the banks[G] and washed him with salt water.[59] Katherine Grant (1623) caused a distempered cow to be pushed backwards into the sea until it was washed by

---

A. Spleen.
B. Cardialgia: pain or discomfort from the heart. Wallace on page 33 of his *A Description of the Isles of Orkney* printed in 1693, records 'Others there be also that use Charms for the curing the Heart-ake and Rickets, but these are much curbed by the careful industry of our pious Ministers'.
C. Lead was often employed to heal.
D. Circular top.
E. An elaborate operation used to cure consumptive complaints or jaundice believed to be brought on by some evil enchantment which caused the heart to waste away. *The Folklore of Orkney and Shetland*, E. W. Marwick, 1975, p.133.
F. Ascertainment of its nature and the cure of the disease went hand in hand. *Primitive Beliefs in the North-East of Scotland*, J. M. MacPherson, 1929, p.255.
G. Raised ground bordering the seashore.

nine surges. Three handfuls of each wave were laved over its back (3 × 9 = 27), which was then brushed with a bunch of burned malt straw.⁶⁰ Jonet Forsyth, of Westray, (1629) healed Robert Reid, who was taken ill at sea, by throwing a bucketful of salt water over him.⁶¹

The wresting thread^A was greatly believed in, in conjunction with the 'Oor Saviour rade' charm quoted earlier. This was used by Kathareen Mansone, of South Ronaldsay (examined by the kirk session at Burrik, 20 April 1660).⁶² Her version was:

> The Lord God
> Be this threid red
> And foale's footestaide.^B
> The Lord God light it^C
> And foale's foot right it^D
> And put it lith to lith^E
> And bone to bone. Amen.

Katherine Caray (why were so many witches named Katherine?) also used the wresting thread and a corrupt version of the charm.⁶³ Helene Isbuster (1635) utterly ruined a man by casting nine knots on a blue thread and giving it to his sister.⁶⁴

The transference of disease from person to person, or from person to animal, was one of the witch's arts. Katherene Bigland cast a sickness on her master, cured him by laying it on his man servant, then laid it back again on her master.⁶⁵ Jonet Forsyth transferred a man's sickness to a mare, which died as he recovered, nothing being found in place of her heart 'bot ane blob of watter'.⁶⁶ Katharine Greive (1633), called on to help Elspeth Tailyeour, who was 'deadlie diseasit', took the sickness from her and cast it on a calf, 'and immediatlie the calf died'.⁶⁷ It was equally possible to transfer disease from

---

A. In innocent hands it was usually a home-spun thread of black wool which in order to effect a cure was tied around a strained muscle or ligament and an appropriate incantation repeated. In Shetland it was known as a *wrestin treed*; wrest: to sprain; *The Folklore of Orkney and Shetland*, E. W. Marwick, 1975, pp.132, 133. However in the hands of a witch the thread could also be red or blue and might possess more sinister powers; MacPherson, *Primitive Beliefs in the North-East of Scotland*, 1929, pp.183-185, gives *reisted* as bewitched or arrested and states p.184 'not only could the witch "reist" men and animals, but her power in this respect extended to the inanimate creation'.

B. Probably foot slid. The more familiar version of this rhyme says:
> Our Saviour rade
> His foal's foot slade
> Our Saviour lichtit doon.

A similar charm appears on p.24.

C. Alighted.
D. Righted.
E. Joint or limb.

animal to animal. Elspeth Cursetter (1629) was called to a sick cow. What happened is told in her indictment:

> You took a cog of water out of the burn before William Anderson's door—and when you came back took three straws, one for William Anderson's wife, one for William Coitt's wife in Warbuster, and one for William Bichen's wife, and put them in the cog with the water: and put the same upon the back of the cow: which three straws danced in the water, and the same water bubbled as if it had been boiling—and therefter you took a little quantity of the said water, and put them in the mouth of the cow, and pushed your arm to the elbow in the throat of the cow: and immediately she rose up, and is as well as ever she was; and at the same instant she was made whole, William Anderson's ox, from before whose door the water was taken, his ox being on the hill shot to death.[68]

In other words, the ox died suddenly and was thought to have been shot by the fairies: 'elf shot'.

Memories of the very oldest beliefs are seen fleetingly in the witch trials. The disastrous practice of doing anything against the sun's course, that is 'withershins' or 'witherways', was used to harm certain people. Margaret Wick, of Shapinsay (examined by the kirk session in 1659) went 'against the sun about the township' and 'glomered[A] with her hands', with the result that her victim's mother, brother and sister all took to bed, and four beasts died.[69] Marion Cumlaquoy of Birsay 'turned herself three several times witherways, about the fire' in Robert Carstair's house, and that year his crops were rotten.[70] Jonet Forsyth 'measured a stack of bere, of seven fathoms, belonging to Michaell Reid, and she took away the substance of the corn thereof'.[71]

There is even the smell of ancient sacrifice, although there is little direct evidence. A proprietor in Birsay, who had been losing a lot of sheep, was advised by the same Jonet 'to take ane beast at Alhallow evin[B] and sprinkill thrie dropps of the bluid of it ben by the fyre'.[72] Near the mid-nineteenth century, a farmer whose animals were all developing disease 'consulted a wise woman who had come from the Black Isle. She said they were bewitched. To counteract the evil influence, he must take the best beast, and burn [it] in a kiln with a roaring fire of peats. This was done with beneficial results'.[73]

Little that is unique in spells and charms can be found in the indictments, but there are interesting variations of those common elsewhere. To a woman who asked how to get back the 'profit of her whole milk', Marion Richart said, 'Go thy way to the sea, and tell nine bores of the sea come in, that is to

A. Groped.
B. Hallowe'en.

say, nine waves of the sea, and let the hindmost of the nine go back again; and the next thereafter, take three handfuls of the water and put within thy bucket, and when you come home, put it within your churn, and you will get your profit again.'[74]

When Anie Tailzeour was asked how she took the profit off people's cattle to give to others she replied 'it was to take three hairs of the cow's tail, three of her member's, and three of her udder's, and go wonderways[A] about the cow, and stroke her on the left side, and cast the hair in the churn, and say thrice, "Come, butter, come".'[75] The same witch tried to cure the sick wife of Stevin Tailzeour, in Papa Westray, by 'measuring the woman, laying one hand on her head, and another on her foot crossways,[B] saying "Mother's blessing to the head, mother's blessing to the feet, and mother's blessing to the heart".'[76] When the Minister of Westray's horse was 'forspoken', or bewitched, and Christian Gow (1624) was asked to cure him, she used this charm:

> Thrie thinges hath the forspoken,
> Heart, tung, and eye, almost;
> Thrie thinges sall the mend agane,
> Father, Sone, and Holie Ghost.[77]

A very similar charm used for curing bewitched milk was recited by Anna Whittle during the Lancaster Trials of 1612:

> Three Biters hast thou bitten,
>   The Heart, ill Eye, ill Tongue;
> Three bitter shall be thy Boot,
>   Father, Son, and Holy Ghost
> a God's name.
> Five Pater-nosters, five Aves, and a Creed,
> In worship of five wounds of our Lord.[78]

Katherine Grant, brought in to help a sick child, asked for a cup of water and a knife. When she got these she moved the knife in the water, spat into the cup, 'gantit'[C] over it and said:

> The dead uprose,
> To the cradle she got
> To mend the bairn

A. Anticlockwise.
B. Across the body. A person accused of witchcraft was sometimes required to undergo ordeal by water. Tied 'crossways', i.e., the right thumb to the left big toe, and the left thumb to the right big toe, the accused was thrown into water. Innocence was proven by sinking, and floating established guilt.
C. Yawned, or blew into it.

> That bitten was,
> In the name of the Father,
> the Son and the Holy Ghost.[79]

(Once again, twenty-seven words). Then she ordered the water to be cast out of the cup. The child recovered.

Elspeth Cursetter told a man who was in bad health to 'Get the bones of ane tequhyt[A] and carry thame in your clothes'.[80]

As a remedy for a hurt or ulcer, Katherine Caray prescribed earth from the spot where a man had been slain.[81] Katherine Cragie gave Jonet Ingsger a dead woman's snood[B] to bind round her husband's waist, 'and if it war the dead manis sting[C] which trublit him, it wold cuir and heale him'.[82]

Curiously, there is little reference in the seventeenth century trials to use of herbs, but also in Katherine Cragie's indictment was the charge that Annabell Murray 'contracted a lingering disease, and never recovered thereof until she died', her offence being that she made known the existence of 'three grasses bound in a knot' within a clout,[D] which lay in Katherine's house. The grasses were probably not a medicine but a charm.[83] One of the few genuine examples of herbal treatment was mentioned in the trial of James Knarstoun (1633), who rubbed the arms and legs of a woman who had sciatica with an 'oyle, made of mekillwort'.[E]

The Book of the Black Art

A text-book of witchcraft much disdussed at one time in Orkney, and firmly believed to exist, was the Book of the Black Art. It is difficult to determine whether this was a single book or whether there were numerous copies in circulation, but it was certainly a dangerous possession. On its owner's death it was reclaimed by the Devil, who also collected the soul of the person who had used it. Desperate attempts were therefore made to get rid of it in time, but it could only be disposed of by being sold to someone else. A few accounts say that the price received had to be smaller than its last owner had paid. In any circumstances it was difficult to sell, for it was of

---

A. Linnet.
B. Or sneud: a string or ribbon used by females for tying their hair.
C. The meaning is uncertain. The treatment suggests that the trouble was abdominal, e.g. gall or kidney-stones, appendicitis, colic or the like. The words may perhaps indicate pleurisy or any malady producing a severe stabbing pain, where *sting* might derive from O.N. *stingi*, Icelandic and Faeroese *stingur*, a stitch or sudden pain in the side. But the term may be a synonym for the phrase *deadman's nip* in Shetland or *deadman's pinches* in Ulster, applied to a skin eruption or ulcer of unknown origin, ascribed to the trows. See James R. Nicolson *Shetland Folklore*, 1981, p.168.
D. Cloth.
E. The plant belladonna or deadly nightshade.

distinctive appearance, the pages being black and the printed characters white, and none but the most foolish or foolhardy would have anything to do with it.

One of the last people believed to possess it was a Sandwick man, who tried in vain to destroy it. It would not burn, and if he tried to tear it to pieces, leaf by leaf, it miraculously united itself. On one occasion he took it out to sea, tied up in a sack with a big stone, and plumped it overboard. When he got home it was still there. At last he summoned up courage to take it to the minister, the Rev. Charles Clouston, who bought it from him and then buried it deeply in the manse garden.

Recently, a somewhat similar story came to me from Sanday. In this instance the book belonged to the witch Recchel. She persuaded a young girl (whose name I was given) to become the owner of it. When this girl found out the character of the volume she was greatly alarmed, and tried in vain to persuade the witch to take it back. Then someone advised her to throw it over a cliff known as Gronafea Head. She did so, but when she got home it was lying on her bedroom table. Again it was the minister, this time the Rev. Matthew Armour, who managed—in some unspecified way—to put the book safely out of circulation. An interesting thing about these stories is how recent they are: Mr Clouston died in 1884 and Mr Armour around 1903.

One is forcibly reminded of the *svarteboker* (black books) of which there are many accounts in Norway. In 1607, an un-named Dane put together, chiefly from foreign sources, a book of wizardry ascribed to a famous medieval wizard named Cyprian. This was quickly distributed in transcriptions throughout Denmark and Norway, and its contents formed the nucleus of the printed 'black books', which also included a whole series of charms and spells taken from oral tradition. An ancient book of magic is still in existence: it was found in Vinje Kirk in the Telemark, and had obviously belonged to one of the last Catholic priests of that church. The general legend of the Book of the Black Art may well be derived from Norway, for there was frequent communication between Orkney and Norway until the latter half of the eighteenth century. While I have not discovered so far an insistence on black pages and white print in the main Norwegian accounts of *svarteboker*, two tales from the Lofoten Islands which speak of black books contain the idea. In one of these tales 'the pages were black, and the letters were white and red'; in the other 'the pages were of black parchment, and the writing was red—written with blood'.[84] It is possible that genuine copies of the old books of magic found their way to Orkney, but it is quite conceivable that old black-letter books, written in Latin or some foreign tongue, were regarded by ordinary people as copies of the dreaded volume. An amazing collection of books which came to Orkney in the sixteenth century could have provided the superstitious with just the kind of volume they would have identified as the Book of the Black Art. In September 1557 a ship carrying goods to the Hanseatic merchants in Bergen from Rostok in the north of Germany was seized unlawfully by a French vessel and brought to 'the port of Orkney', presumably Kirkwall, where she was disposed of to a consortium of lairds and merchants, mainly from the South Isles. The large and rich cargo was 'masterfully robbed'. Among other things, it contained 'books in Latin, Greek, German and Danish, large and small, to the number of three thousand volumes and more'.[85]

Other powers: looking, 'ganting' and touching

While the reputed witches used most frequently material objects and magical formulae to achieve their ends, they seem also to have depended on their physical faculties, for both destructive and benevolent purposes.

The mere act of looking could be disastrous.[A] We have read already how the Devil told Jonet Irving to look on people 'with opin eyes' and pray evil for them. Christian Marwick looked over a byre door, 'whereupon the calf died presently and the cow fell sick'.[86] Katherine Grant went to Henry Janie's house 'with a stoup[B] in her hand, with the bottom foremost and sat down right opposite the said Henry, and breathed thrice on him: and going forth he followed her; and being on the pavement, she looked over her shoulder, and turned up the white of her eye, where by her devilry, there fell a great weight upon him, that he was forced to set his back to the wall; and when he came in, he thought the house ran about with him; and thereafter lay sick a long time'.[87]

Here, looking is allied with 'ganting'. The word normally means yawning, but in this context blowing out one's breath on the person seems to be what is meant. A charge against Marion Richart was that she took water in a cup, put something into it that looked like 'great salt', spat several times into the cup, and 'when you had so done, you *aundit in bitt* (which is a Norn term),

---

A. In every parish there were people who were called 'ill-fitted' (ill-footed). If one met such a person when starting on a journey, it was most unfortunate and unlucky. The only way to break the spell was to go home and eat some bread, then start off again. Not long since, a woman told me that, as a girl, she accompanied a North Ronaldsay farmer's wife on a journey that was to take them to the other end of the island. On the way they met a certain man. The local woman immediately returned to her home, remarking that no good would come of that journey. To meet that particular man was a bad omen. Another North Ronaldsay man who was regarded as uncanny, and avoided for that reason, once complained bitterly to a neighbouring farmer that the latter always met him 'with iron in his hand'. It was a mere coincidence that the farmer was carrying a file with which to sharpen the knife of his reaper; but undoubtedly the complainer considered that the farmer believed the idle tale and carried iron to protect himself against sorcery. (EWM)

B. Wooden pail.

that is to say, you blew your breath therein...'⁸⁸ When William Mylne was 'deadlie seik, and the winding scheit laid at his head to be put on him', Christian Gow brought him instantly back to health, 'be ganting and whispering over the said diseased persone'.⁸⁹

In the act of cursing or bewitching, a woman would pull her hair loose, an action which seems to have been frightening to the victim. In Hoy, Margaret Mudie's cow trespassed on Bessie Skebister's (1633) corn. 'Ye sat doun' reads Bessie's indictment, 'and taking of your curtch,^A sheuk your hair lous, and ever since shoe [Margaret] hes bein so vehementlie pained, that shoe ... hes nevir bein weill since ye curst hir, or sheuk your hair lous'.⁹⁰ The sickness of the 'good man of Noup', in Westray, seems to be connected in Jonet Sinclair's trial (1643) with certain actions she performed 'with hir hair about hir lugis'.^B,⁹¹ An unpleasant person named Helen a Wallis (Helen of Walls) was so furious when a neighbour's cattle grazed on a field whose ownership was disputed that, in what looks like a frenzy of anger, she 'raif the curtch aff hir heid, and put it vndir hir belt: shuik hir hair about hir luidgis: ran to the Ladie Chappell hard by, and went thryse about it vpoun hir bare kneis, prayand cursingis and maledictiones [to] lyght vpoun the said William: and thairefter cam to his hous, and yeid sa about his fyir syd, and did the lyk: and thairefter cuming furth quhair his gudis was pasturing said thir wordis following:

> Gleib wind luik in the air of the lift
> And never have power to eat meat'.^C,⁹²

It is interesting to note how religion was united with paganism and wrath in the circling of the old chapel, while she *prayed* curses and maledictions.

Touching could also be potent for good or evil. When Cirstane Leisk (1643) spread her hand on a man's back he fell sick, but when she repeated the action he immediately became well.⁹³ Christian Marwick 'straikit^D hir hand' over Margaret Craigie's breast, and that same night Margaret died.⁹⁴ Agnes Scottie (1616) touched a man, and gave him many 'injurious wordis', after which he 'conceivit ane great fear and trembling, contractit seiknes, and within dayis thairefter dyit'.⁹⁵ Marion Cumlaquoy hit a cow thrice 'with the

A. A woman's cap.
B. Ears.
C. Tore the curtch off her head, and put it under her belt: shook her hair about her ears: ran to the Lady Chapel close by, and went thrice about it upon her bare knees, praying curses and maledictions to light upon the said William: and thereafter came to his house, and went so about his fireside, and did the same: and thereafter coming forth where his cattle were pasturing said these words following:
> Glebe wind look in the air of the sky
> And never have power to eat meat.
D. Stroked.

skirt of her coit,[A] and instantly the kow was struckin with a strange seikness'.[96]

Second-sight

If the witch had the second-sight her prestige, or notoriety, was the greater. As far as I can judge, the people who were supposed to have this faculty were the least malevolent of the witches. Despite the tale told about the Hoy witch, Bessie Skebister, shaking her hair loose, and the allegation of a man who in delirium imagined she was riding him to Norroway[B] and other places with a bridle in his mouth, the charge against her was mainly that she was a 'dreamer of dreams'. All the honest men of the island said that it was the usual thing when boats were in danger to ask Bessie whether they would come home safely or not, and that the common proverb was 'Giff Bessie say it is weill, all is weill'.[97] Once James Chalmers found her 'weiping for the boittis',[C] but she told him that this was not because they would not come home safely, but for 'the truble they wer in'. They all came home by the route she had predicted. When the oar of a boat which had been driven out to sea came ashore at Walls, the goodwife of the Bu, whose eldest son was on the boat, sought reassurance from Bessie, who answered that 'they ar all weill, and will be home or they sleep', which duly happened.[98]

Bessie Skebister might be harmless, and possibly well enough liked by her neighbours, but the possession of the strange power of predicting events was enough to make the issue of her trial certain: she was strangled and burned. The same fate overtook Elspeth Reoch, who 'saw Robert Stewart natural son of the late Patrick sometime Earl of Orkney with Patrick Traill to whom she was with child and certain others with ropes around their necks in Edmond Callendar's house at their afternoon's drink before the Earl of Caithness's coming to the country'.[99] Elspeth also was harmless, a poor deluded creature much abused by men whom she took to be fairies.

There were pretenders no doubt whose knowledge of events came from people who did not realise that they were passing on useful information. Margaret Craigie testified against Katherine Cragie that if she had been in the farthest part of the isle, she would reveal on coming home exactly what Margaret had said in the privacy of her house.[100] Elspeth Cursetter was able to describe all that there was to eat at a banquet she had not attended, as well as the subjects of conversation, but declared that she had been 'on the buird in

A. Coat.
B. Norway.
C. Boats.

liknes of a bie'.[A],[101] Several witches were credited with having revealed the whereabouts of articles that were lost. There is no mention of unwitting informers such as servants or children, but these, skilfully manipulated, may sometimes have been the source of the witch's knowledge.

A type of woman much consulted in the islands has become known in popular tradition as a 'storm witch': one who pretended to control the weather. There were general practitioners, like the often mentioned Katherine Cragie, who would peddle a fair wind or a love charm with the same wheedling insistence, or like Anie Tailzeour, who was said to have raised a great storm for the purpose of washing away Annie Peace's peat-stack,[102] but the real storm witches seem to have been specialists who flourished at a period later than that covered by the witch trials, and who lived mainly in Stromness and Hoy.

The Stromness storm witches included Bessie Millie (made famous by Sir Walter Scott), Effie Gray and Mammie Scott. To their company Mattie Black of Brims deserves to be added. She lived in a tumble-down cottage near Skeppegeo, and apparently had a Red Indian mother. Once two Caithness lads, over in Brims with the father of one of them to buy a calf, went to Mattie's house, without the old man's knowledge, and purchased a fair wind home. Mattie gave them three straws, each with an inch or two of coloured wool tied to it. She informed them that they would have a fair wind to Cantick, but if they thought it insufficient, they were to throw a straw over the side of the boat, which would give them a smart breeze to the Tarf of Swona. Here the wind would drop, but they could throw over the second straw to ensure a following wind to the Caithness coast. The third straw was not to be thrown overboard until the mast was lowered, if they did not want a trip back to Saltness.[B] Everything went as Mattie said, with the old man quite innocent of what was taking place. Near the end of the voyage, however, he noticed the third straw lying in the boat, recognised it for what it was and flung it over the side, shouting 'Till 'e devil wi' a witch's win'.

A. 'On the table in likeness of a bee'. Until recently a fly or bluebottle was often described in Orkney as a bee.

B. It is interesting to compare this story with a description in Richard Eden's *History of Trauayle*, 1577, of how Lapland magicians raised winds:

> They tye three knottes on a strynge hangyng at a whyp. When they lose one of these they rayse tollerable wynds. When they lose another the wynde is more vehement; but by losing the thyrd they rayse playne tempestes as in old tyme they were accustomed to rayse thunder and lyghtnyng.

In other accounts it is affirmed that the secret power over the wind possessed by Laplanders depended entirely on the nativity of the magician: he had an absolute power over the particular wind which blew the moment he was born; thus one would be master of the north wind, another of the east wind, and so on. Lapps frequently sold winds, in the shape of three knots on a string, to sailors credulous enough to buy them. (EWM)

Immediately the wind veered, increased to a gale, and eventually brought the boat, which could only run before it, back to Brims.[103]

Mammie Scott was supposed to have taken a terrible revenge on some men who angered her as she sailed across the Pentland Firth to Caithness. At a house where she made a halt she asked for a wooden bowl, or 'bummie', and set it floating on a tub of water. With a finger she agitated the water until the bowl capsized. As it did so she exclaimed, 'Aye, there they go, but I'm sorry for the puir strange lad that's wi' them'. That same evening a Walls man and his two sons, the objects of her fury, were drowned with the stranger they were ferrying across the Firth when their boat was overturned.[104] I have heard a similar story in Sanday, and in Shetland.

Anyone eating an egg pushed his spoon through the shell when he had finished, and no-one threw an egg shell into the fire without first crushing it. If the shell was left whole, the witches (some said fairies) would use it as a boat and sail out to sea to wreck the first ship they met. Witches were said also to put limpet shells in the fire, meanwhile chanting an incantation, to bring about shipwreck.

At one time Orkney had an unenviable reputation among sailors as the veritable home of witches. Walter Traill Dennison, the Sanday writer already mentioned, was born in 1826. As a boy he was taken to see the docks and shipping of Leith. An old sailor whom he encountered took him on his knee and began to tell him stories. But when the sailor heard that the boy belonged to Orkney, he shrank from him, exclaiming, 'O, my lad, you hail from that lubber land where so many cursed witches dwell'.

Who were the witches?

It is difficult to tell from the heavily biased language of their indictments what sorts of women were included among the witches. A few most certainly were embittered old women, who reacted to the provocations of their neighbours with furious unguarded words. Such people lived by themselves in houses that no one entered, and with each passing year grew queerer and more mysterious. But these, I imagine, were not typical.

Then there were the vagabonds, very like the tinkers of later times, but less law-abiding, who wandered from island to island, getting food and a bed where they could, and living entirely on their wits. Where they found credulity they would exploit it, cajoling the strong, scaring the weak. Such were the Faw family (1612), charged with murder, incest, adultery, theft and sorcery.[105] Such too was William Scottie (1643) 'vagabound' and 'warlache'.[A,106] In her indictment Jonet Rendall was described as 'a poor

---

A. Warlock.

77 Tinker family near the old slaughterhouse, Cairston Road, Stromness, c.1900

78 Road workers breaking stones, c.1905

79 Steam-powered road roller, c.1905

vagabond with[in] the pochin[A] of Rendall'.[107] Constant references to 'beggeris' and 'vagabounds' may be found in the old 'Country Acts'. Shetland was much tormented by vagabonds from 'Orkney Caithness and other foreign places who abuse, beg and overlay the country begging picking stealing and oppressing the inhabitants thereof'.[108] There was another reason why some alleged witches were continually on the move. Numbers of them who had escaped the stake were punished by banishment from their native county. In the old Caithness Church Records there is the entry: 'WICK, October 12th, 1698. Being informed likewise that sorcery and witchcraft abound so much in the said parish—that sorcerors banished out of Orkney lurke there—they recommended seriously to the heritors and magistrate forsaid to banish all such out of the town and country, which they promised to do'.[109] Three years later (5 October 1701) Wick Kirk Session decided that 'a person suspect of sorcrie' must 'procure a testimony from Orkney other wayes to be banished'.[110]

How these women were hounded from place to place may be inferred from an individual case. On 5 July 1658, the kirk session meeting at Burrik, South Ronaldsay, directed that 'Eupham Rosie' who had ten years ago been delaited[B] with witchcraft in Stroma, be 'appointed to goe out of the Isle'.[111] Later in the month (19 July 1658) Canisbay Kirk Session recorded that 'Effie Rosie flitting frome Stroma to Orkney wes sent back to gett hir testificat, but sche being before this tyme slandered with witchcraft be Wm. Rosie. She, being called, compeired,[C] and being accuised, confessed that hir daughter-in-law said that sche was so weil learned that sche culd mak hir stoup[D] goe and milk the cow'. Another daughter-in-law testified that when her father went to sea, Effie prayed that his boat should become a hood to his head, which happened and he was lost.[112] What the session decided to do does not seem to be minuted.

Probably the most troublesome and typical witch was the resident one, who was not necessarily the lonely spinster of tradition. Information about individual circumstances is meagre, but from a list of seventeenth century witches which I have compiled it is clear that at least four were married women; two others had daughters, another had sons, and still another a grandson, and these also might have been married or widows.

There were families, it would appear, that practised witchcraft as an art and passed on their secrets to their descendants. Such a family were the Knarstouns. Alexander Knarstoun, 'in Skaill in Tuskebister', and James Knarstoun were both tried on the same day in February 1633. The house

A. Or parochin—parish. (EWM)
B. Charged.
C. Appeared.
D. Wooden pail.

called Bokan, according to a Sandwick folklorist,[A] 'was long inhabited by a race of witches—Warsetter or Marsetter to name—who kept little images like "dolls"[B] in recesses or "amery presses"[C] in the house, which they were in the habit of consulting at the wishes of "dupes". The "amerys" or presses were in the walls of the old ruins which are now pulled down. In this house very long ago the famous soothsayer Sati sometimes resided, who was well known for fortune-telling over all Orkney. His place of concealment beneath the floor was found some 70 or 80 years ago [written circa 1900], where he issued some of his soothsayings prophecies &c'.[113]

In the 1595 *Rentale of the King and Bischoppis Lands of Orkney*, a 1 farthing land in Wosbustar, South Sandwick, 'perteining to Elspet Marsetter, witche', is mentioned; and in the same Rental a 1 farthing land in Halkland, Rendall, is entered as 'perteining to Anne Marsetter, witche'.

If from the evidence available one could make what modern policemen would call an 'identikit' picture of a witch, that is a composite picture, it would be something like the following.

She is a person who is both poor and something of a misfit in the community.[D] Better-off and better favoured women marry happily and have children who take up most of their time and attention. She may have a quick temper, and may have become embittered by her circumstances, so that she is morbidly ready to take offence and ruthless in repaying injury, real or imagined. Her only way of exercising power over her neighbours is to pretend to supernatural knowledge. Brought up in a superstitious age, she believes that such knowledge is available. She may set about acquiring it by picking up and memorising all the spells and charms that are current in her neighbourhood, using them in charlatanic fashion with much invented hocus-pocus. Or she may become so obsessed that she may actually try to sell herself to the Devil, using any formula she can discover, and may bring herself to believe that she has actually made a pact with him. If she manages to consort with other witches, she may even meet a person who purports to be the Devil.

Witchcraft, besides being a means to power, probably becomes her way of life, and (because she is poor and obsessed and not the kind of person that anyone cares to employ) her only means of livelihood. She finds that there are two ways in which she can get alms or payment from her credulous neighbours: the one by offering to confer favours, the other by suggesting that she can be a danger to those who repulse her.

    A. George Marwick, whose unpublished folklore is now generally regarded as suspect.
    B. Idols.
    C. Cupboards.
    D. Unusual personal appearance such as hairiness could single out someone for classification as a witch. In Orkney there was a saying 'A hairy wife's a gairy wife, a hairy wife's a witch'. Gairy—greedy, covetous, parsimonious.

Disease is of constant occurrence among men and animals. When she hears of a case she contrives at once to visit the household, insinuating that she is able to offer a cure. Her fame may become such that she is actually sent for by people in extremity. She probably has to make in addition what might be termed begging visits from house to house. When she is sent away empty-handed, she may utter veiled or specific threats, such as people will remember a short or even long time afterwards when some disaster overtakes them. Her projection of her personality may be so terrifying that fear of her may cause weak-minded people to become ill. Part of her livelihood may come from what present-day racketeers would call 'protection money', in other words, a number of her neighbours may give her frequent gifts of food or clothes to prevent her from exercising her evil art on themselves. For instance, Jonet Rendall asks from Gilbert Sandie 'ane plack[A] of silver in almis fra him for his mearis,[B] that they might be weill over the year'.[114]

Besides pretending to cure or cause disease, avert death or bring it, she may dabble in all kinds of minor matters. She may offer to obtain a new husband for a widow, sell a fair wind, bring back prosperity, or 'profit', when that has been lost, tell a young girl's fortune, decide which is the most propitious day for attempting a new venture, blight someone's crops—there is no end to her possible activities.

She may know just where to stop, making herself as much of a blessing and nuisance as the island or parish will tolerate. But she may become intoxicated by power and such a menace that urgent complaints are made to the kirk session, and she is ordered to be examined by that body. At such a crisis, if she is unlucky, she will be handed over to the civil authorities for trial.

The Orkney trials

That is a severely rational picture of a witch, divested of uncanny features. Not everyone will agree that it accounts for all the odd stories which were told at the trials, even if the laws of evidence were disregarded—as they nearly always were—and the witnesses were actuated by fear and credulity. But the inescapable fact remains that at their trials the witches were powerless; nearly always bewildered, and sometimes as ready to confess as to deny; incapable of injuring their tormentors or of enlisting their sympathy. It was not that the judge and jury were calmly sceptical or immune from suggestion: it was merely that in her turn the accused witch was completely overawed and her pretensions vanished. Occasionally she became a poor babbling creature, like an animal in a trap, trying desperately to see where her

A. A sum of money.
B. Mares.

safety lay. There are revealing annotations on some of the indictments: 'The pannell denyet not, scho said scho was vncouth, and wist not quhat to say'.[A,115]

Many, perhaps most, of the charges were absurd falsehoods, but one cannot refrain from believing that most of the women were guilty on one count, that of 'giving your self forth to have such craft and knowledge'. Deceivers, if only self deceivers, they paid a terrible price for their arrogant claims. Fundamentally, it was not the business of the courts to decide whether they had exercised their supposed powers mainly for good or evil: it was the possession of unnatural powers that was the crime. The 'using and practising of witchcraftis, sorceries and divinationes', pretending to have the infernal knowledge, and 'keeping company and society with the devill', were the matters on which the person was arraigned. Flagrant and malicious actions might aggravate the crime, or provide circumstantial evidence, but witchcraft itself was a mysterious crime against God—a teaming up with his eternal enemy—which was far more appalling than any of the actions by which it might be accompanied. Even when the action might seem benign, like a spectacularly successful cure, the jury was asking itself if such a miracle was possible without the aid of the Devil. Against such a minor charge as that made in Katherine Cragie's indictment, accusing her of knowing what was said in a house when she was absent, there is the annotation 'Devilish revelation',[116] whereas the allegation that she was responsible for inflicting a woman with a lingering and mortal disease incurs no harsher comment than 'Strong presumption [of witchcraft]'.[117]

It would be tempting to suppose that the heretical nature of the crime and the interest of the Church in its punishment were the reasons why trials were sometimes held in St Magnus Cathedral, but there was in fact no special significance in the use of that building. Courts of various kinds were held there over a longish period. The courtroom was frequently referred to as the Wallhouse. This designation is thought to apply to the south transept chapel, which may have replaced a former apse, and which, being built on to and out from the cathedral wall, could easily have been named the Wallhouse. The chapel would have made a cramped courtroom, but if, as seems probable, the whole front of it was unscreened, the adjacent transept would have provided all the accommodation required. That both chapel and transept were used may be inferred from the headings to various trials. In quaint Latin, the place where the court assembled is described as *insula vocata de Wallhouse, in Templo St Magni*.[118] Here we have an extension of the name to the aisle (or transept)—*insula* being pressed into service as meaning 'isle'! This is undoubtedly the place referred to in other trials as St Columba's Aisle, or perhaps

---

A. The accused denied not, she said she was uncouth, and did not know what to say.

Scapa Bay, 1869

Sam Bough, RSA, RSW, 1822–1878

more correctly St Colmus Aisle (Colmus being a shadowy Celtic saint designated as Apostle of the Orkneys).

It may well be that another of the Cathedral's functions was that of a prison. The space between the south transept chapel and the side wall of the building was built in and roofed over to form a dark narrow cell, traditionally known as 'Marwick's-hole'. Other possible places of confinement are the small second-storey rooms over the north and south chapels.

The extent to which torture was used to extract confessions cannot even be guessed at. Certainly confinement in Marwick's hole would break the spirit of a nervous individual, even if the jailers used none of the horrid instruments that were available to them in that barbarous age. The only person whose sufferings we know of in some detail is Alysoun Balfour, of Ireland, Stenness (1594),[119] who was accused of complicity in a plot to murder Earl Patrick Stewart.[A] She had been consulted, it was averred, on how to bewitch the earl. A confession was extracted from her under violent torture. She was kept in some fiendish contrivance called the *caschielawes* for forty-eight hours. This was perhaps a method of causing unbearable pain by stretching out the body using a system of weights.[B] Her husband was tortured at the same time in the *lang irons*.[C] Their son was placed in the 'buitis,[D] with fiftie sewin straikis',[E] and their daughter, aged only seven, was tormented by some kind of thumb-screw named *pinny winkis* or *pilliewinks*. Alysoun, who was taken several times out of the *caschielawes* unconscious and returned to it again for prolonged torture, was subjected to the additional agony of seeing her family painfully maltreated. When she was taken at last to the 'heiding hill',[F] she protested her complete innocence, saying that she had only confessed because of the unendurable torment, and because of a promise of her life from the parson who attended her.

One hesitates to say more about the damnable cruelty of such proceedings. Perhaps they were untypical: the awful vengeance of a frightened tyrant exercised through brutal underlings. It was seldom, however, that a witch—brought to trial and confronted with a band of credulous witnesses, ready to swear solemnly to the most improbable happenings—escaped with her life.

A. See also *The minister and the witch*, p.403.
B. An iron framework which encircled the leg, and was then placed in a moveable furnace. See John R. Tudor's *The Orkneys and Shetland*, 1883, p.368.
C. Fetters.
D. Boots or bootikins which 'extended from the ankles to the knee, and at each stroke of a large hammer (which forced the wedges closer), the question was repeated. In many instances, the bones and flesh of the leg were crushed and lacerated in a shocking manner before confession was made'. See Pitcairn's *Criminal Trials*, vol. i, 1833, p.373 *et seq.*
E. Fifty-seven strokes.
F. Probably the place of execution, which in Kirkwall was at the top of Clay Loan, a location known as Gallowha'.

Marable Couper, Katherene Bigland, Marion Richart, Jonet Forsyth, Jonet Reid, Jonet Rendall, Bessie Skebister, Issobell Sinclair, and many others, were sentenced to be 'wirried to the death,[A] and burnt in ashes'.

A few, for a first offence, and where the evidence was notably weak, were sentenced to banishment. Branding and scourging were occasionally resorted to. At her first trial in June 1640, Katherine Cragie, of Rousay, had the astonishing good fortune to be absolved; but she was back before her judges in July 1643 with a number of additional items on the charge-sheet. It is impossible to decide whether she was temperamentally unable to limit her pretensions or whether witchcraft was her sole means of livelihood.

Occasionally a witch may have been the victim of summary justice meted out by cruel and superstitious neighbours. One such was Scota Bess, who was beaten to death in the barn of Huip, Stronsay. Her murderers used flails which had been dipped in the water in which communion vessels had been washed. Bess was buried in a field to the south-east of the present farmstead, but her body would not stay in the earth. Although it was deeply interred on the evening of her murder, it lay on the surface of the field next morning. The following night it was carted to the Muckle Water in the central part of the island. After being sunk in the loch it was covered with load after load of turf carried by several boats from the loch shore. In this way, it is said, the only island in the loch was formed. A swan nests on it each year.

A suggestion of mob violence is contained in a tradition attached to a small cleft on the Birsay shore, known as Baabie Tait's Clive. Babbie, who lived at Howaquoy, was supposed to be a witch, and is said to have been drowned at the 'clive'.

It took a long time to erase the fear of witches from the mind of the ordinary man, but by the end of the seventeenth century the presbyteries, although they still probed deeply into accusations of witchcraft, were less inclined to accept the evidence of frightened or fanatical witnesses. In 1688 an Orphir man, Heugh Moare, was imprisoned in Marwick's Hole in the Cathedral to await punishment for declaring that Barbara Huitchisone of the same parish, whom he had personally seen in the company of the fairies, had borne four dead children fathered by them, and that she and her mother had taken to themselves the whole 'profit' of the Bu of Orphir, a neighbouring farm. The presbytery was anxious that Barbara should be 'restored to her good name'.

Nevertheless, the clergy were not by any means free from superstition, and in the year following, thought it expedient to make Thomas Swintone 'answer for his scandall in raising the wind that stormie Sunday'.

A. Strangled.

In July and September 1708 the Kirk Session of Birsay considered the case of Katherine Taylor, a cripple beggar-woman from Stromness, who was supposed to have washed a sick man, William Stensgar, with water which she later emptied at a 'common Slap[A] in the high way'. The inference was that the disease which had been taken away from William in the water would be transferred to the person who next went through the gateway.

Katherine insisted that what she had done was to 'tell out the paine' in William's knee, which had become powerless, using the following formula:

> As I was going by the way I met the Lord Jesus Christ in the likeness of another man, he asked me what tydings I had to tell and I said I had no tydings to tell, but I am full of pains, and I can neither gang nor stand.
>
> Thou shalt go to the holie kirk, and thou shalt gang it round about and then sit down upon thy knees, and say thy prayers to the Lord, and then thou shalt be as heall[B] as the hour when Christ was born.

We are not told what happened. It would have been difficult to fault a farrago of sentiment so impeccably pious.

The fear of witchcraft has not completely disappeared in Orkney, although spells and charms, to the best of my knowledge, are no longer used. A very few people are believed to have uncanny, but entirely unspecified powers, and some care is taken not to offend them. A generation or two ago, certain well-known tinkers, now dead, took advantage of their supposed knowledge of sorcery to sell their wares to superstitious country folk. Muttered curses, and even actual threats like 'I'll witch your coo,[C] mistress', are remembered.

Earlier this century, a much respected Orkney lawyer, Duncan J. Robertson, related to Orkney Antiquarian Society (1924) some of the witch stories he had collected on his journeys through the islands. One of these concerned a 'famous witch-doctor in Papa Westray who used to be brought over to Westray in a six-oared boat to visit the sick'. Often she attributed her patient's malady to the malevolence of some person recently dead. In such cases she recommended that a spoonful of earth from that person's grave should be mixed with every meal the patient ate.

Once Mr Robertson spoke sharply to a reputed witch, to the manifest discomfort of an island ground officer who was with him. This man told the lawyer's clerk that the woman had already drowned three men, and he was worried that, after offending her, Mr Robertson had to set sail for another

A. Gate.
B. Whole.
C. Bewitch your cow.

island, although it was the calmest of June days. 'The curious thing is', Mr Robertson related, 'that our boat was very nearly capsized by a sudden squall'.

As manager of a certain estate, Mr Robertson was asked to find a fresh croft for a man who had angered a local witch. The woman said, or did, something on the farm after which the tenant lost animals of all kinds and 'nothing throve[A] for him'.

List of Reputed Witches

A date in brackets is that of the trial, or public examination, of the person named. An unbracketed date preceded by c. (circa) means that the supposed witch was probably at the prime of her activity around that period.

Witches named in Sagas, and referred to in the Text

Heimskringla	Eyvind Kellda
	Queen Gunnhild
	Rognvald Rettilbain
Njal's Saga	Sorcerer-Hedin of Kerlingardale
	Svan of Svanhill
Orkneyinga Saga	Eithne
	Ragna of North Ronaldsay
	Ragnhild
	Sweyn Breastrope

Orkney Witches from the Sixteenth Century Onwards, Mentioned in the Preceding Pages

The places or island in which the witch had a home is given, where known. The appellation 'wanderer' means that the person was a beggar or vagabond, frequently moving from place to place:

Agnes Scottie (1616) Probably wanderer
Alexander Knarstoun (1633) Tuskerbister, Orphir
Alysoun Balfour (1594) Ireland, Stenness
Anie Tailzeour (1624) Sanday
Anne Marsetter c.1595 Halkland, Rendall
Annie Caird c.1755 Stromness
Anno (or Annie) Swannay c.1880 Sanday

A. Prospered.

Baabie Tait (?) Birsay
Barbara Boundie (1643) Wanderer
Bessie Millie c.1814 Stromness
Bessie Skebister (1633) Walls
Christian Gow (1624) Possibly wanderer
Christian Marwick (1643)
Cirstane Leisk (1643)
Effie Gray c.1860 Stromness
Elspet Marsetter c.1595 South Sandwick
Elspeth Cursetter (1629) Probably wanderer
Elspeth Reoch (1616) Wanderer
Eupham Rosie (1658) Stroma/South Ronaldsay
Faw family—John Faw, etc. (1612) Wanderers
Geillis Sclater (1616) Wanderer
Helen a Wallis (1616) Walls
Issobell Sinclair (1633)
James Knarstoun (1633) Tuskerbister, Orphir
John Sinclair (1633) Hoy
Jonet Drever (1615) Westray
Jonet Forsyth (1629) Westray ('vagabound, dochter to umquhile[A] William Forsyth in Howrnes within the Isle of Westray')
Jonet Irving (1616)
Jonet Reid (1643) Sandwick
Jonet Rendall (1629) Rendall
Jonet Sinclair (1643) Westray
Kathareen Manson (1660) South Ronaldsay
Katherine Grieve, alias Millar? (1633) Sanday (erroneously called an Evie witch by George Petrie—*Orcadian*, 21 July 1860—and a Rendall witch by W. R. Mackintosh—*Around The Orkney Peat-Fires* var. ed.)
Katherene Bigland (1615) Westray
Katherine Caray (1616)
Katherine Cragie (1643) Rousay
Katherine Grant (1623)
Katherine Taylor (1708) Stromness; wanderer
Magnus Linay (1616) Wanderer
Mamie Scott c.1850 Stromness (earlier in Flotta)
Marable Couper (1624) Birsay ('Spous to Johne Spens in the North-syd of Birsay')
Margaret Sandison (1635) Sanday

A. Daughter to the late.

Margaret Wick (1659) Shapinsay
Marion Cumlaquoy c.1630 Birsay
Marion Richart (1633) Sanday
Mattie Black c.1850 Brims
Recchel Tulloch c.1870 Sanday
Scota Bess c.1630 Stronsay
Thomas Swintone (1689)
William Scottie (1643) Wanderer

Some other Orkney Witches not mentioned in the Foregoing Text

These names and references have been taken from various sources, written and oral 'They are documented in the same way as in the general Notes.

c.1595   'Alisoun Margaret's daughter [Thurvoe, Walls] burnt for witchcraft', *Rentals of the Ancient Earldom and Bishoprick of Orkney*, collected by Alexander Peterkin. Edinburgh, 1820, Section II, page 103.

c.1595   'Jonet of Cara [South Ronaldsay] who was burnt for witchcraft'. Ibid., p.94.

c.1595   'Robert Ness, witche'. Ireland, Stenness. Ibid., p.38.

(1616)   Agnes Yullock [Probably Tulloch] (Rec. Ork., f.74 and v., quot. Dalyell, p.62). Touched a woman, who afterwards recovered her health; and caused the 'whole strength' of a farmer's tilth[A] to decay.

(1616)   Oliver Leask (Rec. Ork., f.65 v., quot. Dalyell, p.126) 'On a deficiency of milk, grass, taken from the spot whereon the pail stood, was to be thrown among the milk to avert recurrence of the like'.

(1616)   William Gude (Rec. Ork., f.63 v., quot. Dalyell, p.32) 'Prayit evill', so that sheep and cattle died.

(1633)   Christiane Dauidsone (Sanday?), spouse to William Harper, 'that took grass and baked a bannock, and gave to the goodman of Papa his grieve, who died; and the dog that got the bannock died. The bannock was for keeping their profit'. This witch was incriminated by Marion Richart at her trial. A.C.M., trial Richart, p.163.

A. Land under cultivation.

(1633) Elen Forster (Sanday?), spouse to James Burgar, 'can mend both the heartcake[A] and beanschaw[B] and put down horses to the goodman of Langskaill'. Mentioned in a memorandum on manuscript of M. Richart's trial. A.C.M., trial Richart, p.163.

(1635) Helen Isbuster (Rec. Ork, f.97, quot. Dalyell, pp.270, 305, 307, 388). Charmed mice into a corn stack; charmed a glaid[C] so that it sat on the ridge of a roof until it died; utterly ruined a man by nine knots cast on a blue thread.

c.1643 Marjorie Paplay. 'Thomas Lentron, his being put to death by Marjorie Paplay her witchcraft, by putting a white thing like chalk in his drink'. Orkney Presbytery Book 1639-1646, November 9, 1643.

(1643) Cristane Poock [Poke] (Rousay) 'late servant to Henrie Ingisgar in Papa, and now with Kowie Ingsgar, can charm the worm and the falling-sickness; and that she used the said falling-sickness to an ox in H[S]avaskaill, and that she got for doing this a plate of meill and a blood-pudding upon the head of the plate'. Incriminated by Katherine Cragie at her examination on 12 July 1643. A.C.M., trial Cragie, p.171.

(1643) Helen Hunter, 'Inswoman in Brugh'. (Rec. Ork. f.262-265, quot. Dalyell, pp.256, 392). Injured cattle by spinning with a black rock. A 'foirspoken'[D] horse was 'nyne tymes foirbitten'[E] by her and made an immediate recovery.

(1643) Jonet Thomeson, or Greibok (Rec. Ork. f.255 and v., quot. Dalyell pp.58, 59, 266, 271). Charged with causing and curing sickness, tainting corn, and causing by sorcery a bird to make a desperate attack on a person she disliked.

(1643) Margaret Ranie, alias Todlock (Rousay ?), 'Healed a cow of John Bellis in Quoyskowis of the baneschaw'.[F] Also incriminated by Katherine Cragie. A.C.M., trial Cragie, p.171.

(1643) Thomas Cors. (Rec. Ork. f.261, quot. Dalyell, pp.492-493). Described as a 'warlock'. Burst into a torrent of imprecations against James Paplay and his wife, who would, he said, 'be fain to

---

A. Cardialgia: pain or discomfort from the heart.
B. Sciatica.
C. Kite.
D. Bewitched.
E. Charmed.
F. Sciatica.

	eat grass under the stanes and wair under the banks',[A] which, with other predictions, came to pass.
Early 19th century (?)	Merro o' Midgar (Sourin, Rousay). Was blamed for having forspoken cattle, and was credited with the power to 'draw milk out of bourwood'.[B]
c.1850	Jenny Young (Rackwick, Hoy). Regarded in the neighbourhood as a benevolent witch with a gift of healing. She seemed to have some knowledge of hypnosis. Once, when a local laird annoyed her at a dance, she fixed him with her eyes and commanded him to take off his clothes. She only broke the spell when he had danced round the room in nothing but his shirt, to the accompaniment of derisive laughter from the other dancers.
c.1850	Scapa witch (See *Orkney Herald*, 23 February 1910). A Shetland woman 'prayed that no more whales would be sent to Scapa'. She went a few paces into the sea near Nether Scapa, and pushed a thimbled finger into the sand, withdrawing the finger and leaving the thimble. Then she pronounced a 'malison'[C] and proclaimed that whales would never again be captured in Scapa Flow until the thimble was found.
c.1850	Tammy Gibbon (Deerness). Was said to possess the Book of the Black Art, and to be able to turn himself into a cat. Stories are still told of how he was observed early one morning on the Eastside links performing some kind of dance ritual.
c.1893	Belle o' the Slap (Wasbister, Rousay). Was thought to have put a curse on a local family, so that the steamboat *Fawn*, which was taking them and their possessions to Evie, almost foundered as she approached the pier. Belle's method of cursing was to walk across the road twice in front of the line of carts and animals as they left the Rousay farm. A sudden surge of cattle prevented her from crossing the road a third time. It was firmly believed that if she had been able to do so the steamer instead of righting herself would have sunk.
Date quite uncertain	An unnamed Birsay witch, wife of a grieve at Boardhouse (See *Orcadian*, 10 April 1924), tried to make the gift of a child, her stepdaughter, to the Devil, but was foiled through her husband overhearing her as she made the pact at an old house up the Mill Burn. The man laced the little girl tightly into her corset (which

A. Be compelled to eat grass under the stones and seaweed at the shore.
B. Elder tree.
C. A malediction or curse.

The Big Tree, Albert Street, Kirkwall, 1888   Arthur Melville, RWS, RSW, RP, 1855-1904

prevented the stepmother and the Devil from abducting or injuring her), and then informed the authorities in Kirkwall, who apprehended the woman. She was tried and condemned to death.

Date uncertain   Felkyo. In *The Orkney Norn*, page 40, Dr Hugh Marwick refers to this person as 'a witch who used to live in the Hill-side district of Birsay'. He writes that the word is 'obviously related to the O.N. *fjolkyndi* or *fjolkyngi*, the black art, witchcraft'.

NOTES

1. Kristofer Visted, *Vor gamle bondekultur* (Kristiania, 1923), p.285.
2. *Comedy of Errors*, William Shakespeare, scene III, lines 10-11.
3. *Encyclopaedia Britannica*, 11 ed., vol.19, p.806.
4. *Danske Studier*, 1919.
5. p.96.
6. Kirkwall, 1961.
7. *Orkney Folklore and Traditions*, Walter Traill Dennison, p.19.
8. This story, told by Dennison, op. cit., corresponds closely with a version heard in Evie by the late Robert Spence of Vassquoy, Birsay, when he was a boy.
9. Ed. of 1700, pp.60, 61.
10. Ibid., p.61.
11. Quoted in *The Story of our Kayak* by William Clark Souter (Aberdeen University Press, 1934), p.14.
12. Laing's tr. Everyman's Library No.847, p.349.
13. Taylor's ed., pp.194, 195.
14. Ibid., pp.238, 243, 244.
15. *Orkneyinga Saga*, Taylor's ed., p.262.
16. Magnusson and Palsson's ed. (Penguin Books, 1960), pp.58, 219.
17. *The Orcadian Sketch Book*, p.164.
18. See Kristofer Visted, op. cit., p.276.
19. *Two Norse Lays* (Kirkwall, 1872).
20. Records of Orkney Sheriff Court in manuscript, f.74, v., quoted by Dalyell in *The Darker Superstitions of Scotland* (1834), p.236. Many extracts from this manuscript source are printed in the book. Further extracts will be noted thus: Rec. Ork., f.ooo, quot. Dalyell, p.ooo, or Ibid., etc.
21. *Acts and Statutes of the Lawting Sheriff and Justice Courts within Orkney and Zetland, MDCII-MDCXLIV* (Maitland Club, Edinburgh, 1840), p.XXIX.
22. Printed by William Mackenzie in his *Gaelic Incantations, Charms and Blessings of the Hebrides* (1885).
23. *A View of the Ancient and Present State of the Zetland Islands*, A. Edmonston (Edinburgh, 1809).
24. *An Etymological Dictionary of the Scottish Language*, John Jamieson, 1879.
25. *The Works of Sir David Lindsay*, Vol.I, 1931, p.371, line 5849 of *The Monarche*.
26. *The Witch-Cult in Western Europe*, M. A. Murray (Oxford, 1921), Introduction, pp.9, 11.
27. No.51, Vol.2, part 1.
28. Vol 1, Edinburgh, 1837.
29. Edinburgh, 1967.
30. 1834.
31. Edinburgh, 1886.
32. *Abbotsford Club Miscellany* (hereafter A.C.M.), trial Richart, pp.157, 158.

33. Ibid., trial Reid, p.182.
34. *County Folk-Lore III*, Orkney and Shetland (London, 1903), p.103.
35. Rec. Ork., f.60, quot. Dalyell, p.7.
36. A.C.M., trial Couper, p.139.
37. Orkney Presbytery Book 1639-1646, p.256.
38. MS Folklore of the late John Bremner.
39. MS Records of the Bishop of Orkney's Court, f.49, v., quot. Dalyell.
40. *Acts and Statutes*, op. cit., p.XXXI.
41. Rec. Ork., f.86, quot. Dalyell, p.470.
42. *Acts and Statutes*, op. cit., p.LIV.
43. A.C.M., trial Tailzeour, p.144.
44. Ibid., trial Richart, p.160.
45. Ibid., trial Cragie, p.178.
46. p.234.
47. Robert S. Barclay ed., *The Court Books of Orkney and Shetland 1614-1615*, p.19.
48. George Marwick's unpublished folklore.
49. A.C.M., trial Cragie, pp.175, 176.
50. B. H. Hossack, *Kirkwall in the Orkneys* (Kirkwall, 1900), transcription of trial, p.257.
51. A.C.M., trial Tailzeour, pp.144, 145.
52. Ibid., trial Cragie, pp.173, 174.
53. Rec. Ork., f.94, quot. Dalyell, p.510.
54. Ibid., f.99, quot. Dalyell, p.388.
55. A.C.M., trial Reid, p.183.
56. See Lynn Thorndike, *History of Magic*, i, 1923, pp.69, 592.
57. A.C.M., trial Reid, p.184.
58. *Old-Lore Miscellary of Orkney, Shetland, Caithness and Sutherland* (Viking Club, 1907-1908), vol.I, pp.162, 163.
59. Robert S. Barclay ed., op. cit., p.19.
60. Rec. Ork., quot. Dalyell, p.393.
61. Ibid., quot. Mackintosh, *Around The Orkney Peat-Fires* (Kirkwall, 5th ed, p.280).
62. Rev. J. B. Craven, *Church Life in South Ronaldsay and Burray in the Seventeenth Century* (Kirkwall, 1911), pp.29-31.
63. Rec. Ork., quot. Dalyell, p.118.
64. Ibid., f.97, v., quot. Dalyell, p.307.
65. Robert S. Barclay ed., op. cit., pp.19, 20.
66. Rec. Ork., f.223, v., quot. Dalyell, p.107.
67. Dalyell, pp.106, 107.
68. Rec. Ork., f.50, v., quot. Dalyell, p.389.
69. Rev. J. B. Craven, *History of the Church in Orkney 1558-1662*, p.225.
70. Rec. Ork., f.272, v., quot. Dalyell, p.459.
71. Ibid., f.234, v., quot. Dalyell, p.259.
72. Ibid., f.294, v., quot. Dalyell, p.184.
73. Rev. J. M. MacPherson, *Primitive Beliefs in the North-East of Scotland* (London, 1929).
74. A.C.M., trial Richart, p.159.
75. Ibid., trial Tailzeour, p.144.
76. Ibid., p.147.
77. Rec. Ork., f.68, v., quot. Dalyell, p.27.
78. Quoted in Geoffrey Parrinder's *Witchcraft: European and African*, London, 1958 and 1963.
79. Ibid., quot. Dalyell, p.124.
80. Ibid., f.51, quot. Dalyell, p.150.
81. Ibid., quot. Dalyell, p.118.
82. A.C.M., trial Cragie, p.177.
83. Ibid., p.178.

84. Dagmar Blix, *Draugen Skreik: Tradisjon fra Lofoten*, Norsk Folkeminnelags Skrifter 93 (Universitetsforlaget, Oslo, 1965), pp.22, 27.
85. *The Men of Noroway*, W. C. Fairweather and R. Meldau, *O.L. Miscellany*, op. cit., vol.x, pp.36-42.
86. Rec. Ork., f.263, v., quot. Dalyell, p.5.
87. Ibid., f.177, 178, quot. Dalyell, pp.7, 8.
88. A.C.M., trial Richart, p.158.
89. Rec. Ork., f.68, v., quot. Dalyell, p.124.
90. Ibid., f.90, v.
91. Ibid., f.264, quot. Dalyell, p.451.
92. Ibid., quot. Dalyell, pp.451, 452.
93. Dalyell, p.61.
94. Rec. Ork., f.263, v.
95. Ibid., f.72, r., quot. Dalyell, p.52.
96. Ibid., f.272, v., quot. Dalyell, p.390.
97. Ibid., quot. Dalyell, p.491.
98. Ibid., f.89, v., quot. Dalyell, p.474.
99. *Acts and Statutes*, op. cit., p.LIII.
100. A.C.M., trial Cragie, p.177.
101. Rec. Ork., f.51, v., quot. Dalyell, p.564.
102. A.C.M., trial Tailzeour, p.146.
103. John Bremner's unpublished folklore.
104. R. Menzies Fergusson, *Rambles in the Far North* (Paisley, 1884), p.70.
105. *Acts and Statutes*, op. cit., p.XXIX.
106. Rec. Ork., f.256, 257, v.
107. B. H. Hossack, op. cit., p.256.
108. *Acts and Statutes*, op. cit., p.XLIX.
109. Caithness Presbytery Records, quoted in 'Some References to Witchcraft and Charming' *O.L. Miscellany*, op. cit., vol.II, p.111.
110. Wick Kirk-Session Records, ibid., vol.II, p.111.
111. Rev. J. B. Craven, *Church Life in South Ronaldsay and Burray*, p.25.
112. Canisbay Kirk-Session Records, quoted in 'Folk-Lore Notes from John o' Groats', *O.L. Miscellany*, op. cit., vol.V, p.133.
113. George Marwick's unpublished folklore.
114. B. H. Hossack, op. cit., p.257.
115. A.C.M., trial Tailzeour, annotation, p.144.
116. Ibid., trial Cragie, annotation, p.177.
117. Ibid., p.178.
118. See instance in Rev. Dr Barry's *History of the Orkney Islands* (2nd ed., London, 1808), p.469.
119. See *Pitcairn's Criminal Trials*, vol.i, part 2, pp.386-388, 392-397.

TALES
FROM THE PAST

TALES FROM THE PAST

1	A memory of 1066	387
2	St Magnus	389
3	The last sea king	392
4	When Orkney went to Bannockburn	397
5	The belted knights of Stove	399
6	Island of Dons and Angels	401
7	The minister and the witch	403
8	Orkney and 'the Englishes'	406
9	Margaret Halcro of Evie—mother of a Scottish Church	409
10	Kirkwall's flood	411
11	Orkney memories of Nelson and Napoleon	413
12	The day that Kitchener died	419
13	The role of Scapa Flow	424

I

A memory of 1066

It is nine hundred years since '1066 and all that', and since we like to think of the past as neatly packaged in centuries, we have been reading and hearing a lot about the Norman Conquest.

I wonder how many of you know that, while Duke William was getting ready in Normandy for his invasion of England, we in the Northern Isles were also getting ready to invade, and that if our invasion had been successful the whole of English history might have been changed.

I should like to tell you about this; but mainly so that I can put on record a little human story, which has been preserved in a mere line or two of our island saga,[1] but which is as tender and moving as a flower seen in an arid desert of war and bloodshed. It concerns the Norse king, Harald Hardrada, and his daughter Maria; but I must tell you first of all about Harald.

The Norse were great givers of nicknames, and 'Hardrada', which is usually translated 'stern', really means obstinate. Harald was a half-brother of Olav the Saint, and he fled to what is now Russia when Olav was defeated at Stiklestad. He was received by the Grand Prince of Kiev, known as Yaroslav the Wise, one of whose daughters became Queen of France. The young Norwegian (he was only in his teens) was captivated by another daughter, Ellisif.[2] He wanted to marry her, but Yaroslav insisted that he must win his spurs, and prove himself a man, before he gave his consent.

Harald needed all his obstinacy, or doggedness, to make his way in a world where strength of body and indomitable courage were the great qualities. He went to Constantinople, served in the Varangian Guard,[3] and was in many a skirmish in the Mediterranean and North Africa. Returning at last, rich in gold and jewels, he married Ellisif. She gave him two daughters, Maria and Ingigerd, and Maria was the apple of his eye.

The day came when Harald was able to go back to Norway, of which he

1. *The Orkneyinga Saga.*
2. Elizabeth.
3. The bodyguard of the Byzantium Emperors in the late tenth and eleventh centuries. It was composed mostly of Norsemen and latterly some Anglo-Saxons.

eventually became sole king. But Harald had seen great kingdoms, and he decided that he must add a wealthier land to his poor, mountainous kingdom of Norway. In 1066 he and Duke William both had the same idea—to annex England.

Harald acted first. He came to the Orkney Islands with a great army, which he increased by recruiting Orcadians. Then he sailed for England.

He had taken with him to Orkney his wife Ellisif and his daughters. They probably lived in the Orkney earls' weather-buffeted hall on the tiny island of the Brough of Birsay. We are not told of Harald's parting from his intensely loving elder daughter Maria, but we can imagine it. We can also imagine how day after day she watched from the island for a ship bringing news of her father.

At first Harald was successful: he conquered the whole north of England. But when he met Harald Godwinsson of England on 25 September 1066 at Stamford Bridge, it was the English who won, and Harald Hardrada of Norway was killed.

This is where our sad little human story comes in. Hundreds of miles away in Orkney, where Ellisif and her daughters were waiting, by some strange power of the affections Maria was knitted to her father in death. 'The same day and at the same hour as King Harald fell,' says the saga, 'his daughter Maria died, and it is said that they had but one life.'

80 The Evie coach setting out from John Street, Stromness, c.1900

81 The Orkney Motor Express leaving Harbour Street, Kirkwall for Stromness, c.1905

82 Orkney's first motor car in Harbour Street, Kirkwall, 1901.
A Daimler-Benz, people were impressed by its maximum speed of 14 mph.

83 Early motor vehicles near the Kiln Corner, Kirkwall, c.1905

2

St Magnus[1]

I wonder how many of those who read in the sagas that St Magnus was 'most noble of race' take the words literally. They may sound like romantic phrase-making, yet they are true in the completest historical sense.

St Magnus was a descendant, through both parents, of that great Norwegian Earl, Rognvald Eysteinsson, Earl of Möre, who was given the islands of Orkney and Shetland by King Harald Fairhair. This Earl Rognvald (not to be confused with the later Rognvalds) was not only the progenitor of the Norse earls of Orkney, but also an ancestor of William the Conqueror, and through him the Norman kings of England. I suppose one can claim that both Olav V, King of Norway, and our own Queen Elizabeth II are among Rognvald's descendants.

The greatest of the Icelandic chieftains could also claim Rognvald as their ancestor, including Hall of the Side, whose adoption of Christianity did much to bring about the conversion of the Icelanders. Through Hall, Earl Magnus could trace his descent a second time to Rognvald Eysteinsson, for Magnus's mother Thora was a great-great-granddaughter of Hall's.

There was also a royal Scottish connection. Magnus was the great-great-grandson of King Malcolm II of Scotland, and the connection was restored when the widowed grandmother of Magnus, Ingibiorg, married King Malcolm III (Canmore). Moreover, as the late John Mooney[2] pointed out, Matilda, queen of Henry I of England, was a kinswoman of St Magnus, both being descendants of Malcolm II. In his youth, Magnus received a welcome as a kinsman at both the Scottish and English Courts.

Early writers were not unmindful of the nobility of St Magnus's ancestry, and it may have been partly due to this that his fame spread so rapidly through the Scandinavian world. It was an unheard-of thing for a man of such proud and honoured birth to choose to die as Magnus did. Any other would have challenged Hakon to a duel to the death, instead of kneeling to the axe. The

1. See also *Viking and saint*, p.457.
2. Eminent Orcadian historian (1862-1950) and author of, among other books, *St Magnus, Earl of Orkney*, 1935.

Norwegian writer Alf Högh is surely right in observing: 'The manner of his death is not only the high point of the Orkneyinga Saga, it is entirely unparalleled in Norwegian history. Earl Magnus was a child of his age, a saint before his time, and by his life and death a living witness to Christianity's power to transform mankind. His own time needed such a witness—our time and we ourselves need it just as badly.'

The lesson Magnus had to teach was a hard one to learn. Norway's St Olaf died on the field of battle. Norsemen could understand the Church militant far better than the Church magnanimous. One wonders if it was merely an accident of history, or the result of the overshadowing of Olaf, or if there was some deeper reason for the fact that the first St Magnus Kirk in Norway was only consecrated in December 1957, 842 years after Magnus's martyrdom. It is situated at Lillestrøm, and is a very modern, flat-roofed building, with squarish windows and a tall, free-standing cross. Magnus, it is true, had been honoured at an early date by an altar in Trondheim Cathedral, and his feast days were kept, but it is strange that, as one of the principal saints of ancient Norway, no church was named after him. In Iceland no fewer than seven churches were dedicated to him, as Dr Alexander Bugge[1] pointed out. There were at least five St Magnus churches in Shetland. It seems that veneration of St Magnus was so strong in Shetland that five or six hundred tons of red sandstone were imported from Orkney to beautify and enrich the church at Tingwall which bore his name.

Some noble Latin hymns were written about St Magnus, for use on the feasts commemorating his death and translation. It seems a pity that they are not used in English versions. One of these (in rough paraphrase) begins:

> Exultingly our ringing voices blend
> In praise of Magnus, since whose holy end
> Are wonders done which all our thoughts transcend.
> The urn is broken, but the fragrance steals
> To sick and suffering, whom its odour heals:
> Swift comes the answer when the suppliant kneels.

There is one rather beautiful Gaelic Hymn to St Magnus. Very appropriately, it was discovered in Orkney itself, having remained in the memory of a farmer who had come to the islands from Kildonan, Sutherlandshire: a Mr George Gunn who lived in the parish of St Ola. The poem appeared in the first volume of Dr Alexander Carmichael's *Carmina Gadelica*, and there has been more than one translation into English. Here is a rendering which has not been previously published:

---

1. *Norges Historie*, II, 2, p.179. Bugge is quoted by John Mooney in *St Magnus, Earl of Orkney*, p.277.

ST MAGNUS

O Magnus, thou hast all our love,
    And thou wilt be our guide.
O fragrant body filled with grace,
    We in thy care confide.

Keep us in mind, thou saint of power,
    Encircling us around,
That even in our darkest day
    Thy presence may be found.

Pasture our cattle on the hills,
    The wolf and fox restrain,
Guard us from ghost's and giant's rage
    And from oppression's bane.

Encompass thou our flocks and herds,
    Surround our lambs and sheep;
From field vole and from water vole
    All creatures safely keep.[1]

Bring healthy dews upon the kine,
    Cause corn and grass to grow,
Give sap to cress and rush and dock
    And bid the daisies blow.

O Magnus of the high renown,
    Upon the crested wave,
In heroes' bark, on sea, on land,
    Wilt thou defend and save.

---

1. The reference to the voles may seem odd, but both the water rat and the field vole were regarded as very destructive, particularly of young tree life.

3

The last sea king

In 1263 some skirmishes with Norwegians led by their king, Haakon Haakonson, took place in the vicinity of Largs, and Scottish tradition (assisted by some historians) has magnified these as The Battle of Largs.

An older generation in Orkney knew Haakon, a trifle romantically, as 'the last of the sea kings', and could recite John Stuart Blackie's 'Death of Haco':

> Woe is me for Haco,[1] Haco!
>   On Lorn and Mull and Skye
> The hundred ships of Haco
>   In a thousand fragments lie!

Since then it has become unfashionable to teach Orkney history; and people nowadays can hardly be blamed for asking what it was that happened here seven hundred years ago. Is there perhaps an excuse for retelling the story?

The focal point, first of all, is the Hebrides. These islands had been settled by Scandinavians for centuries and had long been subject directly or indirectly to the Kings of Norway. Early in the eleventh century they apparently formed part of the dominions of Earl Thorfinn the Mighty, one of Orkney's greatest Norse earls, and in the last decade of that century the Norwegian King Magnus Barelegs reasserted sovereignty. Alexander II of Scotland tried to come to an arrangement with King Haakon IV of Norway, even offering to buy back the Hebrides, but Haakon replied scornfully that he was not in want of money.

Alexander was stung by this reply, and decided that negotiation was futile. He collected a fleet in 1249 to attack the islands, but he became ill on the voyage and died on the island of Kerrera, where he had been put ashore. His son, Alexander III, made up his mind to accomplish what his father had failed to do. Like his father he tried to bargain with Haakon, was repulsed,

---

1. Haco and Hacon are versions of Haakon.

and proceeded to give at least tacit support to chieftains like the Earl of Ross who were harrying the isles.

The Norsemen in the Hebrides, with cattle slain and homesteads burning, sent appeals for help to King Haakon. These appeals he was almost in honour bound to heed, although he must have known the difficulty of maintaining Norse colonies so near the Scottish coast. Perhaps this very difficulty made it seem essential to him to plan an expedition on the grand scale, and to give Scotland such a taste of Norwegian power, and with it such a fright, that the Hebrides would be left thereafter in peace. Moreover, he must have felt compelled to uphold the dignity of an empire to which Iceland and Greenland had just made submission.

Much work was spent in fitting out a magnificent fleet of over a hundred ships, possibly the greatest fleet then existing in the world. Perhaps the fitting out took too long, for it was already high summer in that year of 1263 when the fleet sailed from Bergen. It reached Shetland after two nights at sea and remained there a fortnight, then sailed for Orkney. The point chosen for assembly was Elwick Bay in Shapinsay. Near the end of July the hundred warships anchored there, with Haakon's great warship, the Christ-ship, bearing dragon's heads of gold at stem and stern, towering over them all.

On 28 July, the Eve of St Olaf, in a tent on Shapinsay, mass was celebrated; and to mark the occasion the ordinary folk of the island were shown over the king's ship. With preparations for the main part of the expedition made, the fleet sailed round to Rognvaldsvoe (or Rognvaldsvagr), identified as St Margaret's Hope, and again dropped anchor. It was there for almost another fortnight. These delays have seemed inexplicable to some historians, but the reason for them may have been simple enough. It appears to have been a bad summer, cold and boisterous. While the ships were at South Ronaldsay an eclipse of the sun on 5 August terrified the superstitious, who saw in it a bad omen. It took some days to quiet their forebodings, and even then the weather may not have been propitious. Presumably, Haakon's advisers thought that the expedition could not be further delayed. On Friday, 10 August, it set sail. There is perhaps a question as to whether the ill-assorted warriors under Haakon's command were agreed on strategy, or indeed on anything else. Perhaps some of them regarded the whole expedition as a large-scale viking foray, with booty, rather than a pitched battle, as its most rewarding consequence. However that may be, Haakon's Saga[1] says that the king 'had had during the summer great watchings and much care; he was often called up, and had little peace from his men.'

For the best part of two months the fleet made its way down the western coast of Scotland. It lay for a while at Gigha, then moved to Lamlash Bay

---

1. *The Saga of Hacon*, p.366.

and finally to the sound between the Cumbraes and the Ayrshire coast at Largs. What Haakon expected the Scots to do seems mysterious. They did not possess a fleet capable of meeting him. There was not much point in manning the wild west coast, where a landing by the Norwegians would achieve little beyond scaring handfuls of peasants. The fortified castles near the sea had been reinforced, and could hold out for a long period. Alexander calculated that he could concentrate what forces he had on the lowlands of Ayr, where a landing might most effectively be made. Meanwhile, he used his ships discreetly to watch the Norwegians.

Alexander knew that delaying tactics were safest. It was near enough to the September gales for him to hope that they would come early and do mischief to the Norwegian fleet. Accordingly, he kept emissaries going between himself and Haakon with suggesions for a treaty. Apparently Haakon took these overtures seriously, instead of making a swift and concentrated attack. He may also have been plagued by his men's predilection for plundering expeditions, perhaps encouraged by their Hebridean compatriots. The whole fleet was well south before the end of September, but the bargaining went on, until at last Haakon brought it to an end—too late.

The storms were delayed, but at last they came with prodigious fury. A two-day storm at the very beginning of October did much damage to the Norwegians: some ships were wrecked on the Ayrshire coast, others foundered at sea. Many of the shipwrecked Norwegians were slain at once; but a fight between a larger body of Norwegians, who had come ashore to help their wrecked comrades, and a superior number of Scots who drove them back to the sea, has been called The Battle of Largs. This skirmish, even if a hot encounter, was only incidental to the defeat of the Norwegians, which came about partly by Alexander's strategy, partly by their own indecision, but mainly, like the destruction of the Armada, by sea and tempest. It would have taken Haakon a long time to get his fleet back into fighting trim, and to combat the defeatism of his followers; moreover, he was already a sick man. He decided to sail back to Norway.

At an anchorage in the north of Sutherland, probably Loch Eriboll, Haakon made a halt, then crossed the Pentland Firth to Longhope on 29 October. Some ships preceded him, and had a bad passage. A ship from Rygjafulk was lost with her crew. John of Hestby's ship just missed being drawn into the Swelkie.[1] St Margaret's Hope, then called Rognvaldsvoe, was again the place of assembly. Some ships sailed for home without Haakon's leave, others he allowed to depart, but still others, twenty in all, he commanded to stay the winter in Orkney. With them remained some of his loyal supporters.

1. A whirlpool in the Pentland Firth which is particularly dangerous in certain states of the tide.

After All Saints Day[1] King Haakon sent his own ship to Houton to be laid up for the winter. Each captain did likewise with his ship, some laying them up beside the king's ship, some nearer Scapa. Haakon had gone to Kirkwall, but was at Houton on Saturday, 10 November, to see that his ship was properly cared for. He was very sick that night aboard his ship, but was able to go ashore next day, Martinmas, to hear mass sung for him. Recovering somewhat, he made his way back to Kirkwall, where he was staying with the bishop in the great house whose foundations are partly incorporated in the present Bishop's Palace. In the hall were two long tables, the bishop's and the king's, where their respective followers sat to meals, but the king took his food in his room: sick and weary, but still anxious to put his affairs in order.

As he sat at his window, looking across to the Cathedral, still unfinished after a century and a quarter, he made arrangements for the support of his chief men and their bands, and allotted them quarters for the winter. Most of the ships' captains were sent to farms in the country, but a few faithful men were to stay in Kirkwall. The sickness which afflicted King Haakon did not at first seem deadly. He was a strong man: even if he was popularly known as 'Haakon the Old', he was no more than fifty-nine. After three weeks in bed he felt better, and rose. The first day he paced around his room and through his lodging. The next day he felt able to hear mass in the bishop's chapel. The third day he ventured further, walking across to the Cathedral and around the shrine of St Magnus. When he returned he bathed and allowed himself to be shaved.

It was a brief interlude. That night he felt worse than ever. He was ill and could not sleep. During the days and nights that followed he listened, at first respectfully, to the priests who read from their Latin books. But he found the Latin more and more difficult to understand and ordered them to read from the Norse instead. So, during the next weeks, there were read in the king's sick-chamber all the sagas of the Norse saints and kings, while Haakon listened and nodded between his bouts of pain.

The sickness grew until it was seen to be mortal, and the king made his final arrangements. He divided his silver and plate between his bodyguard and serving men. To King Magnus, his son, he had letters written concerning the things that were to be done in Norway.

The saga[2] says, 'King Hacon was annealed[3] one night before Lucy's Mass.[4] The bishops were there present: Thorgils bishop of Stavanger, Gilbert bishop of Hammar, and Henry bishop of the Orkneys; and abbot Thorleif,

---

1. 1 November.
2. *The Saga of Hacon*, p.367.
3. Received extreme unction.
4. 13 December.

and many other learned clerks. And ere he was anointed then those men kissed him who were by. The king was then still speech-hale.'

In answer to questions he swore that he had no son but Magnus; and then lay back to hear the Saga of Sverrir.

Later, on the evening of Saturday, 15 December, he lost his speech. Near midnight the droning voice of the reader had just finished the saga. As midnight passed 'Almight God called king Hacon from this world's life.'

Four trusty men were with the king at the last: Brynjolf John's son, Erling Alf's son, John queen, and Rognvald ork. Around them were the serving men who had nursed the king during his sickness.

Soon the bishops and clerks came to say the mass for the dead; then Bishop Thorgils and some others prepared the king's body for lying in state. The upper hall of the Bishop's Palace was made ready and a splendid bier erected. On Sunday, 16 December the king's body nobly clad, with a garland on the head, was laid upon it. Round it stood the torch-bearers, their torches filling the hall with light. The great folk and ordinary folk of Kirkwall came silently up the stairs to look at the great warrior. And, says the saga, the body 'seemed to be all bright and comely, with a fair ruddiness on the face as of a living man. It was a great comfort to men for their great grief... to see so fair a corse[1] of a dead man and their own lord.'

That afternoon a solemn mass for the king's soul was sung; and all through the night the bodyguards kept their places beside the bier. Two days later the king was buried with much ceremony in the steps of the choir of St Magnus Cathedral, before the shrine of the saint. A guard was maintained at the grave.

The king had ordered that a Christmas feast should be held. As he had wished, it took place in the palace, with Bishop Henry and Andrew Club-foot as hosts.

The months dragged by. At last on Ash Wednesday[2] the coffin was taken out of the earth and carried across to Scapa, where the king's vessel, the Christ-ship, had been made ready.

After a rough passage the ship reached Bergen, where with great honour Haakon the Old was gathered to his fathers.

1. Corpse.
2. 5 March 1264.

84 A Crossley tourer, BS 1 at Longhope, 1952. It had a canvas hood, and twin tyres on the rear

85 Carrying water from the pump in Broad Street, Kirkwall, *c.*1860

86 Pumping water from a country well, *c.*1900

87 The sacred well, Bigswell, Stenness, 1985

4

When Orkney went to Bannockburn

On Wednesday, 24 June 1964, all Scotland celebrated the victory of King Robert Bruce at Bannockburn, 650 years ago. It might be thought that Orkney, which was part of Norway in 1314, and for another century and a half, would have little interest in this. But the odd thing is that Orkney, remote as it may appear to some, has a knack of getting tangled up in the affairs of its neighbours.

In the translation of Torfaeus' *Ancient History of Orkney, Caithness and The North*, which was made by the Rev. Alexander Pope of Reay, it is confidently asserted that 'The Laird of Halcro commanded three hundred men at the battle of Bannockburn, and fought like a hero. He afterwards returned to Orkney with great honour.' Another historian, Tudor,[1] speculated on whether any of the relics of St Magnus were borne before the Scottish army at Bannockburn. It is not impossible, but there is no proof.

Sir Walter Scott, when in Orkney in 1814, amplified the Bannockburn tradition, by writing, 'The Orcadians say that a Norwegian prince, then their ruler, called by them Harold, brought 1,400 men of Orkney to the assistance of Bruce and that the King, at a critical period of the engagement, touched him with his scabbard saying, "The day is against us." "I trust," returned the Orcadian, "your Grace will venture again"; which has given rise to their motto and passed into a proverb.' Thus, with romantic inaccuracy, wrote Sir Walter; but it is certainly true that the motto of the Halcros of Coubister in Orkney was 'We'll put it to a venture', and that they cherished a similar tradition.

Why should Norwegian Orkney be interested in furthering the cause of Robert Bruce? There are several reasons. King Robert's sister, Isabella Bruce, had been Queen of Norway, and was now living in respected widowhood there. The Bishop of Norway had been excommunicated by the Pope for condoning the murder of Comyn by Bruce. Then despite what our school history books took for granted, it is almost certain that Bruce spent his most

---

1. *The Orkneys and Shetland* by John R. Tudor, 1883.

unhappy winter of 1306 not in Rathlin Island but in Orkney. If he ever took a lesson from a spider, it was probably in the Bishop's Palace at Kirkwall.

The friendship between Robert Bruce and Orkney, which seemed to be sealed when King Robert confirmed an annual grant to St Magnus Cathedral of three chalders[1] of corn and one cask of wine from the farms of Aberdeen, was sometimes disturbed by the king's subjects. There was an agreement, signed two years before Bannockburn, between Bruce and the King of Norway, regarding mutual compensation to be made in respect of the depredations of the 'wild men' of both countries; and in later years there was a complaint by King Robert that Orkney was sheltering his enemies.

Nevertheless, Bannockburn was pleasing to Norwegian Orkney. Old legends say that, on the day of the battle, a rider in shining armour announced the Scots victory in Aberdeen, and later, beyond the Pentland Firth. This supernatural horseman, everyone whispered, was Orkney's own St Magnus.

---

1. An obsolete measure of capacity. In Scotland a chalder of corn was sixteen bolls.

5

The belted knights of Stove

One spring morning, at some time during the first half of the sixteenth century, John Kirkness of Stove in Sandwick, who had steeped some bere seed in the burn preparatory to sowing, was taking the seed out of the burn when a pleasant-looking wanderer with red hair falling to his shoulders came to him and asked for work. He was obviously not an Orcadian, and John Kirkness, who probably had reason to dislike the Scottish adventurers who were finding their way to Orkney, decided to send him packing. The old man was already doing this when his daughter, who liked the looks of the personable youth, interrupted him with a plea on the stranger's behalf. She said that he could look after the geese, of which the farm had a large flock. With some reluctance old John agreed, and the young stranger was sent down to the meadows of Stove to herd the geese.

He was a quiet man, unwilling to discuss himself, and he was the subject of much local curiosity. He would sit pensively on a large stone in the meadow lost in reverie, while the people around observed him furtively. One day he was seen to pull out a gold comb and comb his hair with it. From then on a closer watch was kept on him, and it became evident from his manner that the stranger was a man of high degree. This fact caused the neighbours to pay him exaggerated deference, which the stranger noted and appeared to find irksome.

He prepared to leave Stove, but before doing so he told the family that he was indeed a person of consequence. Turning to John Kirkness he thanked him for his kindness, then asked him to kneel down. Touching the old man's shoulder with his stick he said, 'Rise, Sir John Kirkness, you and your descendants shall always after this be known as "The Belted Knights of Stove".' And so they were, generation after generation. They pointed to the stone in the meadow, which they called 'The King's Stone', and described in detail the appearance of the stranger, never doubting that he was indeed James the Fifth of Scotland.[1]

> 1. James V is popularly supposed to have wandered in disguise around his Kingdom. He did pay an official visit to Orkney in the summer of 1540 during a cruise in May–July. He came with a fleet of twelve ships *en route* to the Western Isles.

Two years ago I investigated the story. I found that the stone on which the King was supposed to have sat is built into a corner of the present barn of Stove. It was originally taken from the meadow as a corner-stone for an earlier barn, and when the new barn was built it was removed as a corner-stone for it. The word KING, most probably a relatively late addition by someone who knew the story, could be deciphered carved on it. Unfortunately, I did not see the stone, as it had been harled[1] with the rest of the barn.

Around the same time I had the privilege of calling on an intelligent and humorous lady in her mid-eighties, who had been born in the house of Stove, and who could claim to be the last Kirkness of Stove to bear the name in Orkney. This lady could confirm that her family were very proud of being the 'belted knights' and she corroborated the fact that the King's Stone is built into the barn. With engaging good nature, she gave me a pleasant family addition to the story. She had heard that when John Kirkness was engaging the stranger he quibbled with him about the wage, whereupon the impatient daughter said, 'Daddy, fee him daddy, for a pound o' more fee. Dinna stand wae him.'[2]

1. Roughcast.
2. 'Father, hire him father, for at least a pound. Don't haggle with him.'

6

Island of Dons and Angels

Up in the Northern Isles we like to say that we are Norse; and indeed most of us can claim descent from the Scandinavian farmers and vikings who began to come west-over-sea nearly twelve centuries ago. The vast majority of our farms have Norse names. For instance, Thor and Odin, old Norse gods, are common enough in place-names even today.

But we are, as an Orkney poet has said, 'a fine mixter-maxter'; for the islands have been visited by men from all the great sea-faring nations, many of whom have settled here; and to us have been sent in turbulent times, with fine impartiality, criminals and covenanters, along with many an odd political refugee.

A wonderful example of how strangers have found a foothold in these far-flung isles, and have mingled their blood with ours, is the island of Westray, one of the most northerly in Orkney. With a little pardonable exaggeration, you could call it the 'Island of Dons and Angels'.

First, the Dons. Perhaps you know that one ship of the Armada, *El Gran Grifon*, was wrecked on Fair Isle. Another ship, dismasted and completely disabled when north of Orkney, was hurried by fierce tides towards the rocks. The crew took to the only two remaining boats. One of these was quickly swamped; the other, as by a miracle, managed to reach the island of Westray.

The Spaniards were hospitably received, and they took kindly to the island. They taught themselves to be first-rate fishermen; they built a settlement of houses beside the shore; and they married island wives. The Dons prospered, they were active and daring, and in later times expert smugglers.

After that first union with Orcadian girls, none of the Dons was allowed to marry outside their community. They kept up this prohibition for over one hundred and fifty years. Long since, the community was assimilated into the common stock, but there is even now no difficulty in knowing a Don. They are dark-eyed, fidgety and restless, and far more given to gesticulation than our easy-going Orcadians.

The Angels all came from a single stem—a little boy who was the only person to be saved when a Russian ship ran on the rocks to the north of the island. There was no clue to his identity, but a piece of wood bearing the name of the ship's home port, Archangel, came ashore. So they called the child Archie Angel, and brought him up an island child[1]. He spoke the local dialect, and no one bothered about his origin. The male line died out years ago, but, under other surnames, there are still Angels in Westray.[2]

1 For an account of the shipwrecked boy and of his descendants in Westray, see *The Orcadian* of 1 November 1990, p.9.
2. A great-great-granddaughter of Archie Angel, Mary Angel was the last person in Orkney to bear the surname. She married Henry Mason and died on 1 October 1938 at 7 Clay Loan, Kirkwall, aged eighty-seven.

7

The minister and the witch

I have had occasion to undertake a task which involves some research into Shetland history and tradition. In doing so I have been reminded, by a terrible act of vengeance which took place on a remote Shetland headland nearly four centuries ago, of an episode from Orkney's past which is now almost forgotten. It is a strange story, interesting enough to tell in full.

At the centre of it is a minister, Henry Colville of Orphir, a pleasant, compliant man who, prior to the 1590s, seems to have led an unexceptional life, seeking to promote the cause of the Reformation in Orkney, studying and annotating pious Lutheran commentaries, and sitting so easy to his benefice that he let the teinds,[1] great and small, to his wife and children, with the full concurrence of bishop and chapter.

On the whole, he took his religious duties lightly, only being spurred into activity now and then by the more militant; as when, for example, he served (along with Earl Robert Stewart) on a committee to deal with Jesuits and seminary priests in Orkney, where they were reported to have a hideout.

Earl Robert liked having Harry Colville around: he probably made a good amanuensis, and he was willing to undertake commissions of a delicate character. He was a favourite, too, with Robert's son Patrick, and their friendship continued after Patrick became Earl in 1592. No doubt Patrick, used to experiencing the animosity of the large family among whom he was brought up, was glad to have a confidante.

Colville encouraged Patrick in his schemes, perhaps discussed with him his dreams of a great palace in Kirkwall, and certainly set his signature to the contract when Earl Patrick sent William Irving of Sabay to see how much he could secure of the ordnance of the ship of the Spanish Armada which had been wrecked there a few years before. Whether he helped to obtain for the Earl various small farms in Orphir, from which their rightful owners were turned out, no one can now say.

---

1. The Scots word for tithes.

All went well until 1594 when Earl Patrick had a fearful scare. His precious brothers, John, James and William, with one or two like-minded friends, were apparently plotting his murder. They were not quite sure whether to poison him at a banquet or to come on him suddenly in his bed at Birsay. Patrick was not a young man to trifle with, and things might go wrong. Then, it appears, they heard of a woman in Ireland, Stenness, named Alison Balfour, who was reputed to know all about sorcery. It occurred to them that it would be far safer to bewitch the Earl first of all. There were several consultations with Alison, with what result one cannot say. Patrick continued to flourish, but Alison was taken to Kirkwall for trial.

It was at this point that Harry Colville became deeply involved. As a clergyman, and as a loyal friend of Patrick, he endeavoured to wring the truth out of Alison. It was essential to get enough evidence to implicate Patrick's brothers and put them out of harm's way.

Alison was persuaded to tell her story by forty-eight hours of torture in an instrument called the caschilawes,[1] and by seeing her elderly husband, eldest son, and daughter of seven, subjected to other forms of pressure, as various as they were terrible. Colville acted alternately as interrogator and spiritual comforter. At last, by promising her that her life would be saved, he managed to obtain from her a confession of sorts, sufficient to enable the court, regardless of the pledges he had made, to sentence her to be strangled and burned for witchcraft.

She was taken, as many a later witch was to be, to the head of the loan (the top of the present Clay Loan), and there in the presence of Colville and four other ministers she was asked to make a dying disposition for the Notary Public. With her end near, Alison's courage came back. She protested her innocence. Before ministers, lawyer and gaping rabble, she told what she had suffered in prison—perhaps in the Cathedral itself. But soon the noose tightened, the fire was kindled, and Alison Balfour was reduced to ashes.

Patrick's brother John was tried in Edinburgh for his part in the plot. He escaped by the skin of his teeth. There was the confession extracted by Colville as evidence against him, but Alison's dying declaration, telling how the evidence had been obtained, saved his life. Free once more, John Stewart allowed himself many private thoughts about the engaging parson who had been such a friend of the family in Kirkwall.

Meanwhile, Colville busied himself about Earl Patrick's affairs. For some reason Patrick required business transacted in Shetland, and sent his obliging friend to Nesting, where he seems to have stayed at some windy habitation on the top of the Noup.

Edinburgh was far from Orkney in those days, and further from Shetland,

---

1. An iron framework which encircled the leg and was then placed in a moveable furnace.

but somehow news of Harry Colville's whereabouts got to John Stewart. This was in 1596, and the Master of Orkney, as John was usually called, lost no time. With thirty friends, who for one reason or another had little love for the Orphir minister, he made his plans. A party of them—including John himself, an Edinburgh lawyer, and a Gilbert Pacock, who had actually watched Alison's burning at Kirkwall—set sail from Montrose and headed north.

They made one break in their journey, at Gairsay. At Langskaill they picked up from William Bannatyne as much fresh provisions and arms as he could supply. In Shetland they took care to make a landfall well away from the place where Colville was living, and continued their journey overland. They took the minister by surprise, and, on a bright July day, 'maist schamefullie, crewallie and unmercifullie slew him.' The only one to suffer for the deed was Gilbert Pacock, a sorry scapegoat who was probably a spy and hireling of John Stewart. Pacock was beheaded at the mercat cross of Edinburgh.

I have spoken of the Minister of Orphir with some restraint, but it seems poetic justice that Alison Balfour was so thoroughly avenged.

In Shetland, the minister's slaying became something of a folktale. There the tradition is that four brothers from Orkney, named Sinclair, whose land Colville had helped the Earl to appropriate, were responsible for his savage death. Indeed, this tale suggests that they were inspired by such ferocity that one of them drank Colville's heart's blood, a vow that he had made and was determined to carry out literally.

This tale seems unlikely, but in the 1595 Rental of Orphir there are two tantalising entries. One refers to a farm in Ingamyre, 'fallen in escheat to my Lord for theft, perteining to the Sinclairs', and the other to a piece of land in Swanbuster 'escheat for theft pertaining to the Sinclairs'.

Whatever the truth, it was a sordid end for the agreeable and personable minister, whose cousin was Abbot of Culross. In one of his books, signed by him 'Henricus Colvill, praecentor Orchaden', Harry Colville underlined the verse from the Book of Job: 'But he saveth the poor from the sword, from their mouth, and from the hand of the mighty.'

How impossible to foresee, that day in the 1580s when he read the words in his quiet manse in Orphir, the last violent scene on the Noup of Nesting.

8

Orkney and 'the Englishes'

A matter which is occupying many Orkney minds at the moment is the pawning[1] of the islands to Scotland five centuries ago, and the gradual infiltration of Scots folk into the county, bringing with them their laws, customs and language. We almost always forget that for a short period neither Norwegians nor Scots were rulers of Orkney, but the people known here as 'the Englishes'. For Cromwell's soldiers found their way after 1650, doubtless unwillingly, to Kirkwall, where the Protector quartered a garrison and erected forts on either side of the harbour. He is still commemorated in Kirkwall to this day by the street known as Cromwell Road.

There was throughout the period of the Protectorate a military governor in Orkney, who sat on the bench with the Sheriff. The names of some of the governors are remembered: Watson, Cooper, Sauray, Powell. They seem to have usurped little of the Sheriff's duty, except when someone spoke, as people occasionally did, 'to the prejudice of the Commonwealth of England'. This was usually the hot-headed son of a laird, but occasionally it was a shrill tongued woman.

Naturally, it was not until the Restoration that people let themselves go, and then the offences of 'the Englishes' were recited with what Shakespeare would have called 'advantages'. They had pulled down the kirk-yard dyke round the Cathedral to build their forts, and had furnished them with wood from Cathedral pews. They had quartered their horses in the kirk. (The writer conveniently forgot that earlier in the century the local administration had

---

1. In 1468 King Christian I of Denmark and Norway pledged Orkney as part of his daughter Margaret's dowry on the occasion of her marriage to the son of King James II of Scotland, afterwards James III. The islands could be redeemed on payment of 50,000 florins of the Rhine, part of the 60,000 florins which formed the whole dowry. King Christian was able to pay only 2,000 of the 10,000 florins still due in 1469, when Shetland was pledged for the balance. There was formal recognition that the islands were held on redeemable wadset of Denmark as late as 1667 in the Treaty of Breda.

used the same building for their more lurid witchcraft trials.) But to go on with the offences of the Cromwellians: they found some base use for the venerable marble slabs of Bishop Tulloch's tomb, where for generations money borrowed by anyone in the town was formally repaid. They stole the bells from the old two-towered church of Deerness. Indeed, one writer has said that 'they were nearly as useful as scape-goats in Kirkwall, as the cat is in lodging-houses.' Of course, the basic grievance was that the Protector's levies of men and money fell very heavily on Orkney, which saw no reason why it should pay for the maintenance of 'the Englishes'.

Yet human nature is always much the same. Just as in the past two world wars British soldiers became the friends of many folk in Orkney, so it happened with the Cromwellians. There were farmers and tradesmen in Cromwell's army, and they taught the Orcadians what they knew about the mechanical arts including the construction of locks, and gardening—particularly the growing of cabbage.

Some of the soldiers stayed behind when the Protectorate ended.[1] Sergeant William Emmerson took up his trade as a shoemaker and became Deacon of the Corporation. His surname survived in Orkney until a generation ago. Harry Erburie became a prosperous merchant. He built a lovely house, with an oriel window, in Broad Street, which the bad taste of last century saw fit to destroy. In 1671, when the Cathedral was struck by lightning and the steeple set on fire, people rushed across to Harry's shop and got from him seventeen salted cowhides to place on the 'highest lofting', to save the bells if they fell. This precaution, and the heaping of earth on the floor, saved all the tumbling bells except one, which was cracked.

Not all the soldiers liked Orkney, and one of the most pungent reminders of the time is an anonymous poem called *The Character of Orkney*, which is the most scurrilous attack ever made on the islands. Little of it is quotable, but at its end the sadly fed-up soldier recounts:

> Butt heere's enough of this, you may conclude
> With mee, the people here are something rude;
> Ill bred (except in breeding lice) ill made
> And nott too cleanly: butt, itt might bee said,

---

1. St Magnus Cathedral's baptismal register records the names of many of Cromwell's soldiers. Hossack, p.432, states 'In the last three years of Cromwell's rule, no fewer than fifteen of the English soldiers stationed in Kirkwall married Orcadian wives; and, as it is only of these three years we have any record, it is fair to infer that other Englishmen married in Kirkwall.'

and concludes with heavy irony:

> Had wee nott conquer'd Orknay, Cromwell's story
> Had cleart noe more of honour in't, and glory
> Then Caesar's; butt with this conquest fell
> Under his sword, The forlorne of Hell.[1]

---

[1] The author is alleged to have been J. Emerson, one of Cromwell's soldiers and certainly that name was included in the Orkney garrison. James Maidment, 1795-1879, an advocate, an important editor of ballad literature, and an antiquarian researcher, described the work as 'coarse but clever ... one of four accounts of travel in Scotland which are vulgarly coarse.' The poems were issued 'From my Cave called the Otter's Hole, in the third month of my banishment from Christendome, September 9, 1652.' The sentiments correspond with those contained in *The Bloody Orkneys*, doggerel penned by a disillusioned serviceman in the Second World War and attributed to one Captain Hamish Blair.

9

Margaret Halcro of Evie—mother of a Scottish Church

I don't know if my native parish of Evie, lying quiet and remote between the Mainland hills and Eynhallow Sound, knows that it is linked with one of the great freedom movements in the Scottish Church. But it is, for it was the fate of a shy Evie girl, Margaret Halcro, to become the mother of the two men who were the chief founders of the Secession Church, Ebenezer and Ralph Erskine.

There is no memorial to Margaret Halcro in Evie, but a Church certificate exists, given at the Kirk of Evie on 27 May 1666, which links her well and truly with the parish. A Church certificate in those days was a mixture of passport and testimonial, and Margaret's one, shorn of its official beginning and ending says:

> Margaret Halcro, daughter of the deceased Hugh Halcro in the Isle of Weir, and Margaret Stewart his spouse, hath lived in the Parish of Evie from her infancy in good fame and report, is a discreet, godly young woman, and to our certain knowledge free from all scandal, reproach or blame. As also, that she is descended by her father of the house of Halcro, which is a very ancient and honourable family in the Orkneys, the noble and potent Earl of Early and the Lairds of Dun in Angus, and by her mother of the Lairds of Barscube in Galloway.

Margaret met her destiny when she left Evie to pay a visit to her kinswoman the Countess of Mar. It was in the Countess's home that she met the Rev. Henry Erskine, and when she consented to marry him she knowingly connected herself with the troubles in the Scottish Church, but also unknowingly with a weird happening about which I shall tell you presently.

As for the Church troubles: Henry Erskine was one of the 2,000 ministers of 1662 who were ejected from their pulpits and manses by the Act of Uniformity. His life had been one of persecution, imprisonment and piverty. It was only after the Revolution that briefly things became more settled, and he was appointed to a Berwickshire parish, where Margaret's son Ebenezer was born.

That very day, 22 June 1680, Richard Cameron and Donald Cargill[1] posted their famous Declaration of Sanquhar Cross. Henry Erskine was implicated, and arrested for 'withdrawing from ordinances, keeping conventicles, and being guilty of disorderly baptism.' Margaret had the agony of knowing that her husband was subjected to the torture of the thumbscrews, but nothing would make him recant. His proud defiance has echoed through Scottish history:

> My lord, I have a commission from Christ, and though I were within an hour of my death, I durst not lay it down at the foot of any mortal man.

Much persecution was to follow before calmer days arrived.

Now for the weird story to which I referred. An old lady in Evie told me long ago that it was once common knowledge there. Sometime between the births of Ebenezer and Ralph, that is between 1680 and 1684, Margaret died—at least to all outward appearance—and was buried. The sexton, knowing that there remained on her finger the valuable gold ring which Henry Erskine had given her, entered the vault at night, raised the lid of the coffin, and used his knife to remove the ring. To his horror, Margaret Halcro suddenly sat bolt upright. When she recovered somewhat, she made her way, shivering in her shroud to the manse and knocked on the door. Her husband was sitting at the fireside with a friend who had called to comfort him. He said 'If I did not know Margaret was dead and buried, I should have said that was her knock.' He went to the door and there was Margaret, very cold, a little frightened, but wonderfully self-possessed.

And self-possessed the discreet Evie girl remained during further adventures in a very troubled age.

---

1. Two extreme covenanters.

10

Kirkwall's flood

When I walk to work in summer through the trees at the Willows and over the Papdale Burn, there is often only the merest trickle of water under the bridge, and even now, in winter, after a lot of heavy rain, the burn isn't all that fierce—the culverts carry it easily under the houses and streets of Kirkwall into the sea.

So it is rather difficult to realise that this same burn was responsible for Kirkwall's flood: 'the greatest' a newspaper said 'that possibly ever befell it since the flood of Noah.' Traditionally, and to a fairly late date, there was a mill on the side of the burn, and at one time there were two dams, fairly large ones. It was the bursting of both these dams, in 1788, after a day or so of heavy rain, that caused the disaster.

Everyone was asleep on a Sunday night in October, when without warning a torrent of water, approaching like a wall, swept down on Kirkwall. There were several houses in the way, particularly near the back of the present Temperance Hall.[1] One of these houses, occupied by a weaver, Robert Drummond, was completely swept away, and the weaver himself, his wife and his son-in-law were drowned. Their bodies floated up the street, then down Mounthoolie Lane, and were found next day in the Peerie Sea. Another victim was Helen Hunter, an old woman, who was drowned in her bed, her house having been overtopped by the water. A number of people saved their lives by hanging on to the cross-beams of their roofs, remaining there for hours in complete darkness waiting for the water to go down. A few, who were good swimmers, made for safety on the higher ground. One of the survivors was a cow, which, although much bruised, was thrown up the street with a chair securely impaled on her horns.

There was a high tide that night, which prevented the water from dispersing. In the Broad Street it was two feet deep, and it overflowed the greater part of the town. The bridge, which still gives its name to Bridge Street, was greatly damaged. In all, about 200 houses and shops were flooded.

1. In Mill Street. Now the Kirkwall Arts Theatre.

A reporter of the period described graphically the material damage. 'Goods were washed out of (the houses) and vast quantities of furniture, meal, malt, barrels, tubs, bedclothes, etc. etc., totally destroyed. Every merchant's shop has suffered considerably, some of them newly entered into business. Garden dykes, doors and walls of homes, and cabbage ground washed away; and Drummond, that unhappy weaver who perished with his family, had his loom and web in it, carried up almost to the Broad Street. Many of the sufferers are reduced to great extremities and the damage is computed to exceed £2,000 sterling.'

Luckily there is nothing that could be called a dam on the Papdale Burn now, and Kirkwall can sleep in peace. Like others, I protest, and exclaim, when we get three inches of water on the Back Road, but sometimes I remember our flood, the greatest since Noah, and have the grace to stay silent.

11

Orkney memories of Nelson and Napoleon

I spent some months, as a very little boy, in the cottage of a maiden aunt. Her parlour was also her spare bedroom, and it had a cavernous box bed, closed during the day by a set of panelled doors. From this recess, vast but comfortable, the last thing my eyes rested on, ill-lit as it was by a flickering oil lamp, was a huge coloured print of the Death of Nelson.

It wasn't the famous painting by Devis, but a far cruder thing, showing the scene on the deck of the *Victory* at Trafalgar just after Nelson fell. Its somewhat lurid colouring disturbed me as much as its subject matter. And I simply couldn't get away from it: it occupied in its dull gilt frame the greater part of the wall. The stricken Nelson was undoubtedly a noble figure, but there were nasty splotches of blood, and some of the sailors seemed villainous. I suppose the artist meant them to appear heart-broken, yet determined to pay out the French, I don't know if they frightened the Frenchmen, but as Wellington would have said, they terrified me.

I discovered later on that the print was extremely popular in the Orkney Islands, having the place of honour in many a home. You might wonder why its subject made such an appeal in isolated islands on the outermost fringe of Britain, until I tell you that these islands played a vital part in the Napoleonic wars, providing out of their small population perhaps two thousand men for the Navy, something like a twelfth of the total population. So the picture which scared me told a story, familiar to many Orkneymen. It was almost a piece of family history.

In one home in Kirkwall, it was regarded more as a family portrait, for to every visitor the woman of the house would point out a shadowy figure, a man named Cooper, who helped to carry the dying Admiral into the *Victory*'s cockpit. He was her father. Had I known things like that as a child, I might have identified some of the other sailors who scared me with families and places with which I was entirely familiar.

Among them would be James Leith of Stenness, a gunner, whose

Trafalgar medal I saw only the other day. James valued his medal, as his descendants still do, so he did not throw it overboard like other sailors did when they found that the medals were made of pewter instead of silver. Between decks on the *Victory*, James contracted tuberculosis. He came home to his native island to die, but the strong northern air restored him and he lived to be a bane and portent to the pension officer. He died at 94, but he had added ten years to his age on joining the Navy. Thus to the officials he seemed to be going strong when well past a hundred. They paid his pension with grudging and awe.

Somewhere on the *Victory*'s deck would also have been John Gaudie of Birsay and George Gaudie of North Ronaldsay. All I know about John Gaudie is that he came back to the moorland farm of Surtadale, from which an improving landlord evicted him. George Gaudie had an even harsher fate. He had taken part in nearly all of Nelson's battles. Most of the time he was a quarter-master belonging to Nelson's barge. Lady Hamilton declared that he was the finest-looking fellow in a crew of picked men.

George served in the Navy until the peace of 1815. When he left the sea he had saved over a thousand pounds. With a job assured at the Portsmouth dockyard, he married a pretty, apparently pious girl, and was happy until she, having obtained control of his money, silently disappeared. The shock quite unbalanced the quiet red-haired Orkneyman. Back home in Orkney, he took to wandering all over the islands. With his troubled blue eyes, the man in the Scotch bonnet and brown monkey jacket was known everywhere. He slept in the fields in summer, in barns in winter, eating when and how he could. He was completely harmless and inoffensive, but one thing angered him—the offer of money. He loathed the sight of it.

You will notice that I have spoken of these simple islandmen who shared Nelson's glory as if it all happened yesterday. So it seems, for local memory is long. Another Nelson touch which came my way recently was in the island of Rousay. A lady there was telling me about her great-grandmother, a wise and imaginative woman, whose stories of the past left an indelible impression on her mind.

One man, with the surname of Kent (fairly common, as it happens, in Orkney) came striding purposefully out of the remembered tales. A taciturn crofter he was, who remembered every few months that he had once been a seaman. He would go quickly past with an empty spirit keg on his back. Over the water in Kirkwall he would get it filled, and collect his pension.

'Who was he?' I asked.

My ignorance could be excused in one not born on that island. My friend explained patiently, 'He was Nelson's cabin boy,' and she went on to say, 'He was with Nelson in the West Indies when Nelson took very ill with a fever. He thought he was dying, and so did everyone else, so he ordered his coffin to be made. Shortly after it was delivered Nelson got better, but he liked the coffin so much that always afterwards he kept it in his cabin. One of the cabin boy's jobs was to keep it spruce and clean and polish the handles.'

Probably that Orkney cabin boy saw Nelson laid at last in his coffin—not the shining one which had stood in the cabin, but a chest of lead, later to be broken in pieces and sold as souvenirs.

From the Orkney Islands had gone these hundreds of ordinary sailors to fight alongside Nelson. With them was a sixty-year-old Orkney admiral, Alexander Graeme. As Commander-in-Chief at the Nore he became intimate with Nelson, who wrote once to his 'dearest Emma', 'Today I dined with Admiral Graeme, who has also lost his right arm (Nelson had lost his at Santa Cruz); and as the commander of troops has lost his leg, I expect we shall be caricatured as the lame defenders of England.' The Orkney admiral described Nelson after Trafalgar as 'the most extraordinary man this country ever produced.'

Looking around the islands for stories of Nelson, one also comes across stories of Napoleon. Two extremely interesting links with Napoleon have rewarded me. I had heard of a teacher in one of our country schools, dead for over a decade, who used to preface his history lessons on the Napoleonic Wars with this preamble: 'The great Napoleon made his final surrender to James Tait of this parish, and his great-granddaughter is sitting among you.' Somewhat heady stuff for an imaginative girl.

Alas, this piece of 'history' was only partly true. But the schoolmaster could hardly be blamed, for the encounter between Quartermaster James Tait, of Deerness, and Bonaparte acquired over the years so much impressive detail and seemingly authentic dialogue that none but a historian would have questioned it. It was eventually written down by the local poet, a man who once sat with his neck in splints for three weeks, believing he had broken it, and on another occasion declared his intention of marrying a mermaid who was repeatedly seen off the coast. Little wonder if his history of James Tait was partly fabulous.

Tait, the story went, was ashore at Rochefort for water with part of the crew of the *Bellerophon*, when Napoleon came up to him and introduced himself. Tait gave the salute due to a superior officer.

But Napoleon said, 'I see you are a courteous man, but you are to be my superior officer now; here is my sword, for I surrender unconditionally and must obey your orders now.'

To which Tait replied, 'Well, my orders are that you keep your sword until we come to Captain Maitland, and then hand it over to him.'

There is much more dialogue, but I think some of it must be true. At any rate it deserves to be true. Listen to this:

'What is the reason,' asked Napoleon, 'that you all treat me so kindly and look on me, an enemy, in such a kindly and respectful manner?'

'Do you remember,' asked Tait, 'one time when you sent an English sailor over the Straits of Dover because he attempted to escape from France in a queer little boat which set the Frenchmen laughing, and telling the joke until you heard of it?'

Napoleon said, 'I remember the queer little craft and the brave man who attempted to cross to England in such a wherry.'

And then the great Napoleon laughed like a boy at the remembrance, and the kindly sparkle of his eye transformed his usually stern countenance as he gazed at the men who thus acknowledged their admiration of a kindly action performed by him when he had such power as few men ever had.

So much for the local poet's account. What I believe really happened is that Quartermaster Tait was in command of the barge which went out from the *Bellerophon* to take Napoleon and his suite off the French brig, which had taken them from Aix roads: thus Tait would have been the first to make contact with the Emperor. On the slow journey to Elba with its many delays Napoleon spoke much with officers and crew, so that Tait brought back with him to Orkney memories of several conversations. He also took back a more tangible token of the Emperor's regard—a greatcoat which Napoleon gave him. If it had been today, that greatcoat would have been put in the museum in Kirkwall; but James Tait wore it year after year through the cold island winters for the excellent purpose of keeping himself warm. Our Orkney farms, after centuries of a most primitive agriculture, were then in process of improvement, and Tait had to build walls and dig drains, often donning Napoleon's greatcoat. No one knows whether coat or quartermaster survived the longer.

By an amazing coincidence another relic of Napoleon came to Orkney, also brought home by a quartermaster. But let me tell you the story, as I have heard it several times, of Napoleon's window.

It began on the battlefield of Waterloo, after Napoleon had fled, abandoning his private carriage. That, by the way, is the subject of another well-known picture, by Ernest Crofts, which is owned by the Walker Art Gallery in Liverpool. In it you can see Napoleon just stepping from his carriage to take possession of a spirited white horse held by one of his officers.

The picture is a dramatic one: a horse-drawn field gun thunders by on the left; on the right soldiers of the famous Old Guard stand with their faces towards the advancing Prussians; all around are wounded or dying men. And there in the centre of the picture, in the middle distance, stands the abandoned

Lobster Fishermen, Rousay, c.1950

Stanley Cursiter, RSA, RSW, 1887-1976

carriage with its door wide open, and in the upper part of the door a square window. It is about that window that my story tells.

In the advance which followed Napoleon's defeat a young British soldier fell, shot through the knee. Darkness came on without any appearance of rescuers, so he dragged himself to the Emperor's carriage and spent the night on its comfortable cushions. He felt better in the morning, and determined to provide himself with a souvenir. The only thing that seemed accessible and portable was one of the thick panes of glass that formed the windows. These had in the centre a plain Roman 'N', Napoleon's monogram.

With his bayonet the wounded man prised the piece of glass from its mountings, and placed it later in the wooden box with which soldiers were then issued.

Soon afterwards he was found by the ambulance corps, who put him on board the *Rochefort* for transportation to England. He became very ill during the voyage, his wound having become septic. It was soon obvious that he would not recover.

With other badly wounded men he was put in the charge of the quartermaster, William Swanney, who came from the little Orkney island of North Ronaldsay. Swanney did what he could to ease the lad's misery. As a gesture of gratitude the dying soldier gave Swanney his field-box and its contents.

This was Swanney's last trip: after Waterloo he was paid off. Although he could have obtained another berth, his wife, who had travelled all the way from Orkney to Portsmouth in search of him, persuaded him to return home. She is still remembered in the island as a masterful woman, whose nickname was 'muslin Meg', allegedly because she had stolen some muslin for which crime she spent some time standing at the Cathedral door in Kirkwall, locked in the branks.[1] Swanney went back with her to North Ronaldsay, with a pocket full of prize money and the box containing Napoleon's window.

In his native island he built himself a new house. Because he was a careful man, who didn't like to waste anything, he used the pane of glass for a skylight. There it remained during his own lifetime and that of his wife.

By the 1870s the house was in the possession of another man, who had a visit one day from a friendly but persuasive American who had heard of Napoleon's window. He saw the piece of glass, now stained by weather and encrusted at the edges with lichen. But it was completely authenticated by the deeply etched Roman 'N'. He coveted the souvenir greatly, and the easygoing islandman let him have it. Indeed, out of the goodness of his heart he constructed a strong box out of driftwood and provided the straw in which Napoleon's window was carefully packed for its long journey to America.

1. Also known as a scold's bridle, it consisted of an iron frame for the head with a metal gag to restrain the tongue.

It was on display in the editorial rooms of the San Francisco *Examiner* in 1887. *The Orkney and Shetland American* of October 1887 reported that the glass which was then in the *Examiner* editorial rooms, belonged to the same carriage which was on exhibition at Madame Tussaud's rooms in Baker Street, London (1887), and was twelve and three-fourths inches long, ten and three-fourths inches broad and one-fourth of an inch in thickness. It bore engraved in the centre of the glass a plain Roman 'N' which Napoleon invariably used for his monogram [N] and carried the marks of the violence which forced it from its original position, as well as having some of the putty still adhering to it which kept it in place in the ruined hut in the far-off Orkneys.

The building in which the relic might have been housed in the 1880s is no longer in existence, nor are two subsequent *Examiner* buildings. All were destroyed in the 1906 earthquake and fire, so we will never know the truth of this colourful but by no means improbable story.

12

The day that Kitchener died

On Monday, 5 June 1966, exactly half a century had passed since the cruiser *Hampshire*, with Field-Marshal Earl Kitchener on board, struck a mine off Marwick Head, Birsay, and sank before any aid could reach her. The repercussions of that explosion sounded around the world in a way that it is difficult for anyone in our own day to realise.

Just a week or two ago, when the Norwegian archaeologists were in Orkney, one of them touched my arm in Birsay and asked, 'What is that great tower?' I told him. 'Ah,' he said, 'Feltmarsjal Kitchener; how well I remember as a boy of eighteen, in Norway, my father rushing in with a white face and saying, "Kitchener is dead!"'

The whole western world was stunned; for Kitchener's reputation—as Secretary of State for War—was almost as great as that of Winston Churchill in the Second World War. A week after he died, at two-mile intervals all the way from the sea to the Somme battlefield, British soldiers bade a *vale* to him. Queen Alexandra placed herself at the head of a national memorial fund which brought in £700,000.[1]

The shock of the great man's death was even more numbing in Orkney itself. I had not realised how great an effect it had had on people on the west coast of the Mainland until, in 1957, Donald McCormick asked me to interview some of those intimately connected with the tragedy for his projected book, *The Mystery of Lord Kitchener's Death*. I found then that forty years had hardly blurred the sharp impact of the tragedy on people's minds. They could remember details with an icy clarity, and their feelings about the

---

1. In 1988 equivalent to £15 million. At the outset the money was used for the relief of severely wounded men. After the Government assumed that responsibility, the idea was conceived of financing the university education of sons of men who had served in HM Forces. Daughters are now eligible. The Fund has been supplemented from time to time by further appeals. In 1986-87 there were 155 Kitchener scholars studying for degrees at Universities and Polytechnics. A Kitchener Medical Prize is awarded annually on the nomination of the Faculty of Medicine of Khartoum University, and over the last decade Kitchener European Scholarships, specifically for business studies, have been available. All scholars may join the Kitchener Scholars Association, which is a living memorial to the Field Marshal.

official reaction to the occurrence, and the blunders made by the wartime authorities, were still sharp and bitter.

I believe, personally, that no event in the history of the parish ever had such an effect on Birsay; and it is noteworthy that the first proposals about a local memorial to Lord Kitchener were made at a special meeting held at Twatt not long after the loss of the *Hampshire*. Birsay would have gone ahead on its own if necessary, but it was felt that all Orkney should be asked to contribute to a worthy memorial, and future meetings were held in Kirkwall.

The first suggestion was lacking in imagination—a stained glass window in St Magnus Cathedral—and there was so much protest that it was dropped hastily. At a later meeting, held on 7 September 1916, the idea of 'a massive stone tower on Marwick Head' was put forward, and this was unanimously acclaimed. Something big, eye-catching and enduring, it was felt, was necessary to commemorate so great a man. The completed tower is certainly big: forty-eight feet high, and twenty-three feet wide at the base; but, although it appears very imposing from the land, it is astonishing how small it looks when viewed from the same angle as the great cliff rampart underneath, as many a photographer has discovered.

Some people find the tower ugly. I have never thought it so. It is unpretentious and uncompromising—a proper landmark. The architect was Mr J. M. Baikie of Kirkwall, and the contractor Mr William Liddle of Orphir.

It is not easy to discover what local difficulties prevented the tower from being built for nearly a decade. It was only completed in 1926, and it was unveiled in July that year by General Lord Horne of Stirkoke, Caithness.

The feeling about Lord Kitchener at the time of his death was fairly reflected in a poem by David Horne, the Kirkwall poet:

> ... against the cloud
> Of cruel war
> We see afar
> A countless host come marching on,
> The like the world ne'er looked upon;
> Mile after mile of armed men
> March past, march past, march past, and then
> Still greater hosts unnumbered come
> Out of the gloom into the light.
> Such a sight
> The world ne'er saw.
> Called into being by his word,
> His word which ever was the law,
> In this great isle set in the sea—
> The throbbing heart of liberty,

88 Demolition in Broad Street, Kirkwall, c.1884. The house on the left was built by Harry Erburie, one of Cromwell's soldiers who settled in the town and became a flourishing merchant.

89 The Earl of Mar and Kellie lays the foundation stone of Kirkwall Town Hall, 20 August 1884

90 Unveiling of Kitchener's Memorial by Lord Horne, Stirkoke, Caithness, 2 July 1926

91 Field Marshal Earl Kitchener

92 Kitchener Memorial, Marwick Head, Birsay

> But now the lone Orcadian shore
> Echoes! echoes!
> 'Nevermore
> Shall he lead on this mighty host!'

Lord Kitchener had called to the colours from every part of the Commonwealth a host, such as the world had never seen, of five million armed men. The great cry on his death was: Who will now direct their fortunes? The power of his personality, which his intimates considered stiff and withdrawn, had become a legend all over the world.

He was actually on board the channel boat on his way back to Egypt on 3 August 1914, when he had an order to return to England. Three days later he was Secretary of State for War; to find that, in his own words, 'There is no army.' He determined to create an army of seventy divisions, calculating that its maximum strength would be reached in the third year of war. His military thinking was unorthodox; it was much derided; but it was right. In the early months of 1916, Kitchener could affirm that sixty-seven divisions were afoot, and that three were in the making. He had great difficulty in obtaining the necessary munitions, but he managed somehow until the amazingly dilatory Ministry of Munitions took over. All the time he had his troubles with generals and politicians. Jealous colleagues were continually sniping at him; but the faith in him of the ordinary soldier and man-in-the-street was complete.

The contribution of Russia to the allied cause, through the inefficiency of the Czarist government and the shortage of guns and ammunition, had been woefully disappointing. Kitchener, whose name was greatly respected in Russia, made the unusual decision to go to Russia himself to confer with Czar Nicholas, and to attempt to set the military house there in order. His journey was to be secret—on a cruiser from Scapa Flow to Archangel....

Lord Kitchener stepped on the train at King's Cross Station in London on the evening of Sunday, 4 June 1916. Early next morning, 5 June, he was in Thurso, looking across to Orkney, with a big sea running in the Pentland Firth and the barometer falling. He crossed with his party in HMS *Oak*, and by lunch-time was sitting with Admiral Jellicoe in his flagship *Iron Duke* in Scapa Flow. No doubt they talked of the Battle of Jutland, just five days past, with its results still uncertain, and of Kitchener's sense of the urgency of his mission.

But Jellicoe was worried by the increasing gale. He knew that, outside in the Atlantic, the weather was very bad. Another thing which bothered him was that the channel through which it had been decided the *Hampshire* should sail had not been swept for mines. No minesweepers could attempt to operate until the storm died down.

He talked of these things with Kitchener, trying to persuade him to postpone sailing, but the War Minister's overriding sense of the shortness of the time at his disposal overcame every consideration. By early evening the *Hampshire* was out at sea west of Orkney, heading north through the storm. She had a titular escort of two destroyers, *Unity* and *Victor*; but as the cruiser's safety was considered to lie in her speed, she soon left them behind. They could not keep up in the heavy seas with the *Hampshire*'s 18 knots. Even when the cruiser reduced speed considerably they found the going too hard, and very soon were ordered to return to base.

The *Hampshire* went on alone, keeping as close as she dared in the lee of the land to allow her famous passenger some comfort. When she was passing Birsay she was roughly a mile and a half from the shore, in a depth of at least thirty fathoms. It was very wild, an Orkney summer storm, cold and desolate. Water was washing over the deck; but everything around seemed more or less safe, although so comfortless, when, shortly before eight o'clock, there was a devastating explosion. In some parts of the cruiser, what with the raging of the wind and sea, it was hardly heard, but the *Hampshire* was vitally injured. The boiler room had been badly holed, and the mass of water which poured in caused the bulkheads to collapse. Some men were terribly mutilated.

Those who could do so found their way to the deck, where it was obvious that the *Hampshire* was sinking rapidly. Lord Kitchener came out of his cabin and made his way slowly to the quarter-deck. He stood there watching, without betraying any obvious sign of dismay, while the men tried to launch the boats—a hopeless task in such a sea. It is said that the Captain, trying desperately to get a boat safely into the water, shouted to Lord Kitchener to come to him, but the War Minister, deafened by the storm, did not hear. In any case it did not matter, for Kitchener—almost sixty-six and a tired, ailing man—could never have stood exposure in an open boat, even if the boat had got away.

Those who managed to leave the ship before she sank did so on a type of raft known as a Carley float. These rafts, tossing on the waves, and constantly drenched by the seas, drifted down the coast in the direction of Sandwick. Many men soon succumbed to exposure. It was well past bedtime when the rafts drifted on the rocks to the north of Skaill Bay. By that time a large number of sailors were already dead, but one here and two there managed to pull themselves to shelter in farmhouses, where they raised the alarm. Only twelve men survived.

The sinking of the *Hampshire* was seen by eyewitnesses in Birsay and reported to Kirkwall. In Stromness[1] too, the naval authorities were informed. Two charges have repeatedly been made: that official help came far too late,

---

1. See also 'The story of the Stromness lifeboats, 1867-1967, p.67.

and that the local people were prevented by the wartime authorities from helping to locate survivors. This is a subject far too complicated and serious to tackle in an anniversary article. Attempts have been made to assess the evidence, notably by Donald McCormick; but no one has yet written from a full acquaintance with Admiralty records which remain unpublished, or after a complete investigation in Orkney. Indeed, there are still people in Orkney who have intimate knowledge of some of the events of that fateful night of 5 June 1916, but who are unwilling to make public their knowledge. Quite understandably, for the controversy was so bitter and personal.

For many years after Kitchener's death the wildest rumours were current. In several parts of the world people declared that they had seen him alive. An odd, but influential, journalist, Frank Power, produced a coffin which, he said, contained Kitchener's body. It was opened in the presence of Sir Bernard Spilsbury and the Westminster Coroner. The coffin was empty.

Anyone who reads the files of *The Orcadian* from the nineteen-twenties will find that public interest and curiosity was forever being whetted by the most unlikely rumours. As in life, so in death, Kitchener became a legend.

For some time now it has been possible to estimate his virtues and his defects in ordinary human terms. In the main, despite the detractors, history has decided that he was a fine soldier, a man of vision, and a loyal servant of his country. Orkney need make no apologies for honouring him.

13

The rôle of Scapa Flow

If you look at a map of Orkney you will see that Scapa Flow lies like a landlocked Mediterranean to the South of the Mainland. Indeed, ancient writers, impressed with the resemblance, called it the Orkney Mediterranean. It has its interior islands and islets, and its Pillars of Hercules in the Kame of Hoy and St John's Head, but quite apart from the geographical resemblance, half of Orkney's history is cradled in the Flow.

Scapa Flow, and its history, are a culmination of many myths: the concept of Herrenvolk countered by the concept of the Hun as barbarian; the myth of Deutschland uber alles in conflict with the myth of Britannia as Ruler of the Waves. But older than them all is a myth that is only remembered in the north, and which seems to symbolize the role, and perhaps the destiny of Scapa.

It is in the form of a story. Long, long ago a princess was abducted. Her prince carried her through Scapa Flow to the island of Hoy. Her angry father would have no offers of peace. His army and the army of the prince did battle on Hoy. But the story has no happy ending . . . indeed no ending. For the princess was no innocent, loving girl, but a Valkyrie[1]—a Chooser of the slain. Every evening with her magic she restored the dead to life and renewed their weapons; and each morning they rose to fight again. The old storytellers called that conflict beside Scapa Flow 'The Everlasting Battle', and they insisted that the strife would continue until the end of all things, until the Weird of the Gods.[2]

To those who know their Orkney history it sometimes seems as if The Everlasting Battle of the myth contains in some mysterious way the truth of Scapa's story. The warriors rise and fall, but century after century they fight

1. Divine maidens who, sent by Odin, determined the course of battles and selected brave warriors for Valhalla.
2. This was Ragnarok: the twilight of the gods; the doom or ultimate fate of the gods. It involved mighty earthquakes, darkening of the sun, the breaking loose of various monsters from their bonds, and a final conflict which ended with the death of the gods and the monsters. However, the sons of the gods survived, to rebuild the earth in a new morning after the night of Ragnarok.

again, and every time that their weapons are renewed they are more deadly.

On a dark October night in 1154 there was a sea battle in Scapa Flow, when Orkney's last great Viking Sweyn Asleifson came suddenly through wind and driving sleet with seven ships and completely defeated the island Earls'[1] fleet of fourteen. In 1263 Haakon Haakonson, the last sea king of Norway, assembled a great fleet in the Flow, before setting out for Largs.[2] His ships returned, battered by storms, and crippled, to shelter there for the winter. He rested his own sick body, and pulled up his fine vessel, the Christ-ship with its dragon's heads of gold at stem and stern, on the Orkney Mainland.[3] In 1529 a fleet sailed over the Flow to invade Orkney; it was manned by hundreds of Caithnessmen who had come to teach rebellious Orkneymen a sharp lesson. By all the laws of warfare, the Caithnessmen should have won; but the hastily summoned and poorly armed Orkneymen believed that dead warriors were fighting on their side. They claimed to see the island saint, St Magnus, in the thick of the battle, and their valour was terrible. Five hundred Caithnessmen and their Earl lay dead on the field of Summerdale and only a handful went back over the Flow.

The Norsemen used Scapa Flow as a base for their warships. They were particularly fond of a little harbour they called Midlands Haven, a place that became known as Houton to thousands of sailors in the two world wars. From Scapa Flow the Norse chieftains of Orkney set out on crusade to the Holy Land. These men in their, to us, incredibly small longships, got to know the Aegean; they sailed round Famagusta; they saw Byzantium,[4] indeed more than one of them served in the Varangian Guard.[5] They set out from Scapa also on their raids on England and Ireland.

Centuries later, long after Norwegian Orkney had become part of Scotland, and Scotland part of Great Britain, men's minds turned again to Scapa. It seemed to a maritime surveyor, called Graeme Spence, an ideal 'Northern roadstead for a Fleet of Line-of-Battle Ships'. He wrote a Memorial[6] of between four and five thousand words to explain his views to the Lord Commissioners of the Admiralty. He instanced the Scandinavians, who he said had 'not only conquered Orkney and the Hebrides but, for a time, all Britain and Ireland and became the Masters or rather the Tyrants of the Surrounding Seas.'

1. Earls Rognvald and Harald.
2. See also *The last sea king*, p.392.
3. At Houton.
4. Constantinople.
5. The bodyguard of the Byzantium Emperors in the late tenth and eleventh centuries. One of the most famous Varangians was Harald Hardrada who invaded England in 1066 with a Norse army. He was defeated by the English king, Harold Godwinson, and killed at the battle of Stamford Bridge, near York.
6. Dated 4 June 1812.

Having got himself thoroughly enthused over the Norsemen, as I too may have done, he even went a bit further, writing a paragraph which I must quote entire:

> Nay even the Romans so famed for their choice of eligible military stations, thought the Orkneys of so much importance that on the Division of the Empire among the sons of Constantine the Great, the Kingdom (as it was then called) of the Orcades, fell to the share of Constantine—a tacit proof that these Islands would not have had such honourable mention made of them if that politic Nation had thought as little of them as we ignorantly do now.

But, to leave romance behind, as Graeme Spence eventually did, and to get down to brass tacks: this protagonist of a Scapa Flow base pointed out first of all the tremendous mischief which could be done to the country by an enemy who captured Orkney. This may have seemed at the time a remote possibility, but in our own century it has twice been a likelihood that our strategists have had to reckon with, more particularly after the German invasion and capture of Norway in 1940.

Spence argued too that a fleet at Scapa Flow would 'intercept and prevent all the Enemy's Trade North-about Britain to Russia, Sweden, Norway, Denmark, Holland and Flanders, a Route which those Nations often take especially in War time.' So you can say that this pioneer strategist anticipated the total blockade, which became one of the Allies' strongest weapons in the First and Second World Wars.

The specific advantages of Scapa Flow as an anchorage were, Spence said, the amount of shelter it gives from the prevailing winds, its large size (about fifty square miles), the depth of its water, which is from ten to twenty fathoms all over the Flow, and the fact that there are adequate entrances and good easy access.

Probably Spence's long report was pigeon-holed, as so many excellent memoranda have been since then. The only thing that happened was that two Martello towers were built between 1813 and 1815, one at each side of the entrance to Longhope. These were connected neither with Spence's proposals, nor with the fear of French sea power, but were a protection to the northern convoys that assembled at Longhope against American commerce raiders, which became very active during the Anglo-American War of 1812-1814. The towers, at Hackness[1] and Crockness, are still in excellent condition, and are to be restored and eventually opened to the public by the Department of the Environment. There is a most interesting little book about them, called

---

1. This tower has been restored and is open to the public.

The Longhope Battery and Towers, by R. P. Fereday.[1] The towers, I may say, were only completed as the danger from America ended.

There were obviously many good reasons why the Admiralty did not act on Spence's report. Our traditional enemies had been France and Spain: it seemed, particularly as the century advanced, that the threat of attack from the north could be discounted. The idea of a friendly Germany was not easily discarded, althoug has time went on some strategists had grave misgivings.

It was not until 1871 that the German Empire, with William I, King of Prussia, as Emperor, was proclaimed. From then on the German mercantile marine grew very quickly, as Germany rapidly became the greatest industrial country in continental Europe, more dependent on overseas countries for her supplies of raw materials, and on foreign markets for her exports. She needed spheres of investment abroad for her surplus capital. She developed an appetite for colonies, and, with her increasing overseas commitments and merchant fleet, a desire for sea power. She felt she had a claim to be an imperial and naval power, and resented the role of the British Navy, which prevented her from extending her influence over non-European politics.

The purposeful building of the German Fleet began with Tirpitz's naval laws of 1898 and 1900. The work proceeded with some caution. Germany was at pains to maintain that she only wanted purely defensive naval armaments. Count Bulow declared in 1904, 'I cannot conceive that the idea of an Anglo-German war should be seriously entertained by sensible people in either country.' But the strengthening of the German Navy proceeded methodically. In 1907 the active German naval forces were given the name of the High Seas Fleet. Capital ship construction increased from two to three ships a year, and then, between 1908 and 1911 to four heavy ships a year. Tirpitz managed to convince the Germans of their need for a powerful fleet by his *risk theory*. To put it simply this meant that the German Fleet was to constitute such a risk for the strongest opponent, that even if that opponent won it would have been so badly reduced in strength that it would be too weak to take on another opponent. In other words, it would be bad strategy to challenge such a fleet as he visualised, even if this fleet could not hope to equal in strength those of the other great powers.

Of course, when war was declared in 1914, the German Navy, secure in its bases in the Heligoland Bight, constituted a real and continuous threat to the safety of Great Britain. The High Seas Fleet was not able to operate against British sea communications, but it could send out submarines and commerce raiders, which took a heavy toll, and its presence at the other side of the North Sea—as the German Ocean immediately became known—kept a great part

---

1. 1971.

of the British Fleet bottled up in northern bases, when it could have been doing more profitable work elsewhere.

When the First World War broke out, a safe commodious base in Scotland became immediately necessary. Even in 1903, Col. A. Court Repington had explained forcefully in *Blackwood's Magazine* the need for controlling from Scapa Flow the water area extending past the Shetland Islands to Norway. But the Admiralty had seemed loth to commit itself, even though the Home Fleet began to use the Flow each autumn as an exercise ground. Undoubtedly there were experts who thought, both for strategic reasons and in the interests of naval personnel, that Rosyth or the Cromarty Firth were far enough north.

In 1909 a large fleet had rendezvoused at Scapa for some months, and there were persistent rumours that the Admiralty contemplated the establishment of a base. Northern members of Parliament championed the scheme, but came to the conclusion, perhaps wrongly, that the First Sea Lord was not impressed with its advantages.

A much more definite proposal was made in 1912 to construct defences at Scapa Flow, but this was abandoned the following year owing to a factor that the pioneer strategist Graeme Spence could not have foreseen—the cost of providing adequate protection from enemy submarines. The money allocated for Scapa Flow was used instead to erect a wall along the top of the Dover breakwater to keep out the spray. Thus, when Britain declared war on Germany in 1914, absolutely no preparations had been made for the use of the Flow as a wartime base.

Even then, there were those who wanted a more southerly base, but Admiral Jellicoe preferred Scapa, and on Saturday morning 1 August, three days before the declaration of war, Orcadians rubbed their eyes to see the Flow filled with the ships of the Grand Fleet.

It was an amazing decision: the Fleet were here with, so to speak, all the doors open, and the anchorage was excessively vulnerable to submarine attack, or even to night attack by destroyers. The work of defence had to begin without an hour's delay.

There was little casual labour in Orkney, so the Orkney Territorials, mobilised on the Sunday, had not only to man the Flow's first defences but also to build them. Their multifarious tasks included the landing of 12-pounder guns from the ships (for the defence of the entrances), and the commandeering on the island of Flotta of ox-carts for transport. Most of the farmers lent their oxen and carts willingly, but one old lady absolutely refused; she was sure the soldiers would be unkind to her ox, which she treated as a child. Finally, a corporal and four men were sent to commandeer the ox, but even then the old woman would not release the animal unless she was allowed to lead him. So for days on end, the island enjoyed the spectacle of old Betty, in her brown shawl and long red and white striped petticoat, walking resolutely at the ox's

93 The battle cruiser *Hindenburg*, 1930

94 The battle cruiser *Seydlitz*, 1928

95 The *Royal Oak* sunk in Scapa Flow by German submarine U47 on 14 October 1939 with the loss of 24 officers and 809 men, out of a ship's company of 1,400.

96 109 Construction of No 1 Barrier looking from Lamb Holm towards St Mary's, 1943. The First World War block ship *Numidian* is on the left.

head, followed self-consciously by a corporal and a few men, who loaded stones at a quarry and unloaded them at the site of a gun battery.

During the first winter a hundred-miles-an-hour gale devastated the whole area of tents, and the Territorials had to live for weeks in dugouts cut into the cliffs. Later on, marines and civil contractors arrived to build more permanent defences.

For months the Fleet was uneasy in its unshielded harbour and only stayed for brief periods. This meant among other things that men from the base establishment—who had still to be accommodated afloat—often had unwelcome trips to sea when the Fleet left at short notice.

For months the unpreparedness of the anchorage was a source of perpetual worry to Admiral Jellicoe. He knew what havoc a few determined German submarines carrying mines and torpedoes could cause. In January 1915 he wrote to Lord Fisher: 'If you could only just compare the orders for the protection of the High Seas Fleet[1] . . . with the arrangements here you would be horrified. I wonder I can ever sleep at all. Thank goodness the Germans imagine we have proper defences. At least so I imagine—otherwise there would be no Grand Fleet left now.'

Everyone concerned had got a severe fright on the night of 16/17 October, when someone reported that there was a submarine in the anchorage. The general hullabaloo caused by the ships racing around, shooting, dropping depth charges, and sweeping the water with their searchlights, came to be known rather facetiously as 'The Battle of Scapa Flow'. Jellicoe immediately took the Fleet to Loch Swilly in the North of Ireland, while Winston Churchill at the Admiralty wrote that 'every nerve must be strained to reconcile the Fleet to Scapa.' He insisted (as he was to do again a quarter of a century later) that nothing must stand in the way of the equipment and security of the anchorage. He demanded a report of progress every third day.

Impressed with the urgency shown by the Government the men worked like slaves on the defence works. The narrower channels on the east of the Flow were blocked by sinking old ships in them. The problem of the wide entrances at Hoxa, Switha and Hoy Sounds was solved with drifter net-boom defences.[2]

1. The German Fleet.
2. These consisted of submarine nets—steel nets with a mesh of two or three feet. The nets were suspended from large iron buoys, roughly ten feet by six, and were anchored on the sea bottom by concrete sinkers weighing eight or ten tons. At either side of the gate in the booms was a ship, usually a drifter or trawler. The gate would have been approximately eighty feet wide and consisted of buoys and nets as in the rest of the boom, but with no concrete sinkers. It was opened by one of the ships dragging it with a hawser fixed to the bottom of the nets. When a vessel had gone through, the other ship immediately pulled it shut with another hawser. In case a submarine might have attempted to pass into the Flow after a ship, a depth charge was sometimes

At last the time came when Scapa Flow could be regarded as secure. Only a month or two after war began, the base was moved from Scapa Bay to Longhope. It remained there until April 1919, when it was moved to Lyness, further up the coast of Hoy, where extensive preparations had been made. At an early stage seaplane bases were established, and navigation in the waters around Orkney was very severely regulated. The infiltration of German spies into Orkney was always regarded as a threatening possibility, and a large part of the North of Scotland was proclaimed a prohibited area. A very popular novel written in the islands by the Orkney novelist J. Storer Clouston concerned the adventures of a German spy in the vicinity of Scapa; it was called *The Spy in Black*, and when eventually made into a film it had its premiere in Kirkwall.

Kirkwall became an examination centre where ships were searched for contraband. Stromness was the headquarters of the Western Patrol.

A further word about the Navy's rôle at Scapa. The basic strategy was to keep the concentration of the main fleet in the north to guard the exit of the North Sea. It was felt that by carrying out this strategy the fleet could perform several tasks: it could cover the trade routes, cut off Germany from the ocean, protect the coast line against invasion, and secure the transport of the army. An important result of the strategy, it was felt, would be the early defeat of Germany by an effective blockade. What the general public, and the Navy itself, wanted badly was a chance of bringing the German High Seas Fleet to battle. This fleet was very securely based in its harbours at Wilhelmshaven, Bremerhaven and Cuxhaven, protected by a maze of difficult channels, a fringe of islands, and an excellent backdoor to the Baltic—the Kiel Canal. Britain had what appeared a wonderful initial success on 28 August 1914,

---

exploded in the wake of the entering ship. There was a double gate at Hoxa and off Flotta, also anti-submarine nets right around some of the big battleships when at anchor.

Once a destroyer coming in at Hoxa heard what sounded like a midget submarine immediately behind her. She dropped a depth charge. The gate-ship had also heard the 'submarine' and pulled shut the gate. To avoid running into the gate, the destroyer had to go suddenly astern and reversed over her own depth charge. The explosion blew the keel to within six feet of the deck, and over ninety men trapped inside the destroyer were lost. The midget submarine turned out to have been a basking shark.

The booms were so constructed that if anything struck the nets a marker came to the surface at that point, and a warning was recorded at the shore end. A watcher had the means of exploding a mine at the place where contact had been recorded. The ship *Hoy Head*, which did the service run, had to ask for permission each day to pass through the boom. On a misty day she went close to the fence and then sailed until she found the gate. On one such day she was about an hour early. Visibility was very poor and she struck the boom. The man on shore was just about to pull the switch which set off the mine, when he thought the ship's engines had a familiar sound. He held his hand, and the *Hoy Head* and her crew were saved. (EWM)

when Beatty and Tyrwhitt made a dramatic swoop into the Heligoland Bight and sank three German light cruisers. This victory, along with Beatty's success over a German battle-cruiser squadron off the Dogger Bank on 24 January 1915, was dearly bought, for it convinced the Germans that a strictly defensive strategy was the right one, and it led them to concentrate on the development of submarine attack. As a direct result of her setbacks, Germany also proclaimed the water around the British Isles to be a war zone where all ships, enemy or neutral, would be sunk on sight. In this she overreached herself, for the sinking of the *Lusitania* on 7 May 1915, with the drowning of 1,100 people, paved the way for America's entry into the war.

But, in so far as Scapa Flow was concerned, the developments I have mentioned meant that, apart from an occasional foray, life for the ordinary sailor was incredibly dull. He was far away from the bright lights; he was confined for the most part on his ship; sometimes the weather could be frightful; and above all, as he read about the terrible battles on the Western front, with the deaths of hundreds of thousands of soldiers, he could not feel that the routine jobs of the Navy in northern waters were comparable in danger or as effective in result. The sailors were never idle, for Jellicoe was a strict disciplinarian, but even so they were often driven hard back on their own resources. Eventually a good deal was done to relieve the tedium: ships had their bands, their dramatic companies, their sports clubs, their opportunities for gambling in quite a big way (one man cleared £870 in the three years he was in the Flow) and often their own magazines. The island of Flotta became the playground of the Grand Fleet. It saw hugely attended football and boxing matches, with sometimes ten thousand spectators. There were sailing and pulling matches, some golf and rough shooting for the officers, and each summer the Naval sports day. With it all, some men came to the end of themselves. Some saved their reason by watching the birds, others by writing scurrilous poems.

To Orkney the presence of the Fleet in the Flow was a strange experience. At night you looked out over the quiet water, to see the lights of a strange shimmering town, and you told yourself that the greatest armada the world had ever seen was lying there. It was a very hungry armada, which helped to consume monthly the greater part of the Army and Navy Catering Board's estimated 320 tons of meat, 800 tons of potatoes, and 80,000 lbs of bread. Each day on HMS *Imperieuse*, a superannuated ship which became a kind of general headquarters, 50,000 items of mail were sorted and despatched.

Time went very slowly on the Flow; but at last in May 1916 the Navy seemed to be given the chance for which it was waiting. The previous January the German High Seas Fleet had been given a more daring and offensive commander in Vice-Admiral Scheer. Then, owing to a strongly worded American note in April, there was a temporary cessation of submarine activities. The U-boats were free for the moment for operations with the fleet; and Scheer thought out a plan for placing fourteen U-boats off the British coast, and then enticing the British fleet to leave its bases, by letting the High Seas Fleet appear off the Norwegian coast. The British Admiralty had, however, become aware of the submarine movements, and on the afternoon of 30 May the C-in-C was warned of the possibility of the High Seas Fleet coming out. In the event the submarines played little part in the ensuing Battle of Jutland. By midnight the whole British fleet was at sea making for the Heligoland Bight—Jellicoe from Scapa, Beatty from the Forth. For both Germany and Britain a decisive battle at sea was psychologically necessary. Scheer and Hipper did not attempt to evade the British Fleet, but they did not give Jellicoe and Beatty the opportunity to fight a great orthodox action. The Germans appeared and exchanged fierce fire with the big ships for a few minutes, then abruptly turned away in smoke and mist and sent in their destroyers for a torpedo attack. Later when the fleets met again, and Scheer was virtually in an ambush, he made another of his abrupt turns and escaped, while the German destroyers by once more attacking with torpedoes compelled the Grand Fleet to turn away.

It is true that the Germans, who found their way with comparative immunity to their bases, never afterwards came out to challenge the British Navy; but they remained an active, threatening presence, a menace that prevented many British warships from undertaking operations in other theatres of war. As for the actual results in terms of casualties, Britain did not come out too well. It was a bruised and battered fleet that returned to Scapa with its dead. It had lost three battle cruisers, three cruisers and eight destroyers and 6,097 sailors to Germany's loss of 2,551 men. It is true that the majority, of the dead had gone down in their ships, but the entire dockyard staff at Scapa, of all trades, spent a whole night making coffins for the casualties on the ships which returned. These were buried on the island of Hoy, with Jellicoe and Beatty standing with bowed heads in the graveyard.

The Navy had only been back in the Flow a day or two, and had not come to terms with the traumatic experience of Jutland, when it had another shock, the loss off Marwick Head of the cruiser *Hampshire*, with Lord Kitchener on board.[1]

There was another disaster before the end of the war, when HMS *Vanguard* blew up on the night of 9 July 1917, with the loss of over 700 men. No sabotage was suspected; it was almost certainly the spontaneous combustion of cordite in the ship's magazine which caused the fantastic explosion. Parts of the burning ship were strewn over the island of Flotta, off which she was lying, and the heather on the island was set alight. Somewhere on the

---

1. See also articles 'The day that Kitchener died', p.419 and 'The story of the Stromness lifeboats', p.62.

The Bridge of Brodgar, Stenness, 1875

Waller Hugh Paton, RSA, RSW, 1828–1895

island next day a packet of treasury notes was picked up intact. The future King George VI, then Prince Albert, was an officer on HMS *Malaya* and saw the explosion. He immediately asked the Commander if he could take charge of one of the picket boats to search for survivors. 'Certainly not,' the Commander said sharply, and the future King of Britain turned away sadly while another took his place. The Prince was well known in Kirkwall. There is an amusing story of a newsagent who owned a small shop in Albert Street, and who owned a large black dog called Prince. One day the dog had disappeared, and Mr Stevenson stood at the door of his shop shouting, 'PRINCE, PRINCE, PRINCE'. Two young naval officers were passing—one of them broke off and came up shyly to Mr Stevenson. 'Did you wish to speak to me, sir?' he asked.

The loss of the *Vanguard* was the most notable event at Scapa until the historic morning in November 1918, when the German High Seas Fleet, steering north in detached groups, entered the Flow for internment. It was a fleet whose officers and men had been bewildered and stupefied by German reverses in France and by the terrible conditions inside Germany. The German Revolution actually started in the naval base at Kiel on 9 November, and spread from there to Hamburg and Wilhelmshaven. A rumour had spread among the sailors that the fleet was to be staked on a last throw against the British, in which it would fight to the death. As a result the crews hoisted the red flag on the ships and arrested their officers. Some officers who resisted were murdered. It seemed at first that the Allies' demand for the surrender of the High Seas Fleet might not be met owing to chaos and divided councils among the revolutionary elements, but when the Allies declared that they would occupy Heligoland if the ships did not adhere to the sailing date they had been given, the Supreme Workers' and Sailors' Council became alarmed and issued an appeal to all hands in their navy to comply with the Allied orders. 'If we fulfil the enemy's conditions,' they said, 'the ships will return when peace is concluded. If we do not, the British will come, deprive us of our Fleet forever, and shell Wilhelmshaven.'

It is important to remember that the faith which upheld the best and most patriotic elements among the skeleton crews which took the ships to Scapa and stayed with them was that they were keeping the ships in German hands until a peace treaty decided their fate. Vice-Admiral von Reuter wrote in his book *Scapa Flow*, 'My object was, henceforward, to preserve this assembled portion of the High Seas Fleet for the German State, whose property it was.'[1] This was very far from being the position of the Allies, who were determined that a fleet big enough to be a threat to them must not remain in German hands. The British wanted to destroy the whole fleet; France wanted to enlarge her own fleet with a share of the German ships. There was considerable

---

1. *Scapa Flow 1919*, p.44.

argument, and when the Germans eventually scuttled their fleet in the Flow on 21 June 1919, many Frenchmen, and indeed others of our Allies were sure that Britain had connived at the operation.

I think a dispassionate observer at this date would say that the Germans came out of this matter of the internment of the fleet with a better record than the Allies. The Germans themselves got rid of unreliable elements on their ships, and for the most part maintained a wonderful standard of discipline. To them Scapa Flow was altogether a prison. Admiral Friedrich Ruge, looking back on Scapa Flow after fifty years has written, 'The region did not appear very enticing as we entered. Under a grey sky there were bare islands of rock, covered only here and there with undergrowth and heather, a few huts, many sheep, very few humans, and great swarms of seagulls and cormorants in the air and on the water.'[1] During the seven months that the ships were at Scapa the Germans were never once allowed ashore. All the food they ate had to come from Germany in spite of the difficulties involved, and a hunger blockade that was still in force. Sometimes the only foods in plentiful supply were pearl barley and jam made from beet.

During the early part of 1919 there was considerable trouble on the battleships from revolutionary elements, whose Sailors' Council sought to take over the functions of the officers. Things were so bad on the flagship *Friedrich der Grosse* that Vice-Admiral von Reuter transferred to the light cruiser Emden on 25 March.

In May the men of the German High Seas Fleet at Scapa learned of the peace conditions of the Allies. There was considerable shock. Admiral Ruge wrote: 'This was not the peace for which we had gone into the internment. One thing had been achieved: we were absolutely clear about the spirit of this Treaty and the fate of the fleet. There was no longer any hope of bringing a single boat home. So there was no point in keeping our vessels right up to the mark and it was doubtful whether bringing them to Scapa Flow had in the slightest bit moderated the enemy's demands.'[2]

The Allies had demanded that the entire Internment Fleet be handed over.

The Treaty proposals seemed to most of the naval men at Scapa so monstrous they could not believe that the German Government would accept them. Cut off as they were from knowledge of what was actually happening in Germany, they were not aware of how weak that Government was, and how impossible it was to resist the Allied demands. From then on it began to be taken for granted by the officers at least that if hostilities recommenced their only course could be to scuttle their ships. Von Reuter's only source of information was copies of *The Times* two or three days old. On

1. *Scapa Flow 1919*, pp.54-55.
2. Ibid., p.100.

17 June *The Times* reported that the Allies had spoken their last word. Unless the Germans accepted their terms, the Armistice would end on Saturday, 21 June and active war would be resumed against Germany. Von Reuter and his colleagues at Scapa decided that they must assume a German refusal of the terms, and on that fateful Saturday the plans which had been carefully laid over the past weeks were put in operation. The signal agreed on—the hoisting of 'Pennant Z', a forked red flag—was given and in every ship the crew set quickly to work to open the sea-cocks and destroy the closing mechanisms.

There are quite a number of people in Orkney who can remember the scuttling. One after the other a great number of the seventy-two ships foundered and went to the bottom. Most of the British Fleet was out of the Flow engaged in gunnery practice. The destroyers and drifters which had been left behind hurried around trying to cope with an impossible situation. Here, they tried to make Germans return on board to close the valves, something that could not be done. There, they picked up boat-loads of German sailors. Sporadic rifle fire came from British naval parties, but for the most part calmer councils prevailed. Eight Germans were killed: Commander Schumann, the commanding officer of the *Markgraf*, and seven Petty Officers and men. Twenty-one were wounded.

A picnic party of Stromness schoolchildren on board the drifter *Flying Kestrel* was in the midst of the ships when they began to sink. It was a lovely calm summer day. Beside them the *Seydlitz* turned turtle. A sailor standing at the stern of another ship was shot and dropped into the water. All around were men on rafts and in little boats. On shore in Orphir a funeral party laid down the coffin it was carrying and stared open-mouthed at what seemed to be a nightmare happening.

When Lizzie Smith, on the little island of Cava, saw boat-loads of Germans coming to land, she locked herself into the lighthouse. British sailors duly came to Cava, and to reassure her she was given a guard of three until the Germans were taken away.

In all something like a quarter of a million tons of shipping had been deliberately sunk. As time passed it began to seem absurd that such a wealth of metal should remain beneath the sea. In 1924, a Wolverhampton engineer, Ernest Cox, decided he would try to bring some of it to the surface. He went to the Admiralty and made his proposals, and bought a great part of the sunken fleet for a sum which has been put at £24,000. It was a venture on which he gambled all his liquid resources, but he was destined to initiate and carry through one of the greatest salvage feats in history. In less than eight years he and his men had salvaged over 170,000 tons of warships, including two great battleships and four battle cruisers. During the thirties the work was carried on by a firm called Metal Industries. Ironically, some of the steel from the first ship raised went back to Germany where it was made into razor blades. One ship, the *Derfflinger*, had been salved and was ready to be towed away when war began. Three employees of the salvage company, Metal Industries, spent the war on a hut on her keel, pumping air into the ship to keep the pressure up so that she would not sink again. During this time the vessel was positioned between Rysa and Pegal burn, Hoy.

A year or two ago some of the steel of the *Kronprinz Wilhelm* was used to shield a diagnostic system installed in the Medical Physics Department of the Western General Hospital in Edinburgh. Steel manufactured so long has negligible radioactivity, whereas steel manufactured today absorbs nuclear fission products from the atmosphere and a certain amount of radioactivity while it is being processed.

In February 1920 the Admiral Commanding Orkney and Shetland hauled down his flag and the dismantling of the base began. It is odd, but true, that in the Munich crisis year of 1938, a party of Royal Marines had just finished dismantling the last of the gun emplacements built during the First World War, while boom defence vessels were making preparations to lay anti-submarine nets at the entrances to the Flow. These nets were in use in the Second World War, which began the following year, on 3 September.

Once again Scapa Flow was sadly unprepared. During the whole year after Munich practically nothing was done to make it a safe and well-equipped base. The Naval Staff had made up their minds that they wanted Rosyth as a main base, but Admiral Forbes, the Commander-in-Chief was determined that it must be Scapa, and when war actually broke out, and Churchill came back to the Admiralty, Forbes had Churchill's wholehearted backing.

There had been block-ships sunk in the eastern entrances to the Flow since the First World War, but some of them had been shifted by storms, causing gaps. There was an obvious gap in the sound between the Orkney Mainland and the island of Lamb Holm; that is, in Kirk Sound. The British noted it, and an old ship was on her way north to be sunk there. But the photographs taken by German reconnaissance planes had also shown that it was a place where a submarine might enter. They could hardly have missed it, for it could be, and frequently was, used by ships of up to 600 tons. Commodore Doenitz, Commander-in-Chief of the U-boats, felt that there was a reasonable chance that a really good U-boat commander might be able to enter the Flow at high water and under cover of darkness. The man chosen for the attempt was Kapitan-Leutnant Gunther Prien of the U-47. In the late evening of 13 October 1939, the submarine nosed her way into the Flow without being detected. Prien had an initial disappointment; he expected to find the main elements of the Home Fleet anchored in the base, but after dark on the previous evening Admiral Forbes, who was most unhappy about the safety of the base, but whose main worry was a massed air attack, had taken the fleet to Loch Ewe. The *Royal Oak*, too slow to keep up with the fast battleships, had been left behind, to act as an anti-aircraft battery for Kirkwall, but more particularly as a guard for the new radar station at Holm, for a time a BBC Transmitting Station. When Prien did not find the fleet, he turned north-eastwards towards Scapa Bay.

There he saw the silhouette of the *Royal Oak*, for it was a clear night, with Northern Lights showing earlier in the evening. The U-boat came up quietly under the cliffs on the east side of the Flow, and fired a salvo of torpedoes at the warship from the landward side. Only one of these hit the vessel, a glancing blow on the forepeak. The crew of the *Royal Oak* thought it might be some small internal explosion, but in case of bombs they were ordered to close up on the guns.

Meanwhile, the U-boat managed to get unnoticed to the other side of the *Royal Oak*, and about twenty minutes later she was able to fire a salvo of four torpedoes straight into the vessel. They made such great holes in her bottom that she sank in less than six minutes. A drifter, the *Daisy*, lying alongside, picked up something like three hundred survivors, and another fifty or so managed to swim ashore. Over eight hundred died.

There was consternation among those responsible for the safety of the Flow. A great deal had to be done before the fleet came back. But it was recognised that the most deadly attack could come from the air. A tremendous effort was made to protect the base with a great ring of heavy and light anti-aircraft guns, searchlights and barrage balloons. When these and the naval guns were firing, the Orkney Barrage, as it was called, was terrifying. The islands shook and reverberated with the multitudinous explosions. Near the end of February, two carefully constructed dummy battleships and a dummy aircraft carrier were brought into the Flow to tempt and test the Luftwaffe. But the Germans did not take the bait. The dummy ships could not keep their secret. Before the day was out, little boys in Kirkwall were shouting to each other, 'Have you seen the dummy fleet at Scapa?' Among other things, these ships had no escort of gulls, like the real warships. Waste food was always pouring from the gash-chutes of the manned vessels, and the gulls were there continually to squabble over it. They had no interest in the dummy ships.

The Home Fleet came back to the anchorage on 3 March. In the next few days there was a spate of German reconnaissance planes, flying very high. On Saturday, 13 March, at dusk, the first heavy air attack came. It was made by about fifty-five planes, coming over in waves of from five to seven. The great barrage opened up, and the fleet was unscathed, but a civilian was killed at the Brig of Waithe in Stenness, where some bombs fell. There was slight damage on land around the perimeter of the Flow. Two more determined attacks were made during the month of April 1940, which did amazingly little damage. The barrage had now grown so deadly that the Germans nicknamed Scapa Flow 'Hell's Corner', and for the rest of the war, apart from high-flying reconnaissance planes, they left it severely alone. But the Orkney defences immobilised, if that is the word, thousands of bored servicemen badly needed elsewhere. There was also the threat from occupied Norway, and a heavy burden was placed not only on the island garrison, but also on the big ships and little ships which ceaselessly patrolled the waters between the islands and Norway.

There was much waiting in the Flow, and occasional drama and great gallantry. It was from Scapa Flow that Captain Warburton-Lee led his flotilla of five destroyers against ten German destroyers lying in the fjord near Narvik. He sank two and damaged three more, but in the course of the raid lost two destroyers and his own life. A house in St Rognvald Street, Kirkwall still bears the proud name of Warburton-Lee.

It was from Hatston aerodrome near Kirkwall, whose planes patrolled the Norwegian coast, that news came that the German ships *Bismarck* and *Prinz Eugen* had slipped out of Bergen and were at large in the Northern seas. And it was from Scapa that the *Hood*, Britain's finest battle-cruiser, went out on her last voyage, for she was sunk by the *Bismarck* with a loss of ninety-five officers and thirteen hundred men.

All the time from soon after the sinking of the *Royal Oak*, that great defence work, the Churchill Barriers, were being built. The work took four years, from May 1940 to July 1944, and cost two million pounds. Four causeways were built on the seabed and these eventually linked the Mainland with the four islands on the east side of the Flow. One of the channels to be closed was half a mile long and in places the depth was fifty feet. The currents in the channels could be twelve knots at times. Owing to the urgency of the work, and to the fact that there was no accommodation available for the men who were to construct the barriers, a 16,000 ton liner, the *Almanzora*, was filled with railway engines and rails, concrete mixers, stone crushers, huts, blankets, stores, and hundreds of tons of crushed stone, sand cement, and sent to Orkney. The workmen lived on her until permanent quarters were erected on shore. In all 580,000 tons of rock, from four Orkney quarries, were dropped into the channels, to be buttressed by 333,000 tons of five- and ten-ton concrete blocks. Five hundred British and Irish workmen and twelve hundred Italian prisoners of war laboured on the barriers. In the course of the work ten men lost their lives.

Some hundreds of the Italian prisoners lived in a camp on Lamb Holm, the uninhabited island nearest to the Mainland. They tried to beautify their bleak, hutted camp. First of all they made a memorial of St George Slaying the Dragon and erected it in their camp square. They much desired to have a church, and with the goodwill of the camp commandant they utterly transformed two nissen huts until they became a chapel of extraordinary beauty, entirely constructed from scrap material. This chapel is still in being, and is still almost as lovely inside as it was when the Italian prisoners built it.

At the beginning of the Second World War, Scapa Flow was about as barren of amenities as it could possibly be. But things quickly improved. The base at Lyness got a cinema and then a theatre was built. The little island of Flotta had its own Garrison Theatre; and so did Stromness, when it dawned upon the authorities that Stromness was not in Iceland, where the theatre had been sent by mistake. Great personalities came and went—Gracie Fields, Francoise Rosay, Gertrude Lawrence, Yehudi Menuhin, Pouishnoff, Beatrice Lillie, Evelyn Laye and many more. Tommy Handley did an ITMA on the Flow that kept King George VI, who was in the audience, in fits of laughter. In the latter part of the war, ships of the American Navy came into the Flow. As the American battleship *Tuscaloosa* came in, she signalled to the Home Fleet, 'How is the second largest navy in the world?' Back came the British Navy's reply, 'How is the second best?'

After the war the base was gradually run down, and the naval part of it was closed on 29 March 1957. Two hundred people were at the Farewell Ceremony, at which the White Ensign and the paying-off pennant, 266 feet long, were hauled down. It gave one an eerie feeling to stand among the acres of empty huts and sheds, which had once been filled with over 3,000 people, and to watch the flags very slowly falling when the bugles called 'Sunset'.

To all intents and purposes, the Everlasting Battle of Scapa Flow has come to an end. But we cannot tell. Oil tanks, and a pipeline, and the great tankers are about to take over. What they will make of the Flow, and of Orkney, is a question we hardly dare to ask.

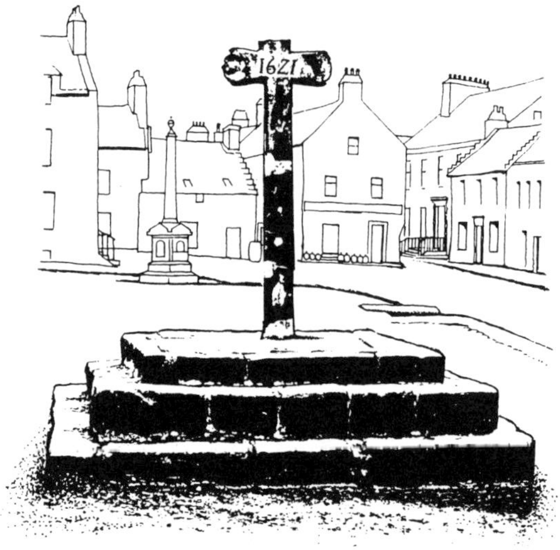
1621

ORKNEY
MONUMENTS

ORKNEY MONUMENTS

1	Treasure troves	443
2	The strongest hold in Britain	446
3	Peterkirk—an island sanctuary	448
4	Chiocchetti and the Italian Chapel	453
5	Viking and saint	457
6	The curious history of the Big Tree	463

I

Treasure troves

The words 'treasure trove' are magical. They recall all the best boys' books from *Treasure Island* onwards. Their magic seems to affect both grown-ups and boys. The excitement caused by the discovery of the St Ninian's hoard in Shetland, and more recently by the finding of a three-thousand-year-old gold torque in England,[1] bears this out.

So far, probably the first collection of things beautiful in themselves to be found in Orkney is the Skaill hoard; and it is over a hundred years, in March 1858 to be exact, since this was discovered. It all began with a boy chasing a rabbit into a hole in the links at Sandwick. At the mouth of the burrow he found a few fragments of silver, scratched up by the rabbits. The news got abroad and people began to dig. Soon a large quantity of silver articles had been unearthed. Luckily, Mr George Petrie of Kirkwall, a prominent Orkney antiquary, who also was one of the first to explore Skara Brae, heard about the find and rushed out to Sandwick. He managed to recover most of the articles. When collected they were found to weigh sixteen pounds. It was an amazing collection. There were ornaments of silver —brooches, arm rings and neck rings—some ingots of silver, and a number of silver coins. The coins, although perhaps the least interesting to an antiquary, would have thrilled a romantic, coin-collecting lad. There was a St Peter's penny, struck in York in the tenth century, a penny of King Aethelstan, and a number of others from the East. These last still had legibly inscribed the places of their mintage—Al-shash, Baghdad and Samarkand.

In all, there were some nine brooches, fourteen twisted neck rings and arm rings, and twenty-three solid armlets. We wonder how many Orcadians have gone to the National Museum[2] to see these treasures?

In Orkney, people are already asking: 'What will be found when the

---

1. Found in 1960 at Moulsford, Berkshire, it dates from the middle Bronze Age, weighs approximately one pound and is now located in Reading Museum.
2. National Museum of Antiquities, Queen Street, Edinburgh. Artefacts from Skara Brae are also on display at Tankerness House Museum, Kirkwall, Stromness Museum, and at Skara Brae.

Skaill sands at Deerness are excavated?'[1] The answer seems to be: traces of a civilisation that the experts will be able to interpret, but not perhaps objects of intrinsic worth or beauty. Still, there is always a possibility.

Coins are naturally the most frequent objects of value to be unearthed. Through the centuries our forefathers buried their money in earthen pots. In Sweden the number of Cufic and Anglo-Saxon coins discovered in hoards numbers nearly forty thousand. As old coins are so numerous, those who find them are often disappointed when they are told that their market value is slight. Museums are packed with Roman coins. I can remember an occasion when I was handed in change a dozen coppers and discovered that one of them was a denarius from the time of Vespasian (AD 69-79).

In 1870, when Mr Petrie was digging at the Broch of Lingro he discovered a number of denarii. They dated from around AD 69 to AD 183, and carried the images of Vespasian, Hadrian, Antoninus Pius, and Crispina. These were interesting enough, but I am sure that Mr Petrie was fascinated in something else from the same site: a playing-dice of bone.

To my mind some of the most valuable discoveries ever made in Orkney were those in the sands at Westray between Pierowall Bay and the farm of Gill. There in 1841, Mr Petrie found the skeleton of a man together with that of a horse in a single grave. There were also some iron boat rivets, which suggested a symbolic ship burial. Graves opened there in 1849 yielded more rivets, shield-bosses, an iron knife, a sword, bone combs, brooches, two more horse skeletons and human skeletons. Further graves discovered in 1851, 1855 and 1863 contained articles of the same type, and in addition an axe, a spear head, a key, a sickle blade, two buckles (all of iron), and a decorated fitting of silver. It is a great pity that the finds are poorly recorded; but even so Professor A. W. Brøgger felt confident about their value. Here were the graves, he declared, of some of the first Norse settlers. 'In other words,' he wrote, 'it is the earliest generations of settlers which are before us, the first and second generations of those who populated the Orkney Islands.' 'Pierowall,' he went on, 'is the "Hofn" of the Saga of the Orkneymen, "the harbour" par excellence, the best and only real harbour in the Orkney Islands, with the old shipping life with its shallow boats. It is quite natural that this place became a centre.'[2]

There are possibly many interesting things still hidden by the Pierowall sands, as there are in many a hillock and mound of Orkney. But we realise

1. The discovery led to a 20-year programme of excavations by the late Peter Gelling, initially on Viking houses and later on prehistoric ones. The Norse part of the settlement was published by him in the National Museum's bicentenary volume— Fenton and Palsson (eds.), *The Northern and Western Isles in the Viking World*, Edinburgh 1984. A brief note on part of the prehistoric material appears in Colin Renfrew's *The Prehistory of Orkney*, Edinburgh 1985.
2. *Ancient Emigrants*, A. W. Brøgger, 1929, p.121.

today that it is much better to leave them there until the experts, with all the resources now at their disposal, can investigate them thoroughly. The artifacts are only part of the story; sometimes the most interesting part is told by the stones and earth in which they are hidden; and this is a tale the ordinary treasure seeker cannot read, and in his untutored eagerness may well destroy.

2

The strongest hold in Britain

It is exactly a century since the last ruins of the Old Castle of Kirkwall were pulled down[1] to make way for the present Castle Street. With walls eleven feet thick, the Castle was 'one of the strongest houlds in Britane, without fellow', as a frustrated besieger remarked.[2] It was built by the great Earl Henry Sinclair in the fourteenth century, when people were still addressing their letters from 'Kirkwall in Norway'.

It stood quietly enough for nearly two centuries. Then, one spring night in 1528, it was taken by surprise by James Sinclair of Brecks in Orkney and his brother Edward. These men, with the backing of many Orcadians, were in revolt against William Lord Sinclair, their cousin, who had been appointed Justice Depute of the islands. In taking possession of the Castle, the attackers killed three of their own nephews. It was certainly a grim family party!

Next year Lord William came with an army of Caithness men to oust the rebels, but his forces were routed by the Orcadians at Summerdale.

In the following century another party of rebels seized Kirkwall Castle. They were commanded by Robert Stewart, son of the notorious Earl Patrick.[3] The quixotic young man was making an attempt to win back his father's forfeited possessions.

The Earl of Caithness, remembering the past reverses of his family, coveted the job of retaking the Castle. He knew its strength and brought great guns from Edinburgh Castle to subdue it. One of these guns was a monster known as 'Thrawn Mouth'. For five weeks in the autumn of 1614 the cannon battered away at the building. They breached it, but could not destroy it. It was only taken at last through the treachery of one of Robert Stewart's friends.[4]

1. In 1866.
2. In 1614 more than two centuries after it was built c.1380, George, Earl of Caithness, who commanded the force which captured and reduced the castle to ruins, wrote that but for securing the services of Patrick Halcro 'it would have been ane langsome siege; for I protest to God the House has never been biggit by (without) the consent of the Divil, for it is one of the strongest houlds in Britane, without fellow.'
3. See *The minister and the witch*, p.403.
4. Patrick Halcro.

The Government decided that it was too strong a building ever again to get into the wrong hands, so it was partly demolished.

All that is history; but I wondered what happened to the building afterwards, and decided to do some detective work. I found that most of the stones of the Castle lie today in Kirkwall's West Pier. They reached it in a roundabout way. They were used to build Kirkwall's Tolbooth in 1742, and then, when the Tolbooth was itself pulled down last century,[1] they were carted to the West Pier, which was under construction.

Right up to 1865, however, a massive fragment of the old wall of Kirkwall Castle dominated the lower end of Broad Street. Did our ancestors of a hundred years ago, I wondered, make any protest about the removal of the historic ruin? The answer is 'No'. Instead, the Town Council voted a hundred pounds towards the making of the new road.[2]

The demolishers got to work. They came upon five of the cannon balls used in the siege, two of them (great 32-pounders) belched forth by 'Thrawn Mouth'. Their most interesting find was the Castle well, beautifully built of freestone, with a fresh spring supplying it with pure water.

No one had the heart to destroy the well. It was covered up, and the roadway made over the top of it. How many of those who drive their fine cars over it today know that underneath is the old well of the Castle of the St Clairs—the Castle of which Sir Walter Scott wrote in *The Lay of the Last Minstrel*:

> Still nods their palace to its fall,
> Thy pride and sorrow, fair Kirkwall.

Last of all, my search took me to the cellars of what was once the Castle Hotel. There I found a funny old-fashioned pump, undoubtedly connected to the well. Near it were traces of building which may possibly be part of the Castle's foundations. I pumped vigorously, without realising that if I had been successful I might have flooded the building above through some old pipe cut off somewhere along its length.

But what a story it would have made, if a present-day householder had found it necessary to mop up water from a well built when Orkney was still a part of Norway.

---

1. In 1890.
2. The remaining wall, some fifty-five feet long by eleven feet thick and of varying height, was removed and used to improve access to Kirkwall Harbour.

3

Peterkirk—an island sanctuary

Many of the old parish kirks in Orkney are close to the sea, but of all the kirks that still stand, in their grey, functional severity, along the island seaboard, Peterkirk in South Ronaldsay has perhaps the finest situation. The road to the kirk drops steeply shorewards between the fields to a sandy beach, with an unbroken horizon of the North Sea, punctuated sharply by two dark headlands. From the road on a wild day the kirk looks as if it is afloat on broken water, like a legendary ark.

Like an ark, too, Peterkirk has stood the assaults of age and fashion. While more than one of the old parish kirks have been declared redundant, in favour of some gaunt structure of Victorian Gothic which the weather has not even mellowed, Peterkirk has just been restored,[1] to become a place in which it is a joy to worship, and the most perfect example in Orkney of its style and period.

The Church of Scotland has been aware for a considerable time of the historical and architectural value of some of its older country churches. Its Committee on Artistic Questions relating to the Church is warmly sympathetic when the restoration of a genuinely interesting building is proposed, so the congregation of St Peter's was able to call on the advice of two experts, Mr J. Wilson Paterson, the architect and ex-chairman of the committee, and Dr Stanley Cursiter, the Queen's Limner in Scotland, himself an Orkneyman.

One is hardly prepared, as one enters the kirk through a low porch and lifts the iron 'sneck' of the main door, for the austere beauty one finds inside. Here is, one might say, a quintessence of Presbyterianism; not grim and off-putting as so many writers would have us believe, but restrained and ordered: the natural expression of a grave, undramatic people and of a tidy, regulated landscape.

White-washed walls and grained woodwork are familiar enough, but it is the layout of the long narrow church that is so attractive. At the centre of one of its walls—the wall with the windows—is a canopied pulpit, its sides

1. 1967.

97 St Peter's Church, South Ronaldsay, 1967. The interior is shown below.

98　The Italian Chapel, Lamb Holm, Orkney, 1944

99　Italian prisoners-of-war at the inauguration of the statue of St George and the Dragon, 1943

of classic panels rising from a high box plinth. Every seat in the building is so situated as to allow its occupants to concentrate their gaze on the pulpit, from the roomy family pews in its near vicinity, with their central tables covered with dark red cloth, to the short 'desk' pews along both side walls.

There would be room for a wide central aisle, but there are, in fact, two narrow aisles with a double line of seats between. These seats are so made that the book-rest of the front seat can fold down; a flap on the back of this seat folds up, and the front seat itself can be pulled forward so that its original front is now its back. This, in effect, gives a double row of seats facing inwards towards the 'flap', which becomes a communion table running the whole length of the church. Here is the old, traditional arrangement of which few examples survive. On Communion Sundays many generations have sat stiffly but reverently at this table, as the elements were dispensed and the unity of word and sacrament insisted on.

At either end of the church are steep galleries, lit by central windows connecting gallery and ceiling. The fronts of these galleries, with their horizontal panels, deep carved plinths and chaste mouldings, give, along with the pulpit, just the right amount of sober ornament. The galleries are reached by unenclosed stairs, with hand rails.

There is need of a few curves to soften the effect of so many straight lines. These are supplied by the round-topped windows, the octagonal pulpit and the hemispheres of the lamp globes, swinging in pairs from elegant wrought-iron brackets along the length of the aisle. The former oil lamps, complete with shining copper bowls and narrow glasses, have been retained, but they are lit by concealed bulbs fed through invisible wires.

Screwed to the front of the pulpit is a bracket font, with its original flat-bottomed pewter bowl, placed high so that the whole congregation might see the minister's hand. At the side of the pulpit, where the minister's door used to be, is a glass-fronted cupboard containing the kirk's wooden collection ladles and the moulds in which were cast its communion tokens.

No-one has written a history of Peterkirk,[1] but fragments of its story can be pieced together from old records. The foundation must be an ancient one. In pre-Reformation times, the Bishop of Orkney was parson of the neighbouring island of Burray and of St Peter's parish, while the Provost or Dean was parson of St Mary's at the south end of South Ronaldsay, and vicar of the two churches on that island and the one in Burray. This had been so since the 'first erection of the bishoprikis and dignities of the chaptor and Cathedrall Kirk of Orknay.'

The present church was built in 1641, as a date over the minister's door

1. This article was written in March 1968. In 1972 the Rev. Stuart D. B. Picken, MA, BD, PhD, wrote *The Soul of an Orkney Parish*, which includes information about Peterkirk from the sixteenth century.

would suggest. It probably had a thatched roof, like many of the island kirks of that day; but as early as 1657 Walter Wooleritch, a slater, was employed to 'mak the roof free of wind and raine', and the various *touns*[1] in the parish were asked to provide between them 500 slates. The roof must have continued to give trouble, for in 1664 it required another '200 slaites . . . to mend all the falts.' The previous year something had had to be done about the kirkyard walls, for 'the beasts and swyne are abusing and digging in the burrials of the dead.'

In the two centuries following the Reformation, there were periods of ecclesiastical activity on the island and periods of scandalous neglect. Near the end of the eighteenth century the walls of Peterkirk had 'for several years stood without a roof exposed to all the winds of heaven.' A programme of rebuilding and restoration in 1801 gave us the church very much as it is today.

Oddly enough, this remote church, with its congregation of fishermen and crofters, and a local laird or two in their box pews, always seemed to keep in touch with national affairs. One of its ministers, 'Maister Walter Stewart', was excommunicated for exhorting his flock to join with the Marquis of Montrose. One day in September 1659, the kirk was gravely affronted when 'two quakers, Inglisch men, troubled the congregatione and abused the people befoir the minister came to the church.' In May 1660, it gave thanks for 'his Majestye's saife and happy returne.' In October 1665, it observed a day of solemn humiliation and fast for the Great Plague in London and the failure of the harvest in Scotland, but 'the people wer not so weell conveined as that dewty requyred.'

The behaviour of the people often gave the pious ministers cause for concern. Around the middle of the seventeenth century they were brought frequently before the session for slander, 'scandalous bedding', sheep-stealing, 'ryots', and 'playing at football or other prophane games.' Their taste for playing at football on the Sabbath is mentioned more than once. For some the punishment was to stand in the *jogges*[2] 'all the tyme of divyne service'; for others the stocks were considered more appropriate. Many had the habit of resorting when ill or in trouble to the old roofless chapels of the medieval church or to holy wells. They were sternly cautioned against 'all charming and charmers (and) haunting of superstitious places, as chappels or weels.' There was a sharp object lesson in 1643 when the presbytery ordered to be burned a wooden figure of St Peter which had long been held in great veneration.

1. For detailed information regarding touns or townships, see 'Farming in Orkney during the last two centuries', p.5.
2. An instrument of public punishment consisting of a hinged iron collar attached by a chain to a wall or post and locked round the offender's neck.

But the Peterkirk folk had many merits. For instance, although they might put a high proportion of spurious coin into the poor's box on ordinary occasions, their liberality could be depended on when there was genuine need. In December 1663, they contributed thirty shillings for some 'Inglisch strangers who had beene schip-broken.' Two years later they raised thirty-two shillings for 'some skippers and sailers who had been taken at sea by the Hollanders and spoyled of their goods and vessell brunt.'[1] This amiable trait continued down the years. In 1830, a congregation which had been content on a former Sunday of bad weather to put $3\frac{1}{2}$d into the offering gave over three pounds for a woman whose husband had been drowned.

The church has had some notable ministers, but none so individual as John Gerard, who occupied its pulpit from 1815 to 1850. Even now, well over a century after his death, his pithy sayings and eccentric doings are related. He would stop a sermon to watch with interest the outcome of a fight between two dogs in the aisle, assuring his congregation that the little one would win; he told the children to let Bible truths stick to their hearts as butter to bere bannocks; he protested his continual fear of 'Deists, radicals, papists and voluntaries'; and he often inveighed against his hearers. But he was happy in his manse in South Ronaldsay, where there was no music 'but the ceaseless growl of Orkney winds, the dashing of the waves at the back of my house, and the birring of the maid's wheel.'

From the high canopied pulpit of Peterkirk came such observations as these:

> 'Brethren, I find the mice have been at this sermon, but I'll just begin where they left off.'
>
> 'It is impossible to live at peace with some men, for there is Willie Sinclair in the gallery, who borrowed a caisie[2] from me six weeks ago, and has not yet returned it. Who could live at peace with such a man?'

And in remonstrance to the Deity during a wet harvest:

> 'Send us a guid soughing wind that will ripen the strae[3] an' winna hairm the heid. But if Ye send us a rantin', reivin', roarin' wind as Ye sent us last time, Ye'll play the verra mischief wi' the aits[4] an' clean spoil a'.'

There was a time when the island of Burray had its own minister and South Ronaldsay two or more. But, with falling population and reduced

1. Burnt.
2. A carrying basket made of straw.
3. Straw.
4. Oats.

manpower in the Church, things have come round full-circle to the situation in old times, and the present minister, the Rev. Stuart Picken, BD, has charge of all churches in both islands. The restoration of Peterkirk has occurred almost at the beginning of his ministry. It has given him great pleasure, and he hopes that the church, which will be open to tourists, will attract many visitors who want to see the kind of setting that Presbyterianism at its best was able, quite unselfconsciously, to provide.

Bowling in Tankerness House garden, 1885

Arthur Melville, RWS, RSW, RP, 1855-1904

4

Chiocchetti and the Italian Chapel

At one minute past midnight on 8 May 1975, the Second World War against Germany will have been over for thirty years. One week later, in Moena, a lovely little Italian town in the heart of the Dolomite country, Domenico Chiocchetti will be celebrating his sixty-fifth birthday. The link between these two anniversaries is Orkney's Italian Chapel, which Signor Chiocchetti designed and painted.

Thirty years have taken their toll of the wartime buildings which were erected all over Orkney: heavy concrete gun emplacements are derelict; observation towers have been scourged by gales, and are doorless and windowless, or have been pulled down; the sites of what were once big, well-appointed camps (such as Caldale) are festering eyesores.

It was a miracle that the Italian Chapel should have been built, for so much depended on what happened to the quiet Italian artist and decorator Chiocchetti, who was flung this way and that by the fortunes of war. He was in the English quarters of a prison camp in Gineifa, Egypt, getting paid in Egyptian piastres for copying and enlarging family photographs, when he was told that his camp was going to be transferred to India. If he, too, had gone east there might be, who knows, somewhere on the hot plains the remains of a church. There is, I believe, an Italian Chapel, also built by prisoners-of-war, at the foot of the escarpment overlooking the Rift Valley, Kenya. The Italians constructed a road there in the 1940s, and their chapel, built solidly in rocks, is (or was) a work of art.

But Chiocchetti did not go to India. At some stage a Scottish corporal intervened, and he was included in a contingent which made the seemingly endless journey, via Durban, Freetown and Liverpool, to Lamb Holm, where hard, tedious work on the Churchill Barriers awaited them.[1] This was their

---

1. They arrived in January 1942, stayed until September 1944 and adapted remarkably well to alien conditions. They believed in self-help and made delightful trinkets, ornaments and metalwork, all of which found a ready local market. The proceeds were a welcome supplement to the daily allowance in camp money of 1/6d for

first impression of Lamb Holm: 'The little island could hardly have appeared more desolate: bare, foggy, exposed to wind and heavy rain. The camp consisted of thirteen dark, empty huts, and mud.' The Italian padre commented ruefully on 'the difference from the African climate to the northern climate of Orkney—nights almost Polar, intense cold, and what storms!'

With the cold and the heavy work, it was difficult at first for the men to summon up energy for other interests. But better days came, and the prisoners set to work to transform Camp 60, as their quarters were named. They managed to get flower seeds and roots of plants, and in the summer they had bright flower beds of many colours. Cement paths led from hut to hut. In the mess hut they built a little theatre, and Chiocchetti designed and painted the scenery for each production. A photograph still extant shows a couple of actors, with very demure-looking 'wives'. Chiocchetti also decorated the recreation hut, and included caricatures of the popular English sergeant, known to everyone as 'Wooden Leg'.

Concrete is an unlikeable material, but the prisoners could do marvellous things with it. They constructed a bowling alley with concrete bowls, and even a concrete billiard table, whose cushions were made from much-folded pieces of army blanket. From cement, too, over a frame-work of barbed wire, was created the well-known statue of St George slaying the dragon, the model of the prancing horse being a picture in a magazine bought in a Kirkwall shop. I have beside me as I write a photograph of the inauguration of the statue. The huts surrounding the statue of St George can be seen, though they are partly hidden by the great crowd of prisoners. Between the huts are lines of washing, but in the foreground are flowers, and the plinth of the monument is covered with leaves and branches.

So much has been written about the designing and building of the chapel, and so many thousands of the guide book have been distributed, that it would be superfluous to re-tell the story. In the last thirty years the place has become a legend. It is possible that up to two hundred thousand visitors have found their way to Lamb Holm. When a visitors' book, covering a few years, was analysed, it was found to contain names of people from seventy-seven countries.

---

skilled men and 1/- for manual workers. A newspaper was printed in Italian by Penn Press, London, entitled *The Newspaper of the Prisoners*, plays and concerts were held and an orchestra formed. After the Italian capitulation in September 1943 more frequent communication was permitted between the two camps, an Italian newsletter *The Saturday Newspaper* was circulated, and reasonable freedom given to move about the islands and to visit Kirkwall. Football was popular, matches being played against Army and Kirkwall teams, and a Sports Day was held at Camp 60 on Lamb Holm in July 1944.

Innumerable magazines have carried pictures of the Italian Chapel, and films have been made. In 1960 a member of the Italian Chapel Preservation Committee took to Moena (Domenico Chiocchetti's home town) a 16mm film made and lent by Mr Douglas Shearer of Kirkwall. In the local cinema there, the Orcadian visitor and Moena's citizens watched the film being shown, to the accompaniment of the tape-recordings of two BBC Italian language broadcasts describing the chapel. Later that evening, the visitor was the guest of honour at a dinner given by the officials of Moena, at which the Mayor made a speech of welcome and sent his best wishes to the committee in Orkney. Most memorable of all, the toast to the guest was proposed by Signor Chiocchetti himself. A permanent token of Moena's interest in the chapel is its gift of the carved figure of Christ crucified which can be seen on the wayside shrine erected in 1961.

Domenico Chiocchetti had always wanted to be an artist, but he was the youngest of twelve children in a peasant family, and there was no money to send him to art school. When he was fifteen, however, he went to study the art of painting statues and decorative work in a studio at Ortisei, where he also went to a technical school. He was actually working on the decoration of a church when he was called up and sent to the Sixth Anti-Aircraft Regiment of the Mantova Division destined for Libya. In his pocket was a little picture of the Madonna of the Olive Branch which was later the inspiration for the central picture above the altar in the Italian Chapel. 'The rest of the picture,' he has written '. . . I created myself. The war was going on and naturally the motif which inspired me was peace. On the left, an angel held in his hand the heraldic badge of Moena—a man rowing his boat out of the storm towards the calm sea. On the right, another angel was sheathing his sword.'

In Moena, after the war, when he could take time from his work as a decorator, Chiocchetti painted landscapes and portraits, holding an exhibition of pictures, often with fellow artists, each summer. The editor of *The Orcadian*, who visited the family in Moena a number of years ago, wrote of him: 'In his own valley and far beyond, his stature has grown, not only for the religious statues he still paints full-time for churches and monasteries in the whole area, but also for his close association with the Chapel in Orkney. . . . As we walked around the little Dolomite resort with its population of some 2,500, swollen by some 8,000 to 9,000 tourists in the peak August month, Domenico could hold his head high. He was universally liked and respected; he was the town artist, the family man, the son of Moena who had returned a symbol of success from Scotland in wartime.'

It was in 1960 that Signor Chiocchetti first returned to Orkney, having been 'discovered' by the BBC a short time before. He came back with his wife, Maria, in 1964, and again in 1970, with his son Fabio and elder daughter

Letizia.[1] On each occasion he did restoration work on the chapel. It was a great joy to him, and his wife, when they were given a civic reception by Kirkwall Town Council in 1964.

These notes, suggested by the thought of the coming anniversaries in 1975, are written in the hope that they make visits to the Italian Chapel a little more vivid to younger Orcadians, who have no memories of the sombre and eventful wartime days.

1. In September 1985 members of the Chiocchetti family visited Orkney and carried out restoration work on two inside windows.

5

Viking and saint

Ever since the eighteenth century, visitors to St Magnus Cathedral, Kirkwall have been shown a loose stone in the massive pillar which once flanked the High Altar. Behind this stone lie some ancient bones now believed to be those of St Rognvald, that personable and accomplished earl. He made a vow, at home in Agder, South Norway in 1136, that if he conquered his ancestral realm in the Isles he would have a church of stone more splendid than any in the land built at Kirkwall, Orkney to be dedicated to his uncle, St Magnus.

The gallant figure of St Rognvald goes marching through Orkney history, fighting battles at sea, founding his cathedral, crusading to the Holy Land, telling stories, writing poetry, making love. He was no plaster-saint, but so bright was his image in the North that a generation after his death he was canonised.

Orkney historians have gloried in retelling Rognvald's story, but no adequate memorial—apart from the bones in their broken coffin—existed to link him vividly with the cathedral he built. This was a sad insufficiency which worried many lovers of the building, including the Orkney artist Stanley Cursiter, who has known the cathedral since, as a little boy, he stood in the dark immensity of the nave, wildly excited by the clanging bells in the tower.

Dr Cursiter conveyed his concern to the Society of the Friends of St Magnus Cathedral, a body formed some years ago to help to preserve the fabric of the great church and to contribute to its enrichment. On the Society's council are represented Kirkwall Town Council (which holds the building on behalf of town and community), the Church of Scotland congregation which uses it for worship, and members of the general public, both in Orkney and far outside the islands. The idea of furnishing the east end of the cathedral (shut away from nave and choir by a tall organ-screen of oak) as a St Rognvald Chapel was readily accepted, along with Dr Cursiter's offer to design suitable furniture.

For a while visitors to Stanley Cursiter's home in Stromness saw in his upstairs studio drawings of pulpits and lecterns, designs in paint and models in plasticine. Dr Cursiter admits that from the time of his earliest suggestion he had his eye on the two essentials of his scheme: a series of old oak panels preserved in the cathedral, and the skill of a young Kirkwall craftsman, Reynold Eunson,[1] who makes traditional Orkney chairs in a little workshop almost under the shadow of St Magnus.

The first things needed were a communion table, pulpit and lectern. Into modern settings of natural oak, panels from centuries-old cathedral furnishings were to be incorporated. Dr Cursiter laid his designs on Mr Eunson's work-bench. Soon his young collaborator was as enthusiastic as himself. Chair-making went on but Mr Eunson, who is not concerned about the number of hours he works in a week, found time for the skilled job he had undertaken, restoring the lovely old panels, shaping and finishing the new oak. The result has been acclaimed a triumph.

The front of the communion table comes from the stall of a bishop, some of its curious foliate panels bearing bunches of grapes. The pulpit also preserves some record of Orkney history. A large frontal panel once graced the pew of Earl Patrick Stewart—'Black Pate' of Orkney tradition—whose arms with the date 1593 it bears. Patrick was a shameless tyrant, but a man of exquisite taste, as his palace across the road from the cathedral still testifies. Eventually he was hanged in Edinburgh, being granted a short reprieve so that he could rehearse the Lord's Prayer, which he seemed unaccountably slow to learn.

Another of the pulpit panels has a coat of arms with the initials of Edward Sinclair of Essenquoy and his wife Ursula Foulzie. Ursula was a daughter of the Rev. Gilbert Foulzie. Gilbert probably began his career as a monk, became Archdeacon of Orkney, and later, being possessed of a convenient conscience, the first minister of Kirkwall after the Reformation. The only lasting boon he bestowed on Kirkwall was a secular one, similar to that of Earl Patrick, for in 1574 Foulzie enlarged and restored the Kirkwall mansion now known as Tankerness House, incomparably the finest dwelling-house in the town, recently reconditioned under the direction of the late Ian Gordon Lindsay.

Other equally artistic, but unidentified, panels complete pulpit and lectern.

The furniture was placed on a low platform underneath the cathedral's east window. This magnificent pointed window has a 'wheel' extending from side to side over four lights.[2] It was a splendid focus for the new chapel, but

1. See also 'The story of the Orkney chair', p.85.
2. The rose window and the four lancet lights below were installed in 1918 in memory of Sheriff George Hunter MacThomas Thoms, Sheriff and Vice-Admiral of Orkney and Zetland and Sheriff of Caithness, Orkney and Shetland 1870–1899. His outstandingly generous legacy enabled the restoration of the Cathedral between 1913 and 1930.

the stone infilling of the arches beneath it, which were to form a background to the furniture, was somewhat poor. Dr Cursiter decided to clothe the wall with a suitable material, and to set against that—one in each arch—figures of the three men most concerned in the foundation of the cathedral. These were St Rognvald himself; his father Kol, who had most to do with the planning and superintendence of the building; and Bishop William the Old, Orkney's first resident bishop, who transferred the relics of St Magnus to Kirkwall.

Now came Reynold Eunson's most demanding assignment. Once again Dr Cursiter brought designs, but Mr Eunson had never before attempted to carve a figure, and could hardly believe that he could do so with success. The determination of the artist overcame the scruples of the craftsman. With Dr Cursiter within call to give advice and encouragement, Mr Eunson began the work. He was starting from scratch, and he taught himself to carve as he went along, mastering the technique of the three-quarter profile, the foreshortened arm. . . .

With patient work, over a period of three months, the figures were completed. They are now in their arches in the St Rognvald Chapel—Kol with scroll and plumbline; Rognvald, the central figure, with a model of his cathedral; Bishop William with his right hand raised in blessing.

To these furnishings have been added a gilded cross, an alms-dish representing a Viking longship (carved from mahogany by Dr Cursiter), and pulpit and lectern falls, knitted in a Fair Isle design by Miss Elsie Linklater, of Stromness. Other items will follow, for the enrichment of the chapel is a long-term project. But each item will be made in Orkney and will have some strong local tradition.[1]

For a proper understanding of what the cathedral, along with the new chapel, means to Orkney some account is needed of the events which led to its foundation. The central figure here is Magnus Erlendson, joint earl of the Isles with his cousin Hakon in the early years of the twelfth century.

'Saint Magnus[2] the isle earl,' says *The Orkneyinga Saga*, 'was the most peerless of men, tall of growth, manly, and lively of look, virtuous in his ways, fortunate in fight, a sage in wit, ready-tongued and lordly-minded . . . quick of counsel and more beloved of his friends than any man.'

When the cousins had ruled the Isles, more or less amicably, for nearly a

---

1. Subsequent embellishments are a prayer desk gifted anonymously and made by Reynold Eunson; three hand-carved oak chairs also made by Reynold Eunson and gifted by Mrs Dora Barclay, widow of Rev. William Barclay, MA, FSA Scot, Minister of the Cathedral 1919-1936; and presented by Mrs M. B. Gorie, Kirkwall, two silk book markers with locally made silver gilt medallions which are replicas of the figures of Magnus and Rognvald incorporated on the Provost's chain.
2. See also article 'St Magnus', p.389.

decade, dissension crept in. Hakon was imperious and a warrior, while Magnus had shown himself a pacifist, and was by nature an ascetic. But Magnus, who was probably everything a true Viking detested, had nevertheless a popularity which irked Hakon. Bad men fanned the flames; good men tried to get them together to settle their differences.

A meeting was arranged at Eastertide, probably in the year 1117, on a little island called Egilsay. Each earl was to have two warships and a stated number of men. Magnus kept his promise; Hakon, surrounded by unscrupulous advisers, broke the agreement and increased his force four times. With Magnus at their mercy, the malcontents refused to have any compromise, and forced Hakon to have him slain.

On the bleak moor Magnus knelt among his enemies, and prayed for them. In the words of *The Orkneyinga Saga* he was 'as blithe as if he had been bidden to a feast.' He crossed himself and bowed himself to the stroke. 'He was struck in the middle of the head with a single blow, and so passed from the world to God.'

Odd things began to happen. 'The spot before was moss-grown and stony; but shortly after, the worth of Earl Magnus shone so bright before God that there grew green sward where he was slain.' To a little island off the coast of Birsay, where his grandfather Thorfinn the Mighty had built a church, Magnus's body was taken. 'A heavenly light was often seen to shine over his grave . . . men who were sick made pilgrimages—both from the Orkneys and Shetland—and they kept their vigil at the grave of Saint Magnus the Earl, and were cured of [all] their diseases.' The tales of miracles multiplied.

Hakon lived for another six years. He sought absolution from the Pope, and ruled humanely. But it was unsafe to mention the miracles while Hakon was alive. Bishop William, a masterful but cautious prelate, would not give them credence. He continued to deplore them when Paul, Hakon's son, became earl. But eventually popular opinion became too strong. A man had a vision in which St Magnus told him that he wanted to be taken to Kirkwall. Despite Earl Paul's displeasure, Bishop William felt he must obey, and a great procession bearing the saint's relics wound its way across the moors to the town on the bay.

If the bishop had one ear open to devout believers in Magnus in the Isles (by whose blazing piety he may have had his own imagination kindled), he may also have heard with the other ear strong voices out of Norway, where Magnus's nephew Rognvald was claiming his share of the island earldom. Rognvald, an athlete and poet, was, says the saga, 'a promising man of medium height, well-made, clean-limbed like the best of men, and with light chestnut hair . . . the most popular of men, and one of the most accomplished of his time.' If Bishop William hoped to reach an accommodation with this gifted

North Aisle of St Magnus Cathedral, 1885
The wooden steps which led to the Town Council gallery were built
about 1850 and removed in the early 1920s.
Arthur Melville, RWS, RSW, RP, 1855-1904

and romantic young man, he did well to give due honour to his sainted uncle.

Rognvald's first expedition against Orkney was the most ludicrous fiasco. Earl Paul surprised him in Shetland and captured his whole fleet. Rognvald returned to Norway dispirited and humiliated. But now his father Kol, a man of the most practical sagacity, put heart into him. He gathered fresh equipment and new ships. Then, mindful of Orkney feelings, and perhaps of the aspirations of Bishop William, he counselled his son to make a vow 'to have a church of stone built in Kirkwall in the Orkneys, when thou gainest that realm, so that there be not a more magnificent in the land; and let it be dedicated to Saint Magnus the Earl thy kinsman. And let it be endowed so that the foundation may increase and that to it may be brought his relics and with them the Episcopal seat.' This vow Rognvald made with due solemnity.

The new fleet made its base in Shetland. Meanwhile, Kol first contrived to have the beacon on Fair Isle lighted prematurely, causing great alarm in Orkney; then, when he was ready to sail, he had it drenched with water so that it could not give warning. So Rognvald landed unexpectedly in Orkney, and Bishop William arranged a truce between him and Paul. While Paul was in Rousay otter-hunting, so that he could meditate on what action to take, his companions were slain and he disappeared. He had been seized and carried hurriedly to Scotland.[1] A new figure, Sweyn Asleifson, destined to become one of the last and greatest of the Orkney Vikings, had taken a hand in the game.[2]

Now was the time for Rognvald to honour his vow. With the help of Kol, he did so magnificently. A ground plan was marked out, builders were gathered, and a glorious church of red sandstone began to grow beside the bay in the little hamlet of Kirkwall—'a burning flower in the astonished North.'

The three great men—Kol, Rognvald and William—worked together with one mind, and before they died a great part of the building was erected. Bishop William, full of admiration for those qualities in Rognvald which led later to his canonisation, loved him like a son, accompanied him on his stirring voyage to the Holy Land, which it must be said included some piracy. They sailed home up the Adriatic to Apulia where they procured horses, and rode first to Rome and then across Europe to Denmark.[3] The bishop outlived

1. He was taken to Athole and it was said that he had voluntarily gone into a cloister. He never returned to Orkney and was probably murdered.
2. He captured Dublin in 1171 but was subsequently ambushed and killed outside the town during negotiations for a ransom. Annually he wintered on Gairsay where he was said to have kept eighty men, and where he had a large drinking hall. Sweyn was known as 'The Ultimate Viking'.
3. Their absence of three years included a stay for several months at Constantinople where they enjoyed the delights of the capital of the Eastern Roman Empire.

the earl by ten years: his episcopate went back beyond the martyrdom of Magnus and it lasted for sixty-six years.

Now at last, in the Cathedral of St Magnus, the three friends are fittingly remembered.

6

The curious history of the Big Tree

The fact that Kirkwall's Big Tree has been given a notional life of only five years,[1] and that arrangements are being made to plant a new tree in its place, has renewed speculation about the history of this famous sycamore.

Its age must continue to be a matter of inference, but it seems that by putting together all the facts that can be found, some interesting deductions may be made. The principal deduction is that the Big Tree could be over 160 years old.

Perhaps the first thing that an amateur detective, investigating the case of the Big Tree, should do is to discover what early writers on Kirkwall had to say about the town's trees. Trees were so scarce here at one time that any of normal growth tended to be regarded as rarities. We can go right back to the Rev. James Wallace, who knew Kirkwall intimately in the latter part of the seventeenth century. In his *A Description of the Isles of Orkney* he wrote: 'There is no Forest or Wood in all this Country, nor any Trees, except some that are in the Bishop's Garden at *Kirkwal*, where are some Ashes and thorn and Plum-Trees. . . .'[2]

Trees were just as rare in Kirkwall a century later; for in 1774 the naturalist George Low observed, apart from some wall fruit trees which 'produce but ordinary apples . . . a few Ashes in the Palace garden, but they are crooked and much deformed by knots, which renders the wood good for nothing.'[3] Twenty years afterwards, the Rev. George Barry declared in his statistical account of the town: 'There are almost no trees in all this country, if we except a few fruit trees in Kirkwall.'[4] A trained observer, John Shirreff, echoed this in 1814.

   1. This article appeared in *The Orcadian* of 18 November 1965. In October 1987 the tree was pollarded in an effort to extend its life.
   2. 1693 edition, p.19.
   3. *A Tour through the Islands of Orkney and Schetland*, published in 1879, p.59.
   4. *The Statistical Account of Scotland 1791-1799*, Vol. XIX, Orkney and Shetland, section on Kirkwall and St Ola, p.47.

Thus we have unanimous testimony that before the nineteenth century there were no trees worthy of the dignity of the name in Kirkwall. But this is not to say that some of the trees which later flourished in the town were not planted before, or soon after, 1800. In 1836 the Rev. C. Lessingham Smith found at Macdonald's Inn at Kirkwall 'a capital garden, in which there are actually several green trees, a sort of sight it does one good to look on.'[1] The Kirkwall trees were much more noticeable in the late 1850s. Then (said the poet Tennyson's brother-in-law, Charles Weld) 'Small courtyards shaded by trees—actual trees, thick with leaves—stood between some houses and the street.'[2]

Daniel Gorrie, an editor of *The Orkney Herald*, published a book entitled *Summers and Winters in the Orkneys* in 1865. In it he said: '. . . in the very heart of the ancient burgh three stately trees, that seem to have wandered from some southern woodland, spread their benignant shadow across the street.'[3]

Here, surely, we come at last to the Big Tree, with its two equally stately neighbours, which stood in a garden in Albert Street until, presumably, the 1870s. Around them was a wall which was, at one end at least, over eighteen feet high. The long house which these trees so effectively screened still stands, not very much altered. Built between 1665 and 1676, it had several owners, but was sold eventually to a merchant named Robert Laing. In this house was born in 1762 one of Kirkwall's most notable sons, Malcolm Laing the historian.

Is it possible that this same Malcolm Laing planted the Big Tree? He often stayed in Albert Street until the year 1805, when, on the death of his father, he sold it to Sheriff Nicolson. What are the inherent possibilities? We know that Malcolm Laing was a keen gardener. When Sir Walter Scott visited him at Papdale in 1814 he found that Laing had made one or two attempts at trees, and that he was so interested in his peas that he had brought a quantity of brushwood two hundred miles from Aberbrothwick to support them. Did his interest in gardening and tree-growing begin at Albert Street? There is the further interesting fact that among the imports into Orkney in 1803 were listed '16 Bundles of young trees'. Was the Big Tree included in one of those bundles?

Experts say that a sycamore lives from 150 to 250 years, and that it attains its full growth in about sixty years. The stately trees in Albert Street were almost certainly fully grown in the 1860s. This would make it possible that they were planted at the time when Malcolm Laing, during prolonged

---

1. *Excursions through the Highlands and Isles of Scotland in 1835 and 1836*, p.205.
2. *Two Months in the Highlands, Orcadia and Skye*, 1860, pp.166-167.
3. Ibid., p.15.

100 The Tolbooth, Kirkwall, built 1740, and demolished 1890, was used for Town Council meetings and Sheriff and Burgh Courts. It also served as prison, guard-house and masonic lodge.

101 St Magnus Cathedral, 1890

holidays in Kirkwall, was completing his *History of Scotland* or preparing a second edition, and seeking in gardening some diversion from his sedentary labours.

When Malcolm Laing sold the Albert Street house it became (after Sheriff Nicolson) the property of the Baikies of Tankerness and, following them, the Heddles of Melsetter. One of the latter, John Heddle, sold it to the Kirkwall chemist Thomas Sclater.

It was with Thomas Sclater that the Big Tree's existence as a separate entity, and a solitary feature in a widened Albert Street, began. Mr Sclater had arranged to pay for the big house he had purchased in twenty annual instalments of £60 each. He had undoubtedly bought the property as a commercial speculation—it was easily divisible into what we would call flats, and it was set well back from the street. Mr Sclater decided to make use of the ground behind the garden wall in Albert Street in a remunerative way. The inference is that it was he who cut down the two tall trees beside the Big Tree which were directly in the way of his scheme; and it was certainly he who took down the garden wall and erected against the front, or street-side, of his house the row of lean-to one-storey shops.

It is doubtful if there now exists an account of Mr Sclater's transactions, or of the attitude of the townspeople, which may indeed have been indirectly responsible for the Big Tree being spared. That there was some trouble, in which the Town Council took a part, is suggested by the following remarkable letter, dated 30 January 1875, which Mr Sclater sent to the Town Clerk:

> Sir,
> To avoid litigation, and by way of compromise I hereby beg to offer to convey to the Town Council of Kirkwall my whole right and interest in and to the large Tree growing in front of my property in Albert Street for the sum of Five Pounds Sterling, the Council undertaking to keep it pruned on the side next my house so that the branches do not reach within six feet of the wall or roof.
> THOS H. SCLATER.

At a meeting on 3 February 'the arrangement come to with Mr T. H. Sclater for the preservation of the large Tree in front of his premises in Albert Street was reported,' and the Treasurer was authorised to send him his five pounds. The Works Committee was instructed to have the tree properly pruned and protected.

There the record ceases for a while. But the Big Tree, standing serenely in the middle of the street, with carts, bicycles and pedestrians passing and re-passing under its shady branches, became famous far beyond Kirkwall.

The Rev. Mr Whyte told an audience in the south that he had been where 'one tree is called a forest'. The rather feeble joke was invented that the tree was taken in each night and set out again in the morning. A lecturer on Orkney said solemnly that, for the benefit of Orcadians who had never seen one and might fail to identify it, a notice was attached to the venerable sycamore on which was printed, THIS IS A TREE.[1] Local wags declared that in 1883 Gladstone cast reflective eyes on the Big Tree.[2] Native Kirkwallians professed to be able to tell a stranger to the town because he passed the tree on the inside (between the tree and the shops) whereas townspeople, used to skirting the garden wall, passed it on the outside. So the legend grew.

A long time ago the Big Tree showed the first signs of decay. Fifty-five years since, in August 1910, Dr Bell told Kirkwall gardeners that unless something was done to preserve it the Big Tree would soon decay and have to be cut down. It apparently had no railing. Damage was done by merchants who piled their empty boxes against the trunk and used it as a lean-to for their barrows. Dr Bell's voice was a powerful one in Kirkwall, so a special meeting of the Town Council was convened to discuss the tree's condition. Inevitably, a committee was appointed to take any necessary steps. Like so many committees before and since, this one proved adept at putting off a decision. Two years, and more, passed without anything having been done; probably because no-one had any idea of what to do with an ailing tree. All that was decided eventually was to erect a railing. The growth of decay gradually became more apparent, but the Big Tree, hardy specimen that it is, has been an 'unconscionable time a-dying'. More than half a century.

For generations it has been an inspiration to Orcadians, so it is not strange that it has found its way into our local literature. Duncan J. Robertson, who passed it every day on his way to his office, celebrated it in a poem, 'To a Street Sycamore', in the course of which he wrote:

> Here in the narrow street you stand,
> Built round about on every hand;
> Only your topmost boughs can spy
> The blue waves breaking on the land . . .
>
> To you with each returning Spring
> The crows their clumsy courtship bring,
> And the blithe starlings come and go
> Among your boughs on restless wing.

---

1. Someone writing a postcard description of a visit to Kirkwall said that all ladies when passing the Big Tree shut their eyes and scratched their right ear. The gentlemen from the Provost down were said to lift their hats.
2. Gladstone had a tree-felling proclivity.

The Kirkwall poet David Horne wrote of it too, in one of the best and imaginative of his poems, which began:

> Auld sycamore, brucked[1] by the world's coorse naevs,[2]
> Gizzened[3] by summer suns, an' stiff wi' rheum
> That gnaws baith man an' tree ye mind the hour
> Th' relentless worms o' time can never cloom[4] . . .

Alas, the 'relentless worms o' time' have almost completed their victory; but the Big Tree, even when it disappears, will be a legend in Kirkwall, which its successor, perhaps by its lack of stature, will help to perpetuate. A phrase which one can imagine rising constantly to the lips of Kirkwall's ancients in far-distant days may be, 'Ah, but you should have seen the Big Tree.'

1. Damaged or bruised.
2. Rough fists.
3. Parched.
4. Devour.

Bibliography

Anderson, Joseph, *The Orkneyinga Saga*, London, 1873.
Asbjornsen, P. Chr., *Norsk Huldre-Eventyr og Folkesagn*.
Barclay, Dr John, Remarks on some parts of the Animal that was cast ashore on the Island of Stronsa, September 1808. Wernerian Natural History Society of Edinburgh, XIX.
Ben, Jo., 'Descriptio Insularum Orchadiarum', in Barry's *The History of the Orkney Islands*, 1805.
Blackie, John Stuart, *Lays of the Highlands and Islands*, London, 1873.
Blix, Dagmar, *Draugen Skreik*, Norsk Folkeminnelags Skrifter 93, Universitetsforlaget Oslo, 1965.
Brand, J., *A Brief Description of Orkney, Zetland, Pightland-Firth and Caithness*, Edinburgh, 1701.
Brøgger, A. W., *Ancient Emigrants, A History of the Norse Settlements of Scotland*, Oxford, 1929.
Brown, James, DD, *The Life of a Scottish Probationer*, Glasgow, 1908.
Calder, J. T., *History of Caithness*, 1861.
Craven, Rev. J. B., DD, *A History of the Episcopal Church in the Diocese of Caithness*, Kirkwall, 1908.
Daiken, Leslie, *Children's Games throughout the Year*, Batsford, 1949.
Dasent, Sir G. W., DCL, Icelandic Sagas, Vol. IV, *The Saga of Hacon* and a fragment of the Saga of Magnus with appendices, London, 1894.
— Icelandic Sagas, Vol. III, *The Orkneyingers' Saga*, London, 1894.
Defoe, Daniel, *An Account of the Conduct and Proceedings of the Pirate Gow*, London, ND.
Dennison, Walter Traill, *Orkney Folklore and Traditions*, Kirkwall, 1961.
— *Orkney Weddings and Wedding Customs*, Kirkwall, 1905.
Douglas, Norman, *London Street Games*, Chatto & Windus, 1931.
Edmondston, Arthur, MD, *A View of the Ancient and Present State of the Zetland Islands*, 1809.
Emerson, J., *The Character of Orkney*, from a Volume of Miscellaneous MS Poems in the Library of the Faculty of Advocates, marked Jac. 5.7.26, small 4to, originally described as *Poetical Descriptions of Orkney MDCLII*.
Eunson, G., *The Ancient and Present State of Orkney*, 1788.
Fea, James, *Considerations on the Fisheries in the Scotch Islands*, 1787.
Fereday, R. P., *The Longhope Battery and Towers*, Stromness, 1971.
— *The Orkney Balfours, 1747-99*, Oxford, 1990.
Firth, John, *Reminiscences of an Orkney Parish*, Stromness, 1920.
Goodfellow, Rev. Alexander, *Rev. John Gerard, Centenary of His Ministry in South Ronaldshay*.
Gorrie, Daniel, *Summers and Winters in The Orkneys*, London, 1868.
Grant, Dr Isabel F., *Highland Folk Ways*, London, 1961.
Hamer, Douglas, MC, MA, ed., *The Works of Sir David Lindsay*, Volume I, 1931.
Hibbert, Samuel, MD, FRSE, *A Description of the Shetland Islands*, Edinburgh, 1822.
Holbourn, Prof. Ian B. Stoughton, *The Isle of Foula*, Lerwick, 1938.
Hollinshead, Raphael, *The Scottish Chronicle, or a Complete History and Description of Scotland*, Volume I, Arbroath, 1805.
Horne, David, *Under Orcadian Skies*, Kirkwall, ND.
Hossack, B. H., *Kirkwall in the Orkneys*, Kirkwall, 1900.
Johnston, Alfred W. and Johnston Amy, ed., *Old Lore Miscellany of Orkney, Shetland, Caithness and Sutherland*, Vols II-VII, Coventry and London, 1909-1914.

Ker's Naval Log, 1778-1782, National Library of Scotland, MS 1083.
Leask, J. T. Smith, *A Peculiar People and Other Orkney Tales*, Kirkwall, 1931.
Low, Rev. George, *Tour Through the North Isles and part of the Mainland of Orkney in the year 1774*, London, 1915.
McCormick, Donald, *The Mystery of Lord Kitchener's Death*, London, 1959.
Mackay, John D., unpublished paper on 'Social and Economic Conditions in Papa Westray during the Nineteenth Century.'
MacKinlay, James M., *Folklore of Scottish Lochs and Springs*, Glasgow, 1893.
McPherson, J. M., *Primitive Beliefs in the North-East of Scotland*, London, 1929.
MacWhirter, A., FSA (Scot.), *Orkney and the Good Templar Centenary*, printed in *The Orkney Herald*, 17, 24 and 31 July 1951.
Martin, M., *A Description of the Western Islands of Scotland*, London, 1703.
Mitchell, Sir Arthur, KCB and Clark, James Toshach, *A Description of the Orcadian Islands by me Jo. Ben, living there, in the year 1529*. A translation from the Latin Manuscript in Barry's *History of Orkney*, pp.433-434, and contained in *Geographical collections relating to Scotland made by Walter Macfarlane*. Vol. III, Edinburgh, 1908.
Marwick, Ernest W., *An Anthology of Orkney Verse*, Kirkwall, 1949.
Marwick, George, *The Old Roman Plough*, a discussion paper read at Dounby, Sandwick on 8 October 1903.
Marwick, Hugh, *Proceedings of The Orkney Antiquarian Society*, Vol. V, 1926-1927.
Mowat, John, *John o' Groats, The House and its Story*, 1930.
MS James 43**, fol.3, Bodleian Library, Oxford.
Nicolson, James R., *Shetland Folklore*, London, 1981.
Omond, James, *Orkney Eighty Years Ago*, Kirkwall, 1980 (reprinted from *The Orcadian*, 8 April and 19 May 1911).
Opie, Iona and Peter, *The Language and Lore of School-Children*, Oxford University Press, 1959.
Pennant, Thomas, *Arctic Zoology*, Vol. I, London, 1784.
Phillips, W. C. (late Chief Shipwright, RN), *The Loss of HMS Hampshire and the Death of Lord Kitchener by A Survivor*, London, ND.
Pitcairn, Robert, *Criminal Trials (Scotland), 1488-1624*, 3 Vols, Edinburgh, 1833.
Priestley, J. B., *Man and Time*, Aldis Books, London, 1964.
Robertson, Duncan J., *Waith and Wrack*, London, 1918.
— *Proceedings of The Orkney Antiquarian Society*, Vol. II, 1923-1924.
Robertson, George S., *History of Stromness*, 1900-1972.
Robertson, John D. M., *Uppies and Doonies*, Aberdeen University Press, 1967.
Robertson, M., ed., *The Collected Poems of Vagaland*, Lerwick, 1975.
Robertson, R. A., *Laeves fae Vagaland*, Lerwick, 1952.
Ruge, Friedrich, *Scapa Flow 1919: The End of the German Fleet*, 1969, English edition, 1973.
Scott, Mary A., *Island Saga: The Story of North Ronaldsay*, Aberdeen, ND.
Scott, Sir Walter, *Northern Lights or a voyage in the lighthouse yacht to Nova Zembla and the Lord knows where in the summer of 1814*.
— *The Pirate*, London, 1903.
Shearer, John et al., *The New Orkney Book*, London, 1966.
Shirreff, John, *General View of the Agriculture of the Orkney Islands*, Edinburgh, 1814.
Sinclair, Sir John, Parish of Canisbay, *The Statistical Account of Scotland*, Volume eighth, 1793.
Smith, Rev. C. Lessingham, MA, *Excursions through the Highlands and Isles of Scotland in 1835 and 1836*, London, 1837.
Spence, John, *Daybook, 1884-1906*.
Stromness News, 18 April 1884.
Sutherland, Elizabeth, Marchioness of Stafford and Countess of, *View in Orkney and on the North-Eastern Coast of Scotland*, 1807.
Taylor, Alexander Burt, *The Orkneyinga Saga*, London, 1938.
Thomas, Lieut. Fred William Leopold, *Account of some of the Celtic Antiquities of Orkney*, Archaeologia, Vol. xxxiv, London, 1851.

Torfaeus, Thormodus, *Ancient History of Orkney, Caithness and the North*, translated by the late Rev. Alexander Pope, 1866.
Tudor, John R., *The Orkneys and Shetland*, London, 1883.
Turville-Petre, E. O. G., *Myth and Religion of the North*, London, 1964.
Visted, Kristofer, *Vor gamle bondekultur*, Kristiania, 1923.
von Reuter, Vice-Admiral Ludwig, *Scapa Flow: the account of the greatest scuttling of all time*, London, 1940.
Wallace, James, *A Description of the Isles of Orkney*, Edinburgh, 1693.
Weld, Charles Richard, *Two Months in the Highlands, Orcadia and Skye*, London, 1860.
West, John F., edited and annotated *The Journals of the Stanley Expedition to the Faroe Islands and Iceland in 1789*, Vol. I, Introduction and Diary of James Wright (Føroya Frooskaparfelig, Torshavn, Faroe Islands, 1970).
Wilson, James D. and Mooney, John, *The Deerness Mermaid*, Kirkwall, 1894.

Glossary

Aak:	Common guillemot.
Ale-kirn:	A container for brewing ale.
Airt:	Direction.
Aits:	Oats.
Ale-y Scones:	See Whey Scones.
Ammery:	Or Amery. A cupboard. Also Almery, Aumry and Aumbry.
Ava:	At all.
Ayre:	Or Aire. A shingle beach, usually separating the open sea from a lagoon and with the sea ebbing and flowing through an opening at one end.
Ba':	The traditional street game played on Christmas Day and New Year's Day between Up-the-Gates or Uppies and Down-the-Gates or Doonies.
Back:	A low isolated wall inside a house against which the peat fire was built.
Back-feast:	Entertainment given by the best man after a wedding.
Baenie:	Or Baenibider. A Dog. (Fisherman's term.)
Baldung:	A turbot. (Fisherman's term.)
Baneschaw:	Or Beanschaw. Sciatica.
Barm:	Yeast.
Batchie:	A card game.
Beesmilk:	The first milk given by a cow after calving.
Beltane:	The first day of May, old style Julian calendar. This was thirteen days later than the new style Gregorian calendar. The calendar was reformed in 1752.
Ben:	The best room or parlour; the inner part of a house.
Bere:	Barley, specifically four- or six-row, hardier and coarser than ordinary two-row barley.
Bere bannocks:	Thick, round scones made from Orkney barley.
Beul:	A stall.
Beyou:	An old-fashioned Orkney scythe mainly used for cutting meadow hay.
Biggin:	Building or dwelling,
Bikko:	A straw dog, usually made from the last of the harvest.
Bink:	A flagstone used for a bench and supported by several other flagstones set on edge; a dresser.
Birtick:	A fire. (Fisherman's term.)
Blaan fish:	Fish partly dried by exposure to wind and sun.
Bland:	A drink made from buttermilk and boiling water.
Blathic:	New buttermilk, or thin watery buttermilk. Also Blathew.
Blidemaet:	Food and drink offered to visitors after the birth of a child.
Blown milk:	Warm cow's milk with a little rennet added to make it curdle. The mixture was then 'switched' with a home-made instrument consisting of a rounded stick with a wheel at the end and a series of spokes. Cow-hair was fixed to the spokes and the stick rotated between the palms until the milk was sufficiently 'blown' or aerated.
Bog hay:	Hay made from marsh grass.
Bogle:	Or Bogie. A terrifying ghost or spectre.
Boneshaw:	Sciatica.
Bonnyhoose:	Seaman's taboo word for a church.
Bonnyman:	Seaman's taboo word for a clergyman.

Borrowing day:	3rd April, when anything given on loan could be regarded as a gift.
Bourwood:	An elder tree.
Bowman:	A farm servant, usually married, who lived in a cottage near the farmhouse.
Bram:	Oatmeal and milk (or buttermilk) eaten uncooked.
Brand-iron:	Gridiron.
Branks:	Also known as a scold's bridle, it consisted of an iron frame for the head with a metal gag to restrain the tongue.
Breeks:	Cod roe boiled and sliced. See also Kilts.
Breer:	The first shoots (of a crop).
Bridescog:	Drinking vessel used at Orkney weddings. Shaped like a small tub with two or three handles (horns) and usually made of alternate staves of light and dark wood, secured with hoops (girds) of wood or metal.
Brochan:	Thin oatmeal gruel.
Brose 'fae the lee side o' the broth pot':	The term used for a dish made with oatmeal and salt and a spoonful or two of the fat that boiled to one side of the pot when soup was being made.
Broust:	A brewing of ale.
Browsy:	Plump, well fed.
Bruck:	Refuse, rubbish.
Brucked:	Damaged or bruised.
Brudge:	To shred.
Buanhoos:	Or Banehoos. A church. (Fisherman's term.)
Buckies:	Whelks.
Buil:	Gather together and enclose for the night; also an enclosure.
Buird:	Sturdy.
Buit:	Boot.
Bummie:	A wooden bowl.
Burd:	Progeny, the young of animals.
Burstin:	Bere dried in a pot until brown, then ground in a quern. It was mixed with buttermilk and supped with a spoon.
But:	The kitchen or outer part of a house.
Bygg:	Bere.
Caisie:	Or Kaizie. A carrying basket made of straw.
Carvey biscuit:	A hard, ship's biscuit with carvey (caraway) seeds baked into it, and containing salt but not sugar.
Cashielawes:	An iron framework which encircled the leg, and was then placed in a moveable furnace.
Ceutikin:	Stockings without feet.
Chalder:	An obsolete measure of capacity. In Scotland a chalder of corn was sixteen bolls.
Chaumer:	One-bedroomed sleeping accommodation.
Chield:	Also Chiel. Child.
Chizzen-maet:	A present of food brought secretly to a mother the day after childbirth by the women who attended the delivery.
Claith:	Cloth.
Clapshot:	Turnips and potatoes boiled in a pot and then mashed together.
Clivan:	Tongs. (Fisherman's term.)
Clive:	Or Clivvie. A cleft or fissure.
Cloom:	Devour.
Cloot:	Or Clout. A cloth.
Clour:	A blow.
Cog:	A wooden container made of staves.
Cole:	Haycock.
Coo-shell:	The larger white bi-valve shell. The Iceland Cyprina.
Cooter-neb:	Razorbill.

Couple-back:	Cross-beam.
Creepie:	A small stool, usually made of straw.
Crossways:	Across the body.
Cruisie:	Or Kruisie. Open, boat-shaped lamp with a reed wick, using fish oil (melted livers) or whale oil. Also known as a Koly.
Cubbie:	A straw basket.
Cuithes:	Saithe or coal-fish.
Curch:	A woman's cap.
Curl-doddy:	Clover head.
Cutty:	A very thick oatmeal bannock, frequently baked on hot embers.
Cutty pipe:	A short, stumpy clay pipe.
Cutty spoon:	A short-handled spoon, usually of horn.
Dagon:	A large piece of anything edible, especially a large piece of cheese.
Daich:	Oatmeal and water mixed to form a stiff dough. Sometimes called rolly-o-daich when it was rolled into a ball.
Damp:	A rope's end. (Fisherman's term.)
Darrow:	A large slice or lump.
Dead man's sting:	The meaning is uncertain. The treatment suggests that the trouble was abdominal, e.g. gall or kidney-stones, appendicitis, colic or the like. The words may perhaps indicate pleurisy or any malady producing a severe stabbing pain, where *sting* might derive from O.N. *stingi*, Icelandic and Faeroese *stingur*, a stitch or sudden pain in the side. The term may be a synonym for the phrase *deadman's nip* in Shetland or *deadman's pinches* in Ulster, applied to a skin eruption or ulcer of unknown origin, ascribed to the trows.
Denty:	Also Dainty. Remarkable, esteemed.
Dian-stane:	Also Darrow-stane. A thin, round disc of stone with a hole near one edge, attached to the beam of the old-fashioned, single-stilted Orkney plough. It was a sun symbol and used to promote fertility and induce the sun's influence into the open furrow. When at sea the crofter hung it round his neck.
Domiless:	Listless.
Down-the-Gates:	Also Doonies. Those who play down-street in the traditional Ba' game played over the streets of Kirkwall on Christmas and New Years' Days. Old Norse: *gata*, a road.
Dwaam:	Daydream; a faint.
Ebb-maet:	Shell fish such as whelks and limpets gathered from the rocks at low tide.
Eekname:	Nickname mainly used in Stronsay. See also teu-name.
Eggalourie:	Eggs and milk boiled together.
Erison:	A short prayer for help.
Faa:	The heart, lungs and other internal organs of a slaughtered animal.
Fael:	A sod or turf.
Faigr:	The sun. (Fisherman's term.)
Falls:	Collars, usually with more than one layer.
Farr:	A boat. (Fisherman's term.)
Finnie:	A fire. (Fisherman's term.)
Fissies:	Chilblains.
Fisting:	Chimney crook. (Fisherman's term.)
Fitless cock:	The remains of stuffing, made into a dumpling and boiled in a pot of soup, but often specially made to take the place of meat.
Fitting:	A cat. (Fisherman's term.)
Flackie:	A straw mat.
Flail:	A staff hinged to a handle by leather and used for beating out grain.
Flaymeur:	See Yarpha-peat.
Fleep:	Turn inside out, peel.

Flesh meat:	Animal meat, as opposed to fish or 'ebb meat' (shellfish).
Foal:	A small bannock.
Foirbitten:	Charmed.
Foodin:	A cat. (Fisherman's term.)
Forspoken:	Bewitched.
Freuteries:	Also Frooterys—superstitious beliefs, notions or customs.
Funa:	A fire. (Fisherman's term.)
Gaa:	Also Gall. A sore.
Gad:	Also Gaad. A rod or pointed stick.
Gadman:	A person who used a stick to direct animals.
Gairy:	Greedy, covetous, parsimonious.
Gant:	To yawn.
Garry-skons:	A sticky pancake or crumpet.
Geyly:	Well.
Gey siccar:	Very strong.
Gird:	A hoop.
Girnel:	A meal chest.
Gissing:	Childbed.
Gizzened:	Parched.
Glaary-kleppo:	A sticky, ill-cooked bere bannock.
Glaid:	A kite.
Gleeds:	Live coals.
Glomer:	To grope.
Gloondie:	Glutton.
Gloup:	A cave which has collapsed at the inner end making the sea visible from above.
Glouricks:	Eyes. (Fisherman's term.)
Gloy:	The straw of oats from which the grain has been removed.
Glunt:	To swallow food ravenously, and without chewing it.
Goaking day:	April Fools Day, 1 April.
Graith:	Urine.
Grimmelins:	Twilight.
Grind:	A gate.
Groat:	A coin of small value.
Grunkies:	Pigs.
Guidwife:	The mistress of a house.
Gundy:	Toffee.
Gundyman:	Toffee seller.
Hadd:	Shelter.
Hairst:	Harvest.
Hallan:	Area of cross-bars below the roof used by hens for roosting.
Hallowmas:	The first day of November.
Hamefare:	A feast held to celebrate a move into a new house.
Hammars:	A mass of stone, or a crag, jutting out of the face of a hill or slope.
Hanlicks:	Mittens. (Fisherman's term.)
Hansel:	A refreshment of bread and cheese offered to the guests at a wedding as they returned from the wedding walk, and before they entered the wedding house.
Hansel-bairn:	The youngest child in the district who was present at a wedding.
Hansel-wife:	An elderly, respected woman who handed out refreshments immediately after a marriage ceremony.
Harled:	Roughcast.
Hart cake:	Cardialgia: pain or discomfort from the heart.
Heaters:	Wedge-shaped buns usually baked in rings of eight. Sugared and glazed on top, these sections resembled the cast iron inserts, or *heaters*, used in laundering irons and by tailors.

GLOSSARY

Heather cowe:	Stalk of heather.
Heckla:	A dog-fish. (Fisherman's term.)
Hemma:	A wife. (Fisherman's term.)
Herdie boy:	A lad employed in summer-time to control stock and in particular to keep animals on grazing and off unfenced cultivated land and crops. Girls were similarly employed.
Heuk:	A sickle, a hook.
Hollands:	A grain spirit manufactured in Holland.
Holy night:	Christmas Eve.
Howe:	A hillock or mound.
Hoydeen:	A minister. (Fisherman's term.)
Ill-wad:	Ill-will.
Jogges:	An instrument of public punishment consisting of a hinged iron collar attached by a chain to a wall or post and locked round the offender's neck.
Johnsmas:	Midsummer.
Kail:	Cabbage.
Kail breu:	The water in which cabbage is boiled, left to cool and drunk as a thirst quencher.
Keedin:	A cheek. (Fisherman's term.)
Kemping:	A competition or contest. When cutting corn each man would have a woman partner and kemping took place to see which couple could complete the greatest amount of work which involved gathering, binding and stooking.
Kilts:	Cod roe. See also Breeks.
Kirking of Kirkwall Town Council:	Ceremonial attendance at St Magnus Cathedral of the incoming Council, normally on the first Sunday after its election.
Kirket:	To attend church on the first Sunday after an event, e.g., an election, marriage, etc.
Kirksucken:	Buried in the churchyard. (Fisherman's term.)
Kirn:	A churn or container.
Kirn-milk:	Buttermilk.
Kirser:	A cat. (Fisherman's term.)
Kishie:	Straw basket.
Kittly:	Tickly.
Klagum:	Pulled toffee. See also Gundy.
Kline:	To cover thickly, e.g., with butter.
Klineoo:	A buttered bannock given as a perquisite to the herd when a cow was served by the bull.
Klounk:	The noise made by swallowing a liquid hurriedly and in quantity.
Knockit corn:	Bere pounded in a large hollowed stone.
Knocking-stane:	A hollowed-out stone in which grain was pounded.
Koly:	See Cruisie.
Koy:	A bed. (Fisherman's term.)
Krackans:	Also Krackling. A dish made by melting suet, taking what remains after the tallow is extracted and cooking it in a pot with oatmeal.
Kraeno:	The common mussel.
Krang:	The flesh of a whale.
Krappin banno:	Cod livers kneaded into bere meal and boiled in a pot with fish.
Kunie:	A wife. (Fisherman's term.)
Kye-kail:	Cabbage suitable for cattle.
Lammas Market:	A centuries-old traditional event when cattle, horses, cloth (especially linen) and various other goods were traded, and cheap-jacks and showmen set up booths on the Kirk Green in front of St Magnus Cathedral. The fair at Lammas was one of three annual events authorised in the town's charter of 1486. At one time the market started on the first Tuesday in August and was restricted to three days. A more recent Lammas Market

of longer duration is recalled by the fact that within living memory the market opened on the first Tuesday after 11 August and finished on Saturday the following week, known as the 'hindmost Saturday'. The Lammas Market has been replaced almost entirely by the Orkney Agricultural Show.

Lang irons:	Fetters.
Leam:	Earthenware.
Leean:	Lying.
Leepid gibbo:	Scalded cat. The name also given to oatmeal mixed with hot buttermilk.
Liveren:	Flour or meal put into soup to thicken it.
Liver heids:	Cod heads and livers, boiled together with potatoes.
Liversoakie:	A gutted sillock filled with livers and roasted.
Loofsfull:	Handfuls.
Loose:	Louse.
Loup:	To leap.
Lowe:	Burn, glow.
Lowts:	Sour cream, ready for churning.
Lug:	An ear.
Lugged sheu:	Shoe with raised or extended sides.
Lum:	Chimney; hole in house roof for letting out smoke and for light and ventilation.
Maat:	Malt.
Matratla-stilhod:	A minister's house. (Fisherman's term.)
Mekillwort:	The plant belladonna or deadly nightshade.
Melder sillocks:	Sillocks dried on top of straw in a kiln.
Mert:	An animal killed in the fall of the year and salted down for household use over the winter.
Mettin:	A seed of grain.
Moo:	Mouth.
Mougelden:	Or Mudyelin. A small sillock rolled in meal and roasted, without being gutted.
Muckle supper:	The feast at the end of harvest for workers, friends and neighbours. Now succeeded by Harvest Home.
Mudveeties:	Swine. (Fisherman's term.)
Mullyos:	The gleanings after crop was cut and sheaves gathered. Also the name given to those who ensured that one farmer did not supplement his crop by purloining that of his neighbours.
Naevs:	Fists.
Napp:	Oatmeal and milk mixed to form a dough.
Neb:	Beak.
Neuk-bed:	Recessed bed of stone, built as an extension to the house.
Nip-a-doons:	Bere bread broken into a bowl of sweet milk and eaten like sops.
Nippin:	Freezing or smarting with cold.
Nogal:	A large piece, a chunk. Also Whuggal.
Norn:	The Norse dialect formerly spoken in Orkney.
Norwast:	North-West Canada.
Norwasters:	Orcadian labourers and tradesmen employed by the Hudson Bay Company. Held in high regard, these men made up three-quarters of the Company's employees at the end of the eighteenth century.
Noust:	A hollow or recess at the edge of a beach into which a boat is drawn up and secured.
Nugged ale:	Mulled ale.
Oot-by:	Outer room or scullery.
Orkneyinga Saga:	Probably written in Iceland in the early thirteenth century, the original title was *Jarla Sogur*, viz, the (Orkney) Earls' Sagas. The Saga is the history

GLOSSARY 479

of the earldom of Orkney from the end of the ninth to the early thirteenth century. It records oral traditions supplemented by skaldic songs concerning events which occurred in much earlier times.

Orra-house:	Shed where miscellaneous items were stored.
Owsen:	Oxen.
Partan:	An edible crab.
Pauntree:	A beam over the fire from which a pot, kettle or griddle was suspended.
Peedie:	Also Peerie. Small.
Peedie folk:	Fairies.
Peuchis:	Tripe.
Pight aits:	(Picts oats.) Wild oats, once common in Orkney.
Pilliewinks:	Or Pinny winkis. A thumb-screw.
Pirraina:	A girl. (Fisherman's term.)
Plack:	A sum of money.
Plankings:	A method of reallocating and dividing land into compact plots which swept away the old run-rig system. The usual Orkney plank was forty fathoms square: 6,400 square yards. From Old French *planche*, a measurement of land.
Plantikreus:	Walled enclosures used solely in the older Orkney economy for the raising of cabbage plants.
Plout kirn:	Butter churn.
Pochin:	Or Parochin. Parish.
Pock:	Also Poke. A bag or pouch, a small sack.
Prestingolva:	A minister. (Fisherman's term.)
Puling:	Sickly.
Purdo in a kloot:	Boiled pudding.
Purr:	Boiled salt herrings. Also Salt Purr.
Quern:	A hand-mill for grinding meal and malt.
Quey:	Also quaig, queyoo, quoy. A heifer; a young cow before she has had a calf.
Rae:	Roe-deer.
Ragger:	A seaman's taboo word for a knife.
Rame:	Cream.
Ran:	Herring roe.
Ranze:	The roe of a fish.
Rape:	Rope.
Rattan:	Rat.
Reddan:	Cleaning.
Reek:	Smoke; a dwelling-house with a fire burning in the hearth.
Reestid:	Also Reestit. Smoked.
Reestit mutton:	Smoked, dried mutton.
Rems:	Or Remmacks. Oars. (Fisherman's term.)
Restid fire:	Banked fire.
Rig:	Ridge, a plot of land or field.
Riggin:	The ridge of house roof.
Rime:	Hoar frost.
Ringrody:	Or Ringlody. A kettle. (Fisherman's term.)
Riv:	Dawn. (Fisherman's term.)
Rivlins:	Shoes made from untanned hide.
Rolly-o-daich:	See Daich.
Roset:	Resin.
Rost peedie:	Roasted sucking pig.
Rowed:	Wrapped.
Rumbly thump:	Potatoes and kail boiled together in one pot.
Runk:	An old woman. (Fisherman's term.)
Run-rig:	A communal system of land organisation with scattered, narrow strips of

	cultivated land shared among tenants, each getting a share of the good and the poor land. Run-rig holdings often became small, numerous and confused.
Saa:	Salve or ointment.
Saave:	The tops or blooms of heather or common ling.
Sae:	Water tub.
Sae-bink:	Flagstone on which buckets or tubs were set.
Saetro:	Counting-out rhyme.
Sain:	To make the sign of the cross.
Sargas:	An unpalatable mass of food.
Scabbit:	Scabbed.
Scads:	Hurts.
Scorrie:	Young gull.
Seal burd:	Seal pup.
Seggie-boat:	Toy boat made from an iris leaf.
Selkie:	Seal.
Sellar:	A bedroom leading off from the living room.
Sheun:	Shoes.
Shorn:	Curdled.
Sids:	Oats.
Sillock:	Young coal-fish.
Skirlies:	Fried onions or shallots, with oatmeal sprinkled over them.
Skrae:	A two-year-old coal fish split and dried.
Skroo:	Old Norse: *skrufr*, a corn rick.
Skunie:	A knife. (Fisherman's term.)
Slap:	A gate, usually in a field.
Sholtie:	The common top-shell.
Smurslin:	The truncated gaper-shell.
Sneck:	Latch.
Snoddy:	A very thick oatcake.
Snood:	Or sneud. A string or ribbon used especially by young, unmarried women for tying their hair.
Sooans:	Fine flour attached to the inner husk of oats.
Soolen:	The sun. (Fisherman's term.)
Soor-dook:	Buttermilk, or sometimes sour milk.
Sooros:	Green leaves of sorrel.
Soo-shell:	The truncated gaper-shell.
Soyndick:	Eye. (Fisherman's term.)
Spaeman:	Or Spaewife. A person with the gift of second sight; a fortune-teller.
Speun-cubbie:	A small straw basket for horn spoons.
Spleuchan:	Tobacco pouch made of seal skin.
Spooter piece:	Or Splootero. Bread on which liquid butter has been spread or splootered from the mouth.
Spoots:	Razor fish.
Sploot ebb:	A spring tide when the sea retreats and uncovers stretches of sand containing spoots.
Steidstane:	Foundation stone.
Steng:	A mast. (Fisherman's term.)
Steul:	A straw stool or chair. In their original state these were almost completely made of straw and were of three kinds: a low, backless stool; a low-backed stool; and a high-backed or hooded stool. They were the predecessor of the present Orkney chair.
Stoor:	Dust.
Stoup:	A wooden pail.
Strae:	Straw.
Straik:	To stroke.

GLOSSARY

Straikan graith:	Stale urine.
Suids:	Husks of oats.
Suntags:	Eyes. (Fisherman's term.)
Swack:	Active, lithe.
Swap-net:	A net with a triangular frame, mounted on the end of a long, thin bamboo pole. It was used for catching birds on cliffs.
Swats:	When suids (husks of oats) are steeped in water the sooans sink to the bottom of the jar and the liquid that is left is the swats.
Sweet bed:	Or Sweet haep. The heap of bere before it is sent to the grinding mill to be dried.
Sweetie-folls:	A sweet biscuit containing ginger and treacle and decorated on the top with sugared caraway seeds.
Swelkie:	A whirlpool in the Pentland Firth, particularly dangerous in certain states of the tide.
Sye:	To strain.
Sype:	To drain.
Taand:	A firebrand. (Fisherman's term.)
Tailing day:	2 April. The practice, almost now disappeared, of pinning a paper tail on an unsuspecting passer-by.
Taize:	Tease.
Tammy-norie:	Puffin.
Tattie-masher:	Potato masher.
Tatties and point:	Potatoes, especially new potatoes, dipped in butter.
Tattie shaws:	The stalks and leaves of potato plants.
Teeack:	Lapwing.
Teu-name:	Nickname. See also Eekname.
Tevrdin:	Thunder. (Fisherman's term.)
Thoomb piece:	Or Toomb piece. Bread which has been buttered using the thumb.
Three-taed pot:	Three-toed pot.
Throve:	Prospered.
Tirl:	The act of rotating, turning, twirling.
Tirlie:	Something whirled round, usually by wind.
Tizing:	Coaxing.
Toomal:	The best land in the toonship.
Toom piece:	See Thoomb piece.
Toonship:	An area of good, easily farmed land with a boundary wall of turf and stones separating it from the waste land outside.
Trilso:	Toddler.
Trow:	Also troll. A supernatural being or goblin; a mischievous fairy. There were hill trows or hill folk, and sea trows.
Trowy:	Sickly.
Trulla-scud:	A witch. (Fisherman's term.)
Tusk:	A ling-like fish of the cod family.
Twa-built hoose:	A long building consisting of two farm houses with their stables etc. built end-to-end.
Tyno:	A skewer or thin wire.
Tyno sillocks:	Sillocks dried hung on a thin wire until they were very dry and hard.
Up-the-Gates:	Also Uppies. Those who play up-street in the Traditional Ba' game on the streets of Kirkwall on Christmas and New Years' Days. Old Norse: *Gata*, a road.
Ungadrengur:	A young man. (Fisherman's term.)
Upstanda:	A minister. (Fisherman's term.)
Vamm:	To bewitch. (Fisherman's term.)
Venga:	A cat. (Fisherman's term.)
Voaler:	A cat. (Fisherman's term.)
Waand:	A bamboo pole.

Waar cowes:	Lengths of large, broad-leaved seaweed.
Wame:	Belly.
Ware:	Seaweed (the kind used as manure).
Wash cog:	A small wooden basin.
Weird of the Gods:	Ragnarok. The twilight of the gods; the doom or ultimate fate of the gods.
Wented milk:	Sour milk.
Whey scones:	Also Ale-y scones. Large pancakes baked of oatmeal soaked in cheese.
White money:	Silver.
Withershins:	Or Witherways. Doing anything against the sun's course.
Whuggal:	See Nogal.
Wonderways:	Anti-clockwise.
Wort:	The liquid at an early stage of brewing to which hops are added.
Wrest:	To sprain.
Wresting thread:	Or Wrestin treed. A home-spun thread of black wool which in order to cure a complaint was tied around a strained muscle or ligament and an appropriate incantation repeated.
Wummle:	An auger.
Yappie:	A hen. (Fisherman's term.)
Yarpha-peat:	Rough, fibrous peats. Also known as flaymeurs.
Yera:	An ear. (Fisherman's term.)
Yetlin:	An iron griddle.
Yink:	A lover. (Fisherman's term.)
Yirnings:	Part of the stomach of a calf salted, dried and soaked in water.
Yole:	A small, undecked, two-masted fishing boat.
Yunsie:	A hen. (Fisherman's term.)

Index

The numbers in italics give the pages facing the relevant illustrations.

Aaks, as food, 103, *164-5*, *172*
Adventure, wreck of, 62
Aff-shaering, 22
Agricultural improvements, 10, 11
Agricultural Society,
　South Ronaldshay, 136
　Stronsay, 9
Agricultural Society, Stronsay, 9
Aith's Bank, 335
Albion, wreck of, 62
Ale, 19, 191
　brewing, 103-5
　Yule, 128
Alexander II, King of Scotland, 392
Almanzora, 438
America, influence of, 82
Ammery, 96
Angel family, 401-2
An Anthology of Orkney Verse, xv
Archery, 182
Arcturus, wreck of, 63
Armada, Spanish, 401, 403
Askham, Captain, 39-40

Ba' Game, 129, 140, 180-2, *224-5*, *240*, *298*
Bacchante, HMS, 31
Back-feast, 105
Balfour, David, 53
Balfour Hospital, *173*
Balfour Mains, 22
Baltic, trading with, 7, 19
Banks, *Sir* Joseph, 310
Bannockburn, Battle of, 397
Bannocks,
　bere, 19, 106
　from last sheaf, 23
Barley, *See* Bere
Barry, Rev. George, 463
Batchie, 220
Beards, sailors, 33
Beatty, Admiral, 431-2
Bedded (harvested crop), 23
Beesmilk, 106
Bellerophon, 415-16
Beltane, 14, 139, 305
Beowulf, 334
Bere, 7, 19
Beuls, 95
Beyou, 21
Big Tree, *381*, 463-7

Bignold Park, 185
Bigswell, 304-5
Bikko, 22
Bink, 96
Birmingham, 33
Birsay, palace at, 26
Bisgeos, *288*
Bishop of Orkney, 449, 459-61
Bishop's Palace, 395, 398
Bismarck, 438
Blaan fish, 106
Blakeley's Well, 303
Bland, 106
Blathic, 106
Blidemaet, 106
Blown milk, 107
Boars of Duncansby, 60
Boats, launching, 34
Bog-hay, 231-2
Bonfires, 139-41
Book of the Black Art, 362-4
Book-shop experiences, 242-51
Bottles, messages in, 74-5
Boundary walls, 6
Boys' Ploughing Match, 134-6
Braga, 63
Bram, 107
Brand-iron, 107
Branks, 417
Breckness, 63, 65
Breeks, 107
Bridescake, 107, 120
Bridescog, 107, 121
Bridge of Brodgar, *433*
Broadcasting, xvi
Brochan, 108
Brose, 24, 108
Brough, 303-4
Brown, George Mackay, xv, xix
Brownstown well, 303
Bu, The, 9
Burgar's Bay, 205
Burray, 9, 129
Burstin, 108
Burwick, ferry to Huna, 56
Buses, 241, *388*
But and ben houses, 95-7
Bygg, 19

Cabbages, 26, 27

484 INDEX

Caithness, Earl of, 446
Caldale, 453
Calendars, Gregorian & Julian, 14
Calving, 13
Cameron, Richard, 410
Canada, xvi
  migrations to, 8
  trading, 81
Cargill, Donald, 410
Carmania II, wreck of, 69
Carvey biscuit, 108
Castle, Kirkwall, 446-7
Castle well, 447
Chair, Orkney, 85-7, 458
Chapel, Italian, 438-9, *449*, 453-6
Chaumer, 97
Childhoods, 214-15
Chiocchetti, Domenico, 438-9, 453-6
Chizzen-maet, 108
Churchill Barriers, 56, 61, *429*, 438, 453
Churchill, Winston, 429, 436
Circle of Loda, *309*
Civil List, xvii
Clapshot, 108
Clouston, David, 65
Clouston, J. Storer, 430
Coastguards, 63
Cod, fishing, 7
The Coffin, 32
Coffin, Nelson's, 414-15
Coffins, 83, 124
Collector of Stamp Duties, 38
Colville, Henry, 403-5
Commissioners of Supply, 11
Concerts, 186-7, 189-90, *269*
Cooter-nebs, as food, 103
Corrigall, as toonship name, 6
Costa Head, 68
Covens, 349
Craa'nest, *133*, *140*
Craftsmen, 81-4, *112-13*, *132*, 226
Creatures of Orkney Legend, ii
Creepies, 96
Cricket, 184-5
Crockness, Tower, 426
Croft houses, 95-7, *133*
Crofting, 11, 12, 95-7
Cromwell, Oliver, 27, 406-7
Crossikeld, 303
Cubbie Roo, 258-9
Cubbies, 96
Cuithes, 34, 109
Curling, 182
Currency, Scots, 20
Cursiter, Stanley, 90, 457-9
Cutty, 108

Dagon, 108
Daich, 108
Dale of Woodwick, 258
Darrow, 108
Davidson, Thomas, 50, 209-10
Day-books, 81-4
de Groot, John, 55
Deepdale, 287
Deerness, parish, 5
Deerness Mermaid, 285
Defoe, Daniel, 43
Dennison, Walter Traill, xvi, 261, 276-7, 318, 336, 341, 344-5
Description of the Isles of Orkney, 26
Devil, 349
Devil's hand, 17
Dialect, xviii
Dian-stane, 15
Din King, 283
Diss, 22
Doenitz, Commodore, 436
Dog-fish, 108
Dounby, 5
Dovrefjell, wreck of, 59
Down-the-Gates, 140, 180
Draughts, 145-6
Drinking, 191-3
Druids, *308*
Drummond, Robert, 411-12
Dulse, 109
Duncansby Head, 60, 61
Dundas, Lord, 9
Dwarfie Hammars, 265
Dwarfs, 265
Dwarmo, 265

Eagles, 297-8
Earl Sigurd, (ship), 54
Earl Thorfinn, SS, *44*, 54
Ebb maet, 109
Echna Loch, 258
Eday,
  calving, 13
  capture of John Gow, 42
Edda, 257
Edinburgh University, Honorary degree, xvii
Eels, 172
Egg industry, 11
Eggalourie, 109
Egilsay, 460
Elections, 211-13, *352*
Elf-arrows, 270
Elves, 268-72
'Englishes', 406-8
Entertainment, 186-8, *260-1*, *268-9*
Erison, 13
Erlendson, Magnus, 459
Erskine, Henry, 409-10
Ettan's Pow, 258
Eunson, George, 37-8, 192
Eunson, Reynold, 86-7, 458-9
'Everlasting Battle', 424, 439

Evie, xv
  introduction of scythes, 21
Evie Hills, 258
Evil eye, 364-5
Eynhallow, 91, 276-7, 305, 317-18, 336
Eynhallow Sound, 259

Faa, 109
Faely fights, 146
Fair Isle, 461
  trips to, 52-3
Fairies, 269-73, 279-81
Farming, 5-15, *16*, *17*
Fea, James, 42-3
Fea, Jennie, 100
Feeders, 237-8
Feu-duty, 10
Field sizes, 5
Fin Folk, 276
Finger-steen, 258
Finn Wife, 336
Finns, 334-7
Finstown, 5, *177*
Fish, in wells, 305-6
Fishing, 7, 9, *76*, *77*, *96*, *97*, *416*
Fitless cock, 109
Fitty Hill, 258
Flail, 7
Flett, J. G. S., 25
Flooding, Kirkwall, 411-12
Flotta, Grand Fleet at, 431
Flying Dutchmam, 31
Foal, 109
Fodder, 231-2
Folklore, Myths and Legends of Britain, xvi
The Folklore of Orkney and Shetland, xvi
Food, 103-13
Football, 179-82, 450
Forbes, Admiral, 436
Forbes, Bishop, 60
Foulzie, Gilbert, 458
France, wars with, 8, 9
Freuteries, 13-15, 98-100, 122-3
Frodi, 259-60
Frooteries. *See* Freuteries
Fullarton, John, 44-5
Fulmars, 58
Funerals, 124, *208*
Fursakelda, 272, 305
Fursan, xv

Gairsay 23, 461
Games, 145-181, *145-83 261, 268*
Garry-skons, 110
Gaudie, George, 414
Gaudie, John, 414
George V, King, 31, 141
George VI, King, 433, 439
Gerard, John, 451
German Ocean, 427

German Navy. *See* High Seas Fleet
Gigs, 222
Girnel, 96
Gladstone, 466
Gloup, The, 58
Goats, feral, 60
The Good Shepherd, 65-6
Gorrie, Daniel, 464
Gow, John, 42-4
Graeme, Alexander, 415
Graemsay, 259
Graham, John, 211
Graham, Sister Margaret Manson, 24
Graith, 14
Grand Fleet, 428-9, 431
Greentoft (Eday), 22
Greig, Robert, coxwain, 66
Grettir the Strong, 145
Grimness, 20
Grinds, 7
Grotti, 60, 259
Grottie-hoose, 32
Groundwater, as toonship name, 6
Guides & Brownies, *286*
Guizing, 132
Gunnhild, Queen, 335, 340
Gypsies, 342-3

Haakon Haakonson, 392-6, 425
Hackness, Tower, 426
Hair eels, 172
Hairst roses, 24
Hakon, Earl, 459-60
Halcro, Margaret, 409-10
Halcro, Patrick, 397, 446
Hallan, 95
Hallowe'en, 137-8
Hallowmas, 139
Hamefare, 110
Hamilton, Lady Emma, 414
Hammars o' Syraday, 306
Hampshire, sinking of, 67, 419-23, 432
Hansel, 110
Hansel-wife, 120
Harald, Earl, 425
Harald Hardrada, 387-8, 425
Harray, toonships, 6
Harvest bannocks, 23
Harvest feasts, 25
Harvest Home, 25
Harvest knots, 24
Harvesting, 6, 7, 19-25
Hatching eggs, 14
Hatston aerodrome, 438
Haymaking, *340*
Heaters, 221
Heather ale, 193
Hebrides, 392
Heddle, John, 465
Heimskringla, 335, 337-8

Helbeck, Hans, 19
Heligoland Bight, 427, 431, 432
Henry Sinclair, Earl, 446
Herbalists, 100
Herring fishing, 7
Herston, 61
Hether Blether, 276-7
Heuks, 20, 21
Hibbert, Samuel, 46
High Seas Fleet, 427, *428*, 429-32
   internment of, 433-5
   salvage, 435-6
   scuttling of, 435
Hildaland, 276
Hill-folk, 219
Hill-trows, 123, 263, 267
Hills of Hoy, 259
Hogboon, 267
Hogmanay, 129-30
Holland (Stronsay), 22
Hollinshead's *Chronicles*, 191
Holms of Ire, 296
Hood, 438
Horne, David, 467
Horse and plough festival, 134-6
Horse hair, 172
Horseman's Society, 18
Horseman's word, 16-18
Hourston, as toonship name, 6
Houses, 95-7, 218-19
Houton, 425
Howe of Hoxa, 56
Hoxa Head, 57
Hoxa Sound, 429
Hoy, naval burials, 432
Hoy Head, (ship), 430
Hoy Head, shipwrecks, 69
Hoy Sound, 429
Hudson's Bay Company, xvi, 8, 217
Huip, 22
Huldrefolk, 274-7
Huna, ferry, 56

Illness, and witchcraft, 353-62
Imperieuse, HMS, 431
Instabilie, 17
Internment Fleet, 433-5
Iona, SS, *36*
Isbister, as toonship name, 6
Italian Chapel, 438-9, *449*, 453-6

James III, King of Scots, 19
James V, King, 399
Jamieson, Thomas, 20
Jarlshof, seal bones at, 47
Jellicoe, Admiral, 421, 427-9, 431-2
JJKSW, 68-71
Johanna Thorden, wreck of, 58
John A. Hay, 66-8
John o' Groats, 57, 58, 60, 61

Johnston, William, coxwain, 68, 70
Jotner, 257-8, 259
Jotun, 257-8
Journey from Serfdom, xvi
Jutland, Battle of, 421, 432

Kail breu, 110
Kailyards, 26, 28
Kairi Keld, 305
Kame of Hoy, 424
Keelilang Hill, 183
Keldamurra, 305
Kelday, 301
Keldraseed, 302, 305
Keldro, 301
Kelp, uses of, 7-9
Kemping, 21
Kennedy's Tomb, 60
Keppel, Captain, 44
Kierfea Hill, 258
Kirbister and Corrigall Farm Museum, 95
Kirk Rocks, shipwrecks, 69
Kirk Sound, 436
Kirking, 90
Kirkness, toonship, 264
Kirkness, David M., 86
Kirkness, John, 399
Kirkness, William, 90, 91
Kirkwall,
   Arts Theatre, 411
   Ba', 129, 140, 180-2, 224-5, 240, *298*
   Big Tree, 463-7
   Broad Street, *396*, *420*
   Castle, 446-7
   export trade, 19
   Fair, *xxii*
   flood, 411-12
   harbour, 69, *221*
   historical, 5
   Lammas Market, 52
   Marwick becomes Freeman, xvii
   move to, xv
   Papdale House, xvii
   Shore Street, *81*
   Summerhouse, *33*
   Tolbooth, *464*
   Town Council,
     & Cathedral, 457
     customs officers, 38, 90, 91
     Kirking, 90
     reception for Chiocchetti, 456
Kirn-milk, 28, 110
Kirning, 13
Kissing meat, 120
Kitchener, Lord, 419-23, *421*, 432
Kites, 178
Klaqum, 110
Klineoo, 110
Kloss, 97
Knitting, 7

Knockit corn, 110
Kol, 459, 461
Korn, 19
Krackans, 110
Krang, 110
Krappin banno, 110
Kringlafiold, 140
Kruisie, 95
Kye-kail, 27
Kyerrin, 132

Lady Well, 304
Laing, Malcolm, 464-5
Laing, Samuel, 212
Lairds, 5, 7
Lamb Holm, 438, 453-4
Lammas Market, 52
Land improvements, 9
Landlords, 9, 10, 11, 12
Langskaill, 23
Largs, Battle of, 392, 425
Last sheaf customs, 22, 23, 24
Law, udal, 6
Lectures, 187
Legendary creatures, 257-78
Leicester City, wreck of, 70
Leith, James, 413-14
Life in the Orkney Islands, xvi
Lifeboats, Stromness, 62-73, 422
Limpets, as bait, 34
Lindsay, Maurice, 58
Linen industry, 9
Linklater, Eric, xix
Links of Hunton, 302
Liver heids, 110
Liversoakie, 110
Livestock, 5
Loch of Boardhouse, 258
Loch of Knitchen, 274
Loch Ness, 282
Loch of Scockness, 258
Longhope,
 farming, 14
 Fleet base, 430
 lifeboat, 73
 Martello Towers, 426
Looking Around, xvi
Lord Devonport, wreck, 69
Loss of profit, 13, 353-5
Low, George, 307, 312, 463
Lowts, 111
The Luggage Boat, 32
Lusitania, 431
Lyness,
 Fleet base, 430, 439

Maat, 103-4
Macdonald's Inn, 464
MacGillivray, Evan, 81
MacKay, Captain, 312-13

Mackenzie, Sir George, 346
Macnab, Clan, 203-4
Maeshowe, 267-8
Magnus, Saint, 389-91, 397, 425, 459-62
Malaya, HMS, 433
Malcolm Canmore, King of Scotland, 389
Man from nowhere, 288-9
Manswal, 301
Marbles, 177
Martello Towers, 426
Marwick, as toonship name, 6
Marwick Head, 432
 Tower, 419-20
Marwick, Ernest Walker
 birth, xv
 in bookshop, xv
 broadcasting, xvi
 broadcasts to Canada, xvi
 death of, xvii
 Honorary Freeman, xvii
 television, xvi
 visits to Norway, xvi
Marwick, George, 370
Marwick, Janette, xviii
Mary, Queen, 345
Medicines, 101-2
Meedoo, 231-4
Meedoo-sweet, 233
Melder sillocks, 111
Mert, 111
Mester Ship, 324
Michaelmas customs, 25
Midlands Haven, 425
Midsummer, 139
Mill Loch, 307
Miller's Word, 16
Mills, 82-3
Moena, 453, 455
Motor cars, 239-40, *389*, *396*
Mougelden, 111
Mound-dwellers, 266-7
Muckle supper, 25
Muir, Edwin, xix, 233
 autobiography, 31
 tutor, xv
Mullyos, 21
Mummies, Stroma, 60

Napoleon Bonaparte, 415-18
Napoleonic Wars, 8, 9, 413-18
Napp, 111
Narvik raid, 438
Nature Conservancy Council, 46
Naval blockade, 426, 430
Nelson, Admiral, 8, 413-15
Ness, 63, 65
Neuk beds, 95-6
The New Orkney Book, xvi
New Shetlander Writing, xvi
New Year customs, 129-32

New Year Song, 129
Newark Bay, 285
Newbattle Abbey, xv
Nip-a-doons, 111
Nisse, 266-8
Njal's Saga, 340
Nor-wasters, 8
Norfolk, HMS, 39
Norman Conquest, 387
Norn, 6
Norse legends, 424
Norway,
  Marwick visits, xvi
  trading with, 7, 19
Nottingham, 33
Nowlan, Willie, 216
Nowt Bield, 259
Numerology, 15

Oatmeal, 20
Oats, 7, 19
Odal. *See* udal
Odin Stone, 42, 309-21, 337
Olav, Saint, 387, 390
Omond fiddle, 88-9
Omond, James, 20, 24, 88-9
Oon, 22
Orcadia, SS, *37*, 50-4
The Orcadian, xv, xvi
Orkney Barrage, 437
Orkney Belle, 31
Orkney chair, 85-7, *132*, 458
Orkney dialect, xviii
Orkney Folklore and Traditions, xvi
The Orkney Herald, xv
Orkney Heritage Society, xvi
Orkney Steam Navigation Co., 53-4
Orkney Territorials, 428-9
Orkneyinga Saga, 81, 114, 258, 316, 338, 340, 387, 390, 459-60
Orphir, parish, 5
Orra-house, 97
Outdoor games, 176-9
Outer Kirk Rocks, 63
Oven pot, 11

Packet boats, 50
Papdale, xvii, 411, 464
Parish annals, 218-27
Parishes, 5
Partan, 111
Patrick, Earl, 403-4
Paul, Earl, 461
Pauntree, 96
Peace's Orkney Almanac, 207-8
Peat, 114-115, *193*, *208*
Peerie folk, 13, 120
Peerie fool, 290-2
Peerie Sea, 411
Pegal Burn, 274

Pennant, Thomas, 48
Pentland Firth, voyaging, 55-61
Pentland Skerries, 59
Peterkirk, 448-452
Petrie, George, 443-4
Peuchis, 111
Phantom ships, 31-3
Picken, Rev. Stuart D. B., 449
Pickie aets, 20
Picts, 20, 193, 264
Pierowall, 267, 444
Pilots, Pentland Firth, 55
Piracy, 42-5
Plankings, 10, 21
Plantikreus, 26, 27, 28, *32*
The Play o' de Lathie Odivere, 47
Ploughing, 14, 15 134-6, *241*
Point of Oxan, shipwrecks, 62
Point of Spoil, 65
Population, 11
Porteous Mob, 36
Poverty, 228-30
Prien, Kapitan-Leutnant Gunther, 436-7
Primula scotica 59
Prinz Eugen, 438
Prisoners of war, 438, *449* 453
Privateering, 44
Protectorate, 406-7
Provost's Chain, 90-1
Pulsekerry, 63
Purdo in a kloot, 111
Purr, 111
Putting, *261*

Quarrying, 235-6
Queen Mother, 86
Quern-trows, 263-4
Querns, 7, 60, 96

Rae, Dr John, 183
Ragnarok, 424
Rame, 111
Ranze, 111
Reaping machines, 22, 23
Red Head of Eday, 259
Redware, 70
Reestid, 111
Reformation, 450
Rendall, 203-4
Rendall, Robert, xv, 145
Rental of Orphir, 405
Reuter, Vice-Admiral von, 433-4
The Revenge, 42-3
Rhyming games, 159-72
Richan, Captain William, 39
Riddles, 173-6
Rigs, 20
Rip, 22
Road-making, 235-6, *369*
Robert Bruce, King, 204, 397-8

Robert Stewart, Earl, 26, 403
Robertson, Captain Robert, 50-4
Robertson Duncan J., 466
Robertson, John D. M., 81, 182
Robertson, T. A., xvi, 19
Roeberry, 56
Rognvald Eysteinsson, 389
Rognvald, Saint, 145, 425, 457-62
Rosie James, 57-8
Rost peedie, 111
Rothiesholm Head, 284
Royal Oak, sinking of, *429*, 437-8
Rumbly thump, 111
Runrig, 6, 20

Saave, 105
Sabbath, harvesting on, 21
Saetros, 170-2
Saga of Eirik the Red, 340
St Angus, 32
St George, statue, 454
St John's Head, 424
St Kilda, 74-5
St Magnus, 301
St Magnus II, SS, 44
St Magnus Cathedral, *frontis.*, xvii, 348, 398, 457, *461*, 465
St Magnus Cricket Club, 184-5
St Margaret's Hope, 394
St Mary's Church, 449
St Ninian's Well, 301
St Ola, 390
St Ola I, SS, 37
St Ola Cricket Club, 184
St Olaf (ship), 64
St Peter's Church, 448-52
St Rognvald Chapel, 457-9
Saltaire, 64
Sanday, 6
Sands, John, 74-5
Sandwick, 13
Sanquhar Cross, Declaration of, 410
Sator's Stone, 307
Scapa Bay, *372*, 430, 437
Scapa Flow, 17, 56-7, *305*, 424-39
 bombing of, 437
 closing of base, 439
 gun emplacements, 57
 Lord Kitchener at, 421
 phantom ships, 32-3
Sclater, Thomas, 465
Scott, *Sir* Walter, 43, 297, 397, 447, 464
Scottish Salmon Net Fishing Association, 46
Scythes, 15, 21
Sea monsters, 282-7
Sea-trows, 262
Seal meat, eaten in Lent, 48
Seal stories, 295-6
Seals, 58
 culling, 49

 grey, 46-9
Seaweed, as manure, 7, 27. *See also* Kelp
Secession Church, 409-10
Second-sight, 366-8
Selkies, 46-9
Selkies Hellier, *160*
Sellar, 95-6
Shakespeare, wreck of, 65-6
Shaw, George Bernard, 240
Sheaf-getting, 22
Shearer, Douglas, 455
Sheaves, tying, 20, 21
Shell-games, 145
Shirreff, John, 463
Shops, *141*, *192*
Shows, *260*
Sickle 20
Sids, xv, 111
Sinclair, Edward, 458
Sinclair, Henry, 446
Sinclair, William, 446
Singing games, 147-59
Skaill, 21, 74
Skaill Bay, 422, 444
Skaill hoard, 443
Skara Brae, 95
Skare, 22
Skatehorn, 205-6
Skatt, 10
Skelwick, 266
Skippigeo, *64*
Skipping, 178
Skirlies, 111
Skrae, 111
Skroo, 22
Slaps, 7
Smart, Billy, 239
Smith, Adam, 36
Smith, C. Lessingham, 464
Smugglers, 36-41
Snoddy, 111
Sooan scones, 112
Sooan Sids, xv
Sooans, 111
Soor-dook, 112
Sooros, 112
South Ronaldsay, 134-6
South Ronaldshay Agricultural Society, 136
Southampton, 32
Spence, Graeme, report on Scapa Flow, 425-6
Spence, John, 21, 81-5
Spies, 430
Spinning, 7
Spleuchans, 49
Splooter piece, 112
Spoots, 76-7, *96*, 112
Stamford Bridge, battle of, 388, 425
Standing stones, 258, 307-8, *316-7*
Stanger Head, 57
Steam ships, 50-4

Steuls 85-6
Stewart, Earl Patrick, 446, 458
Stewart, Earl Robert, 26, 403, 446
Stewart Earls, 6
Stone of Odin, 42, 309-21, 337
Stone of Quoyboon, 258
Stone-breaking, 235-6
Stones of Stenness, 309
Stoor Worm, 282-3
Story-telling, 323-30
Stove, belted knights of, 399-400
Straw dogs, 22, 23
Straw-plait industry, 9
Stroma, 58-60
Stromness, xvii
  anniversary, 216
  historical, 5
  lifeboat, 62-73, 422
  Masonic Hall, 63
  prosperity of, 8
  Town Hall, 12
The Stromness News, 216-17, 353
Stronsay, 6
  land improvements, 9
  lifeboat, 73
Sturluson, Snorri, 335
Submarine nets, 429
Submarines, 428-9, 431-2
Substitute words, fishing, 34-5
Summerdale, battle of, 425
Superior duty, 10
Superstitions, 98-100
  farming, 13-15
  fishermen, 33
  marriage, 122-3
  sea, 31-5
Swanney, William, 417
Sweetie-folls, 112
Swelchie, 260
Swelkie, 60, 394
Sweyn Asleifson, 425, 461
Switha Sound, 429
Swona, *45*, 57-8

Tailing day, 133
Tait, James, 415-16
'Taking the profit', 13, 353-5
Talk of the Town, xvi
Tall stories, 323-30
Tammy-nories, as food, 103
Tangy, 262
Tankerness House, *286*, *452*, 458
Tatties and point, 112
Teeacks, 98
Teeve Well, 302
Teevick Well, 302
Television, Marwick on, xvi
Temperance, 192, 195-9, *276-7*, *284*
Temperance Hall, 411
Theatre, 187

Thoms, Sheriff, 458
Thomson, Mr (lawyer), 12
Thorfinn Skull-splitter, 56, 340, 392, 460
'Thrawn Mouth', 446-7
Threshing, 7
The Thrymquilda, 342
Tinkers, *368*
Tithes, fish, 33
Tolbooth, 186, 447
Toomal, 6
Toonships, 5, 6, 20
  boundary walls, 6
Toothache, 99-100
Torf-Einar, 114
Torture, 373
Tounships, 450
Trading, 7, 8, 19
Trafalgar, 413
  battle of, 8, 413
Traill, Thomas, 53
Tratland, 301
Travelling shop, *14*
Treasure, 443-5
Trees, 463
Trip-trap-truisky, 146
Trolls, 259-60
Trowie Glen, 260
Trows, 123, 127, 260-5
  hill-, 13
Tuscaloosa, 439
Twa Tammies, 32
Tyno sillocks, 113

Udal, 6
Udallers, 6
Uniformity, Act of, 409
Unstan Cairn, 19
'Up-the-Gates', 140, 180
Uppies-and-Doonies, 140, 180, *See also* Ba' Game
Uranium mining, xvii

Vagabonds, as witches, 368-9
'Vagaland', xvi
Valkyrie, legend, 424
Vanguard, explosion of, 432-3
Varangian Guard, 387-8, 425
Velzian, 13
Veto Poll, 196-9
Victory, 413-14
Violins, 88-9

Wages, harvest hands, 21, 22
Walking, 183
Wallace, Rev. James, 26, 309, 463
Ward Hill, 259, 349
Warebeth, 65
Warrenfield, 141
Wars, Napoleonic, 8
Water carrying, *396*

Water of Hoy, 274
Water-horses, 274
Waterloo, battle of, 416-17
Watsone, Alister, 20
Weaving, 7
Wedding customs, 119-121, *209*
Wedding superstitions, 122-3
Weld, Charles, 464
Well of St Mary, 304
Wells, 301-6, *397*
Wells of Kildinguie, 302
Wells of Swona, 57
Wentid milk, 113
West Mainland, 5
West Pier, 447
Western Patrol, 430
Whaling ships, 8
Whey scones, 113
Whisky, *277*
Whisky Jock, 217
White House of Breck, 203
White Worm, 333
Wideford Hill, 31

Widewall, 56
William the Old, Bishop, 459-61
Winds, buying, 33
Winster's Well, 303
Witch trials, 345-8
Witchcraft, 333-83, 404
Witchcraft trials, 371-6
Witches, lists, 376-81
Witch's cat, 350-2
Women, as farm workers, 9
Woodwick, 265
Wooleritch, Walter, 450
World War I, 428-33
World War II, 242-51, 436-9
Wyre, 258

Yappies, 14
Yarpha peats, 28, 114
Yesnaby, *212*, *349*
Yetlin, 96, 113
Yetnasteen, 258
Yirnings, 113
Yule, 127-8, 133, 139, 191